PATHS OF THE MESSIAH

BARGIL PIXNER

PATHS OF THE MESSIAH

and

Sites of the Early Church from Galilee to Jerusalem

Jesus and Jewish Christianity in Light of Archaeological Discoveries

Edited by Rainer Riesner

Translated by Keith Myrick and Sam and Miriam Randall

IGNATIUS PRESS SAN FRANCISCO

Original German edition:
Wege des Messias und Stätten der Urkirche.
Jesus und das Judenchristentum im Licht neuer archäologischer Erkenntnisse.

Cover photograph © by iStockPhoto.com

Insert: Photograph of mosaic depiction of Christ
by Brother Lawrence Lew, O.P.

Cover design by John Herreid

ISBN 978-0-89870-865-3
Library of Congress Control Number 2007927426
Printed in the United States of America ♾

To Gerlinde Hartmann

*In gratitude for her generous help,
which made possible the translation of this work*

CONTENTS

EDITOR'S INTRODUCTION

The life of the author, which was to lead him to faraway places, began in Untermais near Meran in the heart of an almost paradisiacal part of Central Europe. Bargil Pixner was born on March 23, 1921, as the oldest of eight children in the family of the local sexton.[1] At his baptism he was named Virgil after the third bishop of Trent, who was stoned to death by pagans in the Rendena Valley probably in A.D. 405.[2] From earliest childhood, the firm faith of his parental home, especially the profound piety of his mother, made its impression on Bargil Pixner. The inherited faith soon had to be proven as his own. After World War I, the right of self-government was withheld from the German-speaking inhabitants of South Tirol. After Mussolini seized power, they suffered in particular under the chauvinistic politics of the Fascists.[3] When Hitler occupied Austria in 1938, the two dictators reached an agreement in which the affected South Tyroleans had no say, i.e., that whoever identified himself with ("opted for") Germany should be resettled in the German Reich.

With such men and women motivated by Christian values, a resistance movement started, first against Italian Fascism and then, after the occupation of South Tyrol by the German Wehrmacht, also against Nazism. Bargil Pixner became involved in these activities. After finishing the gymnasium Johanneum in Dorf Tirol (near Meran), in 1940 he attended the priest seminary in Trent and then the seminary of the

[1] Short biographies: "Provocative Thinker", *Jerusalem Post*, November 4, 1993, international edition, 12; J. INNERHOFER, "Sohn der Freude", *Katholisches Sonntagsblatt* (Diocese of Brixen) 14 (April 6, 1986): 5; H. SHANKS, ed., *Who's Who in Biblical Studies and Archaeology*, 3rd ed. (Washington, 1993), 234f.

[2] Cf. A. AMORE, "Virgil", in *Lexikon für Theologie und Kirche*, vol. 10 (Freiburg, 1965), 789.

[3] The Fascist policies of suppression are reliably and comprehensively documented in O. PARTELI, *Geschichte Tirols*, vol. 4, pt. 1, *Südtirol in der Zeit von 1918 bis 1970* (Bozen, 1989), although his evaluations are controversial in detail.

Missionaries of Saint Joseph in Brixen. In 1944 Pixner was called to the German army. Together with some others he convinced his comrades to refuse the oath of allegiance to Hitler. It happened only once in the Third Reich that a whole regiment refused to take that oath. All were disarmed, and Pixner was transferred to a delousing unit in Silesia. Here he had to face much prejudice because of his known pro-Jewish sympathies. He was even threatened with a court-martial. He has written about this difficult time in one of his popular books for Holy Land pilgrims.[4]

After the end of World War II, Pixner helped in his hometown, Meran, founding a Christian political party representative of the German-speaking population of South Tyrol. A political career was open to him, but instead he followed his inner calling and finished his theological studies. In 1946 he was ordained a priest and joined an English missionary order, the Mill Hill Fathers, which served in the Philippines. There he was the director of the Santa Barbara leper station on the island of Panay. Because of his meritorious work he was able to become a U.S. citizen. After 1956 Pixner worked as spiritual adviser for other priests in the United States, in Italy and in France. In 1969 a long-time dream became true for him: he could go to Israel. He was one of the founders of the peace village Neve Shalom, near the New Testament site of Emmaus (Lk 24:13). Later on, Pixner, with the help of politicians from South Tyrol, tried to bring together Israeli and Palestinian leaders for discussions and negotiations. In Jerusalem Pixner studied Hebrew and biblical archaeology and geography at the Dominican École biblique and the Studium Biblicum Franciscanum.

In 1973 Bargil Pixner joined the Benedictine abbey Dormitio Mariae on Mount Zion in Jerusalem. Very early, this convent showed an interest in the long-neglected Jewish Christian studies. The abbot, Leo Rudloff, was one of the supporters of the Institute of Judaeo-Christian Studies, which was founded in 1953 by the priest John M. Oesterreicher, who emigrated from Vienna to the United States. The then abbot of Dormition Abbey, Laurentius Klein, charged Father Bargil with investigating the Jewish Christian traditions connected with Mount Zion. In 1977, together with the Israeli archaeologists Doron Chen and Shlomo Margalit, Pixner succeeded in the sensational rediscovery

[4] *With Jesus in Jerusalem: His First and Last Days in Judea* (Rosh Pinna, Israel: Corazin, 1996), 9–11.

of the Essene Gate, mentioned by the Jewish historian Flavius Josephus in his description of Jerusalem (*War* 5.145). This gate led to the Jerusalem quarter occupied by this special Jewish group that has become famous through the discovery of the Dead Sea Scrolls near Qumran. From his room in the Dormition Abbey, Pixner could daily look on the former Essene quarter with its remaining large ritual baths. The famous Qumran researcher Professor James H. Charlesworth (Princeton) is only one of the experts who underlined the importance of Pixner's discoveries.[5] The traditional Cenacle [Upper Room] is located very near the Dormition Abbey. Pixner was able to find new arguments supporting as reliable the local tradition that this place was the first center of the Primitive Community. From all this there developed new and interesting views on the life of this community, to which Mary and other members of Jesus' extended family belonged. Pope Benedict XVI, in his book on Jesus, has accepted the thesis of the neighborhood of the Jerusalem Essene quarter and the Cenacle.[6]

Part of his time Father Bargil lived in the Benedictine Monastery of Tabgha, situated near Capharnaum at Lake Gennesaret. Here he was able to do research on the traditions of the Jewish Christians of that region. He could show that these believers lived there at least until the fourth century and faithfully remembered the places connected with the ministry of Jesus. Besides the exploration of Tabgha, Pixner was involved in the excavations on the hill of et-Tell, where some scholars locate the New Testament town of Bethsaida.[7] It was a special joy for Father Pixner that he could present to John Paul II a key found there from New Testament times when the Pope was on a pilgrimage in the Holy Year 2000. Father Pixner guided thousands of pilgrims and tourists from various countries and denominations through Galilee and Jerusalem. Through the holy places and his lively personality, he was able to create for many an interior meeting with Jesus Christ, to whom he had dedicated his own life. In addition to these activities, Pixner was teaching biblical topography and archaeology at the Theological Faculty of the Dormition Abbey, where, with the permission of the Vatican, Catholic and Evangelical students can study together for one year. In his last years Father Bargil was invited to

[5] *The Pesharim and Qumran History* (Grand Rapids, Mich.: Eerdmans, 2002), 53.

[6] *Jesus of Nazareth* (New York: Doubleday, 2007), 224–25.

[7] R. Arav and R. A. Freund, eds., *Bethsaida: A City by the North Shore of the Sea of Galilee*, 3 vols. (Kirksville: Thomas Jefferson University Press, 1995–2006).

present the results of his investigations at several international congresses and at some universities in Europe and the United States. Well prepared, he died in firm faith on April 5, 2002, and he was buried on the cemetery of the abbey in his so deeply loved city of Jerusalem.

This volume of collected essays is the fruit of our working together for more than twenty years. In 1979 Father Bargil lectured at the University of Tübingen, where I was finishing my doctoral dissertation on the first oral Gospel tradition. The old Catholic monk and the young Evangelical exegete soon formed a deep friendship. We discovered that we had three important things in common: the belief in the resurrected Son of God, the trust in the substantial reliability of the Gospels, and scientific interest in the investigation of ancient Jewish Christianity. The research of Father Bargil stirred some discussions, but he also gained important consent. I have documented this in an article for the centenary jubilee volume of Dormition Abbey.[8] Now, when an English edition of these collected essays can appear, great gratitude goes to several persons. Christoph Cardinal Schönborn of Vienna made the contact with Ignatius Press. Keith Myrick, an Evangelical Free Church pastor, and Sam and Miriam Randall, an English Anglican priest and his wife, worked on the translation. The staff of Ignatius Press has been very patient and helpful. This book would not have been possible without the generous donation of Dr. Gerlinde Hartmann (Passau, Germany), who helped—and not for the first time—to sponsor Father Bargil's work. Rightly, this book is dedicated to her.

Professor Dr. Rainer Riesner
University of Dortmund
November 2009

[8] "Essener und Urkirche auf dem Südwesthügel Jerusalems: Zion III", in N. C. Schnabel, ed., *Laetare Jerusalem* (Münster: Aschendorff, 2006), 200–234.

ABBREVIATIONS

Ant.	Josephus. *Jewish Antiquities* (*Antiquitates Judaicae*)
BA	*Biblical Archaeologist*
BAR	*Biblical Archaeology Review*
Baldi	D. Baldi, *Enchiridion locorum sanctorum: Documenta S. Evangelii loca respicientia*, 3rd ed. (Jerusalem, 1982; orig. pub. 1955)
BiKi	*Bibel und Kirche*
CD	*Damascus Document*
CNfI	*Christian News from Israel*
CSCO	Corpus scriptorum christianorum orientalium
DJD	Discoveries in the Judean Desert
EA	*Erbe und Auftrag*
ESI	*Excavations and Surveys in Israel* (Jerusalem)
GBL	H. Burkhardt et al., *Das große Bibellexikon*, 3 vols. (Wuppertal and Gießen, 1987–1989; 2nd ed., 1990)
GCS	Die griechischen christlichen Schriftsteller
Geyer	P. Geyer, *Itinera Hierosolymitana saeculi III–VIII*, Corpus scriptorum ecclesiasticorum latinorum 39 (Vienna, 1898)
HE	Eusebius of Caesarea, *Historia ecclesiastica*
Hennecke-Schneemelcher	W. Schneemelcher, ed., *Neutestamentliche Apokryphen in deutscher Übersetzung*, 5th ed.,

	vol. 1, *Evangelien* (Tübingen, 1987). Eng. trans. of earlier edition: *New Testament Apocrypha* (Philadelphia: Westminster Press, 1963–1966)
HlL	*Das Heilige Land*
IEJ	*Israel Exploration Journal*
EncJud	*Encyclopaedia Judaica* (Jerusalem, 1971)
Klijn-Reinink	A. F. J. Klijn and G. J. Reinink, *Patristic Evidence for Jewish-Christian Sects* (Leiden, 1973)
Klostermann	E. Klostermann, *Eusebius Werke*, vol. 3, pt. 1, *Das Onomastikon der biblischen Ortsnamen*, GCS 11/1 (Leipzig, 1904)
MB	*Le monde de la Bible*
PEFQS	Palestine Exploration Fund, *Quarterly Statement*
PG	Patrologiae cursus completus: Series graeca
PJB	*Palästina-Jahrbuch*
PL	Patrologiae cursus completus: Series latina
PO	Patrologia orientalis
POC	*Proche Orient chrétien*
RB	*Revue biblique*
RQ	*Revue de Qumrân*
SBAZ	Studien zur biblischen Archäologie und Zeitgeschichte
SBFCMa	Studium Biblicum Franciscanum, Collectio major
SBFCMi	Studium Biblicum Franciscanum, Collectio minor
SBFLA	Studium Biblicum Franciscanum, *Liber annuus*
SC	Sources chrétiennes
War	Josephus. *Jewish War* (*Bellum Iudaicum*)
WUNT	Wissenschaftliche Untersuchungen zum Neuen Testament
ZDPV	*Zeitschrift des Deutschen Palästina-Vereins*

PART ONE

The Birth of the Messiah

1. The Nazoreans, Bethlehem and the Birth of Jesus

I. The Journey to Bethlehem

1. The Nazoreans and Nazareth

"And Joseph also went up from Galilee, from the city of Nazareth, to Judea, to the city of David, which is called Bethlehem, because he was of the house and lineage of David, to be enrolled with Mary his betrothed, who was with child." Such is the account of Luke's Gospel (Lk 2:4). In those days Nazareth was a mere hamlet cradled in the foothills of Galilee (illus. 12), unknown to either the Bible or history. For many generations, it had been the residence of descendants of the household of David. They apparently called themselves Nazoreans (Ναζωραῖοι [*Nazōraioi*]; נוֹצְרִים [*Nozrim*]), after the words of the prophet Isaiah (11:1): "There shall come forth a shoot from the stump of Jesse, and a branch [נֵצֶר (*nezer*)] shall grow out of his roots."

It was after this *nezer* that the village of Nazareth was apparently named. According to the author Julius Africanus (ca. A.D. 220) of Emmaus (modern-day Latrun), these descendants of David lived in villages bearing messianic names such as Nazara ("village of the branch") and Cochaba ("village of the star"; cf. Num 24:17 [כּוֹכָב]) (Eusebius, *HE* 1.7.14f.). A village of the latter name existed north of Nazareth, and there was a second one in the Bashan region, a short walking distance from Bethsaida.[1] There, according to Africanus, the Davidic family kept the genealogical records used to prove its royal descent.

In this way the Nazoreans lived in the pious expectation that one day the Anointed of Israel, the Messiah, would arise from their midst.

[1] Cf. B. Pixner and R. Riesner, "Kochaba", in *GBL*, 2nd ed. (1990), 2:801ff., and chapter 13 below, "Batanea as a Jewish Settlement Area" (pp. 169–76, esp. pp. 173–75).

In a manner similar to that of the Qumran Essenes,[2] they liked to apply the words of the prophet in respect to themselves: "Your people shall all be righteous [צַדִּיקִים (*zaddiqim*)]; they shall possess the land for ever, the branch [נֵצֶר (*nezer*)] of my planting, the work of my hands, that I might be glorified", and "The Spirit of the Lord GOD is upon me, because the LORD has anointed me to bring good tidings to the afflicted" (Is 60:21; 61:1). Jesus too quoted this text from Isaiah when preaching in the synagogue in his native town. He, however, gave a vastly different interpretation from the one the status-conscious Nazoreans would have liked (pp. 381–85). Jesus refused to restrict the benefits of his wondrous powers to his ambitious kinsmen, with the result that they drove him out of the town (see Lk 4:16–30).

Joseph the carpenter and his betrothed wife Mary were also Nazoreans (Lk 1:27; 2:4). Through God's miraculous intervention, Mary had become pregnant, and both knew that the soon-to-be-born child would be the Messiah of Israel (Mt 1:20–23; Lk 1:30–33).[3] From the ancient prophet Micah they also knew that the Messiah would not be born in Galilee but rather in Bethlehem (Mic 5:1), and they decided to move there. A contributory reason for their decision was the census ordered by Emperor Augustus, who wanted to streamline his revenue-collection system (Lk 2:1–5). Thus, Joseph and his heavily pregnant wife set out on a long and arduous journey to Bethlehem. To a historian such as Luke, it was important to stress this fact in order firmly to associate the Incarnation of the Son of God with the great historical figures of his time.

2. *From Nazareth to Bethlehem*

After fierce internal struggles, Emperor Augustus had achieved the peak of his power. He was the brilliant architect of the *Pax Romana*, which for some years had reestablished peace and security in his domain. In Jerusalem, Herod was his crafty but devoted vassal, but the people hated this Judaized Idumaean, who had become a Jew only by way of his father. In the year 37 B.C. he had finally defeated Antigonus, the last king of the Hasmonean priestly dynasty (*War* 1.238ff.). Herod the Great was a much-feared tyrant, personally courageous but cruel,

[2] Cf. B. GÄRTNER, *Die rätselhaften Termini Nazoräer und Iskariot* (Uppsala, 1957), 5–36.
[3] Cf. the following chapter, "Mary in the House of David" (pp. 23–37).

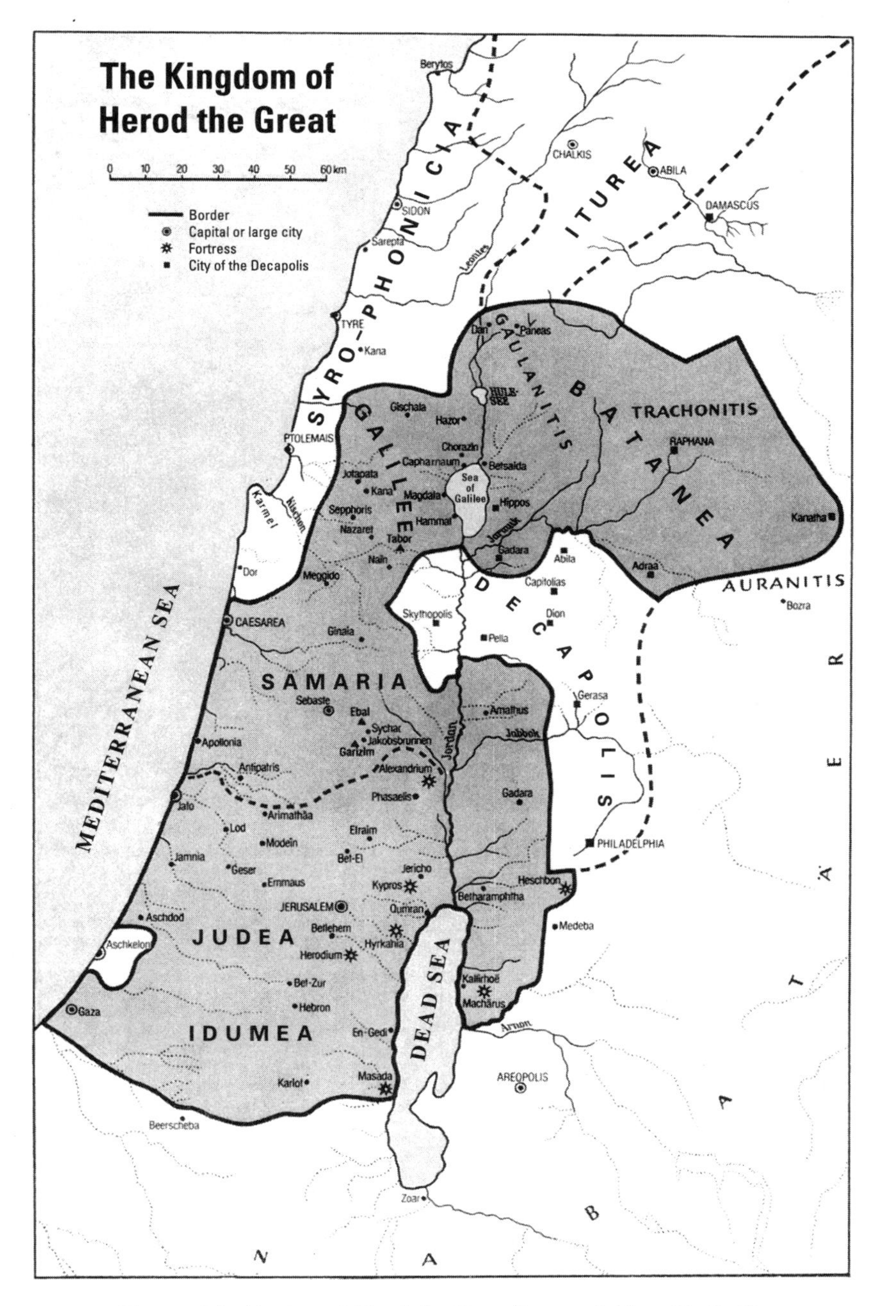

Illus. 1. The kingdom of Herod the Great (d. 4 B.C.) (from G. Kroll).

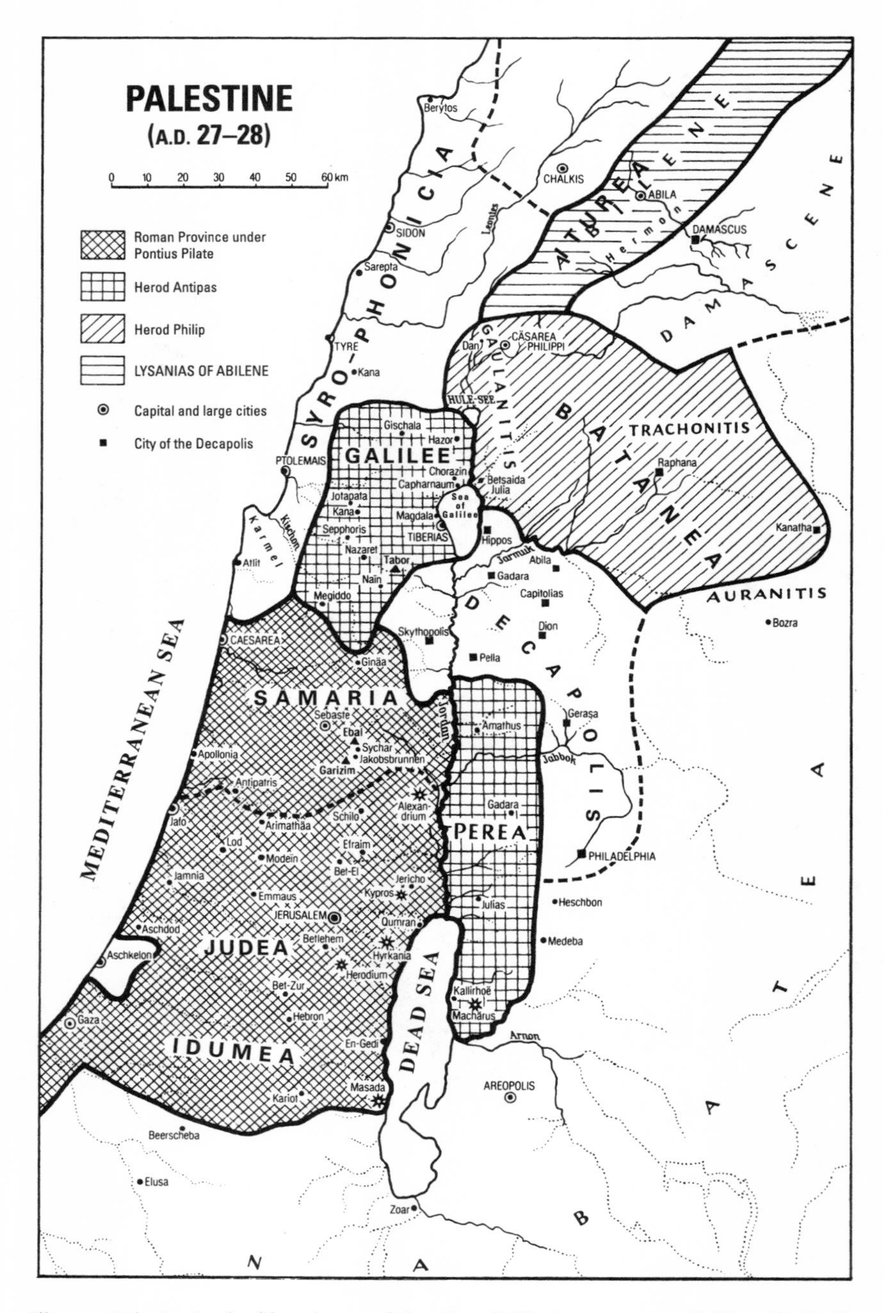

Illus. 2. Palestine in the fifteenth year of the reign of Tiberius (A.D. 27–28) (from G. Kroll).

intensely jealous and plagued by distrust. In 23 B.C. Herod built himself a royal palace in the northwestern corner of the city of that time (pp. 269–70) for himself and his numerous wives and children. Here he received an endless stream of guests from all the corners of the world (*Ant.* 15.317f.; *War* 5.156–83). There he was visited by the magi from the East who, guided by the star, had set out to find the newborn King of the Jews (Mt 2:1–9).

Joseph and Mary must have passed the palace on their way to Bethlehem through Jerusalem (illus. 58). Did Mary, riding on her mule or donkey, perhaps look up at the imposing edifice already sensing the dangers posed to her child by the powerful man behind these forbidding walls? Having left Jerusalem behind, their path led past Beth-Hakerem, the site of the present kibbutz Ramat Rachel. According to a legend related by Theodosius (ca. 530),[4] whose roots go all the way back to the Protoevangelium of James in the second century,[5] they rested at a well just before reaching the ridge near the present Mar Elias Monastery. Even today, a well situated about 500 m in front of the monastery on the left side of the modern highway to Bethlehem is called in Arabic Bir el-Kadismu ("well of the repose"). Unfortunately, a large water conduit now stretches over the well, whose mouth has been sealed with a concrete slab. The reappearance of the star of the magi (cf. Mt 2:9) is commemorated there. The Arabic name indicates that the oldest church dedicated to Mary stood nearby.[6] It was built at this very sacred place and named Kathisma (καθίσμα) after the place where Mary sat.

Upon reaching the ridge, the view of the small town presented itself to them. This was Bethlehem Ephrathah, their ancestral home.[7] A deep joy and a sense of pride may have welled up within them at the sight of it. To the east, the craggy slopes of the Judean Mountains descended steeply to the Dead Sea. On the horizon, the mountains of Moab glowed purple in the rays of the setting sun. In those far-off mountain regions, their ancestor Ruth was born. She had come to Bethlehem with her mother-in-law Naomi at the beginning of the harvest season. As was the custom of the poor, Ruth would follow

[4] *The Topography of the Holy Land* 28 (J. WILKINSON, *Jerusalem Pilgrims before the Crusades* [Jerusalem: Ariel, 1977], 70–71).

[5] *Prot. Jas.* 17:2 (Hennecke-Schneemelcher, 1:345).

[6] Cf. chapter 3, "The Kathisma Church (Mary's Repose) Rediscovered" (pp. 38–49).

[7] Cf. R. RIESNER, "Bethlehem", in *GBL*, 2nd ed. (1990), 1:196–97.

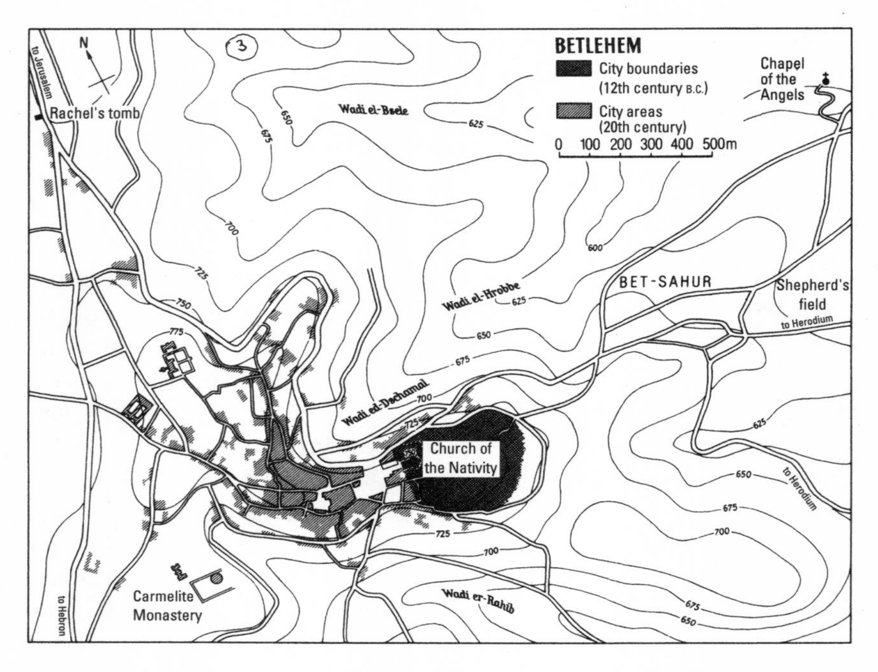

Illus. 3. Bethlehem and its surroundings (from G. Kroll).

along behind the reapers to gather what stalks they had left strewn about. Boaz, the owner of the fields, fell in love with Ruth and took her as his wife. Ruth gave birth to a child. "They named him Obed; he was the father of Jesse, the father of David" (Ruth 4:17).

With these concluding words of the book of Ruth, the man is introduced through whom Bethlehem would become world famous, i.e., David. This shepherd from Bethlehem rises like a star of the highest magnitude over Israel's horizon. When God became disappointed with King Saul, he sent the prophet Samuel to Bethlehem to select the future king of Israel from among the eight sons of Jesse. After the seven oldest boys had passed before him, Samuel requested to see the youngest, who was tending the sheep in the fields. This is how the Bible describes him: "Now he was ruddy, and had beautiful eyes, and was handsome. And the LORD said, 'Arise, anoint him; for this is he.' Then Samuel took the horn of oil, and anointed him in the midst of his brothers; and the Spirit of the LORD came mightily upon David from that day forward" (1 Sam 16:12f.).

Such thoughts might have come to Mary and Joseph's mind when they descended the heights of Mar Elias into the region of Tantur, where a center for ecumenical studies is now located. There, where from time immemorial the trail from the main road over the ridge of the Judean mountain range had bent down toward Bethlehem, the tomb of Rachel was already on display in those days (cf. Mt 2:16–18).[8] It was here that Jacob had buried the wife of his first love, Rachel, who died giving birth to their son Benjamin. In a remark added later to the book of Genesis, we read: "So Rachel died, and she was buried on the way to Ephrath (that is, Bethlehem), and Jacob set up a pillar upon her grave; it is the pillar of Rachel's tomb, which is there to this day" (Gen 35:19–20).

After Joseph and Mary had passed this point, they approached the hometown of their lineage. They sought shelter for the night, but "there was no place for them in the inn" (Lk 2:7). Was it because they were too poor, or were the usual caravan lodgings overcrowded? There was more likely no suitable room where Mary could give birth to the promised child in privacy. Being familiar with the City of David, Joseph remembered a shepherds' cave just outside the town on the western slope of the hill. There he took Mary, and it was there that Jesus, the Messiah, was born.

II. The Birth of Jesus in Bethlehem

1. The Report about the Birthplace of Jesus

Was Jesus actually born in Bethlehem, as had been prophesied by the prophet Micah (Mic 5:1)? Several modern scholars have tried to disprove this. They point out that none of the early New Testament sources, such as the Epistles of Saint Paul or the Gospel of Mark, make any mention of Bethlehem, but what does this prove? There have been countless other great historical figures whose place of birth is unknown. People in antiquity became famous as a result of what they said or did in the course of their lives, and that is what was written about. Therefore, it is not surprising that the earliest authors do not mention Jesus' birth in Bethlehem, even assuming the authors could hardly have remained unaware of the fact.

[8] Cf. J. JEREMIAS, *Heiligengräber in Jesu Umwelt* (Göttingen: Vandenhoeck und Ruprecht, 1958), 75–76.

The disciples and Apostles spoke of what they had themselves seen or heard, beginning with the preaching of the Baptist and continuing until Jesus' crucifixion and subsequent Resurrection (Acts 1:21–22). This is the framework within which Mark, the author of the earliest Gospel, places the life of Jesus, and John does the same. We have no information that Jesus ever returned to Bethlehem, not even during his public ministry. However, his Davidic lineage is repeatedly pointed out in the Gospels (Mt 9:27; Mk 10:47; etc.). The earliest indication of this comes from Paul himself, who in his letter to the church in Rome (ca. A.D. 57) takes for granted that this is known when he writes, "Concerning his Son, who was descended from David according to the flesh" (Rom 1:3).

Shortly after the death of Jesus' "brother" James in A.D. 62, a heresy was being propagated in Jewish Christian circles, according to which the "prophet" Jesus was adopted as God's son at the time of his baptism in the river Jordan (cf. Mk 1:9–11). These same circles rejected the virgin birth, claiming that Jesus was the natural son of Joseph and Mary (pp. 409–11). This heresy would later be known as Ebionism. Matthew's and Luke's versions of the Gospel were attempts at countering this heretical current by emphasizing the apostolic doctrine of the preexistence of the Son of God (cf. Phil 2:5f.). Both of them, independently of one another, made use of family tradition for the story of his conception and birth.

Matthew might have received his information from relatives still living in southern Syria, perhaps in the Nazorean village of Cochaba ("village of the star"; see p. 31). Stories in haggadic[9] style circulated there about magi from the East (Mt 2:1–12) who had followed a star and had found the newly born King of the Jews in Bethlehem.[10] Luke, on the other hand, "having followed all things closely for some time past" (Lk 1:3), may have consulted close relatives such as Simeon Bar Cleopas—Jesus' cousin and the second bishop of Jerusalem—for his source material about the early days of Jesus' life.[11] Certain reminiscences of Mary, who until her death lived among the first Christian

[9] A Haggada is a story in which an Old Testament message plays a great role. This kind of story was very popular among the rabbis.

[10] Cf. A. Strobel, *Der Stern von Bethlehem—ein Licht für unsere Zeit?* (Fürth: Flaccius, 1987); K. Ferrari d'Occhieppo, *Der Stern von Bethlehem—Legende oder Tatsache?*, 4th ed., SBAZ 3 (Gießen: Brunnen, 2003).

[11] Cf. chapter 33, "Luke and Jerusalem" (pp. 423–32).

community on Mount Zion,[12] were also handed down, perhaps as a written Aramaic Haggada. Luke skillfully integrated these family traditions, according to which Jesus was born in Bethlehem, into the third Gospel. This gives us two witnesses who, independent of each other, researched the issue and made known that Jesus was born in Bethlehem.

2. *The History of the Cave of the Nativity*

Following the Edict of Milan (A.D. 313), Christianity emerged from the catacombs. At last, Christians could openly identify with the sites that they considered holy. In the year 326 the pious empress Helen, mother of Constantine the Great, embarked on a pilgrimage to the Holy Land. Immediately after her arrival, she instigated the construction of basilicas at the site of three "mystical grottoes"[13] revered since the early days of Christianity. These were the grotto of Jesus' burial at Golgotha (pp. 303–8), the Cave of the Disciples (Eleona) on the Mount of Olives (pp. 233–34), and the Cave of the Nativity in Bethlehem. The question remains, however, whether the latter indeed marks the site of the manger in which Mary laid the infant Jesus (Lk 2:7). In this case, there is a tradition that can actually be traced back to the time of the relatives of Jesus.

The first leader of the Christian community in Jerusalem was James, the "Lord's brother" (Gal 1:19). He was succeeded by his and Jesus' cousin Simeon Bar Cleopas, who is supposed to have been crucified in around A.D. 100, at an advanced age, because he was of Davidic descent and was a Christian.[14] Jesus' Mother, Mary, lived among the community until her assumption in about A.D. 50. The words "Mary kept all these things, pondering them in her heart" (Lk 2:19) show that she reflected on the events that had taken place during Jesus' youth. We can well be certain that she visited nearby Bethlehem, only 8 km away, rather often. Local traditions stemming from her were able to survive in the Jewish Christian community in Jerusalem, which, according to Eusebius, was very large up until the Bar Kokhba revolt (A.D. 132–135).[15] Already Justin Martyr, born around the year A.D. 100

[12] Cf. chapter 30, "Mary on Zion" (pp. 398–407).
[13] Eusebius, *De laudibus Constantini* 9.17 (PG 20:1371; Baldi, 86).
[14] Cf. chapter 31, "Simeon Bar Cleopas, Second Bishop of Jerusalem" (pp. 408–14).
[15] *Demonstratio Evangelica* 3.5 (GCS 23:131; Klijn-Reinink, 138).

in Neapolis (Nablus), knew of a grotto in Bethlehem in which Jesus had been born.[16]

It is one of the ironies of history that the definite identification of many Jewish and Christian holy sites is owed to a pagan Roman emperor. Following the bloody repression of the Jewish Bar Kokhba insurrection (132–135), Emperor Hadrian reacted with the utmost severity to suppress any Jewish-inspired messianic movement. The Jews were expelled from Jerusalem, and all known Jewish and Jewish Christian holy places were paganized by erecting pagan sanctuaries on them. These were built on such sites as the temple, the pool of Siloam, the Bethesda pool, and Mamre, near Hebron. At the site of the Holy Sepulchre arose a temple of Venus, and over the Grotto of the Nativity, the Romans planted a grove dedicated to the god Tammuz-Adonis.[17]

Origen appears to have visited this pagan cult place in the year 220, at which time he was also shown the place of Jesus' birth. He writes: "In Bethlehem the grotto was shown where, according to the Gospels, Jesus was born, as well as the manger in which, wrapped in swaddling clothes, he was laid. What was shown to me is familiar to everyone in the area. The heathens themselves tell everyone who is willing to listen that in the said grotto a certain Jesus was born whom the Christians revered."[18] The Christians apparently did not allow the pagan cult of Adonis to deter them from visiting the grotto. Around A.D. 315, 10 years before the construction of the Basilica of the Nativity, the future bishop of Caesarea, Eusebius, wrote: "Up till the present day the local population [of Bethlehem] bears witness to the ancestral tradition and proceeds to show visitors the grotto in which the Virgin gave birth to the Child."[19] This means that Emperor Constantine could refer to a foundation in tradition and fact when in 326 he decided to found the Basilica of the Nativity on this spot.

3. The Church of the Nativity

The present Church of the Nativity is one of the earliest Christian structures. The original basilica, erected in the fourth century by Constantine the Great, was enlarged and embellished by Emperor Justinian

[16] *Dialogue with Trypho* 78 (PG 6:657; Baldi, 83–84).
[17] Cf. Jerome, *Letter 58* 3 (PL 22:581; Baldi, 91).
[18] *Contra Celsum* 1.51 (PG 11:755; Baldi, 84).
[19] *Demonstratio Evangelica* 7.2.15 (PG 22:540; Baldi, 85).

(527–565) after it had been severely damaged by hordes of rebellious Samaritans that stormed across the land pillaging and plundering.[20] In the course of time, the complex was expanded by the addition of several chapels and monasteries. On the south side, churches and monasteries belonging to the Armenian and Greek Orthodox churches are adjoined to the masonry of the ancient basilica; at the northern end, it is abutted by the structures of the Franciscans.

About a quarter of the church's facade is covered by a fortresslike supporting wall that cradles the crumbling masonry as if to prevent it from falling down. The facade at one time was decorated with a colorful mosaic, which saved the church when, in the fateful year of 614, almost all sanctuaries in the Holy Land were destroyed by Persian invaders. How this happened is described in a letter from the Jerusalem Synod of the year 838: "When the Persians, after having sacked all the towns in Syria, reached Bethlehem, they were greatly surprised to discover a representation of the magi from Persia. Out of reverence and respect for their ancestors, they decided to honor these sages by sparing the church. And this is how it has survived until this day."[21]

When some 200 years later the country was overrun by the Islamic Arabs, the fate of the church appeared once more in the balance. But their leader Omar decided that the place where their prophet Issa (Jesus) had been born of the Virgin Mariam (Mary) deserved to be protected, and legend had it that he knelt down in the southern apse of the church to pray to Mecca.[22] The Mosque of Omar with its fine minaret that rises at the western end of the church plaza commemorates this gesture of the prophet Muhammad's immediate successor.

First impressions notwithstanding, the impregnable-looking church facade is of interest to the observant pilgrim. The original church had three entrances, two of which have been bricked up. The central and highest portal of Justinian's church was lowered during the Middle Ages; the resulting pointed arch is still visible today. During the Ottoman era, this arch was further reduced, leaving the present low and narrow opening that can be passed only when the visitor bends his head and knees. It is as if it wants to caution him: "Lower yourself, you proud one, if you want to approach God, who for your sake came to us as a child."

[20] Cf. G. Kroll, *Auf den Spuren Jesu*, 11th ed. (Stuttgart: Katholisches Bibelwerk, 2002), 34–52.

[21] Baldi, 105, n. 2.

[22] Euthychius of Alexandria, *Viae regnorum* (Baldi, 105).

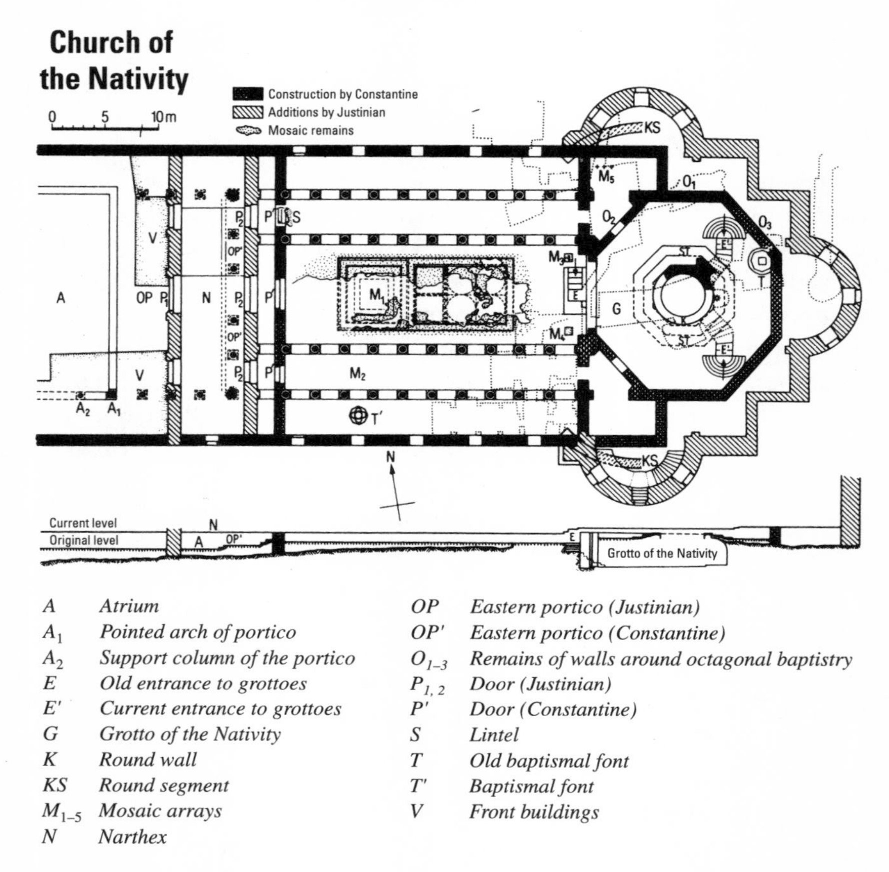

Illus. 4. Plan of the Church of the Nativity from the time of Constantine (A.D. 326) with the additions of Justinian (A.D. 530) according to the results of the 1933–1934 excavations (plan according to E. T. Richmond; L.-H. Vincent, O.P.; and B. Bagatti, O.F.M.) (from G. Kroll). Only the eastern part of the atrium is shown. The subterranean grottoes are indicated by dots, as are the retaining walls and porches (V) on the west facade; for the exact location of the grottoes, cf. illus. 5.

Immediately behind the entrance is a vestibule, the former narthex of Justinian's imposing church. The opposite door leads directly into the main body of the basilica. The interior, whose hallowed antiquity cannot but inspire the visitor with awe, is divided into a central nave and two side aisles. The stone for the numerous "golden-hued" supporting columns described by the Jerusalem patriarch Sophronius[23]

[23] *Anacreontica* 19 (PG 87/3:3811; Baldi, 97).

(580–638) was quarried in Bethlehem, where Justinian's architects also made the pillars for Jerusalem's greatest church dedicated to the Virgin Mary, the "Nea" (pp. 281–84).

The limestone columns that aroused the admiration of the patriarch were adorned during the Middle Ages with frescoes of the Apostles that unfortunately have faded almost completely. The clerestory windows below the elevated roof of the nave provide a bright illumination of the church interior. The remaining mosaics on the side walls and floor attest to the former splendor of this sanctuary. Since the removal of the decorated flat ceiling built by Justinian, the original pointed roof structure from the days of Emperor Constantine is once more visible.

From the year 326, the empress mother Helen zealously pursued the construction of the basilica at the site of the grotto. The place of the present sumptuous iconostasis (a decorated screen across the width of the sanctuary) originally contained an octagonal apsidal structure. Apparently, a baldachin supported by columns covered the grotto below, into which the pilgrims could probably look through a large circular opening. Justinian's architects replaced the polygonal choir area with the transept that characterizes the present edifice. They also facilitated access to the crypt by building two sets of stairs flanking the altar, which are still used by visitors.

On Christmas Day of the year 1100, the church was the scene of the festive coronation of the Crusader king Baldwin I. The Russian abbot Daniel, who visited the Church of the Nativity about that time (1106), describes it thus: "A large church in the form of a cross with a wooden roof rising above the Grotto of the Nativity. The roof is entirely covered with tin, and the interior is ornamented with pictures in mosaic. It has fifty monolithic marble columns and is paved with white slabs. There are three doors. Its length to the great altar is 50 *sagenes*, its width 20. Under the great altar is the Grotto of the Manger, where Christ's Nativity took place, forming a fine and spacious cavern." [24]

4. The Grotto of the Nativity

There are few places in the Holy Land more capable of arousing profound emotions within the pilgrim than the grotto in Bethlehem where,

[24] Baldi, 110.

one silent, mysterious night, some 2,000 years ago, the events took place that changed the course of world history. "Hic de Virgine Maria Jesus Christus natus est"—"Here Jesus Christ was born to the Virgin Mary", reads the inscription on the fourteen-pointed silver star embedded in the white marble on the spot where Jesus entered the world. No one can ever forget this place after seeing it. This is the origin of all the portrayals of Christmas and all the manger scenes found in Christian families.

Another corner of the grotto, down three steps and opposite the Altar of the Nativity, contains the manger. Hewn out of the living rock, its sides were already in the time of Jerome faced with marble.[25] Stone troughs for feeding animals are quite common in this part of the world, even today.[26] The pilgrim, on contemplating the manger, will no doubt be reminded of the words the angel spoke to the shepherds: "For to you is born this day in the City of David a Savior, who is Christ the Lord. And this will be a sign for you: you will find a babe wrapped in swaddling cloths and lying in a manger" (Lk 2:11–12). An old Eastern liturgy says: "In this place heavenly love became manifest in our world. Hope was reborn, and peace embraced the earth."

5. Three Times Christmas in Bethlehem

As each Christian church tends to cling to its own ancient traditions, it is not so surprising that many of the denominations represented in the Holy Land also follow their own religious calendar. The Catholics and other Western churches celebrate the birth of the Savior on the night before the twenty-fifth of December. The Latin patriarch is welcomed by the citizens of Bethlehem and conducted in festive procession to the Church of Saint Catherine. The festivities include caroling by choirs from many countries. The bells ring out, and the Christmas message is broadcast by radio throughout the Western world. The midnight celebrations reach their climax when, amid the rejoicing of the congregation, the patriarch carries an image of the Christ child to the manger in the crypt below the Church of Saint Catherine. The Greek Orthodox and other Eastern churches celebrate the Nativity thirteen days later, on January 7, as they still follow the old Julian calendar.

[25] *Homilia de Nativitate Domini* (Baldi, 91).

[26] Cf. R. Riesner, "Krippe", in *GBL*, 2nd ed. (1990), 2:847.

This colorful ceremony is celebrated in the festively decorated Church of the Nativity. The Armenian Christmas celebrations are held, according to an ancient Eastern tradition, on Epiphany, January 6 of the Gregorian calendar, which corresponds with January 19 of the Eastern calendar. Their patriarch, too, is officially received in Bethlehem, and during the subsequent celebrations the much-tried Armenian people commemorate the appearance of God's Son at his birth, and his subsequent baptism in the river Jordan. Such is the perennial, mystifyingly magnetic attraction of this small town in the Judean Mountains on the hearts and minds of Christians from every region and tradition.

6. *The Adjacent Grottoes*

In A.D. 386, the Dalmatian priest Jerome arrived in the small town of Bethlehem from Rome. He secluded himself in a cave near the Grotto of the Nativity (illus. 5) to study the Bible and try to understand its deeper meanings. In Rome, his strenuous activities as secretary to Pope Damasus had left him no time to pursue his scholastic ambitions. However, even there a circle of pious noblewomen had formed around him, who desired to strengthen the foundations of their belief biblically. One of these, a patrician lady called Paula, and her daughter Eustochium, followed Jerome to Bethlehem, where they founded a convent near the Cave of the Nativity.

Jerome, who had been taught Hebrew by one of the remaining Jewish Christians,[27] now began to translate the Bible from the original text into common Latin. The outcome of his work, the famous Vulgate ("common", "popular"), would form the official Bible of the Roman Catholic Church for the next fifteen hundred years. Employing his extensive biblical knowledge, Jerome also wrote numerous commentaries. He and the two Roman noblewomen were utterly devoted to Bethlehem. Upon her arrival in Bethlehem, Paula had said: "Yes, this will be my resting place; since the Redeemer himself has chosen this as his residence, this is where I too want to stay."[28] Her wish was carried out, and the graves of Saint Paula and her daughter, as well as that of Saint Jerome himself, can be found in the same crypt, close by

[27] Cf. I. GREGO, *I Giudeo-Cristiani nel IV secolo* (Jerusalem: Franciscan Printing Press, 1982), 193.

[28] *Letter 108* 10 (PL 22:884; Baldi, 90). Cf. H. DONNER, *Pilgerfahrt ins Heilige Land* (Stuttgart: Katholisches Bibelwerk, 1979), 156–58.

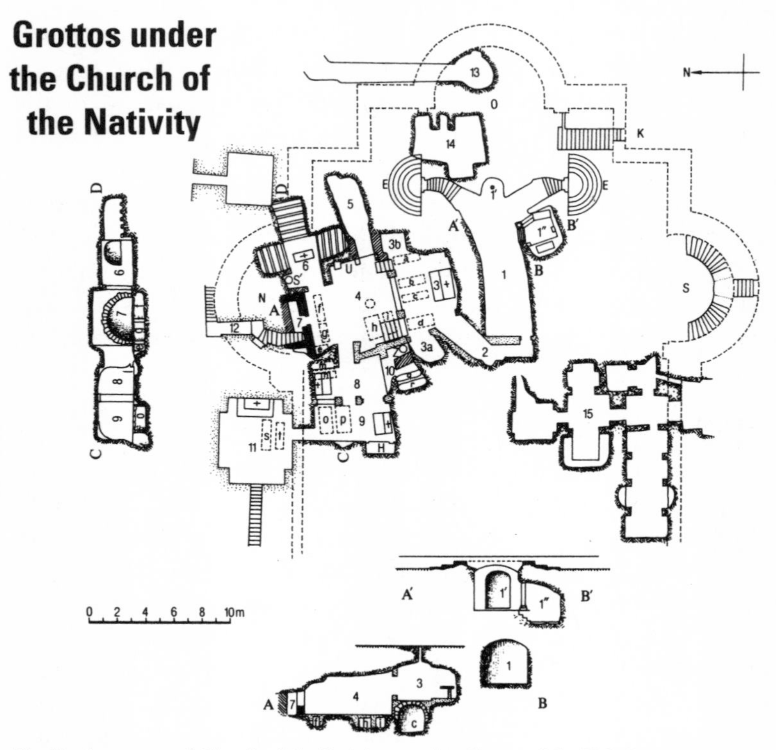

N *Northern apse of Church of the Nativity*
O *Eastern apse*
S *Southern apse*
E *Steps to the grotto*
K *Greek Orthodox chapel*
Z *Well*
1 *Grotto of the Nativity*
1' *Altar*
1'' *Grotto of the manger*
2 *12th century entrance*
3 *Altar of St. Joseph with rock tombs (a–d) in the floor*
3a *Arcosolia*
3b *Arcosolia*
4 *Large grotto with original entrance (u) and five underground graves (e–i)*
5 *Grotto of the Holy Innocents*
6 *Grotto with arcosolia and altar of the Holy Innocents*
7 *Pre-Constantinian arch and Constantinian foundation*
8 *Grotto of saints Eusebius, Paula and Eustochium*
9 *Grotto of St. Jerome with cenotaph (H) and two underground rock tombs (o, p)*
10 *Well (2) with two rock tombs (q, r)*
11 *Cell of St. Jerome with two graves under the floor (s, t)*
12 *15th century entrance*
13 *Grotto with water reservoir*
14 *Cistern of the Wise Men*
15 *Grotto with tombs*

Illus. 5. The grottoes underneath the Church of the Nativity (according to B. Bagatti, O.F.M.) (from G. Kroll). The illustration shows (1) the position of the Grotto of the Nativity and the adjacent grottoes in relation to the floor plan of the Church of the Nativity, (2) the double cross section A–B, A'–B', and (3) the lengthwise cross section C–D. The explanations apply to the adjacent grottoes only.

the Grotto of the Nativity. The Grotto of Jerome is reached by way of a staircase descending inside the Church of Saint Catherine.

The Church of Saint Catherine, also called "Ecclesia ad Praesepe" ("the church by the manger"), was expanded by the Franciscans in 1888. In the course of the accompanying excavations, remains of Crusader buildings were discovered, which were incorporated into the new structure. In 1852 Napoleon III, who considered himself successor to the French Crusader king Louis IX of France, canonized as Saint Louis, had declared the Church of the Nativity French property. This had embroiled him in a dispute with Russia, which espoused the rights of the Eastern Orthodox churches; the resulting conflict became one of the causes of the Crimean War. Although Napoleon was still unable to enforce his claim to the Church of the Nativity, he succeeded, however, in the case of the adjoining Church of Saint Catherine.

In 1975 this church underwent another renovation with great attention to aesthetic detail. Several years earlier (1962–1964) the Cave of Saint Jerome and the adjacent Cave of the Holy Innocents had been similarly restored. An archaeological survey undertaken during the restoration revealed that these caves were already in pre-Byzantine days a choice place for the burial of Christians, because of their location near the Grotto of the Nativity on the north side.[29] One of these, the Cave of the Holy Innocents, was named in memory of the children of Bethlehem who fell victim to Herod's paranoid fear and cruelty (Mt 2:16–18). There is no suggestion, however, that these children were ever buried here; the proximity of Jesus' birthplace may be considered sufficient justification for a memorial at this site. The burial caves found there appear to have once belonged to a large network of grottoes, of which the Grotto of the Nativity in its present situation was only a part. The discovery during the excavations of traces of an entrance with a threshold confirms an earlier theory that these caves on the north side formed the original entrance to the Grotto of the Nativity.

The main altar in this impressively illuminated complex is devoted to Joseph, who raised Jesus. He had selected this place for the birth of the Messiah. It was here that he is said to have had the dream that caused his decision to flee to Egypt in order to safeguard the Child that had been entrusted to his care. "Now when they [the magi] had departed, behold, an angel of the Lord appeared to Joseph in a dream

[29] Cf. B. Bagatti, "Recenti scavi a Betlemme", *SBFLA* 18 (1968): 181–237.

and said, 'Rise, take the child and his mother, and flee to Egypt, and remain there till I tell you; for Herod is about to search for the child, to destroy him.' And he rose and took the child and his mother by night, and departed to Egypt, and remained there until the death of Herod" (Mt 2:13–15).

III. Christian Zion and Bethlehem

Few biblical places other than Jerusalem have exercised such a powerful attraction for the faithful as has this small town in the Judean Hills. Jews know it as the town where the matriarch Rachel is buried and as the ancestral town of Ruth and King David. The name "Bethlehem" pulls on the tenderest heartstrings of Christians. Every year for 2,000 years, great numbers of pilgrims have traveled to Bethlehem. Anyone who has visited Jerusalem will also have seen Bethlehem. Ever since the earliest Christian times, close ties have existed between these two places.

Instrumental in this was another message of the prophet Micah: "And you, O tower of the flock [מִגְדַּל עֵדֶר (*migdal eder*)], hill of the daughter of Zion [עֹפֶל בַּת צִיּוֹן (*ophel bath-ziyyon*)], to you shall it come, the former dominion shall come, the kingdom of the daughter of Jerusalem" (Mic 4:8). The Davidic blood relatives of Jesus, who led the Jewish Christian church from Mount Zion in the first century A.D.,[30] recalled this prophetic word with joy (pp. 389–90). Both the Jewish Christian historian Hegesippos (ca. A.D. 160; see Eusebius, *HE* 2.23.7) and Epiphanius, the bishop of Salamis (ca. 370),[31] inform us that Jesus' brother James was given the honorary title of "Oblias" (Ωβλίας), "because the prophet had foretold him as such".[32] Such Davidic exuberance also sounds forth from the praise of Zechariah in the so-called *Benedictus*: God "has raised up a horn of salvation for us in the house of his servant David" (Lk 1:69). With these words, the father of John the Baptist praised the God of Israel, who fulfills his promises. In the primitive church on Zion, this *Benedictus* was probably sung as a hymn (p. 407). The old prophecy of Micah was therefore believed to have been fulfilled in the Davidics Jesus, James and Simeon Bar Cleopas.

[30] Cf. chapter 25, "The Apostolic Synagogue on Zion" (pp. 319–59).

[31] *Panarion* 78.7.7 (GCS 37:457; Klijn-Reinink, 196).

[32] Cf. chapter 28, "James the Lord's 'Brother'" (pp. 380–93), as well as pp. 403–4.

The other place in Micah's prophecy, the Tower of the Flock, was, according to Jerome,[33] situated in the fields a short distance east of Bethlehem (illus. 3),[34] on the spot where the shepherds had been the first to receive news of the birth of the Messiah (Lk 2:8–18) and where Jacob was believed to have put up his tent (Gen 35:21). An echo of those close links between Zion and Bethlehem sounds in the following lines, a greeting to Bethlehem, composed around the year A.D. 420 by the Jerusalem priest Hesychius:

From Zion I greet thee, Bethlehem;
In the daughter I see thee, the mother.

In you a guiding star lit up,
And in this city a multitude of fiery tongues.

The star guided the magi,
The tongues illuminated Parthians and Medes
And all other nations with their redeeming light.

Through you the bread was leavened,
But Zion prepared the meal.

Your manger nourished the lamb,
But Zion led it to the altar.

You wrapped Jesus in swaddling clothes,
But in Zion he bared to Thomas his breast.

You sheltered the virgin womb
Which conceived, yet knew no man,
But here is a bridal chamber,
Which admitted the groom through locked doors.[35]

[33] *Letter 108* 10 (PL 22:884; Baldi, 90).

[34] Cf. R. Riesner, "Migdal-Eder", in *GBL*, 2nd ed. (1990), 2:977–78. At the Latin field of the shepherds, V. Corbo discovered among the ruins of a monastery (fourth to fifth centuries) some remains of a humble shepherd settlement stemming from Jesus' time (*Gli scavi di Kh. Siyar el-Ghanam (Campo dei Pastori) e i monasteri dei dintorni*, SBFMa 11 [Jerusalem, 1955]). In 1994 Frère Michel, O.F.M., uncovered an installation 50 m below these excavations, which might have to do with a ritual bath (*mikveh*).

[35] *Quaestiones in Jacobum fratrem Domini* (PG 93:1444; Baldi, 480–81).

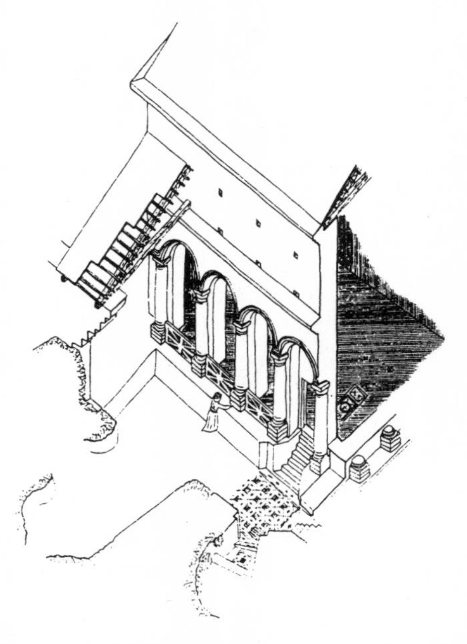

Illus. 6. A "synagogue church" in Nazareth from the fourth century (according to E. Alliata, O.F.M.). The woman in the scene is pointing at the location where the "Mary graffiti" were discovered (illus. 94).

2. Mary in the House of David

I. *The Temple Scroll and the Virgin Birth*

The authors of the first and third Gospels undoubtedly believed in the virgin birth of Jesus. In this event, they found confirmation of the preexistence of the Son of God. Both Matthew and Luke had access to haggadic traditions from sources near the *desposynoi*, i.e., the circle of Jesus' extended family. Matthew may have found such circles in the area of southern Syria (Cochaba in Batanea) (see below). Luke, on the other hand, whose exact knowledge of the topography of Jerusalem and its surroundings can hardly be explained other than by a personal visit to the sacred city, found there in the family circle of Simeon Bar Cleopas, the second bishop of the original church, and Jesus' cousins, the sources for his story of Jesus' childhood and youth.[1]

Religious life in Judaism at the turning point in history was determined by the various Torah schools, the most important ones being those of the Pharisees, the Sadducees and the Essenes. The most influential group politically was that of the Sadducees. Most of them came from the priestly aristocracy. They were attached particularly to the temple cult and considered only the five books of Moses to be binding as the Word of God. They also rejected the belief in a divine righteousness that balances out everything through the resurrection of the dead (cf. Acts 23:8). According to them, God already rewards the just in this life (*Ant.* 18.16–15).

The strict opponents of the Sadducees were the Essenes. The original core of this extremely devout movement consisted of a group of priests under the leadership of the "Teacher of Righteousness" that had left the temple service and withdrawn into the desert around the middle of the second century B.C. They viewed the Hasmonaean high

[1] Cf. chapter 31, "Simeon Bar Cleopas, Second Bishop of Jerusalem" (pp. 408–14), and chapter 33, "Luke and Jerusalem" (pp. 423–32).

priests, whom the Jews had declared the kingly line following the Maccabean revolt (167–164 B.C.; cf. 1 Mac 14:35), as usurpers and their sacrifices in the temple as illegitimate. For cleansing from guilt, the Essenes therefore no longer used the offering of sacrifice but rather ablutions in ritual baths that can still be found in great numbers at the sites of their settlements.

The third and most important Torah school was that of the Pharisees. Like the Essenes, they originally belonged to the Chassidic movement (cf. 1 Mac 2:42), from which they separated in order to develop their own *halakha*, i.e., "way (of the Torah)". From this the name "the separate ones" (פְּרוּשִׁים [*perushim*]) arose, which in Greek became Φαρισαῖοι, "Pharisees". They claimed that their "tradition of the elders" (Mk 7:3) went all the way back to Moses. They were especially zealous in erecting a "fence" around the Torah, as the Mishna (*Aboth* 1:1) puts it. They considered the writings of the prophets to be the Word of God, and they believed in the resurrection of the dead at the end of time (cf. Acts 23:6). Their most famous teachers were the gentle and wise Hillel and the strict Shammai. The Pharisees earned for themselves great merits by strengthening the Jewish self-identity, especially in Galilee, where the population consisted largely of those who, due to the Hasmoneans' policy of forced Judaizing, were second- or third-generation Jews or who had entered the land as immigrants from the Diaspora (pp. 170–71).

What, then, was the religious background of Jesus' family? Luke has handed down to us a saying of Mary that may point to an informative means of answering this question. To the angel's message, "You will conceive in your womb and bear a son" (Lk 1:31), Mary replied, "How can this be, since I have no husband?" (Lk 1:34). The difficulty that Mary mentions sounds strange because it was said a few verses earlier that she was "betrothed to a man" (Lk 1:27). Mary could have easily understood the angel to mean: As soon as you consummate the marriage, you will conceive a son. However, Mary appears not to have seen this as the solution. What justified the raising of such a problem by this betrothed virgin? Had she taken a vow of chastity as the Church tradition has claimed since the time of Gregory of Nyssa[2] and Augustine?[3]

For anyone familiar with modern Judaism, this view appears to be all but impossible. The only surviving form of New Testament Judaism

[2] *In diem natalem Christi* (PG 46:1140ff.).

[3] *De sacra virginitate* 4 (PL 40:398); *Sermo* 291 5 (PL 38:1318).

was Pharisaism. The rabbis succeeded in preserving the essential parts of the traditions of their faith, although Christianity and Islam were growing ever stronger. Today just as then,[4] believers were to fulfill the *mitzvah*, i.e., command and duty that God had given the first human beings to "be fruitful and multiply, and fill the earth and subdue it" (Gen 1:28). Orthodox Jews everywhere are anxious to ensure that the possibility of following this command exists for all their family members in marriage. If any man or woman has remained without a spouse, there is no lack of persons who will not try everything in order to effect a union. In a context influenced by Pharisaic views, Mary's question seems astonishing and incomprehensible.

However, this was not the only Jewish view of marriage in Jesus' day. The Sadducees, who denied the authority of the prophets as well as the belief in a future resurrection of the dead, would probably have had a teaching similar to that of the Pharisees with respect to the command to reproduce (cf. Mk 12:18–27), but the pious from Essenism thought differently. Although their influence on the people was not as strong as that of the Pharisees, there were Essene groups in most of the towns and villages, according to Philo and Flavius Josephus (p. 195). There were celibate Essene monks living in monastic communities such as Qumran or on Mount Zion in Jerusalem.[5] At other locations, however, there were communities of married Essenes who upheld marital abstinence as a religious ideal, whereby sexual intercourse served only the purpose of reproduction (*War* 2:160–61).

What was previously known from ancient writers about the Essenes has been confirmed and supplemented by the scrolls discovered in the caves at Qumran. In the longest scroll from Cave 11, the so-called Temple Scroll, which was published only later, there is a passage (11QTemple 53:16—54:3) that sheds new light on Mary's situation, as she summed it up in the question: "How can this be, since I have no husband?" (Lk 1:34). Most of the scroll has to do with instructions for the construction of the temple and the ordering of its services. The laws, all of which are formulated as direct speech from God, are apparently intended to fill a gap in the legislation of the Pentateuch. Located at the end of the scroll are also general stipulations of the law.

[4] Cf. H. L. Strack and P. Billerbeck, *Kommentar zum Neuen Testament aus Talmud und Midrasch*, vol. 2 (Munich: C. H. Beck, 1924), 372–73.

[5] Cf. chapter 15, "The Essene Quarter in Jerusalem" (pp. 192–219), and chapter 32, "The Jerusalem Essenes, Barnabas and the Letter to the Hebrews" (pp. 415–22).

An explanation of the instructions for the vows in Numbers 30:4–9 is offered here:

> A woman who makes me a vow or binds herself with a formal pledge [17] in the house of her father, with an oath, in her youth, and her father hears the vow or [18] the formal pledge with which she bound herself and her father says nothing about it, [19] all her vows will remain in force and all the pledges with which she bound herself will stay in force. [*Blank*] But if [20] her father forbids her on the day when he heard her, all her vows and all her pledges [21] with which she bound herself formally will not remain in force; and I shall pardon her because he forbade her.

After a lacuna in the text, it is stated with reference to a married woman [16–21] concerning "every oath [to do penance]" that "her husband may sanction [it] or her husband may revoke it the day he hears it; and I shall pardon her." [6] Is it possible that both cases applied to Mary? Do we know anything about Mary's childhood and family background?

II. *The House of David: Exile and Return*

The descent of Jesus from Davidic lineage receives such strong testimony in the Gospels and other early Christian writings that it has to qualify as a fact and cannot simply be brushed aside as a *theologumenon* ("theological statement"). With this expression, many modern theologians intend to say that the evangelists, who were convinced that Jesus was the Messiah, wanted to support this via the artificial construction of his Davidic genealogy. Even older than the witness of the Gospels is that of Paul in the Letter to the Romans from the year A.D. 57. He views himself as an Apostle "set apart for the gospel of God which he promised beforehand through his prophets in the holy Scriptures, the gospel concerning his Son, who was descended from David according to the flesh" (Rom 1:1–3). Outside the New Testament, we have the testimony of Hegesippos (ca. A.D. 160), who reports that under Vespasian, Domitian and Trajan, many relatives of Jesus were persecuted and executed because they were descendants of David (see Eusebius, *HE* 3.12, 19; 32:4).

[6] Text from F. García Martínez, *The Dead Sea Scrolls Translated*, 2nd ed. (Leiden: Brill; Grand Rapids, Mich.: Eerdmans, 1996). Conjectured reconstructions are enclosed in square brackets.

The Davidic dynasty reigned in Jerusalem until 586 B.C. This reign met with a sudden end when, in the year that Jerusalem was destroyed, the members of the royal household along with the aristocratic part of the population were carried off to Babylon (2 Kings 24–25). Furthermore, we learn that around 520 B.C. the Davidic Zerubbabel was released from Babylonian captivity and that the construction of the temple in Jerusalem was begun under his leadership (Ezra 2:2; 3:2; 5:2). In the writings of the prophets of that time, Haggai and Zechariah, the hope shines through that the House of David soon will regain its position of power (Hag 2:20–23; Zech 6:12–13). It may well be that such newly emerging messianic hopes reached the ears of the Persian rulers and that Zerubbabel was called back to Babylon. According to some scholars, this would come closest to explaining his sudden disappearance from Jerusalem.[7] That part of the House of David remained in Babylon can be seen from the fact that Davidics are again found among the group that returned with Ezra to Jerusalem half a century later (about 457 B.C.). Ezra mentions in his book that "of the sons of David, Hattush, of the sons of Shecaniah" had returned to Jerusalem (Ezra 8:2–3). Thus, it may be correctly assumed that many Davidic families had remained behind in the Babylonian Diaspora. It is reported in the Talmudic literature that the famous Rabbi Hillel and Rabbi Chijja were related to descendents of David.[8] It is also claimed for the later exilarchs in Babylon that they descended from the House of David.[9]

The New Testament bears witness that Joseph of Nazareth came from the House of David (Mt 1:20; Lk 1:27). Some things indicate that Mary was also of Davidic lineage. The word of the angel that God would give to Mary's son, not begotten by any man, "the throne of his father David" (Lk 1:32) has always been understood to mean that Mary was also a Davidic.[10] Her kinship with Elizabeth, who belonged to an Aaronic priestly family (Lk 1:36), need not conflict with this. Mary could have been of royal as well as of priestly descent. Indeed, the apocryphal Protoevangelium of James calls her a daughter

[7] Cf. A. VAN DEN BORN, "Zerubbabel", in H. HAAG, *Bibel-Lexikon*, 3rd ed. (Zurich: Benziger, 1982), 927.

[8] Babylonian Talmud, *Ket.* 62b; Jerusalem Talmud, *Taan.* 4:2 (68a).

[9] Jerusalem Talmud, *Kil.* 9:4 (32b); Babylonian Talmud, *Hor.* 11b.

[10] Cf. J. MASSON, *Jésus fils de David dans les généalogies de Saint Matthieu et de Saint Luc* (Paris, 1982), 558.

of David.[11] Ignatius of Antioch[12] at the beginning of the second century and the apologist Justin[13] in the middle of the second century were of the same opinion. Through the marriage to the Davidic Joseph, Mary's son became a full descendant of the royal family.

III. Jesus, the Nazorean

We learn from the Gospels that the family of Joseph lived in Nazareth and that Jesus had the epithet "the Nazorean" (ὁ Ναζωραῖος [but RSV: Nazarene]). According to Luke, Jesus' parents already lived in Nazareth before his birth (Lk 2:4–5), while according to Matthew they first came there after the return from Egypt (Mt 2:19–23). The reason given by the evangelist for the choice of Nazareth as a place of residence sounds almost mysterious, i.e., "that what was spoken by the prophets might be fulfilled. 'He shall be called a Nazorean.'" (Mt 2:23). There has been much guessing at which prophetic word Matthew intended and how it could be connected with Nazareth. Here, the great theologian of the Church, Jerome (349–419), comes to our aid. He mentions in his commentary on the prophet Isaiah that among the Jews who believed in Jesus it was a tradition that the prophecy referred to was in Isaiah 11:1.[14] A "branch", in Hebrew *nezer* (נֵצֶר), is spoken of there, the "branch" from the stump of Jesse whose son was King David. Therefore, the title "Nazorean" does not refer so much to the hometown of Jesus as to his Davidic lineage.

This is how it was understood by the blind beggar on the side of the road to Jericho when someone told him that "Jesus the Nazorean" (Lk 18:38; but see Mk 10:47 [ὁ Ναζαρηνός; Nazarene]) was passing by. His spontaneous reaction was to shout, "Jesus, Son of David, have mercy on me!" (Lk 18:38 and parallels). Hardly anyone could have assumed that the prophecy intended to say anything about the insignificant little village in Galilee. The excavations of the last few decades have revealed that the Nazareth in which Jesus lived had scarcely more than 100 or 150 inhabitants.[15] In those days, this hamlet off the main roads in the hills of Lower Galilee (illus. 12) was more closely associated

[11] *Prot. Jas.* 10:1 (Hennecke-Schneemelcher, 1:342).

[12] *Eph.* 18:2 (PG 5:752).

[13] *Dialogue with Trypho* 45.4 (PG 6:572–73).

[14] *Commentaria in Isaiam* 4 (Is 11:1–3) (PL 24:147ff.; Klijn-Reinink, 222).

[15] Cf. R. Riesner, "Nazareth", in *GBL*, 2nd ed. (1990), 2:1031–37.

with the district of Japhia, a large village located not quite a mile away. According to Josephus (*Life* 230; *War* 3.289ff.), Japhia had played an important role as a strongly fortified town in the great war against the Romans (A.D. 66–70). By comparison, Nazareth was so insignificant (illus. 97) that it is nowhere mentioned in the ancient sources outside the New Testament, neither in the Old Testament nor in Jewish writings.

However, the fragment of a marble tablet from the third century A.D. with a Hebrew inscription was found in 1962 at seaside in Caesarea. It originally contained a list of priestly families that had settled in Galilee during the late Roman period.[16] It also happens to mention a family residing in Nazareth. The discovery was important because it solved an old dispute. It had not been clear from the Greek orthography (Ναζαρέτ[θ], or the variant Ναζαρά) whether "Nazareth" in Hebrew was written with *zade* (צ) or with *zayin* (ז). The clear צ in the inscription supports the connection of the name with *nezer*, "branch". At the same time, another proposal was made invalid, i.e., that the epithet "Nazorean" perhaps had to do with "nazarite" (נָזִיר, Νασιραῖος), someone devoted to God who abstained from every kind of intoxicating drink and did not cut his hair (Judg 13:5, 7).

Therefore, Jesus "the Nazorean" primarily indicates not that Jesus came from Nazareth but that he belonged to the Davidic lineage of the Nazoreans. The word of the prophet is supposed to point to him as the *nezer*-branch from the family of David. However, is it possible for the term to refer to an entire family? We now know from the writings discovered in the caves at Qumran that this was actually the case in those days. From the hymns that are attributed to the founder of the Qumran Essenes, we see that he terms his Essenic group several times as the "branch of divine planting" (1QH 6:15; 8:6, 13). The Davidic clan from which Jesus came will probably have thought in a similar manner. The term "Nazorean", which later was reserved for those who believed in Jesus and for the Lord's "brother" James,[17] was finally extended by the Jews to all who belonged to this new faith (Acts 24:5). The Jews today call Christians *Nozrim* (נוֹצְרִים), and the popular term for Christians among the Arabs is *Nassara*.

[16] Cf. G. Kroll, *Auf den Spuren Jesu*, 11th ed. (Stuttgart: Katholisches Bibelwerk, 2002), 82–83.

[17] Cf. chapter 28, "James the Lord's 'Brother'" (pp. 380–93, esp. pp. 382–84).

IV. The Resettlement of Nazareth

Therefore, one can assume with some degree of certainty that Nazara/Nazareth ("little *nezer*") got its name from a Davidic clan that presumably had arrived from Babylon toward the end of the second century B.C. Many other examples of the transfer of the name of a tribe or clan to a place could be added, such as Dan from the tribe Dan (Judg 18:29), Shomron/Samaria from the clan of Shomer (1 Kings 16:24), Jebus/Jerusalem from the Jebusites (1 Chron 11:4), Manda north of Nazareth probably from the clan of the Mandaeans (p. 172), et cetera. What the original name of the village of Nazareth in the region of Zebulon may have been, we do not know. The old settlement, which had existed since the Bronze Age, was apparently abandoned around the year 733 B.C. At that time, the Assyrian conqueror Tiglath-pileser III invaded Galilee, led most of the Israelites into exile in Assyria (2 Kings 15:29) and created the Assyrian province Megiddo. Galilee had become a land of pagans. The prophet Isaiah lamented this paganizing of the old tribal territories: "In the former time he brought into contempt the land of Zebulun and the land of Naphtali" (Is 9:1). Isaiah speaks of the "*galil* [גָּלִל (i.e., circle)] of the nations" (Is 9:1), but looking into the future, he sees that one day the people will "have seen a great light" (Is 9:2; cf. Mt 4:12–16).

At the beginning of the Maccabean period in the middle of the second century B.C., we find only isolated Jewish groups in Galilee (1 Mac 5:9ff.). This changed drastically with the conquest of the country by the Hasmonean Hyrcanus (134–104 B.C.). He and his successor Alexander Jannaeus gave the inhabitants the choice of either converting to Judaism by being circumcised or of leaving the country (*Ant.* 12.393ff.). At the same time, a strong migration of Jews returning from Babylon and Persia began. Since the results of the excavations in Nazareth suggest that that settlement was interrupted in the Persian and early Hellenistic periods, one may presume that the interruption was ended when a group of the Davidic Nazorean clan resettled the abandoned village in the Maccabean period, probably as a group just returned from Babylonian exile. Because the descendants of David in Nazareth were made up not only of members of Jesus' family but also of other Davidic relatives (Mk 6:3–4 [συγγενεῖς]), and in view of such a small population, it can be assumed that most of the Nazarenes belonged to the same extended family, i.e., to the Nazorean clan.

The writer Julius Africanus, who himself came from Palestine (p. 173), can report at the end of the second century A.D. that the blood relations of Jesus (δεσποσύνοι) in the villages of Cochaba and Nazara (Nazareth) had preserved the Davidic genealogies (see Eusebius, *HE* 1:7.14). This geographic distribution of the Davidics had apparently already transpired prior to the beginning of our era. It is known that families of priestly and royal backgrounds placed a high premium on their genealogies,[18] the former because the validity of their priestly office depended upon them, and the latter because the messianic promises were connected with them. Cochaba was a village located in Batanea, the Old Testament Bashan,[19] an area of Jewish settlements east of the Sea of Galilee (illus. 42), in whose vicinity, according to Josephus, there was a road leading from Babylon to Jerusalem that was used by pilgrims (*Ant.* 17.26).

When the news of the rebuilding of an independent Jewish state reached Babylon, many Jewish families pulled up roots and headed back to the old homeland. Our Davidic clan of the Nazoreans was among them. One can also surmise that some of the Nazorean repatriates first settled in Batanea, as did many other exile groups.[20] They may have founded Cochaba ("village of the star"; cf. Num 24:17 [כּוֹכָב]) in this ancient Israelite region at that time. A part of this clan belonging to the tribe of Judah could have later sought a new home in Galilee in the tribal territory of Zebulon and given their settlement the name Nazara ("village of the branch") from the Hebrew *nezer*. If my interpretation of the Copper Scroll from Qumran (3Q15 8:1—10:4) is correct, various Essene groups appear to have settled in Batanea at that time.[21] Under Herod the Great, the territory was exempted from taxation, and with the newly immigrated "Babylonian Jews", it possessed well-prepared troops for the defense of the pilgrims' road (*Ant.* 17.23–28). It is possible that Essene thought in Batanea influenced the Davidic clan.

In Nazareth, as the report from the Pilgrim of Piacenza suggests,[22] there continued to be Jewish Christians on into the sixth century (pp. 378–79). They apparently still possessed two places of worship

[18] Cf. J. JEREMIAS, *Jerusalem zur Zeit Jesu*, 3rd ed. (Göttingen: Vandenhoeck und Ruprecht, 1962), 308–24.

[19] Cf. B. PIXNER and R. RIESNER, "Kochaba", in *GBL*, 2nd ed. (1990), 2:801–2.

[20] Cf. chapter 13, "Batanea as a Jewish Settlement Area" (pp. 169–76).

[21] Cf. B. PIXNER, "Unravelling the Copper Scroll Code: A Study on the Topography of 3Q15", *RQ* 11 (1983): 323–66 (at 350–53).

[22] *Travels from Piacenza* 5 (J. WILKINSON, *Jerusalem Pilgrims before the Crusades* [Jerusalem: Ariel, 1977], 79–80).

during the Byzantine period.[23] Beneath the Church of Saint Joseph, there are baptismal installations of symbolic significance, which stem from a Jewish ritual bath.[24] A synagogue church of the fourth century underneath the new basilica (illus. 6) was oriented toward the place of the annunciation to Mary (Lk 1:26–38).[25] The greeting of the angel, X[AIR]E MARIA, "Hail, Mary" (Lk 1:28), was found engraved into the base of a column (illus. 94).

Members of Jesus' extended family continued to live in Nazareth at least into the third century. One of them, named Konon, who may be remembered in an inscription in the Church of the Annunciation, died as a martyr in Asia Minor during the persecution under the Roman emperor Decius (249–251).[26]

V. Bethesda and Kosiba

The early Christian traditions concerning the birth and childhood of Mary can be traced back to the so-called Protoevangelium of James. The date of origin is usually assumed to be the mid-second century. James, the brother of the Lord, to whom this work is attributed, was certainly not the author, but in view of the longevity of Eastern family traditions it is not impossible that some elements in it do in fact go back to traditions from the family of Jesus. The Protoevangelium is a narrative about the miraculous birth of Mary, the daughter of Joachim, a wealthy man, and his wife Anna; about Mary's growing up in the temple; and about her virginity, which was not violated by Joseph, a widower from the household of David (pp. 380–81), to whom she had been betrothed by the casting of lots. It also reports that the pious Joachim, who had been despised in the assembly of the sons of Israel because he had no children,

[23] For the excavations in Nazareth, cf. G. KROLL, *Auf den Spuren Jesu*, 11th ed. (Stuttgart: Katholisches Bibelwerk, 2002), 79–92, and R. RIESNER, "Nazarener/Nazareth", in *GBL*, 2nd ed. (1990), 2:1030–37; idem, "Nazarener/Nazareth", in M. GÖRG and B. LANG, *Neues Bibel-Lexikon*, vol. 2 (Solothurn and Düsseldorf: Benziger, 1995), 908–12. On the background of the tradition, cf. R. RIESNER, "Prägung und Herkunft der lukanischen Sonderüberlieferung", *Theologische Beiträge* 24 (1993): 228–48.

[24] J. BRIEND, *L'Église judéo-chrétienne de Nazareth*, 2nd ed. (Jerusalem: Franciscan Printing Press, 1975), 48–64.

[25] E. ALLIATA, "Il luogo dell'Annunziazione a Nazaret", in A. STRUS, *Maria nella sua terra* (Cremisan and Bethlehem, 1989), 25–33.

[26] Cf. B. BAGATTI, *Excavations in Nazareth*, vol. 1, SBFCMa 17 (Jerusalem: Franciscan Printing Press, 1969), 16, 198–99.

retreated in sadness to the wilderness.[27] He pitched his tent there and fasted and prayed forty days and forty nights. A tradition that becomes available for the first time in a Georgian lectionary from the fifth to sixth century claims that this place was in the wilderness of Judah in the Wadi Qelt in the grottoes of Kosiba (illus. 39).[28] A cloister with a sanctuary dedicated to Mary was constructed here around A.D. 470.[29] The place by the Greek Orthodox Saint George Monastery where Joachim prayed and petitioned God to give him a place among the sons of Israel by the birth of a child can still be viewed today. In New Testament times, Kosiba (הכוזבא) appears to have been inhabited by Essenes, for according to a reference in the Copper Scroll (3Q15 7:14–16), it was a place where treasures were kept buried during the war with Rome.[30] Could this also indicate that Mary's parents had ties with the Essenes?

Pointing in the same direction is the Jerusalem tradition that the house of Anna, the wife of Joachim, stood near the pool of Bethesda. John Damascene in the seventh century is the first to speak clearly of the house by the pool of Bethesda, where Mary was born.[31] According to Theodosius (530), there was already in his day a Church of Mary[32] there, and the apocryphal Jewish Christian Pseudo-Gospel of Matthew (fourth or fifth century) assumes that Anna had a home in the area of the temple.[33] After the excavations of the last few decades, there can no longer be any doubt that the pool of Bethesda mentioned in the fourth Gospel (Jn 5:2) was located on the property of the White Fathers north of the temple complex.[34] According to the Copper Scroll (3Q15 11:11–14), there were also various caches of Essene treasure located at Bethesda (בית אשדתין).[35] A residential structure near the pool is also mentioned (3Q15 12:1–3), which could be connected with Anna's living quarters. The Church of Saint Anne is

[27] *Prot. Jas.* 1:4; 4:2–4 (Hennecke-Schneemelcher, 1:340, 342).

[28] Cf. E. Testa, *Maria Terra Vergine*, vol. 2, *Il culto mariano palestinese (sec. I–IX)*, SBFCMa 31 (Jerusalem: Franciscan Printing Press, 1985), 6, n. 20.

[29] Cf. A. Strus, "Santuari Mariani in Palestina nel periodo Bizantino", in *Maria nella sua terra* (see n. 25), 35–66 (at 57–58).

[30] Cf. B. Pixner, "Unravelling the Copper Scroll Code" (see n. 21), 329–30.

[31] *Homilia* 1 (PG 96:670, 678; Baldi, 722).

[32] *The Topography of the Holy Land* 8 (J. Wilkinson, *Jerusalem Pilgrims* [see n. 22], 66); Geyer, 142; Baldi, 722.

[33] *Pseudo-Mt* 3 (Baldi, 721–22).

[34] Cf. R. Riesner, "Betesda", in *GBL*, 2nd ed. (1990), 1:194–95.

[35] Cf. Pixner, "Unravelling the Copper Scroll Code" (see n. 21), 356.

located today at Bethesda. It goes back to the Crusaders, who probably made use of an apparently older Byzantine tradition.[36] The story in the Protoevangelium about Mary, a child consecrated by her parents to the Lord, living in the temple area and working there for the glory of God,[37] had long been considered completely unhistorical prior to the work of the Israeli scholars D. Flusser and S. Safrai, who were able to show that such an institution had indeed existed in the temple.[38]

If Christ was born in the year 7 B.C.,[39] then the year of Mary's birth could have been 25 B.C. In 19 B.C. Herod the Great began to remodel the temple that the Davidic Zerubbabel had rebuilt 500 years earlier in order to turn it into a stately Hellenistic complex (*Ant.* 15.380ff.). Some of the more recent researchers believe that the ideal plan presented in the Temple Scroll from Qumran (11QTemple 30–46) played a pivotal role in the layout of this new structure. Today it is becoming clearer that Essene classes of priests participated in the work, since the construction of the inner sanctuary had to be carried out exclusively by priests (*Ant.* 15.390, 420–421).[40] This is very possible in view of the cessation of Essene opposition to the temple once the naming of a high priest from the family of Boethos ended the control by the illegitimate Hasmonean high priests. At the beginning of his reign, Herod had appointed Simon the Alexandrian, son of Boethos, as high priest and had married his daughter Mariamne (*Ant.* 15.320). According to our new archaeological discoveries, the Essene quarter on Jerusalem's southwest hill was founded in the early Herodian period, as well (pp. 203–5).

The temple service of the priest Zechariah (Lk 1:5–23), the father of John the Baptist, could have something to do with the reorganization of the temple services at that time. Where "in the wilderness" (ἐν τῇ ἐρήμῳ [Lk 1:80]) did the young son of Zechariah and Elizabeth go? He probably joined an ascetic group. The Baptist was influenced

[36] Cf. N. VAN DER VLIET, *Saint Marie où elle est née et la Piscine Probatique* (Paris and Jerusalem, 1938).

[37] *Prot. Jas.* 7–10 (Hennecke-Schneemelcher, 1:341–43).

[38] Information not published. Cf. now C. SAFRAI, *The Status and the Role of Women in the Second Temple of Jerusalem* (Berlin and New York: De Gruyter, 1996), and also F. MANNS, *Essais sur le judéo-christianisme*, Studium Biblicum Franciscanum: Analecta 12 (Jerusalem: Franciscan Printing Press, 1977), 106–14.

[39] Cf. A. STROBEL, *Der Stern von Bethlehem—ein Licht für unsere Zeit?* (Fürth: Flaccius, 1987).

[40] Cf. M. DELCOR, "Is the Temple Scroll a Source for the Herodian Temple?" in G.J. BROOKE, *Temple Scroll Studies* (Sheffield: Sheffield Academic Press, 1989), 67–89.

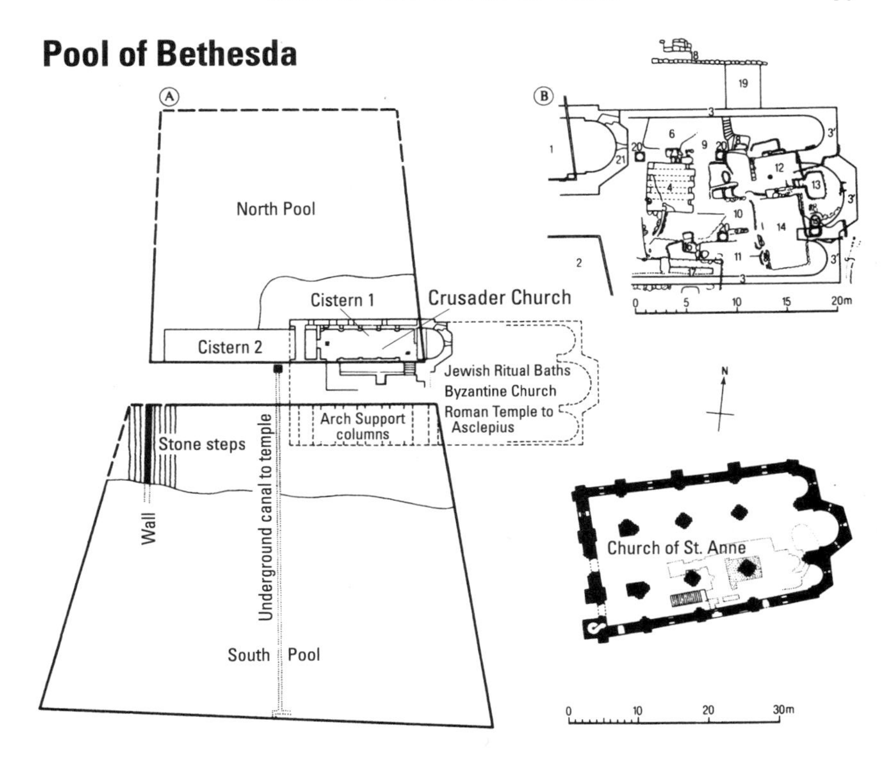

Illus. 7. The plan of the pool of Bethesda (according to J.-M. Rousée, O.P.) (from G. Kroll). Secondary drawing B:

1 North pool	*7, 8, 15, 16 Jewish ritual baths*
2 South pool	*9 Cisterns*
3 Walls of the Byzantine basilica	*10, 11, 12, 14 Underground chambers*
4 Original natural cave (later Roman temple of Asclepius)	*17, 18 Late Roman walls*
5 Entry canal	*19 Mosaic of the Byzantine Martyrion*
6 Further natural caves	*20 Column bases of the Byzantine basilica*

Under the Crusaders' Church of St. Anne (to the lower right), there is also a cave complex.

by the Essenes.[41] For this reason many researchers think of Qumran (pp. 193–94), or could it have been in Kosiba as well? This opens the door to further hypotheses. Of course, the new clues do not provide any security, but they do suggest that there are historical elements that lie hidden behind the stories of the Gospels.

[41] Cf. D. Flusser, *Jewish Sources in Early Christianity* (Jerusalem, 1993), 45–48.

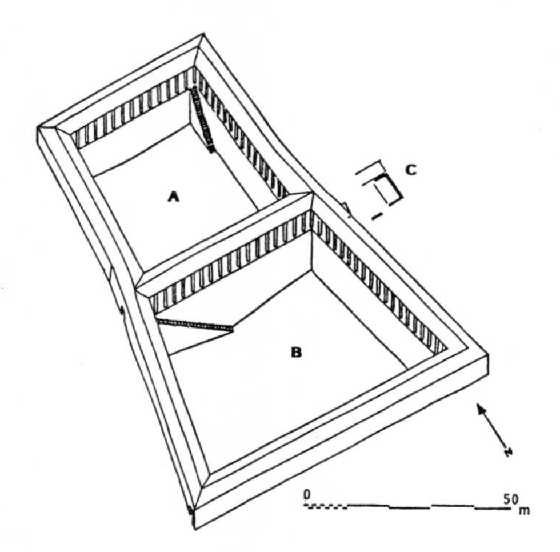

Illus. 8. The Sheep pool with its five colonnades in New Testament times.
A North pool
B South pool
C Jewish bath complex (Bethesda?)

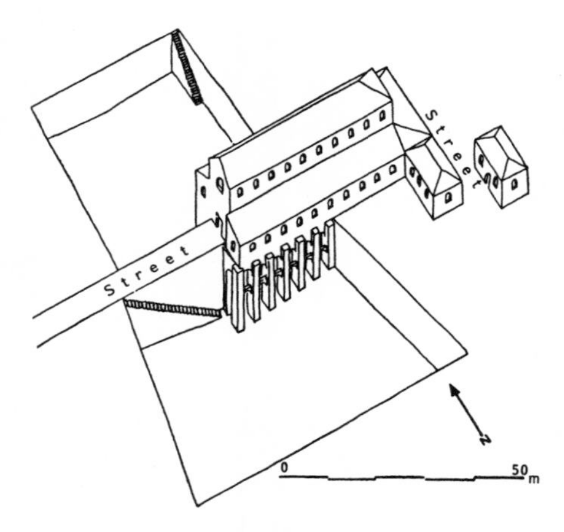

Illus. 9. Byzantine St. Mary basilica at the Probatica (Sheep pool).

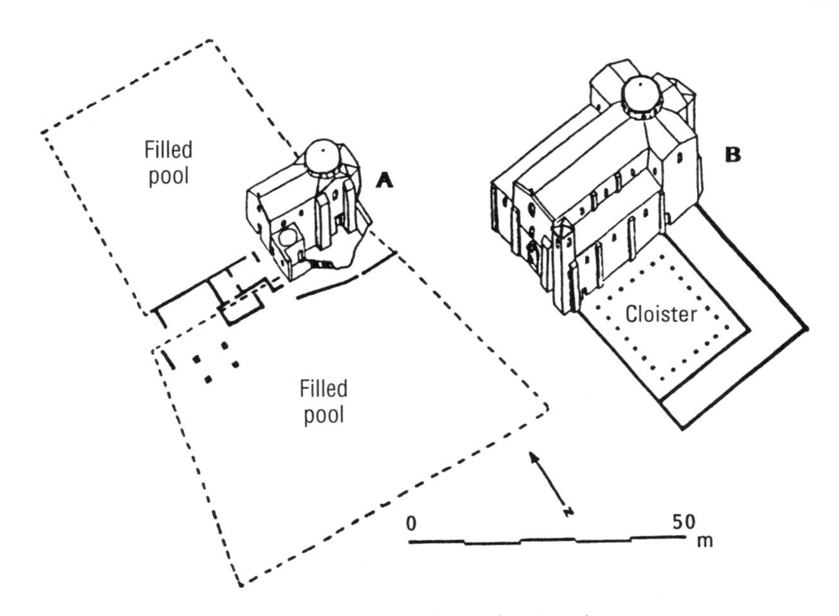

Illus. 10. Bethesda during the Crusades.
A Probatica Cloister
B Church of St. Anne

3. The Kathisma Church (Mary's Repose) Rediscovered

I. A Sensational Discovery

In the fall of 1992, a large bulldozer that was being used in the widening of the highway from Jerusalem to Bethlehem began to rip open the ground in an olive grove 170 m in front of the Mar Elias Monastery and suddenly found itself pushing up a Corinthian capital and several beautifully cut ashlars. That was the beginning of an archaeological discovery that brought to light something sensational. After I had noticed the construction work the year before, I had informed friends in the Israeli Department of Antiquities and also in the Greek Orthodox patriarchy to whom the property belonged that great care must be taken with this planned widening of the road, because an important old station for pilgrimages was suspected there. I had previously surveyed the surface and discovered stone mosaic tiles in various colors and several pieces of well-polished marble. Nearby is the mouth to the cistern of the Bir el-Kadismu. Through study of the pilgrim literature, I was convinced that the famous Kathisma Church must have been located near it[1] and not on the hill of the kibbutz Ramat Rachel to the northeast as had been believed since the investigations by A. M. Schneider and the excavations by Y. Aharoni (1954–1962).[2]

The bulldozer halted its destructive digging, and my friend V. Tsaferis, the responsible official from the Israeli Department of Antiquities, appointed the young archaeologist Rina Avner to search the site for remnants of antiquity in a so-called salvage excavation. What she found was far greater than I had expected. The foundations of a long-lost

[1] *The Glory of Bethlehem* (Jerusalem: Jerusalem Publishing House, 1981), 12–14.

[2] Cf. O. Keel and M. Küchler, *Orte und Landschaften der Bibel*, vol. 2, *Der Süden* (Zurich and Göttingen: Benziger and Vandenhoeck und Ruprecht, 1982), 602–5.

church were uncovered next to the sealed Bir el-Kadismu. So far, only part of the area could be excavated, i.e., the area that was foreseen for road construction. However, it was possible to see that the structure unearthed had been a very large, octagonally shaped church (illus. 11). The mosaics found on the floor of the church were approximately 70 cm below the surface. Some of them show geometric figures, others decorative images of plants. The remains of the walls were built with well-hewn stones. Later, the remains of the highly revered stone of the *Kathisma* (καθίσμα), the seat of Mary, were uncovered in the center of the church octagon.[3]

On December 30, 1992, the Greek Orthodox patriarch Diodoros in the company of his clergy together with the mayor of Jerusalem, Teddy Kollek, visited the excavations.[4] Both the ecclesiastical and the secular authorities considered the new finds to be very important. The patriarch announced that he wished to bear the costs for the entire excavation and restoration of the cloister portion of the Kathisma. The *Kathisma palaion* (the Old Seat), as he said, should again be a center for pilgrims as in times past.

II. Legends Surrounding Kathisma

Since ancient times, there had been on the way to Bethlehem, about halfway between Jerusalem and the Grotto of the Nativity, a cistern that offered tired travelers and shepherds with their flocks both water and a welcome rest. In the Christian era, it was surrounded by many pious legends.

1. An event was connected with this place that is mentioned in the Protoevangelium of James (17:1–3), which was written around the middle of the second century A.D. The Protoevangelium tells the following story about Mary and Joseph's trip to Bethlehem:[5]

> Now there went out a decree from the king Augustus that all (inhabitants) of Bethlehem in Judaea should be enrolled. And Joseph said: "I shall enroll my sons, but what shall I do with this child? How shall I enroll her? As my wife? I am ashamed to do that. Or as my daughter? But all the children of Israel know that she is not my daughter.

[3] Cf. R. Avner, "Jerusalem, Mar Elias", *ESI* 13 (1994): 89–92.

[4] Cf. H. Shapiro, "Ancient Church-Monastery Uncovered near Bethlehem", *Jerusalem Post*, January 9, 1993, international edition.

[5] On the question of whether Jesus was really born in Bethlehem, cf. chapter 1, "The Nazoreans, Bethlehem and the Birth of Jesus" (pp. 3–22).

> The day of the Lord himself will do as [t]he [Lord] wills." And he saddled his ass [his she-ass] and sat her on it; his son led it, and Samuel [Joseph] followed. And they drew near to the third mile(stone). And Joseph turned round and saw her sad, and said within himself: "Perhaps that which is within her is paining her." And again Joseph turned round and saw her laughing. And he said to her: "Mary, why is it that I see your face at one time laughing and at another sad?" And she said to him: "Joseph, I see with my eyes two peoples, one weeping and lamenting and one rejoicing and exulting." And they came half the way, and Mary said to him: "Joseph, take me down from the ass [from the she-ass], for the child within me presses me, to come forth." And he took her down there and said to her: "Where shall I take you and hide your shame? For the place is desert" [cf. Gen 25:23] [cf. Lk 2:34].[6]

Mary is supposed to have sat down on a stone that was shown to pilgrims near the cistern.[7] For this reason, the stone was called *Kathisma palaion* (καθίσμα παλαιόν), i.e., the Old Seat (of Mary, later named "Mary's repose").[8] Another variation of the legend says that the Holy Family came by this well on their flight to Egypt, rested there and drank from it.[9]

2. In the Middle Ages, we find that another addition had been added to the legends surrounding Kathisma. There, or in its vicinity, a story in the book of Genesis is supposed to have taken place.[10] Abraham had set out from the wilderness near Beersheba with his son Isaac to carry out on Mount Moriah God's command to offer a sacrifice (Gen 22:1). The Jewish, Christian and Islamic traditions held the Temple Mount to be Mount Moriah. "So Abraham . . . arose and went to the place of which God had told him. On the third day Abraham lifted up his eyes and saw the place afar off. Then Abraham said to his young men, 'Stay here with the donkey; I and the lad will go yonder and worship, and come again to you'" (Gen 22:3–5). There at the well the young men are supposed to have waited for Abraham's return.

[6] R. Cameron, ed., *The Other Gospels: Non-Canonical Gospel Texts* (Philadelphia: Westminster Press, 1982), 117. According to the Protoevangelium, Joseph was a widower whose four sons by his first wife were called the "brothers" of Jesus (Mk 6:3; pp. 380–81).

[7] Theodosius, *The Topography of the Holy Land* 28 (J. Wilkinson, *Jerusalem Pilgrims before the Crusades* [Jerusalem: Ariel, 1977], 70).

[8] Cf. E. Testa, *Maria Terra Vergine*, vol. 2, *Il culto mariano palestinese (sec. I–IX)*, SBFCMa 31 (Jerusalem: Franciscan Printing Press, 1985), 153–54.

[9] *Pilgrim from Piacenza* 28 (J. Wilkinson, *Jerusalem Pilgrims* [see n. 7], 85).

[10] Daniel Abbas (1106/1107) (Baldi, 109).

3. From the thirteenth century on, a new Kathisma legend appears involving the Wise Men from the East (Mt 2:1–12).[11] The Wise Men had come to Jerusalem in search of the newborn King of the Jews, but they lost sight of the star during their visit at Herod's palace. Here at the Kathisma well, the star suddenly reappeared to them. "When they saw the star, they rejoiced exceedingly with great joy" (Mt 2:10).

III. The History of the Kathisma

The veneration of the Mother of Jesus received new momentum in the entire Christian world through the Council of Ephesus (A.D. 431), at which the title *theotokos* (θεοτόκος), the Mother of God (literally "God-bearer"), was conferred upon Mary. At that time there lived in Jerusalem a pious, wealthy woman named Ikelia who desired to build a church in honor of Mary at the site where the latter had rested. Ikelia had been the wife of a high imperial official. Later, she became a deaconess of Christ. Cyril of Scythopolis writes of her that she was "richly blessed in the things of the world, but even richer through her Christ-oriented lifestyle."[12] It was during the time of Archbishop Juvenal (422–458) that she covered the stone seat of the Kathisma with the dome of a beautiful octagonal structure dedicated to Mary (ca. 440). Because Cyril's report designates Juvenal as archbishop, it can be assumed that the church was built before the Council of Chalcedon (451), at which Juvenal received the title patriarch of Jerusalem.

It is remarkable that in the Armenian lectionary, which describes the Jerusalem liturgy in the years from 417 to 439, a feast of "Mary *theotokos*" was scheduled for August 15 at a location 3 miles outside of Bethlehem (therefore Kathisma).[13] The prescribed liturgical texts listed are Psalm 131 (Ps 132 in the Septuagint), Isaiah 7:10–16a, Galatians 3:29—4:7 and Luke 2:1–7. There is not yet any mention of either the consecration of a church or of the *koimesis* (the death of Mary). Ikelia's church, which for some reason was already consecrated on August 13, was dedicated to the *theotokos* in general. This can be seen from the Georgian lectionary that has the following note for August 13: "On the road to Bethlehem at the Kathisma at the third milestone

[11] Cf. C. Kopp, *The Holy Places of the Gospels* (New York: Herder and Herder, 1963), 33, n. 64.

[12] *Vita Theodosii* 1 (A.J. Festugière, *Les moines d'Orient*, vol. 3 [Paris: Gabalda, 1963], 109).

[13] Baldi, 96, n. 1.

near the hamlet of Bet-Ebri, the consecration of the church of the *theotokos*."[14] Both dates of the Jerusalem liturgy, August 13 and August 15, were thus recorded. Only gradually did August 15 become the day of the remembrance of the receiving of Mary into heaven.

M. Jugié is of the opinion that August 13 in Kathisma was a type of vigil for the Feast of Mary on August 15, which migrated to the Tomb of Mary in Gethsemane (p. 402).[15] In this way, the end of Mary's life, the *koimesis*, or *dormitio* (the deathbed), and the *transitus* (the crossing over) were celebrated two days apart, as were the death (Good Friday) and the Resurrection (Easter Sunday) of Jesus. This would explain the choice of readings that are scheduled for August 15 in the Georgian lectionary, i.e., Galatians 3:24–29 and Luke 11:27–32 (the praise of Mary by a woman from the crowd and the sign of Jonah).

M. van Esbroeck, in a study on the double date, reaches the following interesting conclusion: "The proof that the thirteenth of August originally belonged to a Christmas cycle lies in the founding of the Church of the Kathisma by Ikelia under Juvenal at the third milestone between Jerusalem and Bethlehem at the place where the Virgin Mary had rested before she gave birth. Thus, August 15 was originally the Feast of the Nativity in the Orient, for it is known that December 25 is of Western origin in connection with the feast of *sol invictus* (the invincible sun)."[16] The emperor Maurice (582–602) was the first to set the celebration of the assumption of Mary definitively for August 15 for the entire empire. Thus, in the former Jerusalem liturgy, there are traces of Kathisma that had an effect on the form of the present calendar of feasts.

IV. The Monks of Kathisma

Ikelia had won a number of monks for the maintenance of the Kathisma Church, among whom the monk Anthos is mentioned by name. On the initiative of the pious Ikelia, the custom of monks and the faithful

[14] Baldi, 100.

[15] *La mort et l'Assomption de la Sainte Vierge*, Studi e testi 114 (Vatican City: Libreria Editrice Vaticana, 1954), 181–83.

[16] "Les textes littéraires sur l'Assomption avant le 10me siècle", in F. Bovon, *Les Actes apocryphes des Apôtres* (Geneva: Labor et fides, 1981), 265–96 (at 284).

carrying burning candles in the procession in the Kathisma Monastery on the Feast of the Presentation of Jesus in the Temple (Lk 2:22–24) was introduced for the first time.[17]

Because Ikelia wanted to win more monks for her cloister, she turned to the old and honorable abbot Longinus, whose monk's cell was near the Tower of David (at the modern Jaffa Gate; see illus. 67). We learn from Cyril of Scythopolis, the author of the biography of the famous cenobiarch Theodosius, that the latter (born ca. 423) came from his home in Mogarissus, a town outside Caesarea of Cappadocia, to Jerusalem during the time of the emperor Marcian (450–457). There, Theodosius placed himself under the leadership of the aged monk Longinus. Upon Longinus' kind recommendation, the matron Ikelia brought him to the Kathisma Monastery, where he did the community of monks a great service as cantor because of his marvelous voice. When Ikelia died some time thereafter, Theodosius became the administrator of the entire monastery. He soon found a friend in the like-minded Anthos.

After the *hegumenos* (abbot) died, Theodosius was unanimously chosen as successor, but when he heard about this, he feared the great dangers of the office and fled. His friend Anthos had already retreated to the wilderness of Judah and became a follower of the great abbot Saint Sabas. Theodosius, too, now found refuge there. He retreated at once as a hermit to a cave in a hill lying 35 stadia (about 6 km) away from the Great Laura of Sabas (today, Mar Saba). According to a legend, the Wise Men from the East had hidden there[18] in an effort to evade King Herod's schemes and "departed to their own country by another way" (Mt 2:12). At the request of the numerous pupils who flocked around him, Theodosius founded at his hermitage the *coenobium Theodosii* (now called "Der Dosi"), named after himself. Unlike the monks in the Laura of Sabas who lived as hermits, the monks here lived as cenobites in communities according to language family, although all the communities often came together for joint prayer sessions.[19]

[17] Cyril of Scythopolis, *Vita Theodosii* (A.J. FESTUGIÈRE, *Moines d'Orient* [see n. 12], 3:58).

[18] Theodoros of Petra (mid-sixth century), *Vita Theodosii* 6 (A.J. FESTUGIÈRE, *Moines d'Orient*, 3:109–10; Baldi, 93–94).

[19] Symeon Metaphrastes (PG 114:476). Cf. H. USENER, *Der heilige Theodosios* (Leipzig: Deichert, 1890), 12–13.

V. The End of the Kathisma Church

Ikelia's church, which stood on the pilgrimage road to Bethlehem, received many visitors in Byzantine times. The people gathered there on Christmas Eve, because from there the patriarch of Jerusalem began his festive entry into Bethlehem.[20] We do not know exactly how long the Kathisma Church remained standing. It is assumed, probably rightly so, that this church, too, was destroyed in the Persian invasion (614). The only church to survive the vandalism of the Persians was the Church of the Nativity in nearby Bethlehem (pp. 12–15). The traditional explanation for this is that the Wise Men in the large mosaic on the facade were wearing the clothing of Persian kings.[21] From the following reports of pilgrims, we conclude that the Kathisma Monastery continued to be visited for a long time. The well of Mary's repose remained unforgotten among the people as "Bir el-Kadismu".

VI. The Reports on Kathisma from Pilgrims

Although these reports vary greatly and sound peculiar in their details, they nevertheless prove that a Kathisma Church must have once stood at the location where the excavations recently took place.

1. The archdeacon Theodosius reports (ca. 530) in his work about the Holy Land, "Three miles from the city of Jerusalem is the place where our Lady Mary, the Mother of the Lord, on her journey to Bethlehem got off her donkey and sat down on a stone and blessed the same."[22] Following this report, Theodosius tells an unusual, improbable-sounding miracle story that was probably for the edification of gullible pilgrims. He tells of an otherwise unknown Urbicius who was "superintendent to seven emperors. He himself crowned the heads of these emperors, removed their crowns, and chastised them."[23] This superintendent Urbicius had the stone (Kathisma seat) removed and hewn into an altar stone with the intention of bringing it to Constantinople. The transport got as far as Saint Stephen's Gate (now called the Damascus Gate) in the Holy City, where the oxen were no longer

[20] Cf. M. Jugié, *La mort et l'Assomption* (see n. 15), 183.

[21] Baldi, 105, n. 2.

[22] *The Topography of the Holy Land* 28 (J. Wilkinson, *Jerusalem Pilgrims* [see n. 7], 70).

[23] Ibid., 70–71.

able to move the stone forward. Therefore, it was brought to the Church of the Holy Sepulchre and installed there behind the Lord's tomb. In Constantinople, under the emperor Anastasius (419–518), Urbicius died and was buried. However, because of his sacrilegious attempt to remove the seat of Mary, "the earth would not receive Urbicius, but three times his tomb cast him out."[24]

2. A pilgrim from Piacenza, whose name is unknown, visited the Holy Land around 570 and made the following report:

> On the way to Bethlehem, at the third milestone from Jerusalem, lies the body of Rachel, on the edge of the area called Ramah. There I saw standing water which came from a rock, of which you can take as much as you like up to seven pints. Every one has his fill, and the water does not become less or more. It is indescribably sweet to drink, and people say that Saint Mary became thirsty on the flight into Egypt, and that when she stopped here this water immediately flowed. Nowadays there is also a church building there. From there it is 3 miles to Bethlehem, which is a most renowned place.[25]

After the Persian invasion (614) and the Muslim occupation of the land (beginning in 636), the reports become less frequent; however, they become numerous again during the days of the Crusaders.

3. At the beginning of the twelfth century, the Russian abbot Daniel reports (ca. 1106–1107):

> The holy town of Bethlehem lies 6 versts [a Russian unit of measurement: 1 verst = 500 sagenes (1.067 km)] away from the holy city of Jerusalem toward the south. It is 2 versts across the plain to the place of Abraham's dismounting, where he left his servant with the donkey behind. . . . From there it is approximately 1 verst to the place where the holy God-bearer saw two kinds of people, one laughing and the other weeping. A church had been built here—the cloister of the holy God-bearer—but today this place stands in ruins, destroyed by the pagans. The distance from there to the tomb of Rachel is 2 versts. From there it is 1 verst to the spot where the holy God-bearer got down off her foal of a donkey when that which was in her womb compelled her, for it wanted to come forth. Here,

[24] Ibid., 71.
[25] *Travels from Piacenza* 28–29 (J. Wilkinson, *Jerusalem Pilgrims* [see n. 7], 85).

> there is a large stone upon which the holy God-bearer rested after she had dismounted the foal. And after she got up from the stone, she went on foot to the holy cave, and here the holy God-bearer bore Christ.[26]

Here, a distinction is made between the location of Mary's vision (Kathisma) and her repose (near Bethlehem's Grotto of the Nativity).

4. The Rhineland Crusader Theoderich wrote in the year 1172, "Whoever goes out through the western city gate [of Jerusalem] by the Tower of David and turns toward the south passes first through the Valley of Hinnom that encloses the city on two sides, reaches after a distance of over a half mile a highly revered chapel honoring our holy Lady Mary where she often paused on the way to Bethlehem to rest. Outside there is a cistern where the passersby used to quench their thirst."[27]

5. Ricoldus de Monte Crucis (1294) says in his description of the area around Bethlehem, "We went along a road that leads to Bethlehem . . . , which was traveled by Joseph with Mary, who was expecting, and found the place not far from Bethlehem where Mary and Joseph, who were both tired and thirsty, found rest. There we were shown the spring that sprang forth there and offered its water to the pregnant Virgin."[28]

6. Fra Niccolo de Poggibonsi (1347) was one of the first Franciscans who spent a longer amount of time in the Holy Land. He reports: "On a straight road that leads from Jerusalem to Bethlehem, there is about halfway a beautiful cloister called Saint Elijah. On this side of Saint Elijah, about a stone's throw in the direction of Jerusalem on a level spot, there used to be a church, but now there is only a tiled floor of the mosaic style. When the magi came to Jerusalem, the star disappeared, but once they were outside the city, it reappeared at this place and escorted them to Bethlehem. It is 5 miles from Bethlehem to Jerusalem."[29]

7. The Russian pilgrim Grethenius (1400) describes the road from Bethlehem to Jerusalem as follows: "Halfway, there is the cloister of

[26] *Itineria rossica: Altrussische Reiseliteratur* (Leipzig: Reclam, 1986), 62–63.
[27] Baldi, 113.
[28] Baldi, 122.
[29] Baldi, 127.

the holy Elijah the prophet. On the road leading to it is the tomb of Rachel, the mother of Joseph. A little farther is a field that once yielded peas, which are now turned to stones; one can also see the stone on which Mary rested."[30]

8. The Dominican Felix Fabri, who was in the Holy Land twice (in 1480 and 1483), describes his walk to Bethlehem thus:

> We descended from Mount Zion over the south slope, crossed the valley between the pools and ascended over the Gyon Ridge ... and on the rise, we passed by walls that surrounded lovely gardens. After we left the gardens, we came to a place with the remains of walls where we were told that there is supposed to have been an inn at which the three kings found shelter. As we continued along, we reached a stony place where it was said that the Virgin Mary, who was with child, sat down and rested; we were shown the place where she sat. Continuing, we observed a cistern at which the star seen in the East reappeared to the three Wise Men.[31]

9. The Franciscan custodian of Mount Zion Francesco Suriano (1488) writes: "From Jerusalem to the place where the magi found shelter, it is a half mile. The place where the star reappeared to them is halfway from Jerusalem to Bethlehem. When they saw the star again, they dismounted their animals, prayed and thanked God Almighty. As a sign that their prayers had been heard, three springs came forth at the site where they knelt. Presently, however, [the springs] dried out, but traces of them are still visible today."[32]

10. The Franciscan Bonifacius de Stephanis, who was custodian of Mount Zion from 1552 to 1564, reports: "On the way from Jerusalem to Bethlehem, one comes to a large terebinth under which the Virgin Mary rested when she brought Christ to the temple.... Somewhat farther south of that by the road there is a cistern that today is called the 'well of the magi' or the 'well of the star'."[33]

11. The Franciscan Franciscus Quaresimus (1618) wrote in his book about the Holy Land[34] that this terebinth near the Kathisma well was

[30] B. KHITROWO, *Itinéraires russes en Orient* (Geneva, 1889), 181; Baldi, 134.

[31] Baldi, 139.

[32] Baldi, 145–46.

[33] Baldi, 149.

[34] *Historica, theologica et moralis Terrae Sanctae elucidatio*, 2:601.

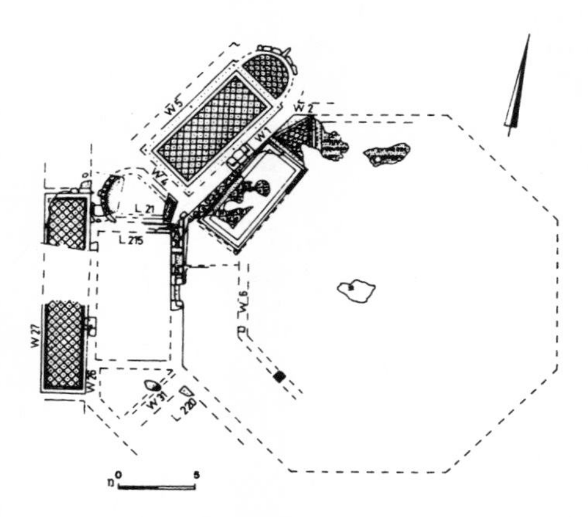

Illus. 11. Remains of the Byzantine Kathisma Church from the fifth century (according to R. Avner, 1993). The revered stone is in the center of the octagon.

held in honor under the name *terebinthus Mariae* ("Mary's terebinth") because the Mother of God rested there in its shade when she offered the sacrifice in the temple on the fortieth day after the birth of the Lord (cf. Lk 2:22–24). In 1645 the terebinth was burned down by an Arab who wanted to keep the pilgrims from setting foot on his field.[35]

VII. Conclusion

From the reports above, we see that the memory of the Kathisma Church with its legendary history remained alive for a long time. Therefore, it is a joy for all those who love the Holy Land that this long-lost sanctuary has now been rediscovered. The excavations, still in their beginning phase, already show that in the case of this sanctuary, we are dealing with a beautiful, relatively large church. Like many Byzantine memorial structures, it was laid out as an octagon, in the center of which stood the Kathisma stone. The well of the Kathisma still exists, although it is presently sealed with a cement cover. Previously, only the part of the site intended to be expropriated for road construction could be excavated. It is hoped that the Greek Orthodox patriarch will also permit excavations on the adjacent part and, as was

[35] Cf. R. Ries, "Kathisma palaion und der sog. Brunnen der Weisen bei Mar Elijas", *ZDPV* 12 (1889): 17–23 (at 23).

announced, will see to it that the Kathisma Church rises up again in new blossom.

Kathisma was the first sanctuary devoted to Mary in the region of Jerusalem. The thirteenth of August as the day of its consecration is very closely related to the great Feast of Mary on August 15, which is celebrated by the Eastern churches as well as Western Christendom. In the Jerusalem church, both feast days even appear to have originally belonged to the Christmas cycle. The motif of "Maria Kathisma" ("Mary rest") was brought to Europe by Crusaders returning home, and it provided the impetus for the construction of rest chapels or churches at many locations. The founder of the cenobite monks, the famous Theodosius, was one of the first monks who looked after the Kathisma Monastery.

Mary's passing by Kathisma and her probable rest there when coming from Bethlehem to present Jesus in the temple gave the pious lady Ikelia the idea of introducing the procession of lights on the Feast of the Presentation (February 2, Candlemas), a practice that gradually found acceptance in the entire world. Finally, the ride of the Catholic patriarch to the Grotto of the Nativity in Bethlehem still begins today, just as in ancient times, on Christmas Eve there near Kathisma. Thus, there are many historical reasons for reviving this long-lost sanctuary.

PART TWO

The Messiah in Galilee

4. Jesus' Routes around the Sea of Galilee

There is not only such a thing as salvation history but also "salvation geography". The Incarnation of the Son of God happened not just anywhere, but at a specific location, and the Kingdom of God was proclaimed in a precisely outlined region.[1] The communities and the roads that bound them and their inhabitants together influenced the form of the revelation of God's saving will. The more we know about the salvation history background, the clearer our understanding of the working of God among the people will be. Thus, the terrain of the Holy Land as a stage for the events surrounding Jesus can be understood as a "fifth Gospel", an expression used by the French author Ernest Renan. The message of the four Gospels reveals itself with new clarity to whoever has learned to read this book of biblical landscape.

The attempt to outline a portrait of the historical Jesus is still usually met with skepticism by historical-critical exegesis. To be sure, there are understandable reasons for such an attitude, but on the other hand, it is obvious that it is becoming ever more difficult for many exegetes to let the message of Jesus come to life as a whole, beyond the analytical elaboration of layers of tradition and the search for the underlying theology of the community. Only this can explain the attacks by E. Drewermann on conventional exegesis and the approval he receives for such. It is against this background that one should read the following insights that have been gained from a familiarity with that small corner of Palestine where Jesus lived. Knowledge of this land's geography and history at the beginning of the first century makes it clear

[1] A former professor at Jerusalem's École biblique, F. Dreyfus, has examined Jesus' high degree of self-confidence (*Jésus savait-il qu'il était Dieu?* [Paris: Cerf, 1984]). The longtime dean of the Dormition Abbey L. Volken in his work *Jesus der Jude und das Jüdische im Christentum* (Düsseldorf: Patmos, 1983) describes Jesus' Jewish roots. I myself attempt to portray Jesus' development in "Jesus and His Community: Between Essenes and Pharisees" in J. H. Charlesworth, ed., *Hillel and Jesus* (Minneapolis: Fortress, 1997), 193–224.

that the story of a specific person is told in the Gospels and that this was not an "ideal type" constructed at a desk somewhere. There will certainly be dispute about the historicity of some incidents, but it should become clear that the narratives of the Gospels often reflect great familiarity with the Galilean landscape. At times, it is obvious that the topography is interpreted theologically, but that in no way means that it is therefore arbitrary.

I. The Evangelical Triangle

The Gospels often report that large crowds from Galilee and the surrounding regions flocked to Jesus to hear him; for example, "Jesus withdrew with his disciples to the sea, and a great multitude from Galilee followed; also from Judea and Jerusalem and Idumea and from beyond the Jordan and from about Tyre and Sidon a great multitude, hearing all that he did, came to him" (Mk 3:7–8; cf. Mt 4:25; 8:1; Lk 6:17; Jn 6:2, 5). One of the reasons that Jesus left Nazareth to settle in Capharnaum[2] (Mt 4:12–17) was certainly his desire to meet people, for which this northwest corner of the lake was very well suited. The German exegete F. Mußner likes to refer to this corner as the "evangelical triangle". In the middle of the base of this triangle stood Capharnaum. To the west along the shore was Tabgha, the isolated region with springs and the mountain to which the Lord often retreated;[3] toward the east beyond the mouth of the Jordan was Bethsaida-Julias;[4] and on the rise north of Capharnaum lay Chorazin. These are the three locations of Jesus' most intensive activity named by Matthew and Luke (Mt 11:20–24 / Lk 10:13–15). A good network of roads leading to faraway lands characterizes this region.

We want to try first to understand the course of the most important highways and roads that ran alongside the lake or to it. Then we will examine them to see which ones Jesus could have used, according to the Gospels.

[2] This spelling more closely corresponds to the original Hebrew form (כְּפַר נַחוּם) and the usual transcription (Καφαρναούμ) in the Greek New Testament. The conventional form "Capernaum" arose through the influence of the Latin translations. "Capharnaum" is chosen here because the town continued to be inhabited almost exclusively by Rabbinic and messianic Jews for three hundred years after Jesus. Cf. chapter 8, "Riddles of the Synagogues at Capharnaum" (pp. 115–27).

[3] Cf. chapter 5, "Tabgha, the *Eremos* of Jesus" (pp. 77–99).

[4] Cf. chapter 9, "In Search of Bethsaida" (pp. 128–42).

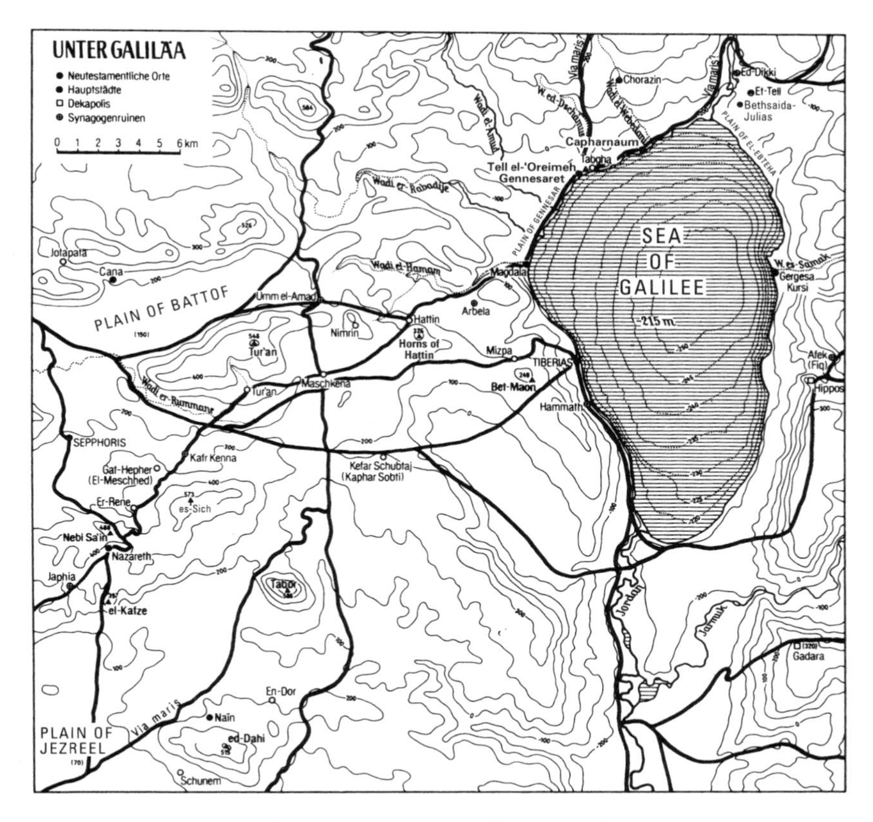

Illus. 12. Lower Galilee (from G.Kroll).

II. The Roman Highways and Roads

1. The So-Called Via Maris

The most important road in this region was the great overland highway from Egypt to Syria, which led from the Nile Delta along the northern coast of the Sinai Peninsula, past Caesarea on the Mediterranean and the pass south of Megiddo to Scythopolis (Beth Shean). From there, Damascus could be reached via two routes. The road then divided south of the Sea of Galilee. One branch ran along the west shore of the lake to Tiberias, Tarichea (Magdala) and Capharnaum, crossed the Jordan at Bethsaida-Julias and led across Gaulanitis to Damascus. The southern branch crossed the Jordan, ran along the southeast corner of the lake, climbed the steep incline of the Golan Heights south of Hippos (Susita),[5] and brushed by the Batanea at Caspin on its way to Damascus. Flavius Josephus describes the last part of this road as a pilgrimage route. It was used by Babylonian Jews coming "to sacrifice in Jerusalem" (*Ant.* 17.26). The other branch of the so-called Via Maris had followed a different route in the Bronze Age and Iron Age during the heyday of the cities Chinnereth (el-'Oreimeh near Tabgha) and Hazor. In the era of the Umayyads and the Crusaders, from whom the term *Via Maris* based on Matthew 4:15 (see pp. 61–62) originated, it followed another course than that of Hellenistic and Roman times. In those days, the road appears to have crossed the Jordan at Bethsaida-Julias. The Roman milestone discovered at Capharnaum and now on display in the garden of the Franciscans is an important witness to an imperial highway going by there in the days of Emperor Hadrian (A.D. 117–138).

Only the upper portion of this milestone was found.[6] The inscription reads: "IMPERATOR CAESAR DIVI TRAIANI PARTHICI FILIUS DIVI NERVAE NEPOS TRAIANUS HADRIANUS AUGUSTUS" ("the Emperor Caesar Trajan Hadrian Augustus, Son of the Divine Trajan Parthicus and Nephew of the Divine Nerva"). The inscription points to an imperial highway because the name of the emperor appears in the nominative case. The route of the Via Maris must have been near the site of the discovery about 200 m northeast of the synagogue in Capharnaum. As we know it from the Via Appia and many other Roman roads, there was a mausoleum alongside this road. According to the excavators, the Franciscans V. Corbo and S. Loffreda, it is to be dated to the first or second century A.D.[7] It contained at least five large sarcophagi.

It is to be expected that for this imperial road, a ford would not suffice, but rather a bridge would be available for crossing the Jordan. Otherwise, the rushing waters of the Jordan would have made the road impassable for several months in winter and spring. The bases for bridgeheads appear to have existed where the Jordan flows forth from

[5] At least four Roman milestones have been discovered on the length of road on the steep incline at Hippos. One was at the base of the basalt cone of Hippos not far from the modern highway. Three lie on the trail that leads over the ridge to the East Gate of the city.

[6] Cf. S. LOFFREDA, *Recovering Capharnaum*, 2nd ed. (Jerusalem: Franciscan Printing Press, 1993), 18–20.

[7] Ibid., pp. 80–81.

the deep ravine near ed-Dikke (illus. 33).[8] In the ruins of ed-Dikke on the east bank of the Jordan, the German archaeologists H. Kohl and C. Watzinger discovered and described a synagogue from Roman times.[9] In Jesus' day, ed-Dikke was probably a suburb of the city Bethsaida-Julias. It cannot be said with certainty whether King Herod the Great or whether Agrippa I or one of the later rulers built such a bridge over the Jordan in order to connect the northern regions of his kingdom, Batanea and Trachonitis (see p. 171) with Galilee.

From Flavius Josephus' report on his engagements in battle at the Jordan crossing, it is in any case clear that the road crossed it at Bethsaida-Julias. King Agrippa II intended namely in A.D. 66 to erect a blockade around the insurgent cities of Gamala and Seleucia and thereby force them to abandon their rebellion before the arrival of the Roman army. Josephus as commanding officer of the rebel forces in Galilee wanted to break up this blockade, which led to the battle at Bethsaida-Julias (see pp. 135–39). About this he says, "At that point forces came from the king, both cavalry and infantry together with their commander Sulla, the captain of the bodyguard. He set up camp 5 stadia [ca. 900 m] from Julias and posted guards on the roads, i.e., on those that led to Seleucia and to the fortress of Gamala, in order to prevent supplies from Galilee reaching the inhabitants" (*Life* 398–99).

From this, it can be concluded with a high degree of probability that the northern route of the Via Maris at that time did not cross the Jordan at the "Bridge of the Daughters of Jacob"[10] farther north, as has been presumed, e.g., by M. Avi-Yonah.[11] It would have been useless to guard the road at Julias, i.e., the road that led to Seleucia and stood, according to Josephus (*War* 4.2), on the lake Semechonitis (Baheiret el Huleh), if another bridge had existed farther to the north. It is most probable that Vespasian also used this road when his three legions broke camp at Hammath-Tiberias late in the summer of A.D. 67 in order to subdue Gamala. In any case, we know from Josephus' report (see above) that a road led from the Jordan crossing at Julias to this city. In order to move such an army across the Jordan, it can

[8] On an excursion with Prof. Dr. Rainer Riesner (University of Tübingen, now the University of Dortmund) in March of 1982, we found pavement stones *in situ* on the west slope of the Jordan ravine right before the drop.

[9] *Antike Synagogen in Galiläa* (Leipzig, 1916), 112–24.

[10] The name probably stems from that of a convent located nearby during the Crusades.

[11] *Erez Yisrạel biymey ha-bayit ha-sheni* [map] (Jerusalem, 1964).

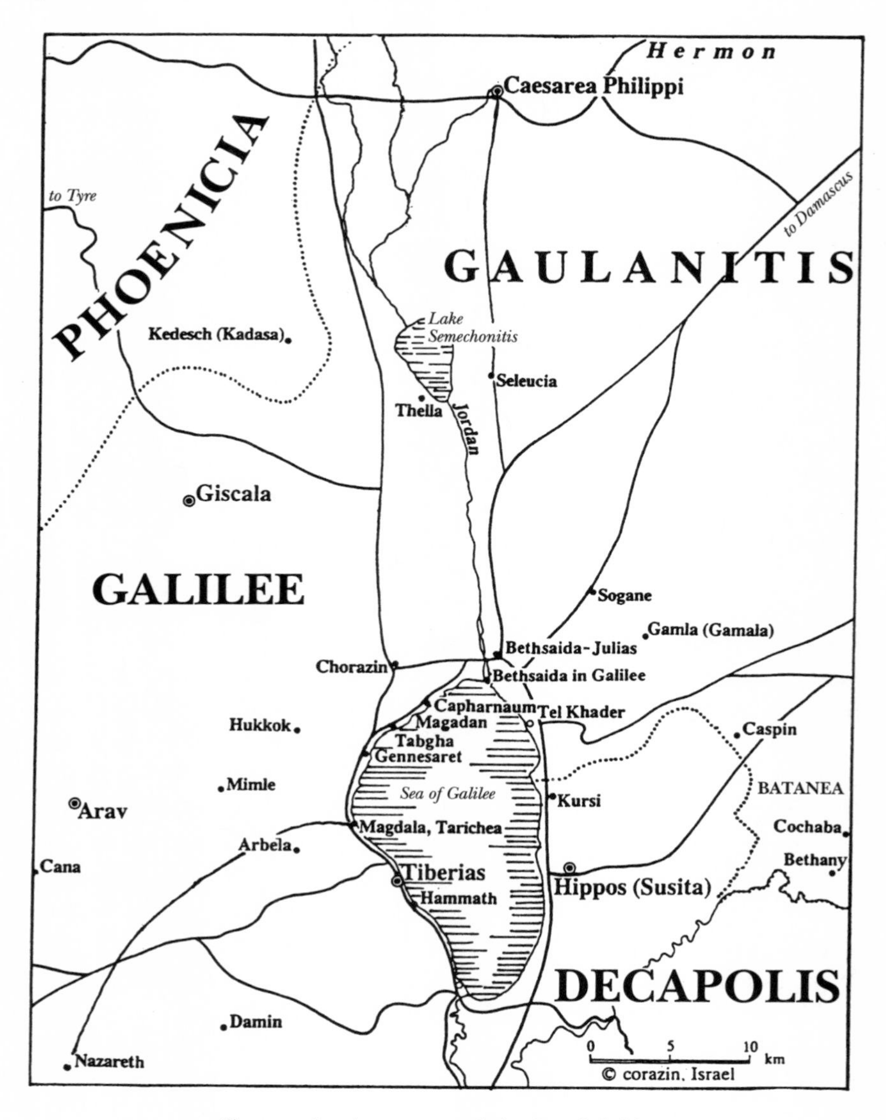

Illus. 13. Jesus' routes around the Sea of Galilee.

probably be assumed that a bridge existed at least as early as then. At the beginning of October, the Roman army reached the plain above Gamala, today the Arabic Deir Karruk (i.e., the Monastery of Gregory), and pitched camp there (*War* 4:13).

2. *Roads at Bethsaida-Julias*

The report about the battle at Bethsaida-Julias tells us that another road led to Seleucia (*Life* 399). This north-south connection thus led past Lake Semechonitis—today all but a small portion, Lake Huleh, has been drained by the Israelis—and finally reached Caesarea Philippi (Panias). This route certainly existed at the time of the tetrarch Philippus named in the New Testament (Lk 3:1) in order to connect his capital city with the second most important city of his kingdom, Bethsaida-Julias, elevated by him to city status (*Ant.* 18.28). There he erected a mausoleum, in which he was later buried (*Ant.* 18.108).

A Roman road led from Julias across the southern Golan into Batanea. At Caspin, it crossed the road that stretched from Scythopolis past Hippos to Damascus, the passageway for Jewish pilgrims leading from Babylon, according to Josephus (*Ant.* 17.26). The route taken by the road leading from Julias was investigated in 1985 by the Israeli archaeologist Z. Maoz of the Golan Survey. He was able to determine that this road is today still evident from the Golan Heights as far as Kibbutz Ramot. Although the northeast shore of the Sea of Galilee is referred to as an uninhabited area (ἐρημία [Mt 15:33 / Mk 8:4], it is nevertheless likely that there was already a road at that time that formed a connection along the eastern shore between Julias and the Decapolis village of Kursi, which belonged to the city of Hippos (see pp. 148–50). Thus, in New Testament times, Bethsaida was the crossing point of several important roadways.

3. *Routes around Chorazin*

As I was examining a ruin east of Chorazin together with Z. Maoz in 1984, we noticed a Roman road that up to that time had remained unknown. It runs along a straight line between Chorazin and Bethsaida-Julias (et-Tell) and is still clearly identifiable for a stretch of about 1 km. This section leads from the rise of el-Kafri, which lies about 1.5 km east of Chorazin (coordinates 205 257), in a straight line to the Wadi Turki, crosses the wadi at Khirbet Umm el-Maras and stretches in the same direction as far as the Wadi el-Musallaka. This wadi runs west of the Israeli settlement Almagor and flows into the Sea of Galilee. The road originally led straight to the Jordan, and its course can still be made out at the end of the Wadi Qil^{c}ai (208 257). Nearby, there was a ford across the Jordan. However, at a certain point in time, this road appears to have to have run behind Tell el-Mutilla (northeast of Almagor) in a northeasterly direction down the slope in order to cross the Jordan via the suspected Roman bridge (208 259).[12]

There are also signs that a roadway led from Chorazin in the direction of Tabgha, where it joined the Via Maris. A road also ran northward via Chorazin, probably through the Wadi Hazor to Giscala,[13] today the Arab Christian village of el-Jish, from where it continued on to Tyre in Phoenicia. From Tyre, there was with certainty a road leading to Cydasa, the modern Kedesh Naphtali very near Giscala. Impressive Roman ruins can still be seen today in Cydasa.[14]

Titus took the road from Bethsaida-Julias to Giscala when he headed out after the capture of Gamala with his thousand cavalrymen to take this last bulwark of the Galilean revolt (*War* 4.87). While Titus spent the night with his troops in nearby Cydasa, the leader of the Zealots, John, son of Levi, fled to Jerusalem (*War* 4.106). The large number of women and children he had taken with him had to be left behind about 3.5 km after starting out. Josephus' report says that in the panic that followed, "many strayed from the way, and on the highway many were crushed in the struggle to keep ahead" (*War* 4.109). Thus, there was also a road across the mountains of Upper Galilee.

III. The Routes Taken by Jesus

From the Gospels, we hear that Jesus traveled a lot. "And he went throughout all Galilee, preaching in their synagogues" (Mk 1:39). The starting point of Jesus' ministry was certainly Capharnaum. Matthew expressly states that he left Nazareth "and dwelt in Capernaum by the sea, in the territory of Zebulun and Naphtali" (Mt 4:13). In this way, Capharnaum became "his own city" (Mt 9:1). If we try to understand Jesus' wanderings within the framework of the network of roadways described above, two difficulties arise. First, we do not always know whether the roads that existed at a particular point in the Roman period were already present in Jesus' time. However, we can assume that connecting trailways were already present in places where the roads

[12] See the aerial view of the region in B. Pixner, "Searching for the New Testament Site of Bethsaida", *BA* 48 (1985): 207–16 (at 210).

[13] Cf. R. Riesner, "Gischala", in *GBL*, 2nd ed. (1990), 1:468.

[14] Cf. idem, "Kedesch", in *GBL*, 2nd ed. (1990), 2:770–71.

later stood. Second, we do not always know whether the evangelists, for certain reasons, gave the various stages of Jesus' travels an order different from that of their sources. Luke has apparently done this with reference to Mark.[15] Thus, the picture of the routes taken by Jesus that we are trying to visualize will initially be that which the writers of the Gospels, especially Mark and Matthew, had in mind. In the process, the possibility that they used older pieces of information is not to be excluded.

1. The Road from Nazareth to Capharnaum

The road that Jesus took when he left Nazareth and moved to Capharnaum (Mt 4:13) can scarcely have been the one leading through Herod Antipas' newly founded provincial capital city of Tiberias. More likely, it was the old road that passed through the Wadi Hammam (Dove Valley) to the sea. From Nazareth to the entrance to Dove Valley, Jesus could pass by the Jebel Turan to either the north or the south. The entrance itself was near a village that today is marked by the ruins of Ammudim (Arabic: Khirbet Umm el-Ammud), among which are the remains of a synagogue from a later period. The road continued from there, made alive by several springs, down the valley and went by the base of the romantically ascending dolomite walls of the Arbela. In 38 B.C. the caves in this rock wall had served as a refuge for rebels. Herod the Great had them smoked out by lowering soldiers from above in crates (*Ant.* 14.420–30). The valley reached the lake by Magdala (Greek: Tarichea). Jesus also probably came through this Dove Valley when he "went down" (κατέβη [Jn 2:12]) to Capharnaum with his Mother, brothers and disciples after the wedding feast at Cana, with certainty the present-day Khirbet Kana,[16] and again when he followed the royal official that had come to Cana to request healing for his son (Jn 4:46–53).

Having arrived in Magdala, Jesus could take the Via Maris that led through the middle of the fertile plain of Gennesaret. On this main road at "Seven Springs" (Tabgha), he reached the district of Capharnaum (cf. *War* 3.519). The people at this time will hardly have called the road "Sea Way", but the evangelist Matthew applies the name to this section of road along the sea. He namely quotes a text from the

[15] Cf. chapter 33, "Luke and Jerusalem" (pp. 423–32).

[16] Cf. R. RIESNER, "Kana", in *GBL*, 2nd ed. (1990), 2:751–53.

prophet Isaiah: "The land of Zebulun and the land of Naphtali, toward the sea [ὁδὸς θαλάσσης], across the Jordan, Galilee of the Gentiles—the people . . . have seen a great light" (Mt 4:15–16; cf. Is 9:1, Hebrew text 8:23). It was as if this prophetic word was tailored to the needs of the evangelist for describing the landscape in which the principal ministry of the Messiah was to unfold. This region did in fact lie in the "land of Zebulun and the land of Naphtali" and included a "sea way" in the form of the overland highway running along the northwest shore of the Sea of Gennesaret, the "Sea of Galilee" (θάλασσα τῆς Γαλιλαίας [Mt 4:18 / Mk 1:16; Mt 15:29 / Mk 7:31]). In the region "across the Jordan" (πέραν τοῦ Ἰορδάνου) stood Bethsaida, the home of several disciples (Jn 1:44; 12:21). Also located near this town was Gamala, a center of the strictly religious, indeed, fanatical, movement of the Zealots (*Ant.* 18.4). Still farther north were the strong Jewish settlements of Batanea.[17]

2. *Matthew's Tax Office*

Mark writes, "He [Jesus] went out again beside the sea; and all the crowd gathered about him, and he taught them. And as he passed on, he saw Levi the son of Alphaeus sitting at the tax office [ἐπὶ τὸ τελώνιον], and he said to him, 'Follow me'" (Mk 2:13–14). The pilgrim Egeria who visited Capharnaum in A.D. 383 reports that Matthew's tax office (*theloneum*) stood on the public road (*via publica*) that went past Seven Springs.[18] However, she does not say whether there was a tradition regarding its exact location. There are two possibilities regarding the type of tax that Levi collected. As I was able to determine in an investigation with the fishing industry expert M. Nun from the kibbutz En Gev, there is a masoned embankment along the shore in Capharnaum that is 700 m long and about 2 m wide. That shows that Capharnaum was a significant trading point for the fishing industry in Roman times. Since we know from Roman sources that fishermen always had to pay a tax on their catch, the tax office could have been a seaside customs

[17] Cf. chapter 13, "Batanea as a Jewish Settlement Area" (pp. 169–76).

[18] Peter the Deacon (A.D. 1137) in a note taken over from Egeria: "Iuxta cuius ecclesiae [Heptapegon] parietes via publica transit, ubi Mattheus apostolus theloneum habuit" (Baldi, 281–82) ("Past the walls of this church goes the public highway on which the Apostle Matthew had his place of custom"—trans. in J. Wilkinson, *Egeria's Travels to the Holy Land* [Jerusalem: Ariel, 1981], 200).

office.[19] The Marcan text may indicate that Jesus, followed by his listeners, walked along the embankment road and came to Levi's tax station at the harbor.

Capharnaum was also a border town. Thus, the tax office could have also served the purpose of collecting taxes on wares that came from the tetrarchy of Philip, the Hauran region (in antiquity, the breadbasket of the coastal region in the west), or Damascus. Then Levi-Matthew's tax station must have been located before the crossing of the Via Maris over the Jordan and thus still in the district of Capharnaum in order to serve its purpose. As we have seen, however, the question remains open whether a bridge crossed the Jordan or only a ford was present at the time of Jesus. Because I consider the latter to be more probable, I would place the tax station at the ruins of Sheik Kilạl, particularly since there is a good spring there.

3. The Three Journeys of Jesus according to Mark

a. Especially Mark betrays a good knowledge of the geography of Galilee in that he portrays a large portion of the evangelistic activity of Jesus in the framework of three journeys. Matthew follows him in this for the most part. All three journeys or trips depart from and return to Capharnaum. The *first journey* is mentioned here only briefly, since it consisted of a round trip across the lake and touched the roadways only in one corner of the Decapolis, in the "land of the Gerasenes" (Mk 5:1; cf. 5:20). A storm arises during the crossing, and with Jesus' first penetration into Gentile territory,[20] a demon-possessed man is healed (Mk 4:35—5:20).

This is the place to say something about Jesus' travels by boat. Through the sensational discovery of a boat from Jesus' time due to the low water level in 1986–1987, we are able for the first time to conceptualize what kind of vessel he and his disciples used.[21] Although they covered long distances on foot, they repeatedly used boats for

[19] Cf. M. Nun, *Ancient Anchorages and Harbours around the Sea of Galilee* (En Gev: Kibbutz En Gev, 1988), 24–26.

[20] Cf. R. Riesner, "Gerasener", in *GBL*, 2nd ed. (1990), 1:442–43.

[21] Cf. idem, "Schiffe auf dem See Genezareth", in *GBL*, 2nd ed. (1990), 3:1371–72. The even lower water level in 1990–1991 likewise brought important archaeological discoveries. Cf. A. Rabinovich, "Kinneret's Lows Are High Times for History", *Jerusalem Post*, April 26, 1991, international edition, 1, 13.

trips in the area of the lake. It must be assumed that even on Jesus' trips to Jerusalem mentioned in the Gospel of John, he completed the first leg of his journey from Capharnaum to the lake's south end by boat. Such a boat may have had dimensions similar to the one found at the kibbutz Ginnosar near ancient Magdala. It could easily hold thirteen men (Jesus and the Twelve; illus. 14). In view of its dating, it is even conceivable that the boat found could have served as the means of transportation for Jesus and his disciples on the first leg of their pilgrimage to Jerusalem.

b. The *second journey* is a long, horseshoe-shaped walking tour from the feeding of the five thousand on the west shore of the lake across the territory of Tyre and the Decapolis to the feeding of the four thousand on a hill in the wilderness of the east shore (Mk 5:21—8:10). We want to attempt to trace this route by turning our attention to the topography. After the disciples around Jesus had been hit by the shocking news about the execution of John the Baptist (Mk 6:17–29), the Master suggests traveling with the boat to a deserted place so they could think over the situation and get some rest (Mk 6:30–32). The crowds look for Jesus in Capharnaum, and when they notice that Jesus' boat is heading for nearby Tabgha, they run down the road for the distance of 2.5 km and are already standing on the shore when the Lord arrives there with the disciples (Mk 6:33). Toward evening, he feeds the crowd with five loaves and two fishes (Mk 6:34–44). The kerygmatic interpretation of this miracle takes note of the twelve baskets that were left over (Mk 6:43). They symbolize the twelve tribes of Israel; thus, we are dealing here with a feeding of God's people under the Mosaic covenant. This is indicated by the seating in groups of hundreds and fifties (Mk 6:40), to which the Israelites were accustomed during the wilderness wanderings (Ex 18:25).

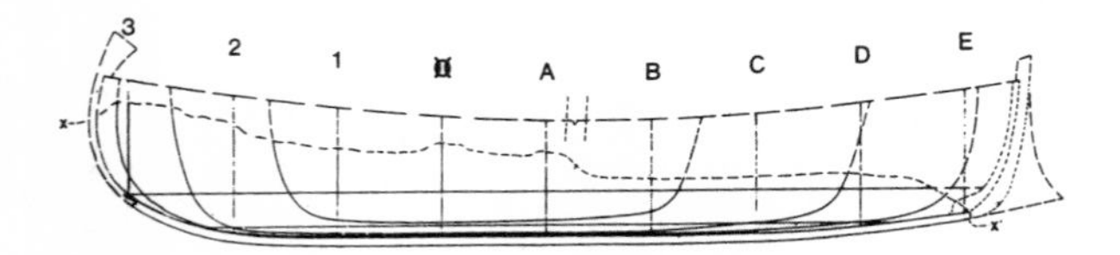

Illus. 14. The boat from Magdala (according to S. Wachsmann, 1990). The broken line marks the recovered portion.

What follows is intimately connected with the sudden awakening of messianic enthusiasm in the crowd (cf. Jn 6:15) and with the danger presented to Jesus (cf. Mk 6:14–16) by Herod Antipas, the "fox" (Lk 13:32), because of it. It may have been in the spring of A.D. 28 that the unsettling news reached Capharnaum that John the Baptist had been executed and that Jesus himself was suspected by the "king" of being a second John (Mk 6:16). While the synoptic Gospels see the main cause of the Baptist's execution in the hate harbored by Herodias, the unlawful wife of Antipas, Flavius Josephus gives us to understand that a political reason was the main motive for removing John. This could have been triggered by the dance of Herodias' daughter at the banquet in the fortress Machaerus.[22] We can better appreciate the danger for Jesus that grew out of the tetrarch's suspicion if we take a look at the report of this Jewish historian:

> Herod [Antipas] had put him [John] to death, though he was a good man and had exhorted the Jews to lead righteous lives, to practise justice towards their fellows and piety towards God, and so doing to join in baptism.... When others too joined the crowds about him, because they were aroused to the highest degree by his sermons, Herod became alarmed. Eloquence that had so great an effect on mankind might lead to some form of sedition, for it looked as if they would be guided by John in everything that they did. Herod decided therefore that it would be much better to strike first and be rid of him before his work led to an uprising, than to wait for an upheaval, get involved in a difficult situation and see his mistake.... John, because of Herod's suspicions, was brought in chains to Machaerus, the stronghold ..., and there put to death.[23] (*Ant.* 18.116–19).

The beheading of John and the suspicion of the superstitious Antipas that Jesus was the Baptist returned to life (John *redivivus*) and would continue the work of the latter meant for Jesus that he himself was threatened by the same fate at the discretion of the tyrant in the fortress of Tiberias. For as large crowds had once assembled around John, so too around Jesus, who now for more than year had been publicly active in Galilee. Jesus' disciples and he himself could have easily come

[22] Cf. R. Riesner, "Johannes der Täufer auf Machärus", *BiKi* 39 (1984): 176.

[23] In L. H. Feldman, trans., *Josephus: Jewish Antiquities; Books XVIII–XIV*, 5th ed., Loeb Classical Library 433 (Cambridge, Mass.: Harvard University Press, 1996).

under suspicion of being close to the Zealots and of forging secret plans for revolt. The "fox" might have gotten the idea that in the case of this popular prophet from Capharnaum it would be better to act quickly while this was still possible. We can see that from now on Jesus avoids anything that could give the ruler of Galilee a reason to throw him into the dungeon. He therefore does not remain in one place very long. After the feeding of the five thousand, Jesus urges the disciples to immediately travel on ahead to Bethsaida (Mk 6:45), thus to an area where the peace-loving Philip ruled (*Ant.* 18.106–7). However, a strong wind (Mk 6:48), probably the notorious sirocco that sweeps in from the northeast in spring and winter, prevented the crossing. Jesus, who spent the night on the mountain in prayer, saw this and wanted to go to his disciples (Mk 6:46–48). The report says that in so doing he walked across the waves. As soon as Jesus took a seat in the boat, the wind subsided and made it possible for them to land on the nearby shore of the village Gennesaret (Mk 6:53; pp. 144–45). The last excavations have shown that in Roman times, the settlement was no longer on the hill Chinnereth (Tell el-'Oreimeh) as it was in the time of the Old Testament (Josh 19:35) but rather at its base not far from Ain et-Tine (Fig Spring).[24]

Jesus now hurried from village to village, probably evading Antipas' spies, in the direction of the Phoenician border. One of these "villages" (Mk 6:56) along the way may have been Giscala, for he presumably took the road described above. We know from its later history that it was strongly interspersed with Pharisees and Zealots (*War* 4.92ff.). Jerome even appears to know that the ancestors of the Apostle Paul came from there.[25] Mark and Matthew insert at this point the discussion about the Jewish dietary laws (*kashruth*) that Jesus abolished (Mk 7:1–23 / Mt 15:1–20). At the time that Mark wrote his Gospel, the question of clean and unclean foods was still very current in the churches, which came in part from Judaism and partly from paganism. Mark has it that Jesus takes a decided stand against a rigorous interpretation of the dietary laws: "There is nothing outside a man which by going into him can defile him; but the things which come out of a man are what defile him" (Mk 7:15). To this, the evangelist adds his

[24] Cf. U. Hübner, "Die 3. Grabungskampagne 1984 auf dem Tell el-Ọreime am See Gennesaret", *HlL* 117, nos. 2–3 (1985): 11–19 (at 16).

[25] *De viris illustribus* 5 (PL 23:646).

own interpretation: "Thus he declared all foods clean" (Mk 7:19). It is interesting to notice that here Luke, who up to this point has almost always followed Mark, goes his own way, since he was apparently of the opinion that the dietary laws had been done away with not by Jesus but rather through Peter's vision in Joppa (Acts 10:9–16).[26] Mark probably inserted the pericope here because Jesus was about to leave Galilee for the first time for a somewhat longer stay with his disciples in Gentile territory.

Jesus crosses the border and now finds himself on Gentile terrain near Tyre, but he forbids the disciples to make his presence known in any way (Mk 7:24). "I was sent only to the lost sheep of the house of Israel" (Mt 15:24). He also utters the hard statement: "It is not fair to take the children's [the Jews'] bread and throw it to the dogs [the Gentiles]" (Mt 15:26 / Mk 7:27). However, at the plea of the Syro-Phoenician woman whose faith had impressed him, he goes beyond this principle and heals the daughter of this Gentile woman (Mk 7:25–30). This is a turning point in Jesus' life, for in this attention given to a Gentile woman Jesus breaks through the bounds of Judaism.[27] He may have been guided by the following thoughts: had his Mother not spoken of the words she always treasured up in her heart and that the old man Simeon had spoken about him in the temple: "My eyes have seen your salvation / which you have prepared in the presence of all peoples, / a light for revelation to the Gentiles, / and for glory to your people Israel" (Lk 2:30–32)? Was he not a "Nazorean" (נוֹצְרִי, Ναζωραῖος), from the lineage of David (p. 29)? And what had the prophet Isaiah said in his second song about the royal servant of God? "It is too light a thing that you should be my servant to raise up the tribes of Jacob and to restore the preserved of Israel [*n^ezurei Yisra'ẹl* (נְצוּרֵי יִשְׂרָאֵל)]; I will give you as a light to the nations, that my salvation may reach to the end of the earth" (Is 49:6).

After this event near Tyre Jesus travels through the region of Sidon, probably continuing on the ancient highway that went from Tyre to Bozrah via Dan and Caesarea Philippi (illus. 2). It was used above all for bringing grain from Hauran to both coastal cities. Jesus ascends the heights of the Golan, nears the Sea of Galilee in the depression

[26] I thank my fellow Benedictine, Brother Vincent Mora, O.S.B. (Jerusalem), for this observation.

[27] Cf. W. Bruners, *Wie Jesus glauben lernte* (Freiburg: Herder, 1988), 77–95.

and finally finds himself in the middle of "the region of the Decapolis" (Mk 7:31).[28] Along the way, more and more people gathered around Jesus. There were probably many non-Jews among these, for the Decapolis named by Mark (Mk 7:31) could have been the district of Hippos that belonged to the Greek free city Hippos located in southern Golan near the lake (close to the modern kibbutz En Gev).[29] A road led from there down to the lake toward a hill covered with ruins located right at the shore and rising about 30 m above the lake. The hill, which used to be called Sheik Chader, is known today as Tell Hadar. On the hill, there was an Israelite city that belonged to the land of Geshur. It was destroyed around 730 B.C. (cf. 2 Kings 15:29).[30] This tell, on which early Arabic pottery shards were found, might possibly have been the location of the feeding of the four thousand (Mk 8:1–20).[31] It lies not far to the north of Wadi Semach, which in those days formed the boundary between the tetrarchy of Philip on its north side and the Gentile Decapolis.

The legendary late Byzantine report in the *Vita S. Helenae et Constantini*, which led the emperor's mother to build churches on several sites, goes back to an older travel log (pp. 92–93) that followed a path beginning in the Jordan Valley on the east bank and continuing around Lake Gennesaret to Tiberias. The first memorial site is the "Dodekathronos", the "throne of the Twelve", "where Christ sat and taught and where he multiplied the loaves and fed the four thousand".[32] The Dodekathronos is normally assumed, without sufficient reasons, to be in Tabgha at the Sanctuary of the Primacy. The beautiful large ashlars from the Iron Age walls on Tell Hadar may have been interpreted for pilgrims as the throne of the end time (cf. Mt 19:18 / Lk 22:30).

According to Matthew, Jesus went up on a mountain or hill (ὄρος) and healed many sick (Mt 15:29). Matthew also implies that the multitudes that had remained with Jesus three days was composed for the most part of non-Jews when he writes that "they glorified the God of

[28] Cf. F. G. Lang, "Über Sidon mitten ins Gebiet der Dekapolis: Geographie und Theologie in Markus 7,31", *ZDPV* 94 (1978): 145–60.

[29] Cf. R. Riesner, "Hippos", in *GBL*, 2nd ed. (1990), 2:581.

[30] Cf. M. Kochavi, "Tel Hadar", *ESI* 6 (1987/1988): 76.

[31] With permission from the Israeli authorities, a stone marker has been erected on this hill in memory of the second miraculous feeding of the multitude. A new park has been opened on the shore (Golan Beach) next to the tell.

[32] Baldi, 278–79.

Israel" (Mt 15:31). Jesus miraculously fed this multitude as well, whereupon this time seven baskets of leftovers were collected (Mt 15:32–39 / Mk 8:1–10). The number indicates the seven Gentile peoples (cf. Deut 7:1; Acts 13:19) that were driven out by the twelve tribes of Israel and were excluded from the covenant with God.[33] Through Jesus, they are now offered the Bread of Life. The contrast between Israel and the Gentile peoples in the two stories is already emphasized in the oldest commentaries on the Gospels.[34]

The common hypothesis that the two stories in Matthew and Mark are doublets, i.e., two different accounts of one and the same event on the east shore of the lake, can scarcely be upheld on the basis of topographical considerations.[35] Whoever is familiar with the area around the lake cannot comprehend how the multitudes of people, who from Capharnaum had watched the route taken by the boat, could have reached the landing point before the boat (Mk 6:33) if they would have had to cross the Jordan in order to reach the east shore. Tabgha and Capharnaum are separated by only 2.5 km. If the feeding of the five thousand had taken place on the other shore, it would have been absolutely impossible to overtake the boat in this manner. Not only the distance (from 20 to 25 km) would have precluded such a possibility, but also the crossing of the Jordan, which rises dangerously especially in the spring after the snow on Mount Hermon melts, would have created major difficulties. As seen above, the strong headwind (Mt 14:24 / Mk 6:48) that blew in the spring when there was "green grass" (Mk 6:39) can only have been the sirocco that sweeps in from the northwest. Therefore, the boat traveling toward Bethsaida (Mk 6:45) must have set sail from the west shore of the lake. Thus, it was there that the feeding of the five thousand took place,[36] in a "lonely place" (ἔρημος τόπος [Mt 14:13 / Mk 6:32]), the one ancient tradition identified with Tabgha, which was probably handed down by the Jewish Christians of Capharnaum (pp. 90–97). Tabgha was surrounded by

[33] Also cf. chapter 11, "Kursi and the Land of the Gerasenes" (pp. 148–55).

[34] Origen, *Commentaria in Evangelium secundum Matthaeum* 11, 19 (Mt 15:32) (PG 13:970–74), and the *Discourse of Barsabbas*, probably stemming from the second century A.D. (M. van Esbroeck, "Discours de saint Barsabée, achevêque de Jérusalem", in *Barsabée de Jerusalem sur le Christ et les églises*, PO 41/2 [Turnhout: Brepols, 1982], 229–30).

[35] Also countering this in recent times is F. Neugebauer, "Die wunderbare Speisung (Mk 6,30–44 parr.) und Jesu Identität", *Kerygma und Dogma* 32 (1986): 254–77 (at 273).

[36] Also cf. B. Bagatti, "Dove avvenne la moltiplicazione dei pani", *Salmaticensis* 28 (1981): 293–98.

farms and villages, where the multitude could have bought something to eat (Mt 14:15 / Mk 6:36). On the other hand, the feeding of the four thousand happened, as we have seen, on the sparsely populated (ἐρημία) northeast shore of the lake (Mt 15:33 / Mk 8:4). Thus, the hearers carried baskets or hampers that had handles (σπυρίδες [Mk 8:8]), like those portrayed, strangely enough, in the mosaics of the Byzantine church of Kursi. The "small fish" (ἰχθύδια [Mk 8:7]) with the bread could have been sardines, as they happen to be very plentiful in the bay of Kursi.

Much more probable than the doubling by Mark and Matthew of a single account of the feeding of a multitude is a summarizing of the two events in one account by Luke (Lk 9:10–17) and the other by John (6:1–13). They did this in such a way that they told of the feeding of the five thousand but did so within the geographical framework of the second event. Luke speaks of a place outside of Bethsaida (Lk 9:10). Since Philip the Tetrarch had elevated Bethsaida to city (πόλις) status around the beginning of the first century (pp. 130–31), the villages all the way to the border of the Decapolis (Wadi Semach) had been included in the district of the new *polis* (cf. *Ant.* 18.28). According to John (Jn 6:3; cf. 6:17, 24), Jesus goes up on a mountain or hill (ὄρος) on the east shore. From the place where the four thousand were fed, Jesus travels by boat to the west shore. Matthew specifies his destination as Magadan (Mt 15:39), and Mark names Dalmanutha (Mk 8:10), but John says Capharnaum (Jn 6:17, 24). The first two terms are probably designations for the region of Tabgha (pp. 77–80).

A location on the west shore, as some scholars propose,[37] is in my opinion not required, in spite of the variants in the codices D and Θ that assume a departure from the region of Tiberias on the west shore. The phrase "Jesus went to the other side of the Sea of Galilee" (πέραν τῆς θαλάσσης [Jn 6:1]) could hardly have reference to Tabgha. A new location for the miracle would be necessary, e.g., in the Arbela region,[38] but the tradition for the Horns of Hattin, where the Crusaders were annihilated by Saladin in 1187, is very late (fifteenth century).[39] When viewed from Tabgha, Capharnaum as a point of departure (ἤρχοντο

[37] Cf. R. E. Brown, *The Gospel according to John*, vol. 1 (London: G. Chapman, 1971), 232, 257–59.

[38] Thus B. E. Schein, *Following the Way: The Setting of John's Gospel* (Jerusalem: Sadan, 1980), 210–11.

[39] Cf. C. Kopp, *Die heiligen Stätten der Evangelien*, 2nd ed. (Regensburg: Pustet, 1964), 268.

πέραν τῆς θαλάσσης εἰς Καφαρναούμ [Jn 6:17]) does not make sense. In that case, the question, "When did you come here?" (Jn 6:25) would not be justified. Why did the multitude need boats to cover the 2 km to Capharnaum (Jn 6:24)? Although there is a reference in Josephus (*Life* 153) where πέραν is used in a verb (διαπεράω) for the trip from Tiberias to Tarichea, it appears to me that *peran* is always to be understood as *on the other side* of an imaginary line between the points of the Jordan's flowing into and out of the lake. One travels by boat to the location of the feeding of the five thousand and goes on foot to the place where the four thousand were fed.

The hill of Tell Hadar fits the account of John well. Jesus goes to the other shore (Jn 6:1), and the multitude follows him on foot (Jn 6:2). Jesus goes up on a "mountain" or hill (Jn 6:3 [ὄρος]), just as at the feeding of the four thousand in Matthew (Mt 15:29). Jesus directs the question of where bread should be bought (Jn 6:6) to Philip, who was from nearby Bethsaida (cf. Jn 1:44). In the evening the disciples go down to the lake (Jn 6:16 [κατέβησαν ἐπὶ τὴν θαλάσσαν]) and sail to the other shore to Capharnaum (Jn 6:17) while Jesus retires deeper into the mountains (Jn 6:15), perhaps along a Roman road in the direction of the Golan Heights. The people "on the other side of the sea" (πέραν τῆς θαλάσσης [Jn 6:22]) saw how the "boats from Tiberias came near the place where they ate the bread" (Jn 6:23), perhaps the harbor of the fishing village of Kursi (pp. 151–52). The great multitude of Gentiles had in the meantime returned to the Decapolis and to Syria. The few inhabitants of the Jewish west shore who remained went back to Capharnaum (Jn 6:24), while the disciples probably had landed in Dalmanutha (pp. 78–80; Jn 6:17).

John did not merge the two events into one without reason. Basically, he reports the feeding of the five thousand, but the location is that of the feeding of the four thousand on the east shore. Since according to the general tradition the earlier miracle was followed by the walk on the water, the fourth evangelist had to make a few minor adjustments in his account. In sailing from east to west the disciples could of course not run into a headwind (the sirocco); therefore, he avoids the expression "headwind" (ἄνεμος ἐναντίος αὐτοῖς [Mk 6:48]) and has the lake simply be stirred up by a strong wind (Jn 6:18 [ἄνεμος μέγαλος]). Furthermore, since the traditional location of Jesus' joining the disciples in the boat after having walked on the water was near Tabgha, he has the boat be from 25 to 30 stadia away from the place where the multitude was fed (Jn 6:18). That is precisely the distance from Tell Hadar to Magadan (Tabgha). One reason why John prefers to stage the multiplication of the loaves on the largely uninhabited east shore is probably that he needed the wilderness scene for his discourse on the heavenly manna in the synagogue in Capharnaum (Jn 6:31–32), and Tabgha is of course not a wilderness. In John's account the bread discourse follows as an answer to the question: "What sign do you do, that we may see, and believe you?" (Jn 6:30). Jesus is also pestered with the request for a sign at his arrival on the west shore in Matthew and Mark (Mk 8:11–13 / Mt 16:1–4). Since the fourth evangelist could record only one of the miracles among his seven "signs", he tries to bring together in it elements from both synoptic stories. John, who in my opinion was writing for Jews, was less interested in the feeding of the Gentiles.

c. Yet a *third Galilean journey* is reported in Mark and Matthew, i.e., the one that led Jesus to the villages at Caesarea Philippi and once more back to Capharnaum (Mk 8:11—9:33). Jesus sails in a boat from the area near Capharnaum (Mk 8:13–21) to Bethsaida (Mk 8:22). There, they could above all stock up on bread for the long trip, for during the crossing, they had remembered that they had taken only one loaf with them (Mk 8:14). Outside of Bethsaida, probably already on the way to Caesarea Philippi (p. 140), Jesus heals a blind man (Mk 8:22–26). After this, he travels through the entire region of Philip, presumably walking along the road on the east slope of the Jordan described above (see p. 59), in order to enter the villages encircling the capital city Caesarea. The Petrine messianic confession and the first prediction of Jesus' suffering (Mk 8:27—9:1; cf. Mt 16:13–28) may have occurred not far from the famous cliff above the source of the Jordan.[40] After Peter's confession, the disciples were surprised by Jesus' peculiar order "to tell no one about him" (Mk 8:30). This secrecy concerning the messianic title, emphasized especially in Mark, may sound strange; however, after the rediscovery of Gamala,[41] located not very far away, we can better understand the reason.

Gamala sat like an eagle's nest on an isolated ridge protected on two sides by steep drops. With its patriotic ideas, the city influenced a large portion of the Jewish population around Lake Gennesaret. Judas

[40] Cf. R. Riesner, "Caesarea Philippi", *GBL*, 2nd ed. (1990), 1:225–26.

[41] Cf. G. Cornfeld, *Josephus: The Jewish War* (Grand Rapids: Eerdmans, 1982), 254–60.

of Gamala, who was probably a Pharisaic scribe, together with Rabbi Zadok, also a Pharisee, had called the movement of the Zealots into being in the year A.D. 6 (*Ant.* 18.4–10, 23–24). His family was from Gamala, and it developed into a dynasty that controlled the Zealots until their demise at Masada (A.D. 73/74). Judas' father, Ezechias (Hezekiah), had been a patriot before him and had been leader of a guerilla gang that rose up against Romans and their friends in Trachonitis (*War* 1.204, 256). In the end, the youthful Herod the Great had taken him prisoner and executed him in short order, which caused an outcry among many Jews. Judas of Gamala taught a radical theocracy, i.e., God alone is the ruler of Israel, not the Roman emperor. Therefore, it was wrong to pay him taxes (cf. Mk 12:13–17). In Acts, it is said of Judas: "Judas the Galilean arose in the days of the census and drew away some of the people after him; he also perished, and all who followed him were scattered" (Acts 5:37). Presumably, Herod had him executed.

Two of Judas' sons, James and Simon, were crucified under the procurator Tiberius Alexander (A.D. 46–48; *Ant.* 20.102). Another son, Menahem, took possession of weapons after an attack on Masada in A.D. 66, entered Jerusalem as if he were the messianic king and seized control of the insurgents; however, he was then murdered by a rival party (*War* 2.433–49). Joseph, the son of the midwife, had inherited the spirit of Judas and led the battle for Gamala at the beginning of the Jewish War (A.D. 66–67) with an unparalleled tenacity that finally ended in mass suicide (*War* 4.11–54, 62–83). Eleazar, the leader of the Zealots at Masada, was also a descendent of Judas of Gamala (*War* 7.304–406). The entire Zealot movement was motivated strongly by messianic expectations. A political messiah was expected who would lead his troops in battle from victory to victory against Rome.

When we hear that after his encounter with Jesus, Andrew of Bethsaida had whispered the good news in the ear of his brother Simon (Peter), "We have found the Messiah" (Jn 1:41), he was definitely thinking in Gamalan terms. One of the disciples that had joined Jesus is expressly called Simon "the Zealot" (Lk 6:15 [ὁ ζηλώτης]; cf. Mk 3:18). It would not be surprising if he were from Gamala. Judas Iscariot (one of the *sicarii*?) was certainly someone whose messianic expectations resembled those of the Zealots. A similar concept of the Messiah will have been shared by more or less all of the disciples. In view of the proximity of the two towns Gamala and Bethsaida, from which most of the prominent disciples came (Peter, Andrew, James, John, Philip; p. 128), this should not be surprising. There was an urgent need for the retraining of the Twelve.[42] Jesus, in searching for his Father's will in prayer, had decided on a messianic concept that sounded very different from what the disciples expected. Certainly, his contemplation of the servant songs played an important role. "And he began to teach them that the Son of man must suffer many things, and be rejected by the elders and the chief priests and the scribes, and be killed, and after three days rise again" (Mk 8:31).

Six days later Jesus goes up on "a high mountain" with three of his disciples (Mk 9:2) and is transfigured in their presence. The Gospels do not say which high mountain is meant. The oldest traditions (from the fourth century A.D.) are uncertain, as they name three different mountains as the location of the transfiguration, i.e., Mount Hermon, Mount Tabor, and the Mount of Olives.[43] The latter is mentioned in the oldest pilgrimage account, that of the Pilgrim of Bordeaux (A.D. 333),[44] but this claim is completely untenable. Subsequently, Mount Tabor[45] generally became the mount of transfiguration; however, there are significant historical reasons that make this unlikely.[46] In A.D. 330 Eusebius, who also wrote the highly respected *Onomastikon* (a record of biblical place-names), still left the question open: "Tabor and Hermon. . . . I think that the wonderful transfigurations [παράδοξαι μεταμορφώσεις] of our Redeemer took place on these mountains."[47] Therefore, many exegetes believe that Mount Hermon or a nearby peak would more likely do justice to the Gospel account.[48]

[42] For more details on this, see my article mentioned in n. 1. On questions of chronology, see appendix 1 (pp. 433–38).

[43] Baldi, 319ff.

[44] *Itinerarium* 18 (Geyer, 23; Baldi, 320, n. 3).

[45] Cf. R. Riesner, "Tabor", in *GBL*, 2nd ed. (1990), 3:1517–20.

[46] Mt. Tabor was an inhabited, fortified mountain prior to and after Jesus. In 218 B.C., Antiochus II had at first conquered the settlement located on Mt. Tabor (Atabyrion) and then fortified it (Polybius 5.70.6). Then the Hasmonaean king Alexander Jannaeus succeeded in assimilating the mountain into his territory (*Ant.* 13.395–96). However, when in 63 B.C. Pompey invaded Jewish territory with his legions, Mt. Tabor became Roman (*Ant.* 14.102). In 67 B.C. Vespasian recaptured Mt. Tabor, which had been occupied and fortified by rebel Jews (*War* 4.54–61; *Life* 188).

[47] *Exposition on Psalm 88[89]:13* (PG 23:1092).

[48] Cf. C. Kopp, *Holy Places of the Gospels* (New York: Herder, 1963), 245–46; cf. R. Riesner, "Hermon", in *GBL*, 2nd ed. (1990), 2:562–63.

Jesus descends from the mount of transfiguration and heals a deranged boy, probably in one of the Jewish villages south of Caesarea Philippi (Mk 9:14–29). After Jesus crosses the Jordan somewhere, he again makes his way in secret through Galilean territory (Mk 9:30). Here, he speaks to his disciples once more concerning his suffering and his Resurrection (Mk 9:31–32). Together with them, he finally returns home to Capharnaum probably by way of Chorazin (Mk 9:33; cf. Mt 14:24–27). The last stretch of the way had once again been used by the disciples to quarrel over rank (Mk 9:34). Soon thereafter Jesus takes leave of Galilee and goes to Jewish land east of the Jordan. The "region of Judea beyond the Jordan" (τὰ ὅρια τῆς Ἰουδαίας πέραν τοῦ Ἰορδάνου) in Matthew 19:1 (cf. Mk 10:1) is in my view not Perea in the southern part of the land east of the Jordan, but like "Bethany beyond the Jordan" (Βηθανία πέραν τοῦ Ἰορδάνου) in John 1:28 (cf. Jn 10:40), it is Batanea with its strongly Jewish population (illus. 41) in northern Transjordan.[49] From there Jesus traveled via Jericho (Mk 10:46–52) to reach the final destination of all the ways he traveled upon, the holy city Jerusalem (Mk 11:1ff.). If we follow the chronology of John, there are interposed between the arrival of Jesus on the Mount of Olives and the festive entry into the city still other events, such as the resurrection of Lazarus (Jn 11:1–44); the outlawing of Jesus by the Sanhedrin (Jn 11:47–52); the hideaway in the village of Ephraim, the modern et Taybeh, "near the wilderness" (Jn 11:54); as well as the anointing in Bethany (Jn 12:1–9). This is all chronologically plausible and does not necessarily contradict the Synoptics.

IV. Summary

The public life of Jesus was a life underway by foot. He walked to meet and help people. He walked to bring his message to them. Finally, he walked to avoid dangers that threatened him, especially from the powerful. He said of himself, "I must go on my way today and tomorrow and the day following; for it cannot be that a prophet should perish away from Jerusalem" (Lk 13:33). The topographical and archaeological investigations of the last several years can help us know the ways of Jesus better. The more we do, the easier it will be for us to

[49] Cf. chapter 14, "Bethany on the Other Side of the Jordan" (pp. 177–91).

place his words in their original context and to begin to comprehend them.

Supplement: In 1991 M. Nun discovered the harbor of the town of Gennesaret, which could shed light on Mark 6:53.[50] The discovery was made possible by the dramatically low water level of the lake. In New Testament times the normal level had been approximately 2 m lower, so that nowadays the old harbors are normally underwater.[51] Around A.D. 1000 a new outlet into the lower Jordan formed near Degania (the onetime kibbutz of Israel's first prime minister, David Ben-Gurion), through which less water could flow off. As late as 1106 the hegumen Daniel saw both of the competing outlets.[52] We know of a total of sixteen ancient harbors and anchorages around Lake Gennesaret.[53] Especially extensive were the wharfs at Capharnaum, measuring up to 600 m in length.[54] After a second low water level, a boat from the time of Jesus (pp. 63–64) was discovered in 1986 at Migdal (Magdala).[55]

[50] Cf. chapter 10, "New Discoveries in Bethsaida" (pp. 143–47).

[51] M. Nun, *The Sea of Galilee: Water Levels, Past and Present* (En Gev: Kibbutz En Gev, 1991).

[52] *Itineraria rossica—altrussische Reiseliteratur* (Leipzig: Reclam, 1986), 89–90.

[53] M. Nun, *Sea of Galilee: Newly Discovered Harbours from New Testament Days* (En Gev: Kibbutz En Gev, 1992).

[54] Y. Stepansky, "Kefar Nahum Map, Survey", *ESI* 10 (1992): 87–90 (at 89–90).

[55] S. Wachsmann, ed., *The Excavations of an Ancient Boat in the Sea of Galilee (Lake Kinneret)* (Jerusalem: Israel Exploration Society, 1990).

5. Tabgha, the *Eremos* of Jesus

I. *Earlier Names of Tabgha*

Hardly any site in Galilee has a wealth of evangelical tradition like the spring-rich region at Capharnaum, which today bears the name Tabgha. This same area had other names in earlier times. The Spanish noblewoman Egeria[1] was an extraordinary woman in the fourth century A.D.: intelligent, pious, enterprising and furnished with excellent letters of recommendation, something especially helpful in view of her extensive pilgrimages. She had not only participated in the liturgies over a period of three years in the holy city Jerusalem but had also visited Egypt and Syria, had climbed the mountains Sinai and Tabor and also, as the abbot Valerius later wrote to his monks, ascended the mountain "called Heremus, on which the Lord taught his disciples the beatitudes."[2] It is all but certain that the Latin place-name *Heremus* was used by Egeria herself, although it does not appear in the brief summaries preserved for us in the collection of old documents of the librarian of the Monte Cassino Monastery, Peter the Deacon, from 1137.[3]

The Greek expression ἔρημος (τόπος) corresponding to *heremus* is used in the Gospels[4] to describe the lonely place to which Jesus loved to retreat near Seven Springs just 2 km southwest of Capharnaum.[5] Jerome, who came to this region in A.D. 386 with the senator's daughter

[1] This is her proper name, not Silvia or Aetheria as was earlier believed. Cf. P. Maraval, *Égérie: Journal de voyage (Itinéraire)*, *SC* 296 (Paris: Cerf, 1982), 16–27.

[2] *Epistola beatissime Egerie laude conscripta fratrum Bergidensium monachorum Valerio conlata* 3 (*SC* 296: 342–43: "aliumque ualde excelsum, in quo Dominus discipulos beatudines docuit, qui appellatur Heremus [v.l. aeremus]."

[3] R. Weber, "Petri Diaconi: De locis sanctis", in *Itineraria et alia geographica*, Corpus Christianorum: Series latina 175 (Turnhout: Brepols, 1960), 98.

[4] Mt 14:13 / Mk 6:32; Mt 14:15 / Mk 6:35 / Lk 4:42; Mk 1:45 / Lk 5:16; Mk 6:31.

[5] Cf. R. Riesner, *Jesus als Lehrer*, WUNT 2/7, 3rd ed. (Tübingen: Mohr Siebeck, 1988), 353–54; A. Niccacci, "Trente ans de fouilles du 'Studium Biblicum Franciscanum' et l'exégèse du Nouveau Testament", *Bibbia e Oriente* 26 (1984): 225–42 (at 227–30).

Paula, called the mountain ridge stretching from Tabgha to the north *solitudo*,[6] which represents the Latin synonym of the expression in biblical Greek. According to Flavius Josephus, the rich springs, whose salt content and temperature vary, contributed greatly to the fertility of the area and were named simply Καφαρναούμ because of their proximity to Capharnaum (*War* 3.519). The water was routed around the slopes of Tell el-'Oreimeh to the plain of Gennesaret via an aqueduct (cf. *War* 3.516–21).[7] Part of this aqueduct can still be seen near the former youth hostel Kare Deshe, which in the past had served as a German hospice for pilgrims and has now taken on this function once more. The extent to which the phenomenon of the Tabgha springs animated the imagination of observers is shown by the fact that Josephus could voice the speculation that these springs abundant with water were connected underground with the Nile.

On top of the tell stood the Old Testament city of Chinnereth on the border of the tribe of Naphtali (Josh 19:35), while the New Testament Gennesaret (Mt 14:34 / Mk 6:53) was located on the plain[8] near the richly flowing spring of et-Tine (p. 66). In the Roman era, the great caravan route that later came to be called the Via Maris went by Tabgha on its way from Egypt to Damascus (pp. 55–58). A small Roman road fort (Khirbet el-Khan) has been found at the base of the east side of Tell el-'Oreimeh near the modern Israeli pumping station (Mobil Ḥaarzi).[9] According to Matthew's Gospel, which quotes Isaiah 8:23—9:1 at this point (Mt 4:12–17), Jesus began his preaching ministry in the "land of Zebulun and the land of Naphtali, toward the sea" (pp. 61–62). With Chorazin and Bethsaida[10] as the other two corners and Capharnaum[11] as the midpoint of the base, Tabgha formed the so-called evangelical triangle (F. Mußner) where Jesus preached and worked more than in any other area (Mt 11:20–24 / Lk 10:13–15).

In the Gospels, this area is apparently also described with the name Magadan and the peculiar designation Dalmanutha. Thus the place where the disciples landed the boat after the feeding of the four thousand

[6] *Letter 108* 16 (PL 22:889; Baldi, 275).

[7] Cf. C. Kopp, *The Holy Places of the Gospels* (New York: Herder, 1963), 175.

[8] Cf. U. Hübner, "Ausgrabungen auf dem Tell el-Ọreime nahe Tabgha", *HlL* 115, nos. 2–3 (1983): 2–9.

[9] Cf. V. Fritz, "Kinneret und Ginnossar", *ZDPV* 94 (1978): 32–45.

[10] Cf. chapter 9, "In Search of Bethsaida" (pp. 128–42).

[11] Cf. chapter 8, "Riddles of the Synagogues at Capharnaum" (pp. 115–27).

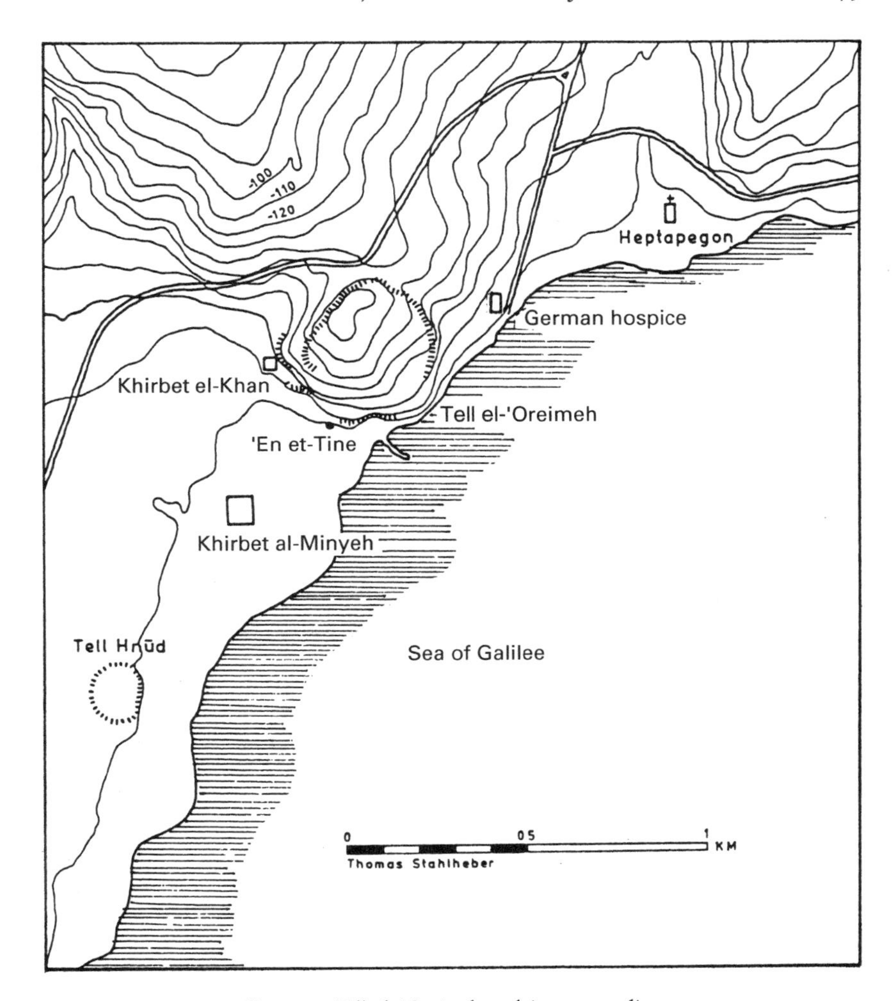

Illus. 15. Tell el-'Oreimeh and its surroundings.

is named in Matthew 15:39 and Mark 8:10. There has been no lack of scholars who have attempted to solve the riddle of the "district of Dalmanutha" (τὰ μέρη Δαλμανουθά).[12] B. Hjerl-Hansen in an article written in 1946 appears to have made an important contribution.[13] Following the speculation of other exegetes, he sees in "Dalmanutha"

[12] Cf. C. Kopp, *Holy Places of the Gospels* (see n. 7), 191.

[13] "Dalmanutha (Marc, VIII, 10): Énigme géographique et linguistique dans l'Évangile de S. Marc", *RB* 43 (1946): 372–84.

a compound Aramaic designation consisting of the genitive particle *dal* (דַּל), i.e., a contracted form of the prepositions *de* (דְּ) and *le* (לְ), meaning "of, belonging to", and the word *mạnutho* (מַעְנוּתוֹ), namely, "his refuge or residence". Hjerl-Hansen rendered the sense of the phrase דלמענתה לגלילא with "la contrée de sa demeure" (i.e., "the region of his home") and saw in it an indication of Capharnaum (cf. Mt 4:13; 9:1).

In my opinion, it alluded more to the area around Tabgha that in those days belonged to Capharnaum. In the innermost circle of the disciples, the phrase "the region of his home" may have been used to refer to the place where the Master spent much of his time. Here, as in other cases (e.g., Mk 5:41; 7:34), Mark appears to have preserved an Aramaic expression that had become commonplace in the original tradition. Matthew, who must have known Mark's text, chose the correct place-name for this area, i.e., Magadan (Μαγαδάν). This name is presumably composed of *may* (מַי), "water", the name of the Canaanite deity of fortune *Gad* (גַּד) and the locative ending *-an* found frequently in Galilee (pp. 131–32).[14] The name "the (happy) water of Gad" (מַי גַּד) would fit well the area around Tabgha with its abundance of springs.

II. *Egeria's Account and the Tradition of the Jewish Christians*

The presence of Jewish Christians in Capharnaum is proven by Jewish sources[15] and now by archaeology as well.[16] The Jewish Christians who lived in this area from the time of Jesus until the fifth century passed on traditions about locations from one generation to another. They regarded three different rock formations as the locations of Gospel events connected with the *eremos* area. The feeding of the five thousand (Mt 14:13–21 / Mk 6:31–46) was commemorated near a boulder lying directly next to the Via Maris, the Sermon on the Mount

[14] The name of the god Gad is also used in other biblical toponyms, such as Baal-gad (Josh 11:17), Migdal-gad (Josh 15:37 [LXX: Μαγδαλγαδ (A); Μαγαδαγαδ (B)]) and possibly Megiddo (?). Comparable to these are names such as "waters of Noah" (מֵי נֹחַ [Is 54:9]), "waters of Nephtoah" (מֵי נֶפְתּוֹחַ [Jos 15:9; 18:15]), etc.

[15] Cf. H. L. Strack and P. Billerbeck, *Kommentar zum Neuen Testament aus Talmud und Midrasch*, vol. 1, *Das Evangelium des Matthäus* (Munich: C. H. Beck, 1926), 159–60.

[16] Cf. G. Bagatti, *The Church of the Circumcision*, SBFCMi 2 (Jerusalem: Franciscan Printing Press, 1971), 128–29; V. Corbo, *The House of St. Peter at Capharnaum*, SBFCMi 5 (Jerusalem: Franciscan Printing Press, 1972); S. Loffreda, *Recovering Capharnum*, 2nd ed. (Jerusalem: Franciscan Printing Press, 1993).

(Mt 5–7 / Lk 6:17–49) at a cave in the nearby mountain slope, and the appearance of the resurrected Christ of John 21 at the stone steps leading down to the lake. Egeria found these traditions already in circulation when she visited the area of Tabgha around the year A.D. 383.[17]

She reported on what she discovered there with the following words:

> Not far away from there [Capharnaum] are some stone steps where the Lord stood. And in the same place by the sea is a grassy field with plenty of hay and many palm trees. By them are seven springs, each flowing strongly. And this is the field where the Lord fed the people with the five loaves and the two fishes. In fact, the stone on which the Lord placed the bread has now been made into an altar. People who go there take away small pieces of the stone to bring them prosperity, and they are very effective. Past the walls of this church goes the public highway on which the Apostle Matthew had his place of custom. Near there on a mountain is the cave to which the Savior climbed and spoke the Beatitudes.[18]

The Byzantines called the place Heptapegon (Ἑπτάπηγον) in Greek,[19] from which the later Arabic form et-Tabgha evolved, of which only the mutilated form Tabgha remains today.

However, not only these three events were commemorated here but in time other Gospel stories as well. Over the course of the centuries, the three old, reliable local traditions were passed on, but they were also expanded and embellished with legends. The locations shifted, and Christian traditions were taken over by the Muslim Arabs and adapted to their views. We now want to investigate briefly the development of the individual traditions in chronological order.

[17] Cf. J. WILKINSON, *Egeria's Travels to the Holy Land*, 2nd ed. (Jerusalem: Ariel, 1981), 237–40.

[18] Ibid., 196ff.; taken from Peter the Deacon (1137): "Non longe autem inde cernuntur gradus lapidei, super quos Dominus stetit. Ibidem vero super mare est campus herbosus, habens foenum satis et arbores palmarum multas et iuxta eas septem fontes, qui singuli infinitam aquam emittunt, in quo campo Dominus de quinque panibus et duobus piscibus populum satiavit. Sane lapis, super quem Dominus panem posuit, est factum altarium, de quo lapide nunc frusta tollunt venientes pro salute sibi et proest omnibus. Iuxta cuius ecclesiae parietes via publica transit, ubi Mattheus apostolus theloneum habuit. Inde in montem, qui iuxta est, est [spelunca], in qua ascendens beatudines dixit Salvator" (Baldi 281–82). There is no reason to change the expression *spelunca* in the only manuscript published by J. F. GAMURRINI (Baldi, 282, n. 1) to *specula* ("height, observation post") as in Geyer, 112.

[19] Cf. Epiphanius Monachus (Baldi, 278).

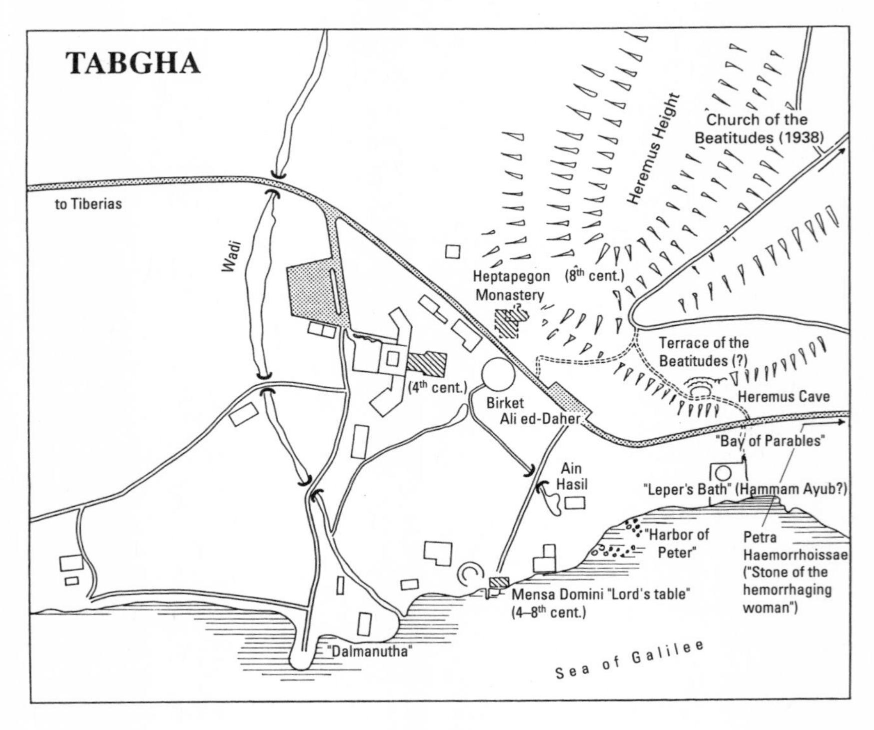

Illus. 16. Tabgha.

III. The Calling of the Disciples

Although a tradition regarding the location of the calling of the first disciples (Mt 4:18–22 / Mk 1:16–21) first appears in medieval accounts, Master Thetmar (A.D. 1217) will probably have hit on just the right place with his localizing of the story of the calling at Tabgha.[20] The bay at Seven Springs was one of the most sought-after spots for fishermen in Jesus' time just as it is today. Especially in winter and spring, the warm springs that pour into the lake attract the tilapia fish, known as "Saint Peter's fish", which prefers tropical temperatures.[21] One of the most knowledgeable persons about fishing on Lake Gennesaret

[20] Baldi, 283–84. An anonymous pilgrim from Gaul (1383) has the calling of Andrew and Peter take place at the *bains de Vertu* ("baths of Virtue", i.e., medicinal springs); Baldi, 288–89.

[21] When the larger part of Lake Huleh north of Lake Gennesaret was not yet drained, it happened in the more severe winters there that some of the St. Peter's fish froze to death.

and a man from whom I have learned much, M. Nun from Kibbutz En Gev, told me on many occasions that Capharnaum's fishermen had their place of work here.[22] For this reason, he names in his study of ancient harbors around the lake a small fishing harbor at Tabgha, "Peter's harbor", that he was able to investigate during the low water level in 1986.[23]

As Jesus was about to begin his public ministry in Capharnaum after the imprisonment of John the Baptist, he called the first four disciples to follow him (Mt 4:12–22 / Mk 1:16–21). We know from the fourth Gospel (Jn 1:28ff.) that he had already met these men from Bethsaida in the company of the Baptist (pp. 182–83). After the wedding feast at Cana, however, they apparently all returned to their usual vocation. Thus we find a small group of fishermen around the boat of Zebedee (Mk 1:20) at Magadan (Tabgha). Fish like to stay among the reeds that grow plentifully along the shores of the modern tongue of land "Dalmanutha" west of the springs. Peter and Andrew stood in shallow water where they were fishing with a casting net, just as I have been able to observe among the fishermen of today. The manner in which Mark describes the handling (ἀμφίβληστρον [Mk 1:16]) of this net (ἀμφιβάλλοντες [Mk 4:18]) indicates exactly this kind of fishing near the lakeshore.

Then Jesus came by after he had gotten on the Via Maris at the mouth of Dove Valley at Magdala (p. 61). He caught sight of the two brothers from the shore and called to them: "Follow me and I will make you become fishers of men" (Mk 1:17). They left their nets and went with Jesus a short distance farther (Mk 1:19a). The small harbor lay 500 m to the east, just behind the Franciscans' modern Chapel of the Primacy. At that time, just as today, a strong waterfall poured out of the easternmost spring into the lake. There the fishermen preferred to wash their nets and then get them ready to be used again. Jesus met John and James just as they were doing this kind of work, and he also invited them to follow him (Mk 1:19b). While the two pairs of brothers were on their way to Capharnaum, Zebedee together with his day laborers gathered the nets together (Mk 1:20), certainly including the net that Peter in his excitement had left lying there.

[22] Cf. M. Nun, *Der See Genezareth und die Evangelien*, SBAZ 101 (Gießen: Brunnen, 2001); *The Sea of Galilee and Its Fishermen in the New Testament* (En Gev: Kibbutz en Gev, 1989).

[23] *Ancient Anchorages and Harbours around the Sea of Galilee* (En Gev: Kibbutz En Gev, 1988), 22.

A very peculiar tradition handed down to us by Theodosius around the year 530 may be connected with the call of the disciples.[24] He claims that the Lord baptized the Apostles at Seven Springs (p. 91). However, this news hardly deserves much trust, as no one else knows anything about it. It probably is one of those curious pilgrimage legends that soon fell into oblivion.

IV. The Sites of the Sermons on the Mount and on the Lake

One reason that Jesus came to Capharnaum from the mountain hamlet of Nazareth, in those days with not many more than from 100 to 150 inhabitants, was very likely that he could much more easily come into contact with people there. We have seen that Capharnaum was located on an important overland highway. The first period of Jesus' ministry, which we also call "the Galilean spring", was marked by many people streaming into Capharnaum, curious and looking for help. The most important words of Jesus to the crowd that came together have been summarized in the Sermon on the Mount (Mt 4:25–8:1 / Lk 6:17–49) and the Sermon on the Lake (Mt 13 / Mk 4), both of which are localized in close proximity to Tabgha.

The pilgrim Egeria already pointed to the traditional location of the Sermon on the Mount with her remark that on the mountainside at Seven Springs was "the cave to which the Savior climbed and spoke the Beatitudes" (p. 81). There happens to be a fairly extensive, grassy area above a cave[25] (plate 3a), which would be excellent for such sermons. Two large basalt blocks mark the place that today is called "Heremus Height". According to Matthew, Jesus climbed a mountain or hill (ὄρος [Mt 5:1]) for the sermon that begins with the Beatitudes (Mt 5:3–12). According to Luke, Jesus came down from the mountain to a level place (ἐπὶ τόπου πεδινοῦ [Lk 6:17]) after a night spent in prayer (Lk 6:12). The traditional Heremus Height actually fits both accounts. It was possible for a considerable number of people to assemble there without trampling the cultivated fields lying all around it.

[24] *The Topography of the Holy Land* 2 (J. Wilkinson, *Jerusalem Pilgrims before the Crusades* [Jerusalem: Ariel, 1977], 63).

[25] Concerning the history of the Cave of the Beatitudes, see R. Riesner, "Die Höhle der Seligpreisungen in Tabgha", *HlL* 121, nos. 2–3 (1989): 16–21.

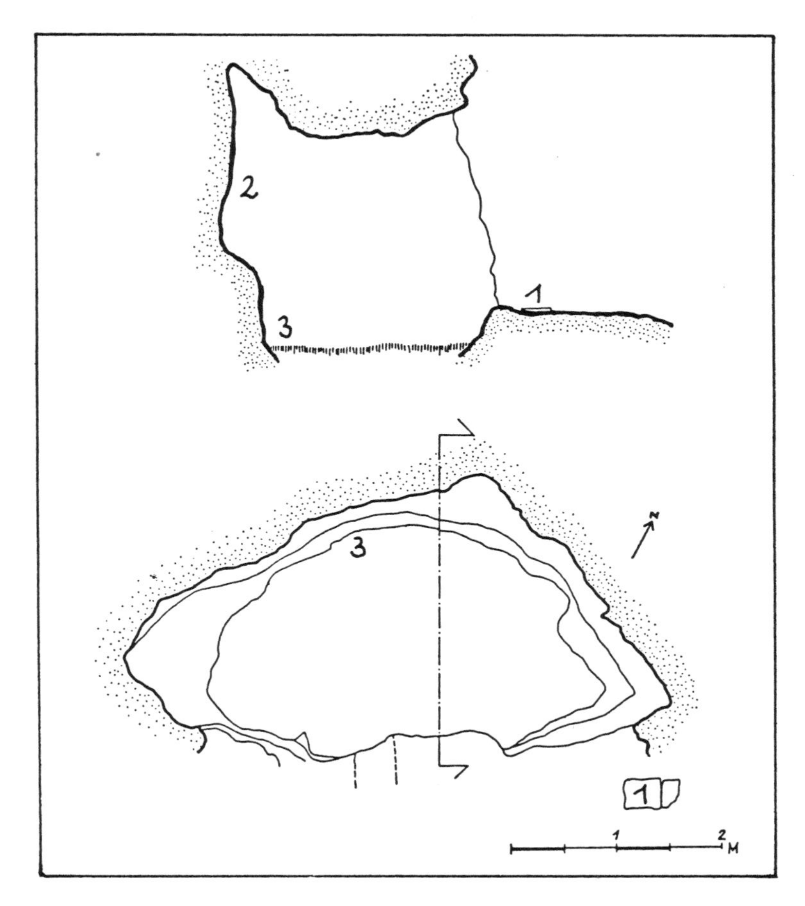

Illus. 17. Tabgha, Heremus Cave (Magharet Ayub) (from D. Chen and D. Milson, 1984). The Leper's Bath is about 10 m away from the lake. Above it in a northeasterly direction (50 m) is the cave above which lies the expanse of the Heremus Height plateau.

1 *Two cut basalt stones (*in situ*) are the remains of a (Byzantine?) wall in front of the entry to the grotto.*

2 *Location of an ancient cross cut into the rock.*

3 *A sidr tree grows from within the cave outward and overshadows the entrance.*

In the spring the hill is a magnificent flower garden filled with anemones and irises, the "lilies of the field" (Mt 6:28), and chirping "birds of the air" (Mt 6:26) hop from limb to limb in the prickly sidr trees. The words about the "city set on a hill" (Mt 5:14) were put in the

Lord's mouth by the splendorous Decapolis city of Hippos (pp. 148–49), which in those days beamed from a rocky vantage point across the lake. Towering above the northeast corner of the lake was the rock fortress of the Jews, Gamala, the Zealots' place of origin with their militant messianism that in forty years would plunge all Israel into ruin. This moved Jesus to bless the peacemakers and the meek, "for they shall be called sons of God" and "shall inherit the earth" (Mt 5:5, 9).

The modern Church of the Beatitudes was erected in 1928 about 1 km farther up on the same ridge of the Heremus Height. Thus, a beautiful vantage point was created close to the Italian pilgrimage hospice that had already been built in 1903. Historically, this was the first church of the eight Beatitudes. It is indeed a pleasant surprise that in all the pilgrims' accounts that speak of the location of the Beatitudes,[26] no church is ever mentioned. Apparently, there was a desire to preserve the site as Jesus had seen it. With the Byzantines' strong policy of sanctuary construction and the same in modern times, this is a good thing. However, the traditional Heremus Height does appear to have had many visitors in antiquity and in the Middle Ages, as pottery fragments are found there repeatedly although no traces of buildings are to be encountered.

Five hundred meters away from the Heremus Cave and the terrace above it in the direction of Capharnaum is a small, well-formed bay surrounded by a theaterlike terrain sloping down to the shore. This is possibly the place where Jesus spoke from a boat to the crowd assembled on the shore. Since this bay is considered to be the location of the Sermon on the Lake (Mk 4:1ff.), experts have tested the acoustics of this natural theater and have found them to be excellent.[27] I myself had the opportunity to confirm with groups the excellent audibility of a voice if Jesus' sermon according to Mark had been delivered from a boulder in the lake. Because Jesus spoke to the people from a floating pulpit in parables (ἐδίδασκεν αὐτοὺς ἐν παραβολαῖς [Mk 4:2]), the place is today sometimes called the "Bay of the Parables".

It may be assumed that Jesus sailed from here on the same evening to the Decapolis, stilled the storm during the crossing (Mk 4:35–41)

[26] *De situ urbis Jerusalem* (1130–1150): "Secundo milario a Capharnaum desensus montis est in quo sermonicavit ad turbas, in quo et leprosum curavit" (Baldi, 281). Also cf. Baldi, 415, 417, 419–20.

[27] Cf. B. C. Crisler, "The Acoustics and Crowd Capacity of Natural Theaters in Palestine", *BA* 39 (1976): 128–41 (at 137).

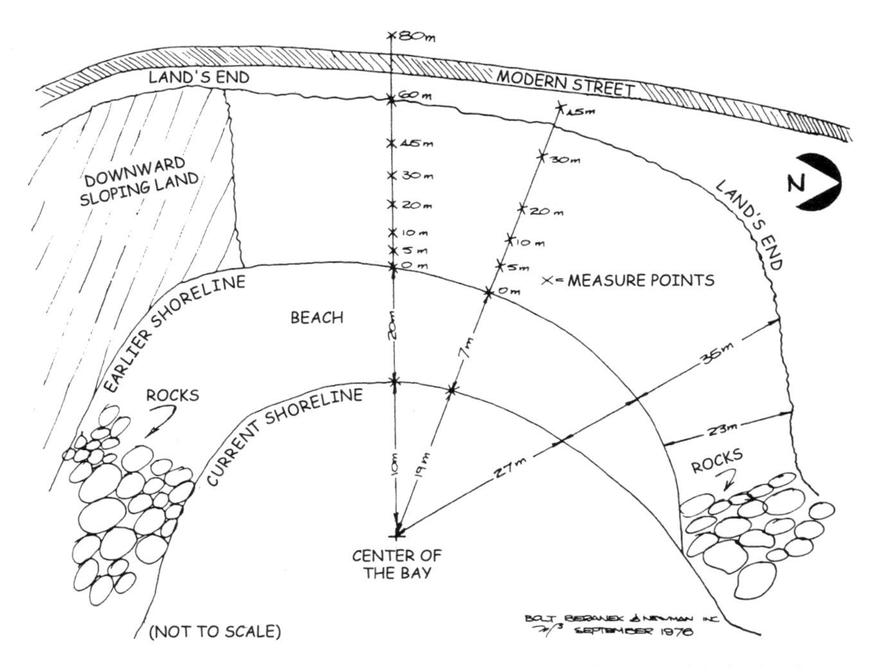

Illus. 18. The "Bay of the Parables". From the given point (in the center of the bay), a human voice can be projected across the water and easily heard by those within this "natural theater".

and banished the demons into the swine in Gentile territory near Kursi (Mk 5:1–20).[28] On the return trip, he is supposed to have landed in this bay, where the synagogue ruler Jairus was waiting for him (Mk 5:21–24). The testimony of late Byzantine accounts tells of a memorial stone located halfway between Tabgha and Capharnaum, which are 2 miles apart.[29] The stone with a cross carved into it was erected at the traditional site where the Lord had healed the woman with the flow of blood (Mk 5:25–34). Jesus was at that time on the way to Capharnaum to visit Jairus, who had begged him to help his little, terminally ill daughter. Today there is once again a memorial stone showing the monogram of Christ and the hand of a woman. Engraved in the block of basalt are the words PETRA HAEMORRHOISSAE ("stone of the hemorrhaging woman").

[28] Cf. chapter 11, "Kursi and the Land of the Gerasenes" (pp. 148–55).

[29] Epiphanius Monachus in the ninth century (Baldi, 277f.); *Vita S. Helenae et Constantini* from the tenth or eleventh century (Baldi, 278f.).

The great Church historian Eusebius (265–340) claims that the healed woman came from Caesarea Philippi (Panias; *HE* 7.18). He had seen her house on a visit there. On a column at the entrance to the house stood a bronze statue of a woman kneeling and pleading, with hands outstretched toward a young man. Depicted are the woman herself and Jesus. Only in a Gentile Christian milieu is the making of such a statue conceivable. Based on this probably genuine tradition, several things become understandable. The woman was a Gentile, apparently a woman of means (cf. Lk 8:43). After the news of the miracle worker in Capharnaum had gotten through to her in Caesarea, she started out to go and find him. She knew how sensitive the Jews were about ritual purity. This woman was unclean for them in two respects: (1) as a Gentile, and (2) as a woman afflicted with a flow of blood (αἱμοῤῥοοῦσα Mt 9:20]). Therefore, she secretly slipped through the crowd to Jesus and said, "If I touch even his garments, I shall be made well" (Mk 5:28). She was in fact healed.

V. The Healing of the Leper

The Heremus Cave below the Heremus Height has an unusually varied history connected with the healing of the leper and woven around with legends. In Matthew the healing of a leper and the return of the disciples to Capharnaum follow the Sermon on the Mount (Mt 8:1–4). "When he came down from the mountain, great crowds followed him; and behold, a leper came to him and knelt before him, saying, 'Lord, if you will, you can make me clean'" (Mt 8:1–2). The oldest traditions about Tabgha go back, as we have seen, to messianic Jews from Capharnaum. According to Jewish law, a leper had to undergo a ritual bath after his healing (Lev 14). It is probably for this reason that the easternmost of the Tabgha springs was called the "Leper's Bath".[30] In the Byzantine period, this esteemed spring was enclosed in a circular structure.

It is speculated that the Old Testament text about the healing of Naaman the Syrian (2 Kings 5:1ff.) found use in the liturgical formation of the memorial for this leper's healing (L. Klein). The seven washings of Naaman in the water of the Jordan were thus transferred to the

[30] Cf. B. Bagatti, *Antichi villaggi cristiani di Galilea*, SBFCMi 13 (Jerusalem: Franciscan Printing Press, 1971), 89–91.

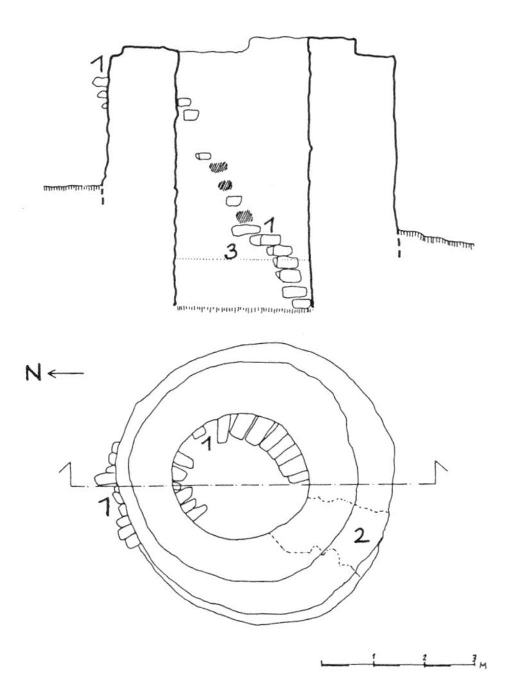

Illus. 19. The Leper's Bath (Hammam Ạyub). Recorded by the architects Dr. Doron Chen and David Milson in January 1984.

1 *Basalt steps fitted into the outside and inside of the circular Byzantine wall.*

2 *Modern breach in the tower wall where the spring water drains off.*

3 *Water line of the spring.*

man healed by Jesus. The speculation is justified that this event had an effect on the name "Seven Springs", where the leper found healing. There are only three large springs (namely, Hammam Ạyub, Ạin Hasil and Birket Ali ed-Daher) plus a great number of rivulets that emerge between these three from the base of the Heremus Mountain. Thus the original name May-Gadan, "water of Gad" (Mt 15:39), was replaced by the Byzantines with Heptapegon (Seven Springs), to which the modern name Tabgha testifies.

In many accounts from the time of the Crusaders, we read about the traditional location of the healing of the leper. As the oldest witness, the standard work from the period, *De situ urbis Jerusalem* (A.D. 1130–1150), reports: "Two miles from Capharnaum is the descent of the mountain [*descensus montis*] from which Jesus preached to the multitudes and at which he healed the leper."[31] This tradition is recurrent in the pilgrimage accounts.[32] However, the development of the legends surrounding the healing of the leper soon took a new turn. The Muslim inhabitants began to take an interest in the healing power of the "Leper's Bath". For them, the leper is no longer the one healed by Jesus but rather is the leper Job (Arabic: Ạyub), who also plays an important role in the Muslim tradition.

In the fourth century A.D. the pilgrim Egeria visited a cave sanctuary of Job in the Syrian Golan at the Springs of Jarmuk (illus. 41), which continued to be venerated by the Muslims after the Arabic conquest in 648.[33] Today the place is still called Sheik el-Meskin ("the unfortunate sheik"). The Islamic legend says that the wealthy sheik Ạyub was tempted by Satan because of his faithfulness to God. After he had lost his possessions and his family, he was also struck with leprosy. He had to leave his home and lived in the Heremus Cave (mentioned above) in the mountainside at Tabgha. The legend says that his entire body was covered with worms. When he suddenly got up one day, several of them fell on the ground. In fear he picked them all up and put them back in place on his body. His wife watched all of this, shaking her head, and he said to her, "If Allah wants them here, then they should remain here." The story typifies many a pious Muslim's devotion to God that often borders on fatalism. However, as the story continues, God finally cared for his faithful servant Ạyub and commanded him to sling the dirt in the cave on himself and to wash himself once a day for seven days in the "Leper's Bath". On the seventh day, his skin became as pure as that of a child. Having been healed, he returned to his home. Therefore, the spring is today called Hammam Ạyub (Bath of Job) in the vernacular and is still visited by Muslims, especially by Druze women, for healing.

VI. The Multiplication of the Loaves

The miracle of Jesus that has been connected with Seven Springs since the earliest times is the feeding of the five thousand (Mt 14:13–23 / Mk 6:31–48). Most exegetes today consider the two stories about the multiplication of the loaves in both the Gospel of Mark and that of

[31] Baldi, 281.

[32] Cf. Baldi, 413, 420, 423.

[33] Cf. J. Wilkinson, *Egeria's Travels* (see n. 17), 108–12.

Matthew to be doublets, i.e., two accounts of the same event. The singular feeding of the multitude would have happened on the east shore of the lake, as assumed by John (Jn 6:1ff.). Thus, the memorial in Tabgha would be at the most for pilgrims for whom the visit to the other side of the lake would have been too difficult.[34] However, anyone who is familiar with the area around the lake has to admit that the description of Mark, the earliest evangelist, is applicable only to the west shore (pp. 69–72). The location tradition of the Jewish Christians was kept alive by two churches from the fourth and fifth centuries, which were the destination of many pilgrims.[35] John and Luke combined the two miracles into one account and reported the event in the geographic context of the second. C. Kopp saw "a mountain north of the Wadi es-Samak in the kingdom of Philip"[36] as the location of the multiplication of the loaves. Tell Hadar, a hill with ruins, is the first to come under consideration (p. 68).

A late Byzantine account, which is dealt with in the following, calls the site of the feeding of the four thousand Dodekathronos (δωδεκαθρόνος), i.e., "throne of the Twelve", because Jesus gathered the twelve disciples around him at this multiplication of the loaves (Mt 15:32 / Mk 8:1; cf. Jn 6:3). The throne of the Twelve is usually assumed to be at the Sanctuary of the Primacy in Tabgha. The text from the *Commemoratorium de casis Dei*, dated A.D. 808, which is used to support this, is mutilated and has only "duodec..."[37] to offer, which could also be emended to read "duodecim apostolorum". According to Theodosius, the "Lord Christ baptised the apostles" at Seven Springs.[38] Daniel Abbas said in 1106 that the Chapel of the Primacy was "dedicated to the holy Apostles".[39] The five heart-shaped column sections and the large plinth, which lie there in the sand and have often been interpreted as the Dodekathronos, are more likely to have made access to the water of the lake possible for pilgrims, as M. Nun believes. According to the late Byzantine account, the Dodekathronos and thereby the site of the feeding of the four

[34] Cf. C. Kopp, *Holy Places of the Gospels* (see n. 7), 214–23.

[35] Cf. chapter 7, "The Churches of the Multiplication of Loaves and Fishes" (pp. 102–14).

[36] *Holy Places of the Gospels* (see n. 7), 214.

[37] Baldi, 277.

[38] *The Topography of the Holy Land* 2 (J. Wilkinson, *Jerusalem Pilgrims before the Crusades* [Jerusalem: Ariel, 1977], 63).

[39] Baldi, 280f.

thousand was on the east shore of the lake, a localization that was later still occasionally recalled.[40]

The *Vita S. Helenae et Constantini* from the tenth or eleventh century describes the journey of the mother of the emperor, the builder of churches, from east to west to the holy sites by the Lake of Tiberias (illus. 13) that at the end of the first millennium could still be found. The following is this important, though somewhat confused, text: "Around the [Lake of] Tiberias are the following sites: the so-called *dodekathronos* where Christ, our God, sat down and taught. On this [hill] he multiplied the seven loaves and fed four thousand [Mt 15:32–39/Mk 8:1–10]." In the following, it appears that a town on the left bank of the Jordan has been confused with another. The town is called Capharnaum, but in reality it has to be Bethsaida. The correct location of Capharnaum was probably no longer known at that time:[41]

> Nearby is the area around Capharnaum where Christ our God lived. The house of John the Theologian is also there [p. 129]. . . . On it she [Helen] crossed the nearby river [Jordan] together with the imperial bodyguard and the respected personalities she had brought with her from Constantinople. She found a stone cross where Christ healed the woman with the flow of blood. She went on from there and came to a fort [καστέλλιον] at which a large spring emerges called Heptapegon, where Christ our God had performed the miracle of the five loaves and two fishes. There she built a wonderful sanctuary and went down to the lake and found the place where our Lord Christ had appeared to the Apostles as they were fishing after the Resurrection [Jn 21]. . . . There she also erected a church in honor of the holy and blessed Apostle."[42]

The author of the *Vita* in his hagiographical fantasy thereby attributed the churches that could be found to the works of Saint Helen. Drawing

[40] The Franciscan custodian of Zion Bonifacius de Stephanis (1551–1564) has preserved part of this tradition: "Not far from Kursi [*Corasain*] are the ten cities, which the Gospel names *Decapoleos*, namely, on the other side of the Sea of Galilee [*et sunt ultra mare Galilaeae*]. . . . Nearby, there is also a mountain and the desolate place where Christ satisfied the four thousand" (Baldi, 291).

[41] Even St. Willibald in A.D. 723 had found nothing more than a house and a wall in Capharnaum, while in Bethsaida he saw the church where the home of Peter and Andrew had stood (Baldi, 266).

[42] Baldi, 278f.

on an older source,[43] he described with relative accuracy the holy sites of the first millennium, in spite of quite a few mix-ups. The two locations where the multitudes were fed had probably even been viewed from a hilltop at Tiberias by Jerome and Paula, who was traveling with him.[44]

However, what had happened to the beautiful, second Church of Heptapegon with the valuable mosaics that were probably donated by the Jerusalem patriarch Martyrios (478–486)? It can be assumed that it fell victim to the destructive frenzy of the Persian hordes, like most of the churches at that time (p. 110). The Christian life that originally blossomed round about the lake died a slow death after the subsequent Arabic conquest (636). Testifying to this gradual decay is the pilgrimage account by the Gallic bishop Arculf, who spent nine months in the Holy Land in A.D. 670. He found no remaining buildings in Tabgha. Only several columns lying strewn about the edge of the spring-fed stream bore witness to the position of the sanctuary of the multiplication of loaves. Arculf is certainly right in claiming that the multitude that was present at the miracle of the loaves quenched its thirst at these springs.[45]

A layer of debris 1.5 m thick accumulated above the costly mosaics over time. This layer was not removed until 1932 during the excavations of the priestly archaeologists A. E. Mader and A. M. Schneider.[46] However, approximately 150 years after the destruction, the memory of the miracle at Seven Springs returned to life in the eighth century. When Charlemagne began to be interested in the location of the holy sites, he ordered the creation of a list of holy places and of the members of orders and priests who lived there. In 808 the *Commemoratorium de casis Dei* came into being. It is said of Tabgha in it, "Above the lake [*supra mare*] of Tiberias is a monastery, which is named Heptapegon, where the Lord fed his people with five loaves and two fishes, five thousand in number. Ten monks live there. Next to the lake [*iuxta mare*], there is also a church, which is named after the twelve Apostles,

[43] Cf. A. M. Schneider, *The Church of the Multiplying of Loaves and Fishes* (London, 1937), 46–48; idem, *Die Brotvermehrungskirche von et-tâbgha am Genesarethsee* (Paderborn, 1934), 44–48.

[44] *Letter 46* 3 (PL 22:491; Baldi, 276): "Inde [from Tabor] ad mare veniemus Gennesareth, et de quinque et septem panibus videbimus in deserto quinque et quatuor hominum milia saturata. Apparebit oppidum Naim."

[45] Adomnan, *The Holy Places* 2.24 (J. Wilkinson, *Jerusalem Pilgrims before the Crusades* [Jerusalem: Ariel, 1977], 108).

[46] See n. 43 for the excavation report.

where the Lord stayed with his disciples. A [rock] table [*mensa*] is there, at which he sat with them. A priest and two clerics are there."[47]

Thus in the eighth century a monastery stood on the rise (*supra mare*) and a church by the lake.[48] This monastery on the mountain in the Carolingian account is certainly identical with the "Kastellion Heptapegon" (καστέλλιον Ἑπτάπηγον) that the monk Epiphanius had found in the ninth century a mile west of the Petra Haemorrhoissae.[49] In this fortlike monastery, so says the late Byzantine account, there was a "large church" (ἐκκλησία μεγάλη). Yet, as the parallel account from the *Vita S. Helenae* cited above shows, Epiphanius added the "large" of the Heptapegon spring to the church. Through the excavations by B. Bagatti in 1935, a small chapel was uncovered, which showed two mosaic periods.[50] However, this was not an original chapel of the Beatitudes, as the excavators believed, but rather a sanctuary that succeeded the Church of the Multiplication of Loaves (pp. 103–5). The Byzantine monastery was directly above the large spring of Tabgha and was connected with the church, as the ancient road was routed below this spring, in contrast to the modern one that goes between the spring and the Kastellion ruins.

With the Kastellion Heptapegon monastery, the location of the multiplication of the loaves now gradually migrated from the plain by the lake to the adjacent rise that was identical with the traditional site of the Sermon on the Mount. The first to report on this move was the Crusader Saewulf (1102): "The mountain upon which the Lord Jesus fed the five thousand with five loaves and two fishes rises not far from the [*castrum*] Gennesaret [Khirbet el-Minyeh?]. This mountain is named the Lord's Table [*tabula Domini*] by the inhabitants. At the foot of the mountain is the Church of Saint Peter, beautiful but almost deserted."[51] The master Thetmar, who visited the land somewhat later (1217), also believed that Jesus fed the five thousand on the mountain "there where he, encircled by his disciples, had preached."[52] Frater Benedict

[47] Baldi, 277. Cf. C. Kopp, *Holy Places of the Gospels* (see n. 7), 221–22.

[48] Some archaeological signs can be interpreted to mean that both churches had been preceded by even older structures. Cf. S. Loffreda, *The Sanctuaries at Tabgha* (Jerusalem, 1978). However, the pilgrimage accounts (Arculf, Willibald) are silent about it.

[49] Baldi, 277f.

[50] "La cappella sul Monte delle Beatitudini", *Rivista di archeologia cristiana* 14 (1937): 1–91.

[51] Baldi, 280.

[52] Baldi, 283f.

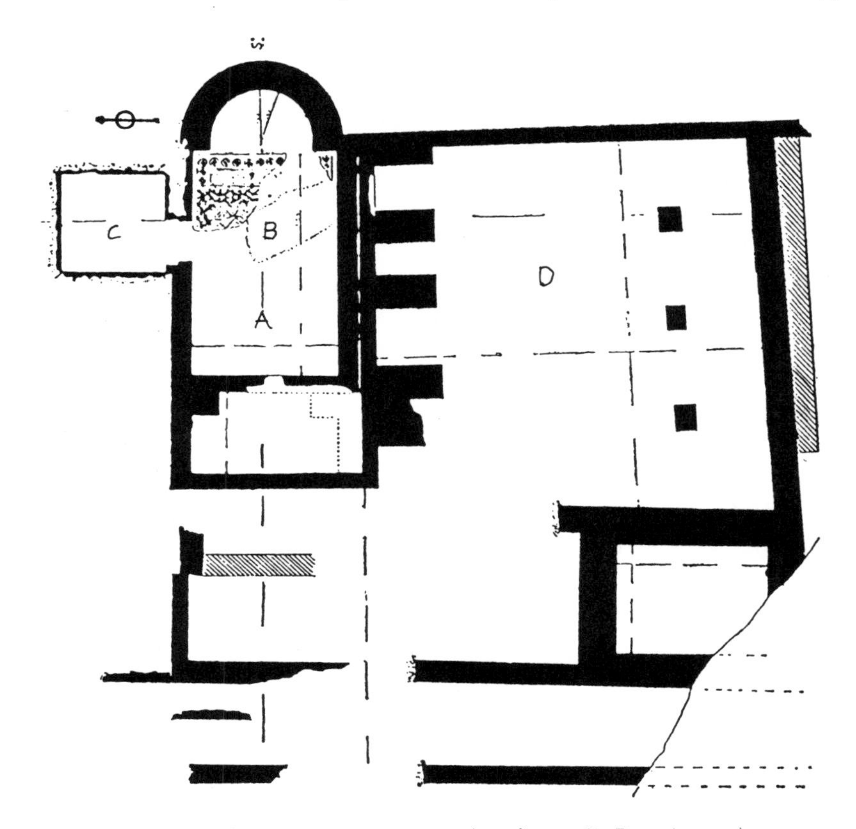

Illus. 20. The Heptapegon monastery (according to B. Bagatti, 1935).
A Chapel
B Cistern
C Sacristy
D Cloister

of Alignano (ca. 1260) was of the same conviction: "There in the vicinity [of Capharnaum] on a mountain in the direction of Tiberias is the place where Jesus fed the five thousand with five barley loaves and two fishes, from which twelve baskets full were left over." [53]

Toward the end of the thirteenth century, the Saxon Dominican Burchard from Mount Zion reports that Christ held the Sermon on the Mount from a mountainside (*ascensus montis*) and also fed the five thousand there. He says Jesus fled to this place when the people wanted

[53] Baldi, 284.

to make him king (cf. Jn 6:15) and spent the night there in prayer (cf. Mk 6:46). He also speaks enthusiastically of the splendid view from this mountain. He adds other interesting details, i.e., that this elevation was as long as the flights of two arrows and its breadth a stone's throw. It was "covered with grass and pleasant, suited for preaching. There is also a stone displayed there, on which the Lord Jesus sat, and with it the seats of the Apostles. (The Christians call the place *tabula* or *mensa*.) At the foot of this mountain near the lake, approximately 30 paces away, is a flowing spring surrounded by a wall." [54] The walled-in spring is certainly the Bath of Job (Hammam Ạjub), and the description of the mountain elevation fits well the site of the Sermon on the Mount mentioned above (p. 84).

Occasionally, pilgrims also sought the place where Jesus met the centurion from Capharnaum (cf. Lk 7:1ff.) near Tabgha.[55] The Lord's walk on the lake is frequently localized here as well.[56] From this mountain Jesus could actually watch how the disciples struggled toward Bethsaida to reach the other shore ahead of him (Mk 6:45) desperately rowing against the strong headwind (the sirocco from the northeast; Mk 6:48). There Jesus walked across the lake to come to their aid. After he had entered their boat, he no longer wanted the tired disciples to cross over to Bethsaida. He had them land where the village of Gennesaret was (Mk 6:53), which in those days was near the Fig Spring (Ạin et-Tine), from which the Benedictine Monastery of Tabgha today gets its good water, no longer on the Tell Chinnereth as in the past (p. 66).

Since Seven Springs with its *eremos* mountain was one of Jesus' favorite places to stay, the assumption is probably not totally unjustified that this is the same "mountain in Galilee" mentioned by Jesus (ἐπορεύθησαν εἰς τὴν Γαλιλαίαν εἰς τὸ ὄρος) to which he sent his disciples after the Resurrection (Mt 28:16): "And when they saw him they worshiped him; but some doubted. And Jesus came and said to them, 'All authority in heaven and on earth has been given to me. Go therefore and make disciples of all nations, baptizing them in the name of the Father and of the Son and of the Holy Spirit . . . ; and behold, I am with you always, to the close of the age'" (Mt 28:17–20). This

[54] Baldi, 285. The sentence in parentheses is probably a gloss.
[55] James of Verona (1335) (Baldi, 286–88).
[56] Master Thetmar (1217) (Baldi, 283f.).

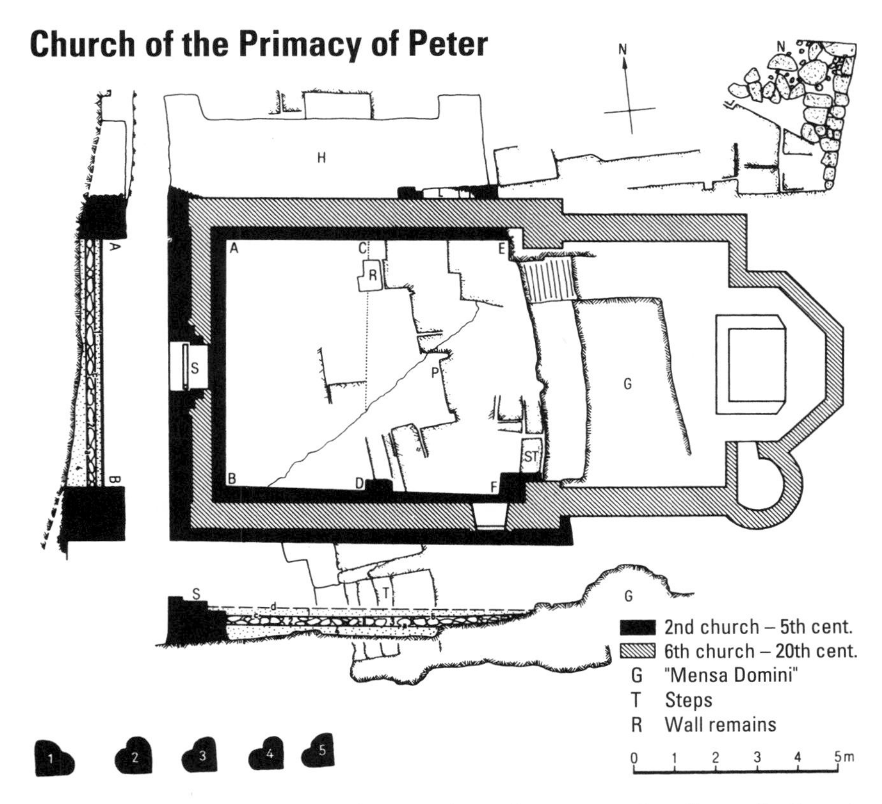

Illus. 21. Church of the Primacy of Peter—plan and excavations (according to B. Bagatti, O.F.M. [1936], and S. Loffreda, O.F.M. [1968]) (from G. Kroll). Ground plan and longitudinal section.

mountain near Capharnaum thus could have been the post-Easter appearance's landscape background that the author of the conclusion of Matthew had in mind.[57]

VII. The Appearance of the Risen One (John 21)

Approximately 200 m east of the Church of the Multiplication of Loaves and Fishes on an outcropping that juts out into the lake stands the Chapel of the Primacy built by the Franciscans. It commemorates the

[57] For the view that it was Mt. Tabor, cf. R. Riesner, in *GBL*, 2nd ed. (1990), 3:1514–20 (at 1519).

appearance of Jesus at Lake Tiberias told in John 21. Just as fishermen prefer this bay in the spring (pp. 82–83), Peter may well have led his six fellow disciples to this place in those days following Easter when he announced to them his decision, "I am going fishing", and received the answer, "We will go with you" (Jn 21:3). Thus we can imagine the risen Lord here on the rock table in the first light of day as he prepared a breakfast of bread and fish for his own (Jn 21:8). In the course of their meal together he tested Peter's love and said, "Feed my lambs, feed my sheep" (Jn 21:15–17) and thereby gave him the highest pastoral office (primacy).

A modern bronze statue serves as a reminder of this event. During the flowering of the Byzantine Age, as long as the beautiful Heptapegon sanctuary existed, the evangelical memorial sites in the area (the *eremos* plateau of the Sermon on the Mount, the holy cave, the Leper's Bath and the place of the post-Easter appearance at the lake) were looked after by the monks. Besides the round tower around the holy spring of the leper and an enclosing wall around the cave, there were originally no other structures at these sites. Thus, the pilgrim Egeria (A.D. 383) does not mention a church at the site of the post-Easter appearance (p. 81). After the destruction by the Persians (A.D. 614) and the Islamic conquest (A.D. 636), lush, rank vegetation covered the ruins for 150 years. The courageous pilgrim Willibald, the later bishop of Eichstätt, who stayed in the Holy Land two years (724–726) and got as far as Bethsaida, Kursi and Panias,[58] did not deem Seven Springs worthy of the slightest mention.

At least when the Kastellion monastery was built above Tabgha's main spring (pp. 103–4), a chapel dedicated to the twelve Apostles was erected 150 m south at the stone steps as well. It was originally planned to commemorate the entire life of the Twelve as fishermen and disciples by the lake; however, the Easter morning meal soon became the focus of the memorial. The rock table was considered the "Mensa Domini" ("Lord's table").[59] This shrine was now visited by many pilgrims, and its tradition came down through history without interruption. The stone steps mentioned by Egeria may have already served fishermen in Jesus' day and been preserved in the memory of the Jewish Christians of Capharnaum. They continued to be the focal

[58] Baldi, 266, 297f.

[59] First in A.D. 808 in *Commemoratorium de casis Dei* (Baldi, 277).

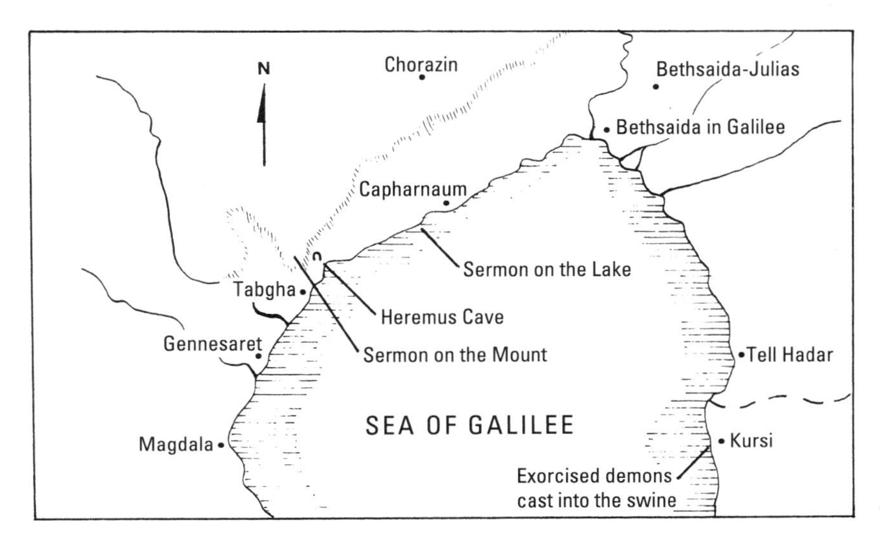

Illus. 22. Tabgha's surroundings (according to C. R. Page, 1995)

point for the pilgrims, even after the chapel was destroyed by Sultan Bibars in 1263.[60] Not until 1933 was the little Church of the Primacy of Peter rebuilt by the Franciscans; in 1985 it was restored in good taste.

The Tabgha area is thus very biblical terrain in its own right. For over fifteen years, I was able to follow the footsteps of Jesus here on the Sea of Galilee while observing the blossoms of tradition and legend that have sprung from the eastern soil alongside the historical traces. I wanted to record some of them here on the occasion of the one hundredth anniversary of the founding of the German settlement in Tabgha (February 6, 1889), before they are swept away in the hectic rush and flurry of change in our present age and fall into oblivion.

[60] Cf. Baldi, 284ff.

6. A Further Port by Tabgha

The place that Jesus and the disciples attempted to reach when they traveled to Bethsaida (Mk 6:45–48)[1] is still uncertain: "And when they had crossed over [καὶ διαπεράσαντες ἐπὶ τὴν γήν], they came to land at Gennesaret [ἦλθον εἰς Γεννησαρέτ], and moored to the shore [καὶ προσορμίσθησαν]. And when they got out of the boat, immediately the people recognized him, and ran about the whole neighborhood [περιέδραμον ὅλην τὴν χώραν ἐκείνην]" (Mk 6:53–55). It is uncertain what is meant by "Gennesaret". Is this perhaps a settlement or a landscape? Josephus mentions a landscape "Gennesar" (Γεννησάρ [*War* 3:516–21]), and the Rabbinic literature a place "Ginnesar" (גינסר).[2] R. Pesch writes in his commentary on Mark: "The indication of the landing (in a port) gives probably the *locality*, not the landscape ahead."[3] The verb προσορμίξεσθαι appears only here in the New Testament (Mk 6:53) and means "to dock in a port". Some believe that the redundant sounding idiom ἐπὶ τὴν γήν was a later added comment.[4]

Perhaps this topographical question will gain new insight through the research of M. Nun. When the water of Gennesaret was particularly low in the year 1991, M. Nun discovered the remains of ports dating from the Roman-Byzantine period. At the east foot of Tell Kinneret (Tell el-'Oreimeh), he also discovered an anchorage site, directly in front of the renovated German hospice (in former times, the Israeli youth hostel Kare Deshe).[5] This port was narrow and had two entrances. M. Nun discovered also a paved beach promenade, which had been

[1] Cf. chapter 4, "Jesus' Routes around the Sea of Galilee" (pp. 53–76, esp. pp. 65–66).

[2] Cf. R. RIESNER, "Genezareth (Ort)", in *GBL*, 2nd ed. (1990), 1:439.

[3] *Das Markusevangelium*, vol. 1 (Freiburg: Herder, 1976), 365.

[4] Cf. C. P. THIEDE, *Die älteste Evangelien-Handschrift?* 4th ed. (Wuppertal: R. Bruckhaus, 1992), 41–43.

[5] *Sea of Galilee: Newly Discovered Harbours from New Testament Days* (En Gev: Kibbuz En Gev, 1992), 36f.

located in the Hellenistic-Roman part of Gennesaret at the south foot of Kinneret. The distance of this port from the village was probably due to soil deposits from et-Tine (illus. 15) around the lakeshore of the village of Gennesaret. The distance between place and port could also be the reason why Mark writes rather pedantically the fact that Jesus first landed and then came to Gennesaret (Mk 6:53).

7. The Churches of the Multiplication of Loaves and Fishes

I. The Church of Joseph of Tiberias

When the pilgrim Egeria visited the Holy Land in A.D. 383, she found in Tabgha a church built above the rock that the tradition connected with the feeding of the five thousand (pp. 80–81). The rock itself had been used as an altar:

> Not far away from there [Capharnaum] are some stone steps where the Lord stood [see Jn 21:4]. And in the same place by the sea is a grassy field with plenty of hay and many palm trees. By them are seven springs, each flowing strongly. And this is the field where the Lord fed the people with the five loaves and the two fishes. In fact, the stone on which the Lord placed the bread has now been made into an altar. People who go there take away small pieces of the stone to bring them prosperity, and they are very effective. Past the walls of this church goes the public highway on which the Apostle Matthew had his place of custom. Near there on a mountain is the cave to which the Savior climbed and spoke the Beatitudes.[1]

The church of which Egeria speaks was the first one on this site and must have been erected around A.D. 350. It was accidentally discovered in March 1936 as the artist B. Gauer dug out the mosaics in front of the altar of the church there at that time. While digging for a solid foundation in which to embed the mosaics restored by him, he found the apse of the oldest church.[2] It was a simple structure in the Syrian style that stood parallel to the old road and was not yet oriented toward the

[1] J. Wilkinson, *Egeria's Travels to the Holy Land*, 2nd ed. (Jerusalem, 1981), 196ff. See Latin text, p. 81, n. 18.

[2] An initial report on this: "Ein neuer Fund in der Brotvermehrungskirche zu Tabgha", *HlL* 80 (1936): 60.

east, as was later customary. It is probable that we know even the name of the builder of this church.

Around the year 370 Bishop Epiphanius of Salamis in Scythopolis (Beth Shean) met a certain Jewish Christian named Josepos who told him his life's story.[3] Born in Tiberias to a respected Pharisee family, Josepos had been sent to collect the offerings of the Jewish communities in Asia Minor. While on that mission, he came to know and esteem a Christian bishop from the region from whose library he borrowed the New Testament. Josepos thus gained a knowledge of Jesus and applied for baptism, having suffered many a persecution at the hands of his former fellow believers. Later, Emperor Constantine took notice of him and granted him the title of *comes*, or count. The emperor also allowed him to build churches in the Jewish Christian communities of Galilee, such as Sepphoris, Nazareth, Tiberias and Capharnaum.

Archaeology has proven that there was not yet a church built over the "house of Peter" in the middle of the fourth century[4] and thus confirms Egeria's statement that "its walls stand until this day as they used to be."[5] We can therefore assume that Constantine's permission to build a church in Capharnaum was finally realized on the outskirts of the town, i.e., in Tabgha.[6] The first tentative excavations in 1911 at Tabgha by P. Karge revealed "under the main entrance, serving as threshold to the cloister, a large basalt slab bearing the funerary inscription in Greek of a certain Josepos."[7] Unfortunately, in spite of repeated searches, this alleged memorial stone (?) of Josepos, which presumably came from the first church, has not been found again.

II. The Hillside Monastery and the Holy Cave

At the beginning of the fifth century, a monastic fellowship was founded in Tabgha. The buildings of the monastery, which were subsequently

[3] *Panarion* 30.4–13 (PG 41:410–17; GCS 25:338–51).

[4] Cf. V. Corbo, *The House of St. Peter at Capharnaum*, 2nd ed., SBFCMi 5 (Jerusalem: Franciscan Printing Press, 1972).

[5] Preserved by Peter the Deacon (1137): "In Capharnaum autem ex domo apostolorum principis ecclesia facta est, cuius parietes usque hodie ita stant, sic fuerunt" (Geyer, 112; Baldi, 299).

[6] Accepted by L.J. Hoppe, *The Synagogues and Churches of Ancient Palestine* (Collegeville: Liturgical Press, 1994), 99.

[7] A.M. Schneider, *The Church of the Multiplying of Loaves and Fishes* (London, 1937), 33. For German ed., see n. 13.

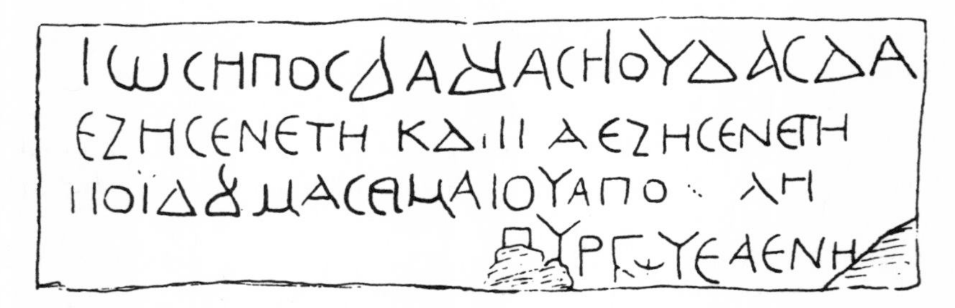

Illus. 23. The Josepos Stone (sketch). It shows traces of later changes.

erected adjacent to the Church of the Multiplication of Loaves, stretched up to the slope of the hill that stood on the other side of the "public highway" (*via publica*). A chapel was built onto the highest part of the monastery. This chapel with mosaics from various periods was excavated in 1935 by the Franciscan archaeologist B. Bagatti.[8] Under the small building, he discovered a cistern cut into the rock with a depth of 3.5 m, a length of 4 m, and a width of 2.2 m, with a typical lime plaster (illus. 20). Therefore, this cistern can hardly be identified with the Cave of the Beatitudes mentioned by Egeria, as has been suggested, because it is unlikely that the monks would have transformed a cave considered by them to be holy into a common water reservoir.

Going from the ruins of this chapel about 200 m eastward, one comes upon a natural cave (illus. 17) that shows traces of veneration from early times.[9] The grotto may have served as a hermit's cave in the Byzantine period (plate 3a). This is suggested by two hewn basalt stones nearby, which were *in situ* as the remains of a closing wall until the cave was devastated in 1986, and a cross hewn into the rear wall, as well as by the pottery found in the area. In the first edition of his anthology of sources *Enchiridion locorum sanctorum*, D. Baldi identified this grotto as the cave mentioned by Egeria.[10] Baldi wrote that the grotto [Heremus Cave] was under the custody of the Franciscans and was called Magharet Ạyub by the local Arabs.

Just below the cave, a constantly bubbling spring of fresh water flows forth (illus. 19). The spring was surrounded by a wall in the Byzantine

[8] "La cappella sul Monte delle Beatitudini", *Rivista di archeologia cristiana* 14 (1937): 1–91.

[9] Cf. R. Riesner, "Die Höhle der Seligpreisungen in Tabgha", *HlL* 121, nos. 2–3 (1989): 16–21.

[10] *Enchiridion locorum sanctorum* (Jerusalem: Tipografia dei PP. Franciscani, 1935), 354.

period.[11] The small plain above the cave was probably identified with the location of the Sermon on the Mount (cf. Mt 5:1; Lk 6:12, 17), while the cave was perhaps considered to be the place to which Jesus withdrew for prayer after the first feeding of the multitude (p. 84). The site where the leper was healed (Mt 8:1–5) was later exhibited here, and in Muslim times it was identified with the patient sufferer Job (p. 90). Here, we have a classic example of how additional traditions are taken on by a genuine tradition, are expanded with legend and are eventually even adopted by the members of another faith.

III. The Byzantine Church of the Patriarch Martyrios

During the second half of the fifth century, the church that marked the site of the first multiplication of the loaves underwent extensive structural alterations. It is unclear whether this became necessary due to the destruction of the first church by an earthquake or if only because the small Jewish Christian shrine could no longer accommodate the large numbers of pilgrims visiting the site. As a first step, the new church was given a proper eastward orientation in keeping with the standard practice at the time in ecclesiastical architecture. Consequently, the rock of the multiplication of the loaves, which had been used as an altar in the first church, was no longer at the center of the building. The rock formation to which the sacred stone originally belonged stood in the middle of the presbytery of the fourth-century church and was exposed in the most recent excavations in 1979.[12] In the later church the altar was erected a few feet to the east and coincided with the wall of the apse of the first shrine. The sacred stone was removed from its original rock setting and installed under the new altar, where it replaced the customary reliquary. It was found in that position by the excavators in 1932,[13] and it lies there to this day.

[11] Cf. S. Loffreda, *Scavi di et-Tabgha*, SBFCMi 7 (Jerusalem: Franciscan Printing Press, 1970), 125–37.

[12] Cf. R. Rosenthal and M. Hershkovitz, "Tabgha", *IEJ* 30 (1980): 207.

[13] Cf. A.E. Mader, "Die Ausgrabung der Brotvermehrungskirche auf dem deutschen Besitz et-Tabgha am See Genesareth", *HlL* 78 (1934): 1–15, 41–66, 89–103, 129–49; A.M. Schneider, *Die Brotvermehrungskirche von et-tâbgha am Genesarethsee* (Paderborn, 1934) (English edition: *The Church of the Multiplying of Loaves and Fishes* [see n. 7]).

The three-nave church was also given a new atrium with a narthex, a prothesis (today's Blessed Sacrament chapel), and a diaconicon (now the sacristy). The two latter rooms were connected by a corridor running behind the apse. The builders of the second church tried to preserve the traditional site of the multiplication of the loaves as much as possible, as is demonstrated by their readiness to make the north wall of the prothesis abnormally oblique on account of the public road that Egeria mentioned. This irregularity was retained during the 1980 restoration. The wedge-shaped room farther to the west, formed by the road and the wall of the church, was adapted by the Byzantines for olive oil production. Since it was a common practice among Eastern pilgrims to acquire a small quantity of oil at the holy places they visited, we may assume that pious Christian visitors who anointed the sacred stone with a few drops and carried the remainder home with them purchased some of the oil produced at Tabgha. An old olive mill and press now stand in the courtyard of the church as reminders of days gone by.

IV. Remarkable Mosaics

The most admirable feature of the Byzantine church is to be found underfoot. The largely intact floor mosaics are very imaginative, lively in conception and of the highest artistic quality. The oldest and best ones date from around the second half of the fifth century. More than one artist's hand can be discerned in them. The first craftsman, wishing to portray flora and fauna found near lakes, drew extensively on Egyptian motifs, presumably because he himself was an Egyptian. He must have been a great lover of nature as well as a keen observer. His representation of a pair of wild ducks perched comfortably on a papyrus plant is particularly charming. Rather terrifying is the depiction of ruthless combat between a flamingo and a serpent. Several medium-sized cormorants raise themselves aloft at the sight of the dreadful duel while a tiny bird hovers above the battle twittering imperturbably toward the sky. Nearby a swan arches its long neck against two reeds while a duck, crouching below, watches a heron stalk past. Many of the scenes are quite humorous, like that of two partridges taking great pains to present a garland of flowers, or the one of a timid and helpless little badger, wearing a collar like a domestic pet, trying to defend itself against the attack of an insolent and angry shorebird.

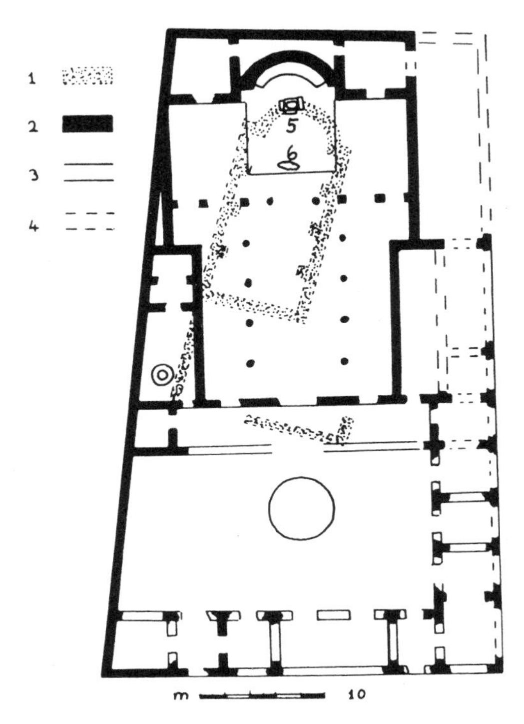

Illus. 24. Plan of the Church of the Multiplication of Loaves and Fishes (according to S. Loffreda, O.F.M., 1978).

1 Plan of the sanctuary from the fourth century
2 Walls of the basilica and the cloister from the fifth century
3 Remains of the foundation
4 Probable course of the wall
5 The position of the stone today
6 Original position of the holy stone

A second mosaic artist, who worked not long afterward but with slightly larger stones, does not seem to have been very well acquainted with Greek spelling. One of his mosaic inscriptions, located in the northern transept in front of the entrance to the prothesis, reads: "Lord, remember Saurus at this holy place [ΤΩΠΩ)". *Tōpō* is written with two omegas, and his own name is written incorrectly with the *OU* ligature instead of a simple *U*. If Saurus was the artist's name, as seems likely since the donor is named in the second inscription, the misspelling is rather surprising. The second mosaic inscription, which is found to the left of the high altar, is important for determining the

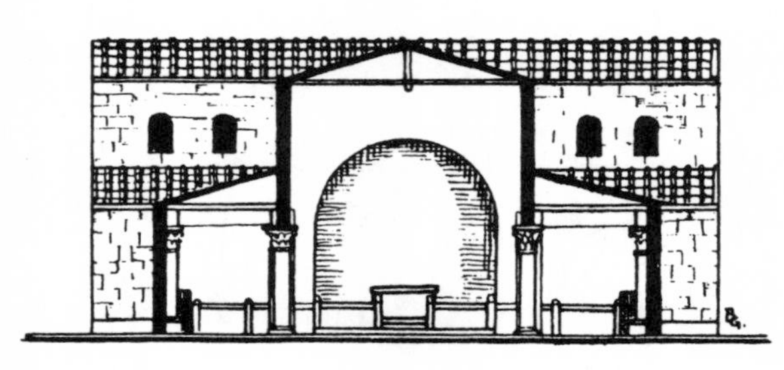

Illus. 25. Byzantine Church of the Multiplication of Loaves and Fishes from the fifth century (according to A. M. Schneider, 1934).

chronology of the mosaics. Although a few letters are missing on the right-hand and bottom margins, the content of the inscription is certain: "To the memory and the repose of the sponsor, the holy patriarch Martyrios". Although only two letters, *M* and *T*, of the patriarch's name have been preserved, there is no doubt that the inscription must have referred to Martyrios, who was patriarch of Jerusalem from 478 to 486 and founder of the large Martyrios cloister east of Bethany.[14] The excavation of the cloister conducted by Y. Magen of Israel's Department of Antiquities is one of the most impressive in recent years.[15] A large mosaic now finds itself in the midst of the new Israeli settlement Maạle Adummim. The patriarch also built a church over the tomb of his teacher and friend, Saint Euthymios. This church is also located in the Judean wilderness at Mishor Adummim, 1.5 km from the Jerusalem-Jericho road. Since the inscription at Tabgha mentions the repose of Patriarch Martyrios, who was the donor of the mosaic floor and presumably also the founder of the church, the mosaic must have been laid out shortly after 486, the year of Martyrios' death.

[14] Episodes from the life of Martyrios are recorded in Cyril of Scythopolis' *Life and Deeds of Saint Euthymius* (PG 114:675ff.).

[15] Cf. F. Comte, "Le monastère de Khirbet-Mourassas", *MB* 38 (1985): 57–59.

It is known that the patriarch lived in Egypt when he was a young monk.[16] If we assume that he brought a prominent Egyptian mosaicist of his acquaintance to Tabgha, it would account for the Egyptian influence manifest in the older layer of mosaics. Much in the mosaics is reminiscent of the Nile landscape. For example, there are depictions of birds commonly found along the Nile perched on stylized papyrus plants, and there is a representation of a nilometer, a pillarlike structure that the authorities employed to measure the level of the Nile. The higher the Nile rose, the higher was the agricultural yield and thus the taxes. The Egyptian origin of the artist would also explain the appearance of birds common to Egypt but rarely or never seen near the Sea of Galilee. The same mosaicist (Saurus?) who laid out the two inscriptions fashioned the famous mosaic of the loaves and fishes that was in front of the sacred stone. The T-shaped plan of the church may have been derived from a North African model. No other churches in Palestine during this period possessed transepts. The second church at Tabgha is unique in this respect. The only contemporary parallels existed in Algeria, southern Egypt and Nubia.

V. The Later History of the Church

Saint Sabas, who along with Martyrios had been a disciple of Saint Euthymios, visited the church at Heptapegon during the fifth century accompanied by monks from the celebrated desert monastery in the Kidron Valley. They sailed in a boat to Kursi (see pp. 150–51) and, after they had visited the holy places along the lake, continued their pilgrim journey to Caesarea Philippi (Panias, today's Banyas).[17] About the year 530 Theodosius, recording geography related to the holy places, mentioned that the seven springs were 2 miles from Magdala and Capharnaum.[18] He even claimed that it was the place Jesus baptized the Apostles (see p. 91). Around 570 the anonymous Pilgrim from Piacenza reported that he visited the site of the feeding of the five thousand and saw extensive fields and groves of olive and palm trees.[19]

[16] PG 114:667.

[17] *S. Sabae Vita* (Baldi, 311).

[18] *The Topography of the Holy Land* 2 (J. Wilkinson, *Jerusalem Pilgrims before the Crusades* [Jerusalem: Ariel, 1977], 63).

[19] *Travels from Piacenza* 9 (ibid., 81).

The basilica was destroyed sometime during the first half of the seventh century during the Persian (614) and Arab (635) invasions that ended the Byzantine epoch in the Holy Land. The Gallic bishop Arculf, who passed that way about 670, found no building standing, only a few fallen columns in the vicinity of the spring.[20] The Persians had vandalized the great basilica of Heptapegon, like so many other edifices. What continued to exist was the unpretentious hillside cloister with the chapel of the Beatitudes and the simple sanctuary of Mensa Domini,[21] which commemorated the appearance of Jesus on the shore of the lake to the Apostles following the Resurrection. In all probability the two remaining holy places of Heptapegon were never destroyed but gradually fell into decay after Islamic Bedouin claimed the land and Christian pilgrims became more and more infrequent. A tower built by the Crusaders to the north of the Mensa Domini site also fell into ruin soon afterward. The basilica itself remained covered by earth and rubble for almost thirteen hundred years.

VI. The Church of Heptapegon Rediscovered

During the late nineteenth century, Europe witnessed a gradual growth of interest in the Holy Land. Long neglect obscured the locations of sacred sites around the Sea of Galilee. Even the site of Capharnaum, the setting of Jesus' adult life and activity, was scarcely known.[22] It was thus good that in order to search for Capharnaum, the Italian Society for the Holy Land, in collaboration with the Franciscan custodians of the holy places, purchased an approximately 2.5-km-long strip of land stretching from Tabgha to Tell Ḥum (Capharnaum). Further to the west the area of Ard es-Siki (illus. 15), with the bay of Minet en-Nachleh and the hill of Tell el-'Oreimeh, was acquired in 1889 by Franz Keller for the German Palestine Society from an Arab effendi residing in Safed and from the Bedouin.[23] The legal validation

[20] Adomnan, *The Holy Places* 2.24.2 (ibid., 108).

[21] Cf. S. Loffreda, *Scavi di et-Tabgha* (see n. 11), 48–105.

[22] Cf. C. Kopp, *The Holy Places of the Gospels* (New York: Herder and Herder, 1963), 171–79; R. Riesner, "Kapernaum", in *GBL*, 2nd ed. (1990), 2:764–68; and chapter 8, Riddles of the synagogues at Capharnaum.

[23] The history of the purchase of the Tabgha property was recorded in the *Nachrichten-Blatt des Deutschen Vereins vom Hl. Lande* (Cologne) 8, no. 2 (1934): 73ff.

of the purchase, however, involved a great deal of trouble. In 1891 a Luxembourg priest, Zepherin Biever, who had been residing at Madaba in Transjordan and serving as chaplain to the Bedouin, came to take over the directorship of the new foundation.[24] The following years were filled with hard work—clearing the land, plowing, sowing and building.

Bedouin camped regularly on a corner of the property near the great spring Ain et-Tabgha (also called Ali ed-Daher). As they pulled out their tent pegs, broken fragments of mosaics emerged. The famous engineer G. Schumacher, planner of the Haifa-Damascus railway and builder of the first hospice at Tabgha, made a survey of the newly acquired property in July 1889 and correctly indicated the location of the mosaics and ruins on a corner of his map.[25] In 1911 Professor Paul Karge investigated the site. He uncovered the ground plan and the place of the altar with the venerated stone as well as some of the Byzantine mosaics, including the famous mosaic of the breadbasket and fish. Professor Karge's excavations, however, were interrupted by the Turkish government and had to be abandoned.[26] Resumption of the work was stymied for a long time by a dispute between the German and Italian societies concerning boundaries. Not until 1932 did the archaeologists Fathers Andreas E. Mader and Alfons Maria Schneider succeed in overcoming all the obstacles, enabling them to carry out serious excavations.[27] They uncovered the wall and mosaics of the fifth-century Byzantine church but knew nothing of the earlier edifice. Only in 1936, in the course of the restoration of the mosaics by Bernhard Gauer, were the foundations of the older church accidentally revealed. While digging for a firm foundation to place the mosaics that he had restored, he found the apse of the older church. In 1970 the remains of the earlier, fourth-century church were freshly examined by the Franciscan archaeologist Stanislao Loffreda.[28] Based

[24] In 1968 Les amis de la Terre Sainte au Luxembourg published a biography of Abbot Zepherin Biever (1849–1916) under the title *Un luxembourgeois prêtre en Terre Sainte.*

[25] Schumacher's note: "Hier sollten Ausgrabungen gemacht werden: Mosaiken und Ruinen." Cf. A. E. Mader, "Die Ausgrabung der Brotvermehrungskirche" (see n. 13), 4.

[26] Unfortunately, an excavation report was never published. Cf. P. Karge, *Rephaim: Die vorgeschichtliche Kultur Palästinas und Phoeniziens* (Paderborn, 1917), 321; A. M. Schneider, *Die Brotvermehrungskirche* (see n. 13), 11.

[27] Cf. A. E. Mader, "Die Ausgrabung der Brotvermehrungskirche" (see n. 13), 10–15, 41–66; A. M. Schneider, *Church of the Multiplying of Loaves and Fishes* (see n. 7), 8ff.

[28] "Sondaggio nella Chiesa della Moltiplicazione dei Pani a Tabgha", *SBFLA* 20 (1970): 370–90.

Illus. 26. Tabgha, mosaic from the fifth-century Byzantine church showing a breadbasket and two fishes commemorating the first miracle of multiplication.

on the find of a single coin, he dates the construction of the church after 395, but this isolated piece of evidence for a late date is outweighed by the historical arguments presented above.

VII. The New German Church of the Multiplication

A temporary church was erected over the site in 1933 in order to protect the mosaics from damage. This church was visited by Pope Paul VI on his pilgrimage to the Holy Land in 1964. The emergency structure, built mainly of timber, grew rickety and unstable. In spite of numerous repairs by volunteer workers, the process of deterioration continued. Visitors frequently remarked that it was inappropriate that one of the oldest and most significant of the holy places should be housed in a decrepit wooden shed. Finally the committee of the German Society for the Holy Land, in conjunction with the Benedictines of the abbey on Mount Zion, who in 1939 had taken over responsibility for Tabgha from the Lazarist Fathers, resolved to create a center of Christian life at the site that would serve the numerous pilgrims who visited it as well as local Arab and Jewish Christians. Thus there arose at the lakeside the *eremos topos*, a serene place of meditation intended for celebrating the Eucharist, for Scripture reading or for quiet contemplation.

Particularly felicitous was the decision to construct the church as a three-nave basilica in the same Byzantine style as the original and to preserve the ground plan of the fifth-century architecture. Two architects from Cologne, Anton Goergen and Fritz Baumann, were entrusted with carrying out the project. They began by familiarizing themselves with the unaccustomed Byzantine style. They visited churches dating from the same period in the Negev and elsewhere and made a thorough study of relevant literature.

What the architects created is a masterpiece of purity and simplicity of line. They had sought to retain, and as far as possible to utilize, whatever was still extant of the original building.[29] A section of the wall that had still been preserved in the apse, in the northern transept and in the prothesis became the base for the new northwestern wall. The altar was reconstructed in accordance with the design of columns still available; one stone from the cornice of the original apse was the model and keystone of the whole series, and the foundation wall of the fourth-century church was made visible in two places through panes of glass. The restoration of the mosaics, carried out in collaboration with experts from the Israel Museum, was undertaken with great attention to accuracy.[30] F. Nastas, a native sculptor from Bethlehem, carved the capitals of the columns out of marble brought from Carrara, Italy, using as a pattern a capital from the Byzantine cathedral of Hippos.

The ceremony marking the laying of the foundation stone of the new Church of Heptapegon took place on May 23, 1980. Exactly two years later the archbishop of Cologne, Josef Cardinal Höffner, solemnly consecrated the completed church and presented it with a magnificent processional cross that is now beside the high altar.[31] The reconstruction of the Church of Heptapegon is an inspiring reminder of the abundant love of Jesus. Upon the site where the

[29] Cf. A. Goergen, "Tabgha am See Genesareth", *Schnell Kunstführer* 1747 (Munich and Zurich, 1989).

[30] Cf. "Tabgha Mosaic Restoration Project", *BA* 45 (1982): 188; J. Shenhav, "Loaves and Fishes Mosaic near Sea of Galilee Restored", *BAR* 10, no. 3 (1984): 22–31.

[31] Cf. "Die Kirchweihe in Tabgha", *HlL* 114, nos. 2–3 (1982): 2–14.

Jewish Christians of Capharnaum commemorated the miracle of the multiplication of the loaves and fishes, the Byzantines erected a splendid church.

This holy place, hidden for over 1,300 years by rubble and debris, has been brought back to life. For the large number of visitors who come there every year from all over the world, this church can become an enduring symbol of Christian hope.

8. Riddles of the Synagogues at Capharnaum

"After he had ended all his sayings in the hearing of the people he entered Capernaum. Now a centurion had a slave who was dear to him, who was sick and at the point of death. When he heard of Jesus, he sent to him elders of the Jews, asking him to come and heal his slave. And when they came to Jesus, they besought him earnestly, saying, 'He is worthy to have you do this for him, for he loves our nation, and he built us our synagogue'" (Lk 7:1–5). Jesus performed miracles (Mk 1:21–28) and spoke his great Eucharistic words (Jn 6:59) in that synagogue. Are there any remains of that synagogue?

Those who have visited Capharnaum will scarcely forget the synagogue ruins that, with their white, limestone blocks, give an impression of the past splendor of Galilean synagogues. The pilgrim Egeria, who visited Capharnaum around A.D. 383, must have had this synagogue, made of white hewn stones, in mind when she wrote: "There [in Capharnaum] also is the synagogue where the Lord cured a man possessed by the devil [Mk 1:23–28]. The way in is up many stairs, and it is made of dressed stone."[1] If this pilgrim at the end of the fourth century could be shown the synagogue, which, as we will see below, had been reconstructed just shortly before her visit, as being that of Jesus' day, then this speaks for continuity in the tradition of the site.

[1] J. Wilkinson, *Egeria's Travels to the Holy Land* (Jerusalem: Ariel, 1981), 196 ("ad quam per gradus multos ascenditur, quae synagoga ex lapidibus quadratis est facta" [Geyer, 112; Baldi, 299]). The expressions "the way in is up many stairs" and "dressed stone" indicate the limestone synagogue. The earlier basalt synagogue, which we shall discuss, stood almost at ground level, and the pavement inside and outside it was almost at the same level. Its walls were made of dressed stone, which was, however, hidden behind the plaster.

I. *The Search for Capharnaum*

In the nineteenth century the exact location of Capharnaum was no longer known. It was supposed only that it must have stood somewhere on the northwest shore of Lake Gennesaret [Sea of Galilee]. In 1838 the famous American scholar E. Robinson identified the ruins named Tell Ḥum by the Bedouin as those of Chorazin.[2] Scholars wavered for a long time between localizing Capharnaum at Tell Ḥum or at Khirbet el-Minyeh (illus. 15) lying farther to the south. In 1894 the Franciscans succeeded in acquiring the field of ruins at Tell Ḥum. Gradually the identification of this place as Capharnaum gained acceptance; today no one questions it. From 1905 to 1921 G. Orfali excavated in the area of the synagogue and began to fit together the many dressed stones lying around into a synagogue structure. Orfali's work was suddenly interrupted when he was killed in an automobile accident. This pious Franciscan was motivated by great enthusiasm, since he always remained convinced that this structure was the synagogue of Jesus.[3]

His conviction proved to be in error, however, just as H. Kohl and C. Watzinger had already proven in their study of the Galilean synagogues. On the basis of comparative studies in style, they believed that the structure had most likely been erected at the end of the second or at the beginning of the third century.[4] Most of the Israeli scholars have come to share this opinion,[5] although the new results based on the last excavations seem to require new solutions.

II. *Controversy over the Dating of the Synagogue*

The Franciscan archaeologists V. Corbo and S. Loffreda suggested a new dating based on their careful excavations.[6] They transpose the construction to the time between the end of the fourth and the beginning of the fifth century. They base their dating on pottery

[2] *Biblical Researches in Palestine*, 11th ed., vol. 2 (Boston, 1874), 403–8.

[3] *Capharnaum et ses ruines* (Paris, 1922), 74–76.

[4] *Antike Synagogen in Galiläa* (Leipzig, 1916), 204.

[5] G. Foerster, "Notes on Recent Excavations at Capernaum", in L. I. Levine, *Ancient Synagogues Revealed* (Jerusalem, 1981), 57–59.

[6] Summarized by S. Loffreda in his article "The Chronology of the Synagogue of Capernaum", in *Scavi di et-Tabgha*, SBFCMi 7 (Jerusalem: Franciscan Printing Press, 1970), 52–56.

and numismatic finds in the layer of filling under the synagogue floor, which is over 1 m deep, though the coins mostly come from the second half of the fourth century. Such coins were found just below the pavement floor; the floor will be discussed later. This new dating was strongly attacked by Israeli scholars because it appeared to destabilize an entire system of synagogue chronology.

In this regard, however, a special position is taken by the Israeli architect D. Chen, who has made a name for himself through his metrological studies on many ancient buildings in Israel. In his analysis of the synagogue at Capharnaum he found that the whole structure was based on the Byzantine foot (32 cm) as the unit of measure, the modulation unit measuring 18 Byz. ft. (5.76 m). In drawing up the building plan, three triangles with the proportions 3:4:5 were taken as the basis. The hypotenuse, here the diagonal of the assembly hall, is 90 ft. wide, i.e., 5 × 18 moduli. The system of design thus follows the Pythagorean theorem. There are also other principles of planning: for example, the distance between columns is 9 ft.; i.e., every two intercolumns correspond to the modulation unit of 18 ft.[7] Because the whole conception of the Capharnaum synagogue is based upon the Byzantine foot, this structure could have been built at the earliest in the Constantinian period, certainly not before that in the late second or in the third century A.D. Other scholars, such as R. Rosenthal,[8] lean toward the late dating of both the Franciscan archaeologists.

III. The Synagogue of the Centurion from Capharnaum

However, where was the synagogue that existed at the time of Jesus in "his city" (Mt 9:1) located? It has long been suspected that the foundations of the New Testament synagogue would have to be sought underneath the present-day synagogue structure. M. Avi-Yonah expressed this opinion repeatedly, referring to the law of the constancy of holy places.[9] Synagogues are built on the site of earlier ones. We get a

[7] D. Chen, "The Design of the Ancient Synagogues in Galilee I", *SBFLA* 28 (1978): 193–202 (at 194–96); idem, "On the Chronology of the Ancient Synagogue at Capernaum", *ZDPV* 102 (1986): 134–43.

[8] "Grundproportionen von jüdischen und christlichen Sakralbauten im spätantiken Palästina", in H. Knell and B. Wesenberg, *Vitruv-Kolloquium 1982* (Darmstadt, 1984), 249–58.

[9] "Some Comments on the Capernaum Excavations", in L. I. Levine, *Ancient Synagogues* (see n. 5), 60–62.

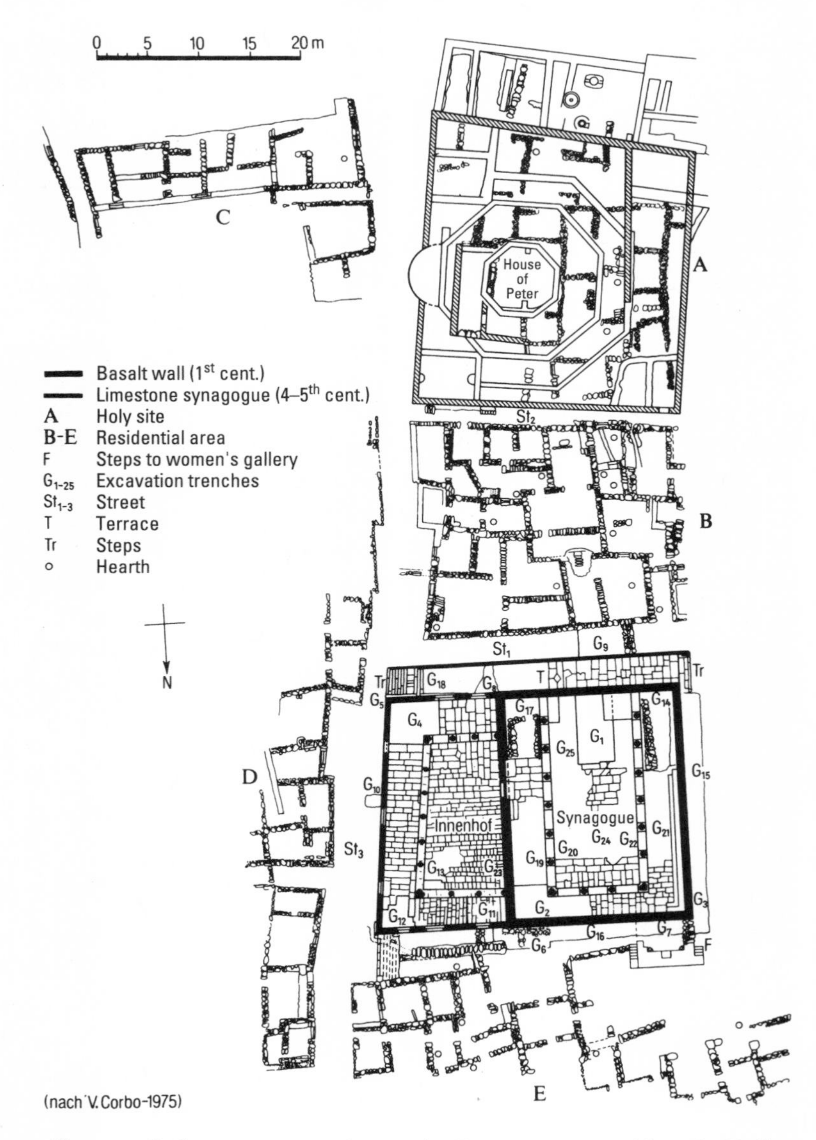

Illus. 27. Capharnaum—excavations on the Franciscan property (from G. Kroll).

glimpse of the uncertain guessing game that has prevailed for decades from C. Kopp: "Wilken . . . thinks that by slight excavations he has proved 'that the foundations of the synagogue undoubtedly belong to the time of Jesus'. I am told that the archaeologist Sukenik dug down

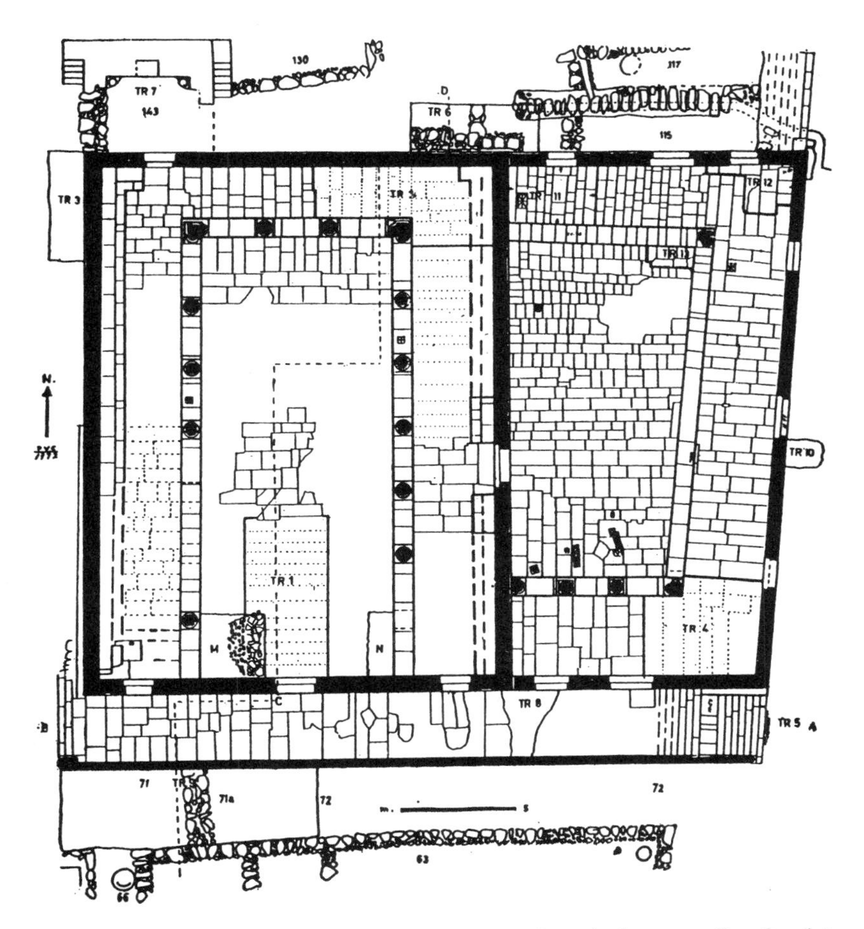

Illus. 28. Plan of the Byzantine (limestone) synagogue. Beneath the west wall, a foundation wall following a deviate course is recognizable.

nineteen and a half feet at one spot, without reaching any older layer beneath the foundations of the synagogue." [10]

Soon after the Six-Day War (1967), the Franciscans wanted to make sure and undertook sample excavations at various spots beneath the synagogue. They gained the impression, however, that the remains beneath the floor of the limestone synagogue were apparently only the continuation of the residential area that had been uncovered south

[10] C. Kopp, *The Holy Places of the Gospels* (New York: Herder and Herder, 1963), 172, n. 8.

Illus. 29. Reconstruction of the Byzantine synagogue according to C. Watzinger (1912). The adjacent courtyard to the east with its surrounding porticoes was the schoolhouse (Beth Hamidrash).

of the synagogue.[11] If not there, then where was the centurion's synagogue? Since no answer to this question was found on the Franciscans' site, excavation was begun in October 1978 on the Greek Orthodox property northeast of it. According to the archimandrite Cyprianos, this excavation had the goal of bringing to light, if possible, the remains of the synagogue where Jesus healed the man with the withered hand.[12] However, no synagogue was found there, nor were there any traces of buildings from Roman times, but it did become clear that Capharnaum's residential buildings had shifted farther to the east in the Arabian period.[13]

In 1980 the sensational news suddenly leaked out to us Benedictines at Tabgha: Corbo and Loffreda believed they had found the New Testament synagogue! It lay exactly under the fourth-century synagogue.[14] Since then, it is no longer a secret, as the find was made public in the summer of 1981. In the meantime, the official

[11] "Sotto la Sinagoga di Cafarnao un'isola della città?" *SBFLA* 27 (1977): 145–55.

[12] *CNfI* 27 (1979): 80.

[13] Cf. V. Tsaferis, "New Archaeological Evidence on Ancient Capernaum", *BA* 46 (1983): 198–204.

[14] *La Terre Sainte* (July/August 1981), 198.

excavation reports[15] and summaries for the general public with pictures, plans and reconstruction drawings have been published.[16] V. Corbo's last excavations brought new light to understanding the stratigraphic structure of the area. Unlike in the residential buildings of New Testament Capharnaum, the basalt walls under the limestone synagogue consist of dressed stones plastered with mortar. The basalt walls are 1.2 to 1.3 m wide and are thus wider than the limestone walls of the synagogue from the Byzantine period. Compared to it, though, the basalt building is about 1 m shorter in length and 0.78 m narrower in width. Beneath the Byzantine floor, a floor paved with basalt was discovered at a depth of 1.1 to 1.2 m, below the nave and side aisles of the limestone synagogue. Corbo assigns the basalt pavement and walls under both the main wall and the stylobates of the Byzantine synagogue to the first century A.D. Assigned by Corbo to earlier structures, another pavement was discovered only 0.2 m deeper under the pavement of the older synagogue, limited to the nave.

With regard to the expansion of the synagogue of the first century A.D., however, the two Franciscan archaeologists are of differing opinions. Loffreda, the excavation team's pottery expert, points out the fact that only the pottery under the lowest basalt pavement comes from the first century A.D., and thus only this pavement dates back to New Testament times. He therefore believes, in contrast to Corbo, that the centurion's synagogue was smaller and covered only the space of today's nave. Loffreda thinks it probable that no expansion of the New Testament synagogue took place until the third century.[17] Both archaeologists want to clarify this by way of further investigations.

IV. The Latest Research Results

New structural elements came to light and others became more visible in the excavations along the west wall of the synagogue already in

[15] S. LOFFREDA, "Ceramica ellenistico-romana nel sottosuolo della sinagoga di Cafarnao", in *Studia Hierosolymitana*, vol. 3, SBFCMa 30 (Jerusalem, 1982), 273–312; V. CORBO, "Resti della sinagoga del primo secolo a Cafarnao", ibid., 313–57.

[16] Cf. B. BAGATTI, "Capharnaüm, la Ville de Pierre", *MB* 27 (1983): 8–16; J. F. STRANGE and H. SHANKS, "Synagogue Where Jesus Preached Found at Capernaum", *BAR* 9, no. 6 (1983): 24–31; S. LOFFREDA, *Recovering Capharnaum*, 2nd ed. (Jerusalem: Franciscan Printing Press, 1993), 32–49.

[17] "Le sinagoghe di Cafarnao", *Bibbia e oriente* 26 (1984): 103–14.

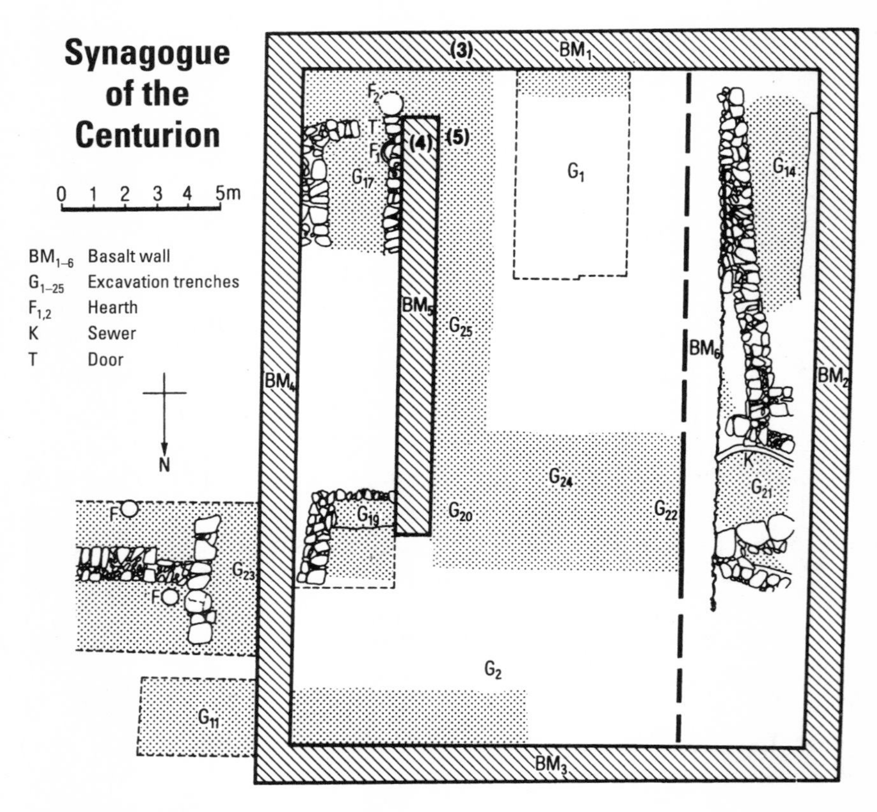

Illus. 30. Plan of the earlier synagogues based on excavation findings (according to V. Corbo, O.F.M. [1982]) (from G. Kroll).

the late summer of 1984. The wall that supports the present synagogue is composed of larger and smaller dressed basalt blocks and shows a still partially visible plaster of mortar. D. Chen remarked to me that this fact alone precluded the possibility of this being simply a foundation wall since foundations are not plastered. In addition, the already-known fact that the lower wall is not aligned with the limestone wall above it can now be more easily observed (plate 3b). Perhaps there was a desire when building the new structure to improve the orientation toward Jerusalem.[18] The wall of the older synagogue rested in turn upon an older wall, this time made of uncut basalt stones. To the

[18] Cf. R. Riesner, "Die Synagogen von Kafarnaum", *Bibel und Kirche* 39 (1984): 136–38.

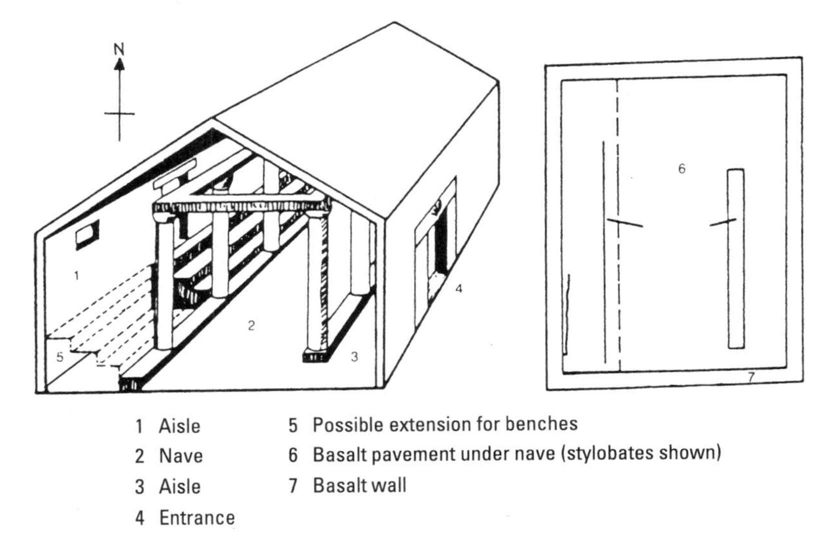

Illus. 31. Reconstruction drawings of the old synagogue in the development from the first to the third century.

west of it lies a pavement that appears to be occasionally interrupted by structures. The latter were probably destroyed in Byzantine times in order to put down a new pavement of uncut basalt stones, reaching up to the lower wall of the synagogue.

Capharnaum also proved to be older than had previously been assumed. There were clear indications that the community had already been settled in the Persian period and not first in the Hellenistic.[19] Capharnaum's network of roads has also become clearer. From the Via Maris (pp. 55–58) that passed by on the north side, the main road (*cardo*) went toward the lake past the synagogue and Peter's house (illus. 27). The Decumanus branched off at a right angle to the main road in an east-west direction and went right by the synagogue. Near this side street, a whole series of beautiful, green glass plates from the first century A.D. was discovered.[20]

The excavations at the Greeks' site also led to new, sensational results in the fourth season in 1985. Near the boundary of the Franciscan property, Vassilios Tsaferis found some typical structures made of dressed limestone and including thermal baths with hypocaust (*caldarium*,

[19] Cf. V. Corbo, "Le origini di Cafarnao al periodo Persiano", *SBFLA* 34 (1984): 371–84.
[20] Cf. S. Loffreda, *Recovering Capharnum* (see n. 16), 23f.

frigidarium and *tepidarium*), which he dated by the pottery to the first century A.D.[21] The entire complex was apparently a Roman garrison installation. It can be conjectured that the pagan centurion lived in this settlement separated from the rest of the buildings of Jewish Capharnaum.[22] In this way his words come alive: "I am not worthy to have you come under my roof" (Lk 7:6).

V. Jews and Jewish Christians in Capharnaum

A very unique phenomenon is presented by one of the four limestone steps that lead to the present synagogue entrance. It was specially hollowed out, apparently to make it unnecessary to destroy the basalt step protruding into it. The beautiful limestone ashlar blocks were mercilessly cut to fit over the not completely horizontal basalt wall of the earlier synagogue, probably in order to preserve the older wall. Here the question arises: When the beautiful Jewish synagogue was built, was consideration shown to an earlier building because Jesus had taught there? Which Jewish group would have done such a thing? Where did the money for building such a magnificent synagogue, whose splendor and size surpass every other in Galilee, come from? Is not a Jewish building on a Christian site unusual in a time when Christianity was already supported by the imperial house? Thus, yet a number of riddles that will busy scholars on into the third millennium are also posed by the limestone synagogue. I tend to agree with my friend Zvi Maoz (Katzrin), the Golan Survey archaeologist, who thinks that the limestone synagogue is a demonstrative synagogue, i.e., an exhibitionary or memorial synagogue. This synagogue would have been built because the Roman Empire had become Christian at that time and the stream of pilgrims to the places in the Gospels continued to grow.

Around the end of the fourth century, Capharnaum was a purely Jewish town in which non-Jews were not allowed to reside. We have a revealing statement in this regard from Bishop Epiphanius of Salamis (315–404). He wrote in his book *Panarion*, published in A.D. 374: "In the towns and villages of the Jews [in Galilee] . . . it was impossible to build churches since no one was allowed to live among them who was

[21] Cf. V. Tsaferis and M. Peleg, "Kefar Nahum", *ESI* 4 (1986): 59.

[22] Cf. R. Riesner, "Neues von den Synagogen Kafarnaums", *Bibel und Kirche* 40 (1985): 133–35; idem, "Kapernaum", in *GBL*, 2nd ed. (1990): 2:764–68 (at 765).

a Hellene [Gentile] or a Samaritan or a Christian [μήτε Χριστιανόν]. This was especially the case in Tiberias; in Diocaesarea, also called Sepphoris; in Nazareth; and in Capharnaum. Close watch was kept that no one settled among them who belonged to another people [τινα ἄλλου ἔθνους]."[23]

Epiphanius had gotten this news for the most part from Count (*comes*) Josepos (Joseph) of Tiberias (pp. 102–3), with whom he had had a long talk in Scythopolis (Beth Shean). This respected Jewish convert had been introduced to Constantine and had been commissioned by him to build churches at the four mentioned locations in Galilee. The one for Capharnaum was to all appearances not built in the village itself, since on her visit (ca. 383) Egeria had still seen the original walls of the house of Peter, over which a Byzantine church was then erected in the fifth century.[24] The Constantinian church seems more likely to have been built at Heptapegon (Tabgha) on the edge of the area of Capharnaum where the feeding of the five thousand (Mk 6:35–44) had taken place.[25]

It may sound surprising that according to the text of Epiphanius it was also forbidden to all Christians to settle in Capharnaum since it has become clear through the excavations of recent decades at the house of Peter that people lived there who believed in Jesus. These believers in Jesus could have been Jewish believers called *minim* (מִנִים) in the Jewish sources and whose presence in Capharnaum in the second and fourth centuries is also reported by Rabbinic writings.[26] These *minim* have never called themselves Christians but rather Nazoreans, Ebionites, or simply Israelites (p. 333). Today we term them actually incorrectly "Jewish Christians". The name "Christians" (Χριστιανοί), first coined at Antioch (Acts 11:25), remained limited to the Gentile Christians during the first century. The word is used here by Epiphanius in the same sense.[27]

[23] *Panarion* 30.11 (PG 41:424; Baldi, 296).

[24] In Peter the Deacon: "ex domo apostolorum principis ecclesia facta est, cuius parietes usque hodie ita stant, sicut fuerunt" (Geyer, 112; Baldi, 299) ["The house of the *prince of the apostles* has been made into a church, with its original walls still standing"—trans. in J. Wilkinson, *Egeria's Travels to the Holy Land*, 2nd ed. [Jerusalem: Ariel, 1981], 194).

[25] Cf. chapter 7, "The Churches of the Multiplication of Loaves and Fishes" (pp. 102–14).

[26] Midrash on Eccl 1:8 and 7:26 (H. L. Strack and P. Billerbeck, *Kommentar zum Neuen Testament aus Talmud und Midrasch*, vol. 1, *Das Evangelium nach Matthäus* [Munich: Beck, 1926], 159f.).

[27] Cf. B. Bagatti, "The Church from the Gentiles in Palestine", SBFCMi 4 (Jerusalem: Franciscan Printing Press, 1971), 71f.

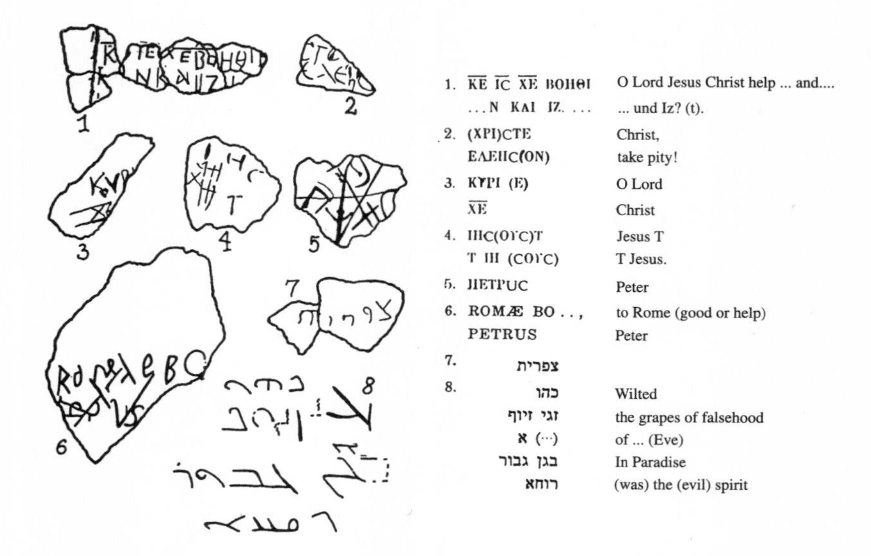

Illus. 32. Graffiti from the House of Peter (according to E. Testa, O.F.M., 1972) (sketch). Inscription no. 8 in Estrangelo is taken from the apocryphal book 3 Baruch 4:9–15: In Paradise Adam and Eve sinned because of the wine offered by the devil. In the future, however, the wine will become the blood of God."

That there were messianic Jews in Capharnaum at least until the end of the fourth century has been clearly confirmed by the graffiti found on chunks of mortar under the remains of the house of Peter. Prayers and invocations of the name Jesus as well as Peter had been carved into the wall of this house, which served as a house church.[28] Judging from the graffiti found, the most frequently used language of the inhabitants and the visitors was Greek, but inscriptions have also been found in the Hebrew language and in Estrangelo, a Syriac script. Astonishingly, the excavators have found Christian symbols, e.g., plates with the Christogram, in very many homes all around the synagogue.[29] It may be assumed that there had to have been a certain symbiosis of Rabbinic Jews and Jews who believed in Jesus, all of whom visited the same synagogue. Moreover, the *minim* had their Eucharistic celebration in the house of Peter, which was surrounded

[28] Cf. S. LOFFREDA, *Recovering Capharnaum* (see n. 16), 58–63, and also J. F. STRANGE and H. SHANKS, "Has the House Where Jesus Stayed in Capernaum Been Found?" *BAR* 8, no. 6 (1982): 29–39.

[29] Cf. S. LOFFREDA, *Recovering Capharnaum*, 30f.

in the fourth century by a kind of ghetto wall. The wall more likely served to protect it from attacks by the powerful Byzantines than from the Rabbinic Jews in their village.

As already mentioned, Egeria remarked that the synagogue she visited was built with squared stone blocks and that several steps had to be climbed to get to it. That has to refer to the limestone synagogue that was new at the time. When Egeria mentions that Jesus healed the demon-possessed man in this synagogue, this proves that this synagogue was considered to be that of Jesus, although it had been renovated and beautified. The archaeological findings agree with this view. Upon closer inspection, it becomes apparent that during the rebuilding, elements that were connected with the activities of Jesus were given special attention: the size and orientation of the synagogue remained the same, and the lower portion of the old synagogue and the old entrance threshold were conspicuously preserved.

All of this justifies us in supposing that this memorial synagogue was built with the aid of imperial subsidies, perhaps jointly by the Rabbinic Jews and the Jews who believed in Jesus. In my opinion this happened during the reign of Theodosius I (379–395), who had churches built at many other places in the Holy Land, such as in Gethsemane and on Zion (p. 349). Because the inhabitants of Capharnaum were exclusively Jews at that time, the emperor wanted to erect a worthy monument to the synagogue of Jesus without disturbing the religious peace. Theodosius was favorably inclined toward the Jews. With new laws, he had tried to stem the ever-increasing tide of anti-Jewish violence at the end of the fourth century. It was emphasized in his legal digest that Judaism was a legal religion (*religio licita*) in the Roman Empire and that it was therefore forbidden to destroy synagogues.[30] Thus, the possibility that the magnificent structure of the limestone synagogue in Capharnaum is to be attributed to the patronage of Emperor Theodosius cannot be ruled out.

[30] *Codex Theodosii* 16.8.9.

9. In Search of Bethsaida

I. The New Testament and the Reports of Pilgrims

Next to Jerusalem, Bethlehem and Capharnaum, the town most frequently mentioned in the Gospels is Bethsaida, the birthplace of the Apostles Peter and Andrew[1] and home of the Apostle Philip (Jn 1:44; 12:21). As part of the so-called evangelical triangle (Tabgha, Chorazin and Bethsaida, with Capharnaum the midpoint of the triangle's base), Bethsaida was situated in that northern area bordering the Sea of Galilee (illus. 13) where Jesus was most active (Mt 11:20–24 / Lk 10:13–15). It was there that a blind man was healed (Mk 8:22–26), and in its vicinity the second feeding of the multitude took place (Mt 15:32–39 / Mk 8:1–10; cf. Lk 9:10; see pp. 68–71). In this miracle story combined by John with the first feeding of the multitude, Jesus requested Philip and Andrew, who knew the bakeries in nearby Bethsaida, to buy bread for the people (Jn 6:5–9). In another episode we are told that the Greeks approached these two Apostles, who have Greek names and must have been familiar with the Greek language in their partly Hellenized hometown, with their request to see Jesus (Jn 12:20–22). Bethsaida was also considered the home of the fishermen Zebedee and his sons James and John (see below) by Theodosius,[2] who wrote around A.D. 530.

Despite Bethsaida's prominence in the New Testament, many people today are not familiar with its name, and hardly any pilgrims have so far visited it. That is amazing in view of the fact that the northwest shore of the Sea of Galilee has been made accessible for visitors since 1967 by the building of new bridges across the Jordan and the construction of roadways. One reason for the neglect of so prominent a biblical site is

[1] Cf. R. SCHNACKENBURG, *Das Johannesevangelium*, 3rd ed., vol. 1 (Freiburg: Herder, 1972), 313.

[2] *The Topography of the Holy Land* 2 (J. WILKINSON, *Jerusalem Pilgrims before the Crusades* [Jerusalem: Ariel, 1977], 63).

the hesitancy of scholars to identify its precise location. The site of Bethsaida, though difficult to reach, was a recognized place of pilgrimage for many early Christians. With the beginning of the twelfth century, the identification of the site became increasingly confused. After the thirteenth century, however, pilgrims to Bethsaida visited a spot near Khirbet el-Minyeh (which is near the big pumping station of the Israel water supply, Mobil Ha'arzi), and because of Mark 6:45 and John 12:21 ("Bethsaida in Galilee"), many scholars in the nineteenth century defended this location.[3] Today this view has lost almost all scientific support.[4]

Around A.D. 530 Theodosius still knew its precise location: "From Seven Springs [Tabgha] it is two miles to Capernaum. From Capernaum it is six miles to Bethsaida, where the apostles Peter, Andrew, Philip, and the sons of Zebedee were born. From Bethsaida it is fifty miles to Panias [Caesarea Philippi]: that is the place where the Jordan rises from the two places Ior and Dan."[5] The monk Willibald, later to become the first bishop of Eichstätt in Bavaria, recorded his visit to this inhospitable and dangerous area in the year 725. The account of his travel says: "From there [Capharnaum] they went to Bethsaida, the city of Peter and Andrew: there is now a church there in the place where originally their house stood."[6] The church mentioned in Willibald's text might have been a successor to the prayer house that was supposedly erected by the Apostle Philip as mentioned in an account ascribed to the Syrian author Simon of Bassora.[7] It was not until the Anglican archbishop Pococke's visit to Palestine in 1738 that a new discussion arose over the location of Bethsaida.[8]

Today there are three main contenders for the site of ancient Bethsaida.[9] They are the Bedouin village of Messadiye (coordinates 209 254), the little ruin field of Khirbet el-Aradj (208 255) and the ruin-covered

[3] Cf. C. KOPP, *The Holy Places of the Gospels* (New York: Herder and Herder, 1963), 180–83; German ed.: *Die heiligen Stätten der Evangelien*, 2nd ed. (Regensburg: Pustet, 1964), 239–43; G. REEG, *Die Ortsnamen Israels nach der rabbinischen Literatur* (Wiesbaden: Harrassowitz, 1989), 533–35.

[4] A rare exception is G. PACE, "La prima moltiplicazione dei pani: Topografia", *Bibbia e oriente* 21 (1979): 85–91.

[5] *The Topography of the Holy Land* 2 (J. WILKINSON, *Jerusalem Pilgrims* [see n. 2], 63).

[6] *The Life of St. Willibald* 96.3–6 (chap. 14) (ibid., 128).

[7] Cf. F. M. ABEL, *Géographie de la Palestine*, 3rd ed. (Paris: Gabalda, 1967), 2:195, and the works cited there.

[8] R. POCOCKE, *Description of the East and Some Other Countries*, vol. 2 (London, 1743–1745), 72.

[9] Cf. C. KOPP, *Die heiligen Stätten der Evangelien* (see n. 3), 233–35.

hill of et-Tell (209 257). Messadiye and el-Aradj have the advantage of being on the Sea of Galilee (ideal places for a fishing village and, therefore, possible locations for the homes of the fishermen Andrew and Peter), while et-Tell lies 2 km from the seashore. Moreover, the few topographers of the past 150 years who picked up samples of pottery from et-Tell's ruins were unable to find any ceramic evidence that the hill was occupied during Roman times. C. Kopp concluded his survey of the scholarly discussion that had taken place until 1961 by quoting E. Zickermann concerning the location of Bethsaida: it is possible "that today its ruins lie beneath the alluvium of the river, which for thousands of years has been depositing masses of earth and gravel." [10] Today, however, there is growing evidence that et-Tell is indeed the site of ancient Bethsaida.

II. The Jewish Sources

Situated in the territory of Philip the Tetrarch, who ruled the territory east of the Jordan from 4 B.C. until A.D. 34 (one of the sons of Herod the Great—see Lk 3:1), the town of Bethsaida was located close to the point where the Jordan River entered the Sea of Galilee.[11] Josephus refers to a development there during Philip's reign: "He also raised the village of Bethsaida on Lake Gennesaritis [κώμην δὲ Βηθσαϊδα πρὸς λίμνῃ τῇ Γεννησαρίτιδι—the Sea of Galilee] to the status of city [πόλις] by adding residents and strengthening the fortifications. He named it after Julia, the emperor's daughter" (*Ant.* 18.28). The beginning of the transformation of a village (Bethsaida) into a city (Bethsaida-Julias), if we accept Josephus' account,[12] must have taken place at the outset of Philip's reign (which began in the year 4 B.C.), because Julia was banished to the island of Pandateria by her father in 2 B.C.[13]

The decision to elevate Bethsaida may have been made because of its excellent location beside the Sea of Galilee, which enabled Philip to provide his territory with a harbor, just as his brother Antipas did

[10] Ibid., 234.

[11] Cf. Flavius Josephus, *War* 3.515; *Ant.* 18.28; *Life* 399; as well as Pliny, *Naturalis Historia* 5.15.71.

[12] However, see p. 146 below.

[13] Cf. E. SCHUERER, *The History of the Jewish People in the Age of Jesus Christ*, vol. 2 (Edinburgh: T. & T. Clark, 1979), 172.

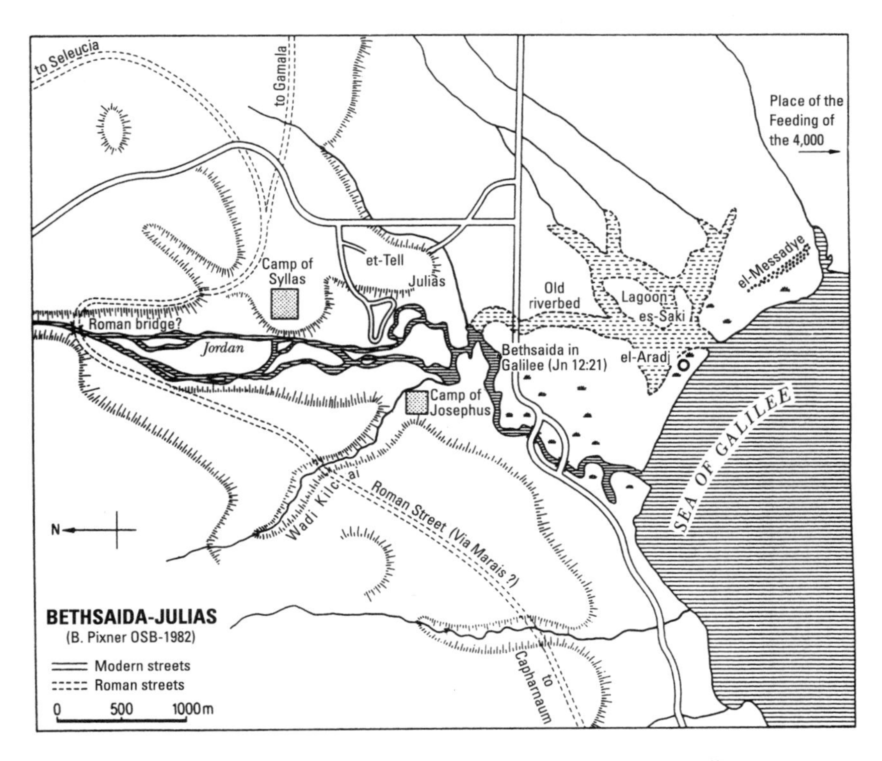

Illus. 33. Bethsaida-Julias and its surroundings (from G. Kroll).

twenty years later by building the city of Tiberias on the opposite western shore (*Ant.* 18.36f.). The inhabitants of Bethsaida were a mixture of Jews, Syrians and Greeks.[14] Philip built himself a splendid sepulcher at Bethsaida-Julias and was eventually buried there when he died following a peaceful reign of forty years (*Ant.* 18.108). That tomb, however, has not yet been discovered. Bethsaida was no doubt considered more advantageous because of its proximity to one of the most important roads in antiquity, the Via Maris (cf. Mt 4:15), which led from Caesarea Maritima to Damascus (see below).

Bethsaida is called Saydan (צַיְדָן) in Rabbinic sources. The Jewish scholar S. Klein confirms that no problem is caused by the omission of the prefix *Beth* ("house") or the addition of the final *n*, as such

[14] Cf. A. Alt, "Die Stätten des Wirkens Jesu in Galiläa territorialgeschichtlich betrachtet", in *Kleine Schriften*, vol. 2 (Munich: C.H. Beck, 1953), 436–55 (at 448).

variations of names are frequent at sites in Galilee.[15] Indeed, in the Greek text of Mark 6:45 and 8:22, the site is called Bethsaidan (Βηθσαϊδαν).[16] The Jerusalem Talmud indicates that Saydan was close to the entry of the Jordan into the Sea of Galilee (*Shekalim* 6:2 [50a]). The name Bethsaida (which in Aramaic is something like *beyt zayda'* [בֵּית צַיְדָא] or *beyt zayyadah* [צַיָּדָא])[17] may be translated as "hunting town" or "fisher town" and reflects the reputation the area seems to have had, and still has, for both wild game and fish. According to the Rabbinic interpretation (*midrash*) of Ecclesiastes 2:8 (*Midrash Kohelet* 2:8), Rabbi Yehoshua acquired pheasants from Saydan for the table of Emperor Hadrian. The rich variety of fish in its waters is also attested by Rabbi Shimon ben Gamaliel: "One day I happened to be in Saydan when they presented me with a bowl of three hundred species of small fishes" (*Shekalim* 6:2 [50a]). Jewish life continued to flourish in this district at least until the fourth century A.D., which is proven by the synagogue ruins of ed-Dikke a little over 1 km northeast of et-Tell.[18]

III. The Location of Bethsaida-Julias

Since 1967, when the region northeast of the Sea of Galilee again became accessible to researchers by the construction of new roads and bridges over the Jordan River, notable progress has been made in the scientific investigation of the Bethsaida-Julias area. I believe there can no longer be any reasonable doubt that Philips' *polis* ("city") is on and around the hill of et-Tell.[19] The main reasons are as follows.

1. As we have seen, topographers were hesitant for many years in identifying et-Tell as Bethsaida because of the lack of Roman pottery on the hill.[20] This negative argument proved to be untenable. Unusual circumstances have led to the solution of the problem. Between 1948

[15] "Hebräische Ortsnamen bei Josephus", *Monatsschrift für die Geschichte und Wissenschaft des Judentums* 59 (1915): 156–69 (at 168).

[16] The proper name, Bethsaidan, is indeclinable. See W. BAUER, *A Greek-English Lexicon of the New Testament*, 2nd ed. (Chicago: University of Chicago Press, 1979), 140.

[17] Ibid., 140; A. SCHALIT, *Namenwörterbuch zu Flavius Josephus* (Leiden: Brill, 1968), 27.

[18] Cf. H. KOHL and C. WATZINGER, *Antike Synagogen in Galiläa* (Leipzig, 1916), 112–24.

[19] Cf. J. F. BAUDOZ, "Bethsaida", *MB* 28 (1985): 28–31 (with supplements by B. PIXNER).

[20] See in particular W. F. ALBRIGHT, "Among the Canaanite Mounds of Eastern Galilee", *Bulletin of the American Schools of Oriental Research* 29 (1928): 1–8 (at 7), and C.C. McCOWN, "Correspondence", *PEFQS* 33 (1935): 144f.

and 1967 the Syrian army crisscrossed the hill (which rises some 30 m above the plain of the Jordan River) with trenches and bunkers, permitting easy access to lower ceramic strata. An initial survey produced several Hellenistic shards.[21] From 1981 to 1984 some of my friends and I gathered samples of pottery, especially from the trenches dug on the highest point of et-Tell. Professor S. Loffreda, an expert ceramicist, believes that the tell shows evidence of an accumulation of pottery similar to the one at Capharnaum. For this reason, it was clear that during the time of Jesus there was a settlement at et-Tell.

2. In 1937 A. Alt wrote the following about et-Tell and its vicinity: "The scarcity of the discovered ruins testifies ... to the modest development and duration of this settlement [Bethsaida-Julias]."[22] As in other cases, such a judgment in contradiction to Josephus' information (*Ant.* 18.28; 20.159) was premature. While inspecting the base of the southern slope of et-Tell, I discovered many dressed stones that comprise a large section of an impressive wall.[23] In the wall, there seems to be a postern that led to a nearby spring (about 10 m away), from which there is an abundant and uninterrupted flow of water. Such a feature made a large settlement on et-Tell possible. Other architectural evidence from et-Tell includes a large, exquisitely worked lintel discovered at the site (and now lying at the northern foot of the hill in the newly developed Jordan Park) and an undressed basalt stone with an engraved cross at its center that I found there in February 1982. The latter seems to testify to a Christian presence on this hill. More systematic excavations at et-Tell might someday unearth vestiges of the church visited by the monk Willibald.

3. According to Josephus, Bethsaida-Julias was situated on the shore of the Sea of Galilee (*Ant.* 18.28) and apparently had a harbor (*Life* 407). However, the present-day distance of et-Tell from the shore is about 2 km. It is a generally known phenomenon that a larger river continually expands its delta by depositing debris. In the case of the

[21] Cf. M. KOCHAVI, ed., *Judaea, Samaria and the Golan—Archaeological Survey, 1967–68* [in Modern Hebrew] (Jerusalem, 1972), 276.

[22] "Galiläische Probleme III: Hellenistische Städte und Domänen in Galiläa", *PJB* 33 (1937): 76–88 (at 85, n. 3).

[23] G. DALMAN, "Bethsaida Julias", *PJB* 8 (1912): 45–48 (at 48), wrote: "Ein Rest der Stadtmauer schien im Nordosten erkennbar" ["A portion of the city wall appeared to be discernable"].

Jordan, however, the alluvium had no effect as long as Lake Huleh, the largest part of which was not drained until the latter decades of the twentieth century, formed a natural drainage basin for silt and debris from the mountains.[24] Just east of el-Aradj, which today is also known as Beth ha-Bek, there is a very large, deep lagoon called es-Saki. In antiquity, this lagoon could have reached all the way to the area of et-Tell (as the eminent topographer Gustaf Dalman once proposed).[25] A geomorphologist, M. Inbar, has mentioned to me privately that this lagoon could have been the former bed of the Jordan River; in fact, C. W. Wilson made the same suggestion when he was working on the survey of western Palestine.[26] At present, the last part of the Jordan flows abnormally far to the west, and there appear to be traces of a now-dry riverbed north of the lagoon es-Saki.[27]

4. If the theory that es-Saki was the old estuary of the Jordan River is correct, then et-Tell, el-Aradj and Messadiye all fit the description of the river passing close by Bethsaida-Julias. However, Josephus seems to indicate that the river entered the Sea of Galilee not at Bethsaida but somewhat below it (*War* 3.515 [μετὰ πόλιν Ἰουλιάδα].[28] This best fits the location of et-Tell. In any case, the ruin fields of el-Aradj and Messadiye are too small for a city that was the head of a toparchy.[29] In fact, there is some question whether Messadiye existed at all during the first century A.D. The plain on et-Tell measures 1.5 hectares (approximately 3.7 acres) and provides the only possible location for a fortified settlement in this vicinity. The more recent findings thus lend further weight to Dalman's opinion[30] that the ancient

[24] In my earlier articles, "Wo lag Bethsaida?" *HlL* 114, nos. 2–3 (1982): 25–31 (at 27), and "Putting Bethsaida-Julias on the Map", *CNfI* 27 (1982): 165–70 (at 166f.), I suggested a lakeshore close to et-Tell and strong alluvion, but see M. INBAR, "River Delta on Lake Kinneret Caused by Recent Changes in the Drainage Bassin", in H. POSER, *Geomorphologische Prozesse und Prozeßkombinationen in der Gegenwart* (Göttingen, 1974), 197–207.

[25] *Orte und Wege Jesu*, 3rd ed. (Gütersloh: Bertelsmann, 1924), 174.

[26] "The Sites of Taricheae and Bethsaida", *PEFQS* (1877), 11–13 (at 13). I was made aware of this by my friend Dr. Rainer Riesner.

[27] See the aerial photograph in B. PIXNER, "Searching for the New Testament Site of Bethsaida", *BA* 48 (1985): 207–16 (at 210f.).

[28] Cf. H. S. J. THACKERAY, trans., *Josephus*, vol. 2, *The Jewish War, Books 1–3* (Cambridge, Mass.: Harvard University Press, 1989), 721.

[29] Cf. A. N. SHERWIN-WHITE, *Roman Society and Roman Law in the New Testament* (Oxford: Clarendon Press, 1963), 131.

[30] *Orte und Wege Jesu* (see n. 25), 173f.

acropolis of Bethsaida-Julias and Philip's palace (*Ant.* 18.108) can be searched for on et-Tell, but on this point, too, excavations will have the last word.

5. A particularly convincing argument against the possibility of el-Aradj or Messadiye having been the main site of Philip's city derives from Josephus' account of the battle of Bethsaida-Julias, which fits in beautifully with the et-Tell location. Dalman had already hinted in this direction (n. 30), but a careful analysis of the account can add further arguments. The battle took place in the late fall of A.D. 66 between the rebel forces led by Josephus and the army of Sulla, the commander of the troops of Agrippa II (A.D. 48–100?). A report of the battle was composed by Josephus himself, who had an intimate knowledge of the area.

IV. Josephus on the Battle of Bethsaida-Julias

The account of the Jewish historian reads: "About this time reinforcements arrived from the king [Agrippa II], both horse and foot, under the command of Sulla, the captain of his bodyguard. He pitched his camp at a distance of five furlongs from Julias, and put out pickets on the roads leading to Seleucia and to the fortress of Gamala, to prevent the inhabitants [of Julias] from obtaining supplies from Galilee.

> On receiving intelligence of this, I [Josephus] dispatched a force of two thousand men under the command of Jeremiah, who entrenched themselves a furlong away from Julias close to the river Jordan, but took no action beyond skirmishing until I joined them with supports, three thousand strong. The next day, after laying an ambuscade in a ravine [ἔν τινι φάραγγι] not far from their earthworks, I offered battle to the royal troops, directing my division to retire until they had lured the enemy forward; as actually happened. Sulla, supposing that our men were really flying, advanced and was on the point of following in pursuit, when the others, emerging from their ambush, took him in the rear and threw his whole force into the utmost disorder. Instantly wheeling the main body about, I charged and routed the royalists; and my success on that day would have been complete, had I not been thwarted by some evil genius. The horse on which I went into action stumbled on a marshy spot and brought me with him to the ground. Having fractured some bones in the wrist, I was carried to a village called Cepharnocus [εἰς κώμην

Κεφαρνωκὸν λεγομένην]. My men, hearing of this, and fearing that a worse fate had befallen me, desisted from further pursuit and returned in the deepest anxiety on my account. I sent for physicians and, after receiving their attention, remained there for that day in a feverish condition; at night, under medical advice, I was removed to Tarichaeae.

Sulla and his troops, learning of my accident, again took heart; and, finding that the watch kept in our camp was slack, placed, under cover of night, a squadron of cavalry in ambush beyond the Jordan, and at daybreak offered us battle. Accepting the challenge, my troops advanced into the plain [μέχρι τοῦ πεδίου], when the cavalry, suddenly appearing from their ambush, threw them into disorder and routed them, killing six of our men. They did not, however, follow up their success; for, on hearing that reinforcements shipped at Tarichaeae had reached Julias, they retired in alarm [about their camp]. Not long after this Vespasian arrived at Tyre, accompanied by King Agrippa [*Life* 398–407].[31]

V. An Analysis of Josephus' Report

In A.D. 67 Gamala, the rockbound fortress overlooking the Valley of Daliot, and Seleucia, on the eastern shore of Lake Huleh, then called Semechonitis (*War* 4.2), were the only towns to the east of the Jordan River that were still in revolt against Agrippa II, who continued to support his Roman allies. Agrippa hoped that by besieging Gamala he would compel its defenders to submit to the Romans. But it was only in November of A.D. 67 that three Roman legions under Vespasian succeeded in breaking the resistance of Gamala after a bloody siege and one of the fiercest battles of the Jewish War (*War* 4.1–83). The town indeed deserved the title of "Masada of the North".[32] At the onset of the siege, King Agrippa sent his commander Sylla to cut off the supply routes from Galilee leading to Gamala.[33] To do that, Sulla pitched camp on a probably semicircular terrace some 5 stadia (about 1 km) north of Bethsaida-Julias (illus. 33). From there he could oversee the traffic moving from the direction of Capharnaum along the

[31] Cf. H. S. J. THACKERAY, trans., *Josephus*, vol. 1, *The Life; Against Apion* (Cambridge, Mass.: Harvard University Press, 146–49).

[32] Cf. G. CORNFELD, *Josephus: The Jewish War* (Grand Rapids: Eerdmans, 1982), 254–60.

[33] Cf. A. SCHLATTER, *Zur Topographie und Geschichte Palästinas* (Stuttgart: Calwer, 1893), 310f.

Via Maris (the ancient highway that connected Egypt and Damascus), and he also could send out a guard to patrol both the route running north to Seleucia and the one branching off from there and ascending the north flank of the Wadi Daliot to Gamala.

It is all but certain that at the time of the second temple, the so-called Via Maris (illus. 12) connecting Egypt with Damascus ran by Bethsaida and not farther north at the later "Bridge of the Daughters of Jacob" (p. 57). It would have made no sense for Sulla to patrol the supply route to Seleucia there[34] if there had been another crossing farther to the north. Furthermore, the milestone found in Capharnaum proves that at least in Hadrian's time an imperial road went by there. Matthew locates the main activity of Jesus along the Via Maris in the region of "Zebulun and Naphtali" (Mt 4:14–17), and the tax station of Levi-Matthew (Mt 9:9f. / Mk 2:13–17) may have stood on this road near the border at the Jordan (pp. 62–63).

In all probability Vespasian used the Via Maris when in the summer of A.D. 67 he advanced from Hammath-Tiberias in order to besiege Gamala (*War* 4.11). It would have been easier by far to cross the Jordan with such a mighty army if there had been a bridge at that time. If there was only a ford through the river, then there was always the danger that the flooding of the Jordan in spring and winter would make crossing impossible. Indeed, there appear to be bridgeheads where the river leaves the deep ravine through the basalt sandbar near ed-Dikke. However, it is impossible to decide whether such a bridge had already been built by Herod the Great to connect his territory in the south with his estates in the north (Batanea and Trachonitis), or first by Agrippa I or a later ruler (pp. 56–57).

At the time of the battle of Bethsaida-Julias, Josephus' headquarters was located at Tarichea-Magdala, the hometown of Mary Magdalen (Mt 27:56, etc.) west of the present-day kibbutz Ginnosar. To reduce the pressure on his beleaguered allies in Gamala, Josephus sent his commander, Jeremias, to their aid. The latter set up camp at a distance of just 1 stadium (184 m) from Bethsaida-Julias, on the western bank of the Jordan River. The encampment, consisting of 2,000 men,

[34] The blockade of Seleucia appears to have had quick success, for Josephus reports: "Now Sogane and Seleucia had quite early in the revolt been induced by Agrippa to come to terms" (*War* 4.4). He thereby thwarted some of the efforts of Josephus, who, upon taking command of the revolt in Galilee, immediately began to fortify Seleucia, Sogane and Gamala (*War* 2.574).

could have been located at the mouth of a ravine (φάραγξ), which can be identified with Wadi Qil[c]ai. These four topographical features—the ravine, the camp, the Jordan River and the site of Bethsaida-Julias—must have been close to one another and oriented in an east-west line. Therefore, according to Josephus' description, neither Messadiye nor el-Aradj are logical sites for the city of Bethsaida-Julias, for there is no ravine or valley in the plain surrounding either site.

However, we now turn to the battle itself. Josephus arrived at Bethsaida-Julias with 3,000 fresh troops. During the night, he placed a large contingent of his men in the ravine (the Wadi Qil[c]ai would be extremely suitable, since his troops would have been well hidden from the view of the men in Sulla's camp). The next morning, Josephus began his strategic maneuver to draw Sulla's forces down from their camp. Toward the end of the dry season, the Jordan River, which divides here into several branches, could easily have been forded even by foot soldiers. The feigned retreat across the Jordan, which was low at that time, brought the enemy near his camp. Then suddenly emerging from the ravine, where they had been concealed, the rebel soldiers attacked Sulla's men on their flank, throwing them into disarray. At that time, Josephus turned his troops around and charged the enemy. Unfortunately, his horse lost its footing in the marshy terrain of the riverbank and threw him to the ground, causing him to wrench his wrist. Seeing their commander injured, Josephus' troops became discouraged and broke off pursuit of the enemy. Josephus was carried to Capharnaum, where physicians treated him and then sent him off to Tarichea.

In the meantime Sulla reorganized his forces and planned a counterattack. Under the cover of darkness, he set up an ambush of horsemen beyond the Jordan River and at daybreak led the bulk of his troops toward Jeremias' camp. Jeremias' men came out of the camp and prepared for battle on the Jordan plain (τὸ πέδιον). (At present there is no plain on the west bank of the river, but if the es-Saki lagoon was the Jordan estuary during the first century, a large plain would have existed between the Galilean hills and the river.) Without warning, Sulla's horsemen stormed down the river valley and attacked Jeremias' troops on their flank. Once again the battle remained undecided because Sulla was forced to withdraw his troops. News reached him that a large contingent of rebel soldiers dispatched by Josephus from Tarichea by boat had landed at Bethsaida-Julias. This last piece of information confirms our belief that the es-Saki lagoon formed the natural harbor of Bethsaida-Julias at that time.

VI. Bethsaida in Galilee

El-Aradj lies on a spur of land that except for a narrow access is completely surrounded by water. Littered across the site are astonishing traces of ancient buildings, among them a synagogue or church, which includes (1) sections of basalt architraves, one with a beautifully formed cornice (plate 4a); (2) a heart-shaped limestone column that I discovered in 1983 together with Mendel Nun, an expert on fishery in antiquity; (3) several capitals that Mr. Nun keeps in the garden of his kibbutz at En Gev; and (4) mosaic pieces shown to me by the family now living in Beth ha-Bek. R. de Haas was presumably referring to the same mosaic when he wrote:

> In October 1929, . . . we happened to just come in time to inspect a splendid Roman Mosaic to the left of the flight of stairs leading up to the house, at a depth of about two metres. Wadih [the administrator of the owner from Damascus at that time] had quite unexpectedly met with it. As it stretched far underneath the main building, he could not properly examine it and had to cover it up again. A sarcophagus not very far away and all sorts of broken columns, capitals and a mass of building stone testify to the wealth still hidden below the surface.[35]

It was related to me that the Syrian army had stored a large amount of ammunition in that building and that Israeli fighter jets had therefore bombed it a long time before the Six-Day War, i.e., in 1956. Because of that operation, the debris of the ancient ruins is scattered over the entire site.

Indication of a settlement at el-Aradj during the time of Jesus was provided by Gustaf Dalman, who found and identified Roman pottery at the site.[36] Some scholars think El-Aradj was the ancient Jewish fishing village, whereas the Hellenistic town was located on the nearby

[35] R. de Haas, *Galilee, the Sacred Sea: A Historical and Geographical Description* (Jerusalem, [1933]), 222.

[36] *Orte und Wege Jesu* (see n. 25), 173.

hill at et-Tell.[37] If the es-Saki lagoon was the ancient Jordan estuary, this would cast light on the mysterious "Bethsaida in Galilee" (Jn 12:21). Bethsaida-Julias was east of the Jordan, i.e., in Gaulanitis. Could it then be called "Bethsaida in Galilee"? When Herod the Great died in 4 B.C., his territory was divided among three of his sons (*War* 2.93–97). Herod Antipas was made tetrarch over Galilee and Perea, while Philip received Gaulanitis and Batanea (illus. 2). The Jordan River was the dividing line between the territories of these two sons. The small fishing village el-Aradj, situated to the west of the Jordan according to our hypothesis, remained in the territory of Galilee, while parts of Bethsaida to the east of the river and concentrated at et-Tell were elevated to the honor of a city by Philip. Thus, it may be that the topography of the Gospel of John, whose precision has been underscored by modern archaeology,[38] also reflects the situation at the time of Jesus' ministry by the lake. The location of both Bethsaidas, one in constant danger of flooding in the Jordan Valley due to the winter rains and the other erected on solid rock, may be the background for Jesus' parable about the houses that were built on sand or on rock (Mt 7:24–27 / Lk 6:47–49). The Jordan River did not constitute the border between territories for long because under Agrippa I and II both riverbanks of the Jordan were in the same territory. Future excavations will show what became of both locations of Bethsaida, et-Tell and el-Aradj, in later centuries.

In recent years, the Israeli government has established a beautiful park in the area between the Jordan River and the hill of et-Tell. In the future, it will be extended to include the historical hill. On the Feast of Saint Andrew (November 30), who was born in Bethsaida (Jn 1:44), the Benedictines of Tabgha erected a memorial stone in 1981 with permission from the Israeli administration. It is only 20 m from the road that leads to the Jordan Park and can be easily visited by pilgrims. The large basalt stone commemorates the miracle of the healing of the blind man, which according to the Gospel of Mark happened outside Bethsaida (Mk 8:23) on the way to Caesarea Philippi (Mk 8:27). The symbols carved into the stone include two eyes—one half-open and one fully open—symbolizing the progression in

[37] For example, F. M. ABEL, *Géographie de la Palestine* (see n. 7), 2:279f.; C. MÖLLER and G. SCHMITT, *Siedlungen Palästinas nach Flavius Josephus* (Wiesbaden: Harrassowitz, 1976), 110.

[38] Cf. especially B. SCHWANK, "Ortskenntnisse im Vierten Evangelium?" *EA* 57 (1981): 427–42.

the recovery of sight. The Hebrew *nezer yishay* ("branch of Isaiah" [Is 11:1: נֵצֶר יִשַׁי]) was a popular Jewish Christian symbol that is found frequently in particular in the Golan Heights (p. 153). The "rainbow cross" [with its three elements: rainbow, points and cross] is reminiscent of the three covenants of God with mankind: the rainbow stands for the covenant with Adam, Noah and Abraham; the twelve points represent the covenant with Israel; and the cross symbolizes the New Covenant.

VII. Supplement: Recent Excavations

After I had published the first edition of these thoughts (n. 24) and after a longer article of mine in an archaeological journal had appeared (n. 27), I had the opportunity in March 1987 to present my thoughts to the "Golan Research Project". In the same year, the young archaeologist Dr. Rami Arav of the University of Haifa carried out test excavations on et-Tell and in el-Aradj.[39] In 1989 the systematic excavations on et-Tell began. These were joined by professors H. W. Kuhn (University of Munich), R. A. Freund (University of Nebraska), and J. J. Rousseau (University of California). After short notices,[40] the first more thorough report appeared in 1991.[41] In 1993 a scientific symposium was held in Münster, the lectures of which are documented in an anthology.[42] In 1995 another symposium, in which I participated, followed in Budapest.[43] The excavations are being continued under the leadership of R. Arav.

Even now, there can hardly be any rational doubt remaining that the *polis* Bethsaida-Julias stood on the hill of et-Tell. The finds in

[39] "Et-Tell and el-Araj", *IEJ* 38 (1988): 187f.; 39 (1989): 99f.; "Et-Tell (Bethsaida)", *ESI* 7–8 (1988/1989): 177f.

[40] H. W. Kuhn, *Betsaida: Ausgrabung einer Stadt Jesu* (68. Jahresbericht 1989 der Gesellschaft von Freunden und Förderern der Universität München) (Munich, 1990), 27–32; R. Arav, "Et-Tell (Bethsaida)", *ESI* 9, no. 2 (1989/1990): 98f.; "Bethsaida 1989", *IEJ* 41 (1991): 184f.; "Bethsaida 1992", *IEJ* 42 (1992): 252–54; R. Arav and J. J. Rousseau, "Bethsaïda, ville perdue et retrouvée", *RB* 100 (1993): 415–28; "Bethsaida 1990/1991", *ESI* 12 (1994): 8f.

[41] H. W. Kuhn and R. Arav, "The Bethsaida Excavations: Historical and Archaeological Approaches", in B. A. Pearson et al., *The Future of Early Christianity: Essays in Honor of Helmut Koester* (Minneapolis, Minn.: Fortress, 1991), 77–106.

[42] R. Arav and R. A. Freund, eds., *Bethsaida: A City by the North Shore of the Sea of Galilee*, Bethsaida Excavations Project Reports and Contextual Studies 1 (Kirksville: Thomas Jefferson University Press, 1995).

[43] Cf. B. Pixner, "Betsaida—zehn Jahre später", *HlL* 129 (1997): 1–16.

three areas (A, B, C) show above all that three settlement periods have to be reckoned with: i.e., the Early Bronze Age (ca. 3050–2700 B.C.), from which the city wall I found probably stems (p. 133); the Iron Age (ca. 1000–587 B.C.); and the Hellenistic–early Roman period. The settlement in the Hellenistic–early Roman period apparently began in the first half of the third century B.C. During this time, quite a sizable settlement was located on et-Tell. Later, there was apparently in the second half of the third century A.D. only a very weak settlement. During the Byzantine period, the hill appears to have been abandoned for the most part. The following chapter contains information about the individual discoveries.

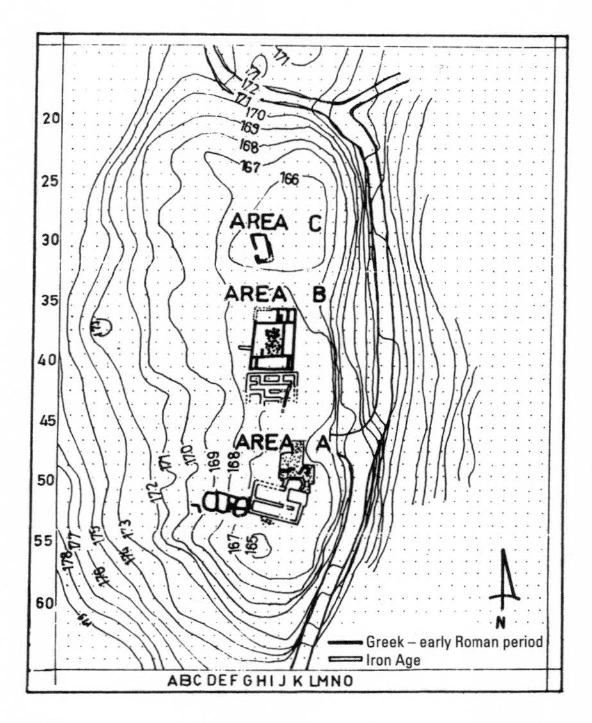

Illus. 34. Excavations on et-Tell (Bethsaida-Julias) as of 1995 (according to R. Arav).

10. New Discoveries in Bethsaida

I. *The Old Testament Period*

The hill of et-Tell measures approximately 400 m in length and is approximately 200 m wide. The settlement area is approximately 8 hectares. The hill rises 30 m above the surrounding area and 45 m above Lake Gennesaret (illus. 33) with the highest point at 166 m below sea level. Most of the highest settlements were removed by Syrian troops and were extended as a fortress before the Six-Day War of 1967. Only the surface lying on top of the hill of this expanded settlement area has so far been partially excavated under the direction of R. Arav.[1] The excavation covers the areas A, B and C (illus. 34) from the south to the north (1995). In area A, Arav found important buildings from the Iron Age (ca. 1000–587 B.C.), and strong walls of a temple complex were excavated. North of this, in area B, a palace building was found, dating from the Iron Age, and between the temple and the palace was a paved square that led to an impressive gateway of the sanctuary and through which a channel ran.

To the east of the temple entrance there was probably an altar, the remains of which are still visible today. The enormous walls of the palace are reminiscent of similar palaces that were from the same period in the south of Turkey and in northern Syria. Such buildings are called *beth-hilani*. However, in the south such palaces have not yet been found. In the palace, large quantities of ceramic containers and also a letter seal (bulla) from the ninth century B.C. were discovered, as the area belonged to the northern kingdom of Israel.[2] Iron Age town

[1] "Bethsaida Excavations: Preliminary Report, 1987–1993", in R. ARAV and R. A. FREUND, eds., *Bethsaida: A City by the North Shore of the Sea of Galilee*, Bethsaida Project Reports and Contextual Studies 1 (Kirksville: Thomas Jefferson University Press, 1995), 3–63.

[2] Cf. B. BRANDL, "An Israelite Bulla in Phoenician Style from Bethsaida (et-Tell)", ibid., 141–64.

walls 8 m thick were discovered; only the eastern side of these has been excavated.

R. Arav assumed that Bethsaida was the capital of the kingdom of Geshur. The Old Testament reports that King David had taken a daughter from King Talmai of Geshur as his wife. Her name was Maacah, and she bore him a daughter, Tamar, and a son, Absalom (see 2 Sam 3:3). When Tamar was violated by Absalom's half brother Amnon, Absalom killed him (2 Sam 13:1ff.), whereupon he had to flee from Jerusalem and stayed three years in Geshur (2 Sam 13:37f.). Probably at that time et-Tell was his place of refuge until he was pardoned again by his father (2 Sam 14:23). Arav believed also that et-Tell is mentioned in the book of Joshua under the name Zer, besides the cities Hammath, Rakkath and Chinnereth (Josh 19:35), which were also at Lake Gennesaret in the area of the tribe Naphtali.[3] Hammath was situated in the south of today's Tiberias, Rakkath by Magdala, and Kinneret on the Tell el-'Oreimeh, south of Tabgha (pp. 78–79).

II. The New Testament Time

For Christian researchers the excavations of the northern part of area B and area C are the most interesting areas in Bethsaida. In area B, a paved yard that was surrounded by dwellings was discovered. The whole area measured 18 × 27 m and had been inhabited at the time of Jesus. It was clear that fishermen had lived there. Hardly anywhere else has such an abundance of fishing remains been discovered. In the yard, where fishnets were spread out, a set of sinkers (i.e., small lead weights that were used with the nets) were found. In the houses, two needles were found, and these were probably used for repairing fishing nets (cf. Mk 1:19). Fishing rods (cf. Mt 17:27) and small portable carved stone anchors of basalt were also found. In contrast, a heavy perforated basalt stone that was used as an altar in a Byzantine church in Tiberias, as the archaeologist Y. Hirschfeld reported, would have been too heavy to have been used as an anchor.[4] M. Nun from Kibbutz En Gev has written a study on the stone anchors and the net weights

[3] "Bethsaida, Tser, and the Fortified Cities of Naphtali", in R. Arav and R. A. Freund, *Bethsaida* (see n. 1), 193–201.

[4] "The Anchor Church at the Summit of Mt. Berenice, Tiberias", *BA* 57 (1994): 122–33.

from Lake Gennesaret.[5] From the New Testament (Jn 1:44; 12:21) and tradition, we know that five of the most important disciples of Jesus, i.e., the brothers Simon and Andrew; James and John, the sons of Zebedee and Salome; and Philip from Bethsaida, were all fishermen.[6] One or more of them could have lived here, on et-Tell.

In the northern area C, an ornate and well-built house was discovered. The original assumption that it must be a synagogue[7] has not been confirmed. Best preserved was a kitchen, which measured 11.3 × 4.5 m; on its left there was a room where, under basalt beams, a cellar was discovered in which different earthenware wine jugs were found. Nearby, an iron scythe was discovered that was used for cutting and collecting grapes. In the kitchen a beautiful golden earring was discovered and also a cosmetic palette, used for coloring eyelashes. Jokingly, I called this house the "dwelling of Salome", the mother who tried to request a special favor from Jesus for her two sons John and James (Mt 20:20–23). To the west of the kitchen there was a 12 × 12.8 m large yard, and north of this there was a small room, in which was discovered a particularly special find: a cross made of clay.

A few meters north of this New Testament housing complex was the northern wall of the town. A partially preserved path, which Jesus and his disciples must often have walked, led from there southward through the settlement. The unusual nature of the excavation in Bethsaida was that here, uniquely, was discovered a Galilean housing complex that looked exactly as it would have at the time of Jesus. It was surprising that in such an important settlement there were hardly any building stones, columns, et cetera, of limestone. Although all around the settlement lava basalt exists, the absence of limestone is remarkable. R. Arav believed that the reason for this was that in several places partly limed pits were discovered that the Bedouin, during their century-long occupation of the hill, used for lime production. Lime pits were also found on the tell. The Bedouin tribe, Tellawīye, took its name from et-Tell and used the hill as a burial place.[8] In the summer of

[5] *Ancient Stone Anchors and Net Sinkers from the Sea of Galilee* (En Gev: Kibbutz En Gev, 1993).

[6] Cf. chapter 9, "In Search of Bethsaida" (pp. 128–42, esp. pp. 128–29).

[7] Cf. U. W. Sahm, "Sensationelle Entdeckungen in Betsaida", *Katholische Nachrichtenagentur (Ökumenische Information)* 52/53 (December 23, 1992): 23f.

[8] Cf. C. Kopp, *The Holy Places of the Gospels* (New York: Herder and Herder, 1963), 184.

1995, at the slope of the hill I found part of a limestone column that seemed prepared for the pits but that had escaped the lime producer.

In July 1993, at the foot of the hill of et-Tell, R. Arav and R. A. Freund found a harbor complex, close by the spring I found northeast of this (p. 133). Josephus mentions that the *polis* Julias (the Roman name for Bethsaida) possessed its own port (*Life* 427). Geomorphologic investigations at the foot of the hills[9] support my view that the lagoon es-Saki (illus. 33) went right up to this site (pp. 134f.). It is possible that the silt deposits of the Meshushim flowing down from the Golan forced the Jordan River, in the post–New Testament period, to move more to the west. Julias, a good place for fishing, could be reached by boat, which explains the many traces of fishermen on the hill. In addition, in area B, a Hellenistic and early Roman seal depicting two men throwing a net (cf. Mk 1:16) was discovered among the coins, two of which were from Tetrarch Herod Philippus (cf. Lk 3:1) and one of which dated to A.D. 29/30.[10] Contrary to the impression given by Josephus (p. 130), the renaming of Bethsaida to Julias apparently happened only at that time, and only after Jesus' ministry in Galilee. Livia Julia, the wife of Augustus, prompted the name change,[11] and it is known that she had good connections to Herod's family (*Ant.* 17.146, 190). A clay figure was found in area A that apparently shows the picture of the empress.[12]

There are possible references to the destruction of et-Tell during the Jewish Revolt of A.D. 66 in Galilee.[13] All evidence points to the destruction of Bethsaida by an earthquake in the first half of the second century A.D. It appears that an earthquake in the year A.D. 115 in south Syria caused extensive damage.[14] A tsunami following this earthquake struck Jaffa and Caesarea, as was reported in Talmudic literature.[15] This earthquake took place allegedly on the night of December 13, A.D. 115, although this date is uncertain. The geomorphologists

[9] Cf. J. F. SHRODER and M. INBAR, "Geologic and Geographic Background to the Bethsaida Excavations", in R. ARAV and R. A. FREUND, *Bethsaida* (see n. 1), 65–94.

[10] Cf. C. MEIER, appendix to chapter 1, ibid., 53–61.

[11] Cf. F. STRICKERT, "The Coins of Philip", ibid., 165–89.

[12] Cf. R. ARAV, "Bethsaida 1989", *IEJ* 41 (1991): 184f.

[13] Cf. R. ARAV and J. J. ROUSSEAU, *Jesus and His World: An Archaeological and Cultural Dictionary* (Minneapolis: Fortress, 1995), 20.

[14] Cf. D. H. K. AMIRAN, E. ARIEH and T. TURCOTTE, "Earthquakes in Israel and Adjacent Areas: Macroseismic Observations since 100 B.C.E.", *IEJ* 44 (1994): 260–305 (at 265, 294).

[15] Jerusalem Talmud, *Moed Katan* 2 (3a); Babylonian Talmud, *Baba Mezia* 49b.

J. F. Shroder and M. Inbar state that an enormous natural catastrophe took place at this time that caused great changes to et-Tell. Not only was Bethsaida completely destroyed, but north of the Jordan Valley, landslides took place, which blocked off the valley. Behind this there formed a lake that burst out with great force and buried the lagoon completely in rubble up to the tell. The latest coin that was found in a house on the tell was of the emperor Trajan (A.D. 98–117), and this fits with the dating of the end of Bethsaida.

III. The Settlement of el-Aradj

An exploratory investigation in el-Aradj, which today is called Beth ha-Bek, made by R. Arav in 1987 revealed only one settlement layer from the Byzantine period, i.e., from the fourth to the sixth century.[16] But the area he investigated (4 × 4 m) was far too small for a conclusive judgment. In earlier investigations some Hellenistic-Roman ceramic shards were discovered.[17] This find has been confirmed recently,[18] so that it was here that the New Testament "Bethsaida in Galilee" (Jn 12:21) was located (pp. 139–40). The extensive archaeological finds from the Byzantine period confirm that there was veneration for this place. However, no traces of a church, which the courageous pilgrim Willibald, later bishop of Eichstätt, visited in the year 725, have yet been found on the hill et-Tell,[19] and the absence of a relevant Byzantine settlement layer means that this situation will not change.

[16] "Et-Tell and el-Araj", *IEJ* 38 (1988): 187f.

[17] Cf. J. F. Strange, "Beth-Saida", in D. N. Freedman, *The Anchor Bible Dictionary* (New York: Doubleday, 1992), 1:692f.

[18] Cf. Y. Stepansky, "Kefar Nahum Map, Survey", *ESI* 10 (1992): 87–90 (at 87); G. Franz, "The Excavations at Bethsaida", *Archaeology in the Biblical World* 3 (1995): 9–11.

[19] Baldi, 266.

11. Kursi and the Land of the Gerasenes

I. The Gospel Reports and Topography

The event of the healing of the demoniac is mentioned by all three synoptic Gospels but with some variation (Mt 8:28–34 / Mk 5:1–17 / Lk 8:26–37): After Jesus went with his disciples in a boat across the Sea of Gennesaret and crossed from the west side to the east, he disembarked in the land of the Gadarenes (εἰς χώραν τῶν Γαδαρηνῶν [Mt 8:28]) or Gerasenes (Γερασηνών [Mk 5:1]), also Gergesenes (Γεργεσηνῶν [textual variant, cf. Lk 8:28]).[1] There he encountered a man possessed by demons, who was living among the graves and in the caves of the mountains. Under the influence of the demons, he tried to prevent Jesus from landing and walking on land that he believed belonged to him. Jesus drove the demons out of the man but allowed them to enter a herd of swine that was grazing in the area. The animals then rushed down the slope into the water of the lake below, where they drowned.

In Jesus' day, the Wadi Semach, which flowed into Lake Gennesaret from the east, represented the boundary between the land of Israel (namely, the tetrarchy of Herod Philip [cf. Lk 3:1]) and the area that belonged to Gaulanitis and that was part of the Hellenistic Decapolis (cf. Mk 5:20). Mark seems to have assumed that the political-geographical boundary represented also a spiritual boundary: God reigned over the land north of the valley, while Satan possessed the pagan south. On the side that Satan ruled, at the outer edge of the Decapolis, lay, according to Origen,[2] a place called Gergesa. It belonged to the region of the Decapolis town Hippos, which is called Susitha (Susita) in Aramaic. The towns of the Decapolis were taken from the Hasmonean kingdom by the Roman legions under Pompey in 63 B.C. and

[1] Cf. R. Riesner, "Gerasener", in *GBL*, 2nd ed. (1990), 1:442f.

[2] *Commentaria in Evangelium Ioannis* 6.24 (Jn 1:28) (PG 14:270; Baldi, 309f.).

were awarded a similar autonomous status to that of the Hellenistic towns (*War* 1.55f.; *Ant.* 14.74f.).[3]

According to the accounts in the synoptic Gospels, Jesus attempted to make his first entry into pagan territory here. That is why the story has a highly symbolic character. The demons and the pigs (the pig is the impure animal par excellence) are the symbols for the power of Satan over the land and its inhabitants. As in the story of the prophet Jonah in pagan Nineveh (Jon 1), the event is preceded by a storm on the lake (Mk 4:35–42). On land, an even more dangerous storm awaited Jesus and his disciples. Satan has been described as someone who, with the help of the possessed, will defend with power his kingly dominion and the land he rules. With the graphic description of the possessed man, Mark describes the nature of paganism (Mk 5:2–7). The possessed one comes out of a cave—he belongs to a spiritually dead world. He is terribly strong and cannot be tamed—the outer power of paganism is insurmountable. He screams and strikes himself with stones—similar to the way the dazed priests of Baal behaved on Carmel (1 Kings 18:28). He complains: "Leave me in peace; have you come here in order to torment me?"—the demons recognize the higher power of God and introduce themselves with the name "Legion" (λεγιών [Mk 5:9]), probably alluding to the power of the Hellenistic towns of the Decapolis founded and protected by the Roman legions.

Why did the pig become the symbol for paganism? The Canaanite people used pigs in their religious offerings, and in Palestine archaeologists have found altars used for such offerings. Since the Jewish people felt that they had a monopoly on bringing offerings to God, this was possibly the principal reason for the Jewish prohibition on keeping pigs and eating pork. In the eyes of the Jews, there existed a particular relationship between pigs and demons. In addition to the background for our story, one of the infamous Roman legions, the *legio X Fretensis*, had a wild boar as its symbol. Apart from this, there are also eschatological undertones. According to Isaiah 65:4, living in caves and graves and eating pork is a distinguishing feature of the apocalyptic denial of God. In one prophecy of Ezekiel it says: "On that day I will give to Gog a place for burial in Israel, the Valley of the Travelers east of the sea; it will block the travelers, for there Gog and all his multitude will be buried" (Ezek 39:11). This was understood

[3] Cf. R. Riesner, "Dekapolis", in *GBL*, 2nd ed. (1990), 1:263f.

by the Jewish community as the area on the eastern side of the Sea of Galilee. Both symbols of heathenism, pigs and demons, are used in the Gospels to demonstrate the power of God: the herd of pigs is drowned in the lake; the possessed man is healed and becomes the first messenger for the Gospels in a pagan country (Mk 5:20).

The banishing of the demons into the herd of pigs did not mean a resolution of difficulties for Jesus. Following this incident, the swineherds fled and told everyone in the town and the villages (εἰς τὴν πόλιν [*polis*] καὶ εἰς τοὺς ἀγρούς [Mk 5:14]). This *polis* can only be the area of the Hippos, a place that functioned as a castle situated on a plateau of a basalt conelike rock. The Hippos is shaped like a horse's head and looks across to the other side of the lake, toward its Jewish rival, Tiberias. The area is described in ancient Jewish sources, traces of which are found in the Jerusalem Talmud (*Shebᶜit* 6:1 [36c]), as also corroborated by Origen (n. 2). Afterward the area would have been inhabited by the Gergesites, who were driven out following the invasion of Joshua of *'erez Yisra'ẹl*. The Gergesites belonged to the seven tribes of the original inhabitants referred to in the book of Joshua: "Hereby you shall know that the living God is among you, and that he will without fail drive out from before you the Canaanites, the Hittites, the Hivites, the Perizzites, the Gergashites [Gergesites], the Amorites, and the Jebusites" (Josh 3:10). Perhaps this puzzling text in Mark, "They came . . . to the country of the Gerasenes" (εἰς τὴν χώραν τῶν Γερασηνῶν [Mk 5:1]), should simply mean that they came into the area of those driven out (גרשים [*geruschim* or *geraschim*]). Origen probably understood the importance of the story with regard to land and its representative and symbolic function. The Hellenistic Gergesites discovered that the loss of the pigs was due to the immense power of the intruding Jewish exorcist, and they then beseeched him to leave the region (Mk 5:17). The banisher became the banished.

II. The Pilgrim Reports

Soon after Jesus' death, Christianity spread across the whole of that region; the leaders of the communities of Hippos appear in the lists of bishops of the first councils.[4] An early shrine was built in memory of

[4] Cf. B. BAGATTI, *Antichi villaggi cristiani di Galilea*, SBFCMi 13 (Jerusalem: Franciscan Printing Press, 1971), 46f.

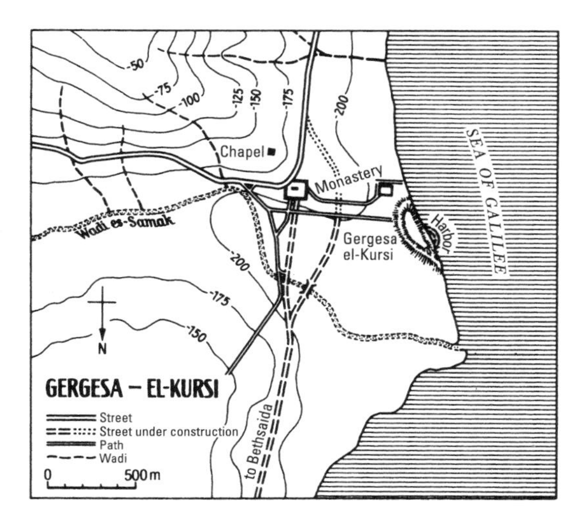

Illus. 35. Gergesa—el-Kursi (from G. Kroll).

the healed possessed man near the mountain cave that was assumed to be his former home. Razor-sharp firestones can be found lying around throughout the area, and this reminds us of the remark of the evangelist that the demon-possessed man struck himself with stones and injured himself (Mk 5:5). In the fifth century a large monastic community was established in the area, and as the shrine on the mountain slope was too small for them, they built themselves a monastery on the plain at the foot of the mountain. Cyril of Scythopolis tells us that in the year 491 the great monastery founder Mar Saba visited the place "Chorsia" and prayed there.[5]

In 723 Saint Willibald, in connection with mentioning our Gospel story, wrote that the Christians owned a church there in which he prayed.[6] Willibald wrongly called the place "Corazaim", a confusion with Chorazin.[7] The area appears on a map dated 1681 that is a reproduction of a much older map and is marked on a mountain east of the village "Kursi". Perhaps it is the Jewish village Kurschi (קורשי),[8] which is mentioned in the Mishna, and in the Talmud. We know that in the

[5] *S. Sabae Vitae* (Baldi, 311).

[6] Baldi, 311f.

[7] Cf. Baldi, 306–8. There shall the Antichrist also be born!

[8] Also M. Nun (see n. 9), V. Tsaferis (see n. 11) and others; G. Reeg, *Die Ortsnamen Israels nach der rabbinischen Literatur* (Wiesbaden: Harrassowitz, 1989), 329f., 556.

fifth century a monastery settlement existed there that was visited by many pilgrims and blossomed until the Persian invasion of the Holy Land in the year 614, after which it subsequently deteriorated. The occupation by the Arabs about twenty years later (638) prevented pilgrimages coming to the area, and Kursi was left almost deserted. In the beginning of the eighth century the church was destroyed by an earthquake, and at the end of that century the monastery was completely abandoned.

III. The Rediscovery of Kursi

For hundreds of years the ruins of the monastery and the church lay hidden. In 1970, as a bulldozer was marking out a new road from Kibbutz En Gev on the east coast of Lake Gennesaret to the new settlement Skofieh on the Golan Heights, the ruins of a Byzantine church were discovered with a wonderful mosaic floor. Further excavations revealed a large fortified monastery with a rectangular support wall of 145 × 123 m together with a protective trench 3 m high.[9] On one side of the church a baptismal chapel was discovered, and on the other side an oil press. At the entrance of the chapel a stone trapdoor was uncovered that led to a vault-shaped tomb of 6.25 m in length and 2.40 m in width with six sarcophagi. The sarcophagi contained the skeletons of twenty-four men of middle age and the bones of one child, all of which must have belonged to the residents of the monastery.[10]

In the year 1979 the Israeli National Park Authority began the renovation of the church and the surrounding walls. The pillar capitals and arches were dug up and reerected, and the arches over the altar were carefully reconstructed. In the process of the archaeological work, a rock above it was also investigated, which was surrounded by a Byzantine construction. V. Tsaferis led the excavation, assisted by D. Gluck. The investigation around the rock revealed a small old chapel,[11] which probably marked the place that commemorated the healed demoniac

[9] Cf. M. Nun, *Gergesa (Kursi): Site of a Miracle, Church and Fishing Village* (En Gev: Kibbutz En Gev, 1989).

[10] Cf. D. Urman, "The Site of the Miracle of the Man with the Unclean Spirit", *CNfI* 22 (1971): 72–76.

[11] Cf. V. Tsaferis, *The Excavations of Kursi-Gergesa* (Jerusalem: Israel Exploration Society, 1983).

(plate 5a). A few steps led up to the chapel, which was blocked off by a whitewashed wall on which crosses and branches were discovered (plate 5b). The branches are probably the *nezer* symbol that represents the Davidian promise of the Messiah mentioned in Isaiah 11:1 (pp. 28–29) and that appears on many Christian monuments on the Golan Heights. The Jewish Christian "Nazoreans" looked upon themselves as the "branch of God's plant" (cf. Is 60:21).[12] A large number of the discoveries are exhibited in the museum of the district capital, Katzrin, in the central Golan Heights.

The floor of the chapel consists of two layers of mosaics, both of which depict a representation of a cross. The existence of the crosses on the two overlaying mosaic floors seems to prove that the chapel must have been erected sometime before the year 427, when the emperor Theodosius II prohibited the use of crosses as floor decorations, in order to prevent their violation by walking on them. The chapel consisted of several pillars and an apse, which had a half-arched stone bench with twelve seats, perhaps the synthronos (σύνθρονος) for the priests.

About 1 km south from this sacred area, there is a rock called el-Kafze. Many believe that it was here that the pigs of the Gospel story were feeding before they threw themselves into the sea.[13] Origen tells us that already in A.D. 248, "a rock lying near the lake was shown over which the demon-possessed pigs had thrown themselves into the lake."[14] It is not certain whether the sloping rock was el-Kafze or whether it was the rock on which the chapel of Kursi stood. Today the ruins of the chapel have been partially restored, and a path leads up the slope. From here there is a good view of the region that is connected with an unusual Gospel narration and makes it more intelligible.

Supplement: For further information, see also Z. Safrai, "Gerasa or Gadara?" *Jerusalem Perspective* 51 (1996): 16–19, and M. Nun, *The Land of the Gadarenes: New Light on an Old Sea of Galilee Puzzle* (En Gev: Kibbutz En Gev, 1996). A German edition of the most important works of Mendel Nun appeared in the series Studien zur biblischen Archäologie und Zeitgeschichte (vol. 10: *Der See Genezareth und die Evangelich* [Gießen: Brunnen, 2001]).—ED.

[12] Cf. R. A. PRITZ, *Nazarene Jewish Christianity* (Jerusalem and Leiden: Brill, 1988), 40f.

[13] Cf. G. DALMAN, *Orte und Wege Jesu*, 3rd ed. (Gütersloh: Bertelsmann, 1924), 191f.

[14] *Commentaria in Evangelium Ioannis* 6.24 (Jn 1:28) (PG 14:270; Baldi, 310).

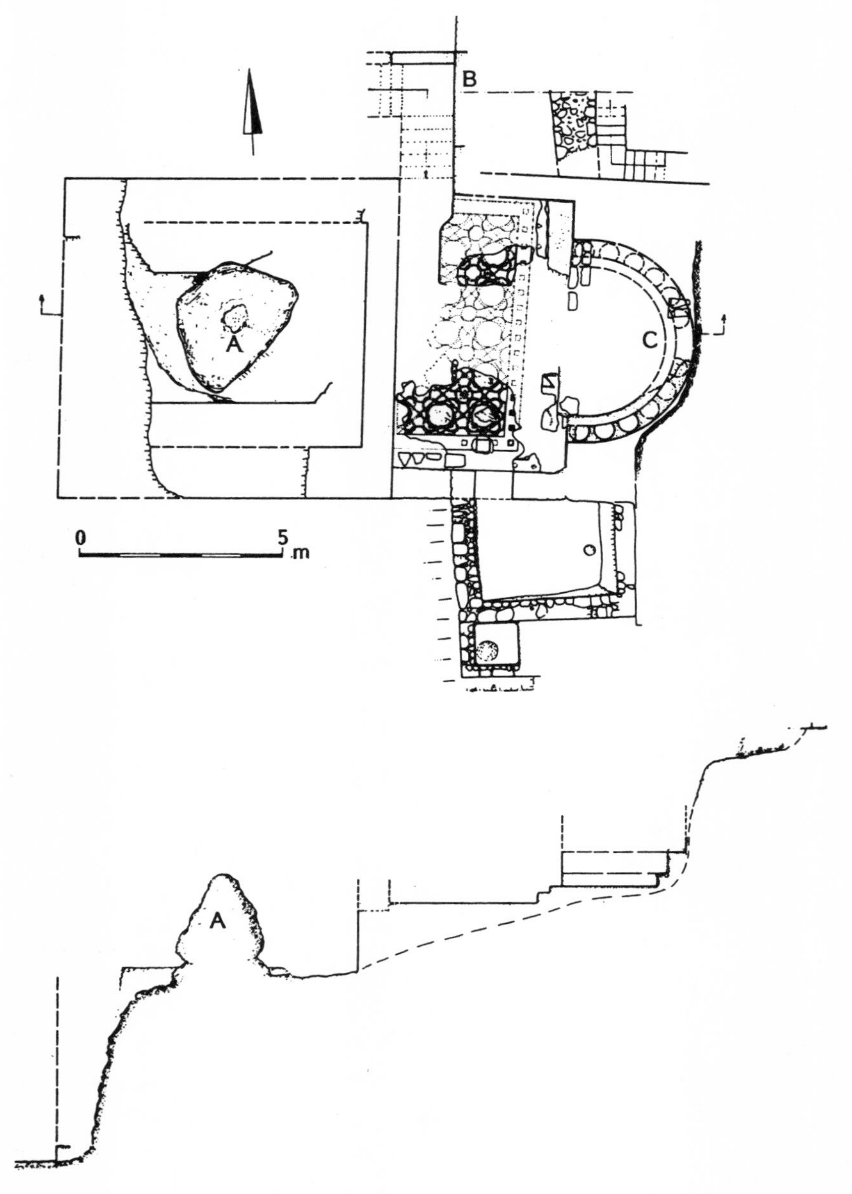

Illus. 36. The hanging chapel (according to V. Tsaferis and D. Gluck, 1975).
A Sacred rock
B Wall with nezer *symbol*
C Apse with twelve seats

Illus. 37. Reconstruction of the hanging chapel (according to V. Tsafaris and D. Gluck, 1975).

PART THREE

The Essenes and Nazoreans

12. The Copper Scroll of Qumran

I. The Discovery of the Copper Scroll

Between March 10 and 29, 1952, an archaeological team from the École biblique and the Albright Institute in Jerusalem, under the direction of R. de Vaux, systematically examined the mountain area west of Qumran. They searched an area 8 km long, looking for natural caves and possible traces of settlement. On March 14, a group led by H. de Contenson discovered some ancient pieces of broken glass in a hollow of a rock. After further investigation the archaeologists realized that a large rock blocked the way into a small cave. After removing this obstacle and freeing the entrance, they revealed a small grotto, which was part of a larger cave that had collapsed. It was here that, on March 20, the archaeologists discovered two copper scrolls, lying one above the other. A photo taken at that time has been frequently republished.[1] Until this discovery, most of the Qumran writings had been located by Bedouin, so this discovery represented a significant success for the archaeologists. Since this was the third Qumran cave in which manuscripts were found, it was called 3Q. Because two copper scrolls, which originally formed one scroll of 2.40 m × 0.30 m, were discovered with fourteen other textual fragments in the same cave, they were all labeled with the seal 3Q15. R. de Vaux regarded the find as a genuine Qumran document[2] and assumed that the rolled-up copper scrolls were left behind by the Qumran Essene community fleeing from the Romans (A.D. 68).[3]

The first one to investigate the unopened scrolls was K. G. Kuhn in 1953. Kuhn's conclusion was that the scrolls contained a list of

[1] *RB* 60 (1953): plate 23.

[2] "Fouille au Khirbet Qumrân", *RB* 60 (1953): 84f.; "Exploration de la region de Qumrân", *RB* 60 (1953): 555–58.

[3] "Exploration de la region de Qumrân", 558.

the hiding places of treasures that have been accumulated by the sect.[4] The only way to open the fragile and oxidized copper scrolls was by cutting them apart into very small segments. This task was undertaken with the greatest care in 1955 and 1956 by Professor H. W. Baker at the University of Manchester.[5] He created twenty-three segments, which were then exhibited at the archaeological museum in Amman.

II. Controversies over the Copper Scroll

The publication for the official text edition was entrusted by the École biblique to the Polish researcher J. T. Milik. The substantial results of his research appeared in 1959 in a journal article,[6] and in 1962 the official text edition was published.[7] The Copper Scroll, in twelve columns, lists sixty-four underground hiding places in different parts of the region. The hidden treasures include gold, silver, exotic delicacies and also scrolls. Milik denied a connection between the list and the Qumran sect. In his opinion, it is a compilation of legendary treasures from a folk tradition that had been edited by someone around A.D. 100.

Not all researchers agreed with this conclusion. J. M. Allegro, who had access to the scrolls in Manchester, published a transcription and interpretation before the official text publication in 1960.[8] In the hope of finding some of the treasures, he put together a team and dug in several places secretly and unscientifically. R. de Vaux expressed the shock by professional archaeologists at the use of such methods.[9] This urgent, but futile, search for the Essene treasures should have been avoided for a simple reason: in the discovered list, an additional detailed duplicate is referred to toward the end (3Q15 12:11–13). If the list at that time had stayed in the hands of the owners of the treasures, they

[4] "Les rouleaux de cuivre de Qumrân", *RB* 61 (1954): 193–205.

[5] "Notes on the Opening of the 'Bronze' Scrolls from Qumran", *Bulletin of the John Rylands Library* 39 (1956): 45–56.

[6] "Le rouleau de cuivre de Qumrân (3Q15): Traduction et commentaire topographique", *RB* 66 (1959): 321–57.

[7] "Le rouleau de cuivre provenant de la grotte 3Q (3Q15)", in M. Baillet, J. T. Milik and R. de Vaux, *Les "petites grottes" de Qumrân*, DJD 3 (Oxford: Oxford University Press, 1962), 198–302.

[8] *The Treasure of the Copper Scroll* (London: Routledge and Kegan Paul, 1960).

[9] *RB* 58 (1961): 146f.

could have recovered all of the treasures following the fall of Jerusalem. Perhaps the priest Jesus, son of Thebutis (*War* 6.387), mentioned by Josephus, was one of the Essene survivors who knew about these hiding places (pp. 409–11).

Researchers less influenced by the sensationalism of hidden treasures and their link to the Essene community acknowledged that the Copper Scroll was a register of genuine treasures but disagreed, however, regarding their true origin. Some, like A. Dupont-Sommer,[10] attributed them to the Essenes. Others thought the documents were linked with the temple treasure,[11] others with the Zealots[12] or other Jewish refugees before A.D. 70.[13] M.R. Lehmann thought it could even be a collection of treasures put aside for the rebuilding of the destroyed temple.[14] Many others thought that they might date from the Bar Kokhba revolt.[15] Even R. de Vaux was not finally convinced that the documents were authentic.[16] H. Bardtke summarized the debate and the uncertainty for the verification of the documents in 1968.[17] In 1983 I myself published a study of the Copper Scroll supporting its authenticity and providing a new topographical commentary on the various hiding places mentioned plus a detailed lexicon.[18] Since then other researchers have again shown interest in the Copper Scroll and have accepted some of my suggestions (p. 165), especially that the scroll is not a later, imaginative work but represents a historical document of the greatest importance.

[10] *The Essene Writings from Qumran* (Oxford: Oxford University Press, 1961), 383–89.

[11] K.G. Kuhn, "Bericht über neue Qumranfunde und über die Öffnung der Kupferrollen", *Theologische Literature-Zeitung* 81 (1956): 541–46; K.H. Rengstorf, *Ḥirbet Qumrân und die Bibliothek vom Toten Meer* (Stuttgart: Kohlhammer, 1960), 26–28.

[12] J.M. Allegro, *The Treasure of the Copper Scroll*, 2nd ed. (Garden City, N.Y.: Doubleday, 1964).

[13] N. Golb, "The Problem of the Origin and Identification of the Dead Sea Scrolls", *Proceedings of the American Philosophical Society* 124 (1980): 1–24; see also idem, "Who Hid the Dead Sea Scrolls?" *BA* 28 (1985): 68–82.

[14] "Identification of the Copper Scroll Based on Its Technical Terms", *RQ* 5 (1964): 97–105.

[15] E.M. Lapperousaz, "Remarques sur l'origine des Rouleaux de Cuivre découverts dans la Grotte 3 de Qumrân", *Revue de l'histoire des religions* 159 (1961): 157–72; B.Z. Luria, *Megillat ha-Nahoshet me-Midbar Jehudah* [in Modern Hebrew] (Jerusalem, 1963).

[16] *Archaeology and the Dead Sea Scrolls* (London: Oxford University Press, 1973), 108.

[17] "Qumran und seine Probleme II", *Theologische Rundschau* 33 (1968): 185–236 (2. "Die Kupferrollen" [185–204]).

[18] "Unravelling the Copper Scroll Code: A Study on the Topography of 3Q15", *RQ* 11 (1983): 323–65; "Copper Scroll", in D.N. Freedman, *Anchor Bible Dictionary* (New York: Doubleday, 1992), 1:1133f.

III. A Genuine Qumran Document

A crucial argument for the authenticity of the Copper Scroll comes from the condition of Cave 3Q and its history. The cave originally contained a set of earthenware vessels with documents, a number of which were destroyed by the collapse of the cave's ceiling.[19] The few remaining fragments[20] are recognized by all as documents originating from the Qumran community. The shape of the cave, the distribution of the earthenware vessels and the hiding place of the Copper Scroll in the furthest corner of the grotto make it impossible that the other documents and vessels were deposited at a later date. The period around A.D. 100 was relatively peaceful in Palestine, and it is incomprehensible that whoever entered Cave 3Q would have left its precious treasure untouched. Most probably, with the approach of the Romans in the year A.D. 68, Cave 3Q was sealed just like the other remaining Qumran caves.

The paleographic dating of the Copper Scroll by J. T. Milik to A.D. 100 is challenged by the recognized writing expert F. M. Cross in the volume of the *editio princeps*.[21] He dates the typescript to the second Herodian period between A.D. 25 and 75 and draws attention to the resemblance of the Hebrew of the Mishna that is paralleled in other Qumran writings. The use of a very valuable material such as copper and the prosaic style of the writing contradict the assertion that it is a mere "folkloric composition". Finally, there is the clear connection to the Essene community, including the mention of ritual baths (3Q15 1:12), hidden scrolls (3Q15 6:5f.; 8:1–3) and priestly articles (3Q15 1:9–12; 3:1–4, 8–10; 8:1–3; 11:1–4, 9f., 14; 12:6f.).

Different historical examples make it possible to assess the total value of the hidden treasures (4,500 talents).[22] In Jerusalem in 63 B.C. Pompey demanded 10,000 talents from the authorities (*Ant.* 14.78). The Essenes lived and shared goods in common and prepared for the

[19] Cf. B. Pixner, "Unravelling the Copper Scroll Code", 334f. According to the Israeli archaeologist J. Patrich, "Judean Desert: Survey of Caves—1985/1986", *ESI* 6 (1987/1988): 66–70, Cave 3Q had collapsed long before the hiding of the documents. Prof. Émile Puech of the Dominican École biblique in Jerusalem, who in 1981 in Paris had a conversation with the discoverer Henri de Contenson about 3Q, could not agree with this assumption. However, it seems that, during a conversation at an archaeological congress in Jerusalem (March 1990), Prof. Patrich managed to convince Prof. Puech to have another look at his proposal.

[20] DJD 3:94–104.

[21] "Excursus on the Palaeographical Dating of the Copper Document", DJD 3:217–21.

[22] Cf. A. Dupont-Sommer, *Essene Writings* (see n. 10), 383f.

eschatological final battle as well as the building of a new temple, as the War Scroll (1QM) and the Temple Scroll (11QTemple) show; it is not inconceivable, therefore, that the community possessed considerable wealth. It is also likely that sympathizers of the Essenes handed their fortune to the sect as a kind of counter to the temple bank.[23]

IV. The Distribution of the Hiding Places

I believe that the Copper Scroll acted as an aide-mémoire for select persons. The descriptions for the hiding places were written in an abbreviated "telegram style", and the merely suggested sites presuppose a specialized local knowledge of the area. Closer details were provided in a duplicate of the document, which was mentioned in the last hiding place of the Copper Scroll (3Q15 12:10–13). These facts make it naturally difficult to identify the various hiding places with any accuracy. All researchers believe that a few hiding places lay around the monastery of Qumran (3Q15 4:13; 5:14). The name Secacah is associated with Qumran (cf. Josh 15:61 [סְכָכָה]), and this name is mentioned four times in the Copper Scroll (3Q15 4:13f.; 5:1f., 12f.).[24] Here is a strong argument for the connection of the scroll to Qumran. With the exception of B. Z. Luria (cf. n. 15), it is accepted by all other researchers that some hiding places lie in and around Jerusalem. Among the locations indicated, there are well-known places that are mentioned in the New Testament such as Siloam (3Q15 10:15f.; Jn 9:7) and Bethesda (3Q15 11:11–14; Jn 5:2).

Most researchers agree with J. T. Milik and J. M. Allegro that the hiding places were distributed relatively irregularly over the whole country of Israel. However, I support a systematic distribution, which relates to the main centers of the Essene settlement:[25] (1) The first seventeen hiding places point to the Essene community settlement on the southwest hill of Jerusalem,[26] in the area mentioned by Flavius Josephus as the "Gate of the Essenes" (*War* 5.145). (2) Hiding places nos. 19–34 (3Q15 4:6—7:16) are situated in Qumran itself and in the area between this Essene settlement and Jericho. (3) Nos. 35–47 (3Q15 8:1—10:4) are to be looked

[23] Cf. B. Pixner, "Unravelling the Copper Scroll Code" (see n. 18), 339f.

[24] Cf. B. Pixner, "Salzstadt", in *GBL*, 2nd ed. (1990), 3:1324; see also "Sechacha", ibid., 3:1418.

[25] Cf. B. Pixner, "Unravelling the Copper Scroll Code" (see n. 18), 341–58.

[26] See chapter 15, "The Essene Quarter in Jerusalem" (pp. 192–219, esp. pp. 215–17).

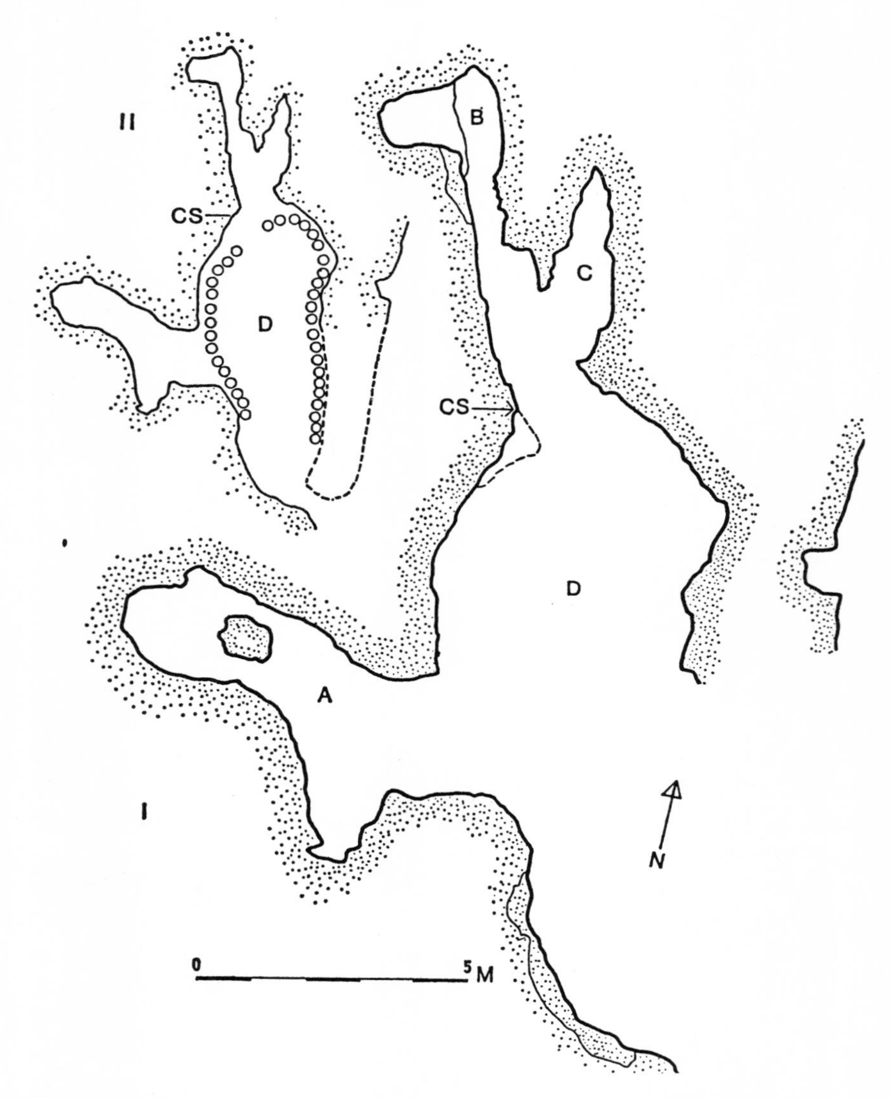

Illus. 38. The Qumran Cave 3Q (according to Doron Chen and David Milson, 1983).
A Steep and narrow ascending side cave
B and C Two extensions of the main cave (approx. 0.5 m high) where the leather scroll fragments were found
D Collapsed main cave. Here the rest of the earthenware vessels were found (see sketch at upper left). The original entrance was obviously in the south.
CS The location of the Copper Scroll. In front of it was a fallen boulder that blocked access to B and C.

for in the area of the Jarmuk River,[27] which corresponds with the "land of Damascus" (אֶרֶץ דַּמֶּשֶׂק) in the so-called Damascus Document (CD 7:15–19), which is not meant as a pseudonym but represents an area of exile for the sect in south Syria.[28] (4) Hiding places nos. 48–60 (3Q15 10:5—12:3) are south and east of Jerusalem, concentrated in the Kidron Valley (pp. 393, 402). (5) Finally, there are three more hiding places to be identified in the north of the country, nos. 61–64 (3Q15 12:4–9).

Regrettably, following Milik's initial verdict, the Copper Scroll had not been the subject of serious and systematic research, but fortunately that situation now appears to have changed.[29] The rather unsatisfactory quality of the original photos of the scroll contributed to the strong differences in their interpretation. We should agree with the demand of A. Wolters that the photographs of the Copper Scroll should be examined by modern procedures in order that it can be made more accessible for further research.[30]

Supplement: Since this was published in German, there has been an increased interest in the Copper Scroll. In the archaeological museum in Amman, new photographs were made, which have served as the basis for an improved text edition. See P. K. McCarter, "The Mystery of the Copper Scroll", in H. Shanks, *The Dead Sea Scrolls after Forty Years* (Washington, D.C.: Biblical Archaeology Society, 1991), 40–54. I still believe that some of the hiding places are located in the area of the Jarmuk. S. Goranson is well informed about the state of research: "Sectarianism, Geography, and the Copper Scroll", *Journal of Jewish Studies* 43 (1992): 282–87. For an appreciation of the connection of Secacah (Josh 15:61) with the Copper Scroll and with Qumran (p. 163), see H. Eshel, "A Note on Joshua 15:61–62 and the Identification of the City of Salt", see *IEJ* 45 (1995): 37–40.[31]

[27] Cf. B. Pixner, "Jarmuk", in *GBL*, 2nd ed. (1990), 2:648.

[28] Cf. chapter 13, "Batanea as a Jewish Settlement Area" (pp. 169–76, esp. pp. 175–76), and also R. Riesner, *Paul's Early Period: Chronology, Mission Strategy, Theology* (Grand Rapids: Eerdmans, 1998), 237–41.

[29] Cf. Y. Thorion, "Beiträge zur Erforschung der Sprache der Kupfer-Rolle", *RQ* 12 (1985): 163–78; A. Wolters, "Notes on the Copper Scroll", *RQ* 12 (1987): 589–96; cf. idem, "The Fifth Cache of the Copper Scroll: The Plastered Cistern of Manos", *RQ* 13 (1988): 167–76.

[30] A. Wolters, "Fifth Cache of the Copper Scroll", 168.

[31] A new edition is J. K. Lefkovits, *The Copper Scroll—3Q15: A Reevaluation; A New Reading, Translation, and Commentary* (Leiden: Brill, 2000). The position of B. Pixner is defended by S. Goranson, "Further Reflections on the Copper Scroll", in G. J. Brooke and P. R. Davies, *Copper Scroll Studies* (Sheffield: Continuum, 2003), 226–32.—Ed.

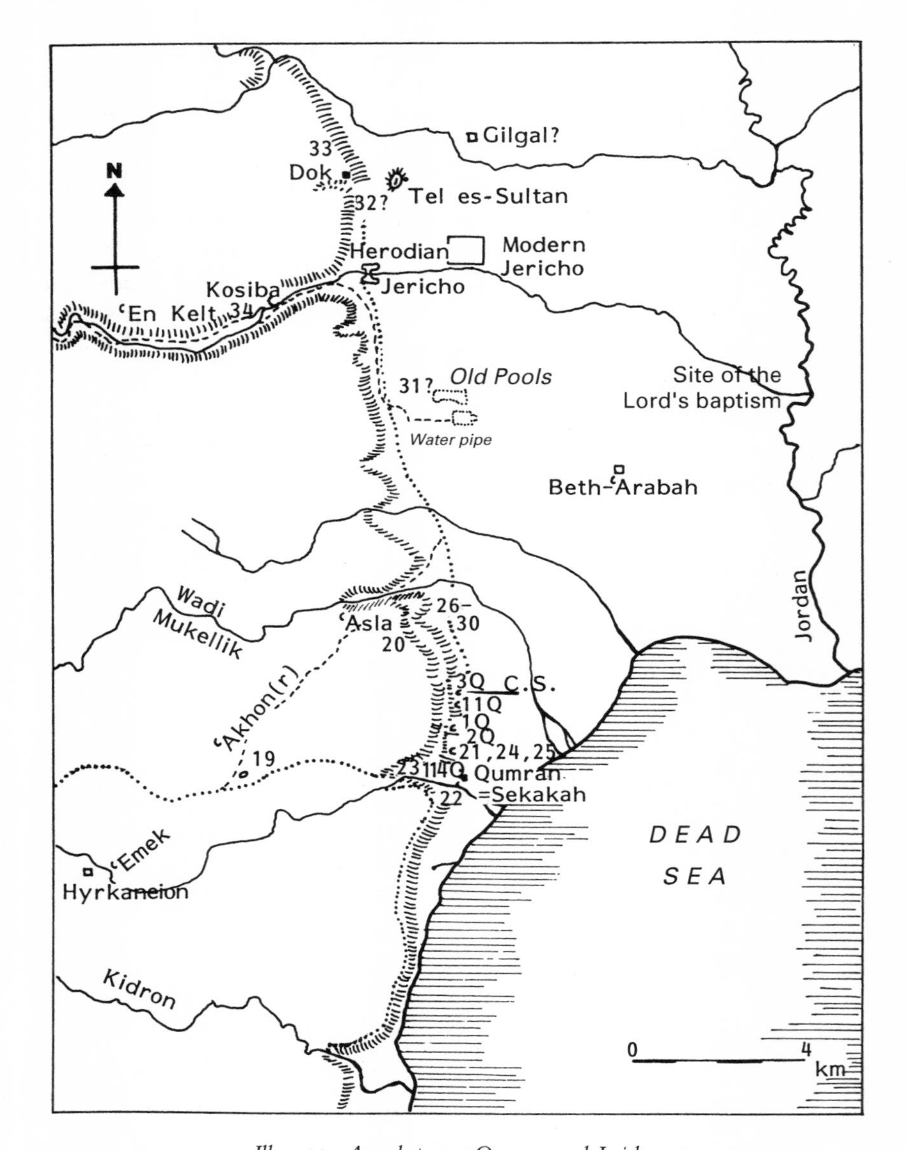

Illus. 39. Area between Qumran and Jericho.
Numbers with Q mark locations where Qumran manuscripts were found. Other numbers indicate proposed sites for the hiding places listed in the Copper Scroll.

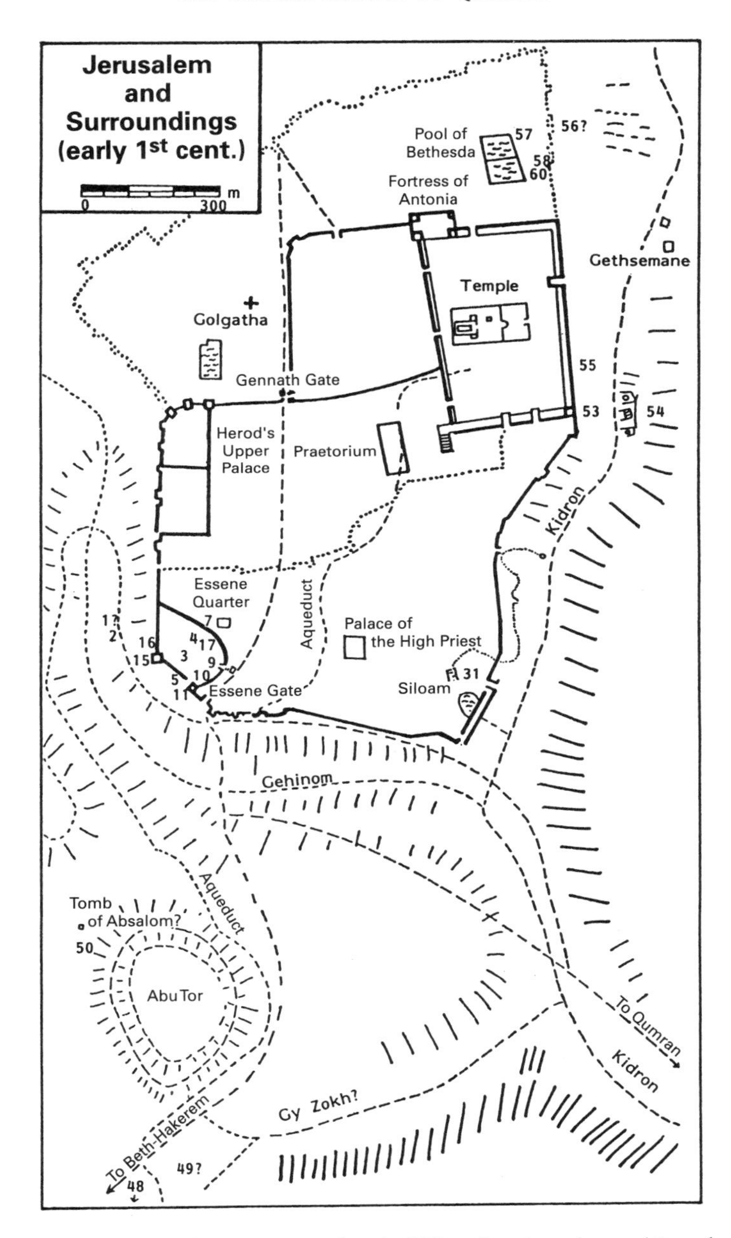

Illus. 40. Numbers mark locations proposed as the hiding places in and around Jerusalem listed in the Copper Scroll.

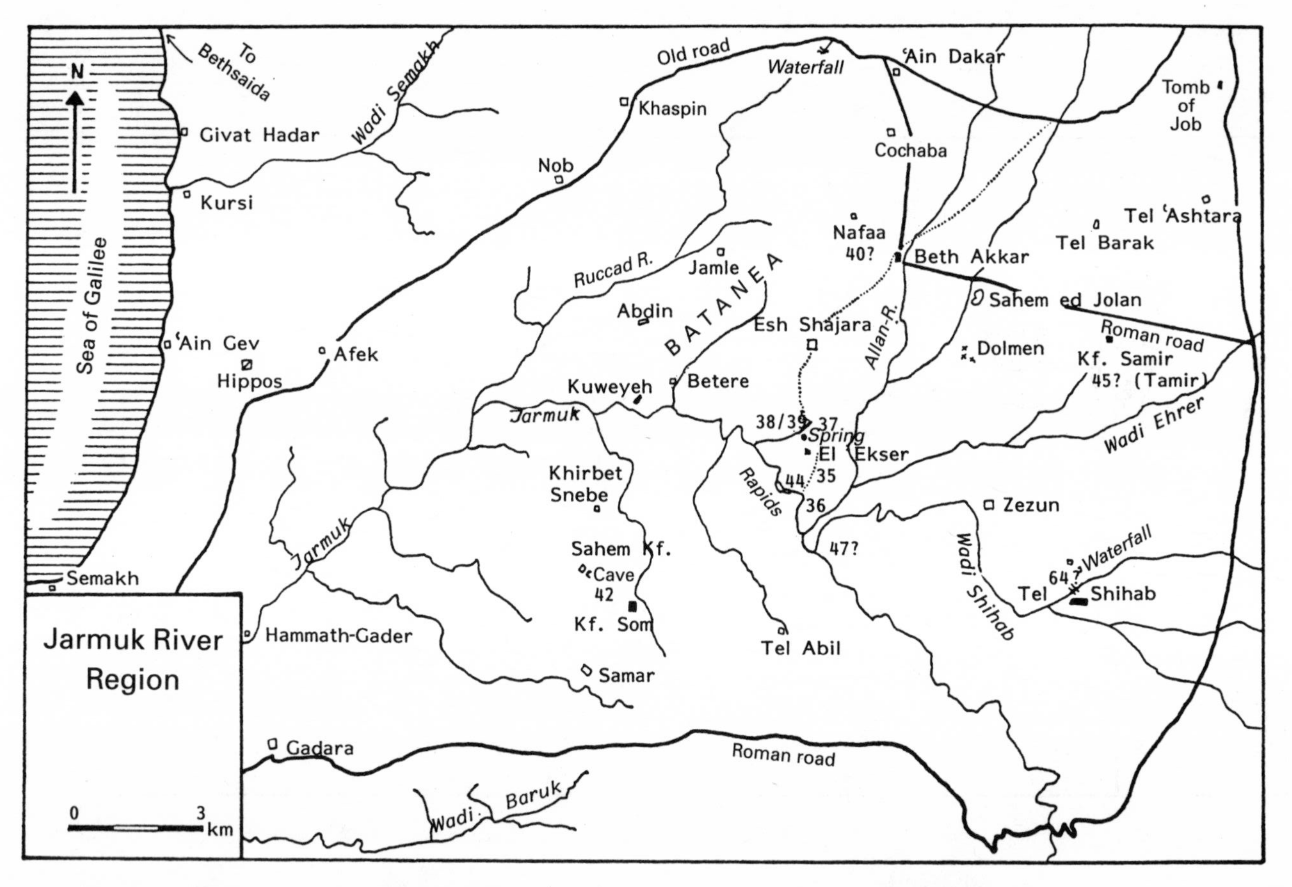

Illus. 41. Numbers mark proposed sites for the hiding places in the area surrounding the Jarmuk River ("land of Damascus") listed in the Copper Scroll.

13. Batanea as a Jewish Settlement Area

The following chapter will focus on the outer edge of the Jewish motherland, "beyond the Jordan" (עֵבֶר הַיַּרְדֵּן [*eber ha-jarden*]; πέραν τοῦ Ἰορδάνου [*peran tou Iordanou*]), where Batanea was located. Eusebius of Caesarea described this area, which is formed by the Jarmuk and its tributary, the river Ruccad (illus. 41), as the "Batanean corner" (γωνία τῆς Βαταναίας).[1] He also mentions a Jewish settlement: Nineveh (today Naveh), which was also part of the "Arab corner" (γωνία της 'Αραβίας).[2] During Jesus' lifetime, the area was governed by the Jewish tetrarch Philip (Lk 3:1), a son of Herod the Great. Batanea was sometimes regarded as belonging to Judea, because the majority of the population was Jewish, and the history of the area was closely connected with that of the main Jewish settlement.

I. The History of Batanea

1. The Old Testament Bashan

This area of land originally belonged to Bashan (Deut 3:10; Josh 13:11). The old "King's highway" from Elath to Damascus went through here (Num 20:17), and some of the stations along the road were mentioned in Egyptian documents of the middle and new Pharonic kingdoms: Astaroth, Bosra, Kanatha and Tobak.[3] One of the kings of Bashan was Og (Deut 2:11; 3:11), whom the Israelites defeated under Moses (Josh 12:4f.). Bashan was subsequently given to the half tribe Manasseh as an inheritance (Num 32:33–42), but a majority of the original inhabitants remained (Num 32:17). Tiglath-pileser III conquered Bashan as

[1] *Onomastikon* (Klostermann, 18, 6) (passages are cited by page and line number).

[2] Ibid., 136, 3; cf. 136, 42.

[3] Cf. A.J. Brawer, "Bashan", in *EncJud*, 1:291–93 (at 292).

well as the Galil (later Galilee) in 732 B.C. (2 Kings 15:29; Is 8:23) and enslaved many of the former inhabitants, transporting them to Assyria. In this newly conquered area, two Assyrian provinces were created, Karnini (Carnaim) and Haurina (Hauran). Under Alexander the Great and his Ptolemaic successors, Bashan was divided into three provinces from the west to the east: Gaulanitis, Batanea and Trachonitis.

2. *Batanea under the Maccabees and Hasmoneans*

In 164 B.C. Judas Maccabees heard of the danger for the Jewish inhabitants of the upper Gilead (1 Mac 5:9–44; *Ant.* 12.330ff.). Encouraged by the Seleucidian army leader Timothy, the local Gentile population wanted to exterminate the Jewish community. Other places in which the Jewish population was in danger included Bosra, Bosor, Alema, Chaspho, Maked and Carnaim—"all these cities were strong and large" (1 Mac 5:26). Judas conquered Bozrah (Basra), then Dateme (?), Alema at the Jarmuk, Chaspho in the southern Golan, Maked, Bosor and the remaining cities of Gilead (1 Mac 5:36). A "ravine" (χειμάρρος) is mentioned, and this was probably the ravine of the Jarmuk (1 Mac 5:40–43). This name comes from ἱερὸς μοῦχος, i.e., *hieros mouchos*, "the Holy Gorge".[4] Strangely, the name of this large tributary for the Jordan is not mentioned in the Old Testament.[5] Judas waded through the brook of the ravine and attacked Timothy's troops (1 Mac 5:42–44), who then attempted to flee into the city of Carnaim, which was, however, also taken by the Jews.[6] This report from the first book of Maccabees suggests that there was a large Jewish settlement in the area, many of whose members were then evacuated by Judas to Judea (1 Mac 5:45–54).

The Jewish king, Alexander Jannaeus, from the newly created dynasty of the Hasmoneans, reconquered Batanea of the Nabataeans at the end of the second century B.C. (*Ant.* 12.393 ff.). They had at that time extended their rule from their capital Petra to Damascus (*Ant.* 12.392). In 63 B.C. Pompey occupied this area (*Ant.* 14.74–76), and he handed Golan (Gaulanitis) and Batanea over to the Itureans and, on the south adjoining area, created the Hellenistic city alliance of the Decapolis (p. 148). The Decapolis includes the areas south from Hippos and

[4] Cf. F.M. ABEL, *Géographie de la Palestine*, 3rd ed. (Paris: Gabalda, 1967), 1:483.

[5] Cf. B. PIXNER, "Jarmuk", in *GBL*, 2nd ed. (1990), 2:648.

[6] Cf. Epiphanius, *Panarion*, 30.2.8 (PG 41:408; Klijn-Reinink, 176).

Gadara to the Sea of Galilee and south of this with Scythopolis (Beth Shean), which is being restored, and even extends beyond the Jordan.

3. Batanea under Herod the Great

The Jewish pilgrim route from Babylon to Jerusalem led, according to Josephus, through the country of Trachonitis (*Ant.* 17.26). It was in this area that the guerrilla leader Ezechias (Hiskia) arose, a forerunner of the later Zealot movement (pp. 72–73). Ezechias was caught and executed around 50 B.C. by the young Herod (*War* 1:204; *Ant.* 14.159). During his reign (37–4 B.C.), Herod gradually conquered the whole area of the earlier Bashan (illus. 1), which had been given to him by Emperor Augustus (*War* 1.398; *Ant.* 15.343–45). Although the Decapolis regained its independence after the death of the Jewish king (illus. 2), Batanea remained under Jewish rule among his successors, Philippus, Agrippa I and Agrippa II (*War* 1.668; *Ant.* 17.189, 319; 20.138).

II. Jewish Groups in Batanea

1. The Return Journey of the Jews

When the area "beyond the Jordan" was governed under Alexander Jannaeus, from Judea, it must have provided a strong migratory pull for Jewish groups. Since the pilgrim road from Babylon led to Jerusalem through Batanea (*Ant.* 17.26), many Jewish groups on their return from Assyria and Babylon settled there. Thus a settlement with the name of Nineveh (today Naveh) was created, which had probably the sole purpose of gathering Jews from the Assyrian Nineveh. Some researchers believe that the famous family of the "sons of Bathyra" (בְּנֵי בַּתִירָה [*bnej bathijrah*]) came from a Batanean settlement with this name (see below), which was to be found in this area.[7] From the Talmud it appears that the elders of Bathyra represented the highest religious authority before Hillel was chosen around 20 B.C. as the leader of the Pharisaic community.[8]

Bashan had always been considered as an area of refuge from Jerusalem. The city Golan, north of Jarmuk, represented one of the Levitical

[7] Cf. Z. KAPLAN, "Bathyra [Sons of]", in *EncJud*, 4:323f.

[8] Palestinian Talmud, *Kila'im* 9:1 (32b); Babylonian Talmud, *Pesachim* 66a; *Baba Mezia* 85a.

places of asylum (Deut 4:43; Josh 20:8; 1 Chron 6:56). Following the murder of his brother, Absalom fled there into this area, i.e., to Geshur (2 Sam 13:37). This was also the place where Elijah fled from Ahab (1 Kings 17:1–6) and hid himself (pp. 184–85). At the beginning of the New Testament period, there were many different Jewish fringe groups that had withdrawn to Batanea.

2. *The Ancestors of the Mandaeans?*

Around 10 B.C. King Herod the Great invited a Jewish clan from Babylon, under the leadership of Zamiris, to establish themselves in Batanea (*Ant.* 17.23–28). This Jewish clan was originally from the Persian Empire and was militarily well equipped, having 500 archers.[9] They were invited to settle in the area to deter criminal activity in Trachonitis. These "Babylonians" selected the fortified locality of Bathyra as their main settlement (*Ant.* 17.26). In the later autobiography of Josephus, the same settlement is called Ekbatane (*Life* 54ff.), after the capital of Parthia (see *Ant.* 10.264; 11.99). The name Ekbatane could have been a derivation of the Old Testament Bashan (בָּשָׁן) from the Greek Basanitis (Βασανίτις), which became Batanea (Βαταναία).

If members of this military clan were called "the Jews of Ekbatane" (*Life* 54), they were still referred to as the "Babylonians" (*Ant.* 17.26:29), which suggests that they had actually emigrated from Parthia. Could this be a Jewish group in which the religious influence of many dualistic ideas from the Persian environment still survived? It is not impossible that these are the Proto-Mandaeans. The Mandaeans settled in this area until the Bar-Kokhba war (135–132 B.C.).[10] They then relocated over the Euphrates into their old tribal area, where they exist today, as a particular baptismal sect that is known for its great devotion to John the Baptist and absolute rejection of Jesus. The Mandaeans' scriptures say that the "upper, clean Jordan" (the "Jarmuk", a source of the Jordan that is called Sheriat el-Menadire in Arabic) was used by them and that the "lying prophet", i.e., Jesus, baptized "down in the dirty Jordan" (near Jericho? [cf. Mt 3:1ff.]).

[9] Cf. J. NEUSNER, *A History of the Jews of Babylonia*, vol. 1, *The Parthian Period* (Leiden: Brill, 1965), 38–41.

[10] Cf. K. RUDOLPH, *Die Mandäer*, vol. 1 (Berlin: Akademie, 1960), 248–52.

3. The Nazorean Settlements

Julius Africanus was a Jewish Christian from Emmaus Nicopolis (today, Latrun) on the Sharon plain who held a Roman government office with connections to Damascus.[11] On one of his journeys, Julius probably came into the Batanea area, where he made some inquiries. Eusebius quotes from a script (ca. 250) by Julius that in the Jewish villages of Cochaba and Nazareth lived blood relatives (δεσποσύνοι) of the Lord Jesus (δεσπότης) who had kept the genealogies of the Davidian family (*HE* 1.7.14). From this it follows that the difference in both family trees, i.e., that according to Matthew 1 and that according to Luke 3, is to be solved by "levirate law" (cf. Deut 25:5–10).

Cochaba was located in the "Batanean corner". Epiphanius of Salamis reported that during his lifetime, members of the Nazoreans (Ναζωραῖοι), which he called a Jewish sect, had settled in Cochaba.[12] He maintained that the Nazoreans originated there, but this hypothesis is doubtful. The Nazoreans, to whom Jesus belonged, according to his "clan name" ὁ Ναζωραῖος (*ho Nazōraios*),[13] seem to have descended from David. From the Old Testament, we know that at the end of the exile, the Davidic clan was found in Babylon (2 Kings 25:27–30; Ezra 1:8). In the second or first century B.C., a group of these Davidic descendents could have emigrated, as did many other Jews, from Babylon and established themselves first in Batanea and from this base established other settlements, e.g., Nazareth in Galilee (illus. 13), which was a hamlet near the large village of Japhia (Josh 19:12).[14]

The names Nazareth and Cochaba could be connected with messianic promises. According to Jerome, the Hebrew-speaking Christians derived the word "Nazorean" from the prophecy in Isaiah 11:1,[15] in which a "branch" (נֵצֶר [*nezer*]) is mentioned. It could be that additionally there is yet another connection to the Hebrew word נצר

[11] Cf. A. Brunot, "Jules Africain: Un laïc chrétien du IIIe siècle", *Le bulletin diocésain* 3 (1975): 105–15.

[12] *Panarion* 29.7 (PG 41:402; Klijn-Reinink, 172).

[13] Mt 2:23; 26:71; Lk 19:37; Jn 18:5–7; 19:19; Acts 2:22; 3:6; 4:10; 6:14; 22:8; 26:9. Cf. chapter 2, "Mary in the House of David" (pp. 23–37, esp. pp. 28–29).

[14] Cf. R. Riesner, "Jafia", in *GBL*, 2nd ed. (1990), 2:641.

[15] *Commentarius in Isaiam* 2.1–3 (Klijn-Reinink, 222). Cf. in addition R. A. Pritz, *Nazarene Jewish Christianity* (Leiden: Brill, 1988), 8–70 (at 54f.).

(*nazar*), which means "preserving, guarding or observing".[16] In Isaiah 49:6 it is said of the servant of God that he not only will raise up the tribes of Jacob but will also restore the "survivors of Israel" (נְצוּרֵי יִשְׂרָאֵל [*n^e zurei Yisra'ęl*]). The passage is concerned with the "holy remainder" of Israel. Isaiah 60:21 describes Israel's final glory: "Your people shall all be righteous [צַדִּיקִים]; they shall possess the land for ever, the shoot of my planting [נֵצֶר מַטָּעַו (*nezer mata'aw*)]", and there is also a possible connection to the "paternal inheritance laws", which Josephus mentions (see below). One controversy has been resolved following the finding of a Hebrew inscription at Caesarea Maritima:[17] "Nazareth" (Ναζαρέτ; נצרת) and therefore also Nazoreans (cf. Mt 2:23) was written in Semitic text with *zade* (צ) and not with *zayin* (ז). The word has nothing to do with the Old Testament Nazirites (נָזִיר; Νασιραῖος) (cf. Judg 13:5, 7), as some Church Fathers and more recent authors had assumed. The name Nazareth following Isaiah 11:1 means "village of the branch". Cochaba is derived from "star"; cf. Numbers 24:17: "A star [כּוֹכָב (*kochab*)] shall come forth out of Jacob."

There were several places with the name Cochaba in Batanea and in Galilee,[18] but it cannot with certainty be confirmed whether these settlements in pre–New Testament times were founded by the Nazoreans. However, the place "Cochaba" recurs in connection with Jewish Christian groups.[19] There were orthodox Nazorean believers[20] and heretical Ebionites living side by side.[21] The name Nazoreans (נָצוֹרָיָא [*nazōrayya*]) applied also to the Mandaeans.[22] There seems to have been contact between the two groups, which is perhaps not surprising given their geographical proximity. The Ebionites demonstrated strong Essene characteristics (pp. 365, 409–11). O. Cullmann,

[16] Cf. B. GÄRTNER, *Die rätselhaften Termini Nazoräer und Iskariot* (Uppsala: Universitets Forlaget, 1957), 5–18.

[17] Cf. G. KROLL, *Auf den Spuren Jesu*, 11th ed. (Stuttgart: Katholisches Biblewerk, 2002), 82f.

[18] Cf. B. PIXNER and R. RIESNER, "Kochaba", in *GBL*, 2nd ed. (1990), 2:801f.

[19] Cf. H.J. SCHOEPS, *Theologie und Geschichte des Judenchristentums* (Tübingen: Mohr, 1949), 270–77.

[20] Eusebius, *Onomastikon* (Klostermann, 172, 1–3); Epiphanius, *Panarion* 40.1 (PG 41:677–80; GCS 31:81): ἐν τῇ Ἀραβίᾳ ἐν Κωκάβῃ; Jerome, *De situ et nominibus locorum hebraeorum liber* 112 (Klijn-Reinink, 206).

[21] Epiphanius, *Panarion* 30.20 (PG 41:437–39; GCS 25:359–61).

[22] Cf. B. GÄRTNER, *Nazoräer und Iskariot* (see n. 16), 24–33.

in an early, pioneering article, proposed an interesting alternative theory regarding Qumran and the New Testament[23] that will be explored in the next section.

4. Settlements of the Essenes?

The Essenes also seem to have experienced part of their historical development in the Batanean region. Batanea was an attractive area as a consequence of the peace and the fiscal privilege it enjoyed, which had come from the settlements of "Babylonian" immigrants into this area, particularly from Jewish groups. These, according to Josephus (*Ant.* 17.26), were a community who "observed the paternal laws faithfully" (τὰ Ἰουδαίων θεραπεύεται πάτρια). The expression θεραπεῦται (*therapeutai*; "servant, observer") is regularly used for the Essene groups in Egypt.[24] Perhaps here is the key to the identification of the "land of Damascus" (אֶרֶץ דַּמֶּשֶׂק) mentioned in the Damascus Document (CD 6:5–19; 7:15–19; 8:21; 19:34; 20:12), copies of which were found in Qumran. I agree with those researchers who believe that "Damascus" functions not merely as a pseudonym for the place of the Essenes' exile (Qumran or Babylon) but can also be understood as a particular topological place.[25]

In a work about the Copper Scroll of Qumran (3Q15), I suggested that some of the hiding places of the treasures mentioned in the scroll, and therefore also an area of settlement for the Essenes, seems to have been in the Jarmuk area.[26] The Hurrites, whose graves were hiding place no. 42 mentioned in the scroll (3Q15 9:7–9), lived, according to the Genesis Apocryphon of Qumran, in the region around Damascus (1QGenAp 21:24–34). The Apocryphon mentions the place *shaweb* (שוה [1QGenAp 21:29]), which also appears in the Copper Scroll (3Q15 8:10–16). This area would seem to relate to the description of the "Nabataean forts" (מצד נאבתי[א]) for hiding place no. 46 (3Q15 9:17—10:2). In the past, Batanea belonged to the area of the Nabataeans (see

[23] "The Significance of the Qumran Texts for Research into the Beginnings of Christianity" [1955], in K. STENDAHL, *The Scrolls and the New Testament* (New York: Harper, 1957), 18–32, 251–52 (at 25).

[24] Philo from Alexandria reports this in his writing *De vita contemplativa.*

[25] Cf. J. MAGNIN, "Notes sur l'Ébionisme II", *POC* 24 (1974): 225–50 (at 232).

[26] Cf. B. PIXNER, "Unravelling the Copper Scroll Code: A Study on the Topography of 3Q15", *RQ* 11 (1983): 323–65 (esp. 350–54).

above), and in the New Testament period, its influence reached to Damascus (2 Cor 11:32f.). There are indications of the presence of the Essenes in Batanea that suggest that this area was a melting pot for different Jewish communities at the beginning of the first century. The "Large River" (נחל הגדול [*nahal ha-gadol*]), is an appropriate name for the Jarmuk (3Q15 10:3f.) under Palestinian conditions.

14. Bethany on the Other Side of the Jordan

I. The Area of Activity of John the Baptist

According to Luke, who knew a number of the traditions about John, who preached and baptized in "the region about the Jordan" (ἦλθεν εἰς πᾶσαν τὴν περίχωρον τοῦ Ἰορδάνου [Lk 3:3]),[1] we get the impression that the Baptist was a "wandering preacher". This is understandable because John, like Jesus, wanted to reach large numbers of people.[2] The area around the Jordan and the rich springs in the nearby area were the normative areas of activity of the different Jewish groups of baptizers.[3] There are at least three places mentioned in the Gospels where John the Baptist had been active.

1. The Baptism Place near Jericho

According to Matthew 3:1, Jesus was baptized by John in the lower reaches of the Jordan, which borders on the desert of Judah (ἐν τῇ ἐρήμῳ τῆς Ἰουδαίας). The oldest tradition is supported by the testimony of the Pilgrim of Bordeaux (333),[4] who probably reliably identified the place of the baptism[5] as the eastern bank of the Jordan, north of Jericho, near the hillock from which it was believed that Elijah was taken up into heaven (cf. 2 Kings 2:5–14): "From the [Dead

[1] Cf. H. Kraft, *Die Entstehung des Christentums* (Darmstadt: Wissenschaflich Buchgesellschaft, 1981), 10.

[2] Cf. R. Riesner, *Jesus als Lehrer*, WUNT 2/7, 3rd ed. (Tübingen: Mohr Siebeck, 1988), 353f.

[3] Cf. J. Thomas, *Le movement Baptiste en Palestine et Syrie* (Gembloux: Duculot, 1935).

[4] *Itinerarium* 19 (Geyer, 24; Baldi, 171).

[5] Cf. C. Kopp, *The Holy Places of the Gospels* (New York: Herder and Herder, 1963), 114–15; German ed.: *Die heiligen Stätten der Evangelien*, 2nd ed. (Regensburg: Puster, 1964), 154–64; D. Baldi and B. Bagatti, *Saint Jean-Baptiste dans les souvenirs de sa patrie*, SBFCMi 27 (Jerusalem: Franciscan Printing Press, 1980), 38–46.

Sea] to the Jordan, where the Lord was baptized by John, it is 5 miles. There, at the river, is a pond and a hill, on the bank of which Elijah had been enraptured. (Inde [a mare mortus] ad Iordanem ubi dominus a Johannes baptizatus est milia quinque. Ibi est lacus super flumen, monticulus in illa ripa, ubi raptus est Helias in cœlo.)" Later the pilgrim site for this event was "moved" to the western bank of the Jordan, where Saint John's Monastery, a Greek Orthodox community, keeps this particular tradition alive. After the peace treaty between Jordan and Israel was signed in 1995, the place could be visited again.

2. *Aenōn near Salem*

According to John 3:23, John the Baptist baptized people at a place where there was abundant water called Aenōn near Salem (ἐν Αἰνὼν ἐγγὺς τοῦ Σαλεῖμ, ὅτι ὕδατα πολλὰ ἦν ἐκεῖ). E. Robinson[6] has proposed that the place was a village by the name of Salem, which is 6 km east from Nablus (Sichem), and M. E. Boismard[7] agreed with him. The supporters of this hypothesis suggest that it is probably the Arabic village with the name Aenun. However, Aenun is quite a distance from the Samarian Salem, and crucially, it is without a spring. B. Bagatti suggests that some disciples of John settled in Samaria and transferred the place-name Salem[8] to this village.

It is probably preferable to support the older traditions, which both Eusebius[9] and Egeria[10] had supported. Today the area is part of Tell Shalem, which is 12 km south of Beth Shean (Scythopolis) and where there is also an abundant spring (Hebrew עֵינוֹן [*ejnon*]?), which is now used for large fishponds.[11] J. T. Milik believes that this is also the location for one of the hiding places mentioned by the Copper Scroll

[6] *Neuere biblische Forschungen* (Berlin, 1857), 438. For other supporters see Kopp, *Heiligen Stätten*, 172, n. 146.

[7] "Aenon près de Salim", *RB* 80 (1973): 218–29.

[8] *Saint Jean-Baptiste* (see n. 5), 69f.

[9] *Onomastikon* (Klostermann, 40f.; Baldi, 214).

[10] *Peregrinatio* 13.1ff. (Geyer, 55; Baldi, 215–17).

[11] Cf. E. Höhne, *Palästina: Historisch-archäologische Karte* (Göttingen: Vandenhoeck und Ruprecht, 1981), Nord F-6. For a description of the place, see F. M. Abel, *Géographie de la Palestine*, 3rd ed. (Paris: Gabalda, 1967), 1:447, 2:441f. It is very difficult to get access to this frontier area. A rare picture is in B. Pixner, *Mit Jesus durch Galiläa nach dem fünften Evangelium* (Rosh Pina: Corazin, 1992), 19; Eng. ed.: *With Jesus through Galilee according to the Fifth Gospel* (Collegeville, Minn.: Liturgical Press, 1996).

from Qumran (3Q15 12:6f.),[12] which underlines the site's importance. As I have previously stated, I believe that the Copper Scroll represents a reliable list of the locations for the Essene treasures.[13] The site might also be the location for the activity of one of the Jewish baptism groups. In addition, near to Salem is Abel-Mehula,[14] which is where Elisha was called by Elijah (1 Kings 19:16–21).

3. Bethany on the Other Side of the Jordan

According to John 1:28, the Baptist ministered at a place (τόπος) called Bethany (Βηθανία; textual variants: Βηθαβαρᾶ, . . . , Βηθαραβᾶ) "across the Jordan" (πέραν τοῦ Ἰορδάνου [*peran tou Iordanou*]). Since Origen (see below), it has been usual to use biblical references to attempt to solve the puzzle of this place's name and its location. There are few other New Testament sites that have caused such debate and where research has reached such considerable differences. All of the various hypotheses create considerable difficulties.[15] Indeed, as a consequence of these complications, it is understandable why N. Krieger suggested that the search should be abandoned, as he believed that the place was fictitious.[16] However, Saint John not only had a very developed theology, but it is apparent from his Gospel that he also possessed a comprehensive geographical knowledge.[17] For this reason and because this place was obviously of great importance to the fourth evangelist, the location for Bethany on the other side of the Jordan should be investigated further and not abandoned as Krieger proposed.

[12] In M. Baillet, J. T. Milik and R. de Vaux, *Les "petites grottes" de Qumrân*, DJD 3 (Oxford: Clarendon Press, 1962), 262.

[13] Cf. B. Pixner, "Unravelling the Copper Scroll Code: A Study on the Topography of 3Q15", *RQ* 11 (1983): 323–61 (particularly 357, n. 50). On the same topic, see chapter 12, "The Copper Scroll of Qumran" (pp. 159–68).

[14] E. Höhne, *Pälastina* (see n. 11), F-6. The original location for this place is directly on the Jordan, while the new Jewish settlement with this name is situated more southwesterly on the road from Jericho to Beth Shean.

[15] Cf. R. Riesner's study, undertaken at my suggestion: R. Riesner, "'Bethany beyond the Jordan' (Jn 1:28): Topography, Theology and History in the Fourth Gospel", *Tyndale Bulletin* 38 (1987): 29–63.

[16] "Fiktive Orte der Johannestaufe", *Zeitschrift für die neutestamentliche Wissenschaft* 45 (1954): 121–23.

[17] Among others, see especially B. Schwank, "Ortskenntnisse im vierten Evangelium?" *EA* 57 (1981): 427–42.

Bethany is the very first place that is mentioned in connection with John the Baptist. It was there that Jesus welcomed his first disciples from John the Baptist's followers (Jn 1:29–51). It was to Bethany that Jesus fled after the lynch mob at the Festival of Dedication in Jerusalem (Jn 10:31–40). It was also there that many more supporters from John the Baptist's circle joined him. "He went away again across the Jordan to the place where John at first baptized, and there he remained. And many came to him; and they said, 'John did no sign, but everything that John said about this man was true.' And many believed in him there [ἐκεῖ]" (Jn 10:40–42). The many references in John's Gospel to Bethany can only mean that at the time of his writing, an important Christian community must have existed there and that the writer had a special connection with this community. K. Kundsin[18] and R. Bultmann[19] both accepted this "special connection" hypothesis. Both of these writers believed that the existence of a Christian community led to the localization there of a ministry of John the Baptist and secondarily of Jesus. But this position has not been properly demonstrated, and the opposite is more plausible.

II. The Necessity of a Northern Location

1. The Oldest Place-Tradition according to Origen

Whoever is concerned with the problem of "Bethany on the other side of the Jordan" must refer to Origen (ca. 185–254), the earliest witness for the identification of John's geographical "problems". Origen had spent much of his life at Caesarea, where he wrote the Hexapla, based on ancient manuscripts. Origen was very interested in the various ancient traditions for the location of particular and significant religious sites. In his commentary on John's Gospel, he remarks that in most of the manuscripts it reads "Bethany" (Βηθανία), but he was convinced that it should rather read "Bethabara" (Βηθαβαρᾶ).[20] The distance between Jerusalem and the Jordan was approximately 32 km. Origen identified "Bethany" (Jn 1:28) as existing on the other side of the Jordan and as the place of Jesus' baptism (Mt 3:1). Most contemporary researchers accept this

[18] *Topologische Überlieferungsstoffe im Johannes-Evangelium* (Göttingen: Vandenhoeck und Ruprecht, 1925), 20f.

[19] *Das Evangelium des Johannes* (Göttingen: Vandenhoeck und Ruprecht, 1959), 64f.

[20] *Commentaria in Evangelium Ioannis* 6.204 (PG 14:269; Baldi, 170f.).

hypothesis.[21] The presence of a Christian community, which seems to have existed in Bethany, rules out any identification of "Bethany" with Wadi el-Charrar, where there was a spring but no trace of a community from the New Testament period.[22] The name Bethabara ("house of transition" [בֵּית עֲבָרָה]? equals ford) was proposed by Origen as a solution to the puzzle because he could not find a village called Bethany on the banks of the Jordan, although he specifically looked for it. Origen's solution does not resolve this particular geographical puzzle because, according to our more extensive knowledge of manuscripts, there is no doubt that "Bethany" (Βηθανία) is the original version of John 1:28, as it appears in the famous papyrus 76 (ca. A.D. 200).

2. *The Distances in John 10–12*

John 11:11–15 assumes that Jesus began the journey to Bethany on the other side of the Jordan (Jn 10:40; cf. Jn 1:28). Lazarus, Jesus' friend, lived in Bethany near Jerusalem (Jn 11:1–18). Jesus reached his destination when Lazarus had already been in his grave for four days (Jn 11:17), that is to say, after four days of travel. We know that on average, walking on foot in Palestine, it was possible to travel around 40 km per day.[23] This would suggest a distance of 160 km between the two places. It is not unreasonable, as S. Dockx proposes, that John 1:28 assumes a place north of Lake Gennesaret [Sea of Galilee].[24] Even R. Schnackenburg, who prefers a site in the southern Jordan Valley, accepts the possibility that the "Bethany" mentioned in John 1:28 could originally have been located in Galilee.[25]

3. *Indications in John 1*

In John 1 there is therefore a strong indication that the location for Bethany must have been in the north, not very far from Lake Gennesaret

[21] Cf. C. Kopp, *Heiligen Stätten* (see n. 5), 153f.

[22] Cf. W. Wiefel, "Bethabara jenseits des Jordan (John 1:28)", *ZDPV* 83 (1967): 72–81 (at 75f.).

[23] Cf. J. Jeremias, *Jerusalem zur Zeit Jesu* (Göttingen: Vandenhoeck und Ruprecht, 1962), 68.

[24] "Bethanie au-delà du Jourdain", in *Chronologies neotestamentaires et vie de l'Église primitive* (Louvain: Peeters, 1976), 12–20.

[25] *Das Johannesevangelium*, vol. 2 (Freiburg im Breisgau: Herder, 1971), 412, n. 1.

(illus. 42). According to Saint John's Gospel, among the disciples that Jesus gained was Andrew and an unnamed disciple of John (Jn 1:35–40). Andrew finds his brother Simon Peter the next day and leads him to Jesus (Jn 1:41f.). On the third day they meet Philip: "Now Philip was

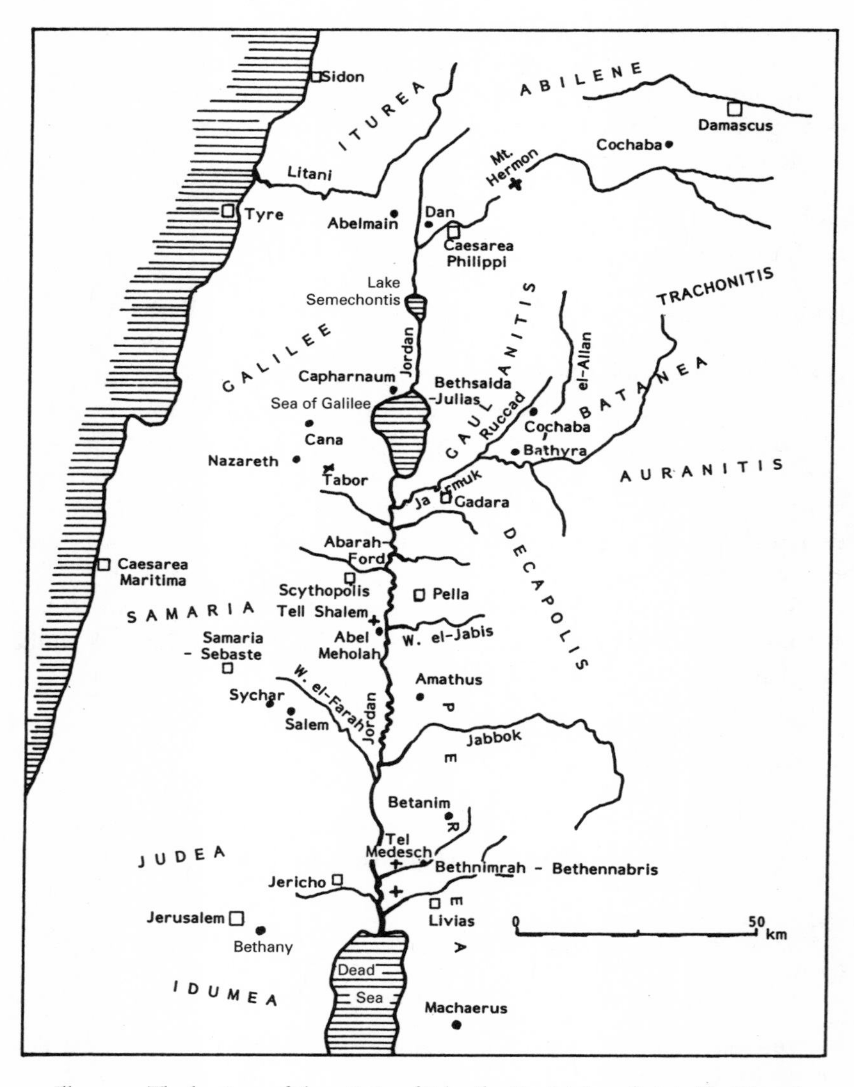

Illus. 42. The locations of the activity of John the Baptist (according to R. Riesner).

from Bethsaida, the city [πόλις (*polis*)] of Andrew and Peter" (Jn 1:44). Within three days Jesus finds three disciples, who all came from Bethsaida,[26] located at the inlet of the Jordan on the north side of Lake Gennesaret.[27] If one agrees with T. Zahn, then John 1:40f. assumes that the unnamed disciple must have brought his brother to Jesus, and this must have been the two Zebedee brothers.[28] The synoptic Gospels indicate that the fisher family of Zebedee came from the north side of the lake (Mt 4:12–22; Mk 1:16–31), and the tradition specifically indicates Bethsaida.[29] That such a gathering of fishermen would come from the traditional "Bethany", which is at the lower end of the river Jordan, seems both surprising and improbable. It is more plausible that this "Bethany" is to be found in the area of Bethsaida, a day's travel away.

4. *The Chronology of John 1–2*

The chronology of John 1–2 according to M. E. Boismard[30] suggests the following account of the first week of activity for Jesus:

Day	John	Activity
1	1:19–28	John the Baptist in Bethany
2	1:29–34	Jesus with John the Baptist in Bethany
3	1:35–39	The calling of the first disciples near Bethany around the tenth hour (4 P.M.)
4	1:40–42	The calling of Andrew and Peter from Bethsaida
5	1:43–45	Departure to Galilee The calling of Philip from Bethsaida and Nathaniel from Cana in Galilee (Jn 21:2)
6	—	—
7	2:1–11	On the third day (calculated from the last mentioned), wedding at Cana in Galilee

[26] The expression used in John 1:44 ("the city of Andrew and Peter") corresponds to the usual Rabbinic way of expressing where a person lives. Cf. R. BULTMANN, *Evangelium des Johannes* (see n. 19), 72, n. 5.

[27] Cf. chapter 9, "In Search of Bethsaida" (pp. 128–42).

[28] *Das Evangelium des Johannes*, Kommentar zum Neuen Testament, 5th ed. (Leipzig: Deichert, 1921), 4:132–35.

[29] Theodosius, *De situ terrae sanctae* 2: "De Capharnaum usque ad Bethsaida milia VI, ubi nati sunt apostoli Petrus, Andreas, Philippus et filii Zebedaei" (Geyer, 138; Baldi, 266).

[30] *Synopse des quatre Évangiles*, vol. 3, *L'Évangile de Jean* (Paris: Cerf, 1977), 99.

The "third day" (Jn 2:1) is, according to typical ancient Christian language usage,[31] the day of Jesus' Resurrection, which was a Sunday. It is understandable that, on the day before, a Sabbath, nothing was reported. Naturally, this chronology had a symbolic meaning for the first Christians. But by his comprehensive topographical knowledge (pp. 71, 139–40, 276) the evangelist has placed a theological construction in a geographically and chronologically possible framework. According to the available time schedule, Jesus finds himself in the morning of the fourth day still in the vicinity of Bethany on the other side of the river Jordan. On the fifth day, he departs finally to Galilee, which he seems to reach on the same day when he called Nathaniel from Cana as his disciple. For the journey to Bethany he would have had only two days, and this fact would contradict again the assumption of Bethany being situated opposite Jericho.

5. The Ministry of John in Batanea

In Greek, "Bethany" (Βηθανία) and "Batanea" (Βαταναία) sound very similar. I wondered whether it was possible that the countryside in John 1:28 "beyond the Jordan" was meant to be the area that all the chronological and geographical indications in John's Gospel seem to suggest. Later I discovered that this had already been suggested by the great English topographer of Palestine C. R. Conder.[32] In fact, a transition from one word to the other is even more likely when one researches the different forms in Aramaic of the Targums for Batanea (e.g., בֵּיתְנַיָּא).[33]

What were the reasons for John the Baptist's ministry so far north in Batanea (illus. 42)? It is remarkable that the two places are associated with baptisms: Jericho and Salem had connections with Elijah traditions (see above). The same is also true for Batanea. The Spanish pilgrim Egeria traveled in 384 from Jerusalem to Carneas (Carnaim) in Batanea in order to visit the grave of Job.[34] On the journey there, she traveled through Tishbe, the hometown of Elijah (1 Kings 17:1) and also through the valley of the Corra (Cherith), where Elijah hid

[31] Cf. Mt 16:21; 17:23; 20:19; Lk 24:7–46; Acts 10:40; 1 Cor 15:4.

[32] "Bethany beyond Jordan", *PEFQS* (1877): 184–86.

[33] Cf. R. Riesner, "'Bethany beyond the Jordan'" (see n. 15), 53f.

[34] *Peregrinatio* 16.1ff. (Geyer, 56ff.; SC 296:191ff.).

from Ahab (1 Kings 17:3–6). J. Wilkinson[35] identified the stream Cherith with the Wadi el-Jabis that led into the Jordan opposite Salem, and so this would correspond to the Old Testament geography. But according to the geographical sequence of Egeria's report, "by the big valley with the strong stream" (*qualis uallis erat ingens, mittens torrentem in Iordanen infinitum*),[36] it is unlikely to be the Wadi el-Jabis that stops behind Tishbe. Rather, it is more likely to be the valley of the Jarmuk on the way to Carnaim. This makes more sense when Egeria sees soon after this "on her left a very big mountain" (*ad subito de latere sinistra . . . apparuit nobis mons ingens et altus infinitum*),[37] which must be Mount Hermon. However, it is impossible to be completely sure because of a missing page in the original document between the mention of Hermon and her arrival in Carnaim[38] in Batanea. As we have previously noted, this region was populated by the Essenes and Proto-Mandaeans and Baptist groups (pp. 172–76), among whom John's mission seems to have found particular support. It is known even today that John enjoys a significant following by the Mandaeans, who have historically rejected Jesus. In their scriptures they say that they had the use of "the clean upper Jordan", and by this they probably meant the Jarmuk (p. 172).

The leaders of the Proto-Mandaeans are significant in this early period. Zamiris, the leader of the clan; his son Jakim (Jacimus); and his son Philippos (*Ant.* 17.29) were all important, particularly Philippos, who in the war of A.D. 66–70 against Rome supported Herod Agrippa II (*War* 2.421; *Life* 46–61, 177–80, 407–9). This Batanean clan remained loyal to the Herodian dynasty. Josephus mentions that it was this group that trained the Herodian soldiers (*Ant.* 17.30f.). Normally the Herodian rulers could rely on the Batanean training camps, but there is a surprising exception. In the year A.D. 36 the Nabataean king Aretas IV took revenge on Herod Antipas because Herod's wife, the daughter of Aretas, who was married to Herod, had fled to her father (cf. Mk 6:17–20). At a battle in Gamalitis (?), Herod Antipas was utterly defeated (*Ant.* 18.109–15). His defeat was caused by the desertion of his soldiers, who originally came from the area of the ex-tetrarch Philip (cf. Lk 3:1). They deserted Antipas and joined his enemies (*Ant.* 17.114).

[35] *Egeria's Travels to the Holy Land* (Jerusalem: Ariel, 1981), 109, 222.

[36] *Peregrinatio* 16.2 (SC 296:192).

[37] *Peregrinatio* 16.4 (SC 296:192).

[38] Cf. P. Maraval, *Égérie: Journal de Voyage (Itinéraire)*, SC 296 (Paris: Cerf, 1982), 193.

People interpreted Antipas' defeat as a punishment by God for the murder of John the Baptist (*Ant.* 18.116ff.; cf. Mk 6:21–29). Could it be that those who deserted Antipas did so because of their devotion to John, whose ministry they had experienced in the north? They would have belonged to those soldiers who came to John and who received the warning: "Rob no one by violence or by false accusation, and be content with your wages" (Lk 3:14).

The tradition of John's stay in the north may also be the reason for the veneration of John in Ramathain in the upper Golan region. Ramathain is a hill with ruins on the road from Bethsaida on the Sea of Galilee to Damascus. Each year, according to C. Dauphin, there was a pilgrimage of Jewish Christians and their disciples. Next to the hill of that town, there is an abundant water pond that could have been used for baptizing and ritual baths.[39]

III. Judea on the Other Side of the Jordan

1. Matthew 19:1, Mark 10:1 and John 10:40

The area of Batanea "on the other side of the Jordan" was an important working area for Jesus at the beginning (Jn 1:28ff.) and at the end (Jn 10:40ff.) of his time of ministry. This also provides the key to another topographical New Testament puzzle. Matthew 19:1 (τὰ ὅρια τῆς Ἰουδαίας πέραν τοῦ Ἰορδάνου) and its parallel passage in Mark 10:1 (τὰ ὅρια τῆς Ἰουδαίας καὶ πέραν τοῦ Ἰορδάνου), both mention that Jesus—after the disappointing failure in Galilee and the sudden breaking off of his mission there, in "Judea on the other side of the Jordan"—opened up another fertile activity: "And crowds gathered to him again; and again, as his custom was, he taught them" (Mk 10:1b). "Large crowds followed him, and he healed them there" (Mt 19:2).

There seems to be two traditions, the synoptic and the one from John's Gospel (Jn 10:40), both pointing to a later ministry of Jesus in the area "on the other side of the Jordan". In both traditions, Jesus retreated from a dangerous area to a quiet place. According to John, Jesus was in danger of getting murdered in Jerusalem at the Hanukkah

[39] "Farj en Gaulanitide refuge judéo-chrétien?" *POC* 34 (1984): 235–45 (at 245). Cf. also C. Dauphin and S. Gibson, "Golan Survey 1988", *IEJ* 41 (1991): 176–79.

feast: "The Jews took up stones again to stone him" (Jn 10:31). "Again they tried to arrest him, but he escaped from their hands. He went away again across the Jordan [πέραν τοῦ Ἰορδάνου (*peran tou Iordanou*)] to the place [εἰς τὸν τόπον (*eis ton topon*)] where John at first baptized, and there he remained. And many came to him" (Jn 10:39ff.). Jesus obviously did not want to experience the same death from stoning as Stephen (Acts 7:55–60) and his "brother" James (pp. 392–93) would later suffer. He decided to retreat to the quiet area of the tetrarchy that belonged to Philip of Batanea. There is a similar incident in Matthew and Mark.

According to Luke, Jesus was warned by some friendly Pharisees (Lk 13:31–33) about threats from Herod Antipas: "At that very hour some Pharisees came, and said to him, 'Get away from here [ἐντεῦθεν], for Herod wants to kill you'" (Lk 13:31). Flavius Josephus has to be believed[40] when he says that the actual reason for the arrest and execution of John the Baptist was because of John's popularity and from an increasing concern by Antipas of an uprising by the people (*Ant.* 18.116–19). As the tetrarch had heard of the increasing enthusiasm of the people for Jesus, he believed at first that Jesus was the resurrected John the Baptist (Mk 6:14f.). Jesus sensed the danger, particularly following the enthusiasm of the crowd after the first feeding (pp. 65–68), and ordered his disciples to cross over quickly to the other bank to Bethsaida (Mk 6:45), where the more tolerant Philip (*War* 18.106f.) ruled. Jesus hastily returned in secret to the area of Tyre (Mk 7:24). This possibility of danger helps explain some of Jesus' other movements. He felt justified to decide himself on the way and time of his death and left the danger zones according to his premonition: "He said to them, 'Go and tell that fox, 'Behold, I cast out demons and perform cures today and tomorrow, and the third day I finish my course. Nevertheless I must go on my way today and tomorrow and the day following; for it cannot be that a prophet should perish away from Jerusalem'" (Lk 13:32ff.). So Jesus left the Galilee of Antipas and wandered on to "Judea on the other side of the Jordan".

Most of the commentators understand "Judea on the other side of the Jordan" to be the area of Perea on the east bank of the Jordan between the Decapolis town Pella and the fortress Machaerus (illus. 42). Perea belonged then to the territory of Antipas, and it was in Machaerus

[40] Cf. H. W. Hoehner, *Herod Antipas* (Grand Rapids: Zondervan, 1979), 124–31.

where John the Baptist was executed (*Ant.* 18.119). Is it possible, however, that Jesus was in the area, where there were Antipas spies and where he could have been caught by "that fox" at any time? Also, nowhere in any of the literature on the history of Perea (Περαία) is there mention of the area being described as "Judea on the other side of the Jordan".

2. *The Origin of the Name*

It is different for the region of Batanea, which belonged to Philip. Batanea and Gaulanitis and Trachonitis as well were governed during the whole first century and afterward, with short breaks, by Jewish kings and tetrarchs (pp. 170–71). At that time the Hasmoneans and Herod the Great described the whole Jewish state as Judea (Ἰουδαία). Adding to this, Flavius Josephus called the whole northern Transjordanian area Judea. In his book the *Jewish War*, Josephus divides the whole of the Jewish settled regions into four areas: Galilee, Perea, Samaria and Judea (*War* 3.35–58). Surprisingly, he also names the eleven Jewish toparchies and both coastal towns of Jamnia and Joppa and also "the areas of Gamala and Gaulanitis, Batanea and Trachonitis, which belonged to the kingdom of Agrippa [I]",[41] as if they had a particular connection to Judea. K. von Raumer wrote: "It seems as if we must accept the position that Josephus proposes, that later northeastern Palestine was included as part of Judea."[42]

In his description, from the view from the Psephinus Tower in Jerusalem, Josephus indicates that the farthest region visible (τὰ τῆς Ἑβραίων κληρουχίας ἔσχατα) was still considered an original Jewish area (*War* 5.160). That probably was the popular assumption at that time, but it is significant that Luke mentions only the territories of the tetrarch Philip, Iturea and the Trachonitis (Lk 3:1) and not the more important regions, such as Gaulanitis and Batanea. This can perhaps be explained if these areas were known in the vernacular simply as "Judea

[41] Josephus, *War* 3.54–56: "The rest of the area, apart from Jerusalem, is divided into the following region of council areas: Gophna in second place, then Akrabata, Thamna, as well as Lydda, Emmaus and Pella, Idumaea, Engedi, Herodias and Jericho. As district towns also Jamnia and Joppa, with the areas of Gamala and Gaulanitis, Batanea and Trachonitis, which were already part of the kingdom of Agrippa" (O. Michel and O. Bauernfeind, *Flavius Josephus: De bello judaico—Der jüdische Krieg: Griechisch und Deutsch*, vol. 1 [Munich: Kösel, 1959], 323).

[42] *Palästina* (Leipzig, 1860), 235.

on the other side of the Jordan" (Mt 19:1 / Mk 10:1) or as "the Jewish land on the other side of the Jordan" (Josephus).

It is possible that the inclusion of that area as part of Judea was inspired by older traditions, which at the Second Temple period were still part of traditional Jewish lore. In Joshua 19:34 there is a description of the boundaries of Naphtali, and it includes the peculiar sentence: "Then the boundary turns westward to Aznoth-tabor and goes from there to Hukkok, touching Zebulun at the south and Asher on the west and Judah on the east at the Jordan [יְהוּדָה הַיַּרְדֵּן] by sunrise." This place, which is found in all the important Masoretical texts, has given the commentators many difficulties. While Napthali in the west touches Asher and in the south Zebulun, how can it be that in the east it meets the Transjordanian Judea? While this statement could easily be dismissed as a textual error, K. von Raumer[43] attempted a solution with the expression *chavvoth ja'ir* (חַוֹּת יָאִיר), "tent villages of Jair", which were found in this area on the other side of the Jordan. Jair possessed sixty towns in Bashan (Deut 3:14).[44] Jerome localized the tents of Jair in the following way: "Havot Jair, qui locus nunc vocatur Golan", and Eusebius spoke in this context of the "Batanean corner" (γωνία τῆς Βαταναίας).[45]

K. von Raumer tried to explain the designation of that area in Joshua 19:34 as part of the house of Judea by pointing to the descent of Jair, whose father's ancestors were from the house of Judah (1 Chron 2:3f.). On his mother's side he was descended from the house of Manasseh and was considered to belong to them. Numbers 36:7 states: "The inheritance of the sons of Israel shall not be transferred from one tribe to another"; it may therefore be the case that some insisted that the *chavvoth ja'ir* were to be counted as part of the house of Judea. So perhaps the description of the area east of Lake Gennesaret as "Judea on the other side of the Jordan" can be traced back to those very old traditions.

3. *Jesus in Batanea*

There is an old Syrian record that Jesus was pursued by Antipas and that he retreated to a Syrian region, where he continued his ministry.

[43] Ibid., 233–41.
[44] Cf. Josh 13:29f.; 1 Kings 4:13; Josephus, *Ant.* 5.254.
[45] *Onomastikon* (Klostermann, 18, 4f.).

According to Ephraim the Syrian, Jesus fled there to work as a spiritual shepherd because this was his paternal tribal area.[46] This tradition is supported by our understanding of "Bethany on the other side of the Jordan" (Jn 10:40; cf. Jn 1:28) and "Judea on the other side of the Jordan" (Mt 19:2 / Mk 10:1). In Batanea Jesus ministered among the disciples of John the Baptist who had been prepared by John's mission. Here Jesus may have met the Essene groups (pp. 175–76), and it is perhaps no accident that the teaching about the "eunuchs for the sake of the kindom of heaven" (Mt 19:12) occurred here. The example of the celibate Essene monks that were familiar to his audience would have been well understood among them.

We can see another possible connection Jesus had with Batanea if we remember that among the Nazoreans were members of the Davidic family.[47] So Jesus may have walked quite often in his youth between Nazareth in Galilee and Cochaba in Batanea (illus. 42) and stayed with relatives there. He could have stayed there after his baptism in the Jordan down by Jericho and later joined the followers of John the Baptist in Batanea. The two disciples who asked him: "Where are you staying?" (ποῦ μένεις [Jn 1:38]) may have accompanied Jesus to his relatives in Cochaba. It was in Judea on the other side of the Jordan that Mark placed the discussion about divorce. The Pharisees turned to Jesus in order to test his position, and they emphasized that Moses (see Deut 24:1) allowed men to write a letter of dismissal and to divorce (Mk 10:1–9). In an authoritative speech, Jesus committed himself more to the position of the Essenes (11QTemple 57:17–19; cf. CD 4:20f.): "What therefore God has joined together, let not man put asunder" (Mk 10:9). Mark continues: "And in the house the disciples asked him again about this matter" (Mk 10:10). Which house is meant here? Is it not possible that he was staying with his relatives in Cochaba?

There are further questions: Could the author of the first Gospel, among the "relatives of the Lord" living on the pilgrim route from Babylon to Jerusalem (*Ant.* 15.26), to which Matthew refers in Matthew 4:16–20 (p. 62), find a memory of the visit of the Wise Men

[46] "Jacob, the son of Isaac, was a shepherd. He had to flee from his brother, who was older than he, and received his Syrian sheep (Laban episode). So Jesus too was a teacher to the Jews, his first sheep, and when he was persecuted by Herod, the king, he became also a shepherd of Syrian brothers." (*St. Ephraim, an Exposition of the Gospel*, ed. G. A. EGAN, CSCO 292/6 [Louvain: Peeters, 1968], 40.)

[47] Cf. chapter 13, "Batanea as a Jewish Settlement Area" (pp. 169–76, especially 173–75).

from the Orient (Mt 2:1–12)? The comment in the fourth Gospel: "And many believed in him there" (Jn 10:42) seems to point to a state that was still true at the end of the first century, when this Gospel was written. We know that at that time there were strong Jewish Christian communities existing there (pp. 173–74). Many commentators assume that the original text of John's Gospel came from that area.[48] The author of the first Gospel could also have been a "priest" from the south Syrian community, which included both believers of Jesus from the circumcision and those from the Gentile community.

Excavations in the year 1999 and following have confirmed that the traditional place of Jesus' baptism on the eastern bank of the Jordan is Wadi e-Charrar (pp. 177–78). See M. Waheeb, Wadi al-Kharrar Archeological Project (al-Magtas), in *Studies on the History and Technology of Jordan* 7 (1998) [Amman: Department of Antiquities, 2001], 591–600; R. Riesner, *Bethanien Jenseits des Jordan: Topographie und Theologie im Johannes-Evangelium*, SBAZ 12 (Glessen: Brunen, 2002), 29–33.—Ed.

[48] Cf. K. Wengst, *Bedrängte Gemeinde und verherrlichter Christus* (Neukirchen-Vluyn: Neukirchner, 1983).

15. The Essene Quarter in Jerusalem

I. The Spreading of the Essenes

1. The Influence of the Essenes

Although the influence of the Essenes was not as extensive across the various sectors of Jewish society as was that of the Pharisees, it does seem that this sect had a considerable influence on Judaism at the time of Jesus. Even if we treat with caution the size of this community that Flavius Josephus proposes, it is still remarkable that he estimated the number of Pharisees as 6,000 (*Ant.* 17.42) and those of the Essenes as 4,000 (*Ant.* 18.29). This estimate (πλῆθος τετραχίλιος) is confirmed by Philo.[1] These numbers represent a ratio of 3 to 2 at the beginning of the first century. The remarkable discovery of the manuscripts in the caves of Qumran could give the impression that the community was confined to the Essene monastery by the Dead Sea, but that community represents only one example of the movement. However, the Essene community in the desert of Judea did possess considerable influence, recognized even by the Roman author Pliny the Elder.[2] There is no doubt that this particular community was more extreme and esoteric than other Essene settlements that existed throughout the country (see below). In spite of the strong spiritual connection with Jerusalem and the temple, the Qumran Essenes lived separately in the desert. The main reason for this separation was the independence of their feast calendar (pp. 242, 362–64, 416–17) and the rejection of this by the Hasmonean priests and royal lineage reigning from 150 until 37 B.C. in Jerusalem and who controlled the temple services.

The Qumran settlement existed approximately from 150 B.C. until A.D. 68, but there is an astonishing gap in occupancy during the time

[1] *Quod omnis homo probus liber sit* 75.

[2] *Naturalis historia* 5.17.73.

of the reign of Herod the Great (37–4 B.C.). Where was the Essene community when it was not at Qumran? To answer this particular conundrum I propose the following hypothesis: Qumran was destroyed in 37 B.C. during the war between the Hasmonean Antigonus and Herod. The Qumran Essenes eventually moved with Herod to Jerusalem, where they lived in an area that later became known as "Zion" on the southwest hill of Jerusalem and where they established a community settlement. About forty years later, during the confusion under Archelaus (see Mt 2:22), Qumran developed once more as an Essene settlement. Archaeological clues seem to suggest that the second settlement period is less significant than the first. It is possible that it was at this new settlement that John, son of the priest Zechariah and Elizabeth, found shelter in an Essene monastery in the desert (see Lk 1:80). John later seems to have separated himself from the Essene community in order to move to the Jordan to pursue his personal mission as preacher of repentance for the approaching Kingdom of God (pp. 177–80). Another Essene-Nazorean group established itself in Jerusalem next to the Essene community, and this became an important part of the subsequent Jewish Christian community. Traces of Essene influence can be identified in the New Testament.[3]

2. *The Relocation from Qumran to Zion*

Archaeological investigation at Khirbet Qumran demonstrated that the Essene settlement had been deserted from about 37 B.C. until the time of Archelaus' reign (4 B.C.–A.D. 6). This absence of almost a generation is even more astonishing when we consider that Herod the Great's government favored the Essenes, and we would therefore expect a flourishing community at Qumran. This favorable disposition toward the Essenes was not for religious reasons but was due to a mutual opposition toward the Hasmoneans, which both the Essenes and Herod considered dangerous rivals (cf. *Ant.* 15.371ff.).

The excavations at Khirbet Qumran by the Dominican R. de Vaux uncovered evidence of extensive destruction by fire of the first

[3] Cf. chapter 18, "The Last Supper of Jesus" (pp. 239–49); chapter 26, "The Essene Quarter and the Primitive Christian Community" (pp. 360–68); chapter 28, "James the Lord's 'Brother'" (pp. 380–93); chapter 30, "Mary on Zion" (pp. 398–407); chapter 31, "Simeon Bar Cleopas, Second Bishop of Jerusalem" (pp. 408–14); chapter 32, "The Jerusalem Essenes, Barnabas and the Letter to the Hebrews" (pp. 415–22).

settlement. Evidence of the fire has also been discovered in many places at the settlement by other archaeologists, and de Vaux originally suggested that this burning had resulted from military activity. This fire must have happened toward the end of the rule of the last Hasmonean, Antigonus, around 37 B.C. Shortly after this destruction, there is evidence around 31 B.C. of an earthquake (*War* 1.370), which further destroyed the buildings at Qumran.[4] R. de Vaux later suggested that the fire might have been caused by the earthquake.[5] However, other researchers have supported his original proposal and believed that the first destruction of Qumran was due to the enemy activity of the soldiers of Antigonus.

I agree with the proposal of enemy activity because the fate of the Qumran Essenes follows a logical sequence of events as described by Josephus. He describes how in the war between Antigonus and Herod, the followers of the Hasmonean high priests around Jericho frequently attacked the followers of Herod (*War* 1.300; *Ant.* 16.458). At that time, "many Jews hated Antigonus and gathered around Herod.... Most of them were driven by a great desire for a change of government" (*War* 1.335). This statement fits well with the antagonism of

[4] "Fouilles au Khirbet Qumrân: Rapport préliminaire sur la deuxième campagne", *RB* 61 (1954): 206–36 (at 235).

[5] *Archaeology and the Dead Sea Scrolls* (Oxford: Oxford University Press, 1973), pp. 21–23. P. R. CALLAWAY, *The History of the Qumran Community* (Sheffield: Sheffield Academic Press, 1988), 29–51, suggests different reasons for the lack of a settlement at Qumran at this time, believing that the evidence from the excavations is not conclusive. Callaway argues that the well-known crack in the giant cistern (ritual bath) that extends to the northeast was probably not the result of the earthquake in 31 B.C. but was due, as the Israeli geologists I. Karcz and U. Kafri have shown, to the regular common geographical phenomena of "swelling, seepage and percolation" (ibid., 45). This regularly occurs in the unstable geological Lisan-Mar plateau, on which the Qumran settlement was established. It is correct that other Dead Sea settlements had not been abandoned (Ain Feskha and Ain el-Ghuwer). But in spite of this I agree with R. de Vaux that Qumran had been abandoned during the Herodian period. I believe this for the following reasons: First, the depth of the sediment (75 cm deep) in the big basin at the mouth of the water system was caused by an obstruction in the water flow after the buildings were burned down and abandoned (R. DE VAUX, *Archaeology and the Dead Sea Scrolls*, 23f.). Second, there is a complete absence of Herodian coins for thirty-three years in the well-documented and dated levels of strata I and II, although other coins from other kings have been found, e.g., forty-three from Alexander Jannaeus (103 B.C.–A.D. 76), sixteen from Archelaus (4 B.C.–A.D. 6) and ninety-one from the Roman procurator (A.D. 6–66). Two Herodian coins were found, but one of them came from a "mixed level", in which coins from the Hasmoneans, of Herod the Great and of the Romans were mixed together. R. de Vaux ascribed the Herodian coins to the beginning of Archelaus' reign, when they would still have been in use (ibid., 22f., 33f.).

the Essenes toward the Hasmoneans, which had intensified following the destruction of Qumran. With the help of various Jewish supporters and the help of the Roman military, Herod managed to capture Jerusalem in 37 B.C. Antigonus was eventually executed, and many of his followers were either killed or dispossessed by Herod. Herod was generous to those who supported him against Antigonus (*War* 1.358; *Ant.* 15.2). It was at this period that the Essenes seem to have achieved their desire to have a place in the Holy City (pp. 196f.) and received an area of Jerusalem that they could then develop according to their own needs and their own halakhah.

II. *The Presence of the Essenes in Jerusalem*

1. *Philo and Josephus*

We know from many different sources that an Essene community had been established in Jerusalem at this time. Philo from Alexandria describes their presence: "They lived together in large communities in several towns and villages of Judea."[6] It is certain that Jerusalem was one of those towns in Judea described by Philo. Josephus mentions that in Jerusalem there was an Essene teacher called Judas, who was a prophet with many followers and close friends (ἑταῖροι καὶ γνώριμοι) who were already in 104 B.C. to be found living near the temple area in the year of the death of Antigonus I (*Ant.* 13.311–13). These Essenes had established a school in order to teach the Essene way of life. To illustrate the close bond between the teacher and pupils, we can point to the rules of the community at Qumran. Mutual discussions and consultations were characteristics of even the smallest groups (1QS 6:3; cf. 1QH 7:22; 9:32f.). The group around Judas must have had their residence somewhere in Jerusalem, although its precise location is uncertain. The prophecy by Judas about the death of Antigonus must have taken place before the persecution by the Hasmoneans. During the Hasmonean reign they probably fled and found refuge in the "desert of Damascus" (pp. 165, 175–76), where they lived in exile until circumstances were more favorable for a return to the "City of Holiness". This period of the Essene history is described by the Damascus Document (CD 1:8ff.; 7:14ff.).

[6] *Apologia pro Judaeis* 1 (Eusebius, *Praeparatio Evangelica* 8.6): "οἰκοῦσι δὲ πολλὰς μὲν πόλεις τῆς Ἰουδαίας, πολλὰς δὲ κώμας καὶ μεγάλους καὶ πολυανθρώπους ὁμίλους" (GCS 43/1:455).

Josephus tells us that when the young Herod was still a pupil, there was a prediction by Menahem, a prophetic Essene, that he would be the future king, and this was the beginning of a long relationship that he had with the community (*Ant.* 15.373–79). Herod must have possessed an unusual trust in those "holy people" because he exempted them from his loyalty oath and gave them the right to assemble, which was strictly forbidden to other religious sects (*Ant.* 15.371). Philo confirms that the Essenes enjoyed the respect and reverence of the political authorities.[7] The dominant obsession for Herod was the fear of the return of the Hasmonean dynasty. The hope for the Essenes of a restoration of the Davidic dynasty was ignored by Herod, perhaps because he thought this too fantastic to represent a realistic danger to his political aspirations. It is reasonable to assume that during the time of Herod's rule and the absence of the Essenes at Qumran, Jerusalem became the Essenes' center.

An unambiguous demonstration of the presence of the Essenes in Jerusalem is the existence of a gate (*War* 5.145). The hypothesis that the Essene Gate at Jerusalem was connected to a specific settlement of the sect was suggested by O. Michel in his notes on the *Jewish War* of Flavius Josephus. He writes: "The Essene Gate has its name perhaps because it was located near the Essene settlement."[8] This will be explored later in more detail.

2. *The Qumran Documents*

Among the many discoveries in Qumran is a hymn that demonstrated the love of the sect for Zion. It is probably one of the most beautiful pieces of poetry from the desert monastery, and it is called the "Apostrophe to Zion".[9] The hymn describes an idealistic "town of the Lord", full of expectation for the "Day of Holiness" and the necessity for cleansing in preparation for that day. When the Chassidim (p. 361), which are mentioned in the hymn, lived as Essenes in Jerusalem, they must have seen themselves, with their own particular purity regulations, as a "blessing" to the town of the Lord and as a source of future

[7] *Quod omnis homo probus liber sit* 89–91.

[8] *Flavius Josephus: De bello judaico—Der jüdische Krieg: Greichisch und Deutsch*, vol. 2, pt. 1 (Munich: Kösel, 1963), 246, n. 41.

[9] J. A. Sanders, *The Dead Sea Scrolls* (Ithaca, N.Y.: Clarendon, 1967), 62f. Previously mentioned in *The Psalms Scroll of Qumran Cave 11*, DJD 4 (Oxford, 1965), 85–87.

hope for Zion. As the text is important for our understanding of the attitude and relationship of the Essenes to Jerusalem, here is its beginning:

> I think of thy blessing, O Zion;
> With all my power have I loved you.
> May your memory be blessed forever!
> Great is your hope, Zion,
> That peace and your long-deserving deliverance may come.
> Generation after generation will live in you,
> And generations of the pious [חֲסִידִים] will be your radiance;
> Those who are preparing for the day of deliverance,
> May they celebrate the greatness of your glory.
> (11QPs[a] 22:1–4)

The Qumran documents also contain texts that seem to support the existence of a settlement in Jerusalem. For example, the author of the War Scroll (1QM 3:10f.; cf. 1QM 7:3f.), writing at the beginning of the Christian era, describes a "community in Jerusalem" (הָעֵדָה יְרוּשָׁלַיִם [*ha^cedah jeruschalajim*]). The Hebrew expression *edah* was used in the Qumran documents to describe a close religious community. From a passage in the Damascus Document we can assume that in the Holy City a significant proportion of this community and also of the one at Qumran must have included those who were celibate: "No man should sleep with a woman in the holy of holies in order not to bring impurity to the town of holiness" (CD 12:1). This extreme attitude seems to suggest that a normal family life was impossible. The Jerusalem community must have been a closed community similar to that at Qumran. Before we further explore the nature of the Jerusalem Essene settlement and further consider the archaeological data, I would like to point to a passage in the Enoch Apocrypha.

3. *The Enoch Apocrypha*

In the Essenes' first book of Enoch, fragments of which have been found at Qumran, the southwest hill (presently called Mount Zion) was treated with particular devotion. In Enoch it says:

> I went from there [paradise] to the middle earth [Jerusalem] and saw there a blessed and fertile place, where trees were growing, with branches cut back, shooting and blossoming. I saw there a holy mountain [the southwest hill, today called Mount Zion], and below the

> mountain, against the east, was water [Siloam], and this was flowing south. Toward the east I saw another mountain [Mount of Olives], higher than that one and between the two was a deep, small gorge [Kidron Valley]; through it was also a stream flowing under the mountain. More to the west from there was another mountain [Abu Tor, "mountain of the menacing counsel"], smaller than that one and more modest in height; between the two was a deep and dry gorge [Gehinnom].... Then I asked [Enoch]: "For what purpose has this blessed land full of trees this cursed gorge in the middle?" And Uriel, a holy angel who was with me, answered: "This cursed gorge is intended for those eternally damned; here will all gather and here is the place of judgment. In the last days, there will be a performance of a just judgment in the *presence of the righteous* taking place; here will the devout of the Lord give praise to the Lord of all holiness, the king to eternity" (1 Enoch 26:15; 27ff.).

Both publishers of the intertestamental Apocrypha, E. Kautzsch[10] and P. Riessler,[11] state in their footnotes to the text that the author of Enoch meant that the "holy mountain" was the present hill of Zion. The Temple Mount was in Enoch's vision the place where the tree of life (Gen 2:9; 3:22) was transplanted (1 Enoch 25). It appears that the Chassidim ("the pious") of Qumran were convinced by the text of Enoch that one day they would be watching from the southwest hill of Jerusalem the punishment of the wicked in Gehenna (Aramaic for Gehinnom) and would be praising God "for his mercy which he has shown to them" (1 Enoch 27:3f.).

III. The Identification of the Essene Quarter

1. The Essene Gate

The best suggestion for the location for the Essene district in Jerusalem is without doubt the area of the gate in the western wall (illus. 58), which Josephus called the "Gate of the Essenes".[12] In the fourth chapter

[10] *Die Apokryphen und Pseudepigraphen des Alten Testaments*, vol. 2 (Tübingen: Mohr, 1900), 255.

[11] *Altjüdisches Schrifttum ausserhalb der Bibel*, 2nd ed. (Heidelberg: Kerrle, 1996), 1293 (first published in 1928).

[12] Cf. R. Riesner, "Josephus' 'Gate of the Essenes' in Modern Discussion", *ZDPV* 105 (1989): 105–9. Already M.J. Lagrange wrote that "il existait dans le voisinage [de la Porte des Esséniens] un couvent de l'ordre [essénien]", in *Le Judaïsme avant Jésus-Christ* (Paris: Gabalda, 1931), 317.

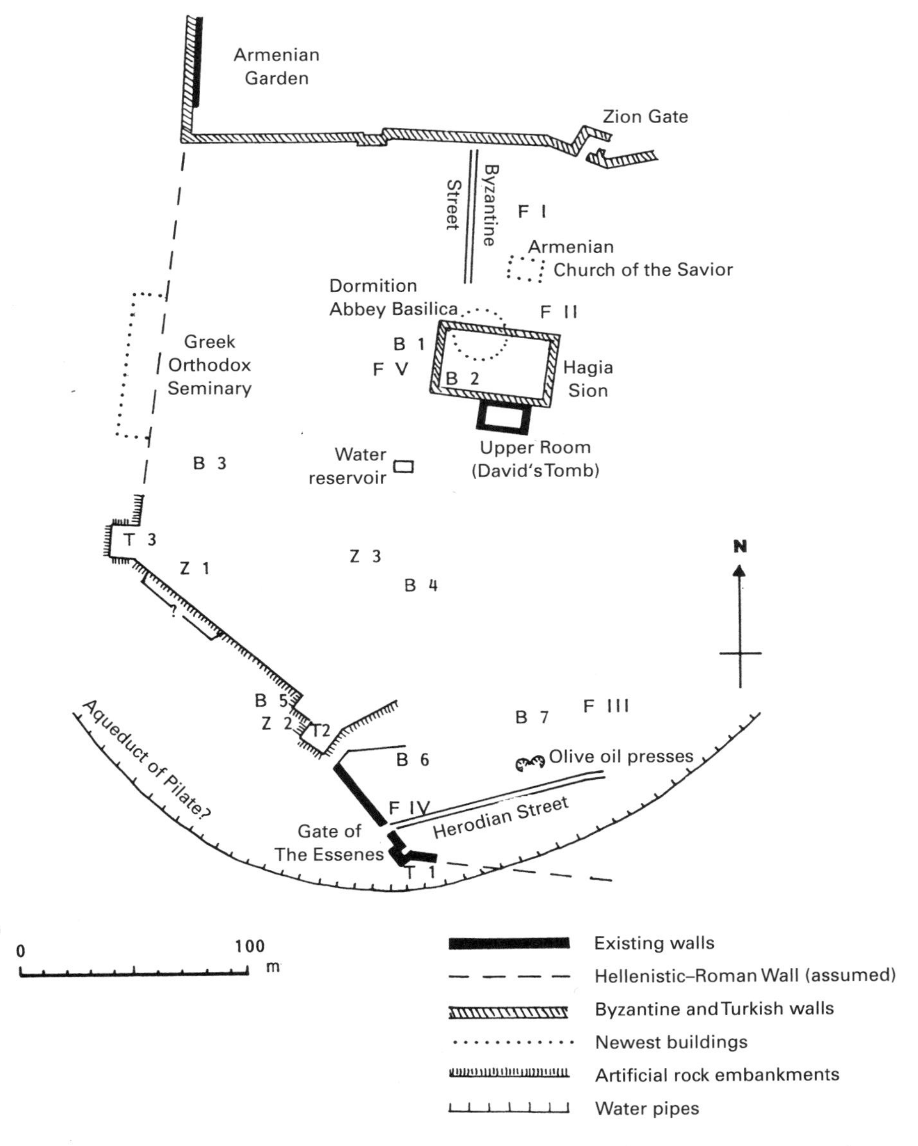

Illus. 43. The Essene quarter in Jerusalem—excavations (according to R. Riesner, 1991)
B 1–7 Jewish ritual baths
T 1–3 Tower or tower platform
Z 1–3 Cisterns
F I–V Excavation areas

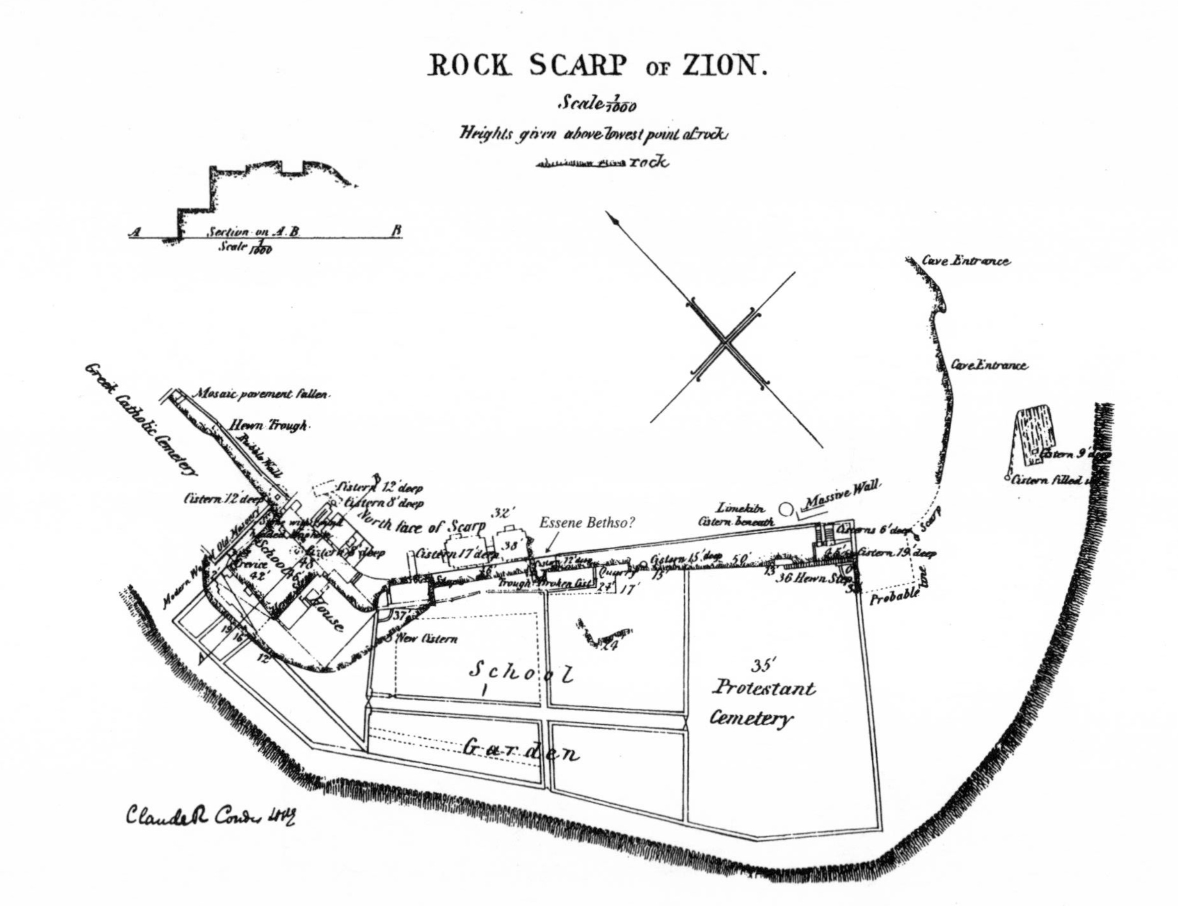

Illus. 44. The rock scarp of the hill of Zion (according to C.R. Conder, 1875). In the middle of the diagram ("trough", "broken cistern") could have been the Essene Bethso.

of the fifth book of the *Jewish War*, Josephus describes that section of the wall as follows: "On the other side, facing west, it [the wall] began at the same starting point [the Hippicus Tower], extended [south] through a place called Bethso [διὰ δὲ τοῦ Βηθσὼ καλουμένου χώρου] to the Gate of the Essenes [κατατεῖνον ἐπὶ τὴν Ἐσσηνῶν πύλην] and turned thereafter facing south [but going east] toward the pool of Siloam" (*War* 5.145). Before the wall sharply curved toward the pool of Siloam, there were two interesting places, namely, the "Gate of the Essenes" and, slightly earlier, "Bethso". The turning point of the wall is still visible today in the southwest tower (Tower 1), which has been dated as Hasmonean. In 1894 the English archaeologists F. J. Bliss and A. C. Dickie discovered in their excavations on the south slope of Mount Zion this tower and the remains of the wall.[13] About 10 m in front of the tower, a town gate was discovered that was particularly interesting because there were four gate thresholds on top of each other, one of which would have been the Essene Gate. In his final report of the excavation, Bliss spoke about his fear that the beautiful lime stones of the four thresholds would soon disappear into the modern buildings of Jerusalem, and he regretted that the gate excavations were left exposed.[14] In fact, soon after these excavations, no trace of the gates seemed to remain.[15]

In 1976 I published an article about the possible Essene quarter on Mount Zion[16] and then received permission in 1977 to undertake another excavation around the area of the gate on the edge of a Protestant cemetery, although at that time this was not too hopeful. I was greatly surprised to discover, 4 m deep, a wall and the gate with the four gate thresholds still on top of each other, just as Bliss had described them, all intact. Also, I found again the excavation trenches that Bliss had made next to the wall. Digging in a still-undisturbed area by the previous excavations, we found pottery remains, which were analyzed. The result justified the preliminary assertion that the lowest door level was from the Herodian-Roman period.

[13] "Second Report on the Excavations at Jerusalem", *PEFQS* (1894): 243–57 (at 242–54); "Third Report on the Excavations at Jerusalem", *PEFQS* (1895): 9–25 (at 12); *Excavations at Jerusalem* (London: Palestine Exploration Fund, 1898), 16–20, 322–24.

[14] *Excavations at Jerusalem*, 324.

[15] A photograph of the area from the time of the excavation by R. A. Mackowski, *Jerusalem in the Time of Jesus* (Grand Rapids: Eerdmans, 1980), 64.

[16] "An Essene Quarter on Mount Zion?" in *Studia Hierosolymitana in onore del P. Bellarmino Bagatti*, vol. 1, *Studi archeologici*, SBFCMa 22 (Jerusalem: Franciscan Printing Press, 1976), 245–86.

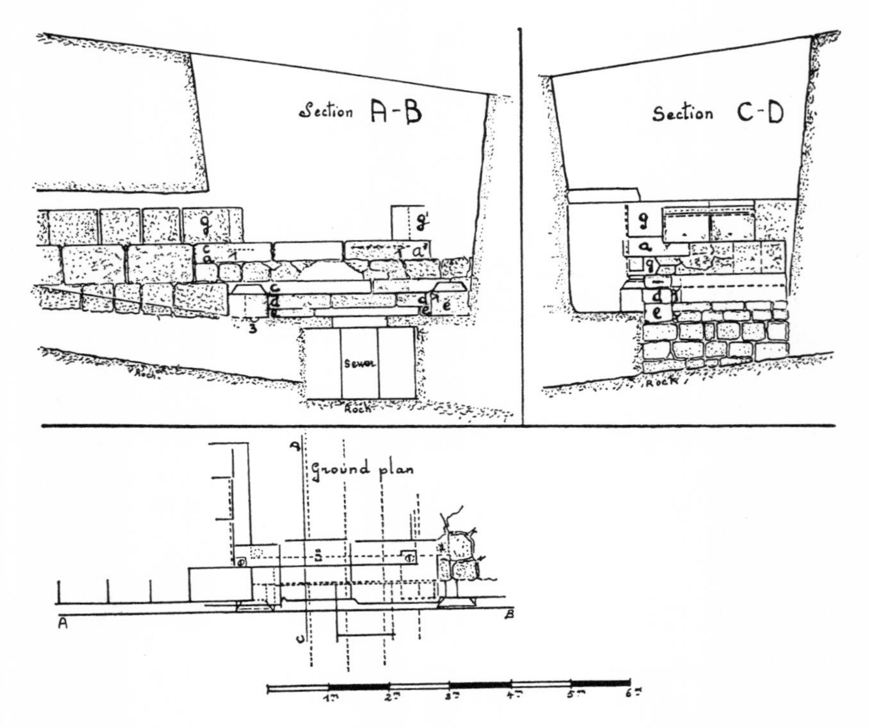

Illus. 45. The Essene Gate (according to F.J. Bliss, 1895) (drawn by T. Sandel). View from outside the gate.

g–g'	*Flank stones for gate posts*	*c*	*Doorstop*
a–a'	*Upper threshold (Byzantine)*	*e–e*	*Lowest threshold (Essene Gate)*
(1–1)	*Gatepost holes*	*e'*	*Flank stone for gatepost*
d–d'	*Middle threshold (late Roman)*	*3*	*Gatepost hole*

From 1979, with the assistance of two Israeli archaeologists, D. Chen and S. Margalit, the excavations were extended (plate 6a). In that year, I was invited by Professor G. Lohfink from the University of Tübingen to present a report on the many preliminary findings.[17] A further, more detailed report about the excavation was published in 1989 in *Zeitschrift des Deutschen Palästina-Vereins*.[18] So far the results could be summarized in the following way:

[17] "Das Essenerquartier in Jerusalem und dessen Einfluss auf die Urkirche", *HlL* 113, nos. 2–3 (1981): 3–14 (at 5–7).

[18] B. PIXNER, D. CHEN and S. MARGALIT, "Mount Zion: The 'Gate of the Essenes' Reexcavated", *ZDPV* 105 (1989): 85–95 and plates 6–16; cf. also the article by B. PIXNER, "The History of the 'Essene Gate' Area", *ZDPV* 105 (1989): 96–104.

1. During the preexilic period, a town wall existed on the southwest hill.[19] The date of this wall was a long-debated question by the archaeology fraternity of Jerusalem, but on October 25, 1988, at a press conference, the results were made public.[20] It was agreed that the wall in question was a section of the wall that King Hezekiah (727–698 B.C.) had built (2 Chron 32:2–5; cf. Neh 3:8 ["the broad wall"]). In 721 B.C. the Assyrian king Sargon II conquered the Israelite northern kingdom (2 Kings 17:5f.), and a considerable proportion of the population fled to the southern kingdom. Among them were many priests and Levites, who were settled by Hezekiah in Jerusalem.[21] Through building the new wall, a part of the western hill got included as a "second [quarter]" (מִשְׁנֶה [*mischneh*]) of the town (2 Kings 22:14). This wall showed many signs of a later destruction by the army of the Babylonian king Nebuchadnezzar in the year 586 B.C. (2 Kings 25:1–10).

2. Some other parts of the town wall date from the Hellenistic period and in particular the period of the Hasmonean kings (150–37 B.C.). This wall went right through the area of our excavation and, according to Bliss, changed direction toward the so-called Tower I" (illus. 46). Here is the evidence that finally refutes the original proposal of the famous English archaeologist K. M. Kenyon that only under King Herod Agrippa I (A.D. 41–44) was Mount Zion included within the town wall.[22] Also untenable is the subsequent[23] opinion of A. D. Tushingham[24] and one of her team workers that the oldest part of the wall at this section, on the southwest hill, dates only from the time of Herod the Great (37 B.C.–A.D. 4).

3. During the Herodian period (37 B.C.–A.D. 70), a gate was added into the Hasmonean wall (plate 6b; illus. 47). Under the road that led to the gate was a big sewage canal. The pottery found under the flank stones of the gate as well as under the big limestone slabs of the canal came originally from Hellenistic-early Herodian times. That the gate

[19] Cf. chapter 16, "The Discovery of Iron Age Walls on Mount Zion" (pp. 220–23).

[20] Cf. A. Rabinovich, "New Jerusalem Archaeological Find Vindicates Maximalists", *Jerusalem Post*, October 26, 1988, international edition, 10.

[21] Cf. M. Broshi, "The Growth of Jerusalem in the Reigns of Hezekiah and Manasseh", *IEJ* 24 (1974): 21–26.

[22] *Jerusalem: Excavating 3000 Years of History* (London: E. Benn, 1967), 155–62.

[23] *Digging Up Jerusalem* (London: E. Benn, 1974), 199–203.

[24] *Excavations in Jerusalem, 1961–1967*, vol. 1 (Toronto: Royal Ontario Museum, 1985), 13–27.

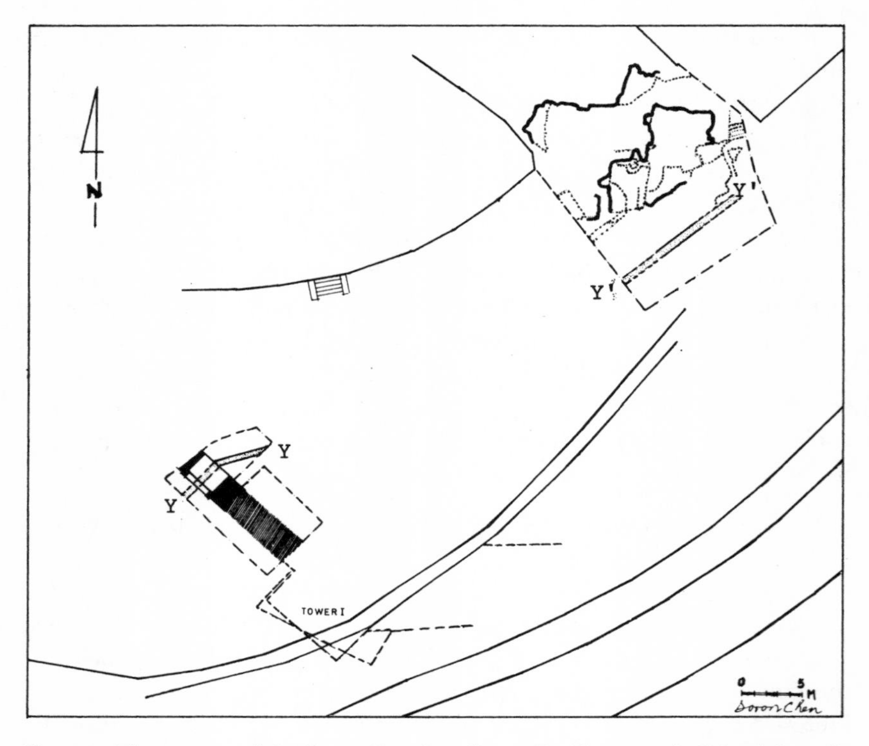

Illus. 46. The area around the Essene Gate (according to D. Chen, 1989). Below left are the gate and the town wall. Above right is a complex of oil presses chiseled into the rock. A sewage channel (Y–Y, Y'–Y') ran through the area.

dates from the pre-Byzantine period is also demonstrated by the different units of measurements used in its construction. The lowest threshold is exactly 9 Roman feet (1 ft. = 0.2957 m) wide. According to Professor B. Mazar, the sewage pipe demonstrates a highly skilled construction typical of workers under Herod the Great.

The gate was built into the preconstructed town wall just as the Essenes settled in Jerusalem. As the Essenes observed very strict purity laws, it would have been appropriate that their district would have its own water supply, with its own gate. Already the distinguished topographer G. Dalman was convinced that the Essenes had their own special access to the town (see below), and this explains why the gate was called the "Gate of the Essenes" by Josephus (*War* 5.145). In A.D 70 this gate, together with the rest of the buildings on Mount Zion (p. 400),

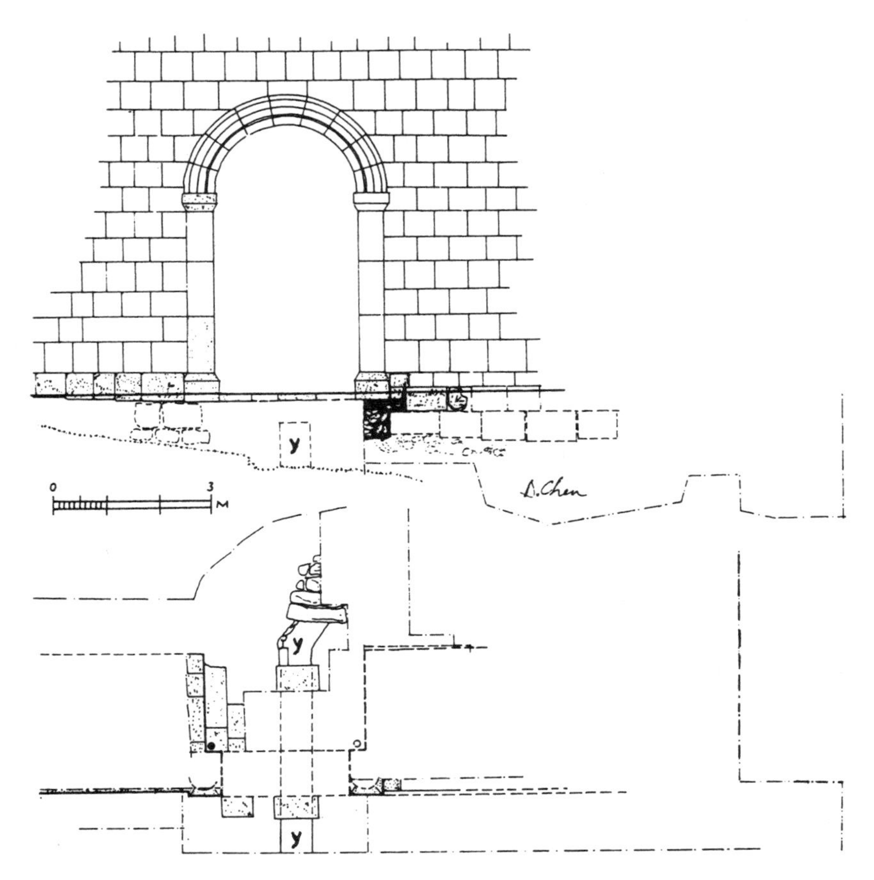

Illus. 47. The Essene Gate—excavation and reconstruction (according to D. Chen, 1989). View from outside the gate. Under the right flank stone, the insertion of the Herodian gate into the Hasmonean wall can be clearly seen.
y Sewage channel

was destroyed by the army of Titus (*War* 6.434). A capital of the Essene Gate discovered during the excavations clearly shows traces of fire.

4. Above the ruins of Herod's gate, there were discovered signs of a primitive passage, built between A.D. 70 and 350. This includes two thresholds, one of which has a dent where the door struck, and this refutes the suggestion of F.J. Bliss[25] that there were two different gates

[25] *Excavations at Jerusalem* (see n. 13), 16.

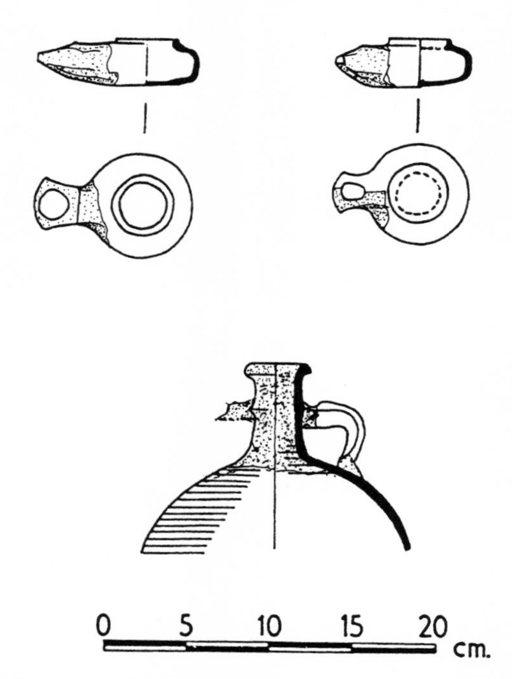

Illus. 48. Pottery discovered by the Essene Gate. Above, Herodian oil lamps; below, a Herodian wine bottle.

in that location. Both of the thresholds are late Roman, from the time of the colony of Aelia Capitolina, and could have belonged to the *murus Sion* of the Pilgrim of Bordeaux.[26] This wall functioned as a ghetto wall (illus. 64), with which the Jewish Christians on the hill of Zion protected their district (pp. 341, 344).

5. In the middle of the fifth century, Empress Eudocia rebuilt the perimeter of the New Testament walls of Jerusalem, as the Pilgrim from Piacenza (570) described.[27] This Byzantine wall was more "cosmetic" than defensive. The new wall was simply placed on the remains of the old one. Also, the gate was renewed by putting 30 cm of mortar on the three earlier thresholds and laying a new one as a new gate, which was slightly moved to the north due to different units of measurement. Also, the road surface had been renewed in certain places.

[26] *Itinerarium* 16 (Geyer, 22; Baldi, 474).
[27] *Itinerarium* 16 (Geyer, 22; Baldi, 469).

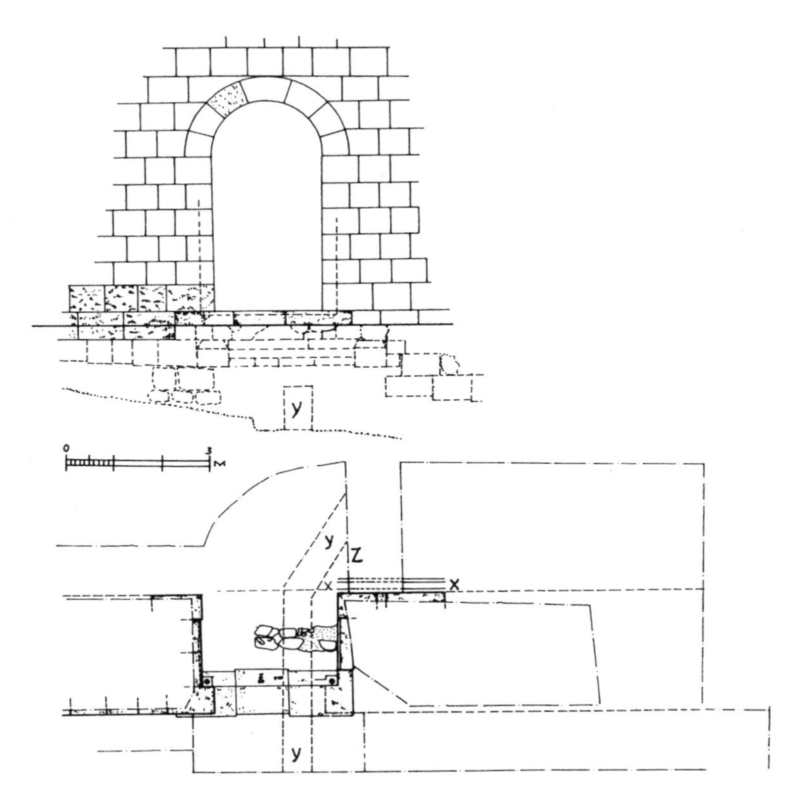

Illus. 49. The Byzantine Gate—excavation and reconstruction (according to D. Chen, 1989). View from outside the gate.
y Herodian sewage channel
x Early Arabian water channel
z Place where Arabic coins were discovered

This explains a Greek cross in a stone pavement that was found by F.J. Bliss.[28] In that period, the gate was used by carts and not just as a pedestrian thoroughfare. In the beginning of the seventh century, the gate was blocked because of the many Arab attacks from Bethlehem, and in the second half of the eighth century it was completely sealed.

Of special interest for our research are also the paths that lead out from the gate. H. Maudslay discovered that the wall of Jerusalem was not directly built on the 6-m-high, artificially created rock slope but stood slightly back so that there was room for a path along the wall in

[28] *Excavations at Jerusalem* (see n. 13), 323f.

the northwest direction.[29] This path led after 40 m to a double bath outside the wall, which is known even today. On the other side of the gate, Bliss found traces of a well-worn path along the town wall that led in a southeast direction to Tower 1, where the path crossed an aqueduct that might have been built by Pilate (p. 270). Bliss assumed with justification that the path from the gate probably crossed the Hinnom Valley like the path today running down from Mount Zion and reaching the road that goes from Jerusalem to Bethlehem.[30] Halfway up the south slope of the Hinnom Valley, a path still exists that continues through the Kidron Valley to the Judean desert and goes to the area of the Essene settlement at Qumran.[31]

G. Dalman believed that it was because of their strict purity laws that the Essenes needed their own access to the Holy City on the southwest hill through the "Gate of the Essenes" mentioned by Josephus (*War* 5.145).[32] To support this view, Dalman points to the Letter of Aristeas, written in 80–63 B.C. in Jerusalem. Besides containing a legendary description of the creation of the Septuagint, the letter provides some valuable insights into the life of Jerusalem during the first half of the first century B.C. It describes the access to the town: "Many staircases lead to the passageways; some people go up, others go down especially if they have a longer way and with consideration for those who follow purity regulations, so that they do not touch anything unlawful" (Pseudo-Aristeas 106).[33] This observation recorded in Aristeas' letter has particular relevance for the Essenes, who believed that they were living in a special state of purity, which they protected and maintained diligently. The text would have confirmed the manner and the high regard in which the Essenes were held and about which Josephus writes (*War* 2.119).

The phenomenon of a particular community settlement giving its name to its principal gate was not unusual. What happened to the "Essene Gate" also occurred to another Jerusalem gate a few centuries later: the Dung Gate. This gate was named in Arabic by the local residents Bab-el-Maghribe (or the "Gate of the Maghrebines"). This

[29] Cf. C. R. Conder, "The Rock Scarp of Zion", *PEFQS* (1875): 81–89 (at 85).

[30] "Third Report" (see n. 13), 13.

[31] A photograph in B. Pixner, "An Essene Quarter on Mount Zion?" (see n. 16), 253.

[32] *Jerusalem und sein Gelände* (Gütersloh: Bertelsmann, 1930), 86f.

[33] P. Riessler, *Altjüdisches Schrifttum ausserhalb der Bibel* (see n. 11), 206. Greek text in A. Pelletier, *La lettre d'Aristéa à Philocrate*, SC 89 (Paris: Cerf, 1962).

gate was named after the Haret el-Maghribe (illus. 70), the district of those Arabs whose ancestors emigrated from North Africa as followers of Abd el-Kadar and settled in the area behind the Dung Gate.[34] Later the Maghrebine community moved to other parts of the town in order to give easier access to the western wall of the temple square (the "Wailing Wall"). The "Maghrebine Gate" is no longer a recognized name.

2. Ritual Baths by the Essene Gate

Further archaeological evidence confirms that the lowest Herodian gate was called the Essene Gate because of the Essene settlement behind it. Not far from the Essene Gate, to the northwest, outside of the old town wall, two ritual baths have been located (plate 7a). C. R. Conder confirmed that the baths originate from the first Roman period (63 B.C.–A.D. 70).[35] It is clear that the users of the gate used the baths in order to fulfill the regulations from Deuteronomy 23:10f.: "If there is among you a man who is not clean by reason of a nocturnal emission, then he shall go outside the camp [מַחֲנֶה (*machaneh*)], he shall not come within the camp; but when evening comes on, he shall bathe himself in water, and when the sun is down, he may come within the camp." As the diligent interpretation of these laws for the Essene residents of the Holy City was required and is stated through the publication of the Temple Scroll (11QTemple 50:15; 51:3), the significance and importance of these baths outside the town wall are clear. The Essenes called their settlements in the desert area and in the towns *machanoth*, which means "war camps" (CD 10:21, 23; 12:10, 20). The *machaneh* at Qumran had a ritual bath (Locus 138) outside this settlement with steps to go in and steps to go out.[36] The "impure" went down the steps and through the bath and out by the opposite steps. Where it was not physically possible to have double steps, one step had a raised middle

[34] Cf. B. MEISTERMANN, *New Guide to the Holy Land* (London, 1923), 213. A further example of a gate that was named after a locality inside the walls is David's Gate, today called the Jaffa Gate, which got its name from the "Tower of David" from the Arab period (Bab Michrab Dawud). The name "David's Gate" was first used by the Pilgrim of Piacenza, *Itinerarium* 21 (Baldi, 484). Cf. Y. TSAFRIR, "Muqadasi's Gates of Jerusalem", *IEJ* 27 (1977): 152–61.

[35] "Rock Scarp of Zion" (see n. 29), 86; cf. also R. REICH, "*Mishna Sheqalim* 8:3 and the Archaeological Evidence" [in Modern Hebrew], in A. OPPENHEIMER, U. RAPPAPORT and M. STERN, *Jerusalem in the Second Temple Period: Abraham Schalit Memorial Volume* (Jerusalem: Magnes Press, 1980), 225–56 (at 238–40).

[36] Cf. R. DE VAUX, *Archaeology and the Dead Sea Scrolls* (see n. 5), 9 and plate 39.

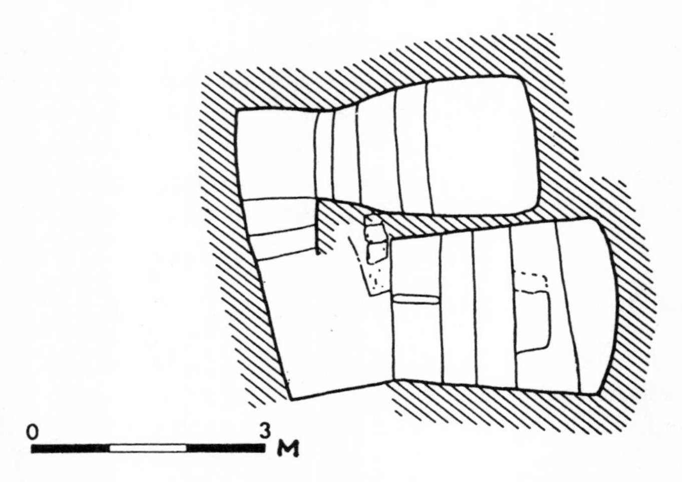

Illus. 50. Double ritual baths outside the town wall (according to R. Reich). The raised divider separating the steps for entering and exiting is on the highest step on the lower bath.

divider to provide for a separation (illus. 50). The Essene community used both methods.

The particular function of the separated steps becomes clear from a papyrus fragment from Oxyrhynchus in Egypt (POxy 840 Z. 7–30). The well-known theologian J. Jeremias considered that the following event was historical:[37]

> And he [Jesus] took them [the disciples] with him to the purity area and walked around the temple square. They met with a senior Pharisee priest by the name of Levi [?], who spoke with them and asked Jesus, "How is it that you enter this area of ritual purity and visit these holy sights without getting cleaned yourself first and even without your disciples washing your feet? How much more have you dirtied this temple square, this pure place, even though nobody who did not bathe beforehand and change his clothes would enter it or dare even to look at this sight." Straightaway Jesus stood still with his disciples and answered, "You are also here on the temple square; are you clean?" He said to him, "I am pure, because I bathed in David's pond and have walked down the steps and up the others, and have put on pure white clothes, and then I came here in order to look upon this holy sight."[38]

[37] *Unbekannte Jesusworte*, 3rd ed. (Gütersloh: Gütersloher Verlagshaus, 1963), 50–60.
[38] Hennecke-Schneemelcher, 1:82.

This passage seems to explain the double stairs, one set to walk down and the other to walk up from the bath. For this reason, only the highest steps have a raised area separating the steps, while the water covered the lower steps and so did not require this. This was the case of both of the baths outside the wall and also of those that were excavated by B. Mazar opposite Robinson's arch on the western side of the temple area.[39] In later development of the Christian baptismal baths, two separate sets of stairs are provided on either side of the pool. In early Christianity it was traditional that the people who were baptized put white clothes on after leaving the pool,[40] as the Essenes used to do after a submerged bath and before their community meals (*War* 2.129).

There was a very important regulation, known from the Qumran literature,[41] that only members of the community, and certainly no non-Jew, were allowed to touch the bath of the Essenes (1QS 5:13ff.; cf. 1QS 6:16f.; CD 10:10–13). The strict purity requirements can be seen in the facts that Josephus provides regarding the Essene novitiate (*War* 2.137–42). The applicant had to live for a year outside the community before he was admitted to the ritual bath, and only after two more years did he become a full member. It is for this reason that I have been unsure for a long time as to where the users of the baths would get the necessary "living water" (i.e., flowing water) that was required for such washing. Subsequent research has provided an answer. In investigating the area, I discovered that the channel leading to the rock-hewn groove led to a Roman cistern. This cistern was about 50 m northwest from there in the bedrock of the Gobat School, which gets its name from a well-known English-Prussian bishop from Jerusalem and where today the American Institute of Holy Land Studies is situated.

This was an important discovery. These cisterns were originally filled with rainwater that came from the roofs of the houses that must have stood where the "Greek Garden" is located today. When we consider how scrupulously the ritual regulations were adhered to by the Essenes, there can be no doubt that the building that housed the ritual

[39] *Excavations in the Old City of Jerusalem near the Temple Mount* (Jerusalem: Israel Exploration Society, 1971), 25.

[40] Cf. J. Daniélou, *Théologie du judéo-christianisme* (Paris: Desclée, 1958), 379f. About the old Christian baptismal fonts, cf. D. Gelsi, "'Date alla chiesa un volto pasquale' (kyrillionas): Alcune considerazioni sui battisteri paleocristiani", *Rivista liturgica* 71 (1984): 571–90.

[41] Cf. E. Lohse, *Die Texte aus Qumran* (Munich: Kösel, 1971), 284, n. 51.

bath water also must have been under some sort of control. That means that the people who gave the name to the gate must also have had a settlement in the area behind the baths. This supports the presence at that time of an Essene settlement in the southwest corner of the walls of Jerusalem.

This conclusion is supported by further evidence. Within the area of the Greek Garden, which must have originally been within the walled area, more ritual baths have been discovered. Where there was no "living water" naturally occurring, such as at Qumran or on Mount Zion, then some had to be created, according to particular halakha regulations. We must search for some comparative regulations in Pharisaic Judaism.[42] As ladled water was not really kosher, it was—according to the regulations of the Mishna—led through a higher "seed reservoir" (אֹצַר זַרְעָא ['*ozar sarᶜa'*]), which contained at least 40 seah (ca. 6,000 L or 1,500 gal.) of unladled rainwater (*Mikwa'oth* 1:7; 3:1f.; 4:4). This method could be repeated as often as renewed water was needed for the ritual bath (מִקְוֶא [*mikveh*]), although the Essene purity baths did not have to follow in every detail the regulations of halakha of the Pharisees, who are described in the Qumran documents as "researchers of smooth things" (4QpNah 1:7). The Essene regulations emphasize that if there is no flowing water, a bath had to be furnished (1QS 3:4, 10; cf. 1QS 4:21). The Damascus Document mentions using a pool in the rock (גֶּבֶע בַּסֶּלַע) as a bath (CD 10:12), and in this respect the installations hewn from rock on the southwest hill of Jerusalem were made even more perfect than the ones made from bricks at Qumran.

So far there have been no systematic excavations in the Greek Garden, but the preliminary excavations made eighty years ago[43] were left exposed until only a few years ago, when the trenches were filled with rubbish. I have been able to investigate them further together with Israeli experts and found three separate indications that a ritual bath installation existed in that area. We discovered (1) a large water cistern, (2) a small seed reservoir and (3) the actual rock out of which the *mikveh* bath had been cut.[44] In the area of the Dormition Abbey,

[42] Cf. E. Kotlar, "Mikva'ot", in *EncJud*, 11:1534–44 (at 1537f.); R. Reich, "Les bains rituels juifs", *MB* 60 (1989): 20–33.

[43] Cf. F.M. Abel, "Petites découvertes au Quartier du Cénacle à Jérusalem", *RB* 8 (1911): 119–25.

[44] Cf. B. Pixner, "Essene Quarter?" (see n. 16), 271–74.

excavations had already been undertaken at the beginning of the twentieth century, and during the excavations in 1983 more ritual baths were uncovered (pp. 399–400). While these baths were small and seemed to have been more suitable for private purposes, the others were obviously community facilities. A similar bath was discovered in our excavations in 1984 of the Nikritia houses. Here we found a ritual bath that in the Byzantine period had been transformed into a cistern.[45] It had been covered by a rock, and the Herodian and Byzantine plaster was very easily distinguishable.

The buildings that were excavated in front of the Dormition Abbey and on the grounds of the Nikritia houses date from the Herodian period and display simple building styles, similar to those that might be expected in a monastic settlement. The houses, which were excavated north of the area of the abbey by M. Broshi, were more "high quality" (pp. 255–257) and were obviously outside the Essene district. Further archaeological investigation would surely reveal more interesting finds, but we are already in a position to declare that the available topographical and archaeological evidence make it very likely that an Essene settlement on the southwest hill of Jerusalem existed.

3. Bethso

In addition to the above, there is the linguistic issue of *Bethso*, although this is probably a triviality. The Βηθσώ mentioned by Josephus (*War* 5.145) is considered by the best authorities—among them J. Schwartz,[46] G. Dalman[47] and Y. Yadin[48]—as nothing more than a toilet installation, and this would include the toilets of the Essene quarter of Jerusalem. Etymologically, *Bethso* is derived from *bejt* (בֵּית), "house", and *zo'a* (צוֹאָ), "excrement". According to Josephus (p. 201), the *Bethso* existed somewhere along the western wall and not far from the Essene Gate near the double ritual bath on the outside of the town wall. The Essenes from Jerusalem would have been keen on observing a regulation from Deuteronomy that calls for the installation of a toilet area

[45] Cf. B. Pixner and S. Margalit, "Mt Zion", *ESI* 4 (1985): 56f.

[46] *Crops of the Holy Land* (Jerusalem: Luntz, 1900), 335.

[47] *Jerusalem und sein Gelände* (see n. 32), 86.

[48] "The Gate of the Essenes and the Temple Scroll", in *Jerusalem Revealed* (Jerusalem: Israel Exploration Society, 1976), 90f. Published earlier in Modern Hebrew in *Qadmoniot* 5, nos. 3–4 (1972): 129f.

outside the camp (Deut 23:12–15). The Essenes could use a hoe that was given to newcomers to the community at the beginning and that was given to be used in designated areas at Qumran, as Josephus tells us (cf. Deut 23:13; *War* 2.147). The reason for giving members a hoe was not only to comply with particular community regulations or simply for hygienic purposes but because members of the community looked upon the settlement as a "war camp [*machaneh*] of God" (see above). Because of the belief that the presence of the Almighty was in their midst, they had to keep the camp pure: "Because the LORD your God walks in the midst of your camp [בְּקֶרֶב מַחֲנֶךָ], to save you and to give up your enemies before you, therefore your camp must be holy, that he may not see anything indecent among you, and turn away from you" (Deut 23:14). A further reason for the strict purity regulations is recorded in the War Scroll: "That the angels of the Holy One will be united with them" (1QM 7:6).

The Temple Scroll provides further regulations for Jerusalem, that near the Holy City the lavatories should be covered with a roof. It goes even further and states that the Essenes were required to go outside the town for the toilet and walk in the northwest direction. The relevant text (11QTemple 46:13–15) says: "And you shall make toilets outside the town, namely, little houses [בתים (*batim*)], with roofs with a trench in which the excrement [צואה (*zo'a*)] can fall, so that it is not visible for an area of 3,000 yards [about 1.5 km] around the town. That is where they should go, outside in the northwest direction of the town."[49] This thesis that the text of the Temple Scroll is to be connected to the Essene Gate was suggested by Y. Yadin, the editor of the Qumran document (n. 48). The only two manuscripts of the Temple Scroll (apart from the large scroll, only a fragment) come from the time of Herod the Great, and this would support this hypothesis. The dating of the composition of the Temple Scroll is controversial, but some think it is also from the Herodian period. The question is as follows: Does the Temple Scroll regulation refer to a topographical issue in Jerusalem, or were the Essene toilet installations designed only to comply with the Qumran halakha? Could the relevant ritual texts perhaps be a later addition?

[49] For the justification of this interpretation according to Y. YADIN, see *The Temple Scroll*, vol. 1, *Introduction* (Jerusalem: Israel Exploration Society, 1983), 302–4; vol. 2, *Text and Commentary* (Jerusalem: Israel Exploration Society, 1983), 199f., digression, cf. B. PIXNER, "Essene Quarter?" (see n. 16), 256f.

Interestingly, the topographical location of the Essene Gate is such that whoever left the town in the direction of the place mentioned by Josephus and called *Bethso* along the town wall had to go in a northwest direction (illus. 43). It is remarkable that this place was the perfect area to comply with the religious requirements because it was the farthest away from the temple area and was also not visible, as the area was on the slope of the southwest of Zion's hill. In 1923 H. Clementz, in his translation of the *Jewish War*, indicated on a map that the *Bethso* lay in the area of the Bishop Gobat School,[50] and this was supported by G. Dalman.[51] C.R. Conder, in his report of the excavations during the building of the Gobat School, described a "buttress of rock, fifteen feet high and about five feet square. At its foot is a niche in the rock."[52] These topographical descriptions (illus. 44) coincide with the remarks of Josephus and the requirements stated in the Temple Scroll. A *Bethso* is possible, at least here.

However, some researchers continue to insist that the Qumran inhabitants were a group sui generis without any relation to other Jewish religious parties, but this hypothesis is not supported by the evidence. The text of the Temple Scroll regarding the toilet installation in the Holy City is interesting for Qumran researchers because the Qumran text and the statements by Josephus about the Essenes can be connected, thus providing a strong argument that the Qumran inhabitants were indeed the Essenes.

4. *The First Three Columns of the Copper Scroll*

There is yet another Qumran document that is particularly interesting in relation to an Essene settlement on the hill of Zion: the so-called Copper Scroll (3Q15). As I previously stated, this scroll consists of two rolls made from copper sheet and was discovered in the year 1953 by a team of archaeologists in one of the many caves in the Qumran area. Along with this scroll, other script fragments were discovered from the Qumran library. The rolls contained a list of sixty-four descriptions of places where treasure was apparently hidden. The list of sites is interesting for information on the topography of the Holy Land. I believe that the text carved into the copper

[50] *Geschichte des Jüdischen Krieges* (Cologne, [1900]), after 695.
[51] *Jerusalem und sein Gelände* (see n. 32); see map within.
[52] "Rock Scarp of Zion" (see n. 29), 84.

functioned as an aide-mémoire for a few select people. The treasures were definitely not, as J. T. Milik[53] believed, merely a legendary fantasy; rather, the descriptions are of hiding places for real treasure that had to be made secure during the war with Rome (66–70 B.C.). This position I have justified in a separate special study.[54]

To summarize my hypothesis: I believe that the list of "hiding places" include the main centers of Essene settlement, which were divided as follows: (1) the settlement on the southwest hill of Jerusalem (illus. 40); (2) the desert around Wadi Qumran, which then had the name of Secacah (cf. Josh 15:61) (illus. 39); (3) the region of Damascus and the slopes north and south of the Jarmuk River (illus. 41); (4) an area of graves in the Kidron Valley just east of the temple; and also (5) a few sporadic places at Garizim by Beth Shean (pp. 78–79) and in the Golan.

If I am not mistaken, the first three columns of the Copper Scroll point to an Essene settlement in the southwest area of Jerusalem. One part of the scroll describes a building on a hill called *kochlit* (כוחלית), where apparently a high priestly piece of clothing and a vessel for tithing have been found (3Q15 1:9–12). Nearby was a rock with a submerged bath cut into it (3Q15 1:12), and a bit further away a silo for salt (3Q15 2:1f.). The importance of this was emphasized in the Temple Scroll (11QTemple 20:13f.). There was also a place called "Manos" (מנש [3Q15 1:13–15]), probably referring to an emergency exit. Under the town wall a large cistern was situated, and next to this there was a projection in which were hidden silver bars (3Q15 2:10–12). This description fits amazingly well with the ground around the double bath outside the town wall (pp. 209–10).[55] On the grounds of the former Nikritia houses, there is a partly exposed staircase[56] that could be connected with the Jerusalem Essene settlement's East Gate, mentioned in the Copper Scroll (3Q15 2:7f.). The jars mentioned in the Copper Scroll that held the priest's tithe (3Q15 1:12; 3:1—4:8–10) point to the fact that the community included priests who exercised

[53] "Le rouleau de cuivre provenant de la grotte 3Q (3Q15)", in M. Baillet, J. T. Milik and R. de Vaux, *Les "petites grottes" de Qumrân*, DJD 3 (Oxford: Clarendon, 1962), 198–302.

[54] "Unravelling the Copper Scroll Code: A Study on the Topography of 3Q15", *RQ* 11 (1983): 323–65. Cf. also chapter 12, "The Copper Scroll of Qumran" (pp. 159–68).

[55] Cf. B. Pixner, "Unravelling the Copper Scroll Code", 344, 346.

[56] Unfortunately, the steps could not be followed further because they continued into the Jewish restaurant Schulchan David. The question as to whether these were the steps that led to the entrance of the Essene *machaneh* remains open, and the above suggestion can at best be a hypothetical solution.

an important role, and this of course was a particular characteristic of the Essene community. However, because of the difficulties with the Copper Scroll, it is probably sensible to exercise caution in any particular interpretation of the scroll and to await further investigation.

V. Summary

To summarize the most important arguments: The most definite clue we possess for identifying an Essene settlement in Jerusalem is Josephus' mention of the "Gate of the Essenes" (*War* 5.145). The situation of the *Bethso* described by Josephus and in the Temple Scroll (11QTemple 46:13–15) is of great help. The ritual baths, which are only 40 m away from the gate outside the wall and were fed through a channel with kosher water, are by my estimation the best clue for the more exact location. The Essenes gathered water from the roofs of their own houses in order to guard the ritual purity of their installation. Other literary and archaeological evidence are a bonus and support the theory for an Essene *machaneh* on the hill of Zion.

Supplement: Archaeological additions to the question of the Essene quarter can be found on page 368 and also on pages 370–74. The location for the Essene Gate, mentioned by Flavius Josephus (*War* 5.145), by the Protestant cemetery has been included in a recent work of the archaeology of the Holy Land (H. Geva, in E. Stern, *The New Encyclopedia of Archaeological Excavations in the Holy Land* [New York: Schuster, 1993], 2:718–28). Given the consensus of opinion by the various experts, it is inexplicable that G.J. Wightman in 1993 could still ignore the most recent excavations and date the gate from the Byzantine period (*The Walls of Jerusalem from the Canaanites to the Mamluks* [Sydney, 1993], 145). In October 1996 there were excavations in the area of the Greek Garden, under the direction of Professor James F. Strange (University of South Florida), who prior to this has worked in Sepphoris. More detailed recent publications about the Essene quarter are as follows: R. Riesner, "Jesus, the Primitive Community, and the Essene Quarter of Jerusalem", in J.H. Charlesworth, *Jesus and the Dead Sea Scrolls* (New York: Doubleday, 1993), 198–234; R. Riesner, *Essener und Urgemeinde in Jerusalem*, SBAZ 6 (Gießen: Brunnen, 1998); and B. Pixner, "Mount Zion, Jesus and Archaeology", in J.H. Charlesworth, *Jesus and Archaeology* (Grand Rapids: Eerdmans, 2006), 309–22.

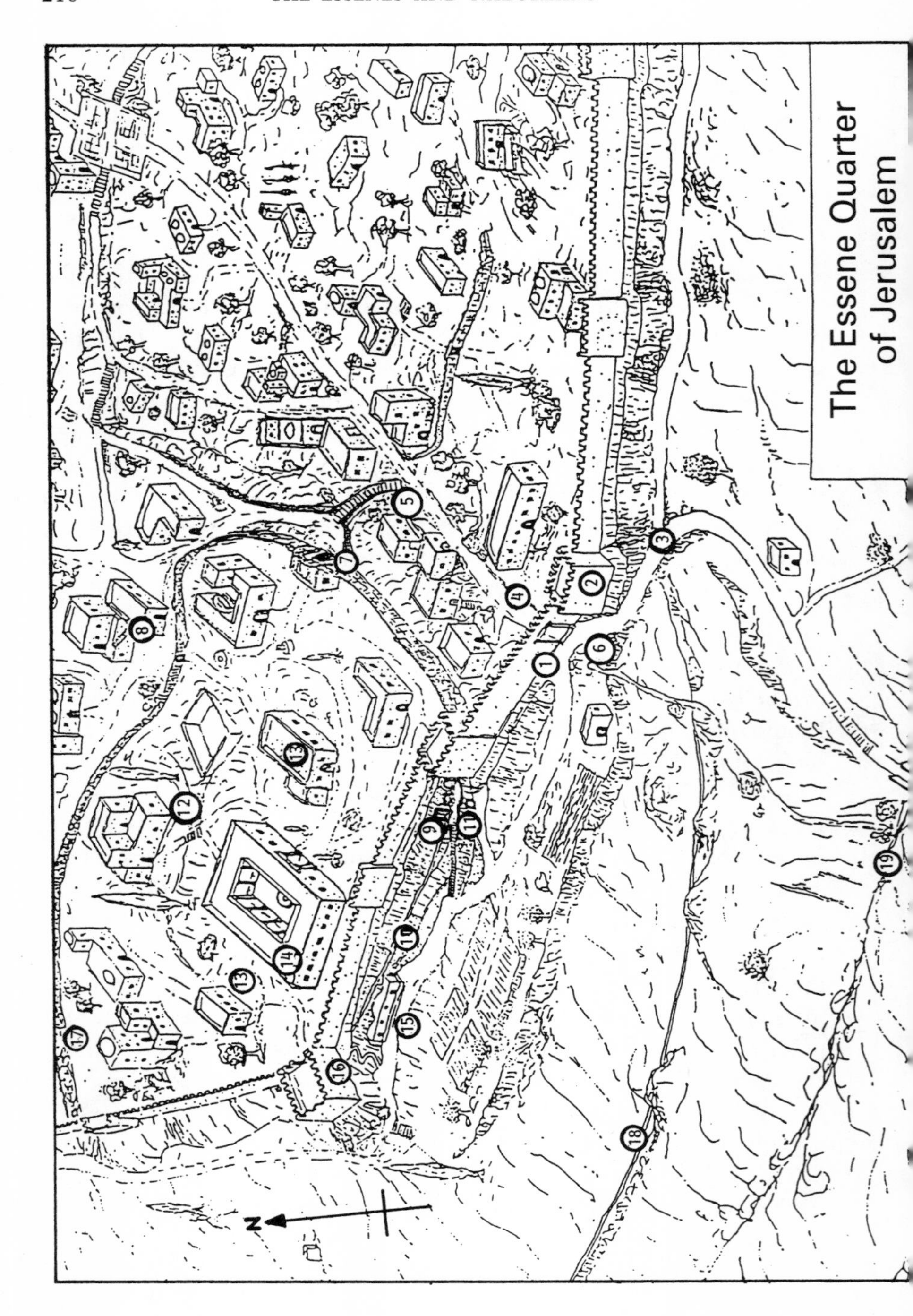
The Essene Quarter
of Jerusalem
N

Illus. 51. The Essene quarter—reconstruction.

1 *Gate of the Essenes (Josephus; archaeology)*
2 *Southwest tower of the town wall*
3 *Path through Gehinnom to Bethlehem, and path along the south wall*
4 *Road from the Essene Gate to the town center (archaeology)*
5 *Oil press and steps (archaeology), which led to the East Gate (Copper Scroll) of the monastic part of the Essene quarter*
6 *Sewage canal, which followed the road (4) and then emptied into the Hinnom River (archaeology)*
7 *Entrance gate to the Essene monastery area (Copper Scroll)*
8 *Guesthouse (*katalyma *[Mk 14:14]) with Upper Room of the Last Supper*
9 *Ritual baths (archaeology) outside the town wall (cf. Deut 23:10) with an emergency door (*Manos*) (Copper Scroll)*
10 *Water pipe to (9) and (11) (archaeology)*
11 *Irrigation cistern under the town wall (Copper Scroll; archaeology)*
12 *Tel Kochlit (Copper Scroll)*
13 *Two ritual baths inside the monastery grounds (Copper Scroll; archaeology)*
14 *Peristyle with large cistern (?) (Copper Scroll)*
15 Bethso *(Essene lavatories) (Josephus; Temple Scroll)*
16 *War tower (Milcham?) (Copper Scroll)*
17 *Wall around the monastery grounds, behind which was the garden area of Herod's palace*
18 *Aqueduct (Pontius Pilate?) to the temple square (archaeology)*
19 *Hinnom Valley (Gehenna)*

16. The Discovery of Iron Age Walls on Mount Zion

I. The Controversy about the Extent of the Walls of Jerusalem

In the year 1977, after the necessary permission had been obtained, I began an excavation on the southeastern slope of Mount Zion in the area of the old Protestant cemetery. This excavation demonstrated three different time periods for the gate belonging to the old town wall, as was evident by three gate thresholds lying on top of each other. The lowest threshold belonged to the Essene Gate (*War* 5.145), destroyed in A.D. 70; the middle was a simple construction from the time of the Roman colony Aelia Capitolina (A.D. 135–325); the third, top threshold belonged to the Byzantine wall from the fifth century.[1] Since 1979 I have been helped by two Israeli archaeologists, Doron Chen and Shlomo Margalit. With the extension of our excavations, we discovered further remains of older town walls (p. 203). These, we hope, will shed new light on the fortification of the city in earlier times.

For many years there has been a lively discussion among the researchers about the location of the preexilic walls. Many believe that the expansion of the City of David (2 Sam 5:9) was very limited and initially included only the hill south of the temple, the original Mount Zion. By building the temple, King Solomon extended the city northward to today's Temple Mount (cf. 1 Kings 9:15; 11:27). But where did the wall lead that encircled the extended city of Jerusalem following the destruction of the kingdom in the north (722–721 B.C.)

[1] Cf. B. Pixner, D. Chen and S. Margalit, "Mount Zion: The 'Gate of the Essenes' Reexcavated", *ZDPV* 105 (1989): 85–95 and plates 6–16, as well as in this book, chapter 15, "The Essene Quarter in Jerusalem" (pp. 192–219, esp. pp. 203–7).

and for which King Hezekiah and his successors were responsible (2 Chron 32:5)? Those who preferred a limited expansion, especially Lady K. M. Kenyon,[2] believed that the expansion of this wall had been hardly larger than that of Solomon. Those who prefer a greater expansion believe that the west hill of Jerusalem, today's Mount Zion, was within the preexilic wall. N. Avigad, in the 1970s, during his excavations of the so-called Broad Wall (cf. Neh 3:8) in the Jewish quarter (illus. 73), found a remaining part of this wall.[3] H. Geva believed that he had also discovered elements of the wall in his excavation in the Citadel.[4]

II. The Iron Age Walls

The evidence provided by the excavation at the southeast corner of Mount Zion led us to believe that we had found the proof for which those who held to a larger expansion were hoping. We discovered the "missing link", the missing part of the wall, which proved the greater expansion and the site of the long-looked-for preexilic wall.[5] During the expansion of our excavation of the Herodian-Byzantine wall (illus. 52a), we tried to extend the excavation outside (*extra muros*) to the natural rock. We found this approximately 2 m below the level of the Essene Gate. During the excavations, which were led by Doron Chen, assisted by David Milson, elements of an Iron Age wall came to light,[6] and later still, a building from the same period (illus. 52c).

In the northwest corner of the city tower (Tower I) were opened up the remains of a wall that stood over 1.5 m high. The foundations formed a perpendicular rock cliff 1.80 m high, above which the wall had been built (plate 9a). We assumed that this wall, constructed from rock from the field, would represent the exterior of an old town wall. This caused us to search for the inside of this presumed wall. When we examined north of it, the layers under the Byzantine wall, we actually found several rows of a wall, built on the rocky ground, which must have formed

[2] *Jerusalem: Excavating 3000 Years of History* (London: E. Benn, 1967), 155–62; *Digging Up Jerusalem* (London: E. Benn, 1974), 199–203.

[3] *Discovering Jerusalem* (Nashville: Thomas Nelson, 1983), 31–60.

[4] "Excavations in the Citadel of Jerusalem, 1979–1980", *IEJ* 33 (1983): 55–67 (at 56–58).

[5] Cf. A. Rabinovich, "New Jerusalem Archaeological Find Vindicates Maximalists", *Jerusalem Post*, October 26, 1988, international edition, 10.

[6] Cf. D. Chen, S. Margalit and B. Pixner, "Mount Zion: Discovery of the Iron Age Fortifications", in H. Geva, *Ancient Jerusalem Revealed* (Jerusalem: Israel Exploration Society, 1994), 76–81.

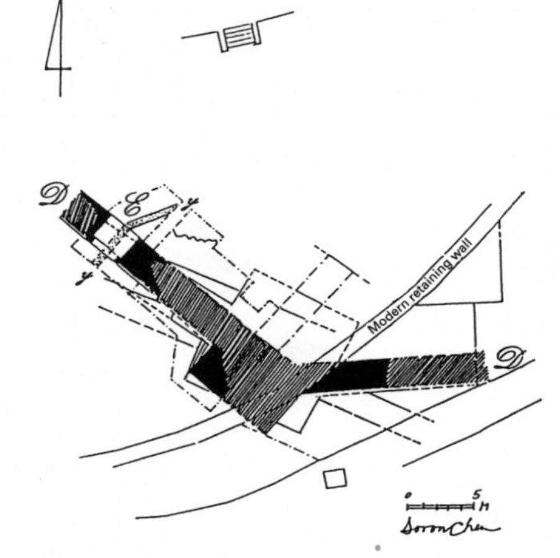

a. Herodian-Byzantine wall (ca. 37 B.C.–A.D. 450).

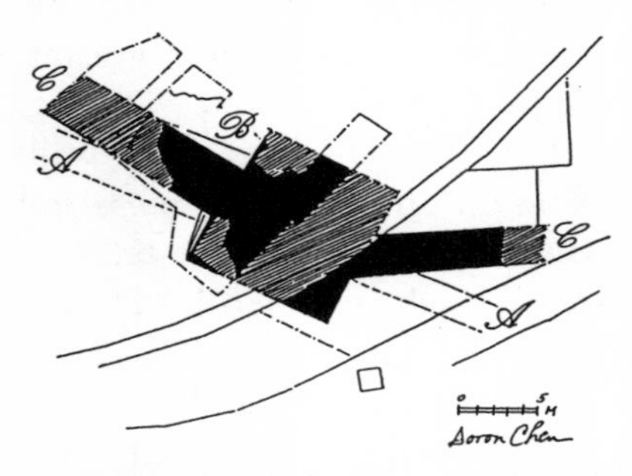

b. Pre-Herodian wall remains (Nehemiah, around 450 B.C.? Hasmonean/Antipater, first century B.C.).

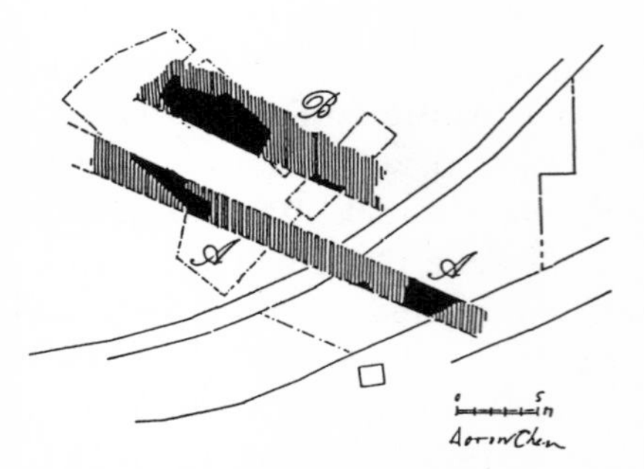

c. Iron Age walls (Hezekiah, eighth century B.C.?).

Illus. 52. The town walls with the Essene Gate (Mount Zion—Protestant cemetery).

A *Iron Age wall*
B *Platform of an Iron Age building*
C *Nehemian (?) Hasmonean wall*
D *Herodian-Byzantine wall*
E *Town gate from three periods (Herodian, late Roman, Byzantine)*
Y *Sewer*

the inside of the old wall. Its total width (A–A) might have amounted to approximately 2.40 m. The stones, which had served for the filling between interior and exterior walls, were removed by later work.

When we expanded the excavation across today's cemetery wall, we found a further section of the same old wall beside the modern road. The length of the whole wall section amounts to nearly 20 m. When the later walls at this southeast corner of Jerusalem were established, a tower was built in the corner, while the oldest wall ran without interruption in a southeast direction. In order to identify the period of this wall, we saved pieces of pottery and of broken glass that had been inserted into the old wall and passed them on to Mrs. Eilat Mazar, an expert in dating pottery. She concluded that all the pieces were typical of Iron Age pottery and dated from the beginning of the eighth to the sixth century B.C.

Parallel to this wall (A–A), at a distance of approximately 3 m, we found three rows of large stones (B), which were the remains of an Iron Age building. Since the majority of building B was still covered by debris, we could not determine at that stage whether it was part of a town wall or another building. The pottery that was found in this structure came from the same period as wall A–A. The Iron Age fortifications, which were excavated by us on Mount Zion, offer the clearest indications that before the Babylonian exile (586 B.C.) the city of Jerusalem had already expanded to include the whole west hill up to the slope of the Hinnom Valley. However, the archaeological evidence is insufficient to determine precisely which of the Davidic kings was responsible for the building of this wall.

III. A Puzzling Wall

In the area between wall A–A and building B, we found a plaster floor with mortar. The expansion of this plaster could not be further examined because the whole space is filled by another large wall (C–C) (illus. 52b). This was temporarily dated to the Hasmonean period, but I believe that the wall might represent remnants of the wall of Nehemiah, who as Persian governor built it with unskilled local labor in the second half of the fifth century B.C. (Neh 1:11—7:4). It is possible that the mortar and plaster of wall C–C represents a renovation attempt by Antipater, the father of Herod the Great (*Ant.* 14.156), following the conquest of Jerusalem by Pompey in 63 B.C. Although one cannot be absolutely sure, I agree with E. M. Laperrousaz[7] that Nehemiah's wall (Neh 3:1–32) followed the same line as the preexilic wall. Here also, however, further excavations and investigations are required.

[7] "Quelques remarques sur le tracé de l'enceinte de la ville et du Temple de Jérusalem à l'époque Perse", *Syria* 47 (1990): 609–31.

PART FOUR

The Messiah in Jerusalem

17. Bethany by Jerusalem—an Essene Settlement?

I. Bethany and the Temple Scroll

In 1983 Y. Yadin published *The Temple Scroll* (11QTemple), following an adventurous discovery in Bethlehem of the hiding place of this valuable leather scroll. Yadin demonstrated that this was by far the longest scroll from the eleventh cave (the site of the scroll's discovery) located near the Essene monastery of Qumran. The Temple Scroll was regarded by the Essene community as an added "Torah", alongside the five books of Moses. In this document, God himself is the speaker, and he presents many regulations regarding the building and the purity of the temple. In the forty-sixth column of the document, it says: "You shall make three places, to the East of the city, separate from each other, to which shall come the lepers, and those afflicted with a discharge and the men who have had an emission of semen.... And the city which I will sanctify to make dwell my name and [my] temp[le within it] shall be holy and shall be clean from any case of whatever impurity with which they could be defiled" (11QTemple 46:16—47:5).[1]

Y. Yadin, in the first edition of *The Temple Scroll*, was of the opinion that the village of Bethany was one of three places east of Jerusalem that the Essenes allocated for people who, because of ritual impurity, could not enter the Holy City and the temple.[2] Later, Yadin wrote:

> This may shed significant light on the celebrated New Testament account of Jesus, on his way to Jerusalem "two days before the Passover", stopping off at Bethany: "And while he was at Bethany in

[1] Translation and text construction according to F. García Martinez and E. J. C. Tigchelaar, *The Dead Sea Scrolls: Study Edition* (Leiden: Brill, 1998), 2:1265.

[2] *The Temple Scroll*, vol. 1, *Introduction* (Jerusalem: Israel Exploration Society, 1983), 305.

> the house of Simon the leper, as he sat at table ..." (Mark 14:3). Bethany is situated at the eastern edge of Jerusalem, on the eastern slopes of the Mount of Olives, and would fit the requirements of an isolation centre for the sufferers of leprosy. If my suggestion is correct, this would prove that Jesus had not happened by chance to find himself in the house of a leper, but had deliberately chosen to spend the night before entering Jerusalem in this leper colony, which was anathema both to the Essenes and the Pharisees.[3]

We know from the Jewish authors Philo[4] and Flavius Josephus (*War* 2.24) that there were Essenes living in most of the villages and towns of the area (pp. 195–96). But Bethany would have had a special meaning for them through "Simon the leper", as there the meal during which Mary from Bethany anointed the feet of Jesus took place (Mt 26:6 / Mk 14:3). What is considered as "pestilence" in the Bible is not necessary leprosy (Hansen's disease) but could be another disease of the skin, perhaps a skin eruption that prevented those affected from accessing the temple. P. Lapide was of a different opinion and suggested that the surname of Simon was a mistranslation from the Hebrew.[5] "Simon the Religious/Essene" (שִׁמְעוֹן הַצָּנוּעַ [*schim*ᶜ*on ha-zanu*ᶜ*a*])—whom Lapide also found mentioned in the Tosephta (*Kelim* 1:6)—which had changed to "Simon the leper" (שִׁמְעוֹן הַצָּרוּעַ [*schim*ᶜ*on ha-zaru*ᶜ*a*]).

II. *Jesus' Friends in Bethany*

Apart from Simon the leper, we know that there were other inhabitants in Bethany whose style of living at that time would have been considered as peculiar. This is true of the brother and sisters Lazarus, Mary and Martha, who were living together unmarried. This was unusual for a Jewish household then because Pharisaic and Rabbinic Judaism considered that their primary responsibility was to "be fruitful and multiply, and fill the earth" (Gen 1:28). However, the Essenes had in this respect a different view.[6] For them, celibacy was held as a virtue, which is what it later became in parts of Christianity. Jesus,

[3] Y. Yadin, *The Temple Scroll: The Hidden Law of the Dead Sea Sect* (New York: Random House, 1985), 177.

[4] *Apologia pro Judaeis* 1 (by Eusebius, *Praeparatio Evangelica* 8.6).

[5] "Hidden Hebrew in the Gospel", *Immanuel* 2 (1973): 28–34 (at 32f.).

[6] Cf. chapter 2, "Mary in the House of David" (pp. 23–37, esp. p. 25).

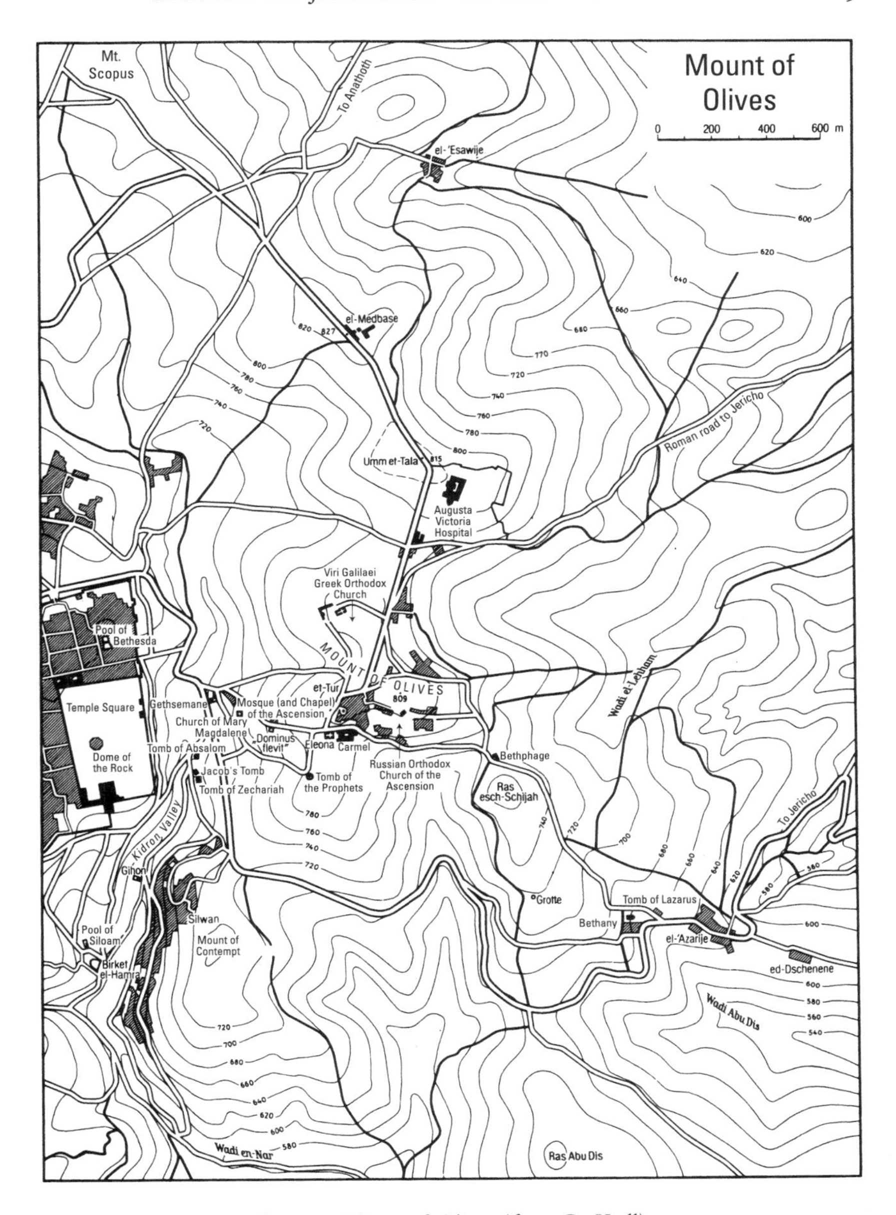

Illus. 53. Mount of Olives (from G. Kroll).

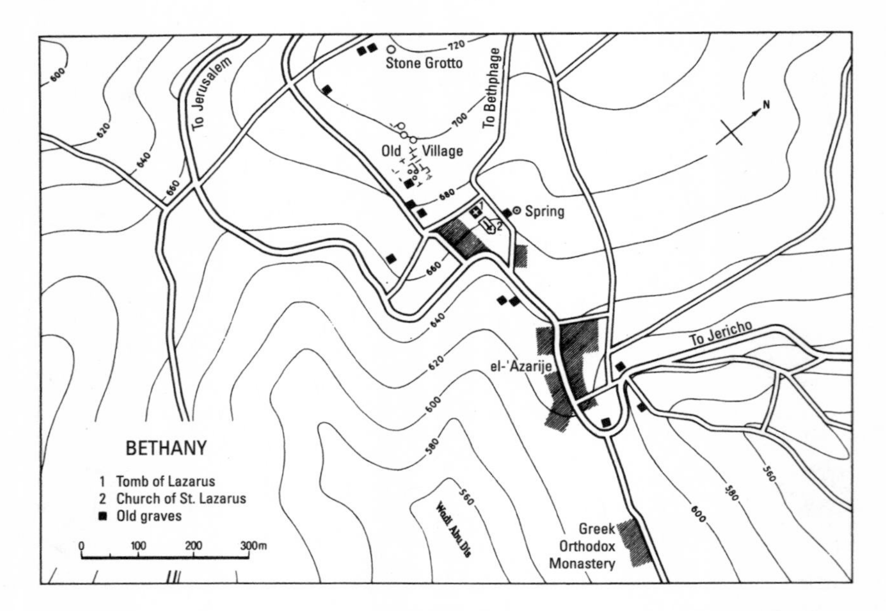

Illus. 54. The old location of Bethany (from G. Kroll).

who was celibate himself, enjoyed being a guest in the house of the brother and sisters.

After the failed assassination attempt at the Hanukkah feast (Jn 10:31–39), Jesus retreated to "Bethany on the other side of the Jordan" (Jn 10:40; cf. Jn 1:28). I am convinced that this Bethany east of the Jordan is identical to Batanea.[7] The Old Testament district of Bashan in Roman times bore the name of Batanea, which was the name of the region and also of the town of Ekbatane (illus. 42). This settlement was founded by the Babylonian Jews as their main settlement at the request of Herod the Great.[8] Their new foundation was named after the Persian capital Ekbatane. After the Roman period the region became popularly known as Bas(h)an or Basanitis.

We may assume that there were connections between the two Bethanies. It is remarkable that the siblings from Bethany by Jerusalem knew of the hiding place of Jesus in the other Bethany, because they had sent a message there to Jesus: "Lord, he whom you love [Lazarus] is ill" (Jn 11:3). Of Bethany on the other side of the Jordan, the evangelist

[7] Cf. chapter 14, "Bethany on the Other Side of the Jordan" (pp. 177–91).

[8] Cf. chapter 13, "Batanea as a Jewish Settlement Area" (pp. 169–76, esp. pp. 171–72).

John says that "many believed in him there" (Jn 10:42). Also, Mark remarks that it was in this place that "crowds gathered to him again; and again, as his custom was, he taught them" (Mk 10:1). After some hectic recent weeks in Galilee (Lk 13:31–33), Jesus found rest and shelter in this south Syrian region (pp. 186–88).

III. Jesus' Last Days in the Essene Surroundings

Jesus had already experienced great opposition at the Hanukkah feast in Jerusalem, but the situation became more critical after the resurrection of Lazarus (Jn 11:1–45). The Sadducee high priestly circles and also some of the Pharisees called a meeting of the High Council (Jn 11:47), in which they decided to kill him (Jn 11:53). Although Jesus was not an Essene, and during his stay in Capharnaum he had kept in touch mainly with the Pharisee teachers, it does seem that during his last activities in Jerusalem he had a special relationship with Essene circles.[9] In both Bethanies, there emerges such a convergence. The period of self-examination that Jesus and his disciples spent in Ephraim (Jn 11:54), which today is a Christian Arabian village, et Taybeh,[10] is to be seen in this light: "The chief priests and the Pharisees had given orders that if any one knew where he [Jesus] was, he should let them know, so that they might arrest him" (Jn 11:57). Jesus knew of these dangers, and it is understandable that he was threatened by them and looked and found protection in the Essene circles, which had rejected official Judaism.

The contact with the Essene groups is particularly important because Jesus did not celebrate his Passover meal according to the dominant "official" calendar (on a Thursday in the year of his death [A.D. 30]) but according to the Essene calendar, on the evening of Tuesday-Wednesday.[11] This proposal by the late Professor A. Jaubert from Sorbonne University[12] is supported by the close proximity between the

[9] I have dealt with the relationship of Jesus to the Jewish religious party in more detail in *With Jesus through Galilee according to the Fifth Gospel* (Collegeville, Minn.: Liturgical Press, 1996). According to the late Prof. David Flusser (Hebrew University of Jerusalem), Jesus had referred to the Essenes as the "sons of light" in Lk 16:8. Cf. A. Rabinovich, "Jesus Knew the Essenes Well ...", *Jerusalem Post* 6, no. 4 (1984): 3.

[10] Cf. R. Riesner, "Ephraim", in *GBL*, 2nd ed. (1990): 1:322.

[11] Cf. chapter 18, "The Last Supper of Jesus" (pp. 239–49).

[12] *La date de la Cène* (Paris: Gabalda, 1957).

location of the Last Supper hall and the Essene quarter.[13] The thesis of the different references about the Passover feast can also provide a solution to the question: Was the meal in Bethany two or six days before the Passover that preceded Jesus' death?

Mark 14:1–3	"It was now two days before the Passover and the feast of Unleavened Bread. . . . And while he was at Bethany in the house of Simon the leper, as he sat at table . . ."
John 12:1–2	"Six days before the Passover, Jesus came to Bethany, where Lazarus was, whom Jesus had raised from the dead. There they made him a supper."

Calculated from Sunday (cf. Jn 18:28; 19:14), it was two days until Tuesday-Wednesday (the Essene Passover) and six days until Friday-Saturday (the temple Passover). The report about the search for a location for the Last Supper, which obviously took place in Bethphage near Bethany (cf. Mk 14:12–16), reveals elements that seem to lead back to a certain tradition that possibly originated from Jewish Christian circles and that demonstrates Essene influence (pp. 239–42). Perhaps the easy way the disciples obtained a donkey in Bethphage[14] for Jesus' entrance into Jerusalem (Mk 11:1–11) is also related to his connections to the Essene community in that place.

IV. Two Holy Caves on the Mount of Olives

During the first four centuries, on the southwest hill of Jerusalem, on Zion, a Jewish Christian community gathered around the "Upper Church of the Apostles", which survived only with great difficulties.[15] This community was poor and constantly threatened through its close proximity to the Gentile colony of Aelia Capitolina and later from the Gentile Christian church of the Byzantine Empire, the latter because of their unorthodox belief, which meant they were regarded as heretical. However, the continual presence on the Mount of Olives of the Jewish Christian community was significant. The inscriptions on some of the ossuaries (containers for bones) that have been found in the installations of graves of the Roman period in the grounds of

[13] Cf. chapter 15, "The Essene Quarter in Jerusalem" (pp. 192–219).
[14] Cf. R. Riesner, "Betfage", in *GBL*, 2nd ed. (1990): 1:196.
[15] Cf. chapter 25, "The Apostolic Synagogue on Zion" (pp. 319–59).

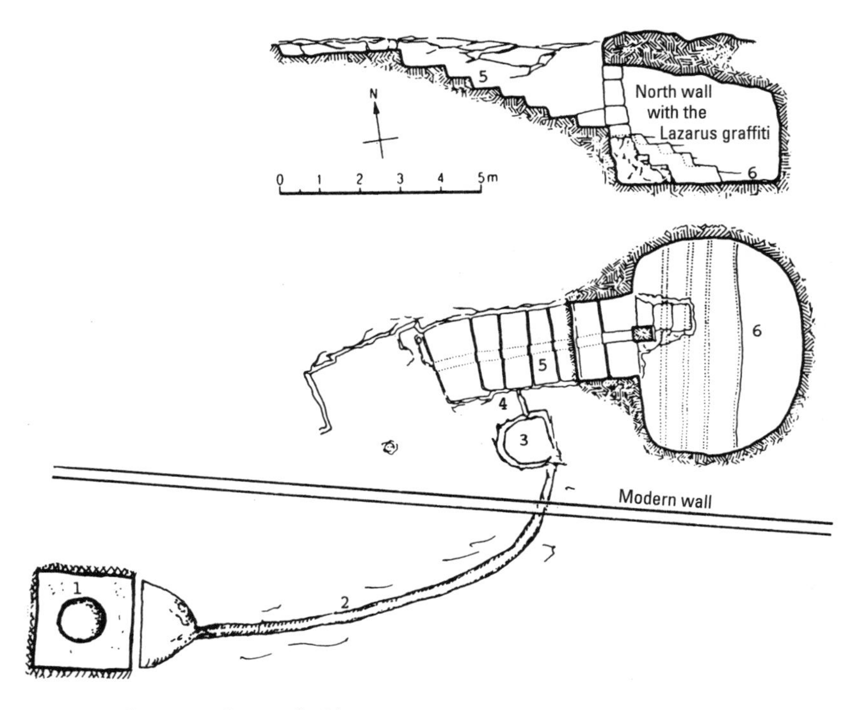

Illus. 55. The Jewish Christian grotto.

1	*Cistern*	*4*	*Connecting channel*
2	*Supply channel*	*5*	*Rock step*
3	*Rainwater reservoir (*'Ozar sar^ca'*)*	*6*	*Ritual bath (*mikveh*)*

the Franciscan monastery Dominus Flevit (cf. Lk 19:41–44), halfway up the Mount of Olives,[16] confirms this.

On top of the Mount of Olives is the grotto of Eleona (illus. 57), whose veneration can be traced back to the early Christian period.[17] This is acknowledged in the work *Demonstratio Evangelica* by Eusebius of Caesarea, whose writing goes back to the time of the Diocletian

[16] Cf. B. Bagatti, "Scoperta di un cimitiero giudeo-cristiano al 'Dominus Flevit' (Monte Oliveto—Gerusalemme)", *SBFLA* 3 (1953): 149–84; B. Bagatti and J. T. Milik, *Gli scavi del "Dominus Flevit"*, pt. 1, *La necropolis del periodo romano*, SBFCMa13 (Jerusalem: Franciscan Printing Press, 1958), 166–82.

[17] The Acts of John, which date from the first half of the second century A.D., confirm the presence of a Docetic Christian sect near this cave (*Acts John* 97) (W. Schneemelcher, ed., *Neutestamentliche Apokryphen in deutscher Übersetzung*, 5th ed., vol. 2 [Tübingen: Mohr Siebeck, 1989], 168f.).

Illus. 56. Bethany—Lazarus graffiti (according to P. Benoit and M. E. Boismard, 1951) (sketch).

persecution (A.D. 312) (pp. 375–76). In the text, Eusebius writes: "The believers will come here from all corners of the world . . . in order to pray at the Mount of Olives opposite Jerusalem. . . . According to the records, the feet of the Redeemer stood . . . on the Mount of Olives by the cave that is shown there. In it, he had prayed, and on the hill, his disciples were told the secrets of the end of the world [Mt 24:3 / Mk 13:3]." [18]

While the "mystic cave" [19] of Eleona was known to all the visiting pilgrims according to pilgrim reports, not far from the eastern slope of the Mount of Olives in Bethany was another grotto (plate 7b), which probably attracted mainly Jewish Christians.[20] This grotto was discovered in 1951 and was researched and described by members of the École biblique P. Benoit and M. E. Boismard.[21] It is found in the garden area of the Sisters of Saint Vincent de Paul and can be visited with permission.

Above limestone, hewn stairs descend into a 5.4 m wide and 4 m deep cave. The stairs were originally part of a wall extension that is clearly visible and is still divided into an entrance and an exit. This wall extension ends by a rock buttress, where the grotto entrance forms two doors, which originally was a narrow staircase that led into the interior. The traces of the stairs are still visible on the south and north walls of the cave. On the walls, one can discern two watertight plasterwork surfaces, one with much graffiti that pilgrims had written in the early Christian centuries. The most important inscription (illus. 56) is on the north wall of the grotto: "Lord, God who has raised Lazarus from the dead, remember your servant Asclepius and your maidservant Chionion."

[18] *Demonstratio Evangelica* 4.I8 (PG 22:457; Baldi, 384f.).

[19] *Vita Constantini* 3.41 (PG 20:1102; Baldi, 386).

[20] Cf. B. Bagatti, *The Church from the Circumcision*, SBFCMi 2 (Jerusalem: Franciscan Printing Press, 1971), 134f., 158.

[21] "Un ancien sanctuaire chrétien à Béthanie", *RB* 58 (1951): 200–251.

The watertight plaster surfaces were later covered over with a lime whitewash, and on them was painted a red cross as well as a more official Greek inscription that, according to the Dominican archaeologist [Benoit], possibly pointed to a particular religious tradition associated with this grotto.[22] Unfortunately, the red inscription on the east wall is now barely legible, but in 1951 it was still possible to decipher the following rows of letters:[23]

. ΘΕ . ΕΙΩΘΕΙ . ΦΕΙΛ. . ΑΛΦ . . .
ΛΟΥΕCΘΕΑ . ΟΥΠΟΔΥCΟΥ . . .

A possible completion may be: God (ΘΕ[ΟΣ]), who are used to being (ΕΙΩΘΕΙ) . . . without clothes (aorist ἀφφεῖλον of ἀφαρεῖν) or without taking care of yourself ([Α]ΦΕΙΔΗCΑ)], bathing (ΛΟΥΕCΘΕ = λούεσθαι), submerging yourself (from ὑποδύειν) . . .

V. A Venerated Ritual Bath from the Days of Jesus

Today it is clear that the grotto contained not only a water cistern but also a Jewish *mikveh* bath for the purpose of ritual washing.[24] A valid ritual bath could be taken only in "living water", which could include spring water, river water, seawater or rainwater. Ladled water was not suitable for such washing. Where there was not such "living water" available, it was possible to create it. A system existed in which available rainwater could be "adapted". Three elements were necessary for this system: (1) a large water cistern; (2) a reservoir for rainwater called by the rabbis *'ozar sar^ca'* (seed reservoir), which must have contained at least 40 seah (about 600 L);[25] and (3) the actual ritual bath, into which a couple of steps for ascent and descent were required (pp. 209–11). Where it was not possible to make two such steps, the step was separated by a raised area in the middle. When the water had to be renewed in the *mikveh*, the old water was taken out and replaced with water from the cistern. As ladled water was unsuitable, the water from the cistern flowed through the rainwater reservoir. The water that was

[22] Ibid., 241–44.
[23] Ibid., 242 (fig. 10).
[24] Cf. R. Reich, "*Mishna Sheqalim* 8:3 and the Archaeological Evidence" [in Modern Hebrew], in A. Oppenheimer, U. Rappaport and M. Stern, *Jerusalem in the Second Temple Period: Abraham Schalit Memorial Volume* (Jerusalem: Magnes Press, 1980), 225–56 (at 253–55).
[25] Cf. Mishna, *Mikwa'ot* 2:1.

flowing out on the other side was considered "living water". Through this procedure, the water could be renewed throughout the long rainless summer months. *Mikva'ot* constructed in this way have been found at Qumran, on Mount Zion, in Jerusalem (pp. 209–13) and also in parts of the temple area. The graffiti bath from Bethany is installed in exactly the same manner as a *mikveh*. By following the supply channel at Bethany from the seed reservoir to the ground of the adjoining monastery, I discovered the large rainwater cistern.

If the red inscription on the east wall was really for the purpose of pointing to the ritual bath, then there was a *mikveh* here that could have been used by Jesus and his disciples before the Last Supper. Would this not shed new light on the words of Jesus as he was about to wash Peter's feet: "He who has bathed does not need to wash, except for his feet" (Jn 13:10)? It is surely right to assume that Jesus and his disciples would have taken a ritual bath before the Passover feast. It is indeed possible that this was the place revered for many centuries as the location for the ritual bath of the Lord and his Apostles, and it is certain that Jewish Christians, who were aware of this tradition, would have wanted to be baptized in such a bath.

The necessity for foot washing is particularly understandable if the Passover meal was taken in a guesthouse of an Essene from Zion (pp. 239–42). Coming from Bethany, the disciples necessarily went on "unclean" paths. Would not the Essene residents have insisted on such a washing, as Jesus himself had done (Jn 13:1–11)? John's Gospel points to the common Jewish practice of ritual baths: "Now the Passover of the Jews was at hand, and many went up from the country to Jerusalem before the Passover, to purify themselves" (Jn 11:55). This would have included a ritual washing before the meal of the feast. May we not assume that close to the place of this bath was also the house of Lazarus, Mary and Martha? Ancient pilgrim graffiti mentioning Lazarus would support this particular hypothesis,[26] and not far from this location, settlement ruins were found of the New Testament village of

[26] After I completed this essay, Dr. Rainer Riesner made me aware of this article: J. E. Taylor, "The Cave at Bethany", *RB* 94 (1987): 120–23. The author believes that the cistern is mentioned by Jerome, *Letter 108*: 12 (PL 22:888; Baldi, 362), as the *hospitium* of Mary and Martha. Mrs. Taylor is in the embarrassing situation of explaining why, according to her opinion on the direct pilgrim route from Bethphage to the Tomb of Lazarus, this is not mentioned in any other source. This seems quite understandable when it concerns the shrine of the Jewish Christians.

Bethany.[27] If the local Jewish Christian community preserved the tradition of Lazarus' grave,[28] then there could also be a tradition associated with this place. If these assumptions are correct, then we can recognize a certain tension in the behavior of Jesus at Bethany. On one hand, he disregarded the strict purity regulations of the Pharisees and the Essenes and frequented the leper colonies, and on the other hand, he took a ritual bath with his disciples in order to celebrate the Passover meal in the Holy City. To be all things to all people was his way.

[27] Cf. S.J. Saller, *Excavations at Bethany*, SBFCMa 12 (Jerusalem: Franciscan Printing Press, 1957).

[28] Cf. G. Kroll, *Auf den Spuren Jesu*, 11th ed. (Stuttgart: Katholisches Bibelwerk, 2002), 278–87.

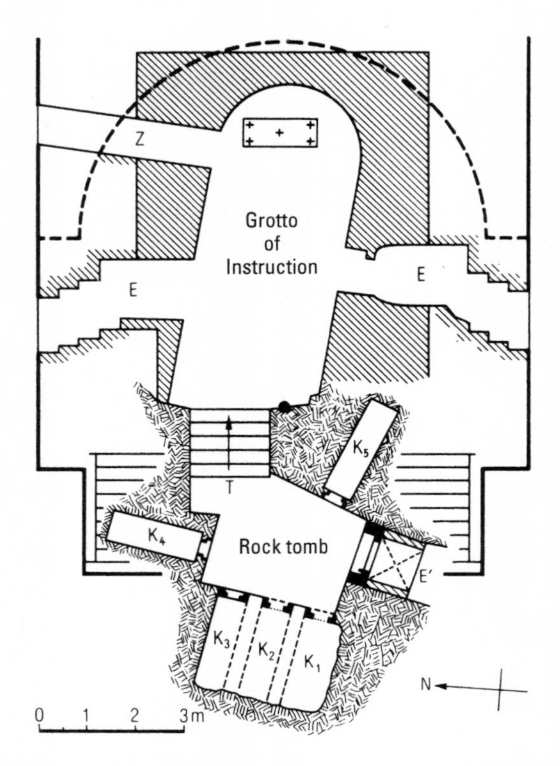

Illus. 57. Grotto under the apse of the Eleona basilica on the Mount of Olives (according to J. Wilkinson, 1978) (from G. Kroll). Originally there was no connection between the grotto and the Jewish kokim *graves.*

Z *Original access*
E *Entrance to the grotto*
E' *Entrance of the rock grave*
K_{1-5} Kokim *("shaft")—graves*
T *Modern stairs*

18. The Last Supper of Jesus

During the New Testament period, an Essene quarter existed on the hill of Zion.[1] Even though the search for the location of this Essene quarter in Jerusalem already forms an important research project, there is further interest because of an ancient established tradition that it was on this same hill that the roots of the original Church began.[2] The question then poses itself: Was there contact between the Essene residents and the original Christian community,[3] and did these contacts include Jesus and his disciples even though they could not have been Essenes?

I. The Search for the Place of the Last Supper

All three synoptic Gospels include a search for a location for the Last Supper (Mt 26:7–19 / Mk 14:12–16 / Lk 22:7–13). John, however, deliberately did not include this. Through the synoptic narrative, did a circle of Essene members from the original Jerusalem community want to emphasize a particular connection of the Lord with their community? The text in Acts 1:13 sounds like the founding narrative (*hieros logos*) for their synagogue, the Upper Room (ὑπερῷον) on Mount Zion. If we take the oldest text, Mark's Gospel, Jesus is somewhere on the Mount of Olives or in Bethany (cf. Mk 13:3; 14:3). As a response to the question by the disciples, "Where will you have us go and prepare for you to eat the Passover?" Jesus sent two of his disciples. Luke specifies that it was Peter and John (Lk 22:8), and the disciples are given the following advice: "Go into the city, and a man carrying a jar of

[1] Cf. chapter 15, "The Essene Quarter in Jerusalem" (pp. 192–219).

[2] Cf. chapter 25, "The Apostolic Synagogue on Zion" (pp. 319–59).

[3] Cf. particularly chapter 26, "The Essene Quarter and the Primitive Christian Community" (pp. 360–68).

water will meet you; follow him, and wherever he enters, say to the householder [οἰκοδεσπότης], 'The teacher says, Where is my guest room, where I am to eat the Passover with my disciples?' And he will show you a large upper room furnished and ready; there prepare for us" (Mk 14:13–15).

I will not analyze the text but only raise certain questions, and I wish to propose some solutions here. First, where could fresh water be found at that time in Jerusalem? The only place is the Siloam pool, which is probably where the encounter happened. Second, what did the man need water for on the eve of the Passover? Third, why was it a man, rather than a woman (if it was for ordinary domestic purposes), who was carrying the jug? Was it perhaps for a prescribed ritual bath? Those who know about the culture of the Middle East know that fetching water was the responsibility of the women. However, was a man carrying water because the regulations of the celibate community on Zion forbade access to women? Was this then perhaps an Essene monk?

The man ascended the road of the steps up to Mount Zion, which today is still partly on the grounds of the Church of Saint Peter in Gallicantu (p. 260). "Wherever he enters, there you ask!" (see Mk 14:14). Were the disciples allowed to go in? Were they forced to ask for the abbot of the monastery, "the lord of the house"? Perhaps it was the supervisor (מְבַקֵּר [*mebakker*]) of the Essene settlement or the monk in charge of guests (cf. *War* 2.125). "Where is my guest room [τὸ κατάλυμά μου]?" the report continues (Mk 14:14). The word κατάλυμά is sometimes translated as the "chamber", but it should rather be translated as the "guesthouse" or the "inn". The Greek word appears only three times in the New Testament: once in this text, then in the parallel story in Luke (Lk 22:11) and finally in the Nativity story of the search for an inn in Bethlehem: "[Mary] laid him [Jesus] in a manger, because there was no place for them in the inn" (Lk 2:7). Was the guesthouse for the Last Supper the *katalyma*, the guesthouse of the Essenes that was normally a side building of the monastery? The Essenes were known for their hospitality (*War* 2.124f.) and maintained a guesthouse in Jerusalem (or several) for groups with whom they wanted to celebrate the Passover feast.

When the text refers to "my guest room", could it in fact simply mean that the room had been previously reserved for Jesus or, also, that the Essene-Christian groups wanted to emphasize the authority of Jesus for their local tradition? The great Upper Room (ἀνάγαιον μέγα)

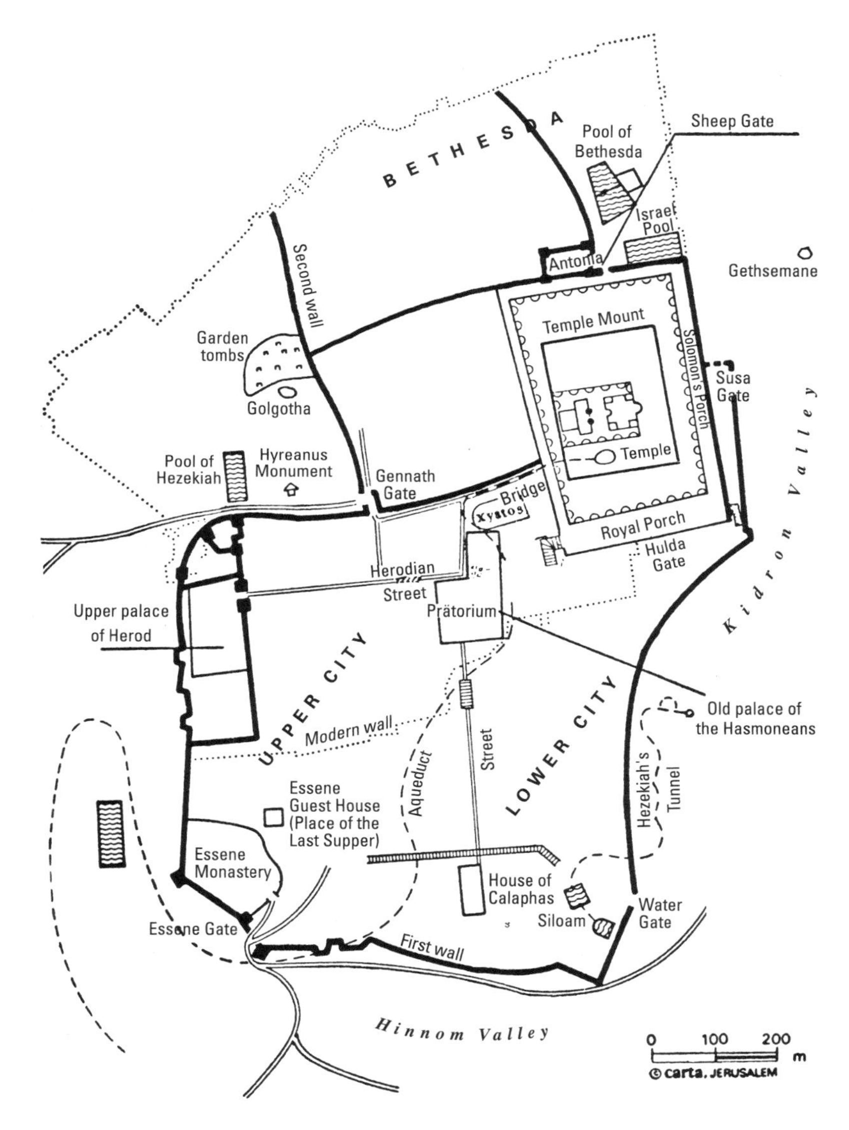

Illus. 58. Jerusalem in the time of Jesus.

in this guesthouse was covered with mats as well as comfortable furnishings and was made "ready" (ἐστρωμένον ἕτοιμον [Mk 14:15]). A Jewish house is ready for the Passover meal when all the bread with yeast has been removed, as the Apostle Paul wrote, "Cleanse out the old leaven"

(1 Cor 5:7). There was a religious obligation for the house to be cleaned from top to bottom; nothing would be left unturned. Still today it is a special ceremony with special prayers. This cleaning was the task of the host, and Peter and John did not need to go looking for old yeast or left-over bread. Mark had said in the beginning of this episode: "on the first day of Unleavened bread" (Mk 14:12). The hall was already *kasher lepesach* (כָּשֵׁר לְפֶּסַח), which means "pure, for the Passover feast". From this follows an interesting conclusion: we know from John's Gospel that the actual official Easter feast was on the first Saturday (Jn 18:28; 19:31). On the Friday, in this case on Good Friday in the afternoon, the house was prepared for the Passover meal. Did the proprietor of the Last Supper hall therefore follow a different calendar? This brings us to the question of the date of the Last Supper.

II. The Date of the Last Supper

Professor A. Jaubert of the Sorbonne University tried to prove that at the time of Jesus in Jerusalem two different calendars were used: the normative lunar calendar (pp. 416–17), which was used in the temple by the Pharisees and Sadducees, and the old priestly solar-lunar calendar, which the Essenes and other religious groups used.[4] If Jesus celebrated the Last Supper in an Essene guesthouse, then Mrs. Jaubert is correct in her thesis that Jesus must have used the Essene calendar. This suggestion was initially well received[5] and has been supported by many commentators, such as B. Schwank[6] and E. Ruckstuhl.[7] R. Schnackenburg also takes this seriously in his commentary on Saint John's Gospel.[8] A plausible solution is provided for the apparent contradiction[9] between the Passion reports of the Synoptics and that of

[4] *La date de la Cène* (Paris: Gabalda, 1957); "Aperçus sur le calendrier de Qumrân", in *La secte de Qumrân et les origines du christianisme* (Bruges: Desclée, 1959), 113–20.

[5] Cf. P. W. Skehan, "The Date of the Last Supper", *Catholic Biblical Quarterly* 20 (1958): 192–99; P. Benoit, *RB* 65 (1958): 590–94 (review of Mrs. Jaubert's book); G. R. Driver, *The Judean Scrolls* (Oxford: Oxford University Press, 1965), 330–35; H. Braun, *Qumran und das Neue Testament* (Tübingen: Mohr, 1966), 2:43–54.

[6] "War das letzte Abendmahl am Dienstag der Karwoche?" *BiKi* 13 (1958): 34–44.

[7] *Die Chronologie des Letzten Mahles und des Leidens Jesu* (Einsiedeln: Schweizerisches Katholisches Bibelwerk, 1963).

[8] *Das Johannesevangelium*, vol. 3 (Freiburg: Herder, 1975), 39–41.

[9] There have been various attempts to resolve this. The Jewish researcher J. Morgenstern assumed in *Some Significant Antecedents of Christianity* (Leiden: Brill, 1966–1968),

Saint John. Presently this thesis is ignored by most commentators. In the light of the new archaeological knowledge about the close proximity of the Essene quarter and the original Christian community on the southwest hill of Jerusalem (the present Mount Zion), Professor Jaubert's hypothesis should receive further acknowledgment. E. Ruckstuhl has particularly provided support for this thesis.[10]

According to the Syrian *Didascalia* (*Didasc.* 5.12–18)[11] and Epiphanius of Salamis,[12] the Last Supper had taken place on a Tuesday evening. In the old priests' calendar used by the Essenes, the fifteenth of Nisan always fell on a Wednesday and with it the Passover meal on the day before, on Tuesday. From the ancient *Teaching of the Twelve Apostles* [Didache], which originated in Syria, we know that the Jewish Christian communities gave up the Pharisaic fast days of Monday and Thursday in order to fast on Wednesday and Friday (*Did.* 8.1), probably in memory of the arrest and crucifixion of the Lord. Many other things seem to suggest that the original church in Jerusalem adapted its feast calendar in order to match it with the that of the Essenes (pp. 363–64).

In the Gospels, we find apparently two different traditions for the Passover: the Synoptics and John. According to the Synoptics the Passover took place two days after the meal in Bethany (cf. Mk 14:1 / Mt 26:2), on Wednesday, but for John it took place six days later (Jn 12:1), on the Sabbath (p. 232). These two traditions must have created confusion in Church practices. Toward the end of the first century, John might have wished to suppress a link to the Essene calendar following the disappearance of the Essene centers and due

8–15, that John followed the official numbering of the days, but the synoptic Gospels used an old Galilean tradition, which counts the days from sunrise to sunrise.

[10] "Zur Chronologie der Leidengeschichte Jesu I–II", *Studien zum Neuen Testament und seiner Umwelt* 10 (1985): 27–61; 11 (1986): 97–129, now in *Jesus im Horizont der Evangelien* (Stuttgart: Katholisches Bibelwerk, 1988), 101–84; "Zür Frage einer Essenergemeinde in Jerusalem", in B. Mayer, *Christen und Christliches in Qumran?* (Regensburg: Pustet, 1992), 131–34.

[11] Text by F. X. Funk, *Didascalia et Constitutiones Apostolorum* (Paderborn: Schöningh, 1905), and A. Voöbus, *The "Didascalia Apostolorum" in Syriac*, vol. 2, CSCO 402 (Louvain: University Press, 1979). For a French translation, see F. Nau, *La Didascalie des douze Apôtres* (Paris, 1912); for a German translation of the relevant paragraph, see E. Ruckstuhl, *Chronologie des Letzten Mahles* (see n. 7), 55–59. The Syrian church was particularly influenced by the Jewish Christian traditions. Also, the Nestorians seem to have adopted a Jewish Christian heritage; cf. J. M. Magnin, "Notes sur l'Ébionisme V", *POC* 27 (1977): 250–76 (at 260–69).

[12] *Panarion* 51.26–27.3 (PG 41:933–36; GCS 31:295–98).

to the fact that their particular way of numbering the calendar was no longer understandable. John and his community in Asia Minor celebrated the Passover (and with it Easter) on the night of the fourteenth and fifteenth of Nisan. It was a fixed date, which was supported as the normative date for the Rabbinic Passover. The reason why the fourth Gospel omitted the words of institution was probably because at that time there was a strong connection between the Christian feast and the Passover celebration, which according to him took place only on the Friday evening (Jn 18:28). Important for John's Gospel was that the death of Jesus coincided with the sacrificing of the lambs in the temple (normally the fourteenth of Nisan [Jn 19:36]). In the meantime, Rome[13] and Alexandria had already made the Essene old weekly calendar the basis for reckoning the arrest of the Lord on Wednesday and his death on Friday in Holy Week (celebrating them through fasting), and for reckoning the Resurrection on an Easter Sunday after a spring full moon. This was the old Jerusalem practice that before A.D. 135 was followed by the Jewish Christian bishops.[14] Both views about the Easter date could provide apostolic endorsement for their particular tradition. This caused one of the biggest crises between the early Christian communities in Asia Minor and the Western churches, the so-called Easter feast debate. Only Emperor Constantine and the Council of Nicea (325) managed to resolve the issue about Easter, proclaiming, in order to reach unanimity and a consensus, that the Roman, or rather the Jerusalem, tradition, which was followed at that time by a majority of the churches, was to be adopted for the whole Church. The celebration for the introduction of Holy Communion on Maundy Thursday is a later practice (fourth to fifth century), and this gave rise to a superficial interpretation of Saint John's Gospel. The three-day chronology of Jesus' trial as the Syrian *Didascalia* describes should probably be given priority (appendix 2 [p. 439]).

[13] D. FLUSSER, "The Temple Scroll from Qumran", *Immanuel* 9 (1979): 49–52 (at 50), drew our attention to another possible liturgical relationship between the oldest Roman church and the Qumran calendar. Through the Temple Scroll, we now know of the first celebration of barley, wheat, wine and oil (11QTemple 18:10—22:11). Bishop Kallistos of Rome (217–222) was meant to have ordered on three Sabbaths (!) a feast of cereals, wine and oil (*Liber Pontificalis* [ed. L. DUCHESNE (Rome: Editrice Vaticana, 1955)], vol. 1, 17.2; Anastasius, *Notitia historica et bibliotheca* [PL 127:1318]).

[14] Cf. Epiphanius, *Panarion* 70.10 (PG 42:356–60; GCS 37:242f.).

III. The Last Supper Room in the Copper Scroll of Qumran?

In this original Qumran document, the treasure hiding places nos. 3–17 (3Q15 1:6—4:2) point to the Essene community settlement on the south-west hill of Jerusalem.[15] There is not total unanimity among researchers who have tried to read and interpret the text about the seventh hiding place. My own solution, if accepted, would provide not only a key to the Copper Scroll but also a possible connection with the details from the New Testament.[16] This would be as follows: "In the cave of the prepared house of Jesus [במערת בית המדחה ישו], under the third layer of plaster: sixty-five gold worked objects" (3Q15 2:3f.). I am interested in the words BM^{c}RT BJT HMDḤH JŠU. I believe that the correct reading of the last Hebrew words should not be JŠN (ישן) but JŠU (ישו). Even J. T. Milik admitted: "Matériellement la dernière lettre est plutôt un *waw*."[17] It is typical for the Copper Scroll that the *ain* (ע) is sometimes missing, as in the northern dialect.[18] In fact, the shortened form JŠU (*Jeshu*) without ^{c}*ain* at the end appears on ossuary inscriptions before A.D. 70.[19]

Who was this Jesus? Josephus mentions a priest with the name of Jesus, son of Thebutis, who, after the fall of Jerusalem, "as the emperor [Titus] had under oath promised protection ... brought two candelabras out from under the temple wall that were very similar to the ones

[15] Cf. chapter 12, "The Copper Scroll of Qumran" (pp. 159–68).

[16] Cf. B. PIXNER, "Unravelling the Copper Scroll Code: A Study on the Topography of 3Q15", *RQ* 11 (1983): 323–66 (at 344–46).

[17] "Le rouleau de cuivre provenant de la grotte 3Q (3Q15)", in M. BAILLET, J. T. MILIK and R. DE VAUX, *Les "petites grottes" de Qumrân*, DJD 3 (Oxford: Clarendon, 1962), 198–302 (at 286).

[18] Cf. ibid., 229. We know from the Jerusalem Talmud, *Berachot* 2 (4d), that men from Scythopolis (near Pella) were not allowed to read in the synagogue services because of their tendencies to pronounce *chet* (ח) as *he* (ה) and ^{c}*ain* (ע) as *'aleph* (א). Cf. E. Y. KUTSCHNER, *Studies in Galilean Aramaic* (Jerusalem: Magnes Press, 1976), 69.

[19] Cf. J. A. FITZMYER and D. J. HARRINGTON, *A Manual of Palestinian Aramaic Texts* (Rome: Pontifical Biblical Institute Press, 1978), no. 106 (233f.). On this ossuary (S. 767), in the Rockefeller Museum, engraved right next to the shortened form JŠU (ישו) is JŠU^{c} BR JHUSP (ישוע בר יהוסף), "Jeshua son of Joseph". The former chief curator of the museum, L. Yitzchak Rahmani, kindly pointed out to me that neither E. L. SUKENIK nor any other serious archaeologist would make the connection to Jesus of Nazareth, as have some sensational reports in the media. Two different forms of names (see also pp. 248–49), namely, MTJH (מתיה) and MTTJH (מתתיה), can be found on an ossuary on another Jewish tomb. Cf. E. L. SUKENIK, "A Jewish Tomb-Cave at the Slope of Mount Scopus" [in Modern Hebrew], *Kovez* 3 (1934): 68f. [The ossuary with the name "Jeshua son of Joseph" made a new pseudosensation with the publication of J. D. Tabor's book *The Jesus Dynasty: The Hidden History of Jesus* (New York: Random House, 2006).—ED.]

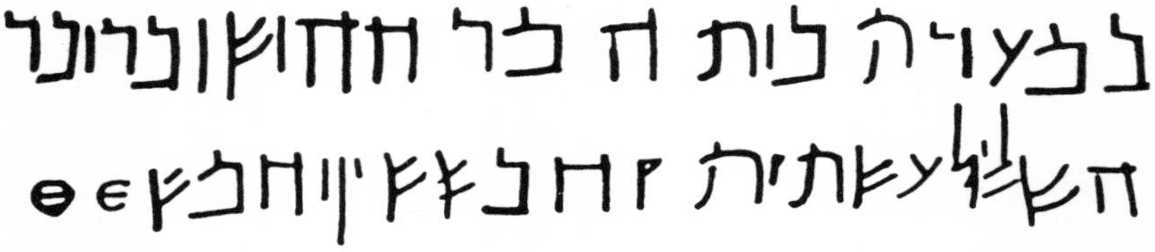

Illus. 59. Copper Scroll, column 2:3f. (according to J. T. Milik, 1962) (sketch). Of particular interest are the last two Greek letters at the end.

used in the temple, also tables, containers all worked out of gold. He also handed over garments: the robes of the high priest with valuable stones and many objects that were used for the holy service" (*War* 6.387). By these acts the priest received his freedom. The temple was consumed in flames (*War* 6.249ff.), as was the fortress Antonia, where the high priestly robes were kept (*Ant.* 15.404–8; 18.93–95) and which had been under the control of the Romans for a long time. The priest Jesus must have found these objects somewhere else. Josephus said with emphasis that the candelabras were not those from the temple but looked very similar. Did the Essenes from Jerusalem take precautions in order to rebuild the ideal temple for God, as had been prescribed in the Temple Scroll (11QTemple 3–11; 30–45)? Was the priest Jesus, son of Thebutis, one of the few who knew the secrets of the Copper Scroll? Could some of the golden objects have come from the seventh hiding place? Hiding place no. 4 (3Q15 1:9–12) seems to have had high priestly robes.[20]

It is yet more amazing that at the end of the hiding place description the puzzling Greek letters ΘΕ were found. I share H. Bardtke's opinion that these peculiar letters would make more sense if the treasures of the Copper Scroll were real and not fictitious.[21] J. M. Allegro[22] had drawn attention to the identification letters in the Mishna[23] and sees in the letters of the Copper Scroll an indication of the origin of the treasures. I would like to suggest a similar solution. The letters were found only in connection with the hiding places around the Jerusalem Essene quarter. The descriptions are also more

[20] Cf. B. Pixner, "Unravelling the Copper Scroll Code" (see n. 16), 343.

[21] "Qumran und seine Probleme II/2: Die Kupferrollen", *Theologische Rundschau* 33 (1968): 185–204 (at 193f.).

[22] *The Treasure of the Copper Scroll*, 2nd ed. (London, 1964), 136, n. 9.

[23] *Ma'aser Sheni* 4:9–11; *Shekalim* 3:2.

detailed than the rest. Could it be a code for the author, whose language was of a northern origin (from the Jarmuk area?) and who knew comparatively well the area of Qumran where the Copper Scroll was hidden but knew Jerusalem less well? Could this have been for his personal orientation, and so he noted the initials of the supervisor of the hiding places of the treasures without revealing their full names? In any case, Josephus has matches of Jewish names for all the initials.[24] It is even more remarkable that the initials for this particular hiding place correspond with the first letters of the father of Jesus the priest, namely, Θε[βουτίς] (*The*[*boutis*]). Was he responsible for the content of this particular hiding place? That the priests Thebutis or Jesus were commissioned with the supervision of these treasures of the Essene community is supported by the community regulations at Qumran: "Only the sons of Aaron should decide about questions of law and possessions" (1QS 9:7). As the name of Thebutis has no parallel in the whole of the rest of the literature, I would like to identify him with the Thebutis who, according to Hegesippos (*HE* 4.22.5), came from a Jewish sect and after A.D. 62 provoked a division in the original church of Jerusalem.[25]

There are questions regarding the expression BJT HMDḤH, "the prepared house" or "the one with the divan covered with rugs". The less common expression, *meducheh* (מְדוּחֶה), is illustrated in Ben-Yehuda's dictionary by a window through which can be seen a hall, with rugs "laid out".[26] There is a comparable expression in Mark 14:15 and Luke 22:12: ἀνάγαιον μέγα ἐστρωμένον, "a large furnished/lined upper chamber". Exactly the same expression that occurs in the Copper Scroll appears in a variant in Luke 22:12: οἶκον ἐστρωμένον (D), "big lined house". Do all these variants with the use of a *terminus technicus* refer to the same building of Thebutis as the Copper Scroll? Is perhaps the text of Matthew 26:18, "Go into the city to such a one [πρὸς τὸν δεῖνα]", a *damnatio memoriae* reminiscent of the negative role that Thebutis played in the original Jerusalem church? The cave (מְעָרָה) that is mentioned in this connection could perhaps be the one that E. Pierotti

[24] Cf. B. PIXNER, "Unravelling the Copper Scroll Code" (see n. 16), 335, n. 32.

[25] Cf. chapter 31, "Simeon Bar Cleopas, Second Bishop of Jerusalem" (pp. 408–14, esp. pp. 409–10).

[26] E. BEN-YEHUDA, *Dictionary and Thesaurus of the Hebrew Language* (New York and London, n.d.), 2:915.

described after two difficult visits.[27] This cave was very large (40 × 15 × 3 m), and the diagram drawn by him shows it directly southeast of the so-called Tomb of David and also of the Last Supper room. According to Pierotti's drawing, the buildings and the cave were connected. But since then this cave has never been rediscovered, and the entrance must have been blocked.

The expression BJT HMDḤH JŠU could also be translated as "the banned house of Jeshu". This could be an allusion to the Last Supper hall, which had become the meeting room of the Jerusalem Jewish Christians. Beth-Jeshu could also be similar to the expressions Beth-Hillel or Beth-Shammai. Beth-Jeshu might mean the supporters of Jesus, the ones who gathered on the southwest hill around the members of his family and who played an important role in the Early Church. Would then "the banned house of Jeshu" hint at the break between the group of Jewish Christians strongly influenced by the Essenes (the Ebionites) and those belonging to Jesus' family group (the Nazoreans) and their supporters (p. 410)?

The preceding hiding place (no. 6) comprised a salt larder (3Q15 2:1f.), the importance of which for the community is emphasized in the Temple Scroll (11QTemple 20:13f.).[28] Hiding place no. 8 is also interesting: "In the subterranean corridor, which was found in the garden of Matthias [היתמ רזחבש]: in a wood pile and in the middle a cistern and in it seventy pieces of silver" (3Q15 2:5f.). With B. Z. Luria,[29] I read MTJH. But J. T. Milik[30] reads BTJH, although he admits that the first letter is a *mem* (מ) rather than a *beth* (ב). Matthias was a common name and was used in priests' families, as Luria has observed. Although it is probably unlikely that this man in the same area of the southwest hill was the same Matthias who was elected as successor of the betrayer Judas (Acts 1:15–26), the possibility cannot be totally dismissed. Researchers have suggested that there are Qumran parallels (1QS 6:16–22; 11:7) for the election procedure of Matthias.[31] We know very little about the Apostle Matthias. A comment

[27] *Jerusalem Explored, Being a Description of the Ancient and Modern City*, ed. T. E. BONNEY (London: Palestine Exploration Fund, 1864), 214–18 and plate 46.

[28] Cf. B. PIXNER, "Unravelling the Copper Scroll Code" (see n. 16), 344.

[29] *Megillat ha-Nahoschet me-Midbar Jehuda* [in Modern Hebrew] (Jerusalem: Magnes Press, 1963), 69.

[30] *"Petites grottes" de Qumran* (see n. 17), 286.

[31] Cf. H. BRAUN, *Qumran und das Neue Testament* (Tübingen: Mohr, 1966), 1:141.

by Clement of Alexandria that Matthias was known for his ascetic way of life[32] is particularly understandable if he had received his original training among the Essenes.

These reflections regarding the Copper Scroll have to remain conjecture. Important support for the reliability of the tradition and for the location of the Last Supper room are the parallels between the circumstances and date of the Last Supper of Jesus and the Essene Passover, as well as the close proximity of the Essene district and the meeting place of the first Christian community in Jerusalem.

[32] *Paedegogus* 2.1.

19. Epiphanius and the Last Supper on Zion

In his new commentary on the pilgrim report of Egeria, G. Röwekamp writes: "The tradition of the Last Supper on Zion appears only in the fifth century."[1] In an otherwise very valuable work about the archaeology of Jerusalem, the opinion was presented that the tradition for this location began only in the fifth century and was developed to satisfy the needs of pilgrims.[2] One reason suggested to support this late dating of the tradition is the scarcity of references in pilgrim records during the fourth century. However, particularly after the Council of Nicea (325), the relative absence of reports is because the Jewish Christians were considered Arians or at least semi-Arians, i.e., denying the full divinity of Jesus. But even during the critical fourth century, we possess traces of a tradition that the Pentecost event (Acts 2) took place on Mount Zion and that this was also the site of Jesus' Last Supper (Mk 14:12–26). Our information comes once again from the well-informed Bishop Epiphanius of Salamis.

Epiphanius, who was probably of Jewish Christian origin (p. 401), around 375 reported on the day and location for Jesus' Last Supper in very careful language in order not to be suspected of sympathies for the Jews. Epiphanius contradicts other views of his time by stating that Jesus celebrated the Passover meal on a Tuesday evening.[3] The research of the late Professor A. Jaubert, of the Sorbonne, suggests that this date was connected to the Essene calendar.[4] The thesis that the Jerusalem meal took place on Mount Zion supports this[5] because

[1] *Egeria: Itinerarium—Reisebericht*, Fontes Christiani 20 (Freiburg: Herder 1995), 60.

[2] K. Bieberstein and H. Bloedhorn, *Jerusalem: Grundzüge der Baugeschichte vom Chalkolithikum bis zur Frühzeit der osmanischen Herrschaft* (Wiesbaden: Harrassonwitz, 1994), 2:118–20.

[3] *Panarion* 51.26 (PG 41:934–36; GCS 31:295–97).

[4] *La date de la Cène* (Paris: Gabalda, 1957).

[5] Cf. D. Flusser, *The Spiritual History of the Dead Sea Sect* (Jerusalem: MOD Books, 1989), 25; J.H. Charlesworth, in J. Murphy-O'Connor, *Paul and the Dead Sea Scrolls*

the proximity of the Essene settlement to the traditional Last Supper room strengthens the assumption that Jesus actually celebrated his last Passover meal according to the calendar of the Essenes.[6] The Jewish researcher D. Flusser provided further corroboration for the Essene context for the meal. Flusser concluded from a study of the liturgical benediction over bread and wine (Mk 14:22f.; 1Cor 11:23f.) that the Early Church had been influenced by the Essene meal ceremony (1QS 6:4–6; 1QSa 2:18–20).[7] Epiphanius did not know the true reasons for the early communion date, but he recorded it faithfully.

It is all the more significant that Epiphanius writes: "For the fulfillment of the Passover, Jesus went on the mountain [εἰς τὸ ὄρος], where he ate the Passover, after he had been in such demand, as he said [Lk 22:15]. There he ate the Passover meal together with his disciples. He carried it out not any differently than them [the Jews], in order also in this case 'not to dissolve the law, but to fulfill it' [Mt 5:17]."[8] From all four Gospels it is clear that Jesus took the Last Supper within Jerusalem (Mt 26:18; Mk 14:13; Lk 22:10; Jn 18:1). If Epiphanius writes that Jesus went "on *the* [definite article!] mountain", then it can only mean Zion, which was at that time the higher west hill. Epiphanius also expressed himself very carefully regarding the Jewish Christian place of Mary's tomb (p. 401), and Zion was also for him in the hands of "those heretics" (p. 347).

Epiphanius reported that in A.D. 130–131 Emperor Hadrian, on one of his trips to Jerusalem (p. 335), visited Mount Zion and discovered a church built there at the site of the "Upper Room" (Acts 1:13).[9] This statement has recently been questioned and the opinion put forth that the Last Supper and the Pentecost event were originally commemorated in the Eleona basilica on the Mount of Olives.[10] Therefore, Cyril of Jerusalem (p. 345) in 348 would have spoken of this as

(New York: Doubleday, 1990), xv; R. ARAV and J.J. ROUSSEAU, *Jesus and His World: An Archaeological and Cultural Dictionary* (Minneapolis: Fortress, 1995), 177–79; C.R. PAGE, *Jesus and the Land* (Nashville: Thomas Nelson, 1995), 134–39.

[6] Cf. chapter 18, "The Last Supper of Jesus" (pp. 239–49).

[7] "The Last Supper and the Essenes", in *Judaism and the Origins of Christianity* (Jerusalem: Magnes Press, 1988), 202–6.

[8] *Panarion* 51.27 (PG 41:936; GCS 31:297f.).

[9] *De mensuris et ponderibus* 14 (PG 43:260–62; Baldi, 477f.).

[10] K. BIEBERSTEIN and H. BLOEDHORN, *Jerusalem* (see n. 2), 3:286.

the "Upper Church of the Apostles".[11] But this is completely improbable,[12] as the "Upper Room" was located inside the walls (Acts 1:12f.). With the restoration of the gothic Last Supper room (1995), many older walls have been uncovered.[13] But even before any further archaeological investigations are undertaken, it can be said that Jesus' journey to the last Passover meal led him onto Mount Zion. The Upper Room became the "mother of all churches"[14] after Easter and one of the most important places of the Early Church.

[11] *Catecheses* 16.4 (PG 33:924; Baldi, 474f.).

[12] Cf. R. Riesner, "Der christliche Zion: Vor- oder nachkonstantinisch?" in F. Manns and E. Alliata, *Early Christianity in Context: Documents and Monuments*, Festschrift for Emmanuele Testa, SBFCMa 38 (Jerusalem: Franciscan Printing Press, 1993), 85–90.

[13] Cf. E. Alliata, "Travaux au Cénacle", *Terre Sainte* (January 1995), 50f.

[14] Cf. chapter 25, "The Apostolic Synagogue on Zion" (pp. 319–59).

20. Where Was the House of Caiaphas Located?

Those who want to visit the places associated with the suffering of Jesus in Jerusalem and wish to find the location of the house of the high priest Caiaphas have two alternatives. One theory, which is still promoted by some pilgrim guides,[1] locates Caiaphas' house in the area of the small "Church of the Redeemer" (Saint Savior's), which lies approximately 20 m north of the church of the Dormition Abbey, within the Armenian cemetery area. The other theory proposes that the house (οἰκία [Lk 22:54]), respectively the palace of the high priest (αὐλὴ τοῦ ἀρχιερέως [Mt 26:3, 58, 69 / Mk 14:54, 66; cf. Lk 22:55; Jn 18:15]), where Jesus was condemned, was at the place where today, on the eastern slope of Mount Zion, stands the Assumptionist church "Saint Peter in Gallicantu" (Saint Peter of the Cock Crow) (illus. 58). The following information might assist visitors to Mount Zion and help to resolve this issue.

I. *The House of Caiaphas on the Hill of Zion*

1. The Armenian Church of the Savior

The oldest report, which describes the house of Caiaphas as close to the basilica Hagia Sion, originates from the hand of the Jerusalem monk Epiphanius, writing in the ninth century. His rather confused record reads,

> Beside the western gate [corresponding to today's Jaffa Gate] of the Holy City is the Davidic tower.... On the right hand of the tower is the Lithostrotos.... On the right of the Lithostrotos is the Hagia Sion.... In the hollow of the Hagia Sion, i.e., the Praetorium, is a small four-column yard with a coal fire stove, where Saint Peter was

[1] Cf. E. Hoade, *Guide to the Holy Land* (Jerusalem: Franciscan Printing Press, 1979), 318.

> questioned by the maidservant, where he denied Christ three times and where immediately afterward, the cock crowed three times. At the same place is also the house of Pilate, Annas and Caiaphas and the emperor [καὶ εἰς τὸν αὐτὸν τόπον ἐστὶν ὁ οἶκος τοῦ Πιλάτου, καὶ τοῦ Ἄννα, καὶ τοῦ Καϊάφα, καὶ τοῦ Καίσαρος]. Outside of the city, on the right-hand side near the wall, is a church, where Peter went and cried, and on the right of the church, three arrow shots distant, is the pool of Siloam.[2]

This "transfer" of Caiaphas' dwelling into the same building where it was assumed in the late Byzantine–Arab period (eighth to eleventh century) that the Praetorium of Pontius Pilate was located represents one of those frequent relocations of significant Christian sites that occurred during a difficult and obscure period. I have described elsewhere the reasons that caused the transfer of the Praetorium of Pilate to Mount Zion.[3] The destruction of the two basilicas, Hagia Maria Nea and Hagia Sophia (the Praetorium church), during the Persian attack and takeover in the year 614 and the occupation of the area south and west of the Al-Aqsa mosque by the Muslims during and after the Umayyad period (eighth century) forced the Christian community to abandon both churches and to look for a new place for the Praetorium (illus. 58). In addition, a paved yard north of the Hagia Sion became the new Lithostrotos. The location for the Praetorium, with its pavement on Zion, was originally a provisional solution, but this eventually became a permanent location, adopted later by the Crusaders.[4]

What was the cause for this late Byzantine relocation of Caiaphas' house to the "replacement Praetorium" on Zion? It is also strange that this site continued to be considered as the high priest's palace and the place where Peter regretted his actions. This "pooling" of the dwellings of Pilate, Caiaphas and the emperor (Tiberius/Hadrian?) into a single building clearly demonstrates relocation. It is possible that one cause for this confusion might be because of a clerical error in the text of the Gospel of Saint John circulating at that time. Where the original text of John 18:28 reads: "and they took Jesus from Caiaphas

[2] Baldi, 564f.; PG 120:261.

[3] "Noch einmal das Prätorium: Versuch einer neuen Lösung", *ZDPV* 95 (1979): 56–86 (at 72–74), as well as in this volume, chapter 21, "The Praetorium of Pilate" (pp. 266–90) and chapter 24, "The Historical Via Dolorosa" (pp. 303–15 esp. 310–11).

[4] Cf. Baldi, 586–88.

to the Praetorium" (ἄγουσιν οὖν τὸν Ἰησοῦν ἀπὸ τοῦ Καϊάφα εἰς τὸ πραιτώριον), variants to the text during this period were extant that read: "and they led Jesus to Caiaphas in the Praetorium" (*adducunt ergo Iesum ad* [instead of *a*] *Caipham in praetorium*).[5] This incorrect version of the text was known to Augustine, who even tried to explain this anomaly in his book *On the Consensus of the Evangelists*: "We understand that something caused Caiaphas to be in the Praetorium ... or that the Praetorium was in his house."[6] The Augustine Choirmasters, who at the time of the Crusades were given the care for the church buildings on Zion, adopted and repeated this variant version of Saint John's Gospel in their Evangeliarium, and their records therefore continued to assume that the Praetorium also served as the dwelling of Caiaphas, an idea supported by the monk Epiphanius. Later, during the time of the Crusades, it was firmly believed that Pilate's Praetorium was at the place of the fortress Antonia (p. 267). The confusion about Caiaphas' house has lasted until very recently, with pilgrims to Jerusalem continuing to assume that it was located on Mount Zion.

2. *The Excavations by the Armenian Church*

In 1971–1972, when the Israeli archaeologist M. Broshi, in his excavations on Mount Zion next to the Armenian Church of the Savior, discovered sophisticated and luxurious buildings from the Herodian period,[7] the location for Caiaphas' house was again discussed. During Broshi's excavations, a paved Byzantine road was uncovered, a road that once came from the north, leading to the Hagia Sion. East of this road, the remains of a house from Herod's time were discovered, which suggests two periods of settlement. According to Broshi, the house would initially have been destroyed by the earthquake of 31 B.C. (cf. *War* 1.370) and then rebuilt. In the debris of this magnificent building, frescoes were discovered that demonstrated a very good artistic hand.[8] Could this be the site for the house of Caiaphas? An unusual characteristic of the frescoes was that they had representations of birds, which was an offense in Judaism

[5] Cf. Baldi, 587, n. 1. Also, a Greek version (ἴσω εἰς τὴν αὐλὴν τοῦ Καϊάφα, ὅ ἐστιν πραιτώριον) of Mk 15:16 (M, Θ) could support this view.

[6] *De consensu evangelistarum* 3.7.27 (Baldi, 587, n. 1; PL 34:1174).

[7] "Excavations in the House of Caiaphas, Mount Zion", in Y. YADIN, *Jerusalem Revealed* (Jerusalem: Israel Exploration Society, 1976), 57–60.

[8] Ibid., plate 3.

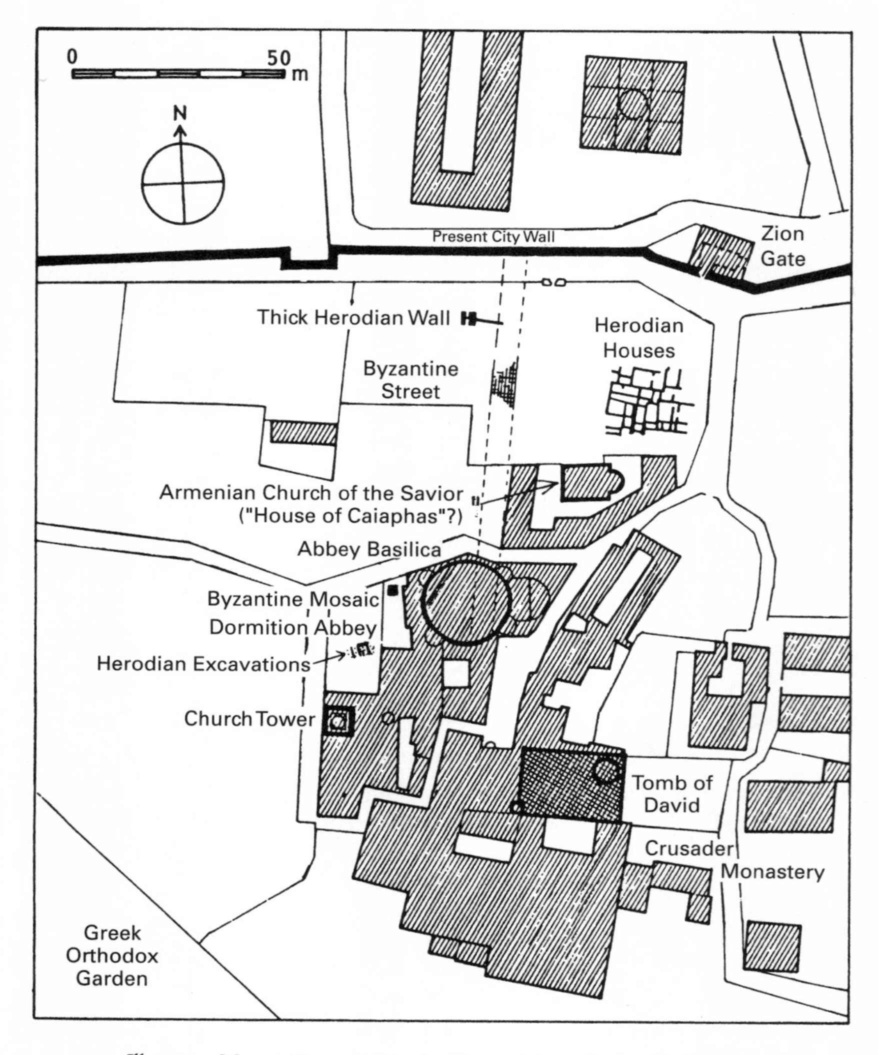

Illus. 60. Mount Zion—"Caiaphas' house" (according to M. Broshi).

because of the Mosaic prohibition on animal illustrations (Ex 20:4; Deut 4:15–19). It would be astonishing to find such a violation of the Torah in the house of a high priest in Jerusalem. While in later Byzantine times, many Jewish synagogues did have representations of animals and people, something like that would have been inconceivable in the period of the second temple. Even Herod the Great, who was not scrupulous in religious observance, avoided such representations in his buildings and palaces, as the excavations at Masada and Jerusalem have demonstrated. I believe that these animal paintings exclude the possibility that Broshi found the high priest's palace on Mount Zion.

What particularly made Christian researchers who were searching for Caiaphas' palace on Zion repeatedly hesitate was the proximity of the Last Supper hall,[9] if the local tradition is considered genuine.[10] It is hardly conceivable that the Last Supper, the Pentecost experience and the regular meeting place of the original community could have been located close to the palace of the high priest. Therefore, all reasons speak against the late tradition for the site of Caiaphas' house at the Armenian Church of the Savior. If we consider the most ancient local reports, it is clear that today's Church of Saint Peter in Gallicantu, on the eastern slope of Mount Zion, most likely represents the correct location of Caiaphas' house.

II. Caiaphas' House on the Eastern Slope of Zion

1. The Excavations Near Saint Peter in Gallicantu

In the year 1888 the area on which is located today's church "Saint Peter of the Cock Crow" was excavated by the Assumptionist Fathers, who discovered the remains of ancient buildings.[11] Important excavation finds had been preserved because above them a church had been built, which was completed and dedicated in the year 1931. The Assumptionist X. Marchet[12] and the Jesuit E. Power[13] were the main supporters for locating Caiaphas' house on the eastern slope of Zion. Their opinion has, however, been persistently resisted,[14] and even today, this resistance has not yet been completely overcome.[15]

[9] Cf. C. Kopp, *Die heiligen Stätten der Evangelien*, 2nd ed. (Regensburg: Pustet, 1964), 404.

[10] Cf. chapter 18, "The Last Supper of Jesus" (pp. 239–49), and chapter 25, "The Apostolic Synagogue on Zion" (pp. 319–59).

[11] Cf. J. Germer-Durand, "La maison de Caiphe et l'Eglise Saint Pierre à Jérusalem", *RB* 11 (1914): 71–94, 222–46.

[12] *Le véritable emplacement du palais de Caïphe et l'église Saint Pierre à Jérusalem* (Paris, 1927).

[13] "The Church of St. Peter at Jerusalem and Its Relation to the House of Caiaphas and St. Sion", *Biblica* 9 (1928): 167–86; "St. Peter in Gallicantu and the House of Caiaphas", *Oriens Christianus* 6 (1931): 182–208.

[14] Cf. esp. L. H. Vincent and F. M. Abel, *Jérusalem: Recherches de topographie, d'archéologie et d'histoire*, vol. 2, *Jérusalem nouvelle*, pt. 3, *La Sainte-Sion et les sanctuaires de second ordre* (Paris: Gabalda, 1922), 482–96.

[15] Cf. also R. Riesner, "Palast des Hohenpriesters", in *GBL*, 2nd ed. (1990): 3:1109f.

The most remarkable discovery was a 6-m-deep and 4-m-broad cistern that had three Byzantine crosses carved in its neck. This cistern is shown today to pilgrims as the "prison of Christ". It has been made accessible to visitors by a break in the south wall. It is always very moving when Psalm 88 is read there, a psalm that is put into the mouth of the imprisoned Lord. However, it is not certain whether this cistern existed at the time of Christ or whether it was built during the Byzantine period. Halfway up the eastern wall there is an opening provided with steps, which is divided into two halves by a pilaster. This was originally the entrance into a Jewish ritual bath (*mikveh*), similar to many that were found in the excavations in

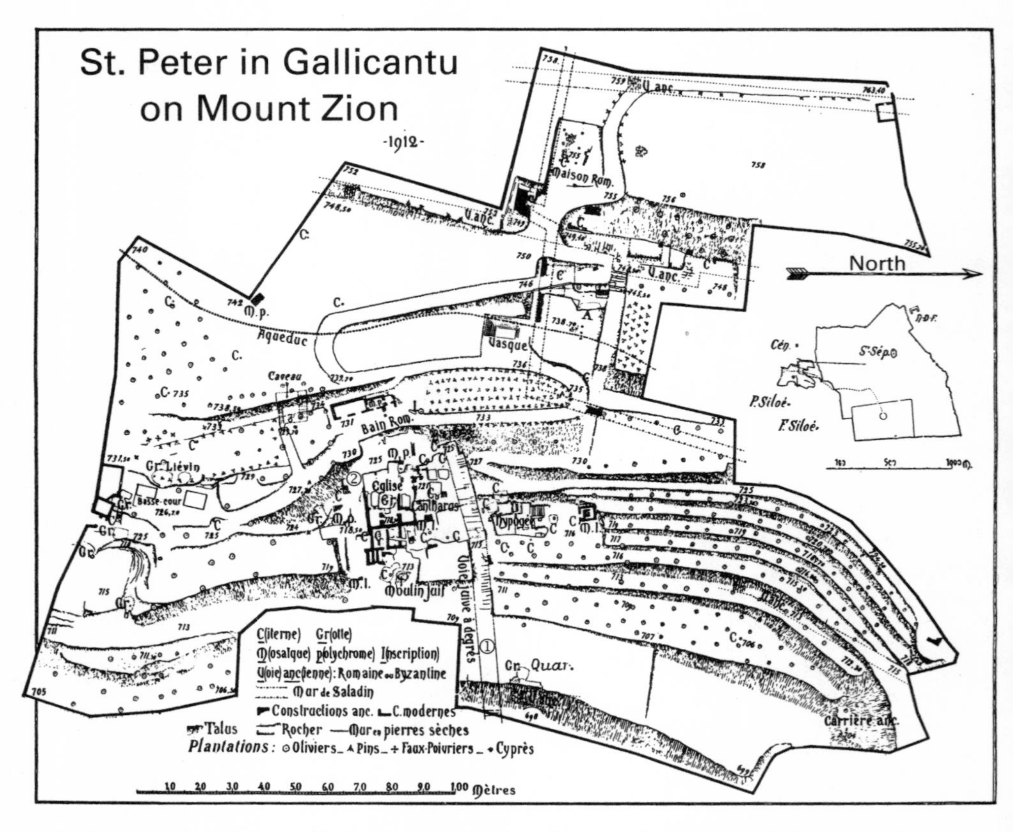

*Illus. 61. St. Peter in Gallicantu—excavations (according to J. Germer-Durand O.S.A., et al., 1912). 1. Stepped path dating from Roman times. 2. St. Peter in Gallicantu (*Église Gr.*). Beneath the church is the cistern venerated as the "Prison of Christ" (*Église Gr.*).*

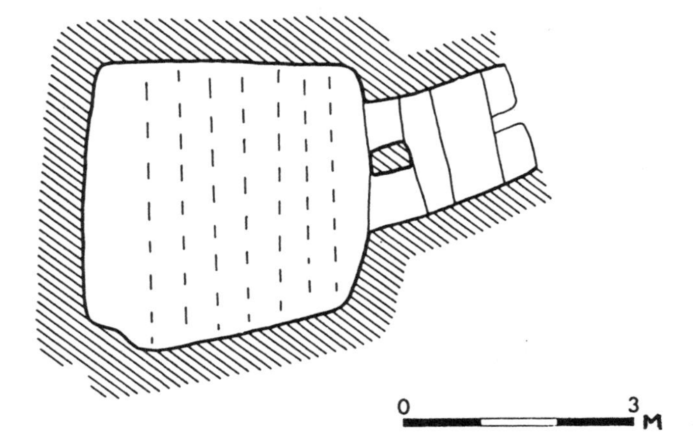

Illus. 62. The venerated cistern, originally a ritual bath (according to R. Reich). The access steps are clearly separated into two halves.

Jerusalem.[16] Such an installation would naturally fit well in a priest's house. It is not possible to determine, however, when the *mikveh* was transformed into a cistern (or maybe a pit or dungeon?). It is more likely that this was the location of the high priest's palace, as a fragment of a door lintel was discovered on which the Aramaic word *korban* (קרבן), "offering" (cf. Mk 7:11), was inscribed.[17] The inscribed stone served later as a door lintel for the gift shop of the Assumptionists.

Another very interesting discovery was the remains of a long outdoor staircase, which perhaps originally led from the pool of Siloam onto the hill of Zion (illus. 61). It is today shown to pilgrims as the stairs by way of which Jesus was led as a prisoner. A close examination reveals that some of these ancient stairs are higher on one side than on the other. If this was a general characteristic of the stairs, it could explain a puzzling remark in Aristeas' letter (p. 208). There it says (Pseudo-Aristeas 106) that some inhabitants of Jerusalem, who followed special purity regulations, reserved a part of the stairs.[18] In the

[16] Cf. R. Reich, "*Mishna Sheqalim* 8:3 and the Archaeological Evidence" [in Modern Hebrew], in A. Oppenheimer, U. Rappaport and M. Stern, *Jerusalem in the Second Temple Period: Abraham Schalit Memorial Volume* (Jerusalem: Magnes Press, 1980), 225–56 (at 241–44).

[17] Cf. J. A. Fitzmyer and D. J. Harrington, *A Manual of Palestinian Aramaic Texts* (Rome: Pontifical Biblical Institute Press, 1978), nos. 107, 234.

[18] Cf. P. Riessler, *Altjüdische Schrifttum zur Bibel*, 2nd ed. (Heidelberg: Kerrie, 1966 [1928]), 206.

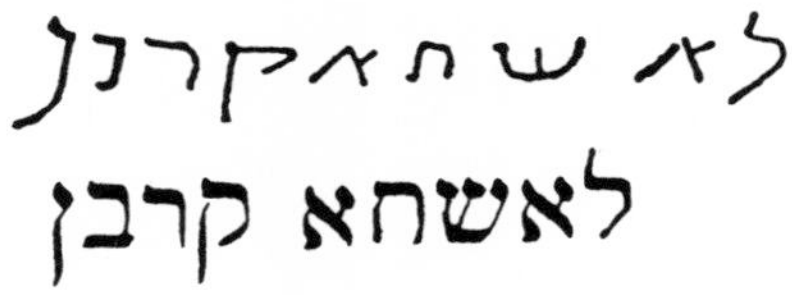

לא שחאקרבן

לאשחא קרבן

Illus. 63. The korban *inscription (sketch).*

New Testament period, the Essene quarter was situated on the southwest part of Mount Zion.[19]

2. The Madaba Mosaic Map

Important support for the proposal that Caiaphas' house is on the eastern slope of Mount Zion comes from the Madaba Mosaic Map, which dates from the middle of the sixth century (plate 1). Today we are able to identify the different churches that are shown on the map in the southern part of the Jerusalem area (illus. 98). It is generally accepted that churches are indicated on the mosaic map with roofs made with red stones. The Hagia Sion and the ancient "Church of the Apostles" (pp. 351–52) are indicated in this way. This is also true of the large Nea church and the Hagia Sophia (pp. 281–82). Unfortunately, the corner of the southeast part of this Jerusalem map, which included the area with the Siloam church and the Tekoah Gate, was destroyed. Fortunately, the Church of Saint Peter in Gallicantu (Caiaphas' house) is still recognizable, although part of it was also lost. Still remaining is the front and part of the roof. For the identification of this building as the Church of Saint Peter, it is of extraordinary importance that two red mosaic stones of the roof are still present. Due to new excavations in the Jewish quarter of the Old City, today we know the exact location of the Nea (pp. 281–83). The location of the fragmentary church on the mosaic map, its distance to the Hagia Sion, to the Nea and to the Sophia leave no doubt. The Christian memorial church was built ca. 450, over the ruins of Caiaphas' palace.[20] The location indicated by the mosaic map corresponds exactly to today's Church of Saint Peter in Gallicantu.

[19] Cf. chapter 15, "The Essene Quarter in Jerusalem" (pp. 192–219).

[20] Cf. already M. Gisler, "Jerusalem auf der Mosaikkarte von Madaba", *HlL* 56 (1912): 214–17 (at 223).

3. The Oldest Pilgrim Reports

Descriptions from the most ancient Christian traditions also point to the area on the east slope between the hill of Zion and the pool of Siloam. In order to be able to understand these reports from the early Christian period, I would like briefly to describe how the topography of Jerusalem at that time looked (illus. 64). The city was twice destroyed, in the year A.D. 70 by the troops of Titus and then again in A.D. 135 by Hadrian's legions. When Hadrian went to Jerusalem in order to rebuild it as a Roman colony, he renamed the city Aelia Capitolina. He flattened the quarry area around the rock of Golgotha in order to construct on it the *forum Hadriani*. Over the place of the crucifixion and Resurrection of Christ, revered by the Jewish Christian community, he established a temple to the goddess Venus.[21] South of it, as has been demonstrated by recent excavations, was the street that followed the same direction as today's King David Street (from the Jaffa Gate to the east) (p. 339). Further to the south was the camp of the *legio X Fretensis*. The western town wall, which was not destroyed in A.D. 70 (cf. *War* 7.1–3), forms part of today's Citadel. This wall ends at an ascent discovered by M. Broshi.[22] This ascent represented the western entrance of the legion's camp.[23] From there, the south wall continued to the southeast corner of the temple. South of this were fields and vegetable gardens, and Eusebius reports that looking at these he could observe how Roman veterans worked in the fields.[24]

On the hill of Zion at that time stood the Jewish Christian synagogue that was built toward the end of the first century (the "Church of the Apostles"). The hill was surrounded by a modest wall, *murus Sion*, described by the Pilgrim of Bordeaux (see below). It seemed to be a kind of ghetto wall that the small Jewish Christian community built for protection against the Gentiles from Aelia and later from the Gentile Christians of the Byzantine city. Around 370 Optatus of Mileve described the topographical situation of Zion in this way: Mount Zion in Palestine "lies somewhat apart, separated from the walls of Jerusalem by a small brook [*parvus rivus*]. Its hill has a not very large, but

[21] Cf. chapter 24, "The Historical Via Dolorosa" (pp. 303–15).

[22] "Along Jerusalem's Walls", *BA* 40 (1977): 11–17.

[23] Cf. B. Pixner, "The History of the 'Essene Gate' Area", *ZDPV* 105 (1989): 96–104 (at 99).

[24] *Demonstratio Evangelica* 6.13.17 (PG 22:636; GCS 23:265).

flat, area."[25] This small, dry wadi, which appears north of Saint Peter in Gallicantu and goes into the Tyropoeon Valley, has been rediscovered in recent excavations.

Following the description of the topography of Zion during the time of Aelia Capitolina, we can understand better the important report of the Pilgrim of Bordeaux, who visited Jerusalem in the year 333. After he had visited the temple square, he says, "One goes from Jerusalem [*exeuntibus Jerusalem*] in order to ascend to Zion, then the Siloam pool is on the left [*in parte sinistra*]." The pilgrim thus left the city by today's Dung Gate and went down to the Siloam pool. After the pilgrim visited the pool, the text continues, "In the same [area] one goes up to Zion [*in eadem ascenditur Sion*], and it becomes visible where the house of Caiaphas the priest was situated [*et paret, ubi fuit domus Caifae sacerdotis*]; there is still the column, where they struck Jesus with scourges. Inside, however, within the wall of Zion [*intra murum Sion*], the place appears where David's palace was located."[26] Caiaphas' house, which the pilgrim visited, was thus on the slope of Zion between the Siloam pool and the wall surrounding the hill of Zion. The south entrance of this wall, by which the pilgrim probably entered the Jewish Christian ghetto, was exposed, following our excavations of the Essene Gate in 1979 (pp. 203–6). After visiting the pilgrim places on the hill of Zion, the pilgrim again crossed Zion's wall (*inde ut eas forum murum de Sion*), and going toward the Neapolitan Gate (in the area of today's Damascus Gate), he saw, toward the Tyropoeon Valley, and to the right, the ruins of the Praetorium of Pilate (*parietes ubi domus fuit sive praetorium Pontii Pilati*).[27] The scourge column mentioned by the pilgrim was brought (between 380 and 390) to Zion and installed in the first Byzantine church (p. 351).

The ruin of Caiaphas' house was so well known by the people in Jerusalem that somewhat later (348) Cyril of Jerusalem preached in the Church of the Holy Sepulchre: "The house of Caiaphas will accuse you. By its current destruction it teaches the power of the one, who, at that time, in this house was condemned."[28] In the background of this sermon are Jesus' prophecies about the destruction of Jerusalem (Mk 13:2). We can assume that in the middle of the fifth century, over

[25] *De schismate Donatistarum* 3.2 (Baldi, 475; PL 11:994).

[26] *Itinerarium* 16 (Geyer, 22; Baldi, 562).

[27] Ibid. For further interpretation of the pilgrim's route, cf. B. Pixner, "Noch einmal das Prätorium" (see n. 3), 66f.

[28] *Catecheses* 13 (Baldi, 563; PG 33:817).

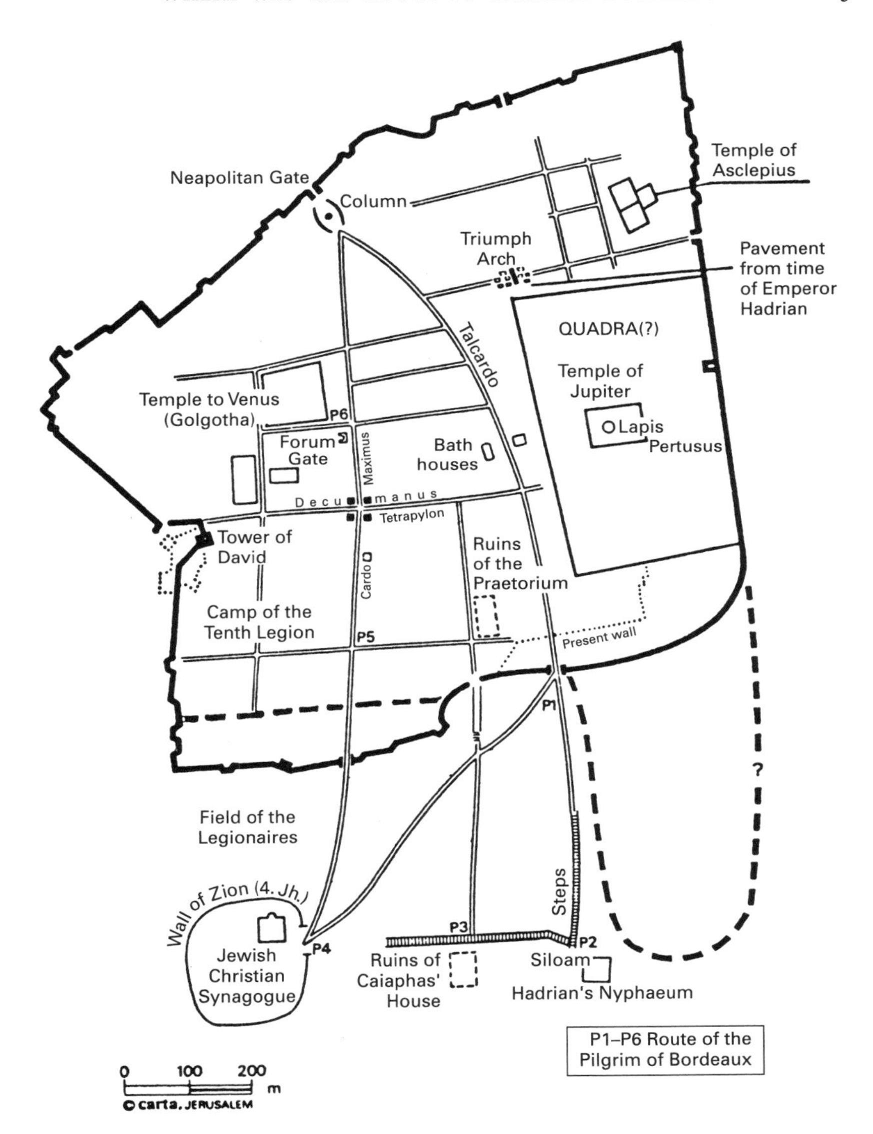

Illus. 64. Jerusalem in late Roman times (Aelia Capitolina, A.D. *135–330/340)*

the ruins of Caiaphas' palace, a church was built that was dedicated to Saint Peter. Possibly this building was also established, like so many other churches, by the empress Eudocia, who during her long stay in Jerusalem felt a special admiration for this Apostle. The Armenian lectionary (Jerusalem 121) at the beginning of the fifth century still mentions the Court of the High Priest, which was included as one of the Stations of the Cross in the large Good Friday procession.[29] The Georgian lectionary, which goes back to the middle of the same century, calls it "the Church of Saint Peter".[30] The description in the Armenian lectionary indicates clearly that the house of Caiaphas cannot have been on the hill but must have been on the eastern slope of Zion in the area of Saint Peter in Gallicantu.[31]

Another important witness is Theodosius (ca. 530), who, in order to measure the different distances between the various holy places, used most probably an "as the crow flies" guess plus the help of an available Jerusalem map. The text reads: "From holy Zion to the house of Caiaphas, which is now the Church of Saint Peter, it is more or less 50 (double) steps [approximately 75 m]. From the house of Caiaphas up to the praetorium of Pilate, there are nearly 100 (double) steps [approximately 150 m]."[32] Also, the author of *Breviarius de Hierosolyma*, who traveled around that time from the Church of Zion, wrote that "the house of Caiaphas, where Saint Peter denied Jesus, is the large basilica of Saint Peter."[33] Around A.D. 870 a monk called Bernhard reported: "Toward the east [*in directum autem ad orientem* (from the Hagia Sion)] is the church dedicated to blessed Peter in the place where he denied the Lord."[34] The text clearly indicates the area of Saint Peter in Gallicantu, while the Armenian Church of the Savior lies to the north of Zion's church.

Testimonies from pilgrims increased during the Crusader period and in the centuries following.[35] The difference between the ancient and

[29] A. Renoux, *Le codex arménien Jerusalem 121*, vol. 2, PO 36:2 (Turnhout: Brepols, 1971), 277–79.

[30] M. Tarchnischvili, *Le grand lectionnaire de l'Église de Jérusalem (Ve–VIIIe siècle)*, vol. 1, CSCO 188 (Louvain: Presses Universitaires, 1959), 188f.

[31] A. Renoux, *Codex arménien* (see n. 29), 2:197, makes an important topographical remark: "Une autre indication topographique montre qu'il faut situer, bien à l'est du Cénacle, la cour du grand prêtre. Après la statio a cet endroit en effet, le seul ms. J. prévoit, pour accompagner la procession jusqu'à *la porte*, le long Ps. CXVIII, psalmodié avec antienne. Si *la cour du grand prêtre* devait être localisée á la *Maison de Caïphe* du Mont Sion, située à 50 mètres de la Porte de Sion, cette prescription serait sans raison." I believe that the reference is to the Balat (i.e., Pilate) Gate (p. 301), so that the long psalm becomes more understandable.

[32] *De situ terrae sanctae* 7 (Geyer, 141; Baldi, 563).

[33] Geyer, 155; Baldi, 563.

[34] Baldi, 564.

[35] Cf. Baldi, 565ff.

the more recent reports is that after the ninth or tenth century there was a duplicating of locations of religious significance. An example of this is the erroneous location of the Praetorium near Zion's basilica, by the house of Caiaphas; another example is that on the eastern slope of Zion, where only the place of Peter's denial was commemorated. There is no doubt that this "doubling up" occurred at a later date and that the ancient recognized place where Jesus was cross-examined by the high priest was in the area where today the church of the Assumptionists, Saint Peter in Gallicantu, stands.

Supplement: Because of the scarcity of archaeological evidence, K. Bieberstein and H. Bloedhorn disagree that the venerated grotto of Saint Peter in Gallicantu was where a previous Byzantine church had existed.[36] It is to be hoped that further excavations will resolve this and continue the work of the Assumptionist archaeologist F. Diaz, which he began in 1993 on behalf of the Spanish Bible Institute. He has discovered, north of the area and near to the staired street Scala Santa, settlement traces from the New Testament period and a plastered square from the Byzantine period.[37]

[36] *Jerusalem: Grundzüge der Baugeschichte vom Chalkolithikum bis zur Frühzeit der osmanianischen Herrschaft* (Wiesbaden, 1994), 3:414.

[37] "Jerusalem, Church of St. Peter in Gallicantu" [in Modern Hebrew], *Hadashot Arkheologiyot* 103 (1995): 68.

21. The Praetorium of Pilate

Archaeologists who examined the places in Jerusalem associated with the Gospels were preoccupied above all by the question: Where was the location of the Praetorium of Pilate, where Jesus was condemned to crucifixion? The answer to this question depends upon the identification of the original Via Dolorosa. Today experts agree where the route to the cross ends: at the rock on the right of the entrance of the Church of the Holy Sepulchre. Modern archaeology has demonstrated that at the time of the Resurrection of Jesus and the old Israeli monarchy, this rock stood approximately 15 m out of an old quarry (pp. 304–6). But if the end of the historical Via Dolorosa is sure, where then was its starting point; or in other words, where was the place of the Praetorium, where Jesus took up his cross?

I. Three Different Praetorium Theories

We can say one thing with certainty: the Praetorium of Pilate was in one of the three palaces of Herod the Great, two of which were built by his predecessors and one that he had built himself (illus. 58). After the death of Herod (4 B.C.) and the banishing of his son Archelaus (see Mt 2:22) in the year A.D. 6, all three palaces were used by the Roman governors before Herod Agrippa I (A.D. 41–44). There was the old king's palace, which had been built by the Hasmoneans. In addition, there was the temple fortress, which was formerly called "Baris" and later "Antonia". The third palace was the upper palace, located in the area of today's Citadel, which was built by Herod in the middle of his reign (about 23 B.C.). The question is, which of these three palaces was the one used by Pilate in the trial of Jesus? Each of the three alternatives has its particular advocates.

1. The Antonia Fortress

Was the Praetorium in the Antonia, as is supported by a late Crusader tradition? Since the twelfth century the Antonia has been the accepted starting point for the Via Dolorosa. L. H. Vincent,[1] the famous archaeologist of the École biblique in Jerusalem, and Sister Marie Aline of the Sisters of Zion[2] believed that they had found archaeological evidence for this tradition when they discovered an impressive limestone pavement under the arches of the Ecce Homo basilica. Unfortunately, their joy to have found the Lithostrotos (Λιθόστρωτος) of John 19:13 was short-lived, because the pavement found there proved to be from a much later time, probably from the time of the emperor Hadrian (A.D. 117–138).

2. The Upper Palace of Herod

Was the Praetorium of the Gospels in Herod's upper palace (the Citadel), as most researchers today believe? Pierre Benoit[3] was of this opinion—in opposition to his teacher and friend L. H. Vincent—for the following reasons: (1) The archaeological arguments for an Antonia Praetorium are not convincing. (2) The Christian tradition for Antonia begins only very late, i.e., in the twelfth century. (3) The historical sources and most significantly the Jewish historical writer Flavius Josephus proved definitely that the Antonia fortress was used neither by Herod the Great nor by any of his successors as a residence. The Roman prefect required a praetorium and a courthouse, and Pilate's residence is described in Matthew 27:27; Mark 15:16; and John 18:28, 33, and 19:9 as a praetorium (πραιτώριον) and in Mark 15:16 as a palace (αὐλή). The greatest obstacle in recognizing the Citadel as the place of the Praetorium is that this hypothesis contradicts the record of the local church in Jerusalem.

[1] *Jérusalem de l'Ancien Testament*, vol. 1, *Archéologie de la ville* (with M. A. STEVE) (Paris: Gabalda, 1954), 193–221; "L'Antonia, palais primitive d'Hérode", *RB* 61 (1959): 87–107.

[2] *La forteresse Antonia à Jérusalem et la question du prétoire* (Jerusalem: Franciscan Printing Press, 1955).

[3] "Prétoire, Lithostroton Gabbatha", *RB* 59 (1952): 531–50; "L'Antonia d'Hérode le Grand et le Forum Oriental d'Aelia Capitolina", *Harvard Theological Review* 64 (1971): 135–67; "The Archaeological Reconstruction of the Antonia Fortress", in Y. YADIN, *Jerusalem Revealed* (Jerusalem: Israel Exploration Society, 1976), 87–89. See also A. VANEL, "Prétoire," *Dictionnaire Biblique* Supplément 8 (Paris: Gabalda, 1969), 513–54.

3. The Hasmonean Palace

New archaeological excavations in the Jewish old town quarter threw new light on the situation of the old Praetorium church in the Byzantine period. As we will see, this new evidence points to an area opposite Robinson's arch and the southwest corner of the temple wall. The arguments for the site of the Byzantine Praetorium have convinced me and a number of researchers.[4] I published an article that included further detail in the scientific journal of the German Palestine Association.[5] Did the Byzantine Praetorium church then really stand at the place of the house of Pilate, or was the whole tradition mistaken?

The ancient Church tradition, which was further supported by new archaeological evidence, points to an area that, at the time of Jesus, belonged to the ancient royal palace of the Hasmoneans. If the Christian community of Jerusalem retained a genuine memory about the place of Jesus' trial, then only the ancient Hasmonean palace is a possibility and warrants further investigation. In order to understand why this ancient tradition, which is based on a whole set of literary sources and supported now also by archaeological finds, is the most likely site, we will now examine the history and the situation of the three alternative places.

II. The Three Castles of Herod

I. The History of the Three Castles

Herod the Great (40 B.C.–A.D. 4), who, following a three-year struggle, gained the throne of the Hasmonean (Maccabean) dynasty, possessed in Jerusalem three castles:

1. The fortress Antonia:[6] On a rock formation directly north of the temple area stood the castle Baris, which had been built by the Hasmonean Hyrcanus I (134–104 B.C.) (*Ant.* 18.91; *War* 1.75). Herod, one of the most

[4] K. JAROŠ, "Ein neuer Lokalisierungsversuch des Praetoriums", *Bibel und Liturgie* 53 (1980): 13–22; A. STROBEL, *Die Stunde der Wahrheit,* WUNT 21 (Tübingen: Mohr Siebeck, 1980), 110, n. 33; E. OTTO, *Jerusalem: Die Geschichte der Heiligen Stadt* (Stuttgart: Kohlhammer, 1980), 152f.; P. BENOIT, "Le Prétoire de Pilate á l'époque byzantine", *RB* 91 (1984): 161–77; R. RIESNER, "Das Praetorium des Pilatus", *BiKi* 41 (1986): 34–37; RIESNER, "Praetorium", in *GBL,* 2nd ed. (1990), 2:1221f. The different opinions are also discussed by E. W. COHN, *New Ideas about Jerusalem's Topography* (Jerusalem: Franciscan Printing Press, 1987), 73–114.

[5] "Noch einmal das Pratorium: Versuch einer neuer Lösung", *ZDPV* 95 (1979): 56–86.

[6] Cf. R. RIESNER, "Antonia", in *GBL,* 2nd ed. (1990), 1:68.

prolific builders in history, altered the old building into an imposing fortress, in order to be able to control the movement of people across the enormous temple square. Antonia was also the place where the high priest's robes were kept (*Ant.* 15.403–8). Herod called the fortress after his Roman friend Marcus Antonius (*War* 1.401). He must have done this before Marcus' defeat of the later emperor Augustus at Actium (31 B.C.).

2. The Hasmonean palace: This palace served the Hasmonean dynasty for over one hundred years as a royal residence. In the year 40 B.C. Herod took this palace from the Hasmonean Hyrcanus II (63–40 B.C.), but he had to surrender it when Hyrcanus' hostile brother Antigonus won the upper hand with the help of Parthian soldiers. In the year 37 B.C., however, when he had been recognized by the Romans as the Jewish king, Herod returned, defeated the last Hasmonean and took up residence in the royal palace once again. Here he lived for one and a half decades. Josephus stresses the fact that during this period (37–23 B.C.) Herod resided only in the Hasmonean palace (αὐλή) and not in the fortress Antonia (*Ant.* 15.292). It is also reported that it was in this palace that he exercised judicial office when he uncovered a conspiracy (*Ant.* 15.286).

The conspiracy investigation led to the execution of Herod's wife Mariamne, and following this, he became ill with despair. When his Hasmonean mother-in-law Alexandra heard that Herod's physician had given up on him, she forged a further conspiracy in order to obtain the palace and also, because of its strategic situation, to obtain the Antonia. Josephus writes: "Here were two [castles]. One of them was in the city, the other near the temple, and whoever possessed them had also power over the Jews. Because without them, it was impossible to bring the daily offerings" (*Ant.* 15.247). Herod discovered this conspiracy and then had Alexandra executed. The Hasmonean palace then had a history as a judicial place, even before the Romans took it over.

3. Herod's upper palace in the area of today's Citadel: In the year 23 B.C., approximately halfway through his reign, Herod's situation became more secure, and he decided, in order to control the whole city, to build his own palace in the area of today's Jaffa Gate. Herod built a magnificent palace. The palace's most beautiful buildings were called Caesareum and Agrippeum, and they were strengthened by three powerful towers in the so-called first wall (Hippicus, Phasael and Mariamne). Here, Herod lived with his women and his large retinue (*Ant.* 15.318; *War* 1.402; 5.177–83).

With the building of the upper palace, however, the lower Hasmonean palace was not deserted, but very probably it continued to be utilized for administrative purposes. A similar development took place in Masada, where the so-called west palace built by the Hasmoneans served as an administration building. Herod renovated this palace and at the same time established for himself and his dependents (on the climatically more pleasant northwest corner of the Masada rock) a beautiful three-story palace for his residence. A similar division between living and administration seems also to have taken place in the Herodian palaces of Jericho and Caesarea Maritima (see Acts 23:35; 24:2, 23f.).

2. *The Use of the Palaces by the Roman Prefects*

When Archelaus was removed in the year 6 A.D. and banished by imperial decree, all of his possessions were confiscated and added to the imperial treasure (τοῖς Καίσαρος θησαυροῖς [*Ant.* 17.344; *War* 2.111]). From this we can conclude that all Roman prefects up to the accession of the Jewish king Agrippa I (A.D. 41–44) were in possession of the three palaces and were using them. Two events during the term of the office of Pontius Pilate seem to indicate the purpose for which he used the upper and the lower Herodian palace. The first episode is reported by Philo of Alexandria. When Pilate had a golden plaque mounted on the Herodian palace (the Citadel), it provoked a riot. This palace was called "the house of the governor" (οἰκία τῶν ἐπιτρόπων).[7]

If the upper palace was used by Pilate as a personal residence (cf. Mt 27:19), then it is very probable that the lower (Hasmonean) palace, only a little way off, was used exclusively for administrative purposes. During his tumultuous term of office, a further event seems to have taken place in the lower palace, which Josephus reported. Pilate had an aqueduct built in order to improve the water supply in Jerusalem. This aqueduct, which came from the Solomon pools at Bethlehem, led through the area of the Hasmonean palace and ended after crossing "Wilson's arch" within the temple area. Its route can still be followed today. In the area where the water pipeline is nearest the supposed location of the palace, a large number of ritual baths were discovered. Josephus reports that the people rose in indignation against Pilate because he had used temple treasury money for the building of

[7] *Legatio ad Gaium* 299–305 (L. COHN and P. W. WENDLAND, *Philonis Alexandrini opera quae supersunt*, vol. 4 [Berlin, 1915], 210ff.).

this aqueduct (*War* 2.175). In an article following the equating of the Praetorium with the Hasmonean palace (n. 4), K. Jaroš suggested that the true reason behind the riot was not because the temple money was taken to improve the water supply of the temple but because this water for the temple was used also by the Roman soldiers in the Praetorium for their baths and thus was "defiled". Cynically, Pilate expected the attack of the crowds and instructed his soldiers to mingle with them in civilian clothes, with hidden clubs. From his "throne of judgment" (ἀπὸ τοῦ βήματος) he instructed his soldiers to attack, and many Jews were killed (*Ant.* 17.60–62; *War* 2.175–77).

The reason Pilate gave his signal from his "throne" was because it was a secure place, easily visible by the soldiers mixing with the crowd. This must have been the same throne of judgment (mentioned in the Gospel of Matthew) where Pilate was sitting (ἐπὶ τοῦ βήματος) when his wife, who had very probably spent the night in the upper palace, sent a messenger because of her dream (Mt 27:19; cf. Jn 19:13). This raises an interesting question: Why did she not inform him directly in the morning? Had Pilate perhaps spent the night in the lower palace? Naturally, we cannot be sure, but it is possible that the governor was with Herod Antipas during the Passover ceremonies. Although Pilate disliked Antipas, diplomacy dictated that he had to offer him, as the tetrarch of a friendly territory, the luxurious comfort of the upper palace. It was here that Antipas had spent most of his childhood. If the trial of Jesus took place in the lower palace, then we can understand the remark by Luke (23:7) that Pilate "sent him up" as an accused to Herod (ἀνέπεμψεν).[8] By this act, their relationship improved: "And Herod and Pilate became friends with each other that very day, for before this they had been at enmity with each other" (Lk 23:12).

An event reported by Josephus (*War* 2.301–8) is often quoted in the controversy over the location for the Praetorium that might challenge the transfer of the Praetorium into the lower palace. The event is a certain parallel to the trial of Jesus and clearly took place in the upper palace. In the year A.D. 66, during the outbreak of the Jewish rebellion,

[8] The other examples of ἀναπέμπειν in Luke are unclear either due to textual variants or mean "to send to a higher authority". The latter is not possible in the case of Pilate, who regarded himself as far superior as province ruler. Cf. C. Mommert, *Das Prätorium des Pilatus* (Leipzig: Deichert, 1903), 22. The expression ἀναπέμπειν would also fit if Antipas had stayed overnight in the Antonia, which represents another possibility.

the governor Gessius Florus came from his usual residence in Caesarea to Jerusalem and moved into the upper Herodian palace. On the next day, he ordered, through hatred of and revenge against the Jews, that the judgment throne (βῆμα) be set before the palace (καθέζεται), and then he ordered that some prominent representatives of the people (*War* 2.301) be cruelly scourged and crucified. There is, however, a significant difference between the situation of Pilate and that of Florus. After the sudden death of King Herod Agrippa I in the year A.D. 44, his son was too young to succeed to the throne, so the Roman governors again took over the responsibility for Judea—but with one exception. The Herodian Hasmonean family of Agrippa retained the Hasmonean palace and also "the jurisdiction over the temple and the money of the holy treasury and the selection of the high priest. This authority remained valid for their descendants up to the end of the war" (*Ant.* 20.16; cf. *Ant.* 20.103, 197, 203).

The Roman governors resided normally only in Caesarea Maritima. Paul was sent there as a prisoner and held in "Herod's praetorium" for two years (Acts 23:35). The upper palace of Herod in Jerusalem was different from the lower Hasmonean palace because it did not possess its own judgment throne. Florus had such a throne set up in front of the palace (βῆμα, without article). Bernice, the sister of Agrippa II, who had dared to walk barefoot in front of the furious governor in order to intercede with him, was ridiculed and mistreated, and with her bodyguard she had to flee and take refuge in the "king's castle". This must have been the Hasmonean palace (*War* 2.309–14).

3. *The Location of the Hasmonean Palace*

The location for the Hasmonean palace could not be identified with certainty until now. The old consensus that this palace must have stood close to the "first [north] wall" is no longer credible because of the thorough excavations of N. Avigad, who was unable to uncover any traces of that building in that area, although a considerable portion of the "first wall" was discovered with a Hasmonean tower.[9] From Josephus (*Ant.* 15.189f.) we can conclude that the palace must have stood

[9] "Excavations into the Jewish Quarter of the Old City of Jerusalem, 1971 (Third Preliminary Report)", *IEJ* 22 (1972): 193f.; "The Jewish Quarter of the Old City, 1975", *IEJ* 25 (1975): 260f.

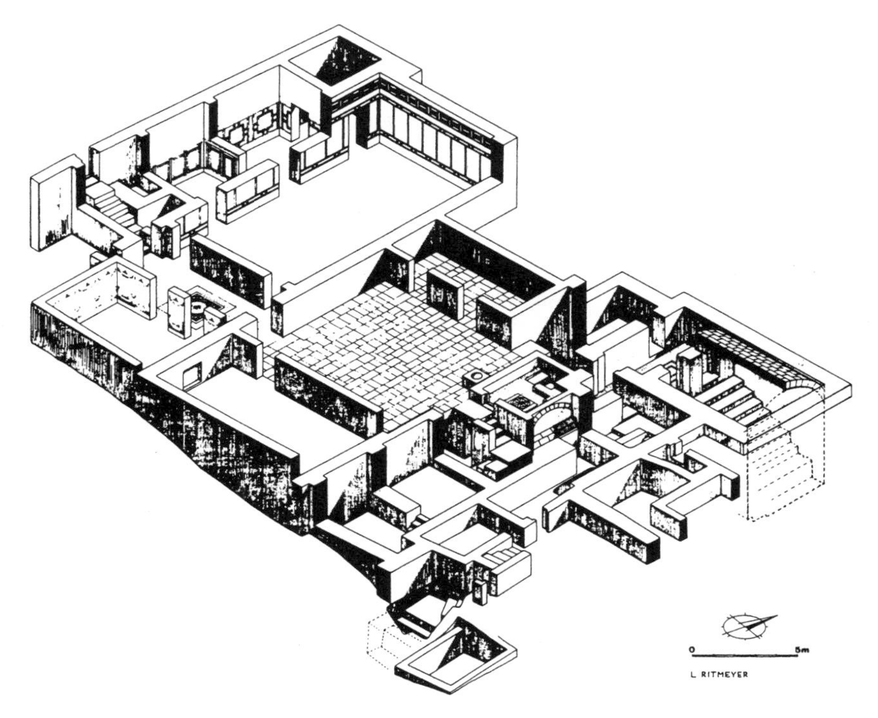

Illus. 65. Isometric representation of the "palatial mansion" (according to the excavations of N. Avigad).

further to the south, to allow King Agrippa II to observe, from a newly built part of the Hasmonean palace, the services of sacrifice in the priests' forecourt. With a more northern location, the high temple building would have obscured the view. Much to the annoyance of the king, the temple authorities prevented this "royal curiosity" by building a wall above the inner hall of the temple.

In another place, Josephus says that the Hasmonean palace stood "at the outermost end of the upper city" (πρὸς τὸ πέραν τῆς ἄνω πόλεως [*War* 2.344]). These topographical details point to a rock projection, which is directly across from the Maghrebine Gate and Robinson's arch. The raised position of this rock over the central city valley (the Tyropoeon Valley), the Temple Mount and the lower part of the city made it an ideal place for a king's palace. The German Order of Knights built its headquarters there in the eleventh century, as well as the church of "Saint Mary in Jerusalem". This church and part of their hospice

Illus. 66. The audience hall of the "palatial mansion" (according to N. Avigad).

have been restored and made accessible for visitors, although they are situated today in the Jewish old town district. The rigorous construction regulations of the German Knights unfortunately completely destroyed all traces of buildings from earlier periods.

With the building of a new large Torah school (Porat-Joseph) at the southeastern edge of the Jewish quarter, the remains of a Byzantine church that was probably the Sophia church have been destroyed (see below). On the eastern side, under the Yeshiva ha-Kotel, there is a wonderful building that dates from the Second Temple period. The excavator N. Avigad believed this must have been a public building, and he called it the "Herodian mansion" or "Palatial mansion".[10] This is the most beautiful building dating from the Herodian period that has ever been discovered in Jerusalem. The large reception hall is particularly splendid. The beautiful mosaic floors of the palace seem to originate from the same art school as those of the palaces of Herod the Great at Masada. The wall frescoes frequently display two layers: one Hasmonean and the upper one Herodian; this later layer is very similar to the wall frescoes of the southwest palace of Masada. The fresco paintings follow a "Pompeian style"

[10] *Discovering Jerusalem* (Nashville, Tenn.: Thomas Nelson, 1983), 95–120.

that was popular in Rome. In addition to beautifully crafted stone capitals, stone tables, etc., a unique rare glass jug was found, one that was signed by the well-known Phoenician master Ennion. All these finds can now be visited in the well-furnished museum under the Yeshiva. In my opinion, there is no doubt that this palacelike building is the remains of the Hasmonean palace.

Approximately 100 m west of the German Crusader Church of Saint Mary, a Herodian road was uncovered that ran in an east-west direction into the axis of Robinson's arch.[11] The large paving stones that were found in this place were probably laid at the time of Herod the Great, in order to connect his new upper palace with the ancient Hasmonean palace. This road may have merged in the east into the Lithostrotos ("pavement"), which is referred to in John 19:13. From here, steps seem to have led into the Tyropoeon Valley. A part of a passage to the valley was found a little north of the massive stairs, which joined Robinson's arch. In the Herodian period, the king's palaces were obviously connected by a road to the temple. There was an exit through the west gate (today's Barclay's Gate), because Josephus writes: "One [road] led to the royal palaces [εἰς τὰ βασίλεια] over a passage [διόδος] by the middle valley" (*Ant.* 15.410).

It is surprising that so much remained from the Hasmonean palace, because during the building of the Church of Saint Mary, to the north, in thorough German fashion, the Crusaders cleared away all ruins right down to bedrock. The explanation for its preservation could be that during the Byzantine period, east of the Sophia church was a public square, and the road to this led from Saint Peter in Gallicantu to the Praetorium. The pavement of this road was found outside of today's old town wall. The Byzantine sewer, which crosses the ruins of the palace, is probably the same one that the Pilgrim of Piacenza mentions (p. 284). It is also not impossible that the so-called Burnt House was part of the Hasmonean palace and that it was likely the palace kitchen. The many stone containers discovered there and the walls with thick soot can hardly be a consequence of the fire in the year A.D. 70 but might rather be characteristic of a kitchen complex.

The identification of the "palatial mansion" with part of the Hasmonean palace, although plausible, must remain hypothetical. Initially,

[11] Cf. N. AVIGAD, *Archaeological Discoveries in the Jewish Quarter of Jerusalem* (Jerusalem: Israel Exploration Society, 1976), 11, 17.

I was alone in my support for a southern location for the Hasmonean palace, but others now agree with this.[12] M. Ben-Dov, the archaeologist of the area south of the temple, not only agrees with my hypothesis but now equates the "Herodian mansion" with the Hasmonean palace.[13] Ben-Dov points out that the discovered weights that bore the name Bar Kathros in the Burnt House do not mean that they necessarily belonged to this family. Bar Kathros was, during the Second Temple period, the name of a well-known priestly family. The family could have supervised the upper markets, which would explain their names inscribed on the weights. Further excavations and exchange of ideas between archaeologists is necessary; in particular, the narrow area between the Burnt House and the Herodian mansion should be excavated.

The location that I am suggesting here for the Hasmonean palace (plate 8a) is consistent with the few topographical data that the Gospels provide for the Praetorium of Pilate. The paved yard named Lithostrotos was located on a higher place according to John 19:13 (Γαββαθᾶ, from the Aramaic גַּבְּתָא).[14] Therefore, the crowd of people who "came up" (ἀναβάς), according to Mark 15:8, probably went from the lower to the upper city. After the death sentence was given, Jesus was led outside of the city (ἐξάγουσιν) to Golgotha (Mk 15:20).

III. The Praetorium in the Christian Tradition

1. The Praetorium Ruins during the Byzantine Period

So far we have tried to demonstrate that in addition to the upper Herodian palace (the Citadel), the Hasmonean palace must also be considered as a possible place for the Praetorium of the Gospels. If the Gospel reports are compared with the historical data, then certain references make this palace more probable than the upper palace as the

[12] Cf. n. 4, mentioning the publications of K. Jaroš and R. Riesner, as well as G. Kroll, *Auf den Spuren Jesu*, 11th ed. (Stuttgart: Katholisches Bibelwerk, 2002), 335–49.

[13] Cf. M. Ben-Dov, *Jerusalem, Man and Stone: An Archaeologist's Personal View of His City* (Jerusalem: Keter, 1990), 161–64.

[14] The old Semitic place-name for the rock cliff opposite the Wailing Wall seems to have been kept until the seventh century. A description that presumably comes from the Armenian monk Anastasios Harutin says: "On the right of Zion is the palace Pilate named Kappata" (Baldi, 585). Cf. R. N. Bain, "Armenian Description of the Holy Places in the Seventh Century", *PEFQS* (1896): 346–49 (at 348); K. Hintlian, *History of the Armenians in the Holy Land* (Jerusalem, 1976), 16.

place for a public tribunal before the year A.D. 44. Additional evidence from local Christian traditions plus new archaeological data make this possibility almost certain. It becomes obvious that only the old Hasmonean king's palace can be meant when the ancient Christian sources speak of the remains of the Praetorium.

The oldest reference to the Praetorium comes from the anonymous Pilgrim of Bordeaux, who visited Jerusalem in A.D. 333 and who supported his account by reference to local traditions. After he had visited the temple area, the pool of Siloam and Mount Zion, which at that time was surrounded by a simple wall (pp. 205–6), he left "Zion's wall" and used a road (probably the Cardo Maximus), which led to the Neapolitan Gate (located at today's Damascus Gate), and found on its right, down to the (Tyropoeon) valley, the walls of the Praetorium, and somewhat further on his left the hill of Golgotha.[15] Even if the newest excavations have made problematic the dating of the Cardo Maximus to the time of Aelia Capitolina, a road nevertheless certainly ran along the eastern border of the camp of the Tenth Roman Legion (*legio X Fretensis*), which is the area of today's Armenian quarter (illus. 64).

The walls (*parietes*) that the pilgrim saw were probably the foundation of the Hasmonean palace, which reached right down into the Tyropoeon Valley. Other ruins of the palace were probably still to be seen along the edge of the slope of the valley. At that time, the area of today's Jewish quarter consisted only of a heap of ruins that lay scattered over the fields and the vegetable gardens of the Roman colony Aelia. Above the destruction layer of A.D. 70, with the remarkable exception of the so-called Tomb of David, archaeologists could not find any remains from the pre-Byzantine period (p. 339), and this demonstrates that the colony Aelia was restricted to the area north of today's King David Street.

Apart from a brief comment in the *Catecheses*[16] of A.D. 348, the palace of Pilate is mentioned another time by Cyril of Jerusalem. The

[15] *Itinerarium* 16f.: "Item exeuntibus Jerusalem, ut ascendas Sion, in parte sinistra et deorsum into valle juxta murum est piscina, quae dicitur Silua. . . . In eadem ascenditur Sion et paret, ubi fuit domus Caifae sacerdotis, et columna adhuc ibi est, in qua Christus flagellis ceciderunt. Intus autem intra Murum Sion paret locus, ubi palatium habuit David. . . . Inde ut eas foris murum de Sion euntibus ad porta Neapolitana ad partem dexteram deorsum in valle sunt parietes, ubi domus fuit sive praetorium Ponti Pilati; ibi dominus auditus est, antequem pateretur; a sinistra autem est monticulus Golgotha, ubi dominus crucifixus est" (Geyer, 22; Baldi, 562, 583).

[16] *Catecheses* 13 (PG 33:817; Baldi, 583).

following quotation seems to confirm that the area of the Praetorium of Pilate was well known at that time in Jerusalem: "The zelatores [οἱ σπουδαῖοι] of the church know the Lithostrotos that is [also] called Gabbatha, which was in the house of Pilate."[17] A special group of well-informed men must have lived at that time in Jerusalem who knew about the traditions of the various holy places.[18] At the time of Saint Cyril and the later visit (A.D. 383) of the pilgrim Egeria to Jerusalem, the ruins of the Praetorium and Caiaphas' house had not yet become places of devotion. We know from the report by Egeria that neither place at that time had been included as part of the Stations of the Cross for the Good Friday procession.[19] In the fourth century this procession followed the way from the Eleona church (on the Mount of Olives) to Gethsemane and then to the Golden Gate (at the eastern side of the temple square), then onto Golgotha (illus. 80).

But soon after this, between A.D. 417 and 439, we find that the Praetorium and Caiaphas' house, although still in ruins, were included in the procession that commemorated Jesus' Passion. Newly discovered Armenian lectionaries (codices Jerusalem 121 and Paris 44) have opened up new sources for the history of the holy places of the Passion by providing fresh evidence about the oldest Byzantine route of the Passion.[20] According to these lectionaries, the procession also included, for the commemoration of Good Friday, a visit to the "Court of the High Priest" (manuscript E describes this as the "House of Caiaphas"). This certainly is to be looked for in the area of the Church of Saint Peter in Gallicantu[21] and led from there to the "Palace of the Judgment" (manuscript E offers "Palace of Pilate"); after this they passed a town gate. From the Praetorium, the route continued to Golgotha.

A further development of the two holy places is reported in the so-called Georgian lectionary, which describes the liturgical ceremony in Jerusalem from the middle of the fifth century A.D. This lectionary describes the two stations between Gethsemane and Golgotha mentioned

[17] *Synopsis Scripturae Sacrae* 77 (PG 28:435).

[18] Cf. B. Bagatti, "La tradizione della chiesa di Gerusalemme sul Pretorio", *Rivista biblica italiana* 21 (1973): 429–32.

[19] *Peregrinatio* 36 (K. Vretska, *Die Pilgerreise der Aetheria* [Klosterneuburg: Österreichisches Bibelwerk, 1958], 222–27).

[20] A. Renoux, *Le codex arménien Jerusalem 121*, 2 vols., PO 35/1 and 36/2 (Turnhout: Brepols, 1968–1971). Cf. also G. Kretschmar, "Festkalender and Memorialstaetten Jerusalem in altkirchlicher Zeit", *ZDPV* 87 (1971): 168–205.

[21] Cf. chapter 20, "Where Was the House of Caiaphas Located?" (pp. 253–65).

above; however, now they were given the name of churches.[22] These two churches, i.e., Saint Peter (house of Caiaphas) and Saint Sophia (Praetorium of Pilate), were probably built around A.D. 450 by the empress Eudocia.

2. *The Praetorium Church and Sancta Maria Nea*

Older than the Georgian lectionary is the report of the visit to the Jerusalem holy sites by Peter the Iberian, who was at that time bishop of Maiuma near Gaza, around A.D. 450. Here it says, "Starting from there, he hurried to holy Golgotha and to the Holy Sepulchre; from there he went down to the church, which was then called Pilate."[23] From the point of view of the topography, it is interesting to notice that the pilgrim "descended" from the Sepulchre to the Pilate church on the slope of the Tryopoeon Valley; this corresponds exactly to the location accepted by us. A church named after Pilate must have seemed strange. Since Pilate's Praetorium was not associated with a saint, the church was soon appropriately called Hagia [Sancta] Sophia (Holy Wisdom) to remind people that in Jesus, godly Wisdom stood before a terrestrial judge.[24]

Around A.D. 510 the Praetorium church is mentioned once more in a short description of Jerusalem: "From there [the house of Caiaphas] one goes to the house of Pilate [*domum Pilati*], where the Lord was scourged and where Pilate handed him over to the Jews. There is also a large church in the area, where they stripped Jesus and where he was also scourged. It [the church] was called Holy Wisdom [*Sancta Sophia*]. . . . If one descends to Siloam, then there is the pit into which the prophet Jeremiah was thrown."[25] The book of Theodosius describing the topography of the Holy Land, written around 530, says: "From holy Zion to the house of Caiaphas, which is now the Church of Saint Peter, it is more or less 50 (double) steps. From the house of Caiaphas up to the praetorium of Pilate, there are nearly 100 [double]

[22] Cf. A. RENOUX, *Codex arménien* (see n. 20), 1:20f.

[23] R. RAABE, *Petrus der Iberer* (Leipzig: Deichert, 1895), 94, 99. Cf. J. WILKINSON, *Jerusalem Pilgrims before the Crusades* (Jerusalem: Ariel, 1977), 58.

[24] Cf. Sophronius of Jerusalem (A.D. 635), *Anacreontica* 20 (PG 87:3821; Baldi, 585).

[25] *Breviarius de Hierosolyma* 5A (Geyer, 155; Baldi, 584). Cf. J. WILKINSON, *Jerusalem Pilgrims* (see n. 23), 60.

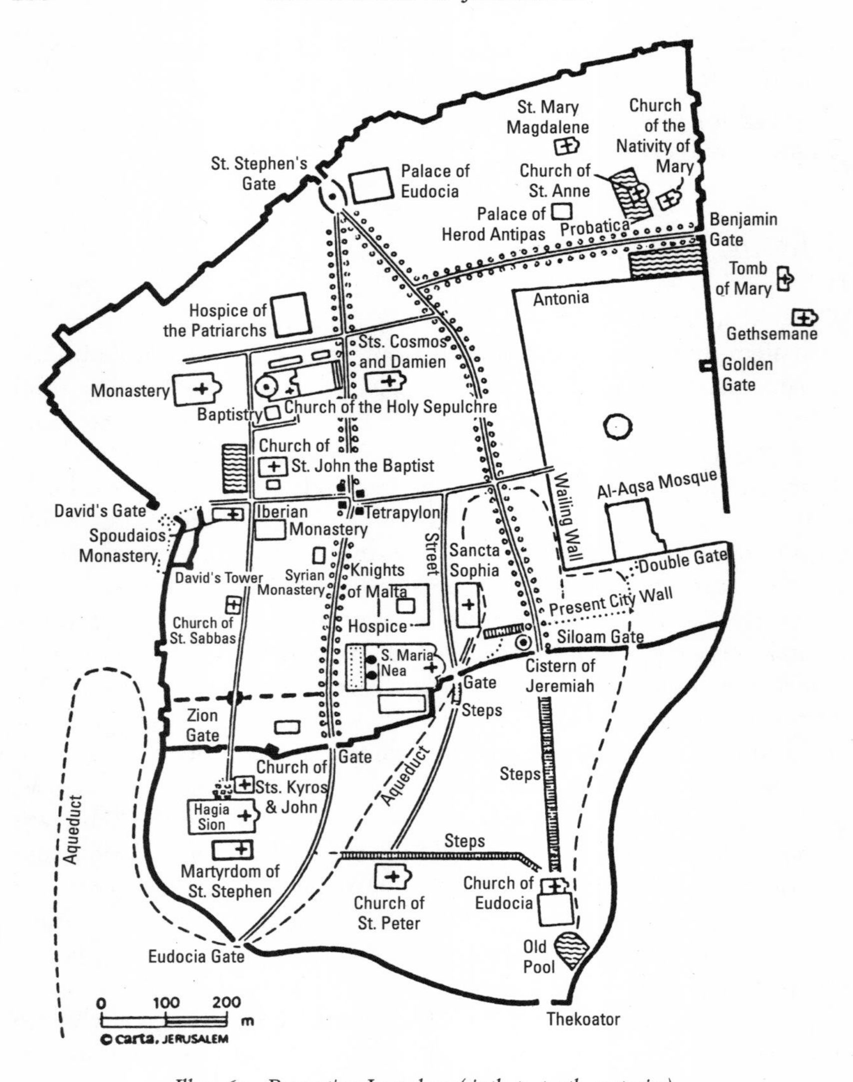

Illus. 67. Byzantine Jerusalem (sixth to tenth centuries).

steps. Here is the Church of the Holy Wisdom, and close by is the pit into which the prophet Jeremiah was thrown."[26]

Emperor Justinian (527–565) ordered the construction, close to the Wisdom church, of pilgrim hospices and hospitals, with thousands of

[26] *De situ terrae sanctae* 7 (Geyer, 141; Baldi, 584).

beds, as well as a new, astonishing church building dedicated to Mary, the Mother of God, that was dedicated in A.D. 543. Procopius of Caesarea (490–562) has left us a detailed description of this basilica,[27] which was called in the vernacular "Sancta Maria Nea", i.e., the new Mary (church), or also simply "Nea". The building of this church is of the greatest importance for the location of the Praetorium church (Sancta Sophia), because from now on, we find the two churches regularly mentioned together, which suggests a close proximity. In the past the proximity of the two churches was not given much attention, as the exact location of both was unknown.[28] However, with the excavations that followed the reunification of Jerusalem in the year 1967, the foundation walls of the Nea were discovered, and so any doubts about its location have been resolved.

In 1970 N. Avigad excavated a wall with an apse oriented in an eastward direction that was one of three belonging to a large church. Later he discovered in the western area of this excavation the remains of a marble-paved narthex with an entrance to the large hall of a basilica.[29] Avigad believed that he had found the long-searched-for remains of the "Nea". In the year 1976, with the investigation of the underground halls, an inscription on a wall was found (illus. 68) that made the identification certain.[30] The Greek inscription reads: "And that is the work that our beloved and pious emperor Flavius Justinianus and the eagerness of Constantinos, the pious-minded presbyter and hegumen [abbott], had completed during the thirteenth acclamation." The

[27] *De aedificiis* 5.6 (H. B. DEWING and G. DOWNEY, *Justinian's Buildings* [Cambridge, Mass.: Harvard University Press, 1996], 342–49). Cf. also F. M. ABEL, *Histoire de la Palestine* (Paris: Gabalda, 1952), 2:359f.

[28] Above all, two locations were suggested: (1) by the Muslim law courts at the Suk el-Kattanin close to the Wailing Wall (F. M. ABEL, in L. H. VINCENT and F. M. ABEL, *Jérusalem: Recherches de topographie, d'archéologie et d'histoire*, vol. 2, *Jérusalem nouvelle*, pt. 3, *La Sainte-Sion et les sanctuaires de second ordre* [Paris: Gabalda, 1922], 571–77; C. KOPP, *Die heiligen Stätten der Evangelien*, 2nd ed. [Regensburg: Pustet, 1964], 419–21); and (2) on the area of the church Notre Dame du Spasme ("our Lady of the spasm") near the northwest corner of the temple square (Arab haram), where the Sixth Station of the Cross is situated (R. ECKART, "Das Jerusalem des Pilgers von Bordeau [333]", *ZDPV* 29 [1906]: 72–92; H. DONNER, "Erwägungen zur Lage des byzantinischen Prätoriums", *ZDPV* 81 [1965]: 49–55).

[29] "Excavations in the Jewish Quarter of the Old City", in Y. YADIN, *Jerusalem Revealed* (Jerusalem: Israel Exploration Society, 1975), 41–51 (at 51); "Excavations in the Jewish Quarter of the Old City of Jerusalem, 1970, Second Preliminary Report", *IEJ* 20 (1970): 129–40 (at 137f.).

[30] "A Building Inscription of the Emperor Justinian and the Nea in Jerusalem", *IEJ* 27 (1977): 145–51.

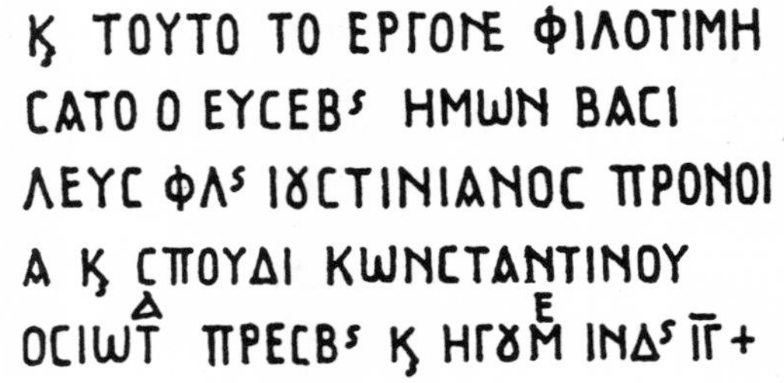

Ϗ ΤΟΥΤΟ ΤΟ ΕΡΓΟΝΕ ΦΙΛΟΤΙΜΗ
CΑΤΟ Ο ΕΥCΕΒ^{s} ΗΜΩΝ ΒΑCΙ
ΛΕΥC ΦΛ^{s} ΙȣCΤΙΝΙΑΝΟC ΠΡΟΝΟΙ
Α Ϗ CΠΟΥΔΙ ΚΩΝCΤΑΝΤΙΝΟΥ
ΟCΙΩΤ^{Δ} ΠΡΕCΒ^{s} Ϗ ΗΓȣΜ^{Ε} ΙΝΔ^{s} ΙΓ +

Illus. 68. Dedicatory inscription of the "Nea" (according to N. Avigad, 1977) (sketch). The third line mentions Emperor Justinian; the fourth, the presbyter Constantinos.

presbyter Constantinos is well known also from other sources as the hegumen of the Nea. In addition, in the excavations at the southern old part of the town wall, M. Ben-Dov[31] found several layers of a powerful retaining wall. This find corresponds perfectly with the report of Procopius that the architect of the Nea was forced to build a solid surrounding wall because the plan sent from Byzantium for the construction of the Nea exceeded the available building area by a quarter more than the allotted space. Hence the location of the Nea is secured, even if there are still particular questions about the reconstruction of its total plan.[32]

The place of the Nea, as it was rediscovered by the archaeologists, corresponds exactly with the place where the Madaba map (plate 1) shows a large church east of the south end of the Cardo Maximus (Platea Centralis). This map, which was found at the end of the nineteenth century, forms a mosaic floor in the sixth-century Church of Saint George in the Jordanian city Madaba. The discovery of the Nea proved once more the accuracy of this mosaic map. The most interesting part of the representation is the section of Jerusalem with its walls, roads and holy places. Very close to the northeast of the Nea, the section shows another church, which was already identified in earlier times by most researchers as the Sophia church.[33]

[31] "Discovery of the Nea Church—Jewel of Byzantine Jerusalem", *CNfI* 26 (1977): 86–90.

[32] In Modern Hebrew, the archaeological magazine *Kardom* 6 (1980): 71f. published two new Nea plans, one by N. Avigad and the other one from M. Ben-Dov.

[33] Cf. G. Dalman, "Die Via Dolorosa in Jerusalem", *PJB* 2 (1906): 15–26 (at 20); idem, *Orte und Wege Jesu*, 3rd ed. (Gütersloh: Bertelsmann, 1924), 358; F. M. Abel, *Sainte-Sion* (see n. 28), 571; P. Thomsen, "Das Stadtbild Jerusalems auf der Mosaikkarte von Madaba", *ZDPV* 52 (1929): 149–74, 192–219 (at 208f.); M. Avi-Yonah, *The Madaba Mosaic Map* (Jerusalem: Israel Exploration Society, 1954), 570.

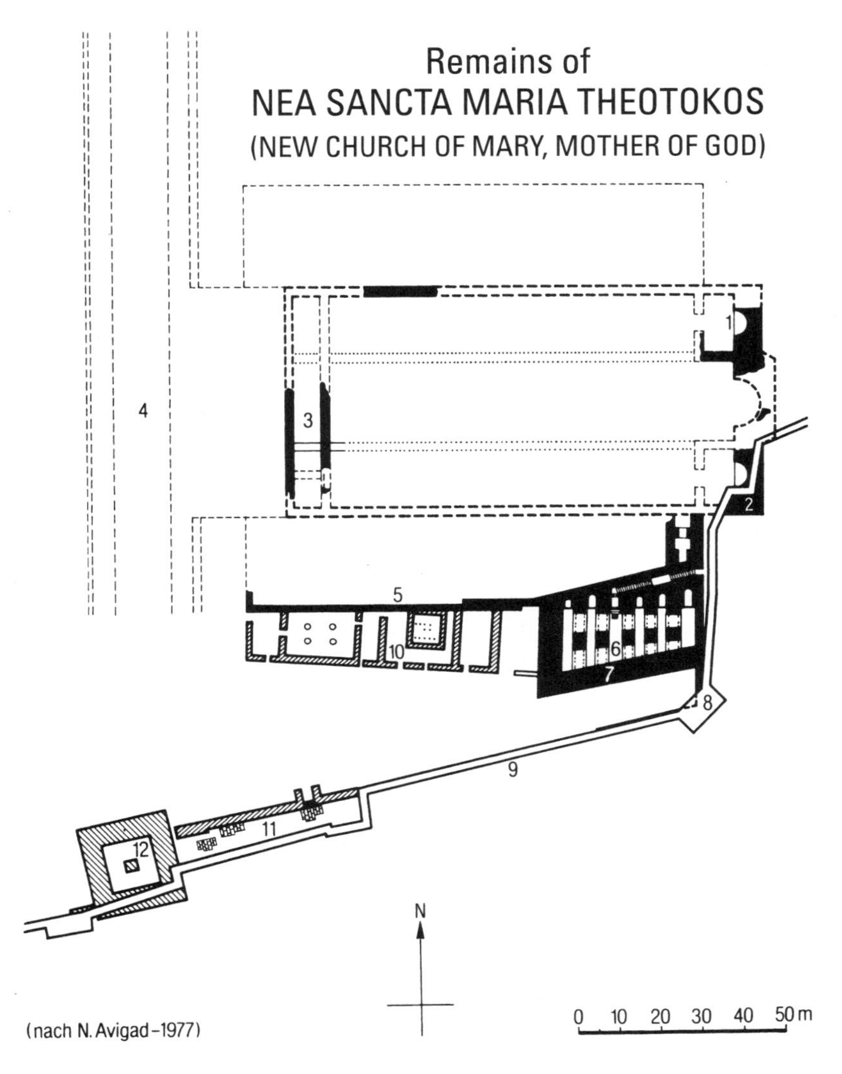

1 Northern side apse
2 Southeastern corner of the church
3 Entrance with narthex
4 Cardo maximus
5 Support wall
6 Vault of underground water reservoir
7 Wall with the Justinian inscription
8 Southeast corner of the support wall
9 Current southern wall of the Old City
10 Buildings from the time of the crusades
11 Byzantine street
12 Gate of Ayyubids

Illus. 69. Plan of the "Nea" (from G. Kroll).

Along the central city valley the map shows a large Byzantine road, the Cardo Vallensis or the Platea Vallensis, with its porticos. The eastern part is shown on the map; the western part was demonstrated by archaeology. The temple area is east; the Sophia and the Nea church are west of the temple area, both churches in close proximity to each other. At the south end, one can see what must depict the "cistern of Jeremiah"; directly beside it, steps descend to Siloam. The corner with the Siloam quarter was unfortunately destroyed on the map.

The same proximity of Hagia Nea and Sophia is shown in many pilgrim reports of the late Byzantine period, from which I want to quote only one example. It is the report from the pen of an anonymous pilgrim from the northern Italian city of Piacenza, who visited Jerusalem around the year A.D. 570. The report is thus contemporary with the Madaba map and can almost be seen as a commentary. The pilgrim writes: "We came [from Zion] to the basilica of Sancta Maria [Nea] . . . and we prayed in the Praetorium, where the Lord was condemned, and where the basilica of the Sancta Sophia is; opposite the ruins of the temple Solomon, under the road, water flows down to the source of Siloam. In the church is the chair on which Pilate sat as he sentenced the Lord."[34] Close to this church on his way to Siloam, the pilgrim went past the so-called *lacus Jeremiae*, which was much visited in Byzantine times and can now be identified.[35]

The proximity of the Sophia and of the Nea churches becomes even clearer in another text by the same author, where he uses the expression "the basilica Sancta Maria with Sancta Sophia, which was the Praetorium."[36] That aqueduct, which the pilgrim saw when passing (*sub platea aqua decurrit ad fontem Syloa*),[37] is of special interest for the location of the Byzantine Praetorium. Up to that time the aqueduct, which brought water from the Solomon pools to the temple square, ran east of the area where it is believed that the Hasmonean palace was located, and this aqueduct was probably built by Pilate. During the Byzantine period, as the temple square was lying desolate

[34] *Itinerarium* 23 (Geyer, 174; Baldi, 584).

[35] Cf. chapter 23, "The Cistern of Jeremiah" (pp. 295–302).

[36] *Itinerarium* 9: "et super basilicam sanctae Mariae ad sancta[m] Soffia[m]" (Geyer, 199) with the variant "super basilicam sanctae Mariae et sanctae Sofiae" (Geyer, 165). Here it almost seems as if the two basilicas were united into one building complex.

[37] *Itinerarium* 23 (Geyer, 174; Baldi, 584). For text reconstruction, cf. B. Pixner, "Noch einmal das Prätorium" (see n. 5), 62, n. 19.

following the prophecy of its destruction by Jesus (Mk 13:1f. par.), the water was rerouted to Siloam.[38]

3. Remains of Sancta Sophia and the Hasmonean Palace?

In the year 1914 L. H. Vincent examined the excavations exposed during the building of a Jewish hospital at the place of today's Porat-Yoseph Yeshiva. He particularly examined the area south of the stairs that lead from the Wailing Wall square to the Jewish quarter. His observations were published in the *Revue biblique*[39] and are of importance for the location of the Praetorium church and the Praetorium. Unfortunately, the ruins were destroyed during the building of the massive Talmud University, so that now only the article with the report remains, as well as the preserved finds of the "Herodian palatial mansion" under the Yeshiva ha-Kotel (pp. 373–75).

Vincent observed that during the building of the aqueduct different structural changes were made, probably by Pilate's builders. He also found a relatively large retaining wall, which he believed belonged, together with other remains, to a Byzantine church. He believed that they belonged to the Nea, but he was hesitant about publishing because the remains did not seem to reflect the monumental character of the building that would correspond to the description of Procopius. Now that we know the exact location of the Nea further southwest, we can be quite sure that Vincent must have seen the remains of the Sancta Sophia.[40] Already G. Dalman regarded this area as a possible location for the Sancta Sophia. Mixed with the debris of the church, Vincent saw a large number of human bones. These discoveries can be explained because both the Nea and the Sophia church were destroyed during the terrible attack by the Persians in A.D. 614. The Christian inhabitants, who looked for refuge in the churches, were slaughtered and buried under the collapsing rubble of the burning churches. During the listing of the dead after this disaster, a certain Kallistos counted 477 victims in the Sophia church alone.[41]

[38] Cf. M. AVI-YONAH, *The Excavations in the Old City of Jerusalem* (Jerusalem: Israel Exploration Society, 1969), 5 and plate 9/2.

[39] "Vestiges antiques dans hâret el-Moghârbeh", *RB* 11 (1914): 429–36.

[40] *Orte und Wege Jesu* (see n. 33), 359, n. 4.

[41] *Alosis* 47 (Baldi, 585, n. 1). Cf. F.J. RHÉTORÉ, "La prise de Jérusalem par les Perses", *RB* 6 (1897): 458–63.

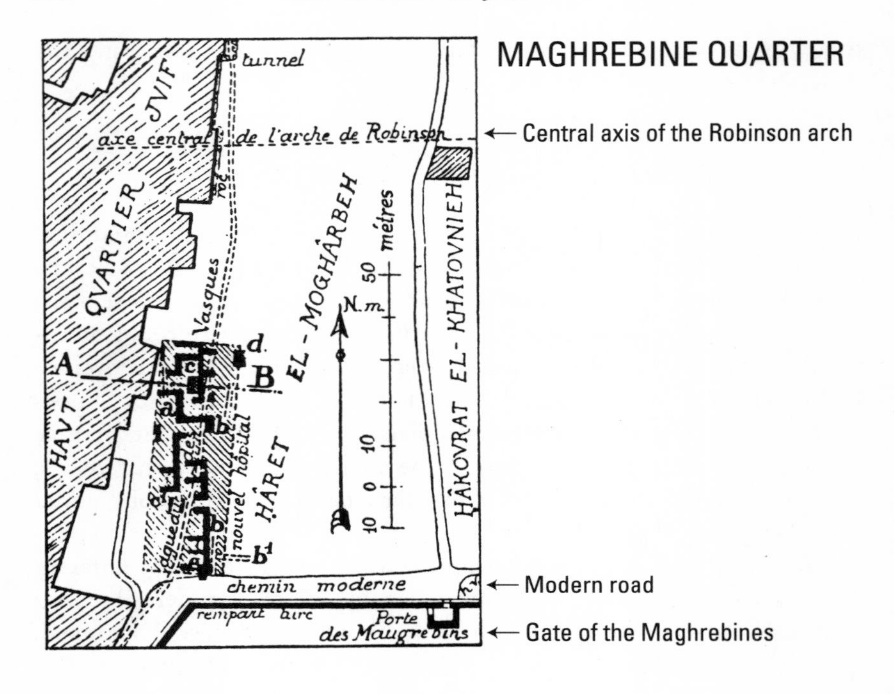

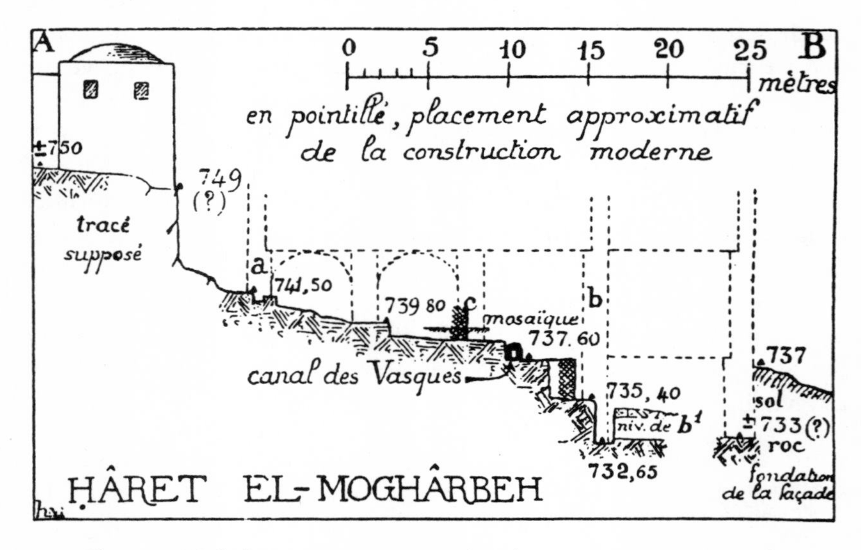

Illus. 70. Maghrebine quarter excavations (according to L. H. Vincent, 1914). Remains found in former Maghreb quarter

In the lower layers of the retaining walls, Vincent discovered much older remains. From ceramic pieces and stonework, he was able to date the artifacts to the Herodian period. He believed that large paving stones at the foot of an old wall were part of the expanded pavement work that dates from the reign of Agrippa II (*Ant.* 20.222). Although Vincent was a supporter of the Antonia theory, by his precise observations he involuntarily pointed to the location of the Sophia church. So we now have archaeological evidence, apart from the historical and literary evidence, that confirms that the Sophia church was located at the place of the Praetorium in the old Hasmonean palace.

Further support for this thesis was provided by the excavations under the house of the Sibenberg family, who have provided a great service for the archaeology of Jerusalem with the preservation of archaeological remains in their cellar and by the creation of a museum. Their building is located in an area south of the "Herodian mansion". In it is an extraordinarily large cistern with Byzantine crosses. This seems to have been partially built with stones and even walls from the Hasmonean period. There are also some interesting smaller objects discovered, which include a seal of King Agrippa (I or II). We must, however, exercise caution with the argument that this proves that the Hasmonean palace used by both Agrippas was located here. The meaning of a board with the label *Chrestos* (ΧΡΗΣΤΟΣ) remains unclear.

IV. Summary

The literary, historical and archaeological investigations of the last decades have demonstrated that the Praetorium, the place of the condemnation of Jesus recorded in the Gospels, was not in the Antonia. The early Christian tradition, which revered a site on the slope of the Tyropoeon Valley, is more likely. With new excavations in Jerusalem, the site for the Sancta Maria Nea is now certain, and with the acknowledged close location of the Nea with the Sophia church as consistent with Christian local tradition, we can be certain today that the Praetorium church must have been on the western slope of the Tyropoeon Valley and not on the eastern slope, as many had assumed.

The history of the liturgical Way of the Cross, including the various memorial places of the Passion on the night of Good Friday, explains why the Praetorium was transferred in the early Middle Ages to Mount

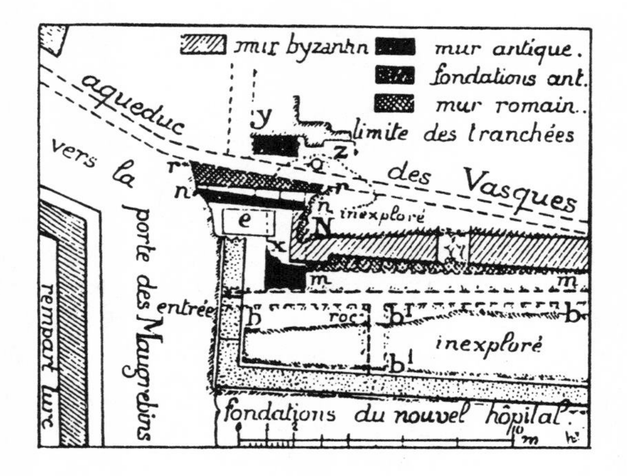

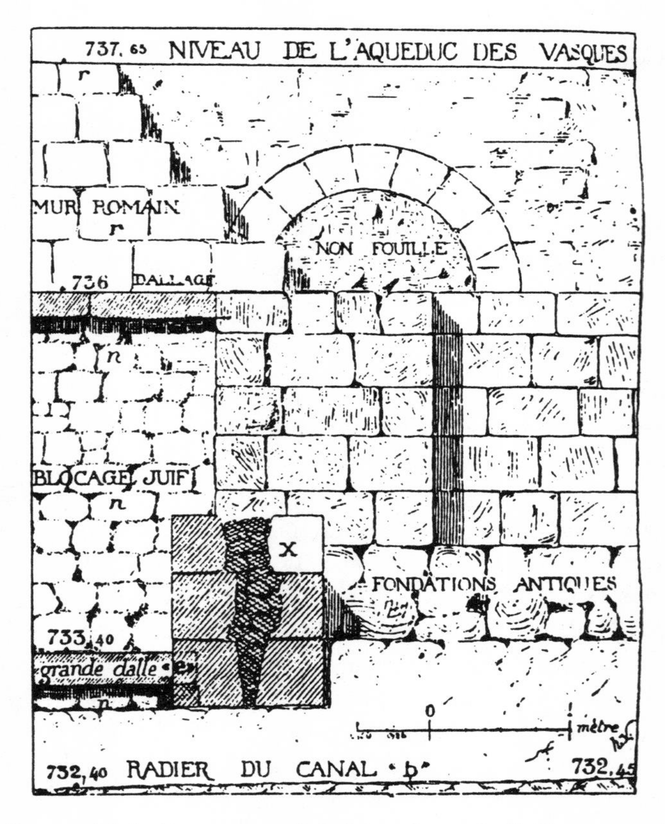

Illus. 71. Maghrebine quarter wall find (according to L.H. Vincent, 1914).

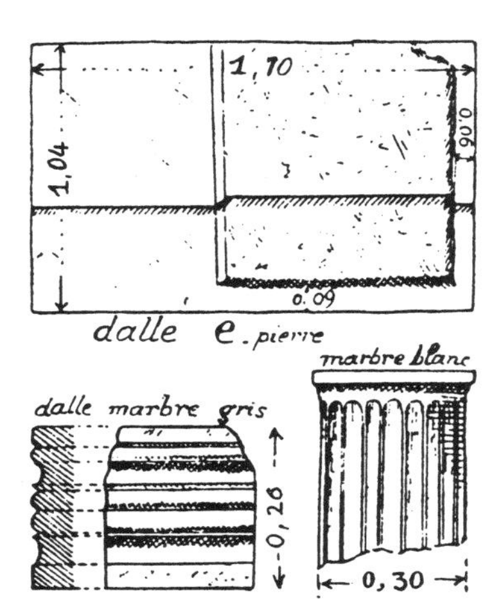

Illus. 72. Maghrebine quarter architectural finds (according to L. H. Vincent, 1914).

Zion and then in the Crusader period to the Antonia.[42] It was those Crusaders who were familiar with Josephus who were dissatisfied with the impossible location of the Lithostrotos on Zion and who believed that the Antonia should be identified with the Praetorium. A more exact reading of Josephus confirms the early Christian tradition that the Praetorium was located in the palace originally built by the Hasmonean rulers and later taken over by Herod the Great. Herod, in the fifteenth year of his reign (23 B.C.), built his own luxurious palace on the highest area of the western hill and used the old king's palace as an administration building and later as the Praetorium. This was done first by Herod and then later by his successor Archelaus (since A.D. 6), as well as by the pre-Agrippan Roman prefects and probably by Agrippa I. After the death of Agrippa I (A.D. 44), the palace remained in the possession of the Herodian-Hasmonean family, which from there administered the affairs of the temple.

As has so often happened, the early Christian tradition of a particular holy place is vindicated. The Praetorium was situated on a hill, west of the "royal (pillars) hall" of the temple, at the edge of today's Jewish quarter. Tradition, history and archaeology meet here, where Jesus stood before Pilate and from which point he carried the cross to Golgotha.

[42] Cf. chapter 24, "The Historical Via Dolorosa" (pp. 303–15).

Supplement: The thesis for the identification of the Praetorium with the former Hasmonean palace has had much support, although my suggestion remained disputed that one could see in the "Herodian mansion" parts of this king's palace. Cf. chapter 22, "Comments about the Praetorium Question" (pp. 291–94), and also R. Riesner, "Nachwort: Ausgrabungen 1989–1996", in H. Blok and M. Steiner, *Jerusalem, Ausgrabungen in der Heiligen Stadt*, SBAZ 4 (Gießen: Brunnen, 1996), 155–68.

22. Comments about the Praetorium Question

In the revised edition of his important book about the archaeology of the New Testament, J. Finegan[1] supports my location for the Praetorium of the Gospels in the Hasmonean palace.[2] R. Jaeckle also agrees with this thesis and, as I do, looks for the Hasmonean palace within the area of the so-called Herodian mansion at the north-eastern slope of Mount Zion in the Tyropoeon Valley.[3] Jaeckle brings some further arguments in support of this view. He quotes a passage in Tacitus that there should be two *praetoria* if the governor has his wife with him.[4] That bolsters my assumption, based on Matthew 27:19, that the wife of Pilate lived in a different place (the upper palace of Herod) from the prefect (pp. 271). Jaeckle also points out that normally the Praetorium would be in the center of the city. This would support a location for it in the Hasmonean palace in the center of Jerusalem rather than in the new upper palace of Herod at the outermost western edge of the city (illus. 58). As the Hasmonean palace was more connected with the older kingdom traditions, the Romans probably preferred to associate the Praetorium with the earlier monarchy.

The important archaeologist N. Avigad (d. 1992), the excavator of the "Herodian mansion" (illus. 65), wrote an outstanding explanation

[1] *The Archeology of the New Testament: The Life of Jesus and the Beginning of the Early Church* (Princeton: Princeton University Press, 1992), 246–50.

[2] Cf. B. Pixner, "Noch einmal das Prätorium: Versuch einer neuen Lösung", *ZDPV* 95 (1979): 56–86; idem, "Praetorium", in D. N. Freedman, *Anchor Bible Dictionary* (New York: Doubleday, 1992), 5:445–47; and in this book, chapter 21, "The Praetorium of Pilate" (pp. 266–90).

[3] "Das Prätorium des Pilatus in Jerusalem", *Jahrbuch des Deutschen Evangelischen Instituts für Altertumswissenschaft des Heiligen Landes* 2 (1990): 51–72.

[4] *Annals* 3.33.

of the finds and how they are wonderfully exhibited in the Wohl Museum. Avigad rejected the theory that this building represents part of a Hasmonean palace.[5] He believed in a priestly palace and suggested that this house was possibly the house of the high priest Ananias, son of Nedebaeus. According to Josephus, this palace was in the upper city on the west hill together with the palace of Bernice and Agrippa II but was burned down by the Zealots in A.D. 66 (*War* 2.426). According to this assumption, it would be possible for the cross-examination of Jesus to have taken place before the high priest (Mk 14:53–65) in the Herodian mansion. However, the most ancient local Christian tradition persistently refers to an area further south and the site where the Church of Saint Peter in Gallicantu is located.[6] Since 1993, excavations in this area have been undertaken by F. Diaz.

Avigad also provided information about the finds from a part of the building that he called the "peristyle building", which might have extended in the direction of the place in front of the Western Wall, the Xystos of Josephus (*War* 5.144; illus. 73). The reader should judge from Avigad's description whether this unusual discovery (illus. 74), a part of the Herodian mansion, could have been part of the Hasmonean palace and thus Pilate's Praetorium:

> The remains of this building represent a structure that differs from all other buildings of the Herodian quarter by its use of the columns.... The traces in the area indicate that they probably belonged to a peristyle (a yard surrounded by columns), which formed a part of a particularly distinguished domicile. That peristyle extended eastward and has not all been (further) excavated.... In the area on the right, a pavement has been discovered of colored stone tiles that have been almost completely destroyed. Some of it was reconstructed due to the remaining tiles and the impressions that the missing tiles had left in the soil, of the corridor. The tiles form a graceful design of connected circles that consist of square black, triangular red and hexagonal white tiles in the center. This pavement technique was well-known as *opus sectile* and was also used in the Herodian palaces in Masada and Jericho.... The discovery of the peristyle building came as a surprise, since nothing comparable in Jerusalem had been found before. The architectural landscape of Jerusalem has

[5] *The Herodian Quarter in Jerusalem* (Jerusalem: Israel Exploration Society, 1991), 76.
[6] Cf. chapter 20, "Where Was the House of Caiaphas Located?" (pp. 253–65).

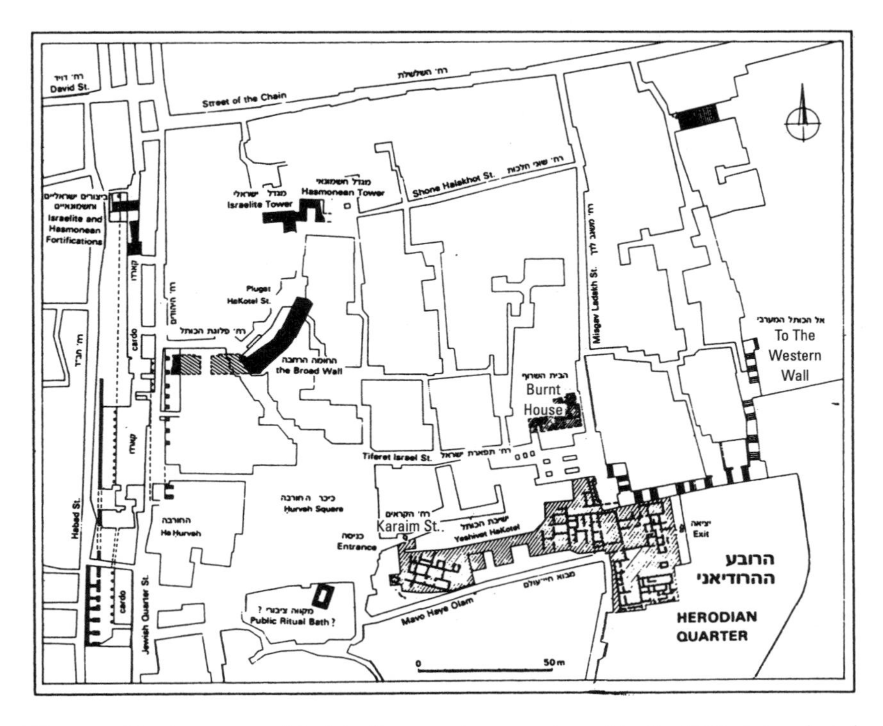

Illus. 73. Herodian quarter. N. Avigad's excavations, now housed in the Wohl Archaeological Museum, are in the lower right shaded area.

been enriched in such a way with a new element, characteristic of the luxurious mansions of Pompeii. This kind of peristyle existed also in the Herodian palaces in Masada, Herodium and Jericho.[7]

[7] *The Herodian Quarter* (see n. 5), 32f., 36f.

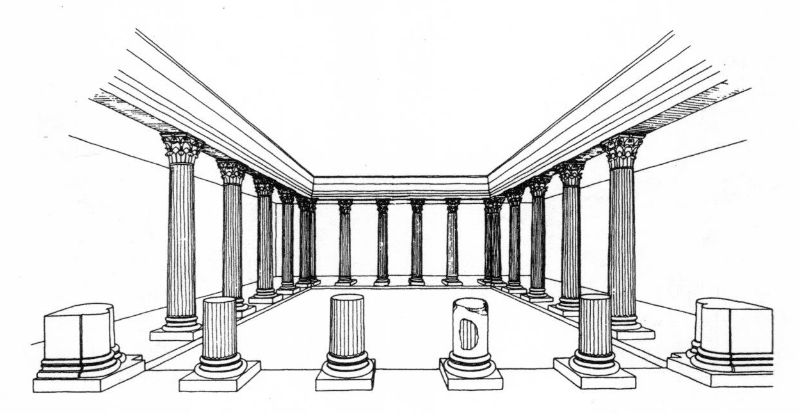

Illus. 74. The peristyle court.

23. The Cistern of Jeremiah

The series of tragic events that afflicted the prophet Jeremiah reached a climax during the Babylonian siege of Jerusalem in the year 586 B.C., when Jeremiah's enemies threw him into a dungeon in the yard of the royal guardhouse, "letting Jeremiah down by ropes. And there was no water in the cistern, but only mire, and Jeremiah sank in the mire" (Jer 38:6). An Ethiopian civil servant of King Zedekiah called Ebed-melech, with the aid of thirty men, pulled Jeremiah out of the pit and saved him from starvation. The pit of Jeremiah became, from the Byzantine to the Crusader period, one of the most visited biblical places in Jerusalem. There are references to it in many pilgrim reports, but eventually the site seems to have completely disappeared.

I. Modern Relocation

Today there is a place in Jerusalem called the "Grotto of Jeremiah"[1] that is almost completely ignored by tourists, pilgrims and visitors. It is located northeast of the Damascus Gate at the edge of the old Arab bus station. This grotto forms part of an old quarry that was carved deeply into the rock and that today is called "Gordon's Calvary" (p. 304). No one seems to know who it was who gave the site the present name, "Grotto of Jeremiah", or when this name was given. Since this place lies outside the walls of Jeremiah's Jerusalem, it cannot be the royal guardhouse or the pit into which Jeremiah was thrown.

Ancient guides locate the Byzantine pit of Jeremiah somewhere in the proximity of Pilate's Praetorium, and some researchers have therefore suggested that the pit was at the present site of the pool Birket Israel, located directly north of the Temple Mount. Other researchers

[1] Cf. Z. VILNAY, *Israel Guide* (Jerusalem: Carta, 1972), 651; J. WILKINSON, *Jerusalem as Jesus Knew It* (Jerusalem: Steinmatzky, 1978), 146.

have proposed the large cistern under the Ecce Homo monastery, based upon alternative theories about the place of the Byzantine Praetorium.[2] J. Wilkinson is perhaps closer to the truth; he writes that it "was looked for somewhere in the southern part of the city, perhaps one of the numerous cisterns near the south-west corner of the Temple area. It was close to the Church of Wisdom (Praetorium) and midway between the Sheep Pool and Siloam. . . . It may have been somewhere near the present Dung Gate." [3]

II. Jeremiah's Pit in the Proximity of the Praetorium

Since I was not satisfied by any of the usual theories about the site for the Praetorium (for example, the Ecce Homo monastery theory, which locates the Praetorium in the Antonia fortress, or the Citadel theory, which places it in the upper palace of Herod), I began my own investigation for an article in 1975. Following the discovery of the Church of Sancta Maria Nea, a new direction was given to my research (illus. 67). The result of this investigation was published in 1979 in the journal of the German Palestine Association[4] and can be summarized in the following manner:

1. Israeli archaeologists rediscovered the Byzantine Nea church.

2. From the literary sources it is clear that the Praetorium church (Sancta Sophia) must have been in very close proximity to this. From the pilgrim reports and liturgical lectionaries of that time and from the sixth-century Madaba Mosaic Map, the Byzantine Praetorium must have been close to the stairs that today lead from the front of the Wailing Wall to the Jewish quarter of the Old City (plate 8a). The most probable place is the area of the Porat-Yoseph Yeshiva, not far from the northeast corner of the Nea.

3. In my opinion the Byzantines followed an old, authentic tradition and built the Praetorium church over the ruins of the former Hasmonean palace, which served both Herod the Great and the Roman

[2] Cf. H. Donner, *Pilgerfahrt ins Heilige Land* (Stuttgart: Katholisches Bibelwerk, 1979), 237.

[3] *Jerusalem Pilgrims before the Crusades* (Jerusalem: Ariel, 1977), 161.

[4] "Noch einmal das Prätorium: Versuch einer Lösung", *ZDPV* 95 (1979): 56–86. See also chapter 21, "The Praetorium of Pilate" (pp. 266–90).

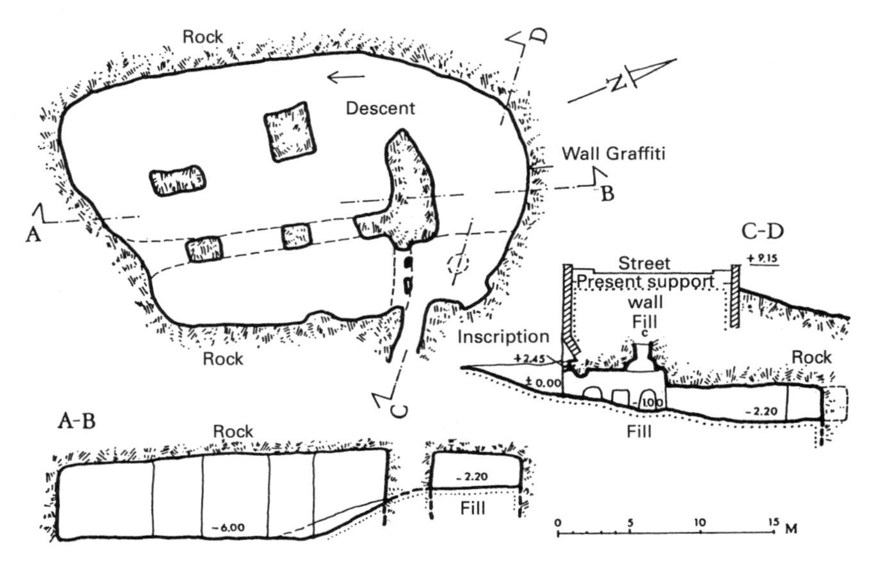

Illus. 75. Cistern of Jeremiah

governors as an administrative seat (illus. 58). At the time of the visit of the Pilgrim of Bordeaux in the year 333, the walls of this palace were still standing and extended down into the Tyropoeon Valley.[5]

In the course of my research for the Praetorium, I spoke with a good friend, the Israeli archaeologist M. Ben-Dov, who was entrusted with the excavations along the southern temple wall and in the Jewish quarter.[6] I asked him, "If I am on the right track with my location for the Sophia church, then Jeremiah's pit must lie somewhere near the Dung Gate. Did you encounter any possible place for it?" He thought for a moment and then said, "There is a possibility. Come and see for yourself, and make up your own mind!" I followed him for approximately 50 m southwest of the Dung Gate to a locked entrance in the rock. After he vigorously shook the door, it opened to a room that seemed to serve as a repository for rusty bedsteads, refrigerators, pots and pans. With the help of a lit candle we found our way to a small inclination of 10 m leading downward to a large grotto, the ceiling of which was supported by some enormous rock columns. The floor of the lower level of the grotto consisted of dried mud.

[5] *Itinerarium* 17 (Geyer, 22; Baldi, 583).

[6] Cf. M. Ben-Dov, *In the Shadow of the Temple* (Jerusalem: Keter, 1985).

When I revisited the grotto several times and examined it further, I found traces of former Byzantine veneration for this place. The rock at the bottom of the entrance arch was decorated with an engraved cross, which is now partly destroyed. Among the graffiti is a Greek inscription, from which the first one and a half lines could be read: KE BOHΘIC TOYC, "O Lord, help those who . . ." This underground grotto was obviously important for visitors during the Byzantine period, and this is confirmed by the graffiti in large Greek letters on the north wall of the descending passage. The rough letters read AKPA, followed by XP, the monogram for Christ. A further XP monogram is chiseled somewhat underneath it. This raises a question: Who left these graffiti? Was it a Byzantine pilgrim who in the fifth century wrote this in order to indicate the direction of the *akra* (Praetorium), Christ's prison, for which the pit of Jeremiah was a *typos*?

In a vestibule behind the entrance, there is a large opening in the ceiling of the grotto. This obviously relates to the original opening of the cistern. On the eastern side of the grotto, there was a large niche cut into the rock, which perhaps served as an apse for liturgical purposes in the Byzantine period. It is to be hoped that the partial steps, which were found during the excavation, will be excavated completely one day. All

Illus. 76. Jeremiah's cistern 1) Inscription above door, 2) Wall graffiti

these described peculiarities seem to correspond very well with the numerous sources from the Byzantine period.

III. Pilgrim Reports

On the basis of the Septuagint, the Greeks called the place *lakkos Ieremiou* (Λάκκος Ἱερεμίου), i.e., "pit or cistern of Jeremiah". The Latin speakers obviously took over the Greek name and called the place *lacus Jeremiae*, although *lacus* in Latin means "lake" or a large water surface. Perhaps they were influenced by the spectacular size of the pit. We find that the Latin form is used in the oldest reference to this place. In his work *De situ terrae sanctae* a certain Theodosius, writing around A.D. 530, provided a list of distances between various holy shrines. After he mentions the Praetorium church, he writes that nearby, Jeremiah was thrown into the *lacus*. The relative distance that Theodosius provides in his text seems to agree quite well with the local situation: "From holy Zion to the house of Caiaphas, which is now the Church of Saint Peter, it is more or less 50 (double) steps. From the house of Caiaphas up to Pilate's Praetorium, there are nearly 100 (double) steps. Here is the Church of the Holy Sophia, and close by is the pit into which Jeremiah was thrown.... The pool of Siloam is 100 (double) steps from the *lacus*, into which the prophet Jeremiah was thrown; this *lacus* is within the wall."[7] The *Breviarius de Hierosolyma*, a pilgrim's diary, written approximately at the same time (between A.D. 510 and 540), specifies, in a longer form, that this *lacus* was close to the Praetorium, where the road descends from the city to the pool of Siloam.[8]

Approximately fifty years later, a pilgrim from Piacenza in Italy visited the Holy Land. His report of the journey (ca. 570), which represents an outstanding commentary that complements the contemporary Madaba Mosaic Map, is very informative. After the pilgrim left Mount Zion, he notes, he came to the Church of Sancta Maria Nea, which was surrounded by thousands of beds and tables from the hospices and hospitals nearby. He prayed in the Praetorium (Sancta Sophia), and his

[7] *De situ terrae sanctae* 7f. (Geyer, 141; Baldi, 584). For the location of Caiaphas' house in the area of the Church of St. Peter in Gallicantu, see chapter 20, "Where Was the House of Caiaphas Located?" (pp. 253–65).

[8] *Breviarius de Hierosolyma* 6A. Cf. J. Wilkinson, *Jerusalem Pilgrims* (see n. 3), 61.

report continues: "From there [the Sophia church] we came to an arch of an old city gate. At this place is the putrid water [*in ipso loco sunt aquae putridae*] into which they threw Jeremiah. From this arch, one descends by way of many steps to Siloam."[9]

If we compare this eyewitness report with the Madaba map (plate 1) and consider some data that recent excavations have offered, then we can draw several conclusions about the topography of the area around the Dung Gate before the Persian invasion of A.D. 614. On one hand there must have been, according to the Madaba map and the pilgrim's report, a large valley route (Cardo Vallensis) that led down from the Damascus Gate (following today's direction of the road el-Wad) to Siloam, where the last part consisted of broad steps. Apart from that, right at the beginning of these stairs is part of a wall that included an archway from the time before Empress Eudocia. As soon as the empress had built the wall continuing further south (ca. A.D. 450), which meant that Mount Zion and Siloam were included in the city, the older wall (perhaps from the time of Constantine) became useless. The pit of Jeremiah lay exactly within these old archways. Besides our grotto, a considerable part of the Cardo valley was discovered. This road was flanked on both sides by porticos. The western colonnade is still *in situ* as the bases of columns suggest and as one column lying close to the pavement indicates, while we recognize the eastern colonnade from the Madaba map. At the southern end of the Cardo, the mosaic shows a place that obviously exhibits an indentation in the center. This part of the representation, which represented a bit of a mystery, can now be identified with the cistern of Jeremiah (illus. 77). The sextant-shaped representation directly beside it may be the archway that the Pilgrim of Piacenza mentions.

The middle of the eighth century A.D. saw the extinction of the Umayyad dynasty and the end of a prosperous time in Jerusalem's history. Afterward the extent and the importance of Jerusalem was reduced to the rank of a provincial town, and the decline began. The wall of Eudocia was given up gradually, as our excavation at the Essene Gate shows (pp. 206–7). The city boundary before Eudocia's time became again the end of the walled city and remained so up to the present time.

[9] *Itinerarium* 24 (Geyer, 174; Baldi, 585).

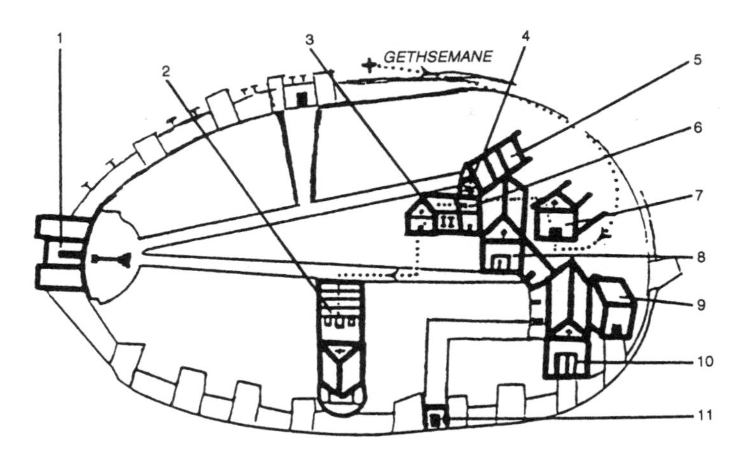

Illus. 77. The Byzantine Way of the Cross on the Madaba Mosaic Map (according to B. Pixner).

1 The Damascus Gate
2 Church of the Holy Sepulchre
3 Sancta Sophia (Praetorium)
4. Jeremiah's cistern
5 Steps to Siloam
6 Gate
7 Saint Peter [in Gallicantu] (Caiaphas' house)
8 Sancta Maria Nea
9 The room of the Last Supper
10 Hagia Sion
11 David's (Jaffa) Gate

In A.D. 985 a Muslim inhabitant of Jerusalem, Al-Mukadassi, numbered the "eight iron gates of the Holy City":[10] (1) Zion's Gate (west of today's Zion's Gate); (2) the Neah Gate (rather than the Teah Gate, at the southern end of the earlier Cardo Maximus); (3) the Balat Gate (perhaps for Pilate or pavement [Lithostrotos]; the road of Saint Peter in Gallicantu to the Sophia church passed this gate); (4) the Gate of the Pit of Jeremiah (in the area of the present Dung Gate); (5) the Siloam Gate (connecting the Al-Aqsa mosque and Siloam); (6) the Jericho Gate (today's Stephen's or Lion Gate); (7) the Gate el-Ammud (the Column Gate, today's Damascus Gate); and (8) the Gate Michrab Dawud (today's Jaffa Gate). The sum total of five gates in the south wall is indeed amazing.[11] The reference can only be to five small gates; each one must have stood at the end of one of the many south-running roads of Jerusalem in the tenth century A.D. As we know

[10] M.J. de Goeje, ed., *Bibliotheca geographorum Arabicorum*, vol. 3 (Leiden, 1879), 167.

[11] Cf. Y. Tsafrir, "Muqadasi's Gates of Jerusalem", *IEJ* 27 (1977): 152–61. The reading Bab En-Nija suggested here was already mentioned by C. Clermont-Ganneau, "La Néa, ou Église de la Vierge de Justinien, á Jérusalem", in *Récueil d'archéologie orientale*, vol. 3 (Paris, 1900), 55–57.

from other sources, the main traffic went through the three gates mentioned last (nos. 6–8). The legendary *Life of Constantine and Helen* from the same pre-Crusader period credits Saint Helen with the building of a shrine close to the cistern of Jeremiah.[12] In the early Crusader period we hear of another pilgrim, a Russian abbot called Daniel, who on his visit was shown the cistern of Jeremiah by a monk from the monastery Mar Saba in the Judean desert.[13] From then on, dust and silence fell over the place. When the Crusaders and then later the Muslim sultan of the Ayyubid dynasty built the town wall, a bit further north, the cistern of Jeremiah was apparently covered with debris and remained buried until it was rediscovered by the spade of the archaeologists.

IV. The Byzantine and Historical Cistern of Jeremiah

If we assume that the long-forgotten cistern of Jeremiah has finally come to light again, then we naturally refer to the Byzantine memorial place. It is easily possible that the people of the Byzantine period decided to venerate the pit of Jeremiah because of its close proximity to Pilate's Praetorium, since the Oriental Christians tended to connect the passion of the prophet with Jesus. Where exactly Jeremiah was thrown into the cistern, nobody knows. The Byzantine location is nevertheless quite reasonable within the location of preexilic Jerusalem. Can it be that the Byzantines followed an old and genuine Jewish tradition? Some very old walls were excavated next to the entrance to the cistern of Jeremiah and under the Byzantine pavement of the Cardo valley. Is it possible that they have something to do with the guardhouse mentioned in Jeremiah (38:6)?

According to the late Professor M. Avi-Yonah of the Hebrew University, there were Jewish tourist guides whose full occupation in early Byzantine times was to lead groups of Christian pilgrims.[14] Were these Jewish leaders in the possession of a valuable tradition that they passed on to their Christian listeners? Perhaps further investigation of the place may yield more answers, just as to other questions of the topography of old Jerusalem.

[12] *Vita S. Helenae et Constantini* (Baldi, 586).

[13] Baldi, 587.

[14] *The Jews of Palestine* (Oxford: Oxford University Press, 1976), 222.

24. The Historical Via Dolorosa

I. *Today's Via Dolorosa*

Each Friday afternoon a procession of Catholic believers reverently singing a processional hymn leave the al-Omariya School, the place of the former fortress Antonia, to make their way toward the Church of the Holy Sepulchre located within the Old City walls of Jerusalem. This solemn procession repeats the final journey of Jesus from the Praetorium of Pilate to the hill of Golgotha. The Franciscans, who since the Middle Ages have encouraged the devotion of the Stations of the Cross (Via Crucis), lead the weekly procession in Jerusalem through the narrow streets of the Muslim quarter on a route called the Via Dolorosa. The procession stops briefly at each of the traditional fourteen Stations of the Cross. In 1964 Pope Paul VI visited the Holy Land and naturally also wanted to follow the Via Dolorosa, together with many thousands of pilgrims, all of whom wanted to follow in the footsteps of Jesus. Today's route has such a venerable tradition that it would be inconceivable to change it simply because of the question of its historical reliability. However, it cannot be doubted that the present "Via" does not follow the route that Jesus actually took. The identification of the end point, Golgotha (Γολγοθᾶ), never changed, but the route "moved" at least twice during its history, because the location of its starting point, Pilate's Praetorium, has moved twice. What determined this relocation, and how did this affect the Via Dolorosa? These questions can be answered thanks to contemporary written sources and fresh archaeological discoveries, all of which throw new light on the actual appearance of Jerusalem at the time of Jesus.

II. *The Unchanging End Point: Golgotha*

In the fourth century the rock of Golgotha had already been identified as the place of the crucifixion of Jesus and was enclosed by the

Church of the Holy Sepulchre. The so-called Garden Tomb located on the Nablus Road, north of the Damascus Gate, is an attractive place for meditation and prayer, but for archaeological and historical reasons, it is indisputably not the place of the crucifixion and the burial of Jesus. During the second half of the nineteenth century, in the days of the English general Charles Gordon, who fell in the fight against the Mahdi, some believed that it was improbable that the place of the Church of the Holy Sepulchre in the year A.D. 30 was outside of the town walls, as the Gospels presuppose (Mk 15:20 par.). It was in this way that Gordon, due to allegorical speculations, believed that Golgotha was to be found on the hill es-Sahira (north of the old Arab bus station).[1] Since then, however, research has made significant progress, and today no serious archaeologist shares this opinion. Today Catholic, Protestant and Israeli archaeologists all agree that the locations for the New Testament places are under the Church of the Holy Sepulchre.[2]

The Church of the Holy Sepulchre now lies within the old part of the town walls, but in Jesus' day, the "place of the skull" (Jn 19:17) was outside the city (illus. 58). Our knowledge of this area has been substantially extended in the last decades by the investigations of Lady K. Kenyon,[3] Mrs. U. Lux-Wagner[4] and Father C. Couasnon.[5] It is now widely accepted that N. Avigad[6] discovered the remains of the Gennath (Garden) Gate, which was, according to Flavius Josephus, where the so-called "second wall" branched from the "first wall" (*War* 5.146). This gate, by which Jesus was probably led from the city (cf. Heb 13:12), lay south of the crossing of today's Suk es-Zeit and King David Street. The "second wall" ran along the line of the Suk to the north and then curved, crossing the Tyropoeon Valley, toward the east, to the Antonia fortress at the northwest corner of the temple square.

The space created by the angle of the two walls, which today is the Muristan quarter, was then a quarry that formed a protection for the west side of the "second wall". Herod the Great created a public park

[1] Cf. J. Wilkinson, *Jerusalem as Jesus Knew It* (London: SCM Press, 1978), 192–200.

[2] Cf. R. Riesner, "Golgotha und die Archäeologie", *BiKi* 40 (1985): 21–26; D. Bahat, "Does the Holy Sepulchre Church Mark the Burial of Jesus?" *BAR* 12, no. 3 (1986): 26–45.

[3] *Digging Up Jerusalem* (London: E. Benn, 1975), 227–32.

[4] "Vorläufiger Bericht über die Ausgrabungen unter der Erlöserkirche", *ZDPV* 88 (1972): 185–201.

[5] *The Church of the Holy Sepulchre in Jerusalem* (London: Oxford University Press, 1974).

[6] *Discovering Jerusalem* (Nashville: Thomas Nelson, 1983), 69.

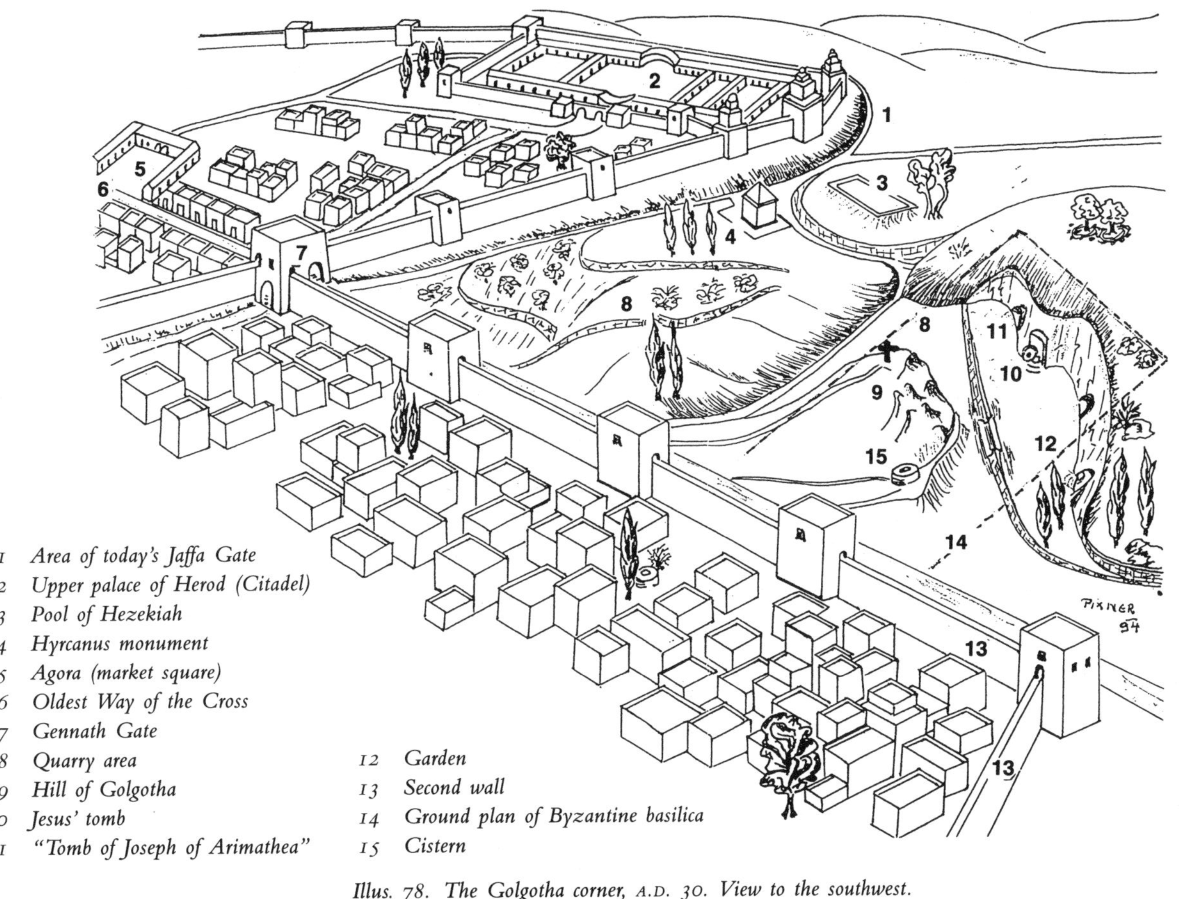

1 *Area of today's Jaffa Gate*
2 *Upper palace of Herod (Citadel)*
3 *Pool of Hezekiah*
4 *Hyrcanus monument*
5 *Agora (market square)*
6 *Oldest Way of the Cross*
7 *Gennath Gate*
8 *Quarry area*
9 *Hill of Golgotha*
10 *Jesus' tomb*
11 *"Tomb of Joseph of Arimathea"*
12 *Garden*
13 *Second wall*
14 *Ground plan of Byzantine basilica*
15 *Cistern*

Illus. 78. The Golgotha corner, A.D. 30. *View to the southwest.*

there, probably as one of his projects for the improvement of the city. That may also explain the name Gennath (Garden) Gate, which led outside, into a garden area. At the north end of this park was a large piece of rock that the quarry workers had left untouched, as it was regarded as useless for the production of stone because of its brittleness. Around this rock, deposits collected, and in time the hill of Golgotha was formed. North of this was a private garden that contained several rock-hewn graves and that was maintained by a gardener (cf. Jn 20:15). One of these graves became Christ's burial place, which is today under the enormous dome of the Church of the Holy Sepulchre.[7]

There is another burial ground nearby that, at the time of Jesus, contained typical graves, tombs (Hebrew *kokim*) and sarcophagi. These can be viewed today, and they are located west of the Tomb of Christ. Not far from this, a third tomb was found,[8] but this is presently hidden under the Coptic monastery. The presence of these tombs is one of the most convincing archaeological indications for the authenticity of the site of Jesus' burial place. The second tomb area lies in a Syrian chapel and is popularly called the "Tomb of Joseph of Arimathea". The foundations of the basilica from the fourth century have cut through this cemetery, which must have existed before A.D. 42. At that time, Herod Agrippa I included this area with the building of the "third wall" of the city, such that no more graves could be added.

There can be no doubt that the places associated with the death and Resurrection of Jesus have been venerated since the very beginning by the Jewish Christians. Emperor Hadrian, following the Bar Kokhba rebellion (A.D. 132–135), "paganized" the Jewish and Jewish Christian holy places by establishing heathen temples (pp. 11–12) on Golgotha and the Temple Mount, which became the center of the new Roman colony Aelia Capitolina. To this end the emperor leveled the quarry so that today the Church of the Holy Sepulchre, the German Lutheran Church of the Redeemer and the Muristan shops stand upon 10–12 m of debris. The quarry area became Hadrian's Forum. This marketplace was overshadowed by the Temple to Venus, which

[7] Cf. R. Riesner, "Golgotha", in *GBL*, 2nd ed. (1990), 1:480–82.

[8] Cf. C. Schick, "Neu aufgefundene Felsgräber bei der Grabeskirche in Jerusalem", *ZDPV* 8 (1885): 171–73.

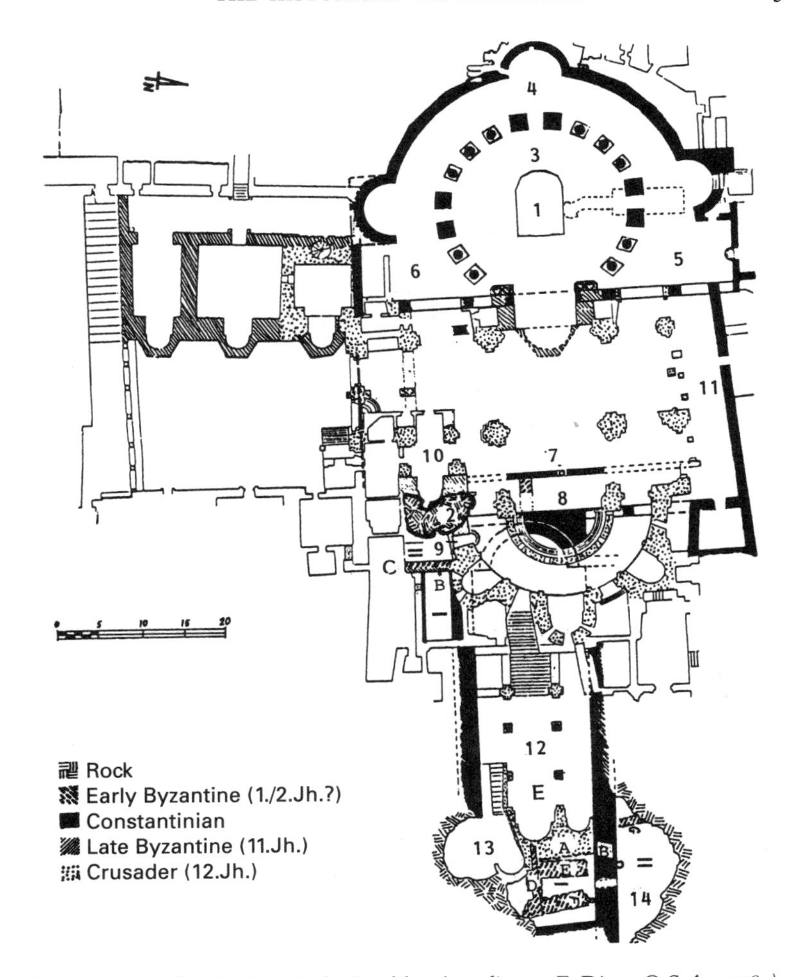

Illus. 79. The Church of the Holy Sepulchre (according to F. Diaz, O.S.A., 1984).

1. *Traditional tomb of Jesus*
2. *Rock of Golgotha*
3. *Rotunda (Anastasis)*
4. *Large apse (Constantine)*
5. *Northern transept*
6. *Southern transept*
7. *Stylobate of the eastern column gallery*
8. *East Wall of church and apse of the Martyrion Church of Constantine*
9. *Jewish Christian cave in the east wall of the rock of Golgotha; Greek Orthodox excavation zones (C I–III)*
10. *Adam Chapel*
11. *Columns of the renovation by Constantine Monomachos (*in situ*)*
12. *Crypt of St. Helen*
13. *Rock chapel of the Finding of the Cross (former cistern)*
14. *Armenian excavations (E I and II)*

B *Wall of the Constantine Martyrion church*

D *Wall with ship graffiti*

was established over the Tomb of Jesus. A marble statue of the goddess came to stand on the rock of Golgotha.[9]

Following the Council of Nicea in A.D. 325, the bishop of Jerusalem, Modestos, asked Emperor Constantine to take care of the places associated with Jesus' suffering, death and Resurrection. From a report by Bishop Eusebius of Caesarea, it is evident that some Jewish Christians in Jerusalem had recorded the tradition for the place of Jesus' tomb.[10] On the instruction of the emperor (*iussu imperatoris*), the pagan temple was destroyed, and below this was discovered the cave of the previously venerated tomb of Jesus, which still remains accessible. Thus we can say, the end point for the path of suffering for Jesus is archaeologically and historically secured.

III. The Movable Starting Point: The Praetorium

The starting point for the historical Way of the Cross, the Praetorium of Pilate, is far more difficult to locate. As I suggested earlier, most researchers reject today for historical and archaeological reasons the belief that the Praetorium was in the fortress Antonia. We will regard later the background of this Christian local tradition, which originated from the Crusader period. The present majority view for the location of the Praetorium of Pilate prefers instead the area of the Citadel near today's Jaffa Gate, where Herod the Great, always anxious about his throne, had built a stately fortress for himself, his family and his successors. However, this place is not the one considered by the early Christian tradition. There is a third castle of Herod in Jerusalem—the old Hasmonean palace, which is all too often overlooked. This stood opposite the southwest corner of the temple in the southeast corner of today's Jewish quarter in the Old City. The evidence that I have previously described leads me to the conviction that this palace was used by Herod and then also by the Roman governors as the central administrative seat. In its walls, Pontius Pilate (A.D. 26–36), probably in the year A.D. 30, condemned Jesus to death. I have already written about this,[11] so a short summary is sufficient here.

[9] Jerome, *Letter 58* 3 (PL 22:581; Baldi, 619, n. 1).

[10] *Vita Constantini* 3.25–39 (PG 20:1085; Baldi, 619–23).

[11] "Noch einmal das Prätorium: Versuch einer neuen Lösung", *ZDPV* 95 (1979): 56–86; cf. in this volume chapter 21, "The Praetorium of Pilate" (pp. 266–90).

The earliest records for the Praetorium of the Gospels by the Pilgrim of Bordeaux (333) and Bishop Cyril of Jerusalem (348) mention only the ruins of the palace. In the fifth century, a church was built above it that received the name "Pilate's church", as Peter the Iberian informs us. But this designation was quickly regarded as misleading, and the church was soon renamed the "Hagia Sophia" (Holy Wisdom), because Jesus, the Wisdom of God, had been condemned here by a heathen judge. We know with certainty from the literary sources that this Sophia church was very close to another famous Byzantine church, the Hagia (Sancta) Maria Nea (illus. 67). The two churches are always mentioned next to each other, e.g., by an anonymous pilgrim in the sixth century from the Italian city of Piacenza, who speaks of the *basilica Mariae ad sanctam Soffiam, quae fuit Praetorium,*[12] "the basilica of Mary near Sancta Sophia, which was the Praetorium." Both churches appear next to each other on the famous Madaba Mosaic Map, also from sixth century (plate 1; illus. 98). After years of scientific speculation regarding their location, the remains of the monumental Nea church were discovered by the archaeologists N. Avigad and M. Ben-Dov on the southeast edge of the Jewish quarter, opposite the temple.

IV. The Byzantine Way of the Cross

Until the end of the fourth century, the Via Dolorosa procession, on the night of Good Friday, ran from Gethsemane through the "Golden Gate" on the eastern side of the temple square to Golgotha (pp. 278–79). Since the beginning of the fifth century, the procession made its way from Gethsemane to the "House of Caiaphas" (in the area of today's Church of Saint Peter in Gallicantu), stopped there, then moved on to the "Palace of the Judge" (Praetorium of Pilate) and finally to Golgotha. At each critical point a suitable Gospel text was read, and along the way psalms were sung. The liturgy of this procession, which is left to us in the oldest Armenian lectionaries, codices Jerusalem 121 and Paris 44,[13] throws an interesting light on the individual places along the route. For example, on the way from the "House of Caiaphas" to the "gate", the procession was accompanied by the recitation of the relatively

[12] *Itinerarium* 9 (Geyer, 599).

[13] A. Renoux, *Le codex arménien Jérusalem 121*, 2 vols., PO 35/1 and 36/2 (Turnhout: Brepols, 1969–1971).

long Psalm 117 [118] (cf. vv. 19–20). The gate mentioned must be from the time before Eudocia (before A.D. 450) and therefore was obviously a considerable distance from the "House of Caiaphas". This gate seems to be indicated on the Madaba map, behind the Nea church and between the Sophia church and Saint Peter in Gallicantu.

The last part of the procession route, from the Praetorium to Golgotha, is the oldest continuous commemoration for the Way of the Cross (illus. 80) and goes back, as we can see, to the first part of the fifth century. This part began by the Praetorium with a reading from Saint John's Gospel about Jesus' trial before Pilate (Jn 18:28—19:16) and stopped at Golgotha with the Lucan report about the carrying of the cross (Lk 23:24–31). If we accept the beginning of this "Way section" within the range of the "archaeological garden", in which are also the ruins of the German Crusader Church of Saint Mary, then the route must have gone first north along today's Misgav Ladach Road, then left through Chain Street, up to the Suk es-Zeit (the former Cardo Maximus) and from there to the Martyrion of the Anastasis basilica and onto the rock of Golgotha (today in the Church of the Holy Sepulchre).

V. A Spare Place for the Praetorium

The destruction of the Christian shrines by the Persian invasion of A.D. 614 left the Nea and the Sophia churches in rubble. In the year A.D. 638, following the Muslim occupation and during the Umayyad period, there evolved great building activity, during which the Al-Aqsa mosque was built on the temple square. A number of magnificent palaces, which were built south of the temple square, were constructed from the stones of the two churches, which had been destroyed. If they had been provisionally restored, then they were destroyed soon again by earthquakes, which were frequent between 746 and 859.[14] Many Byzantine columns from the Christian churches were reused, and these have been discovered within the area of these Muslim palaces. Pilgrims who visited Jerusalem after this period mention neither the Nea or the Sophia church. It seems indeed that the area west of the Al-Aqsa mosque, i.e., the area of today's Jewish Old City quarter,

[14] Cf. D. H. KALLNER-AMIRAN, "A Revised Earthquake-Catalogue of Palestine", *IEJ* 1 (1950/1951): 223–46 (at 226f.).

was settled by Muslims and therefore out of bounds for Christian services.

After the Christian community had lost the real Praetorium with the Sophia church, it "relocated" the Praetorium to Mount Zion. Directly north of the basilica Hagia Sion, the predecessor of today's Benedictine Dormition Abbey, there was a small chapel, devoted to the Alexandrian martyrs Kyros and John; the stone pavement before this became the new Lithostrotos (Jn 19:13), the yard of Pilate's Praetorium. The Good Friday procession then went from Gethsemane to the "House of Caiaphas" and then to the "Lithostrotos" on Mount Zion. From here the route continued through the area of the Armenian quarter to today's Christian Road and then to Golgotha. A place a little east of today's Citadel was pointed out as the place where Jesus met Mary. The chapel that stood next to the replacement Lithostrotos at the place of today's Armenian Church of the Savior took over the location for the "House of Pilate, Annas, Caiaphas and Caesar".[15] This concentration of important names in such a small area is amazing, but the only tradition that remains today relates Peter's repentence to the Church of Saint Peter in Gallicantu (Mk 14:72 par.).

This arrangement of places, which was originally considered as provisional, was regarded and retained by the Crusaders as final. However, not all of them were happy with the improbable location for the Praetorium on Mount Zion. In the year 1172 a knight called Theodoric suggested another possibility.[16] Near the Jerusalem headquarters of the Knights Templars at the north end of the Temple Mount, the ruins of the Antonia fortress had been found. Theodoric stated that this, according to Josephus, had been the authentic palace of Pilate. This "discovery" convinced an increasing number of Christians, and the place on Mount Zion was gradually given up. On the Crusader map of Cambrai from the second half of the twelfth century, one can see within Antonia a small chapel with the name "Church of the Savior" (Ecclesia S. Salvatoris).[17] Only the alleged "House of Caiaphas" remained on Mount Zion.[18]

[15] Epiphanius Hagiopolita (H. Donner, "Die Palästinabeschreibung des Epiphanius Monachus Hagiopolita", *ZDPV* 87 [1971]: 42–91 [at 70, 84]).

[16] Baldi, 588f.

[17] Baldi, 424f.

[18] Cf. chapter 20, "Where Was the House of Caiaphas Located?" (pp. 253–65).

VI. The Via Dolorosa of the Crusaders

This was the beginning of a completely new local tradition. The Franciscan Ricoldus de Monte Crucis was the first to describe the different Stations of the Cross from the Antonia fortress to Golgotha in the

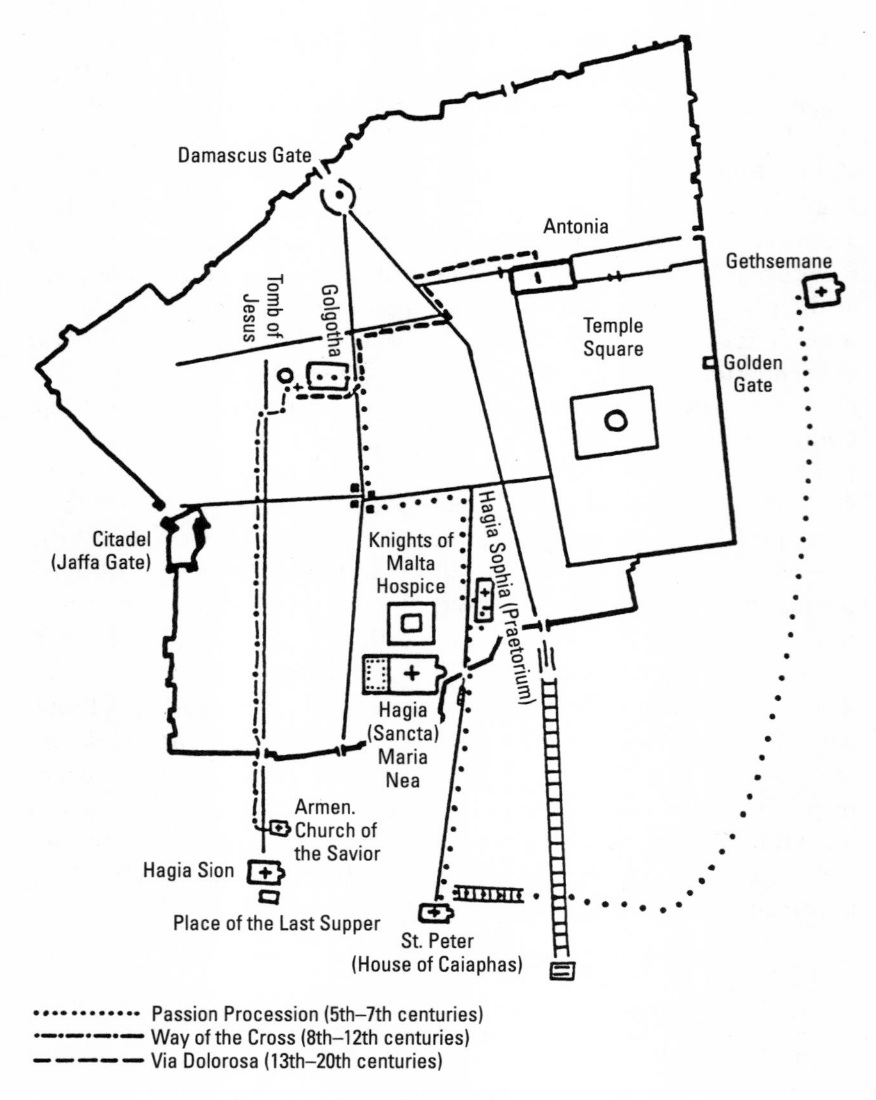

Illus. 80. The development of the Via Dolorosa.

year 1294.[19] He found the place where Jesus met the women of Jerusalem (Lk 23:27–31); a little further, where Jesus met his Mother and where the church "Spasmos Virginis" later stood. Next followed the place where Jesus, exhausted, rested a little; a road crossing was found where he met Simon of Cyrene (Mk 15:21 par.); and then on to Golgotha, the place where the emperor's mother Helen miraculously rediscovered the cross. Over time, all fourteen Stations of the Way of the Cross were established as we now know them.

Possibly a memory of the churches of Sancta Sophia and Maria Nea was retained by the Crusaders. The German Knights, who belonged to the Order of Saint John, built a church, perhaps because they felt somewhat isolated due to their lack of expertise in Latin and French. The project was initiated by a married knight, who is remembered only as *vir Teutonicus, honestus religiosus*, and around 1128 he built a German hospice and a church. When the patriarch of Jerusalem was asked for a title for this church, he gave exactly the same title that Maria Nea had previously carried, that is, the "Holy Mother of God", to this new building (ἅγια θεοτόκος, Sancta Dei Genetrix).[20] This church was rediscovered with the new excavations at the eastern edge of the Jewish quarter.[21] It may be considered as an idealistic successor of "Maria Nea ad Sanctam Sophiam". The Crusader church could stand on the place of the original Gospel "Lithostrotos".

VII. The Historical Via Dolorosa

An attempt to reinstate the original Way of the Cross commemorating the first Good Friday would appear to be a risky enterprise. If we assume that Jesus was led on the shortest route from the Praetorium to Golgotha (which is not certain), then we could imagine that he was escorted across the Herodian paved road, which led from the Hasmonean palace to the west (p. 275), until the procession reached the road that went north to the Gennath Gate (illus. 58). This way Jesus would have been dragged through the area of the "upper market"

[19] Baldi, 593f.

[20] Cf. M. TUMLER, *Der Deutsche Orden im Werden, Wachsen und Wirken bis 1400* (Montreal and Vienna, 1955), 23.

[21] Cf. M. BENVENISTI, *The Crusaders in the Holy Land* (Jerusalem: Magnes Press, 1970), 63f.

(*War* 5.137), which would have been very busy on that day because of the forthcoming festivities. When Jesus came through the Gennath Gate, he could have met the herd of sheep chosen for the Passover offerings in the temple. Here somewhere the execution procession must have come across Simon of Cyrene (Mk 15:21) and the weeping women (Lk 23:27, 31). Jesus was then led on a road that ran between the "second wall" and the quarry. The procession then turned west and arrived on the ground of the old quarry and the rock of Golgotha. Jesus was probably crucified with his face to the east of the town wall and the temple lying behind it, so that the people passing on the road could read the inscription on the cross (Jn 19:20). North of the execution place was a private garden, where Jesus was buried in a newly hewn tomb in the rock (Jn 19:41f.). The memory of this "historical Via Dolorosa" had, according to the Armenian lectionaries, lived on into the fifth century A.D.

Supplement: In the Greek Orthodox area, the summit of the rock of Golgotha is now made visible through a glass plate. With the restoration work, it was discovered that the natural stone was covered by an artificial lime layer, which copied its color and obviously protected the rock. At the traditional place of Jesus' crucifixion, there was a round recess discovered with a half-broken stone ring over it. The Greek excavators G. Lavas and T. Mitropoulos believe that they have identified the historical location of Jesus' cross.[22] However, it is more likely that the stone ring is connected to the votive cross that probably predated Egeria.[23] It was clearly mentioned by the *Breviarius de Hierosolyma* in 530[24] but is also on the Pudentiana mosaic, ca. 400 (plate 2). The building over the traditional Tomb of Jesus was in very bad condition. Before the necessary renovation work was undertaken, a photographic measurement of the building was completed, and one can hope that some of the rock tomb of Jesus remains (M. Biddle). Probably the most accurate reproduction of the Byzantine building of the Holy Sepulchre is to be found in the Capuchin Church in Eichstätt.[25] Also, in

[22] K. H. FLECKENSTEIN, "Israel West Westjordanland Reiseführer" (Lahr: St. Johannis, 1995), 127f.

[23] *Itinerarium* 37.4 (Geyer, 71; Baldi, 628).

[24] Geyer, 153f.

[25] C. KREITMEIR, "Das 'Heilige Grab'" (in Eichstätt), *Im Lande des Herrn* 44, no. 3 (1990): 69–73.

the south Tyrol Passeier Valley there is a copy of the chapel of the Holy Sepulchre, which an ancestor of Andreas Hofer built following a pilgrimage. The archaeological investigations of the last years affirm the authenticity of the Church of the Holy Sepulchre.[26]

[26] J. Patrich, "The Early Church of the Holy Sepulchre in the Light of Excavations and Restoration", in Y. Tsafrir, *Ancient Churches Revealed* (Jerusalem: Israel Exploration Society, 1993), 101–17.

PART FIVE

The Messianic Community

25. The Apostolic Synagogue on Zion

The famous Church of the Apostles, which marks the place to which the Apostles returned from the Mount of Olives, where Christ had been taken into heaven (Acts 1:1–13), can still be found on the southwest hill of the old part of the city of Jerusalem (Mount Zion). Here also was the site of the Last Supper and where Peter held his famous sermon at Pentecost (Acts 2). Strangely, the remains of the Church of the Apostles are now part of a building that is traditionally regarded as the Tomb of King David. However, it is still possible to admire the second floor of this building as the *coenaculum*, the room of Jesus' Last Supper.

I wish to proceed in three steps. The first step is simple and is not denied by any serious historian or archaeologist: the building, in which the so-called Tomb of David lies, is in reality an old synagogue that dates from the Roman period, and it is not the tomb of an Israeli king. By contrast, journalists have attempted to endorse[1] the popular belief about the Tomb of David by referring to the work of the archaeologist G. Barkay. He suggested the possibility of a royal tomb on the western hill of Jerusalem, but this is not supported by any evidence. The second step in my thesis consists of demonstrating that it concerns not a usual Jewish, but rather a Jewish Christian, synagogue. Initially the place for Jewish Christian services was also called a synagogue. Only later, as we shall see, were Christian places of assembly called churches. It was following this later development that the Jewish Christian synagogue on Mount Zion became known as the "Church of the Apostles". Demonstrating this will be the third step in my thesis.

[1] M. Rogoff, "Patchwork of Holiness", *Jerusalem Post*, international edition, June 18, 1988, 6, 18.

I. The Legendary Tomb of David on Mount Zion

The traditional Tomb of David was located on Mount Zion. The Old Testament reports that it was the will of the king to be buried *within* the city. In 1 Kings 2:10 we read: "Then David slept with his fathers, and was buried in the city of David" (עִיר דָּוִד [*ᶜir dawid*]). Normally, graves were almost exclusively *outside* settlements, in order not to contaminate the inhabitants with the ritual impurity of a dead body. An exception to this rule appears for the lineage of the monarchy from David to Ahaz in the history of Israel.[2]

1. The Odyssey of Zion

If today you ask a policeman where Mount Zion is, or if you look on a city map of Jerusalem, you will normally be referred to the broad hill south of the unwalled old part of the Old City. There are two hills that extend from today's Old City to the south and are separated by a valley that in the New Testament period was called the Tyropoeon Valley (*War* 5.140). The western of the two hills has today become Mount Zion (in Hebrew *har zijon* [הַר צִיּוֹן]). This western hill, with steep slopes, is much higher and broader than the eastern one. Until more than one hundred years ago, the researchers were generally convinced that the "City of David" lay on the western hill. There were also few reasons to doubt the assumption regarding the traditional location of the Tomb of David.

But then early investigators and archaeologists questioned these assumptions. In 1838 the American Oriental specialist E. Robinson explored the channel system under the eastern hill, where the water from the Gihon on the eastern slope leads underground to the other side of the hill. What was the purpose of this tunnel under the eastern hill? In 1880 an Old Hebrew inscription engraved on the wall of this tunnel[3] was found, and this helped the German architect C. Schick[4] identify the tunnel as the one that King Hezekiah constructed in the

[2] "And Solomon slept with his fathers, and was buried in the city of David his father" (1 Kings 11:43a). For the later kings, see 1 Kings 14:31; 15:8, 24; 22:51; 2 Kings 12:21; 14:20; 15:7, 38; 16:20.

[3] Cf. G. Kroll, *Auf den Spuren Jesu*, 11th ed. (Stuttgart: Katholisches Bibelwerk, 2002), 107–10.

[4] Cf. A. Strobel, *Conrad Schick: Ein Leben für Jerusalem* (Fürth: Flaccius, 1988), 26; K. H. Fleckenstein, *Wanderer, kommst Du nach Jerusalem* (Freiburg: Herder, 1990), 154f.

late eighth century B.C., in preparation for the Assyrian siege, in order to bring water into Jerusalem (2 Kings 18:13—19:37; 2 Chron 32). But an enigma remained: why under the eastern hill? The following century, with its excavations, demonstrated that the Canaanite (or Jebusite) city, which David conquered around 1000 B.C. and which became "the City of David" (2 Sam 5:7), was situated on the eastern and not on the western hill. The reason for this is clear: the only reliable water source, the Gihon spring, is at the foot of the eastern hill.

Nevertheless, today the western hill is erroneously called Mount Zion, while the eastern hill is correctly called the City of David. Indeed, Zion resembles a moving mountain. The Old Testament reports that David conquered the "stronghold of Zion" (מְצוּדַת צִיּוֹן [*mezudat zijon*]) (2 Sam 5:7). As we have seen, the city is archaeologically confirmed as "David's", and the original Mount Zion (Zion I) was on the eastern hill. Modern excavations by the late Y. Shiloh exposed the foundations of "fortress Zion", a famous building of stairs that, with a height of five floors, represents the highest building from the Iron Age ever found in Israel.[5]

King Solomon, David's son, built his palace and a temple for the Lord on a hill north of the City of David, where still today the Temple Mount is appropriately the jewel of Jerusalem, with the Dome of the Rock at its center. During the biblical period, the location for Zion seems to have moved, because the Temple Mount became known as Zion (Zion II). This shift can already be observed in the later parts of the book of Isaiah (e.g., Is 60:14) and in the Psalms and is apparent in the first book of Maccabees from the second century B.C. (1 Mac 4:37, 60; 5:54; 7:33).

This was the location for Zion until some time before the conquest of Jerusalem by the Romans in the year A.D. 70. At that time the Roman troops destroyed the whole city, including the temple, and with time people reflected on where the old Davidian fortress might have stood. The inhabitants of Jerusalem in the first century A.D. could no longer believe that the splendid palace of David was on the low east hill. General opinion then believed that it must have been located on the western hill on the highest point. Josephus, the Jewish historian

[5] Cf. H. Shanks, "The City of David after Five Years of Digging", *BAR* 11, no. 6 (1985): 22–38.

of the first century, refers to the City of David as on the western hill. Josephus believed that the town wall around the western hill ("first wall") was already built by David and Solomon (*War* 5.143). During the description of the conquest of Jerusalem by David, Josephus suggests that Joab conquered first the lower part of town (the eastern hill) and then the Jebusite fortress (the "stronghold of Zion" [2 Sam 5:7] in the upper city, i.e., on the western hill [*Ant.* 7.62–66]). In this way, a third place, i.e., the western hill, could have been regarded as Mount Zion, and it has remained so until today (Zion III).

2. *The Wanderings of David's Tomb*

Just as Mount Zion undertook migration, so also did David's tomb. When the French archaeologist R. Weill excavated the eastern hill in 1913, he discovered a number of grave caves, among them three beautiful horizontal gallery graves.[6] Weill believed he found the royal tomb in the City of David. Many archaeologists still agree with this.[7] However, even if that was not the genuine location for David's burial, his tomb must be somewhere *on the eastern hill*, within the City of David.

In the past, David's tomb was well known, but it is difficult to infer from the ancient sources its precise location. Nehemiah mentioned David's tomb when he was rebuilding the walls of Jerusalem following the return of the exiles from Babylon in the late fifth century B.C. (Neh 3:16). From this description it becomes clear that he found David's tomb on the eastern hill. It is said, "Shallum . . . repaired the Fountain Gate" and then "the wall of the Pool of Shelah of the king's garden, as far as the stairs that go down from the City of David" (Neh 3:15). Thus David's tomb is clearly situated on the eastern hill. The next verse contains a description of a repaired piece of wall "opposite the sepulchres of David" (Neh 3:16). This tomb must therefore have been within the city, not far from the pool of Siloam but some distance from the Temple Mount, exactly where Weill found the tombs. Josephus reports that Herod the Great (37–4 B.C.) secretly tried to rob the treasures hidden in David's tomb. However, two of his workers died mysteriously, and Herod was seized by fear and arranged

[6] *La Cité de David*, vol. 1 (Paris: Gabalda, 1920), 35–44, 157–73.

[7] Cf. H. SHANKS, *The City of David: A Guide to Biblical Jerusalem* (Washington: Biblical Archeology Society, 1973), 99–108.

to establish at the place a memorial stone (*Ant.* 7.393; 16.179–83). Without doubt Peter referred to this monument when he stated in his sermon at Pentecost: "[King David's] tomb [μνῆμα, i.e., the actual monument] is with us to this day" (Acts 2:29). The Roman historian Dio Cassius (ca. A.D. 150–235) reports that this memorial stone survived the destruction of Jerusalem in the year A.D. 70 but collapsed shortly before the outbreak of the Second Jewish Revolt against Rome under Bar Kokhba (A.D. 132–135).[8]

We know for certain that Rabbi Akiba knew the exact location of David's tomb. Before he was executed by the Romans for his support of the Bar Kokhba revolt, he was asked why it was permitted to put the tombs of David's family in the midst of the city, in spite of their impurity. He answered that the impurity of the graves was taken out of the city by a rock channel from the city into the Kidron brook.[9] This indicates the graves' location because the Kidron lies on the eastern side of the eastern hill. It becomes clear that Akiba accepted the royal burial places on the eastern slope of the eastern hill near the Kidron Valley, exactly where Weill had discovered his grave complex. This confirmation by Akiba provides an additional reason for the acceptance of David's tomb on the eastern hill.

After the Roman emperor Hadrian had put down the second Jewish rebellion, the Jews were banished from the city. Once again Jerusalem was rebuilt, as the Gentile Roman colony Aelia Capitolina. For this reason, the area in which Weill found the royal graves was used as a quarry. It is the opinion of some researchers that the destruction of the graves and the exclusion from the Holy City led many Jews to venerate David's tomb in his birth city of Bethlehem (p. 8).[10] This new location for David's tomb was soon taken over by the Christians, who found support for it in Luke's Gospel, which also calls Bethlehem, Jesus' place of birth, "the city of David" (Lk 2:4, 11), although this name had been originally used only for the eastern hill of Jerusalem.

Eusebius was the first Christian witness to support David's burial place in Bethlehem. In his famous work about the biblical place-names, he wrote (ca. A.D. 330) that both David and his father Jesse

[8] *Historia Romana* 69.14.

[9] Tosephta, *Baba Bathra* 1.11; Jerusalem Talmud, *Nazir* 9 (57d).

[10] Cf. J. JEREMIAS, *Heiligengräber in Jesu Umwelt* (Göttingen: Vandenhoeck und Ruprecht, 1958), 79.

were buried in Bethlehem.[11] In A.D. 333 a man whom we know only as a pilgrim from the French city of Bordeaux visited the Holy Land, and he left a very interesting and reliable report from his journey. In this report, he writes that not far from the Church of the Nativity[12] in Bethlehem is a tomb cave that contains not only the mortal remains of David but also those of Solomon and other members of Jesse's family.[13] Another anonymous pilgrim, from the Italian city Piacenza, came to the Holy Land around the year 570. This pilgrim wrote that "a mile from Bethlehem, in the suburbs, David's body lies buried beside that of his son Solomon."[14]

The Muslims venerated the tombs of David and Solomon in Bethlehem until the fourteenth century,[15] although a new Christian tradition began to develop in the tenth century that located David's tomb on the western hill of Jerusalem, which had been considered for a long time erroneously as Mount Zion. We find the first reference to this relocation in a very confusing document from the tenth century, the *Vita S. Helenae et Constantini*, written for the glorification of the emperor Constantine and his mother Helen by an unknown Greek author.[16]

When the Crusaders conquered Jerusalem in the year 1099, they found the Byzantine basilica Hagia Sion destroyed on Mount Zion (southwest hill, Zion III). They discovered an extension that was in a better condition, where they found not only the alleged David's tomb but also that of his son Solomon and that of the martyr Stephen. Both burial places were connected to that of David.[17] The Crusaders did not continue to recognize the tradition of Stephen's

[11] *Onomastikon* (Klostermann, 42, 12).

[12] Cf. chapter 1, "The Nazoreans, Bethlehem and the Birth of Jesus" (pp. 3–22, esp. 12–16).

[13] *Itinerarium* 20 (Geyer, 25; Baldi, 88).

[14] *Itinerarium* 29 (Geyer, 177; Baldi, 96). Cf. also J. Wilkinson, *Jerusalem Pilgrims before the Crusades* (Jerusalem: Ariel, 1978), 85.

[15] Ali Harad (A.D. 1170) wrote: "Beit Lahem [Bethlehem] is the name of the city where Jesus—peace be with him—was born and where the tombs are from David and Solomon" (*Archives de l'Orient latin* [Paris] 1 [1881]: 605). Ibn Khaldun (fourteenth century) remarked in his historical work: "Then David the prophet died and was buried in Bethlehem" (F. Dunkel, *HlL* 55 [1911]: 25).

[16] Baldi, 495f.

[17] Raymund de Aguilers wrote: "In this church are the following holy shrines: the tomb of King David and that of Solomon and the tomb of the protomartyr, the holy Stephen" (Baldi, 496, n. 1).

tomb at this location, because a Byzantine church with a reliquary of the martyr already stood north of the Damascus Gate (p. 352). Some parts of this basilica, including the mosaic floor, remained and in the nineteenth century became the church Saint Étienne of the French École biblique. The Crusaders directed their attention instead to the tradition of David's tomb, toward Mount Zion, and established a large cenotaph (empty memorial coffin) in order to mark this location. However, for the Crusaders, the Tomb of David was of substantially less significance than the much older tradition that connected this holy shrine with the place of the Last Supper of Jesus, the Jerusalem Resurrection appearances, the pouring out of the Holy Spirit on the Apostles at Pentecost, and the dormition (i.e., the sleep [assumption]) of Mary.

Gradually the false Tomb of David from this newly created Christian tradition was accepted, first by the Jewish community and afterward also by the Muslims. In the years between 1948 and 1967, when the remaining Old City of Jerusalem was in Jordanian control, the site became a special place of interest for the Jews. At that time, the most revered Jewish place, the so-called Wailing Wall or Western Wall (a part of the Herodian west surrounding wall of the temple square), was inaccessible to Jews, while Mount Zion has, since the War of Independence, been under Israeli control.

3. A Mortar Shell and an Emergency Excavation

In 1948 there was substantial fighting on Mount Zion (Zion III), during which a mortar shell exploded in the building that enclosed the traditional Tomb of David. In 1951 the Israeli archaeologist J. Pinkerfeld was entrusted with the task of repairing the damage. While doing this, he gave the building an archaeological examination. His excavation report was, however, published only posthumously, after the author had been killed in 1956 by a terrorist raid on a congress of archaeologists in Ramat Rachel, south of Jerusalem.

Behind the cenotaph of the Crusaders, Pinkerfeld found a niche that was part of the original walls of the building. After he had removed the marble slabs of the floor for the repair work, he dug two exploratory pits, in which he found three earlier floor levels. Approximately 12 cm underneath the present floor, Pinkerfeld discovered the floor of

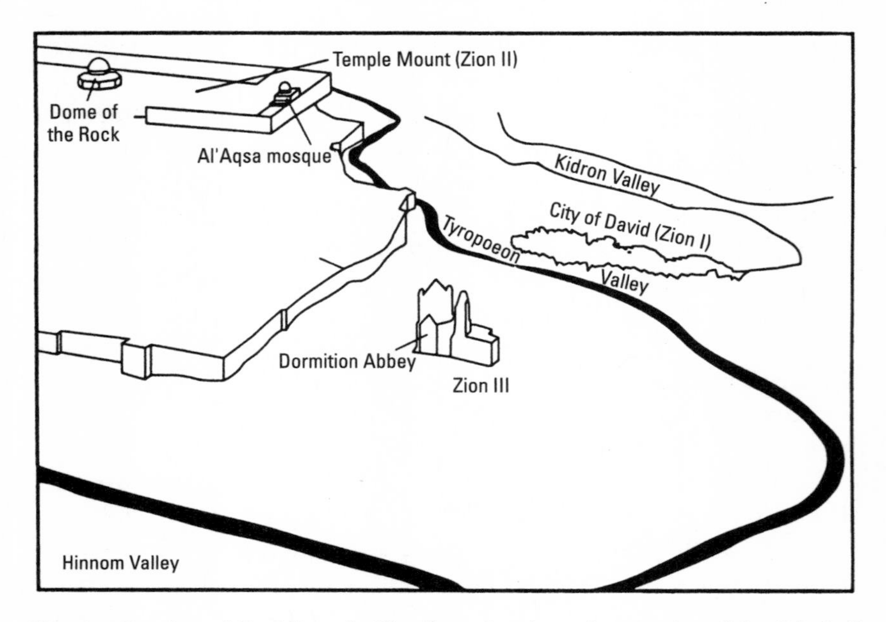

Illus. 81. Locations of David's tomb. The illustration shows the migration of the "idea" of Zion.

the Crusaders. About 48 cm lower, he discovered a late Roman or early Byzantine floor, which consisted of colored mosaic stones in a geometrical design. Then again, 10 cm under that, the excavator found the mortar bed of the original floor as well as obvious remains of a stone pavement.

Pinkerfeld described this original floor in his excavation report as follows: "Seventy centimeters below the present floor level, another floor of plaster was found, quite possibly the remains of a stone pavement. Some small fragments of smooth stones, perhaps the remains of this pavement, were found slightly above the level. . . . It is certain that this floor belonged to the original building, i.e., to the period when the northern barrier and its apse [the niche] were built. This is evident from a section of the wall which shows at that level a foundation ledge projecting into the hall."[18]

As Pinkerfeld discovered, approximately 1.80 m up, in the north wall of the building over the original floor, there was a niche that was

[18] "'David's Tomb': Notes on the History of the Building", *Bulletin of the Louis M. Rabinowitz Fund for the Exploration of Ancient Synagogues*, no. 3 (1960): 41–43 (at 42).

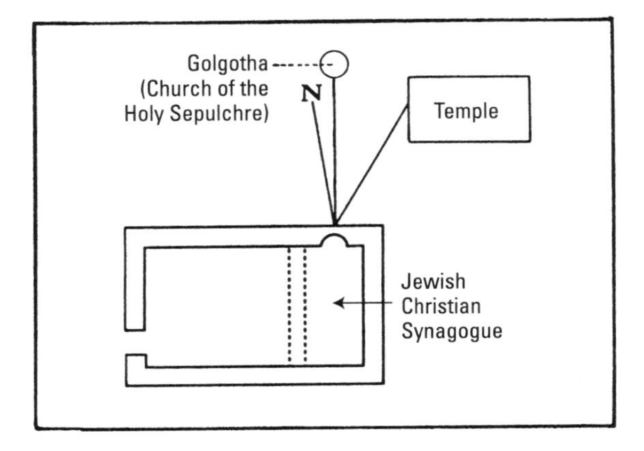

Illus. 82. Orientation of the Jewish Christian synagogue.

part of the original building. Similar niches in comparable height above the floor were found in ancient synagogues and are considered to be repositories for the Torah scrolls. Pinkerfeld assumed that this niche fulfilled the same function. He concluded that this building was originally a synagogue from the Roman period. The fact that this building was actually a synagogue seems now clear, and researchers who examined this are in agreement.[19] The next step consists of deciding what kind of synagogue it was. Was it a usual Jewish synagogue or Jewish Christian?

II. A Jewish Christian Synagogue on Zion

1. The Jewish Christian Synagogues

The first Christians were exclusively Jews. They did not think of themselves as having left Orthodox Judaism. Indeed, one of the first questions for those who were interested in the new religious movement was whether Gentiles were allowed to become Christians at all or whether it was necessary first to become a Jew before one could become a Christian (Acts 15). In the course of this argument, Paul became the principal Apostle to the Gentiles in the Greek-speaking world. We will discuss later the problems between the Jewish Christian community in

[19] Cf. É. PUECH, "La synagogue judéo-chrétienne du Mont Sion", *MB* 57 (1989): 18f.

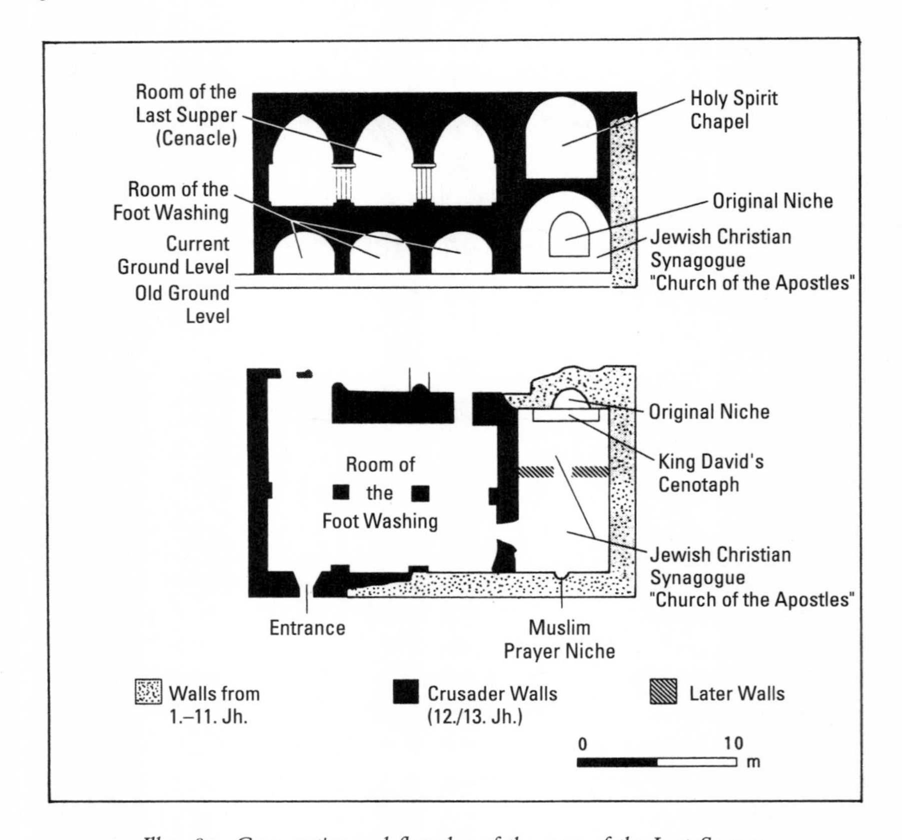

Illus. 83. Cross section and floorplan of the room of the Last Supper.

Jerusalem and the Gentile Christian branch of the Church that developed outside of Palestine.

At the beginning all the Christians originally came from Judaism, and for a long time these Jewish Christians and even some Gentile Christians called their meeting places synagogues.[20] The Jewish house of worship is still today called in Hebrew *beit Knesset* (בֵּית כְּנֶסֶת), which means "house of meeting". Under Hellenistic influence it became *synagōgē*, a Greek word (συναγωγή) that means "meeting". The synagogues were used by the Jewish community for very diverse activities. The principal purpose was, however, as a place for the reading of the

[20] Cf., e.g., Ignatius of Antioch, *Letter to Polycarp* 4.2; *Shepherd of Hermas* 43.9; Justin Martyr, *Dialogue with the Jew Tryphon* 63.5.

Torah; for a translation (*targum*) into the native language; for a reading of the prophets; and, on the Sabbath and festival days, for sermons. The synagogues also served other purposes, e.g., for the study of the Scriptures, for holy meals (particularly on the Sabbath and festival days), as the repository of collections and other community possessions, as a religious court of justice and sometimes even as a guesthouse. The traditional guardian of the synagogue lived nearby.[21]

In order to differ from the Jews, the Gentile Christians began to designate their meetings with the Greek word *ekklēsia* (ἐκκλησία), which means "assembly". The word "church" comes from the Greek word *kyriakē* (κυριακή), which means "belonging to the Lord" (κύριος). From this the English word "church" has been derived.

2. *A Strange Orientation and Informative Graffiti*

We turn again to the synagogue on Mount Zion: was it a Jewish or a Jewish Christian synagogue? Pinkerfeld[22] and also H. W. Hirschberg[23] concluded later that the building was a Jewish synagogue because it is oriented exactly toward the temple, whereas churches were usually aligned toward the east. This, however, is based on at least two errors. In addition, there is further evidence that shows that the building was originally a Jewish Christian synagogue.

The first mistake was the belief that all Christian meeting places were aligned toward the east; this became normative only in the second half of the fourth century (pp. 102–3), after Christianity had become the official religion of the Roman Empire. The building that concerns us here, however, originates from a much earlier time. Second, this synagogue, or its niche, is actually not oriented to the site of the former temple. This can easily be seen from the roof of the "Tomb of David". The niche is actually aligned to the north and not to the northeast, where the temple stood. The difference is small, but significant, because with the Temple Mount visible, the architects were clear about an accurate orientation. Indeed, the synagogue is precisely oriented toward today's Church of the Holy

[21] Cf. L. I. Levine, "Les fonctions de la synagogue ancienne", *MB* 57 (1989): 28–30.

[22] "'David's Tomb'" (see n. 18), 43.

[23] "The Remains of an Ancient Synagogue on Mount Zion", in Y. Yadin, *Jerusalem Revealed* (Jerusalem: Israel Exploration Society, 1976), 116f.

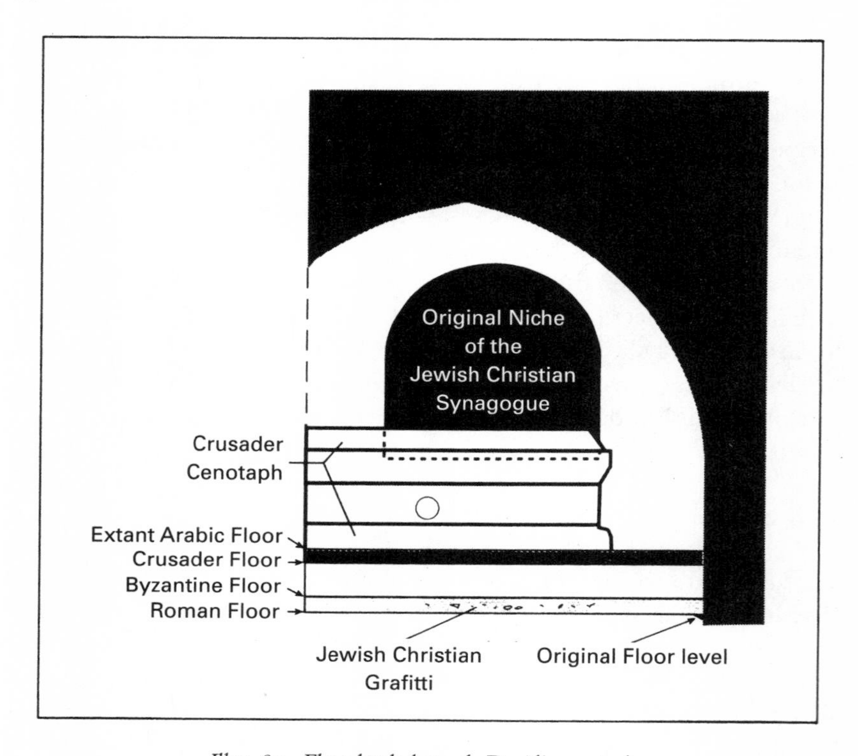

Illus. 84. Floor levels beneath David's cenotaph.

Sepulchre, which was the place of Jesus' crucifixion on Golgotha and of Jesus' tomb.[24]

I believe that this orientation was intentional. It seems logical that Jewish Christians selected an orientation to replace the traditional Jewish orientation toward the temple, particularly after its destruction, with a new focus, i.e., the place of Jesus' burial and Resurrection. This assumption is affirmed by the fact that the Martyrion church, which forms the oldest part of today's Church of the Holy Sepulchre, built by the emperor Constantine in 326, was oriented toward Jesus' tomb. Another holy shrine aligned to Jesus' tomb is the ancient Church of the Tomb of Mary, which already formed a holy place for the Jewish Christian community according to the Franciscan scholar B. Bagatti (p. 404).

[24] Cf. chapter 24, "The Historical Via Dolorosa" (pp. 303–15, esp. pp. 303–8).

There is further evidence: on the lowest floor level, Pinkerfeld found pieces of the original wall plaster of the synagogue, and on this, graffiti were scratched. In his own words: "In the first [Roman] period, the hall was plastered. The fragments were handed over to the late Professor M. Schwabe for examination."[25] However, both Schwabe and Pinkerfeld died before the publication of their investigation. Lastly, the graffiti were published by an expert team of the Jerusalem Studium Biblicum Franciscanum, i.e., by the professors E. Testa and B. Bagatti. They interpreted the graffiti as follows: "One graffito has the initials of Greek words which may be translated as 'Conquer, Savior, mercy'. Another graffito has letters which can be translated as 'O Jesus, that I may live, O Lord of the autocrat'."[26] Perhaps the word *autokratōr* (αὐτοκράτωρ) could refer to King David (cf. Ps 110:1; Mt 22:43). I agree with the Franciscan authors that this was originally a synagogue building and a place of the Jewish Christian cult. As we will see still further, references from later sources call this building the "Church of the Apostles", and this supports its identification as a Jewish Christian synagogue.

3. *The Building of the Jewish Christian Synagogue*

The historical conditions following the Roman destruction of Jerusalem in the year A.D. 70, as well as some new archaeological evidence, demonstrate the circumstances under which this Jewish Christian synagogue on Mount Zion was built. The Roman general (and later emperor) Titus suppressed the first Jewish rebellion in A.D. 70 by burning Jerusalem thoroughly, which also destroyed the temple. Flavius Josephus reports that the destruction reached the most distant corners of the city and was so comprehensive that someone who passed by could not even recognize the earlier existence of a city (*War* 7.3f.).

The destruction included even the city on the western hill (Zion III). In the year 1983, during an excavation in front of the church of the Dormition Abbey, which lies beside the old Jewish Christian synagogue, I found a thick layer of ash covering the steps of a Jewish ritual bath, and in the remains of the fire there were coins dating from the first and second years of the Jewish Revolt (A.D. 66–67 and 67–68).

[25] "'David's Tomb'" (see n. 18), 43.

[26] Cf. B. BAGATTI, *The Church from the Circumcision*, SBFCMi 2 (Jerusalem: Franciscan Printing Press, 1971), 121.

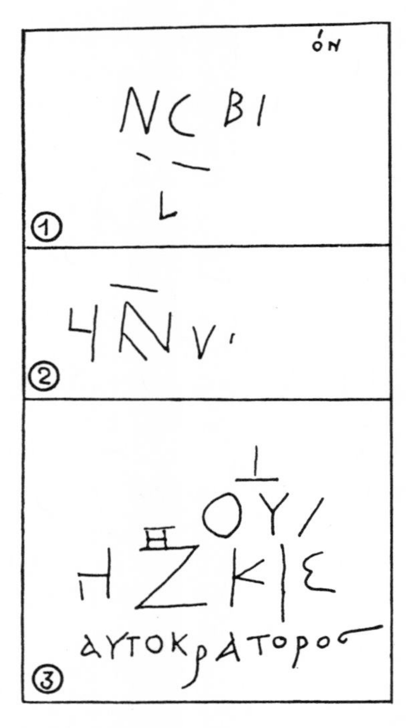

Illus. 85. Jewish Christian graffiti (according to E. Testa, O.F.M., 1962) (sketch). Graffito no. 3 shows, among other things, the words "Live (ZH)*, Lord* (KI[RIO]S) *of the ruler* (AYTOKRATOROS)*".*

It is safe to conclude that at that time, the building that stood at the place of the later Jewish Christian synagogue was also destroyed by the Romans. The Jewish Christian community of Jerusalem fled before this terrible disaster and emigrated to Pella in Transjordan and the surrounding areas of Gilead and Bashan in expectation of the Parousia, the Second Coming of Jesus.[27]

When the Parousia did not happen, the Jewish Christians from Jerusalem decided to return to the destroyed Holy City and reestablish their holy shrine at the place of the "Upper Room", where Jesus held the Last Supper (pp. 412–13). It was also the place where the Apostles returned from the Mount of Olives after the Ascension and awaited the descent of the Holy Spirit at Pentecost (Acts 1–2)

[27] Cf. chapter 31, "Simeon Bar Cleopas, Second Bishop of Jerusalem" (pp. 408–14, esp. pp. 411–13).

and where the community gathered around James "the Lord's brother" (Gal 1:19).[28] There they built a synagogue, which they were able to do because, as Jewish Christians, they possessed a certain religious liberty under the Romans, more so even than the Gentile Christians. The Jewish religion was regarded as permissible by the Roman law (*religio licita*), even when professed by Gentile believers. On the other hand, Gentiles who converted to Christianity could be persecuted by the state until the time of Constantine in the early fourth century. This is perhaps one of the reasons why Jewish Christians did not call themselves "Christians" but "Israelites",[29] "Nazoreans" or "Ebionites" (p. 365).

The archaeological findings support this hypothesis. On the external facade of the synagogue building, stones from the early Roman period are noticeable at the base of the east and south walls (plate 8b), which are still standing at a considerable height.[30] These large stones (e.g., one in the third layer is 0.96 × 1.10 m in diameter) are attributed by most archaeologists to the Herodian period, i.e., before A.D. 70. But these stones were not originally hewn for this building. They were brought here from elsewhere and reused to make this wall. We know this because of the damage to the corners that was caused by their transportation. Different-size rectangular blocks and blocks of irregular heights were also used in the same layer of the east wall. If this were an original Herodian construction, the heights of the stones would be even. Possibly construction occurred during the late Roman period, following the destruction of Jerusalem in the year A.D. 70, and the synagogue building must have been constructed from previously used building material. Who could have done this? I believe that it was the returning Jewish Christians in the late first century and that the so-called Tomb of David was their synagogue. The most probable time for the establishment of such an impressive building was the years between A.D. 70 and 132. At this time a growing Jewish Christian community existed, with a succession of thirteen "bishops of the circumcision" as noted by Eusebius.[31]

[28] Cf. chapter 28, "James the Lord's 'Brother' ", (pp. 380–93).

[29] Cf. Cyril of Jerusalem, *Catecheses* 10:16 (PG 33:681); Epiphanius, *Panarion* 29.6 (PG 41:401f.; Klijn-Reinink, 168); Agapius (Mahbub), *World History* (PO 8:484).

[30] Cf. also G. Kroll, *Auf den Spuren Jesu* (see n. 3), 315–18.

[31] *Demonstratio Evangelica* 3.5 (*GCS* 23:131; Klijn-Reinink, 138); *HE* 4.5:1–4.

Illus. 86. The east wall of the "Tomb of David" and the Last Supper room (according to L. H. Vincent, O.P.) (from G. Kroll). On this part of the east wall, you easily see the position of the windows and relevant areas. The four stone layers (A–D) of large blocks, which remain from the building of the old synagogue, are remarkable. The eight stone layers above probably originate from the Crusader period.

III. The Christian Zion Tradition

1. From the First to the Second Jewish Revolt

Why did later ecclesiastical writers call the old Jewish Christian synagogue on Mount Zion (Zion III) the "Church of the Apostles"? Bishop Epiphanius of Salamis (315–403), who came from the Holy Land

Illus. 87. The Jewish Christian synagogue (first to fourth centuries). An attempt at reconstruction, according to the Pudentiana mosaic (plate 2). The dark stones are from the southeast wall.

(p. 401), described the situation at the time of a visit to Jerusalem by the emperor Hadrian in A.D. 130–131. He

> found the city completely destroyed and the Holy Sanctuary of God razed to the ground, except for a few houses and the small church of God. It stood there where the disciples, returning from the Mount of Olives after the Ascension of the Savior, went up to the Upper Room [ὑπερῷον (Acts 1:3)]. It was erected on that part of Zion [Σιών] that remained undestroyed, together with some neighboring houses and seven synagogues, that stood alone on Zion like huts. One of these survived up to the time of Bishop Maximonas and the Emperor Constantine like a 'hut in a vineyard' in accordance with Scripture [Is 1:8].[32]

The shrine on the hill of Zion mentioned by Epiphanius must have been a Jewish Christian building, because the establishment of a "Christian Church" became possible only after Constantine's Edict of Milan (A.D. 313). Who built this synagogue church, by A.D. 130 on the southwest hill of Jerusalem, as a memorial to the place of the Last Supper and the event of Pentecost? Some information is available that is supplied by a patriarch of the city of Alexandria in the tenth century, Euthychius (896–940). He composed a Church history using available

[32] *De mensuris et ponderibus* 14 (PG 43:260–62; Baldi, 477f.).

older sources,[33] and he wrote that Jewish Christians, who had fled to Pella in order to escape the destruction of the Holy City in A.D. 70, "returned in the fourth year of the emperor Vespasian to Jerusalem and built there their church".[34] The fourth year of Vespasian was A.D. 73, the year when Masada, the last enclave of Jewish resistance, fell into the hands of the Romans (*War* 7.275ff.). The Jewish Christians returned at that time under the leadership of Simeon Bar Cleopas, the second bishop of Jerusalem after James, the Lord's "brother", who, like Jesus, came from the family of David (pp. 408–9).

The Jewish Christians built the synagogue church mentioned above sometime after A.D. 73, and they may have used some of the beautiful stonework from the destroyed Citadel of Herod, which was not far away (pp. 269–70). They may also have used stones from the ruins of the second temple on Zion, hoping to transfer something of the holiness of the old temple to the new, or third, Zion. If this was the case, then we could refer to the apocryphal *Odes of Solomon*, which was written after A.D. 100 by a rival Jewish Christian group: "My God, nobody can change your holy place; for there is no other place to establish it; because there is no authority over it, because you have your shrine planned before those modest places; what is old and venerable cannot be changed by those who come later. You give courage, O Lord, to those whose hope is set on you" (*Odes Sol.* 4:1–3). The "holy place" is the temple (*Odes Sol.* 6:8). If the community on the western hill, under the direction of Simeon Bar Cleopas, did actually use stones from the second temple for their synagogue church, then the accusation of the ode fits well.

After the construction of the building on the southwest hill of Jerusalem, the hill was known as "Zion" (Zion III) among the Christians. The outstanding expert on the topography and history of Jerusalem Professor G. Dalman suggested that the Christian designation of "Zion" not only meant a "migration of the name from the eastern hill to the western hill" but was intended by the Christians to become "a placement of the ideal designation of Jerusalem, on the spot where one imagined the old center [the Early Church] was, before the Roman

[33] The sources of Euthychius are not always reliable, but for the time from the death of James up to the last bishops of the circumcision in Jerusalem, he seems to have had an excellent source at his disposal, perhaps the five books of the work of Hegesippos (cf. PL 111:983–88).

[34] *Annales* (PL 111:985).

Aelia Capitolina."[35] It is possible that earlier there was already a similar Jewish belief because, as we saw, Flavius Josephus looked for Zion on the western hill (pp. 320–22). In the collected messianic sayings of the Qumran Essenes we read, "It is from the branch of David that the researcher of the law will arise ... in Zion at the end of days, as it is written: 'I want the dwelling of David again raised up' [Amos 9:11f.; cf. Acts 15:16 (pp. 390–91)]. That is the ruined hut of David, which will rise and save Israel" (4QFlor 1:10–13). Did the Jerusalem Essenes already regard the southwest hill as the place of the eschatological Zion? Then Hebrews 12:22 could already refer to Mount Zion as the meeting place of the Primitive Community on this hill. In any case, the Letter to the Hebrews compared Zion and Sinai (Heb 12:18–24), as we shall discuss later. This was not just a purely mythical or eschatological belief, as the community of the firstborn, "enrolled in heaven" (Heb 12:23), were real living human beings, who belonged to the community of the original church in Jerusalem.[36]

The oldest reference to new Zion is found in the apocryphal *Life of the Prophets* (*Vitae prophetarum*), whose Hebrew-Jewish source from the first century A.D. was interpolated by a Jewish Christian at the beginning of the second century.[37] These writings are concerned with the location of Isaiah's tomb: "The grave is beside the burial place of the kings, behind the burial place of the Jews on the southern side [near Siloam]. Solomon built the shrine of David in the east of Zion."[38] This corresponds exactly to Zion III, and if this paragraph already belongs to the original source, this would explain the Jewish understanding about Zion during the first century A.D. In the "Life of the Prophet Jeremiah", the narration is interrupted by the following Christian comment: "Then he [Jeremiah] spoke to those around him: 'The Lord went from Sinai into heaven; he will return to Zion with power, as a lawbringer, and that will be the sign for you: all people will venerate a piece of wood.'"[39] The venerated wood is to be understood as the cross. The interpolator of the *Life of the Prophets* is probably the

[35] "Zion, die Burg Jerusalems", *PJB* 11 (1915): 43–84 (at 79).

[36] Cf. chapter 32, "The Jerusalem Essenes, Barnabas and the Letter to the Hebrews" (pp. 415–22).

[37] Cf. P. Riessler, *Altjüdisches Schrifttum ausserhalb der Bibel*, 2nd ed. (Heidelberg: Kerle, 1966), 1321.

[38] *Vit. Proph.* 13 (ibid., 874).

[39] *Vit. Proph.* 14 (ibid., 876).

earliest Christian witness for the interpretation of Isaiah 2:2–5. According to him, the new law of the Gospel sprang from Zion III, the southwest hill of Jerusalem.[40]

Incidentally, coins from the time of the Bar Kokhba rebellion (A.D. 132–135) have a remarkable characteristic.[41] Coins that were stamped at that time take their form and inscription from the coins of the Hasmonean period and the first revolt against Rome, but in the inscriptions, such as *cherut zijon* (חרות ציון), "Freedom of Zion", and *ge'ulah zijon* (גאולה ציון), "Salvation of Zion", the "Zion" of the earlier designs has been replaced with "Jerusalem" or "Israel". Why did that happen? The reason could be that in the eyes of the rebels a new heretical group of Nazorean Jewish Christians, who did not participate in the revolt,[42] had usurped the name Zion.

2. *The Late Roman Colony of Aelia Capitolina*

Professor D. Flusser of the Hebrew University in Jerusalem drew my attention to an ancient text that demonstrates how Isaiah 2:3 influenced the name-giving of the first seat of the Primitive Community in Jerusalem. The text comes from Meliton of Sardes. This bishop of the mid-second century from Asia Minor traveled to Palestine in order to learn about the Hebrew Bible canon from this church (*HE* 4.26.14). He describes the topography of Jerusalem, which floated before his eyes while he delivered his famous Easter sermon in which he blames the Jews for the crucifixion of Jesus "in the center of the city, at the main square" (ἐν μέσῳ Ἰερο[υσαλήμ]).[43] This does not fit with the geographical reality of Jerusalem in the year A.D. 30 but reflects the layout of the city around the middle of the second century, where the site of the crucifixion had actually become at that time the *forum Hadriani*, in the city center.[44] In the same homily we find a further topographical observation. Describing the transition from the old to the new community, Meliton refers to

[40] Cf. in addition W. ZIMMERLI, "Jesaia 2, 2–5" in DORMITION ABBEY (Jerusalem), *Festschrift des theologischen Studienjahres der Dormition Abbey Jerusalem für Abbott Dr. Laurentius Klein, O.S.B.* (St. Ottilien: EOS, 1986), 49–54.

[41] This reference I owe to Prof. Benedikt Schwank, O.S.B. (Beuron).

[42] Cf. Justin, *First Apology* 31.5 (PG 6:376).

[43] *Passah Homily* 39–95 (O. PERLER, *Méliton de Sardes: Sur la pâque et fragments*, SC 123 [Paris: Cerf, 1966], 80–116).

[44] Cf. also R. RIESNER, "Golgotha und die Archäologie", *BiKi* 40 (1985): 21–26, as well as "Golgotha", in *GBL*, 2nd ed. (1990), 1:480–82.

Isaiah 2:3, "The law became Logos [and thus gospel], the old became the new that has gone out at the same time from Zion and from Jerusalem [συνεξελθὼν ἐκ Σιὼν καὶ Ἰερουσαλήμ]." [45]

At that time we have the double identity of Jerusalem (Aelia Capitolina) in the north and Mount Zion in the south (illus. 64). In the area of the Armenian "House of Caiaphas",[46] Israeli excavations by M. Broshi[47] as well as in the Jewish old town quarter by N. Avigad[48] demonstrated that the Roman colony Aelia had been built by the emperor Hadrian north of the lateral valley (the route of today's King David Street), where the *forum Hadriani* formed its center.[49] The colony probably had a wall in the north, but in the south the camp of the Tenth Legion *Fretensis* offered protection (*War* 7.1) and today is found in the Armenian quarter.[50] South and east of this camp, the area was used for agriculture, for fields, vegetable gardens and so on. Zion, therefore, lay far in the south, isolated from the city, and with its own identity: Jerusalem in the north, Mount Zion in the south.

Origen (185–254), a friend of Bishop Alexander of Jerusalem, knew the Holy City from personal experience. Although his allegorical language is difficult for us to understand today, it does show us what kind of picture he had of Jerusalem. In his work *Against Celsus*, he wrote: "And coming from all people, we rise up in these last days to this [raised mountain] and will encourage each other mutually to praise God, who glorified Jesus Christ, because 'this law' proceeded from those who lived on Zion, and went out to us spiritually. Furthermore, 'the word of the Lord' proceeded from Jerusalem ... in order to be spread everywhere." [51] So we have Jerusalem according to Origen, the binary concept of Mount Zion and the reference to Isaiah 2:3. Like Epiphanius in the fourth century (pp. 250–52), Origen seems to assume that it was on this mountain that the last Passion of Jesus took place. In another place he says that the Lord, after the

[45] *Passah Homily* 7 (SC 123:64).

[46] Cf. also chapter 20, "Where Was the House of Caiaphas Located?" (pp. 253–65).

[47] "Excavations in the House of Caiaphas, Mount Zion", in Y. Yadin, *Jerusalem Revealed* (Jerusalem: Israel Exploration Society, 1976), 57–59.

[48] *Discovering Jerusalem* (Nashville: Thomas Nelson, 1983), 207.

[49] Cf. also S. Margalit, "Aelia Capitolina", *Judaica* 45 (1989): 45–56.

[50] Cf. H. Geva, "The Camp of the Tenth Legion in Jerusalem: An Archaeological Reconsideration", *IEJ* 34 (1984): 239–54.

[51] *Contra Celsum* 5.33:17 (PG 11:1232).

Last Supper, crossed to another hill. Origen emphasized that the words Jesus spoke to Peter were said on the Mount of Olives: "He [Jesus] taught; the disciples ... whoever received the bread of the blessing and ate the body of the word, and drank from the cup of gratitude ... to take, eat and be thankful ... to cross over from one hill onto the other hill [*de alto transire in altum*]; because the believer cannot do anything in the valley, he went up to the Mount of Olives." [52]

3. *Eusebius and the Pilgrim of Bordeaux*

The most valuable and the clearest document about the origins of Mount Zion come from Eusebius (260–340), the metropolitan bishop from Caesarea, who knew Jerusalem very well. These documents are very important, because they go back to the pre-Byzantine period and show the old Jewish Christian tradition.[53] A text from *Demonstratio Evangelica* is particularly interesting and was written by Eusebius before A.D. 325 (pp. 275–76). He begins with Isaiah 2:3 and writes:

> For out of Zion shall go forth the law, and the word of the LORD from Jerusalem. He shall judge between the nations, and shall decide for many peoples; all the nations ... shall flow to it, and many peoples shall come and say: "Come, let us go up to the mountain of the LORD, to the house of the God of Jacob.' " But what is that law which proceeds from Zion? It is none other than that which was announced by Moses in the desert on Mount Sinai; it is meant to be the word of the gospel, which came from our Redeemer Jesus Christ and his Apostles from Zion and came to all peoples. It is a well-known fact that it proceeded both from Jerusalem and the nearby hill of Zion [ἀπὸ τῆς Ἰερουσαλὴμ καὶ τοῦ ταύτῃ προσπαρακειμένου Σιών ὄρους], where our Savior and Lord accomplished many acts and taught.[54]

The exact location of Zion is indicated by Eusebius in the *Onomastikon*: south of Golgotha and north of Hakeldama.[55] Zion is therefore identified with the southwest hill.

[52] *Commentarius in Evangelium secundum Matthaeum* 86 (Mt 26:29) (PG 13:1737).

[53] Note especially Eusebius, *Demonstratio Evangelica* 3.5 (PG 22:221); 6.13 (PG 22:432–39; GCS 23:262–67); as well as *Eklogae propheticae* 4.13 (PG 22:1217); 4.15 (PG 22:1220).

[54] *Demonstratio Evangelica* 1.4 (PG 22:431; Baldi, 473f.).

[55] *Onomastikon* (Klostermann, 38, 21; 74, 20).

For Eusebius, Mount Zion was a location separate from Jerusalem. The North African Optatus of Mileve mentioned that around 370 Mount Zion was separated by a small wadi from the walls of Jerusalem.[56] Mount Zion possessed its own circular wall at the beginning of the fourth century, which was different from the wall of Aelia Capitolina. So the Pilgrim of Bordeaux left Jerusalem with his entourage in the year 333 (*exeuntibus ex Jerusalem*), and after an excursion to the pool of Siloam, he went up to Zion, visiting on the way the ruins of Caiaphas' palace (Saint Peter in Gallicantu) and finally reaching the wall of Zion (*murus Sion*).[57] Our excavations of the Essene Gate (*War* 5.145) in the Protestant cemetery confirmed this.[58] This gate in the old west wall of Jerusalem shows three successive, different gate thresholds, one above the other. The lowest threshold (the Essene Gate) is Herodian, and the highest Byzantine (the Eudocia wall, ca. 450). The examination of pottery below the middle threshold showed that this belonged to a gate that was added between A.D. 70 and 350. This was a rather primitive gate, more like a gutter that belonged to a wall or an embankment that had been put around Mount Zion. Over this threshold the Pilgrim of Bordeaux traveled and saw from there some ruins that he assumed to be David's palace (*intus autem intra murum Sion paret locus, ubi palatium habuit David*).[59]

Eusebius had already visited Jerusalem and Mount Zion at the beginning of the fourth century. He tells that there "with his own eyes" he could see how the prophecies by the prophet Micah about Zion had proven to be true: "Therefore because of you Zion shall be plowed as a field" (Mic 3:12; cf. Is 1:8; Jer 26:18). Eusebius had been able to observe how Mount Zion was plowed, strewn with oxen by Romans, probably veterans of the Tenth Legion.[60] That must have been a standard statement about Zion at that time, because Cyril of Jerusalem[61]

[56] *De schismate Donatistarum* 3.2 (PL 11:994; Baldi, 475): "in illo monte Sion, quem in Syria Palestine a muris Hierusalem parvus disterminat rivus; into cujus vertice est non magna planities."

[57] *Itinerarium* 16 (Geyer, 22; Baldi, 474).

[58] Cf. chapter 15, "The Essene Quarter in Jerusalem" (pp. 192–219, esp. pp. 205–6).

[59] *Itinerarium* 16 (Geyer, 22; Baldi, 474). The same tradition can be found in a letter by Jerome, 108.9: "Egrediens [Paula left the Church of the Holy Sepulchre] ascendit Sion, quae in arcem vel speculum vertitur. Hanc urbem quondam expugnavit et reaedificavit David" (PL 22:884; Baldi, 479).

[60] *Demonstratio Evangelica* 7.1 (PG 22:635; Klijn-Reinink, 138).

[61] *Catecheses* 16.18 (PG 33:944).

and Cyril of Alexandria[62] made similar remarks. This agricultural use of the southwest hill at this time is confirmed also by the Israeli excavations of the Armenian and Jewish quarters.

When Eusebius says that Jesus had already ministered on Zion and had taught there, he probably refers to the event of the Last Supper and to the event of the Resurrection at that place. At the time of the pilgrim Egeria (A.D. 383), the custom had been adopted of celebrating the memory of the Last Supper "behind the cross [*post crucem*]" of the hill of Golgotha.[63] The Syrian tradition of the same time speaks clearly of the fact that Jesus had held the Passover on Zion.[64] This local tradition on Mount Zion is enhanced by recognition of the connection between the last Passover of Jesus and the Essene quarter on the southwest hill.[65]

For some of the holy places in Jerusalem before the arrival of Helen in the year 326, and the subsequent building of the first Byzantine shrines (Holy Sepulchre, the Eleona basilica on the Mount of Olives, and the Church of the Nativity in Bethlehem), there are hardly any literary references or records, but we are more fortunate concerning Mount Zion, for which several texts exist. The Byzantine authorities attempted to "control" the tradition and present their own belief, altering local traditions accordingly. Therefore, any records that predate 326 are particularly valuable in describing the local traditions of the population. To summarize, only a few other Christian places in Jerusalem possess such an old local tradition as the southwest hill does as the place of Jesus' Last Supper and the cradle of the primitive Church.[66] No other place is able to make a serious counterclaim.

[62] *Commentaria in Sophoniam* 11 (Zeph 1:13) (PG 71:964).

[63] *Peregrinatio* 37.1 (Geyer, 85; Baldi, 629f.).

[64] *Didaskalia Addai* (A. Vöobus, *The Synodicon in the West Syrian tradition*, CSCO 368 [Scriptores Syrae 162] [Louvain: Presses Universitaires, 1975], 188). The oldest incontestable reference to the Communion on Zion is by Hesychius of Jerusalem (ca. 440), [e.g.,] *Quaestiones in Jacobum fratrem Domini* (PG 93:1480; Baldi, 480f). Cf. also M. Aubineau, *Hésychius de Jérusalem: Homélies pascales*, SC 197 (Paris: Cerf, 1972), 129–32.

[65] Cf. chapter 18, "The Last Supper of Jesus" (pp. 239–49).

[66] Cf. also L. H. Vincent and F. M. Abel, *Jérusalem: Recherches de topographie, d'archéologie et d'histoire*, vol. 2, *Jérusalem nouvelle*, pt. 3, *La Sainte-Sion et les sanctuaires de second ordre* (Paris: Gabalda, 1922), 421–59; B. Bagatti, *Church from the Circumcision* (see n. 26), 116–22; idem, *The Church from the Gentiles in Palestine*, SBFCMi 4 (Jerusalem: Franciscan Printing Press, 1971), 63–65.

IV. The Jewish Christian Community on Zion

1. The Watchtower in the Vineyard (Is 1:8)

On the southwest hill above the destruction layer of A.D. 70, everywhere we can discover Byzantine buildings. There is one exception from the time of Aelia Capitolina. Archaeology has identified a late Roman synagogue building made with large Herodian rectangular blocks. The Church Fathers acknowledged this building standing alone on Zion with a noticeable lack of enthusiasm. What was the cause of this reticence? The answer is connected with the inhabitants at that time of the southwest hill.

When the Pilgrim of Bordeaux, whom we have already mentioned, arrived in the Holy City in the year A.D. 333, he did not go like other pilgrims first to the Holy Sepulchre, but to the temple and from there to Zion (Zion III). According to the opinion of some commentators, this pilgrim could have been a Jewish Christian who was well versed in the writings of the Old Testament and who was led to places that were particularly connected with the history of Israel.[67] On Zion, the pilgrim saw not only the alleged palace of David but also "seven synagogues, of which there was only one left; the others were plowed under, just as the prophet Isaiah had foretold."[68] The pilgrim here was thinking of Isaiah 1:8 (cf. Mic 3:12), according to which there will remain one "watchtower in the vineyard" on Zion. The synagogue that the pilgrim saw on Zion can only have been a Jewish Christian one, since he mentioned briefly before this that admission to Jerusalem for Jews was permitted only once a year. They were allowed to weep then for the destruction of the temple, near a "perforated stone" (*lapis pertusus*).[69] This probably refers to the perforated rock (Arabic: *sachne*) under today's Dome of the Rock.

It is difficult to determine from the text the precise identity of this synagogue. Since we know from archaeology that from the time of the pilgrim's visit there was no other synagogue building than the alleged "Tomb of David", this is surely the synagogue. Epiphanius might describe

[67] Cf. H. DONNER, *Pilgerfahrt ins Heilige Land* (Stuttgart: Katholisches Bibelwerk, 1979), 41f.

[68] *Itinerarium* 16 (Geyer, 22; Baldi, 474): "Et septem synagogae, quae illic fuerunt, una tantum remansit, reliquae autem arantur et seminantur, sicut Isaias propheta dixit."

[69] *Itinerarium* 16 (Geyer, 21; Baldi, 445f.).

this Nazorean Jewish Christian synagogue from another point of view as a "church".[70] According to Epiphanius, it was the custom of the Jewish Christians to call their churches "synagogues".[71] However, it is not entirely impossible that the pilgrim saw the synagogue that was preserved by the emperor Constantine (who died in 337) as well as by Bishop Maximonas (331–349) and that Epiphanius seems to differentiate it from the small Church of the Apostles (n. 70). Possibly it was an Ebionite synagogue, to which was connected a tradition of the house of the Apostle John and the location for the dormition of Mary.[72] According to the witness of the Gallic pilgrim Arculf (670), the northwest corner of the first Byzantine church that was established on Zion after A.D. 381 was revered as the place where Jesus' Mother Mary died.[73] The important point is that both the Pilgrim of Bordeaux and Epiphanius had memories of Jewish Christian settlements on Mount Zion. Traces of the Zion wall mentioned by the pilgrim have possibly been found by the Essene Gate (pp. 205–6). This was probably a primitive ghetto wall built by the Jewish Christians in order to protect themselves against the influence and the attacks of the Byzantines. For similar reasons a square wall existed around the Jewish Christian sanctuary of Peter's house in Capharnaum.[74]

Another possible acknowledgment of the synagogue building of the "Tomb of David" is the testimony of Eucherius, who was an educated Roman senator and later archbishop of Lyon. By relying on Jerome and even earlier sources, he wrote ca. A.D. 440 that "the flat top [Zion III] is occupied by monks' cells, which surround a church. Its foundations, so it says, were laid by the Apostles in reverence for the place of the Resurrection of the Lord [*ecclesiam . . . quae illic fertur ab apostolis fundata per loci resurrectionis dominicae reverentia*]. That is also where they were filled with the Holy Spirit, after the promise of the Lord."[75] The puzzling and difficult expression "in reverence for the place of the Resurrection", which was used by Eucherius to describe the reverence for the Church of the Holy Sepulchre, suggests the orientation of the synagogue church was toward Golgotha (see above, pp. 329–30).

[70] *De mensuris et ponderibus* 14 (PG 43:260; Baldi, 478). Text cited fully above (p. 335).

[71] *Panarion* 30.18 (PG 41:436; Klijn-Reinink, 186–88).

[72] Regarding this whole question, cf. chapter 30, "Mary on Zion" (pp. 398–407).

[73] Adamnanus, *De locis sanctis* 1.18.1 (Geyer, 243; Baldi, 489).

[74] Cf. S. Loffreda, *Rediscovering Capernaum* (Jerusalem: Franciscan Printing Press, 1994), 58f.

[75] *De situ Hierusolimae epistula ad Faustum* 4 (Geyer, 125; Baldi, 479).

In the year 348, just a few years after Emperor Constantine had declared Christianity the official religion, Cyril (later bishop of Jerusalem) held his famous catecheses in the newly built Church of the Holy Sepulchre. In the course of his sixteenth catechesis about the Holy Spirit, he remarked that it would actually be more suitable to speak about this topic at the place where the Spirit descended onto the first Christians, i.e., "in the Upper Church of the Apostles [ἐν τῇ ἀνωτέρᾳ τῶν ἀποστόλων ἐκκλησίᾳ]".[76] At that time the Jewish Christian synagogue was well known as the "Church of the Apostles", not only because they had returned after Ascension Day to this place (see Acts 1:12f.), but also because the building had been rebuilt under Simeon Bar Cleopas, the brother of James and cousin of Jesus who was regarded later as an Apostle (pp. 408–14). From this it is clear why Cyril was not able to teach as a presbyter of the Gentile Christian church of Jerusalem in the "Church of the Apostles", even though that would have been appropriate. He could not teach there because this synagogue church was in the control of the Jewish Christian community, as we have already concluded from the report of the Pilgrim of Bordeaux. By this time, the Gentile Christians and the Jewish Christians had already separated.

2. *Traditions of the Jewish Christian Community in Jerusalem*

How could a Jewish Christian community exist in Jerusalem from the second to the fourth century, as B. Bagatti has assumed?[77] As Ariston of Pella (according to Eusebius, *HE* 4.6.3) reports, Jews by imperial edict were banished from Jerusalem in A.D. 135 by the emperor Hadrian, who suppressed the Second Jewish Revolt. Whether this also included the Jewish Christians is not completely clear.[78] The revolt was led by Bar Kokhba, whose messianic requirements the Jewish Christians could not recognize; therefore, the Jewish Christians were persecuted by him (p. 338). Perhaps they did not have to leave Jerusalem. It is also possible that after the establishment of the Roman colony Aelia Capitolina and under the more tolerant emperor Antoninus Pius (138–161) the community returned to the Holy City on Mount Zion. Their

[76] *Catecheses* 16.4 (PG 33:924; Baldi, 474f.).

[77] *Church from the Circumcision* (see n. 26), 118–21.

[78] One can ask whether Sulpicius Severus, *Historia Sacra* 2.31 (PL 20:147), does not presuppose the presence of Jewish Christians.

retention of Jewish customs alienated them from the Gentile Christians, who possessed their own bishop in the city since the establishment of the Roman colony (*HE* 4.6.1). The schism became an unbridgeable break, and following the Council of Nicea, the Byzantine church took an even more stridently anti-Jewish position.

For the Jewish Christian inhabitants, it is characteristic that not only in Mamre but also on the southwest hill of Zion the memory of Abraham's sacrifice (Gen 22) was celebrated.[79] With his visit to Zion, Eusebius could have also have met with the Jewish Christian owners of the old sanctuary. He seemed to have had them in mind when he said that "the brothers of that tradition [οἱ τῇδε κατὰ διαδοχὴν περιέποντες ἀδελφοί], to this day, are holding highly the throne of James, the first bishop of Jerusalem" (*HE* 7.19). Peter Diaconus reported from an ancient source that this throne was in Zion's sanctuary,[80] and this is confirmed by an inscription in the Church of Saint Martin in Tours from the second half of the fifth century (n. 90). With the continued existence of a unique Davidic tradition on Zion, there may be a connection with Jerome,[81] who described the Jewish Christian synagogue as the "tower of the flock" from Micah 4:8 (p. 20). The fact that the leader of the primitive Christian community came from the House of David could have influenced the designation of the original location for this community as "Zion" (pp. 389–92). Around A.D. 400 an edition of a Jewish Christian Gospel (τὸ Ἰουδαϊκόν), which was perhaps identical to the Nazorean Gospel,[82] was kept at the basilica on Zion. The presence of this Gospel may also refer to the existence then of a Jewish Christian community earlier on the southwest hill.

3. The Cornerstone of the Church

Eusebius did not agree with the tradition of the inhabitants at that time on the hill of Zion. He comments on the verse in Isaiah: "Behold, I am laying in Zion for a foundation a stone, a tested stone, a precious cornerstone, of a sure foundation: 'He who believes will not be in

[79] Cf. Epiphanius, *Panarion* 29.1 (PG 41:260; Klijn-Reinink, 168).

[80] Geyer, 108.

[81] *Commentaria in Micham* 2 (Mic 4:8f.) (PL 25:1191).

[82] Cf. P. Vielhauer and G. Strecker, "Die sog. 'Evangelienausgabe Zion'", in Hennecke-Schneemelcher, 1:126f. J. M. Magnin, "Notes sur l'Ébionisme", *POC* 26 (1976): 293–318 (at 301f.), thought of this as the "Gospel according to the Hebrews".

haste'" (Is 28:16). Eusebius ridiculed the way the local inhabitants of Zion interpreted this text, but their interpretation does throw light on the way that the Jewish Christian community thought: "Is it not childish and truly ridiculous of those fleshly thinking to maintain that one of those valuable and highly honored stones will be laid, according to the Lord's statement, as foundation of the material Zion [τῆς σωματικῆς Σιών] and that those who set their trust in it will never be put to shame, as it was prophesied?"[83] However, such convictions give an additional reason why the Jewish Christians clung to their old sanctuary. Origen's pupil Eusebius says Isaiah's prophecies were meant to be understood allegorically and were fulfilled with the creation of a worldwide church. He calls the literal interpretation that the Jewish Christians upheld similar to Jewish old wives' tales (cf. 1 Tim 4:7), stupid and "judaizing". However, Eusebius' remarks seem to me very valuable in identifying the owners of the synagogue church on Zion.

Soon after this, and particularly following the Council of Nicea (325), from which the Jewish Christian bishops were absent, there seems to have been a crisis for the Nazoreans in Jerusalem. Epiphanius helps us determine the time of this crisis (before 337) when he says that a (Jewish Christian) synagogue continued to exist up to the time of the emperor Constantine and Bishop Maximonas (p. 335). In the light of this the words of Epiphanius can be understood when he wrote around 375: "And the fortress Zion [ἄκρα Σιών] had once priority, but now it is cut off."[84] The sanctuary on Zion was considered by the bishop of Salamis as heretical, and the focus of church devotion had shifted to Golgotha, where a large Byzantine basilica stood. That there was actually a dispute about Zion is confirmed by the Church Father Gregory of Nyssa, who visited Jerusalem in 381. He reported that the place at which the Holy Spirit had first been poured out was now in turmoil and that even an opposition altar had been established.[85] The control of the church in Jerusalem had, however, in an earlier period (around the middle of the second century) been handed over from the Jewish Christian bishops to a Gentile Christian, who was not living "on lonely Zion" but resided somewhere in Aelia Capitolina.

[83] *Eklogae propheticae* 4.53 (PG 22:1217).

[84] *Panarion* 46.5 (PG 41:845; GCS 31:208–10).

[85] *Letter 2* (G. Pasquali, *Gregorii Nysseni epistulae* [Berlin, 1925], 11–17).

Jerome (ca. 386) seemed to know of the existence of the Nazoreans in the Holy City (*in nostra autem Jerusalem*) but accused them, because of their outdated Jewish way of observing the law, of splitting the unity of the Church.[86] From other sources, we know of the particular Jewish customs to which he was referring.[87] The Jewish Christians kept the Sabbath and were, probably since the end of the first century, Quartodecimans;[88] i.e., they were committed followers of the Jewish Passover *quarta decima*, on the fourteenth of Nisan, as the day of the Christian Easter. They ate no pork[89] and were chiliastics, expecting a "thousand-year realm" (cf. Rev 20). They also did not call themselves Christians but rather Israelites or Jews (p. 333). Because the sanctuary on Zion was still under Jewish Christian control, this then helps explain something remarkable. Many, often secondary, places received Byzantine sanctuaries in Jerusalem, e.g., the Eleona cave and the Tomb of Lazarus, but for a long time there was no Byzantine church on Zion, although such a church could have already then had the title "the mother of all churches".[90] When lists are made of the various sacred places in Jerusalem, Zion is always ignored.

V. The Later Churches of Zion

1. The First Byzantine Church on Zion

We do not know exactly how the Byzantines finally brought the old Jewish Christian sanctuary on Zion under their control, and until recently we did not even know when this occurred. The Belgian researcher M. van Esbroeck has published some texts that originated from the Georgian monasteries in the former Soviet Union. They seem to provide some answers. In one of these texts, Bishop John of Bolnisi reports various feasts of dedication: the Anastasis (ἀνάστασις),

[86] *Commentaria in Ezechielem* 5 (Ez 16:16) (PL 25:139); cf. *Commentaria in Isaiam* 10 (Is 32:6ff. [PL 24:369f.]).

[87] Cf. J. Daniélou, *Theology of Jewish Christianity* (London: Darton, Longman and Todd, 1964).

[88] Jerome, *Commentarius in Evangelium Matthaei* 4 (Mt 25:6) (PL 26:192).

[89] Euthychius of Alexandria, *Annales* (PG 111:1012f.).

[90] This title is seen for the first time in an inscription in the Church of St. Martin in Tours: "Sanctissima Christi ecclesia, quae est mater ecclesiarum, quam fundaverant apostoli, in qua descendit Spiritus sanctus super apostolos in specie ignis linguarum. In ea positus est thronus Jacobi apostoli et columna, in qua verberatus est Christus" (F. Diekamp, *Hippolytus of Theben* [Münster: Aschendorft, 1898], 100; cf. Baldi, 483, n. 1).

the rotunda above the Holy Sepulchre, the place of the Resurrection, was dedicated on September 13; the Constantine Martyrion basilica, on September 14; and the Hagia Sion, as the mother of all churches, on September 15. In the bishop's own words, "And on the fifteenth of the same month is the dedication of the holy and famous Zion [church], the mother of all churches, the one founded by the Apostles, which was developed, expanded and honored by Emperor Theodosius the Great, in which the Holy Spirit at Pentecost came down."[91]

The building of the first Byzantine church on Mount Zion had been arranged by Emperor Theodosius I, who ruled from A.D. 379 to 395. This ruler had also established the first church in Gethsemane, the so-called *Ecclesia elegans*. The building of the apostolic synagogue on Zion was left untouched. The new church formed only a kind of vestibule to the old building. We know this because of the representation of the famous mosaic in the apse of the Church of Sancta Pudentiana in Rome, which was built around 400 (plate 2). This mosaic shows not only in its center the Church of the Holy Sepulchre but also on Zion the two buildings, i.e., the new Byzantine church and, directly to the right of it, the old Jewish Christian building.

Reconciliation between Jewish Christians and Gentile Christians was facilitated in Jerusalem by a famous personality of the time, the holy Porphyrios, later bishop of Gaza, who seems to have been of Jewish Christian origin. Porphyrios came from Thessalonica to Jerusalem and could have been a monk on Zion. He was a great preacher who succeeded in integrating the Jewish Christians of the Holy City into the broader Church. Both groups had lived separately from each other, spiritually as well as physically. The reconciliation was sealed, and the bishop of Jerusalem at that time, John II (387–419), blessed the expiation altar (Hebrew: *kapporet*) of the Jewish Christians, which was located now in the church of Theodosius. This occurred on the great reconciliation day (Yom Kippur) of the Jewish calendar, on September 15, probably in the year A.D. 394. On this occasion, Bishop John preached an amazing sermon, full of Jewish Christian symbolism, and in his sermon he praised repeatedly the great services of Porphyrios, who is called "the Israelite".[92]

[91] M. VAN ESBROECK, ed., *Les plus anciens homiliaires géorgiens* (Louvain: Presses Universitaires, 1975), 314f. Dr. Rainer Riesner (University of Tübingen, now Dortmund) made me aware of this title, as well as of those in the following note.

[92] Cf. M. VAN ESBROECK, "Jean II de Jérusalem et les cultes de S. Étienne, de la Sainte-Sion et de la Croix", *Analecta Bollandiana* 102 (1984): 99–133.

The sermon by Bishop John and the Pudentiana mosaic support M. van Esbroeck's[93] proposal that the vestibule church was octagonal. The octagonal form was often used in Christian memorial churches, in this case as a memorial place for the "Church of the Apostles". Other examples of octagonal memorial churches are the church over the house of Peter in Capharnaum, which has extensive remains,[94] and the Constantine shrine over Jesus' birth grotto in Bethlehem (p. 14).

The narrower period for the building of the vestibule church can be estimated. Gregory of Nyssa, during his visit to Jerusalem in the year 381/382, still did not see this church.[95] It was new for the pilgrim Egeria, who visited the Holy City between 381 and 384[96] (*ubi ipsa ecclesia nunc in Syon est*).[97] In order to increase the attractiveness of the church of Theodosius, a column at which Jesus allegedly was scourged, which until then had lain in the ruins of Caiaphas' house,[98] was built into the portico. It was viewed by Jerome and Paula and their retinue in the year A.D. 386 (*columna porticum ecclesiae sustinens*).[99] On the morning of Good Friday, large numbers of people came with Egeria to Zion in order to venerate this column. From Egeria's description of the liturgy, it becomes clear that a double sanctuary existed on Zion, the old "Church of the Apostles" (*quia ipse est locus in Syon, alia modo ecclesia est*) and the new Theodosian memorial church.[100] It seems as though at Pentecost the people congregated in the newly built church, while the presbyters also went to the other church, the former Jewish Christian synagogue. The same recognition of the value of the two buildings and their juxtaposition is demonstrated in a moving passage during the inauguration sermon of Bishop John, in which he asked the priests, the builders and building master to go into the "Upper Room".[101]

[93] Ibid., 125, n. 102.

[94] Cf. J. F. Strange and H. Shanks, "Has the House Where Jesus Stayed in Capernaum Been Found?" *BAR* 8, no. 6 (1982): 29–39.

[95] *Letter 3* (PG 46:1014).

[96] Cf. J. Wilkinson, *Egeria's Travels to the Holy Land* (Jerusalem: Ariel, 1981), 237–39.

[97] *Peregrinatio* 39.5 (Geyer, 88; Baldi, 476).

[98] Pilgrim of Bordeaux, *Itinerarium* 16 (Geyer, 22; Baldi, 562).

[99] *Letter 108* 9 (PL 22:884; Baldi, 479). Prudentius, *Dittochaeum* 41, writes somewhat later (394): "Templumque gerit veneranda columna" (PL 60:108).

[100] *Peregrinatio* 43.3 (Geyer, 93.88; Baldi, 476f.). Apparently these two places are differentiated in Jerome's *Letter 108* 9 (PL 22:884; Baldi, 479).

[101] M. van Esbroeck, "Jean II de Jérusalem" (see n. 92), 124f.

2. *The Extension of the Large Hagia Sion*

On the southwest hill, it appears that Bishop John II also built the large rectangular church "Hagia Sion" (Holy Zion), which can be seen on the Madaba Mosaic Map from the second half of the sixth century and which was described by Arculf at the end of the seventh century.[102] The following entry is found in the old Georgian liturgical calendar: "In memory of John, the archbishop of Jerusalem, who first built Zion, and of Modestos, who rebuilt it after the fire [of 614]."[103] The mention of the activity of John can refer only to the Theodosian church because everyone knew that the Church of the Apostles had already stood for centuries on Mount Zion. The work of John is probably strongly stressed because not only was he the bishop present at the establishment of the vestibule church under Theodosius, but he also substantially extended Zion's basilica. In this, the "pillar of the scourging" did not form a component of the architecture but stood in the center of the church.[104] This situation is shown on the contemporary Lateran Sarcophagus No. 174.[105] Small remains of the Hagia Sion have been found in the excavations that preceded the building of the Dormition Abbey at the beginning of the nineteenth century.[106] In the year 1983 we found a small piece of a Byzantine mosaic (illus. 60) in our small excavation in front of the abbey.[107] H. Renard (n. 106) and L. H. Vincent[108] have suggested two different reconstructions. But Vincent's theory, that the synagogue building was already integrated into the large Hagia Sion, was refuted by M. Gisler.[109] The large Hagia Sion is shown in the Jerusalem section of the Madaba

[102] Adamnanus, *De locis sanctis* 1.18.1–3 (Geyer, 243; Baldi, 489).

[103] G. Garitte, ed., *Le calendrier palestino-géorgien du Sinaiticus 34* (Brussels, 1958), 187.

[104] Pilgrim of Piacenza (570), *Itinerarium* 22: "In ipsa ecclesia est columna ubi flagellatus est Dominus" (Geyer, 573; Baldi, 484); in the plan of the Church of Zion by Adamnanus, sketched by Arculf (670), *De locis sanctis* 1.18.1, the column is located in the center with the remark: "Hic columna in medio marmorea stat ecclesiae cui dominus adhaerens flagellatus est" (Geyer, 243; Baldi, 489); Venerable Bede (around 673): "Columna mormorea in medio stat ecclesiae, cui adhaerens Dominus flagellatus est" (Geyer, 306; Baldi, 489).

[105] Cf. E. Power, "The Upper Church of the Apostles in Jerusalem and the Lateran Sarcophagus No. 174", *Biblica* 12 (1931): 219–32.

[106] Cf. H. Renard, "Die Marienkirchen auf dem Berg Sion in ihrem Zusammenhang mit dem Abendmahlssaale", *HlL* 44 (1900): 3–23 (at 16).

[107] Cf. also E. Eisenberg, "Church of Dormition", *ESI* 3 (1984): 47.

[108] *Sainte-Sion* (see n. 66), 451–55 and plate 69.

[109] "Sancta Sion and Dormitio Dominae. Ihre Verbundenheit im Grundplan", *HlL* 79 (1935): 2–13.

mosaic; south of it and separate from it is the "Upper Church of the Apostles" (plate 1; illus. 98).

After reconciling the original Jewish Christian owners of Zion's shrine and overseeing their absorption into the Gentile Christian church, Bishop John was free to proceed with an ambitious plan for the development of Zion. He was supported in this project in the year 415 by the vision of a monk named Lucian. Lucian stated that by a godly inspiration he had discovered in Kaphar Gamala the graves of Saint Stephen, Gamaliel and Abigo. After the bishop listened to the report, he said jokingly to him: "You see that our city possesses many vehicles, but the largest is missing, the ox. You have now found that."[110]

Lucian understood that the bishop wanted one of the three bodies, i.e., Saint Stephen's, brought to Zion. Stephen would provide the important pilgrim attraction that would complete the large basilica. The relics of this important martyr were brought in a large religious procession into the *sacrarium* of Zion's basilica, i.e., into the former Jewish Christian synagogue. From this date it was called "Martyrium Sancti Stephani" or "Room of the Mysteries" and was reduced to an annex of the wonderful Hagia Sion and served as a diaconicon (side chapel).[111] The transferring of the relics happened on the Feast of David and the Lord's brother James on December 26 (p. 393), A.D. 415, and this day became Stephen's feast day. It was a day of joy for all of Jerusalem, and when after a long draught plentiful rain fell, everybody was convinced that God had blessed their enterprise. The relics of Stephen, whether genuine or not, were not left on Zion for very long. All of the churches in the Byzantine Empire were seized by the enthusiasm for their discovery. When Eudocia, the wife of Emperor Theodosius, came to Jerusalem, she established a new church in honor of Stephen north of today's Damascus Gate, at the place of the École biblique (pp. 324–25). Most of the relics were transferred there in 439; other relics went to Constantinople and others to the Mount of Olives. It seems that only the empty sarcophagus of Stephen remained in the old sanctuary on Zion. Because of the erroneous belief at that time that the City of David was on the southwest hill, two further memorial tombs were installed in the tenth century, one for David and one for Solomon. It

[110] *Epistula Luciani* 6–8 (PL 41:813–15).
[111] Cf. Baldi, 483ff.

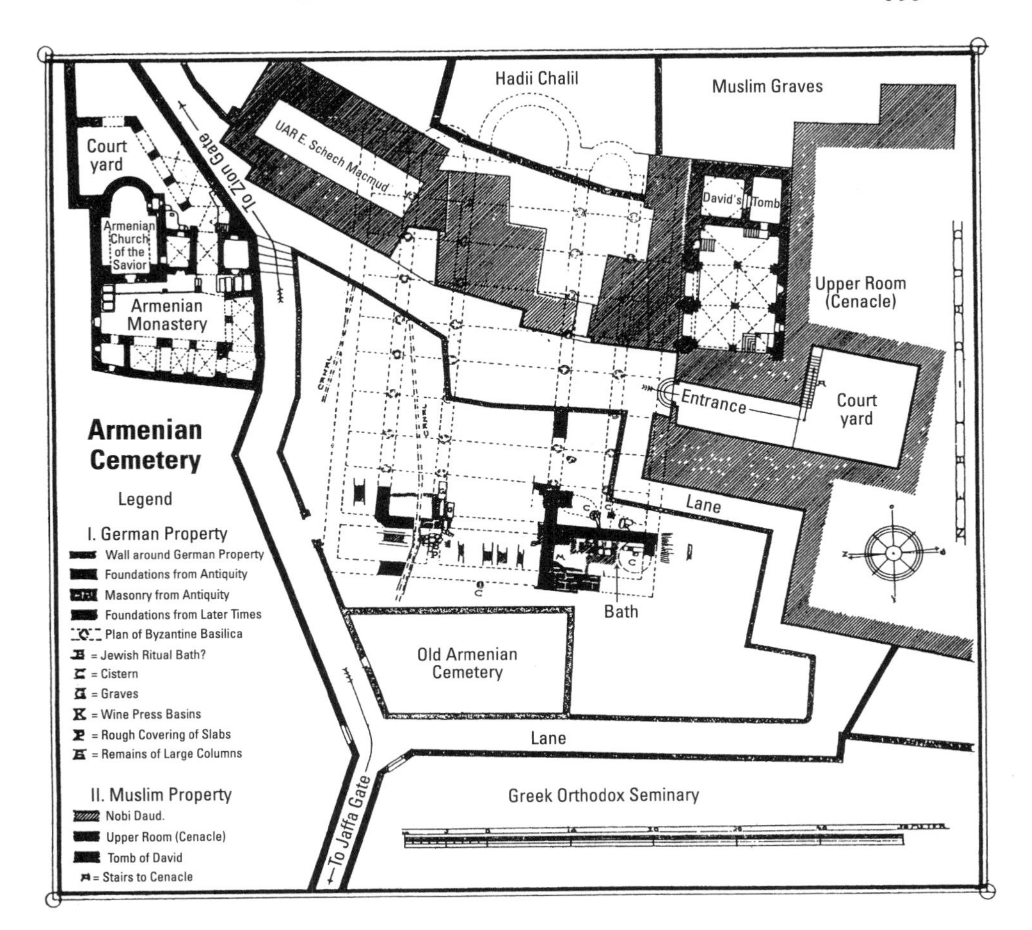

Illus. 88. Dormition Abbey—excavations (according to H. Renard, 1900). The Jewish ritual bath found at that time can be observed.

was these two graves, plus the sarcophagus of Stephen, that were discovered by the Crusaders.

3. From the Crusaders until Today

The basilica Hagia Sion was destroyed during the Persian invasion in the year 614. After Patriarch Modestos had rebuilt it, it was partly destroyed again by Hakim, the Fatimid sultan, in the year 1009. When the Crusaders came to Jerusalem in 1099, they found only a heap of

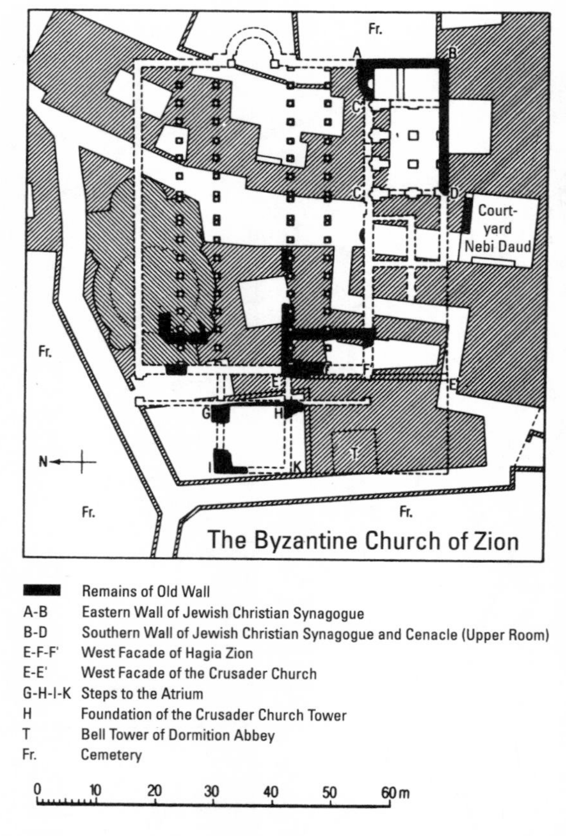

Illus. 89. Reconstructed floor plan of Hagia Sion (according to M. Gisler, 1935) (from G. Kroll).

ruins left of the wonderful Church of Zion. In the southern part of the ruins, in the twelfth century, the Crusaders erected a new church, which they called "Sancta Maria in Monte Sion",[112] in memory of the tradition according to which Mary had lived on Zion following the Resurrection of her Son and had there "fallen asleep".

In the year 1983, when in front of the Dormition Abbey a sewer was built, I took the opportunity to examine the area. It was possible for me to locate the foundation of the front of the Crusader church. The southwest corner of this church is in precise orientation to the

[112] Cf. Baldi, 487ff.

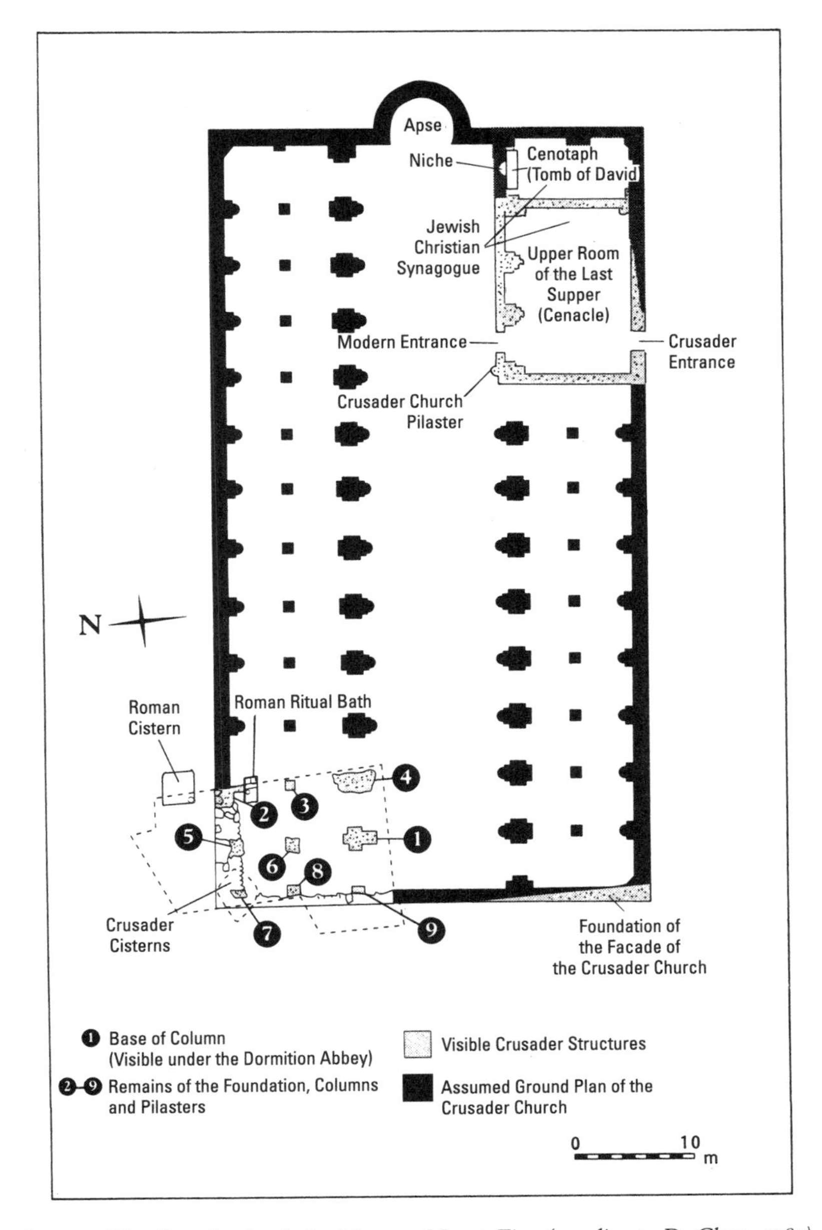

Illus. 90. The Crusader church St. Mary on Mount Zion (according to D. Chen, 1989).

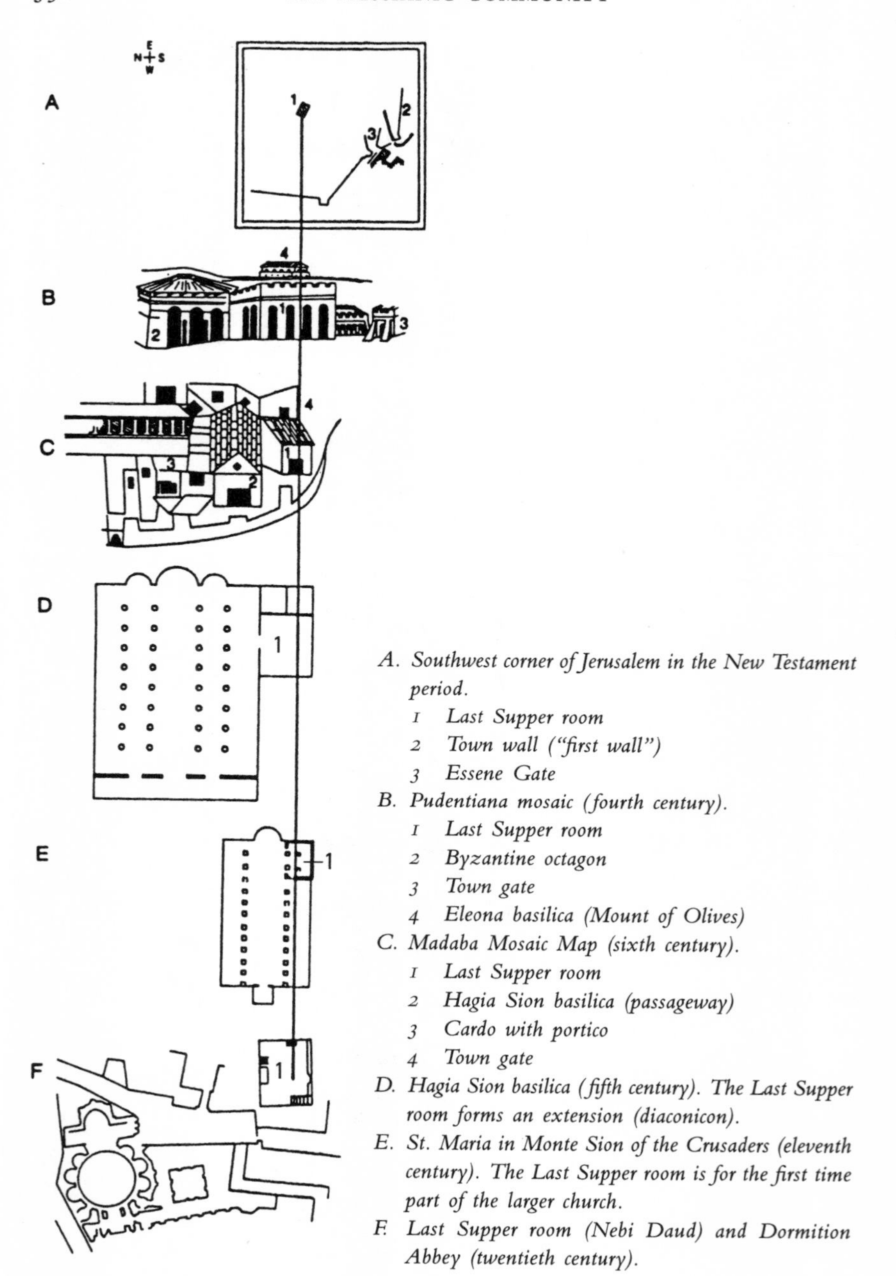

A. *Southwest corner of Jerusalem in the New Testament period.*
   1 *Last Supper room*
   2 *Town wall ("first wall")*
   3 *Essene Gate*
B. *Pudentiana mosaic (fourth century).*
   1 *Last Supper room*
   2 *Byzantine octagon*
   3 *Town gate*
   4 *Eleona basilica (Mount of Olives)*
C. *Madaba Mosaic Map (sixth century).*
   1 *Last Supper room*
   2 *Hagia Sion basilica (passageway)*
   3 *Cardo with portico*
   4 *Town gate*
D. *Hagia Sion basilica (fifth century). The Last Supper room forms an extension (diaconicon).*
E. *St. Maria in Monte Sion of the Crusaders (eleventh century). The Last Supper room is for the first time part of the larger church.*
F. *Last Supper room (Nebi Daud) and Dormition Abbey (twentieth century).*

Illus. 91. The development of the Zion churches (according to R. A. Mackowski, S.J., 1980).

south wall of the Jewish Christian synagogue building. The bases of the nine Crusader pilasters and the western part of the north wall of the Crusader church were found and preserved.[113] It was thus first the Crusaders who incorporated the "Church of the Apostles", the Jewish Christian synagogue, into their church.

The Crusaders established a further floor in the synagogue. The area developed in such a way was called the cenacle (*coenaculum*), which was to memorialize both the Last Supper of Jesus and the location of the Pentecost event. Acts (ὑπερῷον [Acts 1:13]) and the Gospels (ἀνάγαιον [Mark 14:15 / Lk 22:52]) refer to the place of the "Upper Room". On the lower floor, near the alleged Tomb of David, the Crusaders commemorated the place at which Jesus had washed the disciples' feet (Jn 13:1–20). When the Crusaders were forced to leave Jerusalem following their defeat at the Horns of Hattin, close to Tiberias, in the year 1187, they entrusted their church on Zion to the Syrian Christians.[114] The Syrian Christians were forced to leave the Last Supper room and the whole building complex on Zion on the command of the Ayyubid sultan of Damascus, and some years later the building was destroyed. The Syrian Christians transferred thereafter the traditions of Mount Zion to the Church of Saint Mark at the edge of the Armenian quarter, but to this day some of them venerate the Last Supper room.[115] Christian pilgrims of the thirteenth and fourteenth centuries commented in their pilgrim reports that the "Church of the Apostles" and the Last Supper room were in a very poor condition.[116]

At the end of the Crusader period in the Holy Land, there is a report of a journey by a Spanish Jew called Benjamin of Tudela (1167), who draws our attention to the alleged Tomb of David on Zion. Benjamin reports that during his stay in Jerusalem, a Jew called Abraham told him a fantastic story. When Abraham was employed by a Christian patriarch to repair a damaged building on Mount Zion, two other Jewish workers accidentally came into a secret corridor

[113] Cf. the photos of B. Pixner, "Church of the Apostles Found on Mt. Zion", *BAR* 16, no. 3 (1990): 16–35 (at 33), and A. Goergen, *Dormitio*, Kleine Kunstführer 1800 (Munich: Schnell und Steiner, 1990), 9.

[114] Cf. Wilbrandus von Oldenburg (1212) (Baldi, 502).

[115] Cf. J. Murphy-O'Connor, *The Holy Land: An Oxford Archaeological Guide* (Oxford: Oxford University Press, 1998), 68.

[116] Cf. Baldi, 502ff.

and found themselves in a palace with marble columns—the tombs of David and the other kings of Israel! A golden scepter and a golden crown were resting on a table. All around it were objects of wealth lying about. Suddenly the two were attacked by a whirlwind and began to hear voices that instructed them to leave immediately. Confused, they crept back through the secret entrance. They told the patriarch of their discovery, and he wrote a report with the help of Abraham the Jew of Constantinople. After two days one of the two workers was ill in bed, and they refused to go back to the place again. They reported, "We will never go back there, because God does not want any man to see this place."[117] As fantastic and confused as this story may sound, it nevertheless became the basis for the Jewish popular belief that is linked to the tomb of King David.

Between 1335 and 1337 the Franciscans, who had just arrived in the Holy Land, bought the area on Zion from the Saracens.[118] The king of Naples functioned as mediator. Thus Zion became the location of the first Franciscan monastery in the Holy Land. Since this time the Franciscans have been entrusted by the pope with the care of the holy places, and to this day the superior of the Franciscans carries the title *Custos Sancti Montis Sion*. In the fourteenth century the Franciscan brothers repaired the roof of the Upper Room and strengthened it with a gothic serrated roof. South of the *coenaculum*, they built their new Zion monastery, which surrounds an inner court, three sides of which can be seen still today. Apparently, the Franciscans never succeeded in occupying the site of the Tomb of David on the ground floor because it had been previously appropriated by the Muslim community. The Muslim inhabitants of Jerusalem demanded that the local authorities remove the unbelievers from the roof of Nebi Daud (Prophet David). This pressure grew in the Turkish period. In the middle of the sixteenth century (1549), the Franciscans were driven out of Zion by force.

In order to prevent their return, both the "Tomb of David" and the Last Supper room were declared mosques. A prayer niche (Arabic: *michrab*) was inserted into the wall, pointing to Mecca. Thus the building was oriented exactly in the opposite direction (to the south) than it had originally been. Since 1948 Mount Zion has been a part of

[117] Benjamin of Tudela, *Itinerarium* (Baldi, 498f.).
[118] Cf. Baldi, 506ff.

Israel, and the Ministry of Religion now administers both floors of the building. The pseudotomb of David serves as a synagogue, while the Upper Room is open to Christian visitors. Unfortunately, the only archaeological investigation of the building took place during the emergency excavation of J. Pinkerfeld, but it is to be hoped that in the future a thorough investigation can be undertaken. It is also hoped that the question of possession might become part of an international peace treaty. Until then, we should honor this building as the oldest worship place of Christianity and as the "mother of all churches".

26. The Essene Quarter and the Primitive Christian Community

Many researchers have commented on the remarkable similarity in the organization, the service and the social structure of the Essenes and that of the Early Church.[1] If biblical topography can prove the spatial proximity of both groups, then a set of interesting perspectives opens up. Those researchers are quite right who see different groups represented in the Early Christian Community in Jerusalem. Besides (1) the circle of the Twelve, (2) the Lord's brothers (Acts 1:14) and (3) the Hellenists (Acts 6:1), there seems to have been also (4) an Essene group of disciples, since the Early Christian Community with its seat on Mount Zion[2] developed in direct proximity to the Essene quarter[3] in Jerusalem. Are there traces of a tradition that was peculiar to this group in the texts of the New Testament?

I. The Apostolic Synagogue on Zion

We have previously discussed the Apostolic synagogue in the chapter about the search for the Last Supper room.[4] This upper room became the first center for the Early Christian Community and then the synagogue for the Essene Christian group of disciples. The stories about the origins of this early Christian synagogue, as visible in the New Testament, have been told, not just for historical reasons, but also to state the community's possession of an authoritative relationship. The

[1] Cf. K. Stendahl, ed., *The Scrolls and the New Testament* (London: SCM Press, 1957); W. S. LaSor, *The Dead Sea Scrolls and the New Testament* (Grand Rapids: Eerdmans, 1962); K. H. Schelkle, *Die Gemeinde von Qumran und die Kirche des Neuen Testaments* (Düsseldorf: Patmos, 1965); J. Maier and K. Schubert, *Die Qumran-Essener* (Munich: Kösel, 1973), 106–36.

[2] Cf. chapter 25, "The Apostolic Synagogue on Zion" (pp. 319–59).

[3] Cf. chapter 15, "The Essene Quarter in Jerusalem" (pp. 192–219).

[4] Cf. chapter 18, "The Last Supper of Jesus" (pp. 239–49).

group was conscious of its close connection to the Lord and the circle of the Twelve. According to their tradition, the Apostles had come to the city from the Mount of Olives following the Ascension in order to go to the Upper Room (ὑπερῷον [Acts 1:13]). The Upper Room, which was mentioned in the text without any further explanation and with the definite article (τό), was probably a well-known synagogue in the eighties of the first century that perhaps the author of Acts had visited.[5] This group of disciples on the southwest hill obviously had connections before A.D. 70 with the Essene quarter, where the majority of the community were monks and many of them were priests (pp. 196–97). This monastic community had still retained and lived by their own liturgical calendar in a community in which they shared communal goods. They never called themselves "Essenes" in their own writings but were known by this name to outsiders.

II. The "Devout Men" in Luke's Writings

Luke, the Greek author, drew largely from sources that go back to the Essene Christian group (pp. 431–32f.), using a keyword to describe the Jerusalem Essenes and related groups. In my opinion it is a *terminus technicus* that is used only four times and only by Luke: εὐλαβεῖς (*eulabeis*), which is an expression that was already used in the Septuagint and is in Hebrew *Chassidim* (חֲסִידִים), "the pious ones". The designation Essenes (Ἐσσηνοί) or Esseans (Ἐσσαῖοι) is most likely from the Aramaic expression *Chassayya* (חַסָּיָא), and one should therefore actually say "Hesseans". The four persons or groups described in this way by Luke fit well into an Essene context. These were (1) old Simeon (Lk 2:25), (2) the men who buried Stephen and held the lamentation over him (Acts 8:2), (3) Ananias of Damascus (Acts 22:12) and (4) devout Jewish men, "pious men" (ἄνδρες εὐλαβεῖς), who met at the Feast of Pentecost in Jerusalem (Acts 2:5). In my opinion, one can recognize in the text a tradition from the original Essene group of disciples.

III. The First Feast of Pentecost

After the descriptions of the Pentecost event and the assembly place of the 120 of Jesus' disciples (Acts 2:1–4), the narration turns immediately

[5] Cf. chapter 33, "Luke and Jerusalem" (pp. 423–32).

to the surroundings of the house, where a "mighty wind" was to be heard:[6] "Now there were dwelling in Jerusalem Jews, devout men [ἄνδρες εὐλαβεῖς] from every nation under heaven. And at this sound the multitude [τὸ πλῆθος] came together" (Acts 2:5ff.). What did these "devout Jews" do in Jerusalem? Some of them were surely resident there. However, the majority had probably come from far away (cf. Acts 2:7–11) to the Feast of Pentecost, for the Feast of Weeks or of the Firstfruits, as it was called at that time. It is now obvious from the Temple Scroll from Qumran (11QTemple 18:10—19:9) that the Essenes celebrated according to their own solar calendar, which did not agree with the official calendar of the temple hierarchy. It is accepted that the Essenes visited the temple (see *War* 18.19), without sacrificing because of their disdain for the corrupt priests and what they considered to be a contaminated holy sanctuary. They waited for the day when the temple would again be cleansed.

An important occasion for the Essenes was their Feast of Pentecost, which they celebrated throughout their settlements. G. Vermes described its main elements in this way:

> It is not yet possible to say precisely how often the members of the community met, but looking at the community rules and the Damascus writing, the entire sect was obliged to come together at least once a year for the general assembly, at the celebration of the community renewal, which was celebrated in the Feast of Weeks (thus Pentecost). That was the opportunity for new members who desired to join the community to commit themselves by a solemn oath, and at the same time the status of all members was again determined.[7]

If we consider that the meeting at Pentecost was the largest event in the year for the Essene groups, then we can imagine in these days of

[6] If the "mighty wind" (Acts 2:2) not only represents a symbolic event, as many exegetes believe, but an actual wind, then its effect must have been on a limited area. When I lived for several years on Mt. Zion, I often had the opportunity to witness sudden gusts of wind that were sometimes alarming. Such gusts of wind occur on this exposed hill particularly, during the transition period from one season to another, thus, for example, with the change from spring to the summer. It is not clear to me how such a sudden local storm in other parts of Jerusalem, for instance in the lower part of town or the temple district, would have caused a stir. The noise of such a wind, however strong, would only arouse the curiosity of people living near. If the mass of people congregated on Pentecost due to the stormy wind, then it must have developed in the immediate environment.

[7] *The Dead Sea Scrolls* (Baltimore, 1973), 31.

Pentecost the activity in the Essene quarter on Jerusalem's Mount Zion, right next to where the original community gathered.

The fixed ritual is described in such a way at the beginning of the Community Rule from Qumran: "So they are to do year after year, so long as the rule of Belial [thus the devil] lasts. The priests are to enter first, in order according to their spirit, one after the other, and the Levites are to go after them, one after the other, and the people are to enter in the third place, one after the other, to thousands, to hundreds, fifties and tens, so that each man in Israel would know his appointed position in the community for eternal counsel" (1QS 2:19–23). Those who were acceptable to the community "will become clean of all their sins by the Holy Spirit [who] has been given to the community, and by the spirit of honesty and humility their sins are atoned. And if he humiliates his soul under all God's laws, his flesh will be cleansed and he will be sprinkled with purifying water in order for him to be sanctified holy by the water of purity. Then he will steer his steps to walk and change completely and walk in all God's ways" (1QS 3:7–10). Here we are confronted with many remarkable similarities to the first Christian Feast of Pentecost, e.g., the new "covenant" as a background to the celebration; the covenant's reception; the stress of a separation from the condemnation of the old self (Acts 2:40); instruction for the new community (Acts 2:40f.); and baptism after conversion and the outpouring of the Holy Spirit (Acts 2:38).

IV. The Date of the First Feast of Pentecost

The textual variants of Acts 2:1 have been repeatedly discussed by commentators. Most of the texts read: "When the day of Pentecost had come [ἐν τῷ συμπληροῦσθαι τὴν ἡμέραν τῆς πεντηκοστῆς], they were all together in one place." Codex D offers the variant: "And it happened in those days, on the day of Pentecost . . ." Old Latin and Armenian translations and also the Syrian Peshitta used the plural: "And as the days of Pentecost came to an end, they were in one place." The question arises: How could the day of Pentecost come to its end when it says later, "the third hour of the day"—thus it was at nine o'clock in the morning (Acts 2:15)? Could it be that the plural points to a number of Pentecost feasts? The proposal of the spatial proximity of the Essene quarter and the center for the Early Christian Community could throw new light on these questions. And again, the Temple Scroll seems to offer a key.

We know today that at the time of the second Jewish temple in Jerusalem, due to different interpretations of Leviticus 23:15f., three Feasts of Pentecost were celebrated. The passage reads: "And you shall count from the day after the sabbath, from the day that you brought the sheaf of the wave offering; seven full weeks shall they be, counting fifty days to the day after the seventh sabbath; then you shall present a cereal offering of new grain to the LORD. You shall bring from your dwellings two loaves of bread to be waved." Three different interpretations were given for the expression "the day after the sabbath" (מָחֳרַת הַשַּׁבָּת), and the date of the Feast of Pentecost was fixed accordingly: (1) The interpretation of the Pharisees, whose considerable influence at that time determined the behavior of the majority of the pious Jews, is still considered valid today. For them the Passover, regardless on which weekday it fell, was as essential a religious practice as the Sabbath. The Pharisees interpreted "the day after the sabbath" as the first day after Passover. The Feast of Weeks was fifty days after the Passover. (2) The Sadducees, Boethuseans and Samaritans believed that the law indicated the morning after the Sabbath that followed Passover, and they counted fifty days from Sunday after Passover. (3) The Qumran Essenes followed a third interpretation. This is the view of S. Talmon[8] and was confirmed by Y. Yadin[9] from the Temple Scroll (11QTemple 18:10—19:9): the Qumran Essenes counted from the first day after the sabbath but with the following difference. For them it was a Torah-designated Sabbath that followed the eight-day celebration of Unleavened Bread. Thus the Essene Pentecost represented the latest in a series of Jewish Feasts of Weeks. Could the text of Acts 2:1 be connected to this remarkable variant of the different customs of the different groups? Perhaps in the expression of the completion of the Feast of Pentecost, there lay an indication that it concerned the Essene practice?

V. The Early Church Shared-Goods Community

The Early Christian Community accepted a new social structure as part of the conversion experience caused by the Pentecost event. This social structure was not only remarkable but was also typically

[8] In *Memorial Book to Sukenik* (Jerusalem: Magnes Press, 1961), 86.

[9] In *Jerusalem through the Ages* (Jerusalem: Magnes Press, 1967), 77; *The Temple Scroll*, vol. 1, *Introduction* (Jerusalem: Israel Exploration Society, 1983), 99–121.

Essene.[10] The Early Christian Community of Jerusalem was, according to our knowledge, the only New Testament community that maintained this kind of communal living (Acts 2:45; 4:35). We know from some later Jewish Christian groups that these were strongly affected by Essene ideas (pp. 174–75) and that they continued the shared-goods policy of the Early Christian Community in Jerusalem. Obviously, they also took over from the Essenes the name *Ebyonim* (אֶבְיוֹנִים), "the poor". Regarding the Ebyonites (or Ebionites), the Jewish Christian pseudo-Clementine homilies reported that only as much property was permitted as was necessary for life.[11] The shared-goods community was not typically Christian, because there was no express requirement by Jesus for this, even if it corresponded to his teachings (Mt 6:24; Mk 10:24f.; Lk 15:8–12).

We know from Acts that the numerical success of the first mission among the Jews was enormous, if we believe the number given: "So those who received his word were baptized, and there were added that day about three thousand souls" (Acts 2:41). If we assume that a large number of these new converts came from the well-organized Essene community in Jerusalem, then the phenomenon of the introduction of the shared-goods community becomes understandable. The original 120 members of Jesus' disciples [Acts 1:15] took over their social structure, partly by conviction, partly probably for missionary reasons;[12] the numerical weight of the new members being added could also have played an important role: "All who believed were together and had all things in common; and they sold their possessions and goods and distributed them to all, as any had need" (Acts 2:44f.). From this context we can also understand the reason for the discontent of the Hellenists, who either were not allowed or would not participate fully in the "sharing-goods" community: "Now in these days when the disciples were increasing in number, the Hellenists murmured against the Hebrews because their widows were neglected in the daily distribution [of food]" (Acts 6:1).

[10] Cf. B.J. Capper, "'In der Hand des Ananias . . .': Erwägungen zu 1 QS VI, 20 und der urchristlichen Gütergemeinschaft", *RQ* 12 (1986): 223–36.

[11] *Ps.-Clem. Hom.* 15.5–11. Cf. H.J. Schoeps, *Theologie und Geschichte des Judenchristentums* (Tübingen: Mohr, 1949), 351f.

[12] Cf. R. Riesner, "Essener und Urkirche in Jerusalem", *BiKi* 40 (1985): 64–76 (at 76); idem, *Formen gemeinsamen Lebens im Neuen Testament und heute*, 2nd ed., Theologie und Dienst 11 (Gießen: Brunnen, 1984), 30–33.

There was, however, an important difference between the Qumran group and the Primitive Christian Community in the attitude to private property. For the Essenes in the desert monastery, it was a *conditio sine qua non* to hand over everything that they possessed to the community. It was prescribed in the Community Rule: "When someone wants to join the community after having had instruction by the priests and other senior men, then he is to hand over also his possessions and his income into the hand of the man who is supervising the income of the many" (1QS 6:19f.; cf. 1QS 9:8). In the Primitive Christian Community, the handing over of property was on a voluntary basis. This is shown in the words of Peter in the case of Ananias and Sapphira: "Ananias, why has Satan filled your heart to lie to the Holy Spirit and to keep back part of the proceeds of the land? While it remained unsold, did it not remain your own? And after it was sold, was it not at your disposal?" (Acts 5:3–5).

VI. The Priests Obedient to the Faith

There is another possible Essene tradition in Acts 6:7: "And the word of God increased; and the number of the disciples multiplied greatly in Jerusalem, and a great many of the priests were obedient to the faith." The two Jewish groups to which nearly all priests belonged were the Sadducees and the Essenes. It is completely improbable that these converted priests came to Christianity from the group of the Sadducees, who had been responsible for both the condemnation of Jesus and later of James "the Lord's brother" (pp. 392–93). Several commentators have pointed out that these priests were most likely Essenes.[13] We know that priests formed a substantial part of the Qumran settlement and that they were instrumental and prominent members in each individual settlement (מַחֲנֶה [*machaneh*]). If we include the proximity of the Essene quarter in Jerusalem to the first meeting place of the Primitive Christian Community, then this comment is significant. The expression "were obedient to the faith" may contain a certain reservation. Could it be that they recognized Jesus as the Messiah, without separating completely from their Essene brethren? These Essene Christian monks could have been the audience for the Letter to

[13] Literature by H. BRAUN, *Qumran und das Neue Testament*, vol. 1 (Tübingen: Mohr Siebeck, 1966), 153f.

the Hebrews,[14] and James played an important role among this community.[15]

Supplement: In October 1991 a Qumran symposium took place at the Catholic University of Eichstätt. I had the opportunity to give a talk entitled "Archäologische Beobachtungen zum Jerusalemer Essener-Viertel und zur Urgemeinde" (in B. Mayer, *Christen und Christliches in Qumran?* Eichstätter Studien, n.F., 32 [Regensburg: Pustet, 1992], 89–113). Benedikt Schwank, O.S.B., a brother from my order, criticized the assumption of an Essene quarter ("Gab es zur Zeit der öffentlichen Tätigkeit Jesu, *Qumran*-Essener in Jerusalem?" ibid., 115–30). His objections did not convince me. He denied that there was a ritual bath in Qumran outside of the settlement. The large bath at the northwest edge (Locus 138) is surrounded by a small wall that was perhaps intended to stop animals from entering the bath. But this wall differs in strength and height clearly from the wall around the actual area of the monastery (R. de Vaux, *Archaeology and the Dead Sea Scrolls* [Oxford: Oxford University Press, 1973], plates 2, 6 and 17). This means the ritual bath is also situated outside. Also, too little importance is given to the fact that in the southern part of Mount Zion, some poorly built buildings were found in our excavations, unlike the affluent Herodian houses excavated by M. Broshi on Mount Zion; cf. chapter 27, "Notes on the Continuous Existence of Jewish Christian Groups in Jerusalem" (pp. 369–79, esp. pp. 370–74).

[14] Cf. chapter 32, "The Jerusalem Essenes, Barnabas and the Letter to the Hebrews" (pp. 415–22).

[15] Cf. chapter 28, "James the Lord's 'Brother'" (pp. 380–93).

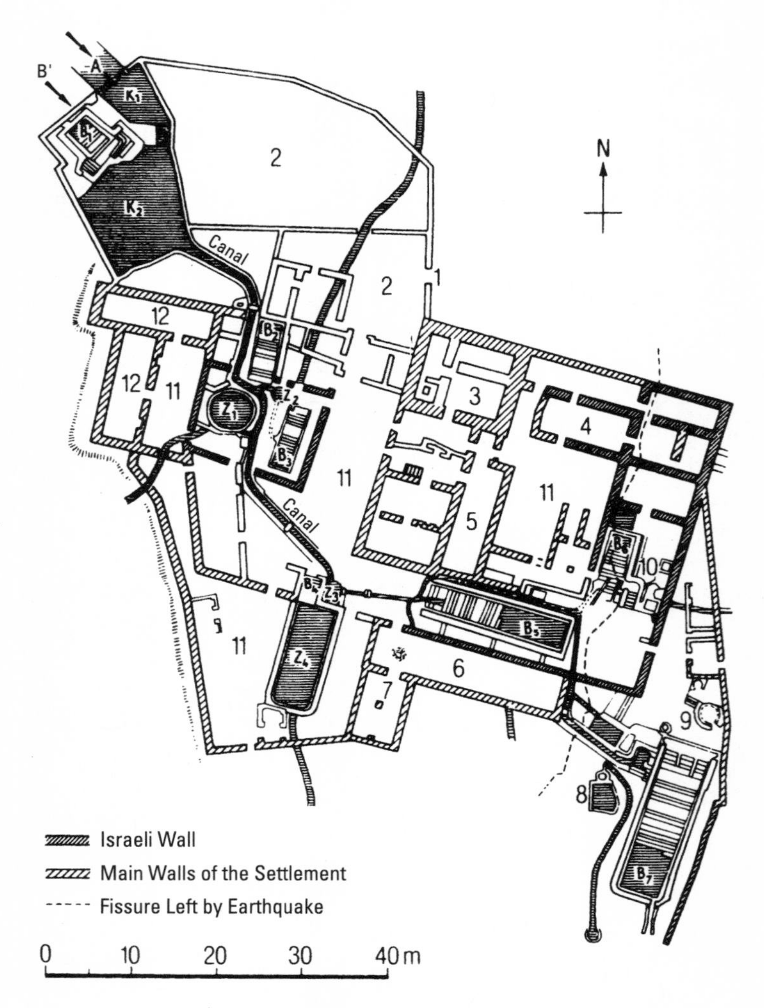

Illus. 92. Plan of the Qumran settlement (according to G. Kroll).
B_1 Large ritual bath northwest of and outside the settlement walls

27. Notes on the Continuous Existence of Jewish Christian Groups in Jerusalem

I. The Settlement on Zion in the First Century A.D.

In an essay on the archaeological evidence for the Jewish Christian community, Mrs. J. E. Taylor categorically denies the existence of an Essene quarter on the southwest hill of Jerusalem and the presence of a Jewish Christian community on today's Mount Zion.[1] This is not the place to restate the literary and archaeological evidence in support of an Essene quarter,[2] which has been consistently confirmed by numerous researchers.[3] Mrs. Taylor's argument,[4] however, is that M. Broshi's[5]

[1] *Christians and the Holy Places: The Myth of Jewish-Christian Origins* (Cambridge: Clarendon, 1993), 207–20.

[2] Cf. B. Pixner, "The History of the 'Essene Gate' Area", *ZDPV* 105 (1989): 96–104; idem, "Archäologische Beobachtungen zum Jerusalemer Essener-Viertel und zur Urgemeinde", in B. Mayer, *Christen und Christliches in Qumran?* Eichstätter Studien, n.F., 32 (Regensburg: Pustet, 1992), 89–113, and in this book, chapter 15, "The Essene Quarter in Jerusalem" (pp. 192–219).

[3] Cf. S. Medala, "Le camp des Esséniens de Jérusalem à la lumière des recentes recherches archéologiques", *Folia Orientalia* 25 (1989): 67–74; J. Finegan, *The Archeology of the New Testament* (Princeton: Princeton University Press, 1992), 218–20; E. Ruckstuhl, "Für Frage einer Essenergemeinde in Jerusalem und zum Fundort von 7Q5", in B. Mayer, *Christen und Christliches in Qumran?* (see n. 2), 131–37; M. Delcor, "A propos de l'emplacement de la porte des Esseniens selon Josèphe et de ses implications historiques, essénienne et chrétienne: Examen d'une théorie", in Z. J. Kapera, *Intertestamental Essays in Honour of Jozef Tadeusz Milik*, vol. 1 (Crakow: Enigma Press, 1992), 25–44; R. Riesner, "Das Jerusalemer Essenerviertel—Antwort auf einige Einwände", ibid., 179–86; as well as "Jesus, the Primitive Community, and the Essene Quarter of Jerusalem", in J. H. Charlesworth, *Jesus and the Dead Sea Scrolls* (New York: Doubleday, 1993), 198–234; idem, "Das Jerusalemer Essenerviertel und die Urgemeinde", in W. Haase, ed., *Aufstieg und Niedergang der Römischen Welt*, part 2, *Principat*, 26/2 (Berlin and New York: de Gruyter, 1995), 1775–1922.

[4] *Christians and the Holy Places* (see n. 1), 208.

[5] "Excavations in the House of Caiaphas, Mount Zion", in Y. Yadin, *Jerusalem Revealed* (Jerusalem: Israel Exploration Society, 1976), 57–60.

discovery in the Armenian cemetery on Mount Zion is evidence for a settlement of upper social classes, an argument that contradicts the theory that this was the principal location of the Primitive Community. Her assertion is based in particular on the presence of a noteworthy dwelling dating from the first century A.D. located in a restricted area near today's Zion's Gate (illus. 60). During our excavations south of this site, under the Dormition monastery and further south, i.e., northeast from the Essene Gate, we discovered some very simple buildings from the same period (illus. 43). The evidence therefore seems to suggest that during the first century A.D. there were three different settlement zones on Mount Zion:

1. In the area of the large ritual baths in the southwest corner of Zion, there was an Essene monastery that, according to the Copper Scroll (3Q15 2:7), was probably unwalled. Similar to the monastery in Qumran (3Q15 4:11f.), this one had a sanctuary at its center (3Q15 1:9; 3:13), known in the Copper Scroll as a *kochlit*, and was presumably the residence of celibate monks (cf. Cairo Document 12:1; 11QTemple 45:11 [Lev 15:18]). This quarter was drained by a set of small channels that flowed into the large sewer that ran below the threshold of the Essene Gate.[6]

2. The next zone, outside of the monastery area, consisted of very poor-quality housing similar in construction to the Essene monastery. Jewish families or groups ideologically sympathetic to the Essenes probably lived here.

3. Beyond this area was a third zone, which extended across the northern part of Zion. In this area were more opulent buildings, and it was this location that was excavated by M. Broshi.

II. Archaeological Traces of the Primitive Community?

I am particularly interested in the area that contained the poorest buildings, which are in remarkable contrast to the magnificent buildings located in the north. So far, not much has been written[7] regarding this area because the results of the final excavation are still to be

[6] Cf. B. PIXNER, D. CHEN and S. MARGALIT, "Mount Zion: The 'Gate of the Essenes' Reexcavated", *ZDPV* 105 (1989): 85–95 (at 89).

[7] Cf. chapter 30, "Mary on Zion" (pp. 398–407, esp. pp. 399–400).

published. In 1983 the Dormition Abbey acquired from the Franciscans a garden that was situated in the front of the church of the Dormition (illus. 60). Since this site was obtained to provide space for the erection of an annex to the abbey, the Israeli Department of Antiquities required that before any construction could begin a scientific excavation needed to be carried out. It was during this excavation, undertaken with the supervision of the Israeli archaeologist E. Eisenberg,[8] that beneath 2 m of earth, including the evidence of an abandoned Armenian cemetery, substantial remains of the church "Sancta Maria in Monte Sion" were unearthed within a Crusader stratum (pp. 353–57).

The layer most interesting for us, however, was the lowest, wedged firmly onto the bedrock of the Herodian Roman period (illus. 93). There we uncovered a row of walls that had belonged to the poorly built houses. These houses, situated along a north-south road nearly 2 m wide, still possessed a well-kept mortar plaster. At the southern end was a rocky elevation where today the tower of the Dormition Abbey stands, and this was presumably the southern end of the housing complex. Also, a number of different cisterns were excavated. The most fascinating structural find was, however, a small ritual bath with steps that ascended eastward. As with at least one other *mikveh*[9] in Jerusalem, in a corner of this ritual bath there was an upright column that perhaps served to provide support for older people as they cleansed themselves.

In the course of the excavation, different coins were found. The most remarkable of them are the coins dating from the Jewish Revolt (A.D. 66–70), which ended in the year 67/68. The inscription on such coins reads חרת ציון שנת שתים, "the liberation of Zion—second year" (A.D. 67/68). When I investigated further the steps of the *mikveh*, I found just such a coin lying on the second step. Over this there was a thick layer of rubble that dates back to the destruction of Zion by the soldiers of Titus in the year A.D. 70. In this layer, I also found a coin of the procurator Valerius Gratus (A.D. 15–26), Pontius Pilate's predecessor. The absence of coins from the last three years of the rebellion seems to suggest to me that these buildings had been abandoned by their inhabitants two years before the destruction of the Holy City.

[8] "Church of Dormition", *ESI* 3 (1984): 47.

[9] Cf. N. AVIGAD, *Discovering Jerusalem* (Nashville: Thomas Nelson, 1983), 140, plate 143.

During his excavation of the Herodian quarter, on the northeastern slope of Mount Zion, N. Avigad found coins from the first four years of the Jewish Revolt; only the extremely rare coins of the fifth year (A.D. 70) were missing.[10]

Who were the inhabitants of these poorly built houses? Naturally, I can only speculate, but my assumption would be that they belonged to members of the Primitive Community. We know that they left the city before the beginning of the struggle for Jerusalem and that under the leadership of their second bishop, Simeon Bar Cleopas, they fled beyond Jordan into the area of Pella.[11] Eusebius (*HE* 3.5.3) and Epiphanius of Salamis[12] reported that they were encouraged to flee the city by a prophecy. This prophecy may be identified as the words of Jesus in chapter 13 of Mark's Gospel, where there is a warning to escape if rumors of war are heard (Mk 13:4ff.). Galilee was in the hands of the Romans in the year A.D. 67, so A.D. 67/68 would be the most reasonable year for the escape of the Primitive Community from Jerusalem.

Also, these simple poor buildings would fit well into a picture of the impoverished Jewish Christian community in Jerusalem, for which Paul organized charitable collections in Greece and Asia Minor (1 Cor 16:1–4; Rom 15:25–28). The situation must have become particularly desperate during the years A.D. 47 and 48, coinciding with the period of the Apostolic Council (Gal 2:10), when in Judea during a Sabbath year, there was a particularly severe famine (*Ant.* 20.101). The experiment by the community of sharing goods (Acts 2:44f.; 4:32–37), which probably was introduced in imitation of the practice of their neighbors, the Essenes,[13] apparently did not work for the early Christians but instead led gradually to a general impoverishment. They were also probably influenced by a belief in the imminence of the Parousia.

The rows of simple houses lying between the Essene monastery and the more affluent buildings in the north went, in my view, from the town wall in the west by today's Greek cemetery across our excavation field and through the area of the Dormition church, where, according to early Church tradition, the house of Mary stood.[14] These houses

[10] *The Herodian Quarter in Jerusalem* (Jerusalem: Israel Exploration Society, 1991), 781.

[11] Cf. chapter 31, "Simeon Bar Cleopas, Second Bishop of Jerusalem" (pp. 408–14).

[12] *Panarion* 29.7.7 (GCS 25:330; Klijn-Reinink, 172).

[13] Cf. chapter 26, "The Essene Quarter and the Primitive Christian Community" (pp. 360–68).

[14] Baldi, 737ff.

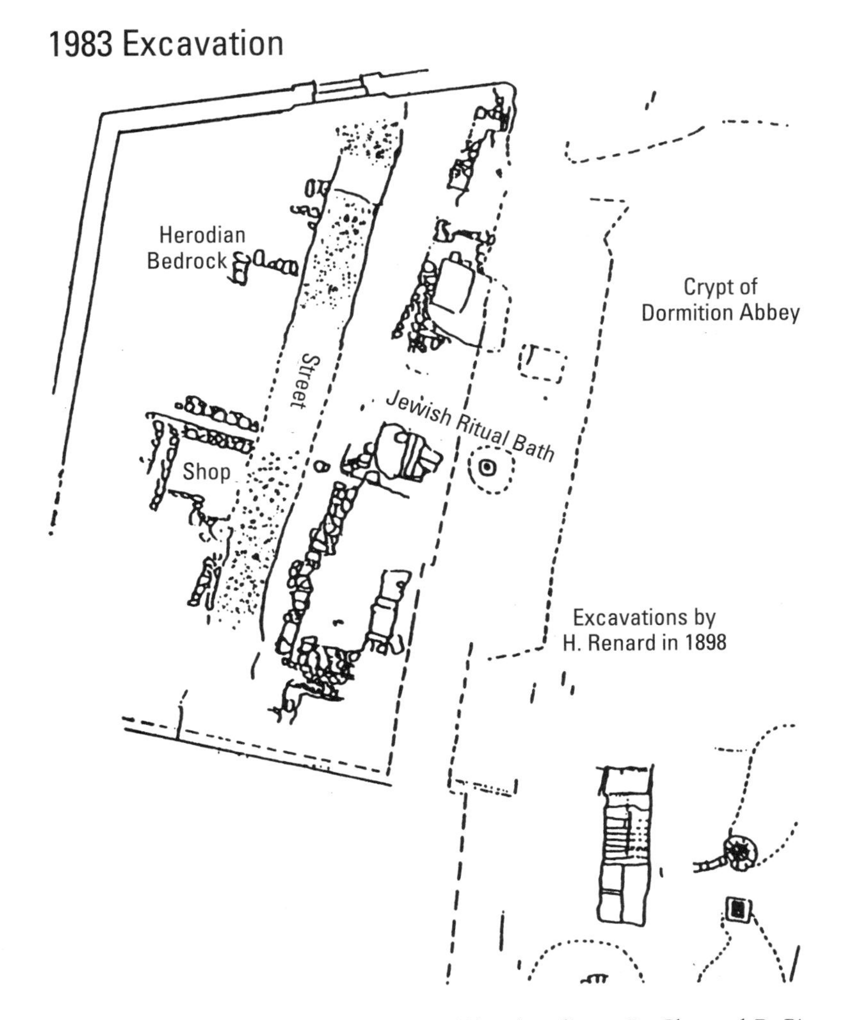

Illus. 93. Excavations in front of the Dormition Abbey (according to D. Chen and B. Pixner, 1991).

included the area of the traditional Last Supper room and extended down toward the Essene Gate (*War* 5.145). North of the road, which led from the city to the Essene Gate (illus. 43), we discovered in our excavations additional simple buildings[15] and another modest *mikveh*,

[15] Cf. B. PIXNER and S. MARGALIT, "Mt. Zion", *ESI* 4 (1985), 56f.

or ritual bath. Beside the road there were oil presses cut into a large rock; these hardly indicate aristocratic inhabitants. To the east of this there were some steps that led from the main road into this ancient residential area.

On a closer investigation of the old excavation plans drawn up in preparation for the building of the Dormition Abbey in the year 1900,[16] I noticed other cisterns and step baths, which we are now able to identify as Jewish ritual baths (illus. 93). Such baths were probably used by the first Christians for baptism because Christian baptism (Acts 2:38) evolved from the established Jewish practice, particularly the Qumran cleansing baths, to which John's baptism (Mk 1:4f.) represented an important link.[17] The buildings in all three areas on Zion suffered from the systematic destruction of the troops of Titus in A.D. 70. Flavius Josephus mentions that the destruction reached every corner of the city (*War* 5.334), and contrary to the skepticism of some modern researchers, our excavations confirmed the record that Zion was included in the destruction.

III. Building Activity at the Essene Gate under Emperor Elgabal

The primitive middle gate, which was constructed from various composite materials, originated, according to pottery remains (illus. 48) found nearby, from the period of the late Roman colony Aelia Capitolina (pp. 205–6). In the debris outside of the gate, approx. 0.4 m above the sewer (illus. 47), earlier a coin of the emperor Elgabal (218–222) was found.[18] The assumption that repairs were made to the gate at the beginning of the third century was confirmed by a further find. After torrential rain in February 1992, I found a coin in the filling behind the wall of the sewer, approximately 1.5 m within the gate complex. After the examination by Mrs. R. Barkay, it was identified also as a coin of the emperor Elgabal.

In my opinion, the middle gate was just a passage through a wall that included the southwest hill. This wall (*murus Sion*) was mentioned

[16] Cf. H. Renard, "Die Marienkirchen auf dem Berg Sion in ihrem Zusammenhang mit dem Abendmahlssaale", *HlL* 44 (1900): 3–23.

[17] Cf. D. Flusser, *The Spiritual History of the Dead Sea Sect* (Jerusalem: MOD Books, 1989), 45–48; O. Betz, "Kontakte zwischen Christen und Essenern", in B. Mayer, *Christen und Christliches in Qumran?* (see n. 2), 157–75 (at 159f.).

[18] B. Pixner, D. Chen and S. Margalit, "Mount Zion" (see n. 6), 88.

in A.D. 333 by the Pilgrim of Bordeaux, who was traveling via the pool of Siloam and, after a visit to the house of Caiaphas, passed through the gate continuing to the isolated settlement on Zion.[19] The buildings that he saw there, probably a synagogue and allegedly David's palace, were in the possession of the Jewish Christians.[20] We do not know precisely whether the decree of Hadrian meant that the Jewish Christians were also obliged to leave Jerusalem (*HE* 4.6.3). If they were included in this expulsion of the Jews, then at the latest they probably returned during the more tolerant reign of Emperor Antonius Pius (138–161) (pp. 345–46). Furthermore, the building activity under Elgabal could point to a later date for a return, because this "Syrian" emperor seems to have been favorably disposed toward Eastern cults, which included the Jews. During this period the Jewish Christians could have erected a wall, on Zion, to create an isolated ghetto existence.

IV. A Source of Pre-Byzantine Traditions

In his *Demonstratio Evangelica*, Eusebius makes reference to the presence and activity of Jesus on Zion (p. 340). When Eusebius writes of "the message of the Gospel ... spread[ing] into the whole world",[21] it is clear that he regarded Zion as the place of the Resurrection appearances and the cradle of the first community. It is important that this represents a pre-Byzantine statement and is therefore unsullied by church politics. *Demonstratio Evangelica* is generally set before the Council of Nicea (A.D. 325) and after the *Praeparatio Evangelica* (ca. A.D. 315–320), but "Eusebius had the main content of this double work already once laid down in former times, during the days of persecution [under Diocletian], before 311."[22] There are even other historians who date the *Demonstratio Evangelica* earlier, i.e., under the persecution of Emperor Decius (A.D. 303).[23] When Eusebius writes about the "brothers" who

[19] *Itinerarium* 16 (Geyer, 22; Baldi, 474).

[20] Cf. chapter 25, "The Apostolic Synagogue on Zion" (pp. 319–59, esp. pp. 341–46).

[21] *Demonstratio Evangelica* 1.4 (PG 22:431; Baldi, 473f.).

[22] O. BARDENHEWER, *Patrologie* (Freiburg: Herder, 1910), 276.

[23] E. L. MARTIN, *Secrets of Golgotha: The Forgotten History of Christ's Crucifixion* (Alhambra, 1988), 91f., suggests some interesting arguments for this date. In the opinion of the same author, Jesus was crucified on the Mount of Olives and buried in the cave of Eleona (pp. 233–34, 338), but this is completely untenable. Cf. chapter 24, "The Historical Via

were still guarding at that time the throne of James the Lord's brother (*HE* 7.19), he very probably meant the Jewish Christians in Jerusalem, who had their center on Mount Zion. Eusebius wrote his polemic against them because he understood Zion as only a spiritual concept (pp. 346–48).

V. The Byzantine Tradition

The fact that Byzantine literature describes Jewish Christian groups negatively and inaccurately, or even ignores them, should not surprise us. The Byzantine Christian emperors instructed that the holy places, which were in their control and often overbuilt by Roman and pagan sanctuaries, should be turned into church buildings. This was true of Golgotha, Eleona, Bethlehem and Mamre. Places that had remained in Jewish Christian possession and were neglected in the fourth century by the Gentile Christians were altered only later, when they became the property of the Church. Texts from A.D. 325 to the end of the fourth century, which tend to display a strong anti-Semitic attitude, also offer a negative impression of Zion, as this had remained in the control of the Nazoreans, who were regarded as heretics by the rest of the Church (pp. 343–48).

The oldest Byzantine texts confirm the Pentecost event occurring on Zion.[24] At nearly the same time we have testimonies of post-Resurrection appearances made by Jesus at that location.[25] The Syrian *Doctrina Addai* is particularly noteworthy, as it identifies the Last Supper and the Pentecost event with the "Upper Room" (Acts 1:13). This tradition dates from at least the fourth century.[26] During the Jewish Christian occupation of Zion, the commemoration of the Last

---

Dolorosa" (pp. 303–15). The same applies to Martin's statement that the pre-Byzantine Christians would have regarded the Mount of Olives as the new Zion and would have established the first church there. Cf. chapter 19, "Epiphanius and the Last Supper on Zion" (pp. 250–52). On the liturgy on the Mount of Olives, cf. R. JAECKLE, "Gottesdienst in Jerusalem in der zweiten Hälfte des vierten Jahrhunderts im Spiegel der Peregrinatio Egeriae", *Jahresbuch von des Deutschen Evangelischen Instituts für Altertumswissenschaft des Heiligen Landes* 4 (1995): 80–115.

[24] Since Cyril of Jerusalem, *Catecheses* 16.4 (Baldi, 474ff.).

[25] Egeria, *Peregrinatio* 39.5 (Geyer, 88; Baldi, 476).

[26] Cf. F.M. ABEL, in L.H. VINCENT and F.M. ABEL, *Jérusalem: Recherches de topographie, d'archéologie et d'histoire*, vol. 2, *Jerusalem nouvelle*, pt. 1, *Aelia Capitolina, le Saint-Sepulcre et le Mont des Oliviers* (Paris: Gabalda, 1914), 453.

Supper was not celebrated there by the Byzantine Christians but in the Church of the Holy Sepulchre (p. 342). Everyone must have known that it was not the original location for Jesus' Last Supper, and this demonstrates that the traditional place (on Zion) was inaccessible. That Jesus' Last Supper with his disciples did not occur on the Mount of Olives,[27] in Gethsemane[28] or Bethany,[29] where various pilgrims report the meals of Jesus, but took place within the city of Jerusalem[30] is clear from the Gospels. "Go into the city" (ὑπάγετε εἰς τὴν πόλιν), Jesus says to those of his disciples who were to prepare for the Passover meal (Mk 14:13).

Mrs. Taylor[31] attempted to ignore Epiphanius' reference to a pre-Hadrian church on Zion,[32] which offers an important link in the tradition between the New Testament period and the Byzantine references. Epiphanius, who probably was born into a Jewish Christian family and only later became an orthodox Christian (p. 401), demonstrated in his writings a good understanding of the Jewish Christian heritage and customs.[33] He even knew of the Last Supper of Jesus on Zion (pp. 250–52). We can therefore support the opinion of many different researchers that Mount Zion was the center for the Early Church and, until at least the beginning of the fifth century, the place where the Jewish Christian community was resident.[34]

VI. The Annex of the Basilica Hagia Sion

The religious sanctuary to the south of the basilica Hagia Sion indicated on the Madaba Mosaic Map (plate 1) is also completely ignored

[27] Petrus the Iberian (F. M. ABEL, ibid., 394).

[28] Theodosius, *De situ terrae sanctae* 10 (Geyer, 142; Baldi, 535).

[29] Euthychius of Constantinople, *Sermo de paschate et de sacra Eucharistia* (PG 86/2:2392; Baldi, 485f.).

[30] Cf. also R. RIESNER, "Der Christliche Zion: Vor- oder nachkonstantinisch?" in F. MANNS and E. ALLIATA, *Early Christianity in Context: Monuments and Documents*, Festschrift for Emmanuele Testa, O.F.M., SBFCMa 38 (Jerusalem: Franciscan Printing Press, 1993), 85–90.

[31] *Christians and the Holy Places* (see n. 1), 210–12.

[32] *De mensuris et ponderibus* 14 (PG 43:2601; Baldi, 478).

[33] Cf. R. A. PRITZ, *Nazarene Jewish Christianity: From the End of the New Testament Period until Its Disappearance in the Fourth Century* (Jerusalem: Magnes Press / Leiden: Brill, 1988), 29–47.

[34] Cf. S. C. MIMOUNI, "La synagogue 'judéo-chrétienne' de Jérusalem au Mont Sion", *POC* 40 (1990): 215–34; R. RIESNER, "Essener und Urkirche in Jerusalem", in B. MAYER, *Christen und Christliches in Qumran?* (see n. 2), 139–55; A. STORME, "Les lieux saints évangéliques XIV: Jérusalem, le Cénacle", *Terre Sainte* (February 1993), 94–107.

by Mrs. Taylor. The red roof tiles prove, as in all other buildings on this map, that this was the location for a Christian church. Due to its location, it is to be identified with today's so-called Tomb of David, and this building cannot have been anything other than an ancient small church (or better, synagogue) of the Jewish Christian community (pp. 351–52). When the powerful Byzantine church acquired this Jewish Christian sanctuary, it is possible that in the year A.D. 415 they placed Stephen's relics in a specially designated niche, which is what Mrs. Taylor believed.[35] However, these relics cannot have been placed then in a sarcophagus but rather in an urn or an ossuary. The sarcophagus present there today, under the niche aligned to the north-northeast, in this pseudotomb of David originates only from the Crusader period.

VII. A Last Testimony for Jewish Christians in Jerusalem?

The report of Adamnanus about the visit of the Gallic bishop Arculf in the year 670 offers a bizarre story about the Jews in Jerusalem, who were in dispute over the cloth of Christ (cf. Jn 20:7).[36] Perhaps the legendary story has a connection to the Shroud of Turin, depicting the image of Christ. A certain support for some historical kernel is the reference to the Saracen king Mavias, to be identified with Mu'awiya (A.D. 658–680), the founder of the Umayyad dynasty in Damascus,[37] who at the time of Arculf's visit was governing Jerusalem. It cannot be dismissed as a pure legendary fabrication, because among the Jews "unbelievers" (*infideles Iudaei*) and "Jewish believers" (*creduli Iudaei, Iudaei vero credentes*) are differentiated, and even "Jewish Christians" (*Iudaei Christiani*).[38]

After the Muslim conquest (A.D. 636) there were obviously still some Jewish believers residing in Jerusalem. This is probable because the anonymous Pilgrim of Piacenza[39] in ca. A.D. 570 assumed that Jewish Christians were living in Nazareth.[40] Individual Jewish Christians

[35] *Christians and the Holy Places* (see n. 1), 219.

[36] *De locis sanctis* 1.9.1–16 (Geyer, 235–38).

[37] Cf. H. Donner, *Pilgerfahrt ins Heilige Land: Die ältesten Berichte christlicher Palästinapilger (4.–7. Jahrhundert)* (Stuttgart: Katholischers Bibelwerk, 1979), 350, n. 35.

[38] Adamnanus, *De locis sanctis* 1.9.2, 9–11 (Geyer, 236f.).

[39] *Itinerarium* 5 (Geyer, 161; Baldi, 4).

[40] Cf. S. C. Mimouni, "Pour une définition nouvelle du judéo-christianisme ancien", *New Testament Studies* 38 (1992): 161–86 (at 180–82).

managed to continue to reside in the Arab area of control until the tenth century,[41] but their connection to the wider Jewish community remained a secret, since their community had been officially merged into the great Byzantine church under Bishop John II at the beginning of the fifth century A.D. (pp. 348–50). This resistance to absorption and the desire to retain their heritage is a typical Jewish phenomenon that was also observed later during the Inquisition period by the Marranos in Spain. If even at the beginning of the Arab period, groups of Jewish Christians continued to reside in the Holy City, then Mrs. Taylor's suggestion of their immediate disappearance from Jerusalem soon after A.D. 70 is completely improbable.

[41] Cf. D. FLUSSER, *Jewish Sources in Early Christianity* (Jerusalem: MOD Books, 1993), 88.

28. James the Lord's "Brother"

I. *The Brother of Jesus*

In 1945 the Gospel of Thomas was discovered in Egypt. There is answered the disciples' question, "Who is it who shall be great over us?" Jesus said to them: "Wherever you have come, you will go to James the righteous for whose sake heaven and earth came into being."[1] This may seem very effusive, but it actually reflects various textual sources that describe the high reputation that the Lord's brother had in the Jewish Christian community. This position of honor is confirmed by the Church historian Eusebius (ca. 330): "The bishop's throne of James, who was the first bishop appointed by the Lord and the Apostles of the church of Jerusalem and, as the godly books teach, was called 'the Brother of Christ', is still admired today by the brothers of that tradition [in Jerusalem]. Thus they express unambiguously the reverence that they demonstrated and continue to hold toward the holy men because of their piety" (*HE* 7.19). The "brothers" that Eusebius mentions were probably the last of the Nazorean Jewish Christians, who at that time still lived on Mount Zion, outside the city of Jerusalem, which at that period had been almost completely abandoned.[2] During the first century, the "synagogue church" still existed (pp. 340–42), which was called by Cyril of Jerusalem (348) "the Upper Church of the Apostles".[3]

The putative letter by Clement of Rome addressed him as "James, the first bishop of the church of the Jews in Jerusalem".[4] But who was

[1] *The Gospel according to Thomas: Coptic Text Established and Translated by A. Guillaumont, H.-Ch. Puech, G. Quispel, W. Till and Yassah 'abd al Masīḥ* (New York: Harper / Leiden: Brill, 1959), no. 12, p. 9.

[2] Cf. chapter 25, "The Apostolic Synagogue on Zion" (pp. 319–59).

[3] *Catecheses* 16.4 (PG 33:924; Baldi, 474ff.).

[4] Pseudo-Clement, *Epistula Clementis ad Jacobum* 1.1 (PL 2:31).

he? In Galatians 1:19 Paul calls him "the Lord's brother" (ἀδελφὸς τοῦ κυρίου). There is disagreement among the traditions of the Eastern and the Western church regarding his relationship to Jesus and how he was a brother of the Lord. All the various Eastern churches, without exception, from the Prechalcedonians to the Greek Orthodox, regard him as one of the sons of Joseph from his first marriage. According to this belief, which is stated in the Protogospel of James,[5] Mary was his stepmother, but the two had a deep and loving relationship. James was educated with his other brothers and sisters as well as with his stepbrother Jesus. Gregory of Nyssa writes that the Mother of God was called "Mother" by James and Joses and that it was she who named James "the Lesser"[6] although they were the sons from the first marriage of Joseph, who had been very young at the time of the death of his first wife.

By contrast the [Roman] Catholic Church relies on the authority of Jerome, who, in his epistle against Helvidius, states that James and the other brothers—Joses, Judas and Simon—mentioned in the Gospel (Mk 6:3) were not actual brothers or stepbrothers of Jesus but, rather, cousins. Their mother was Mary, who is described in Mark's Gospel as the mother of James the Lesser [or "younger"] and Joses (Mk 15:40). This difference between the churches will probably never be resolved. However, both the Eastern tradition and Western research agree that the Lord's brother James was not one of the twelve disciples of Jesus and is not to be confused with the Apostle James, the son of Alphaeus (Mk 3:18). This was also always the position of the Early Church Fathers.

II. Jesus and His Extended Family in Nazareth

Jesus originated from a very pious family. His foster father Joseph is called a "just man" (δίκαιος) (Mt 1:19). A *zaddik* (צַדִּיק) is one within the Jewish community who is considered a diligent faithful observer of the law. Joseph the carpenter (Mt 13:55) and Jesus, who learned this craft from him (Mk 6:3), remind us of a story recorded in the Jerusalem Talmud (*Jebamoth* 8 [9b]): A man comes into a village and seeks someone who could help him solve a problem. He first asks the

[5] *Prot. Jas.* 17:1f. (Hennecke-Schneemelcher, 1:345).

[6] *In Christi Resurrectionem* 2 (PG 46:648).

people of the village whether there is a rabbi present. On receiving a negative answer, he asks: "Is there a carpenter or the son of a carpenter, who can give me a solution?"[7] It seems to suggest that in a small village (like Nazareth), the carpenter was the best informed for halakhic questions. The *zaddik* carpenter Joseph and the *zaddik* carpenter Jesus might have been such men. It would not have been unusual, therefore, that Jesus went regularly to Nazareth to the synagogue (Lk 4:16). The fact that the Nazarenes had their own synagogue, despite the small size of their settlement and a synagogue close at Japhia, could be because they had a different understanding of halakha from their neighbors. The expression "the many" (οἱ πολλοί) that Mark used for those who heard Jesus (Mk 6:2) corresponds exactly to the expression that the Essene documents from Qumran (1QS 6:1ff.) used to describe members of their community (הָרַבִּים [*ha-rabbim*]). We get the impression of a similar environment as from the description in Luke's Gospel of the visit by Jesus to the synagogue there (Lk 4:16–30).

In the Lucan passage the description of the change of attitude by the congregation—from initial enthusiasm to a total rejection of Jesus in the synagogue—is so sudden that many exegetes rightly presume a number of previous visits. He is clearly known to this community. The synagogue service, attended by Jesus on that dramatic Sabbath, consisted as usual of the "Shema Yisra'el" (Deut 6:4ff.), prayers and two readings: one from the Torah of Moses and one from the prophets, the so-called *haftara*. This was followed, if necessary, by a translation into Aramaic (*targum*) and then the sermon.[8] It would seem that an initial glad and enthusiastic reception by a sympathetic audience was followed by questioning, which then degenerated into an attempted assassination.

When Jesus presented himself at the synagogue to speak, he was handed the scroll of Isaiah by the synagogue attendant (see Lk 4:17–20). The *haftara* that Jesus read out was surely longer than the short section Isaiah 61:1f., quoted in Luke (Lk 4:18f.). Since Luke probably used as one of his sources memories of Jesus' family,[9] the quotation, even if shortened, is probably historical. If we include in the Lucan quotation the verses prior to the beginning of the passage (Is 60:20)

[7] Cf. J. Levy, *Wörterbuch über die Talmudim und Midraschim* (Berlin, 1924), 3:338.

[8] For the order of events of the service in the synagogue, cf. R. Riesner, *Jesus als Lehrer*, 3rd ed., WUNT, 2nd ser., 7 (Tübingen: Mohr Siebeck, 1988), 137–51.

[9] Cf. chapter 33, "Luke and Jerusalem" (pp. 423–32).

and additional verses at the end, there is a text that must have had special relevance to the Nazarene community:

The LORD will be your everlasting light,
and your days of mourning shall be ended.
Your people shall all be righteous [צַדִּיקִים (*zaddikim*)];
they shall possess the land for ever,
the shoot of my planting [נֵצֶר מַטָּעוֹ (*nezer mata'o*)], the work of my hands,
that I might be glorified.
The least one shall become a clan,
and the smallest one a mighty nation;
I am the LORD,
in its time I will hasten it.
The Spirit of the Lord GOD is upon me,
because the LORD has anointed me
to bring good tidings to the afflicted;
he has sent me to bind up the brokenhearted,
to proclaim liberty to the captives,
and the opening of the prison to those who are bound;
to proclaim the year of the LORD's favor,
and the day of vengeance of our God;
to comfort all who mourn;
to grant to those who mourn in Zion—
to give them a garland instead of ashes,
the oil of gladness instead of mourning,
the mantle of praise instead of a faint spirit;
that they may be called oaks of righteousness,
the planting [מַטַּע (*mata*)] of the LORD, that he may be glorified.
Is 60:20—61:3

Jesus, who knew his compatriots, must have known that this Isaiah text represented an expression of deep-rooted hope for his extended family. He had probably deliberately looked for this place in the text. No wonder that the eyes "of the many" were directed toward him in the synagogue when he handed the scroll back to the attendant and sat down and began to preach (cf. Lk 4:21).

The text was of particular interest to his listeners, because the third part of Isaiah, the so-called comfort book, describes the eschatological reestablishment of Israel. For the Nazarenes these words had a special relevance. The expression "the shoot of my planting" (Is 60:21) was considered by them to relate to Israel's community. The text was also important to the founder of the Qumran Essene community, the "Teacher of Righteousness", who highlighted this text in the hymns written by him for the community (1QH 6:15; 8:6–10). But the text was even more applicable for the Davidic family in Nazareth because of their ancestral links to David as the "shoot" that came forth "from the stump of Jesse, and a branch [נֵצֶר (nezer)] shall grow out of his roots" (Is 11:1). This text "lived within them" (p. 397). Following the exile and the attempted building of the second temple (Ezra 2:2; 4:2f.; 5:2), the Davidic line suddenly disappeared with Zerubbabel in the dark fog of the Babylonian Diaspora. Although the nation was dispersed and weakened, hope remained that from the Davidic line the Messiah would come. Therefore, in the Batanea area and in Galilee they gave messianic names to their settlements such as Kochaba ("village of the star") and Nazareth ("village of the branch").[10]

The Nazarenes would be this "small remnant" of Israel, through whom the glory of God would shine: "The least one shall become a clan, and the smallest one a mighty nation" (Is 60:22). The Lord would cause it "in its time". Was this now the time? Will this man of their kin, the son of Joseph, of whom they had already heard such marvelous things, be the one to lead them to honor? His speech found initial approval; they were astonished at the way he talked (Lk 4:22). But then suddenly came disillusionment. This son of Joseph had his own plans, if he worked down in Capharnaum under the simple fishermen. Here in Nazareth, in his homeland, he should prove his miraculous ability (Lk 4:23). But Jesus showed them from the history of Israel that God acts differently (Lk 4:24–27). Not to a widow in Israel was Elijah sent but to Zarephath in Sidon (1 Kings 17:9–24), and not a leper from Israel was healed by Elijah but the stranger Naaman the Syrian (2 Kings 5:1–14).

The Nazarenes were bitterly disappointed. They believed that kinship duty laid obligations upon Jesus. But Jesus did not want to make himself available to his kindred for their lofty and future ambitions. The Nazorean clan had for centuries been withdrawn and devoted to the idea of their own role in salvation history, particularly since the influence of Essene ideas. Jesus saw that these beliefs endangered his

[10] Cf. chapter 13, "Batanea as a Jewish Settlement Area" (pp. 169–76, esp. pp. 173–75).

whole project: "No prophet is acceptable in his own country" (Lk 4:24). The congregation became furious. They pushed him out of the town and to a hill, where they wished to throw him to his death. "But passing through the midst of them he went away. And he went down to Capernaum" (Lk 4:30–31a).

III. Jesus and His "Brothers"

After the death of Joseph, James, as the firstborn, became the head of the family, following the old Oriental kinship tradition, and later, it would seem, became also the leader of the whole believing community. Probably by the wedding of Cana (Jn 2:12), but definitely by the time Jesus was excluded from the kinship of the Nazarenes and driven out from Nazareth (Lk 4:16–30), the fate of the youngest was separated from the rest of the clan. Jesus then established himself somewhere around Capharnaum[11] by Lake Gennesaret. It can be assumed that James also moved to Capharnaum to support and protect Jesus (Mk 3:21). James needed to respond to Jesus' assertion that his "true" family were those who did the will of God (Mk 3:31–35). James and his brothers were deeply interested in their brother's success, but they were yet to come to a real faith.

A particularly relevant event is reported in John's Gospel (Jn 7:2–12). "Now the Jews' feast of Tabernacles was at hand. So his brethren said to him, 'Leave here and go to Judea, that your disciples may see the works you are doing. For no man works in secret if he seeks to be known openly. If you do these things, show yourself to the world.' For even his brethren did not believe in him" (Jn 7:2–5). This section highlights two facts: (1) The brothers of Jesus sought to maintain solidarity with their young charismatic brother, despite some disappointment. They showed a personal interest in his work from the natural desire that the work of their brother might be recognized and that they might share something of his fame. (2) The disciples of Jesus in Judea who were faithful to Jesus also retained a link to the influential leaders in Jerusalem.

Who were these Jewish disciples of Jesus? They could have been different families from Bethany near Jerusalem[12] or disciples from

[11] Cf. chapter 8, "Riddles of the Synagogues at Capharnaum" (pp. 115–27).
[12] Cf. chapter 17, "Bethany by Jerusalem—an Essene Settlement?" (pp. 227–38).

Emmaus (Lk 24:13ff.). But in my view it would have included sympathizers from the Essene community on Mount Zion.[13] John reported at the beginning of his Gospel that Jesus drove the dealers out from the temple during the preparation days of a Passover feast (Jn 2:13–23). By this courageous act, many had become aware of him: "Many believed in his name when they saw the signs which he did" (Jn 2:23). It is certain that the cleansing of the temple made a big impact in the Essene community, among whom many were priests (p. 197). The most significant criticism by the Essenes of the Sadducee temple priests was the desecration of the temple. Although the Essenes continued to visit the temple because it was God's dwelling, they refused to sacrifice there as long as it was desecrated (*Ant.* 18.19). They particularly objected that the Hasmonean high priests had introduced for the temple service a calendar of feasts and were no longer using the biblical model but a Babylonian-Persian one (pp. 416–17).

The enthusiasm for Jesus by those Jewish groups who were critical of the dominant temple service did not meet with the expected response from Jesus: "But Jesus did not trust himself to them, because he knew all men and needed no one to bear witness of man; for he himself knew what was in man" (Jn 2:24f.). This statement not only acknowledges a "godly knowledge" but could also mean that he had knowledge of these Essene groups from earlier pilgrim trips to Jerusalem in the company of his brothers. This time, however, was not an occasion for renewed relationship because Jesus understood that the faith he proclaimed represented a significant problem. He was not seeking for "astonished admiration" but discipleship. His brothers wanted to direct Jesus' ministry but not to follow him because at this stage, "his brethren did not believe in him" (Jn 7:5).

From the beginning, commentators have given contradictory answers to the question of the response of Jesus' brothers to his message.[14] This presented for many a difficult and perplexing problem. Jesus announced that he was not going to the Feast of Tabernacles in Jerusalem. However, later he did go to the celebration at the temple, but secretly (Jn 7:2–14). I believe that the best solution for this is that it relates to two different calendars. According to the Qumran finds, we

[13] Cf. chapter 15, "The Essene Quarter in Jerusalem" (pp. 192–219).

[14] Cf. R. Schnackenburg, *Das Johannesevangelium*, 2nd ed., vol. 2 (Freiburg: Herder, 1977), 179f.

now recognize that at the time of Jesus, there were in use two different calendars of feasts. The Sadducees and the Pharisees observed one, and the Essenes and related groups observed another. Jesus, who during his public ministry in Capharnaum went about primarily among Pharisaic groups, observed at this time, with his disciples, the normative temple calendar.

Jesus said to his brothers: "'My time [ὁ καιρὸς ὁ ἐμός] has not yet come, but your time is always here.... Go to the feast yourselves; I am not going up to this feast, for my time has not yet fully come.' So saying, he remained in Galilee" (Jn 7:6–9). Jesus did not use in this case the word "hour" (ὥρα), which is used elsewhere in the fourth Gospel in reference to his hour of death (Jn 2:4; 7:30; 8:20; 13:1), but *kairos*, i.e., "the appropriate time", in order to state that the time for a decision had not yet arrived. In the book of Daniel, in the vision concerning the Syrian king Antiochus Epiphanes IV (175–163 B.C.), who attempted to destroy Jewish worship, it is written: "He shall think to change the times [sacred seasons] and the law" (Dan 7:25). In the Septuagint, the word for fixed times or seasons, i.e., the calendar of feasts, is the same Greek word, καιροί.

The brothers of Jesus therefore went alone to Jerusalem to the Feast of Tabernacles, which was probably not celebrated in the temple area but on the southwest hill of the city. This area was in the settlement area of the Essenes, where the different calendar prevailed (the solar calendar of the Jubilee Book). According to this calendar, the celebrations occurred normally before those in the temple. When the time came for the normative tabernacle celebration, Jesus went up with his disciples to Jerusalem. He celebrated there together with the people in the temple, and it was here that he taught (Jn 7:14). "About the middle of the feast Jesus went up into the temple and taught." He stood next to the altar of sacrifice, where, during the solemn procession, the water for the altar was collected from the pool of Siloam, and he said: "If any one thirst, let him come to me and drink. He who believes in me, as the Scripture has said, 'Out of his heart shall flow rivers of living water'" (Jn 7:37).

It is probable that Jesus suffered from the tension between the two groups, which were both important to him. From a citation in a Jewish Christian Hebrew Gospel that we shall discuss later, we can conclude that James had something to do with the choice of the place for the Last Supper. It is not unreasonable to assume that this deeply religious, ascetic Nazarene was the contact man between Jesus, the Twelve and the Essene Chassidim on Mount Zion. Reconciliation between the religious and physical families of Jesus occurred as he hung on the cross. By his feet there were two people who were particularly close to him but who also symbolically represented the two groups: the Mother of Jesus for his family, and the favorite disciple (John, son of Zebedee) for the disciples. Jesus asked both groups to take care of each other: "'Woman, behold, your son!' Then he said to the disciple: 'Behold, your mother!' And from that hour the disciple took her to his own home" (Jn 19:26f.). From the cross, where he wished to "draw all men to [him]self" (Jn 12:32), he brought reconciliation to these two communities. This reconciliation was a fruit of his death. After the Resurrection of Jesus and his Ascension, both groups united in the Upper Room, i.e., the Eleven, "together with the women and Mary the mother of Jesus, and with his brethren" (Acts 1:14).

IV. The Apostle and the Ascetic

For James the major turning point came when the resurrected Christ appeared to him and made him thereby with the Eleven a witness and Apostle of the Resurrection faith. The Jewish Christian tradition recorded this event in the Gospel of the Hebrews:[15] "The Lord went to James and appeared to him. James had vowed that he would not eat any bread from that hour, since he had drunk from the cup of the Lord, until he would see him rising up from the dead. Shortly thereafter the Lord said: 'Bring a table and bread!' He took bread, said the prayer of thanksgiving, broke the bread and gave it to James, the Righteous, and said to him, 'My brother, eat your bread, because the son of God rose from the dead.'" According to the list of those to whom the resurrected Christ appeared in the First Letter to the Corinthians (1 Cor 15:5–7), James and Peter were the only ones to experience a single appearance.

Thus the Lord's brother steps into the spotlight after the Easter events. He was the only Apostle whom Paul found in the year 37 in Jerusalem, when he lived half a month with Peter (Gal 1:18). An interesting

[15] *Gospel of the Hebrews* 7 (Hennecke-Schneemelcher, 1:147). Cf. also A. F. J. Klijn, *Jewish-Christian Gospel Tradition* (Leiden: Brill, 1992), 79–86.

comment is found in Epiphanius of Salamis (315–403), who shows a Jewish Christian influence (p. 401) that allowed him access to the old traditions from the Jewish Christian groups. Epiphanius says that the three (οἱ τρεῖς) (the sons of Zebedee, James and John, as well as the Lord's brother James) followed the same way of life (πολιτεία): they remained single, "for the sake of the kingdom", wore white linen clothes and lived a hard, ascetic life.[16] This way of life was similar to that of the Essene monks, whose monastery was located near the place of the Last Supper. If "the three" went to live on the southwest hill of Jerusalem—perhaps, however, only after A.D. 70 called Zion (pp. 336–38)—then surely the tradition is genuine that Mary the Mother of Jesus lived there and belonged to this close circle.[17]

V. The First "Bishop" of Jerusalem

In the year A.D. 43 James the Elder (the son of Zebedee) was executed by Herod Agrippa I (Acts 12:1f.), and Peter was released from prison and left Jerusalem (Acts 12:3–17) after giving the care of the church there to the Lord's "brother". "Tell this to James and to the brethren!" was the last command of the departing Peter (Acts 12:17). Although Acts uses the expression "brethren" (ἀδελφοί) normally in the broader sense, apparently as in Acts 1:14, here Jesus' blood relations around James who were influential in the early Christian Church are meant. While the circle of the Twelve resumed the worldwide mission work of the Church, the activity of the Davidic family was limited to Jerusalem and Israel. James was their undisputed head.

His reputation as a law-abiding, pious Jew worked as a "protective wall around his people" (περιοχὴ τοῦ λαοῦ), as Eusebius wrote (*HE* 2.23.7). This was particularly true following Stephen's murder in A.D. 34, the persecution of the Hellenists (Acts 6–8), and the persecution under Agrippa I in the year A.D. 43 (Acts 12). According to the tradition, James had two honorary titles: "the Righteous One" (צַדִּיק [*zaddik*], δίκαιος) and "Obl[i]as" (Ωβλ[ί]ας). The latter, somewhat mysterious, title seems to be important for our understanding of the mentality of the Early Church. Two authors, the Jewish Christian writer Hegesippos from the second century (*HE* 2.23.7) and Bishop

[16] *Panarion* 78.13 (PG 42:720; GCS 37:463f.).

[17] Cf. chapter 30, "Mary on Zion" (pp. 398–407).

Epiphanius from the fourth century,[18] report that the Lord's brother carried this title "because the prophets announced him as such". "Obl[i]as" comes from the Aramaic *ophla'* (עִפְלָא) or Hebrew *ophel* (עֹפֶל) and refers to the prophetic word of Micah: "And you, O tower of the flock, hill [*ophel*] of the daughter of Zion, to you shall it come, the former dominion shall come, the kingdom of the daughter of Jerusalem. Now why do you cry aloud? Is there no king in you?" (Mic 4:8–9a). *Ophel* means "the protected hill", in Greek *akra* (ἄκρα), a word that is used again and again for the hill of Zion (p. 347). James' title thus connects him to Zion.

Only those who understand something about the law-abiding Jew can understand the drastic decision incumbant upon James the *zaddik* when the Apostles met around the year 50 in Jerusalem for the first council (Acts 15; Gal 2:1–10). Peter had come especially to Jerusalem; John was still there. Around the time of the Apostles' council, Mary may have died. The Jewish Christian legend in the so-called *Transitus Mariae* ("Mary's homecoming"), probably used in the liturgy, reports that the Apostles gathered again in Jerusalem around her deathbed.[19]

Barnabas and Paul had stated good reasons that circumcision and observation of the law should not be imposed upon the newly baptized Gentiles. After Peter had spoken, the answer from James was clear and courageous: "Therefore my judgment is that we should not trouble those of the Gentiles who turn to God" (Acts 15:19). It was an event of historical consequence when the three "pillars" (Gal 2:9)—James, Cephas and John—at the end of the Council of Jerusalem shook hands with Barnabas and Paul in recognition of their mission of the "law-free gospel". From then on, two branches of Christianity had begun: the church of the circumcision and the church of the Gentiles (Gal 2:7–9).

The speech of James during the first council contains the famous prophecy of Amos (Amos 9:11f.) about the reestablishment of the House of David, which had been purged (Acts 15:15–18). Although James did not say so, he must have regarded his own leadership position in the community of this New Covenant as a return to the religious meaning of David's house. The Amos quotation was particularly valuable to the Qumran Essenes. We find it both in the Damascus Document (CD 7:16) as

[18] *Panarion* 78.7.7 (PG 42:709; Klijn-Reinink, 196).

[19] *Transitus Mariae* A 1 (Baldi, 737f.).

well as in the so-called Florilegium from Cave 4. This *pesher* (commentary) that expounds on the Amos text is of special interest: "The Lord explains to you that he wants to build a house for you: 'I will establish the throne of his kingdom forever. I will be a father to him, and he shall be a son to me' [2 Sam 7:11–14]. That is the branch of David [צֶמַח דָּוִיד], who together with the interpreter of the law will arise and live on Zion [בְּצִיּוֹן], as it is written: 'In that day I will raise up the booth of David that is fallen. This house of David I will reestablish, in order to deliver Israel' [Amos 9:11f.]" (4QFlor 1:10–13).

If one considers this and other passages from the Qumran writings, we can assume that the Essene converts to Christianity were strong followers of David's descendants, Jesus and James, the Lord's "brother". Members of such Jewish Christian circles, who were strongly affected by Qumran messianic thinking, would have believed that through James, the Davidic rule was restored in a religious sense, so that something of the glory of David lived on. *David ha-melech chay wekayyam* (חַי וְקַיָּם דָּוִיד הַמֶּלֶךְ), "King David lives and exists further": these words are written above the legendary Tomb of David (pp. 322–25) on today's Mount Zion and are still sung today by the Jews. Such thoughts would also be a characteristic of the first Jewish Christians. From this Davidic enthusiasm it was appropriate to call the southwest hill of Jerusalem "Zion", and it was on this hill that the newly anointed Davidic dynasty resided (pp. 336–37).

Local Davidic enthusiasm is particularly evident in the Lucan writings, which often stem from sources that have their origin among the Jerusalem community (pp. 431–32). This is particularly evident in the childhood story of Jesus in Luke's Gospel and in the *Benedictus*: "[He] has raised up a horn of salvation for us in the house of his servant David" (Lk 1:69). The *Benedictus* (Lk 1:68–79) was probably one of the hymns that was sung on Mount Zion (p. 407) before it was taken up into Luke's Gospel. The Davidic renaissance is probably also emphasized in the *Teaching of the Twelve Apostles*, which originated in Syria at the beginning of the second century and which speaks about the "holy vine plant of thy servant David" in the Eucharistic prayers (*Did.* 9–10). If the Mother of Jesus lived in this Davidic family circle, she naturally left her personal memories as hereditary property.

Paul was the acknowledged Apostle for the Gentiles since the Council of Jerusalem but remained connected to the church of the Jews and their leader (cf. Rom 15:25–27). Everywhere he collected eagerly "for the poor among the saints at Jerusalem" (Rom 15:26). He brought the collection around the year A.D. 57 to Zion, where he was received by James and by his whole council, solemnly and in a friendly manner (Acts 21:18ff.). James sought to convince Paul that he should state his loyalty to Judaism because "the crowd [πλῆθος] will certainly gather when they hear that you have come" (Acts 21:22 [papyrus 74; Codex Sinaiticus]). Who is meant by "the multitude", which is also used in Acts (p. 362) and which was involved in important decisions (Acts 15:12)? The word used suggests that the group was similar to an Essene plenary assembly, which in the Qumran writings is called a gathering of "the many" (p. 382). The Jesus believers who originated with the Essenes surely looked to the law-abiding Davidic James (see Acts 11:2f.) as their *mebakker* (מְבַקֵּר). This Hebrew word for the leader of the Essene settlement (e.g., 1QS 6:12ff.; CD 9:18ff.) comes, just like the Greek *episkopos* (ἐπίσκοπος), from a word stem with the meaning "to observe, to exercise supervision". Some commentators understand the Essene *mebakker* as a model for the Christian "bishop".[20]

VI. The Martyr's Ordeal

The probably well-meant advice from James to Paul, to prove his Jewish righteousness by a gesture in the temple (Acts 21:18–26), did not have the desired outcome. The accusations that had preceded Paul from the Diaspora were too persistent (Acts 21:27–36). He was seized in the temple, and only his transfer to Caesarea saved him from certain death (pp. 426–27). But the accusation against Paul as "a ringleader of the Nazorean sect" (αἵρεσις τῶν Ναζωραίων), produced by the high priests and their followers, by which they actually meant the Jewish Christians (Acts 24:5), is now recognized as not directed just against Paul but really focused on the main leader of the Nazoreans on Zion. But the blameless life of this law-abiding Jewish Christian and his reputation with all the people prevented any direct action.

An opportunity was offered at Easter in the year A.D. 62. The high priest Ananos, the youngest son of the high priest Annas and brother-in-law of Caiaphas, before whom Jesus had been judged (cf. Jn 18:12–14), plotted against the Lord's "brother". As Flavius Josephus reported,

[20] Cf. H. BRAUN, *Qumran und das Neue Testament* (Tübingen: Mohr Siebeck, 1966), 2:328–32.

"this violent and bold man" used the interregnum between the two Roman procurators in order to accuse the venerable head of the Jesus community and have him killed (*Ant.* 20.197–203). From Hegesippos we learn that James was thrown from a pinnacle of the temple, where he had given a glowing testimony, and was stoned. With his last strength he prayed for his killers, when he was struck dead with a club (*HE* 2.23.10–19). His corpse was buried on the slope of the Kidron Valley under the temple (illus. 40). Perhaps this grave was already mentioned in the Copper Scroll from Qumran (3Q15 11:1–4) as the "tomb of Zaddok".[21]

In the past the feast of James, as well as the one for King David, was celebrated on Zion on December 26.[22] Today Greek and other Eastern liturgies still dedicate the Sunday after Christmas to the memory of James, Joseph and David. In the Latin liturgy, the Lord's "brother" is unfortunately still in the shadow of the Apostle James, the son of Alphaeus (May 11), but the Benedictine abbey on Mount Zion and the Uniate Eastern rites, together with the members of the Orthodox churches, celebrate on October 23 the feast of this important and fascinating man from the Early Christian Community in Jerusalem.

[21] Cf. B. Pixner, "Unravelling the Copper Scroll Code: A Study on the Topography of 3Q15", *RQ* 11 (1983): 323–65 (at 355f., n. 45).

[22] Hesychius, *Quaestiones in Jacobum fratrem Domini* (PG 93:1480). Cf. Baldi, 481f., n. 3.

29. Jesus and His Life in Light of New Qumran Texts

The belated publication of the Qumran texts and particularly that from Cave 4 led unfortunately to speculations and untenable proposals. Thus it was stated, for instance, that the founder of the Qumran community, the so-called Teacher of Righteousness, might be John the Baptist (B. E. Thiering) or the Lord's "brother" James (R. H. Eisenman),[1] and it has even repeatedly been mistakenly asserted that Jesus was an Essene. Granted, Jesus came from a family that was influenced by the Essene community, but he went his own way. Although by the end of his ministry he was back in touch with the Essene groups in Jerusalem, during his ministry in Galilee he was more inclined to the teachings of the Pharisees of the Hillel school.[2] The recently found Qumran texts should not be misused in order to make sensational and unsubstantiated assertions about Jesus, but these texts can help us understand better the historical context for Jesus, John the Baptist and the Lord's "brother" James.

I. *The Plurality of the Jewish Groups*

Today most reputable Qumran researchers have stopped calling the Essenes a "sect". During the Second Temple period all three principal Jewish groups—which is to say the Sadducees, Pharisees and Essenes—were accepted as valid forms of Jewish living. The autobiography of Flavius Josephus serves as an illustration for this. He was a descendant of an aristocratic priestly family of Sadducees in Jerusalem (*Life* 1–6).

[1] Cf. the refutation in O. BETZ and R. RIESNER, *Jesus, Qumran and the Vatican: Clarifications* (New York: Crossroad, 1994).

[2] Cf. B. PIXNER, "Jesus and His Community between Essenes and Pharisees", in L. L. JOHNS, *Hillel and Jesus: Comparisons of Two Major Religious Leaders* (Minneapolis: Fortress, 1997), 193–224.

He wrote about his youth: "At the age of sixteen I decided to gain personal experience of the different groups into which our people are divided" (*Life* 9). After he had received training in all three religious traditions, he spent time in the desert with an ascetic, Bannus (*Life* 11f.), whose way of life reminds one very strongly of John the Baptist (cf. Mk 1:6). Only after three years of intensive exposure to the various religious traditions did Josephus decide to follow the Pharisees (*Life* 12).

All three religious movements regarded the Torah as their most important law, but each of the groups interpreted the law in their own way. They principally differed in the halakha, i.e., the practical application of the law to life. One other main difference between the groups was the question of the calendar. Philo and Josephus both omitted reporting this, but it has become clearer through a detailed study of the Qumran texts that the calendar disputes were a strong cause for the separation of the Essenes (cf. 1QpHab 11:4–8),[3] which is now confirmed by a halakhic letter from Cave 4 of Qumran called *4Q Miqsat Ma'ase ha-Torah*, i.e., "something of the works of the law" (4QMMT). Several copies of the letter have been found. Many researchers attribute the text to the "Teacher of Righteousness". At the beginning of the letter it states that one may observe only the year of the sun's 364 days (4QMMT A 2f.). For the first time in this letter we encounter the Hebrew verb פרש (*parash*) in the sense of religious "separation", giving the name to the "Pharisee" religious group. The Qumran community says, "We have separated ourselves from the majority of the people" (*paraschnu mi-rob ha-cam*) (4QMMT C 7). The city of Jerusalem is important in this text, and it is described as the "holy [war] camp" (מחנה הקודש [*machaneh ha-qodesh*]) (4QMMT B 60). That helps us understand why the Essenes took the opportunity to return to Jerusalem during the reign of Herod the Great (37–4 B.C.).[4]

II. *John the Baptist and Isaiah 61*

Since Mary, the Mother of Jesus, was related to the mother of John (Lk 1:5, 36), she had intimate contact with a family who seemed to

[3] Cf. chapter 32, "The Jerusalem Essenes, Barnabas and the Letter to the Hebrews" (pp. 415–22, esp. pp. 416–17).

[4] Cf. chapter 15, "The Essene Quarter in Jerusalem" (pp. 192–219).

have Essene inclinations,[5] which we can assume from the background of John the Baptist. As it is evident that John's initial ministry was carried out near Qumran and other Essene and hermit settlements in the area of Jericho,[6] it is not unreasonable to assume that he came from this movement or at least had much sympathy for them.[7] His strong moral demands and his urging for the baptism of redemption (Lk 3:8) point also to Qumran (1QS 3:4–11). However, John must have left the Essene movement at a certain time in order to begin his own ministry, which, unlike that of the Essenes, was directed to "the masses" (cf. Lk 3:7, 10).

How close his thinking was to Qumran's can be deduced from an answer that Jesus gave to a delegation that had been sent by the imprisoned Baptist: "Go and tell John what you have seen and heard: the blind receive their sight, the lame walk, lepers are cleansed, and the deaf hear, the dead are raised up, the poor have good news preached to them" (Lk 7:22). These words resemble surprisingly a fragment from Cave 4 of Qumran, which has only very lately been published:[8] "The Lord will visit the pious [cf. Lk 1:68], and the righteous ones will be called by their names.... He will free the prisoners, make the blind see.... He will heal the wounded and will raise the dead and proclaim good news to the poor" (4Q521 line 5.8.12). The Qumran fragment and the answer Jesus gave refer to the prophecy of Isaiah 61:1f. The Baptist heard these words, which were very familiar to him from his parent's house (cf. Lk 1:78), and they were reinforced during his time with the Essene groups in the desert (cf. Lk 1:80).[9]

III. The Lord's "Brother" James and Isaiah 11

How was it that James, who did not belong to the closest circle of the Twelve, attained such high reputation that the future of the Jerusalem Primitive Community was entrusted to him? It was so outstanding that even Paul, when he was listing the pillars of the Jerusalem

[5] Cf. chapter 2, "Mary in the House of David" (pp. 23–37).

[6] Cf. O. Betz, "Kontakte zwischen Christen und Essenern", in B. Mayer, *Christen und Christliches in Qumran?* Eichstätter Studien, n.F., 32 (Regensburg: Pustet, 1992), 157–75 (at 159–64).

[7] Cf. chapter 14, "Bethany on the Other Side of the Jordan" (pp. 177–91, esp. p. 177).

[8] R. H. Eisenman, "A Messianic Vision", *BAR* 17, no. 6 (1991): 65.

[9] Cf. also chapter 28, "James the Lord's 'Brother'" (pp. 380–93).

community, notes: "And when they perceived the grace that was given to me, James and Cephas and John, who were reputed to be pillars [στῦλοι], gave to me and Barnabas the right hand of fellowship, that we should go to the Gentiles and they to the circumcised" (Gal 2:9). After the escape of Peter from Jerusalem during the Passover feast in the year A.D. 43, the Apostle John apparently remained in Jerusalem.[10] However, it was not he but James who took over the leadership of the Jerusalem community (cf. Acts 12:17). Surely the close relationship of James to Jesus[11] was the main reason for his authority in Jerusalem, but there were also other reasons.

The Qumran writings show us that the Essenes also diligently waited for a Messiah from the House of David. A recently published parchment note from Cave 4 makes clear the importance of Isaiah's prophecy about the "shoot" (נֵצֶר) from the Davidic root (Is 11:1) in their messianic expectations.[12] Even if the part that mentions *nezer* was unfortunately missing, we follow the text reconstruction and translation by Professor G. Vermes of the University of Oxford:[13] "And it will come about that the bud from the roots of Isaiah ... the branch of David [*zemah dawijd*] and they will step into the court hearing ... and the prince of the community, the branch of David, will kill him ... with beatings ... and wounds" (4Q285 lines 2–5). Believers such as the Jerusalem Essene Christian converts who regarded such prophecies very highly must have embraced the royal Davidian origin of James with great enthusiasm and preferred this to the common background of the Twelve.[14] James' strict ascetic lifestyle reported by the Jewish Christian Hegesippos would also have been an influence (*HE* 2.23). This was the position of the Lord's "brother" in the Early Christian Community, and it was very similar to that of an "overseer" (*mebakker*) in the Essene communities (p. 392). It was this that became the model for the Christian bishop.

[10] Cf. Epiphanius, *Panarion* 78.13.4 (PG 42:270; GCS 37:464), and also chapter 30, "Mary on Zion" (pp. 398–407, esp. pp. 403–4).

[11] The assumption that the "brothers of Jesus" were sons of Joseph from his first marriage (pp. 380–81) is now also taken seriously by R.J. BAUCKHAM, *Jude and the Relatives of Jesus in the Early Church* (Edinburgh: T. & T. Clark, 1989).

[12] Cf. chapter 1, "The Nazoreans, Bethlehem and the Birth of Jesus" (pp. 3–22).

[13] "The 'Pierced Messiah' Text—an Interpretation Evaporates", *BAR* 18, no. 4 (1992): 80–82 (at 81).

[14] Cf. chapter 26, "The Essene Quarter and the Primitive Christian Community" (pp. 360–68).

30. Mary on Zion

In the year 1910 on Mount Zion in Jerusalem, the basilica "Dormitio Mariae" was dedicated. The Benedictine monks, who had been entrusted with the church since 1906, believe that this was the place where, after Jesus' Resurrection, Mary the Mother of Jesus lived and also died. I wish to examine whether this widespread tradition is reliable, and I will begin with the archaeological and literary investigations.

I. The Excavations near the Dormition Abbey

In the year 1898 a Catholic association from Cologne acquired the area that had an ancient tradition as the home of Mary (κοίμησις *dormitio*).[1] The memory of the Eastern Christians was linked to a stone cross[2] that the Jerusalem patriarch Sophronius perhaps mentioned in A.D. 635.[3] This stone is today built into the tower of the Dormition Abbey.[4] The excavations that were undertaken during the preparation of the building of the basilica showed that under today's church, the foundations of the famous Byzantine basilica Hagia Sion are to be found.[5] We know from a report of a pilgrimage in the year 670 by the Gallic bishop Arculf that he visited the northwest corner of the large

[1] The traditional testimonies were collected by Baldi, 737–52, and B. BAGATTI and E. TESTA, *Corpus scriptorum de Ecclesia Madre*, vol. 4, *Gerusalemme*, SBFCMa 26 (Jerusalem: Franciscan Printing Press, 1982), 169–87. For the prehistory of the foundation of the abbey, cf. O. KOHLER, "Sancta Sion: Zur Entstehung von Kirche und Kloster Dormitio Beatae Mariae Virginis auf dem Südwesthügel Jerusalems", *Jahrbuch des Deutschen Evangelischen Institutes für Altertumswissenschaft des Heiligen Landes* 2 (1990): 99–119.

[2] Cf. M. GISLER, "Sancta Sion und Dormitio Dominae: Ihre Verbundenheit im Grundplan", *HlL* 79 (1935): 2–13 (5).

[3] *Anacreontica* 20 (PG 87:3821; Baldi, 740).

[4] See a photo by A. GOERGEN, *"Dormitio": Die Basilika der Benediktinerabtei Maria Heimgang—Berg Zion/Jerusalem*, Kleine Kunstführer 1800 (Munich: Schnell und Steiner, 1990), 8.

[5] Cf. H. RENARD, "Die Marienkirchen auf dem Berg Sion in ihrem Zusammenhang mit dem Abendmahlssaale", *HlL* 44 (1900): 3723.

basilica, which was considered and venerated as Mary's "resting place"—the place of Mary's death (*dormitio*).[6]

More than ninety years ago, excavations were undertaken on Mount Zion, but these did not discover any sign of very ancient veneration, comparable to the "house of Peter" in Capharnaum (p. 126). There were some indications nevertheless that this area was held in great veneration. A particular indication is the presence of a burial site. The location considered as the "house of Mary" is surrounded by an ancient Christian graveyard. The phenomenon of burial in proximity to a venerated holy place, such as Bethlehem (pp. 18–19), Gethsemane or the Holy Sepulchre, is a typical Byzantine custom.

More recent excavations were undertaken in 1983. The Benedictine community was able to buy from the Franciscans a small garden in front of the Dormition Abbey in order to build a small porch. According to the law in Jerusalem, the Benedictine community was obliged to conduct an archaeological investigation of the area, right down to bedrock, under the supervision of an Israeli archaeologist.[7] The excavations discovered (1) the foundations of the Crusader church Sancta Maria in Monte Sion (pp. 353–56) and (2) the mosaic from the atrium of the Byzantine basilica Hagia Sion (illus. 60). However, the most interesting excavations were undertaken in the lowest stratum, which was from a period between the first century B.C. and the early first century A.D. (before A.D. 70). This was the time of the oldest Jewish Christian community on Zion.

Approximately 20 m west of the proposed *dormitio Mariae*, the archaeologists were able to expose, in a 4-m-deep excavation, a road hewn into the rock, running from the north to the south. On both sides of the road there were houses that were very simple in design, built from undressed stone. In one of the houses on the eastern side was discovered an interesting Jewish ritual bath (Hebrew: *mikveh* [מִקְוֶא]), which is still *in situ* with half a column still present in its center. Today this kind of ritual bath is well known, since they have been found in many Jewish houses from the time of the Second Temple period.[8] There are records of excavations from the beginning of the century that have discovered other similar ritual baths (illus. 88), even closer to the

[6] Adamnanus, *De locis sanctis* 118 (Geyer, 243; Baldi, 489).
[7] Cf. E. EISENBERG, "Church of Dormition", *ESI* 3 (1984): 47.
[8] Cf. N. AVIGAD, *Discovering Jerusalem* (Nashville: Thomas Nelson, 1983), 139–43.

venerated place of the house of Mary, but they were not recognized as such at that time.[9]

The ritual baths discovered appear much smaller than those that were found further south (illus. 43), in the area of the "Gate of the Essenes" (*War* 5.145), where a monastery similar to the one on Qumran was located.[10] These ritual baths were bigger and better built and probably served a community, i.e., the Essene monks. The much smaller ritual baths that were found in the area of the Dormition Abbey seem to indicate that the inhabitants of this area were poor but pious Jews who had the baths for private use. The majority of the members of the Primitive Christian Community belonged certainly to this category. The so-called *Transitus Mariae*, of which we will hear more of later, says that Mary, when the day of her death was revealed to her, took a bath.[11] These ritual baths stand at the beginning of the tradition of Christian baptism.

All buildings on Mount Zion were destroyed in the year A.D. 70. On one of the steps of the bath that we excavated, I found a coin from the second year of the Jewish Revolt, i.e., from A.D. 67 or 68. The archaeological stratum was from the debris and destruction dating from the year 70 and of the houses destroyed by the soldiers of Titus. There is no doubt that the Last Supper room, the place for the meetings of the first Christians, was also destroyed during this comprehensive disaster. Many ancient sources and archaeological investigations confirm the view that this Jewish Christian meeting place, around the year A.D. 75 and following the return from Pella, was rebuilt as a Jewish Christian synagogue.[12] This Jewish Christian synagogue was partly preserved in the building of the so-called Tomb of David, to which the tradition of the "Upper Room" (ἀνάγαιον [Mk 14:15 / Lk 22:12]; ὑπερῷον [Acts 1:13]), i.e., the place of the Last Supper, clung.

II. Mary's Stay on Zion

John of Damascus, a monk of the monastery Mar Saba in the Judean desert who lived around 700, described the celebration of the Assumption Day of Mary: "Zion, mother of all churches of the world, was

[9] H. RENARD, *HlL* 44 (1900): 16–18.
[10] Cf. chapter 15, "The Essene Quarter in Jerusalem" (pp. 192–219, esp. pp. 209–13).
[11] *Transitus Mariae* A 1 (Baldi, 737).
[12] Cf. chapter 25, "The Apostolic Synagogue on Zion" (pp. 319–59).

the constant domicile of the Mother of God after the Resurrection of her Son. Here on a couch . . . she died a Virgin."[13] This is a beautiful picture: Holy Zion, mother of all churches, was the place of the residence of Mary, the Mother of Jesus. A century before, two patriarchs, who followed each other on pilgrimage in the year 634, described Zion as the place of Mary's homecoming [dormition and assumption].[14] Before these two witnesses from the time of the Arab conquest, we have no reliable records about Mary's homecoming, such as we possess about the place of the Last Supper on Zion.

A very strange but interesting remark was made by Bishop Epiphanius of Salamis (315–403). He originated from Palestine and showed a good knowledge of the local traditions. Probably born into a Jewish Christian family,[15] he joined the large imperial church and became a monk and then the abbott of the monastery of Eleutheropolis (Beth Guvrin) in south Judea. He draws our attention to the fact that Holy Scripture does not say anything about Mary's death. He seems to know, however, that Mary lived at that time with John, but she did not accompany him on his various journeys (see below). Epiphanius mentions that at that time on Zion (and in Mamre) the memory of Abraham's sacrifice (Gen 22) was regularly celebrated.[16] He seems to know even more about the death and tomb of Mary but says: "I do not dare to say anything, and although I have an opinion myself, I prefer to stay silent. Perhaps we will find still somewhere more traces of the holy and blessed Virgin Mary."[17] Why this restraint? He was considered a "defender of orthodoxy" but perhaps did not dare to express himself about a cult place that was still in the hands of Jewish Christian "heretics". The anti-Semitism in the fourth century was so strong that it was directed not only at the Jews but also at the Jewish Christians. We can conclude therefore that during the lifetime of Epiphanius, Mary's tomb was in Gethsemane and the dwelling on Zion was still in the possession of Jewish Christians. They jealously retained those places against the increasing influence of the Byzantine Gentile Christians.

[13] *Homilia in dormitionem Mariae* (PG 96:729; Baldi, 7421).

[14] Modestos, *Economium in Beatem Virginem* (PG 86:3288–99; Baldi, 740); Sophronius, *Anacreontica* 20 (PG 87:3821).

[15] Cf. Agapius (Mahbub), *World History* (PO 8:406).

[16] *Panarion* 18.2.4f. (PG 41:260; GCS 25:216).

[17] *Panarion* 78.11.3 (PG 42:716; GCS 37:462).

About the death and burial of Mary there is another very old, legendary document, which originally came from the synagogue liturgy of the Nazorean Jewish Christians. It is known as the *Transitus Beatae Mariae Virginis*, and it can be summarized as follows: Christ appears to Mary in the shape of an angel and announces that she must leave this life after three days. Joseph of Arimathea lets the other members and the believers know. Mary, who anticipates the arrival of her Son with longing, prepares herself by taking a bath, dresses like a queen and settles down on a couch. The Apostles and the relatives meet. Jesus appears in a bright light and leads Mary's soul into heaven. Her body is washed and dressed by three virgins. The funeral procession, which is to lead from Zion to Gethsemane, is gathering. There then occurs a strange incident, which is represented often in the iconography of the dormition. A Jewish priest seizes the bier of Mary by force in order to throw the body to the ground, but his hands remain stuck to the bier. Moved by fear, he pleads for the Apostle to help him. The prayer of the Apostle permits him to withdraw his hands. He kisses Mary's feet and converts. In Gethsemane, Mary is buried in the lower part of the necropolis.

The *Transitus* seems originally to have been a liturgical text also used by the Jerusalem Jewish Christians, and it exists in various forms. Professor B. Bagatti of the Studium Biblicum Franciscanum in Jerusalem believes that the version of the Codex Vaticanus No. 1982 is the most reliable and retains many elements of the original text.[18] According to Bagatti, a copy of this text could have been taken from Jerusalem to Asia Minor by the bishop Melito of Sardes during his visit to the Holy Land around the middle of the second century. The text is full of Jewish Christian symbols and concepts; e.g., Jesus appears in the shape of an angel, on a cosmic ladder, revealing secrets. It uses a language and concepts that predate the Council of Nicea (325) and that were eventually considered heretical. Professor F. Manns of the Studium Biblicum Franciscanum published a thorough investigation of this important text, which confirms its antiquity and its connection to the Johannine school.[19] The literary sources and the archaeological

[18] "Ricerche sulle tradizioni della morte della Vergine", *Sacra Doctrina* 69/70 (1971): 185–214.

[19] *Le récit de la Dormition de Marie (Vatican grec 1982)*, SBFCMa 33 (Jerusalem: Franciscan Printing Press, 1989).

tradition clearly confirm that after the Resurrection, Mary lived on Zion, and her dormition was also there.

III. Mary and the History of the Primitive Community

This Jerusalem tradition about Mary probably becomes more plausible when study is made of the history of the Primitive Community. Mary was present during the birth of the Early Church on Zion. Acts confirms that on the Ascension Day of Jesus, the disciples returned from Jerusalem, and "they went up to the upper room [ὑπερῷον], where they were staying" (Acts 1:13). Among the 120 believers, two groups became distinctive: (1) the eleven disciples and the women from Galilee (Acts 1:13f.; cf. Lk 8:2f.) and (2) the circle of Jesus' family, i.e., his Mother and his brothers (Acts 1:14). On all of them the Holy Spirit came down (Acts 2), and so Mary stands at the beginning of the Primitive Community. After the martyrdom of Stephen (A.D. 34) the community started to scatter (Acts 7–8). First through the Hellenists (Greek speaking Jews and Christians) and then also through the Apostles, the faith was spread among the Samaritans and then later among the Gentiles. After the persecution of Herod Agrippa I (A.D. 43), Peter also fled from Jerusalem and left the leadership of the church [in Jerusalem] to James, the "brother" of the Lord (Acts 12). The church of the circumcision is in a special way connected with the Davidic family of Jesus.[20]

In the writings of Epiphanius of Salamis, which have many references regarding the situation of the Primitive Community, we find the remark that "the three" (οἱ τρεῖς), i.e., the Zebedee brothers John and James and James the Lord's "brother" (the Lesser), followed an ascetic way of life[21] that was very similar to that of the Essene monks. According to our excavations these Essenes lived in a monastery very close to the Last Supper room on Zion (pp. 415–17). If this is true, then we may conclude that the Lord's "brother" James (the Lesser) and the Zebedee son John, whose brother James (the Greater) was executed in the year A.D. 43 (Acts 12:1f.), lived together on Zion. Since the Lord's "brother" James was the oldest one of the family of Jesus (pp. 380–81) and John as the favorite disciple was connected

[20] Cf. chapter 28, "James the Lord's 'Brother'" (pp. 380–93).

[21] *Panarion* 78.13.4 (PG 42:720; GCS 37:464).

particularly with Mary due to the last will of Jesus (Jn 19:25–27), that suggests that Jesus' family also must have had their dwelling on Zion.

The note from the *Transitus* that Mary was surrounded by all the Apostles on the day of her death,[22] which is contained in all versions of the apocryphal writing, could have a historical kernel. The narration, according to which this unexpected meeting occurred in a marvelous way, with the Apostles arriving in Jerusalem on clouds, is too fantastic to be believed. We do know though that according to Acts, there were a large number of Apostles in Jerusalem in order to decide on the mission methods of Paul and Barnabas (Acts 15:1–34). This meeting in Jerusalem, the so-called Apostolic Council, must have taken place around A.D. 50. Peter came back especially for this, and John was still in Jerusalem. It is not mentioned in Acts, but Paul confirms this in his letter to the Galatians, in which he mentions this meeting: James, Cephas and John, the three "pillars" (στῦλοι) of the Church, offered the right hand of fellowship as a sign to Barnabas and Paul of the goodwill of the community (Gal 2:9). They recommended that Paul take care of the poor in the Jerusalem community (Gal 2:10). The remains of the poor houses that we found on Zion confirm the consequences of the desperate lack of food in A.D. 47 and 48 (*Ant.* 20.101) and the necessity for the large collection, which Paul obtained from other Christian communities for the poor believers in Jerusalem (1 Cor 16:1–4; 2 Cor 8–9; Rom 15:25–28).

We can imagine that Mary's death on Zion occurred during the duration of this apostolic gathering. Around A.D. 50 Mary would have been approximately 70 to 75 years old (p. 34). One assumes with good reason that it was much later (after the outbreak of the Jewish War in the year 66) that John went to Ephesus. It is not very likely that the Virgin at her advanced age could have accompanied him to the Gentile city of Ephesus in order to die alone, far removed from her relatives, as is suggested by a modern interpretation of a vision of Catherine Emmerich. The older tradition is clear that Mary lived and died in Jerusalem. Even after the martyrdom of the Lord's brother James in the year A.D. 62, Jesus' family members continued to play an important role on Zion; thus Simeon Bar Cleopas, a cousin of Jesus, became the second Jewish Christian bishop of Jerusalem.[23]

[22] *Transitus* A 1 (Baldi, 737f.).

[23] Cf. chapter 31, "Simeon Bar Cleopas, Second Bishop of Jerusalem" (pp. 408–14).

His rival candidate for the election was a former Essene priest called Thebutis, probably the founder of the Ebionites, who denied the virgin birth and the preexistence of Jesus. I assume that an element of truth lies in the narration of the *Transitus* concerning the Jewish priest who touched the stretcher. It could be an echo of the opposition of these Ebionite circles against the teachings of the virgin birth. Probably there were already, during Mary's lifetime, among the Jewish Christian groups people with Ebionite sympathies who did not want to accept Mary's testimony. So we can also understand the words of old Simeon in the temple, when he said to Mary: "(and a sword will pierce through your own soul also) that thoughts out of many hearts may be revealed" (Lk 2:35). Thus Mary became, just as Jesus before her, a "sign that is spoken against" (Lk 2:34).

In this case we should follow the famous American commentator R. E. Brown when he says that in Luke's Gospel there are traces of opposition toward the teaching of the Ebionites.[24] By closer investigation of Luke's geographical knowledge,[25] I believe that he did not know Galilee from his own observation, but he demonstrates a good knowledge of Jerusalem and its environment, and I am convinced that Luke had personal knowledge of the Holy City. In the prologue to his Gospel, he emphasizes that "from the beginning were eyewitnesses and ministers of the word" (Lk 1:1f.). When Luke relied on eyewitnesses, he could have found them easily if he was in Jerusalem in the year A.D. 75 and moving among the relatives of Jesus, including Simeon Bar Cleopas. It seems to me that the author of the third Gospel actually made use for the first two chapters of his Gospel of the work of a Haggada, written in Hebrew, which originated from Jesus' family. Only from a source like that could he have gained such intimate facts of the birth and childhood of Jesus.

This message had been hidden perhaps from Mark, Paul and the other Apostles. For a famous person, people are initially more concerned with what he had said and had done and how he died. It was only later that people began to be interested in the circumstances of his birth and his youth. Who else would know Jesus' family traditions better than Mary? If we compare the two childhood stories written by Luke and Matthew, then it becomes clear that the latter's version

[24] *The Birth of the Messiah* (New York: Doubleday, 1979).

[25] Cf. chapter 33, "Luke and Jerusalem" (pp. 423–32).

originated from a completely different family circle than the traditions Luke used. But both traditions are correct at two crucial points: Jesus was born of a virgin,[26] and the place of his birth was Bethlehem.[27] Some speak of a Marian source for Luke and a Joseph source for Matthew.[28]

IV. Mary's Life on Zion

With this historical and topographical background we can imagine Mary's life on Mount Zion following Jesus' Resurrection. We see that Mary probably lived with John. Their neighbors were James "the Lesser" and other relatives from David's house who had moved there from Nazareth. Their dwellings, as we saw earlier, were probably poorer than the average houses in Jerusalem. In the Last Supper room Mary could meet with the others for prayer and for the "breaking of bread", the Eucharist (Acts 2:42). Frequently she visited the temple (cf. Lk 24:53; Acts 5:12), particularly on the Sabbath. In time, the first day of the week, on which Jesus had risen, became the "Lord's day" (Rev 1:10; *Did.* 14.1). The Essenes, who lived in that area, also held the first day of the week in great reverence (pp. 417–18), because on the first day of creation, light and darkness were separated by God (Gen 1:3–5; cf. *War* 2.128).

Certainly Mary would have kept all the Jewish celebrations: the important Feast of Reconciliation (Yom Kippur) with its solemn fasting (Lev 17), the Feast of Tabernacles (Lev 23), the Feast of Weeks (Pentecost) and above all the Passover feast (Easter). Wednesday was the day of the Essenes' Easter, but the Christian community fasted on this day (*Did.* 8.1), on which, through his imprisonment, the Bridegroom was taken away (see Mk 2:20). Also on Friday one fasted, because the Lord was executed on that day.[29] On the night from the Sabbath to Sunday, they also fasted as an act of remembrance of the Lord's silence in the tomb and the Resurrection. It was on this "night of nights" that the Jewish Christians expected Jesus' return, the Parousia.

Mary probably lived in a quite secluded way on Zion. Other people from the outside would hardly have noticed her presence, but the

[26] Cf. chapter 2, "Mary in the House of David" (pp. 23–37).

[27] Cf. chapter 1, "The Nazoreans, Bethlehem and the Birth of Jesus" (pp. 3–22).

[28] Cf. W. Feneberg, *Jesus der nahe Unbekannte* (Munich: Kösel, 1990), 9–14.

[29] Cf. chapter 18, "The Last Supper of Jesus" (pp. 239–49).

whole community was influenced by her demeanor and her religious observance. James and the other Apostles made the decisions about the development of the Church, and Mary celebrated their successes but suffered also the fears of persecution. She was certainly a thoughtful and meditative woman. Luke stressed that very strongly: "Mary kept all these things, pondering them in her heart" (Lk 2:19; see also 51). It is from Luke's Gospel that we have the memories and meditations of Mary in the light of the Resurrection of her Son. These memories were passed on at first secretly within the family, then collected and made into the form of a Hebrew Haggada. Luke has taken up this Haggada in his Gospel together with the songs of the Jewish Christian community on Zion, such as the *Benedictus* (Lk 1:68–79), the *Magnificat* (Lk 1:46–55) and the *Nunc Dimittis* (Lk 2:29–32). So Mary became also the Mother of the Jerusalem Primitive Community and the heart of the developing Church. Zion became the cradle of Christianity. Mary stood beside the cradle of the mystical Christ, as she had stood next to the cradle of the God-man Jesus at Bethlehem.

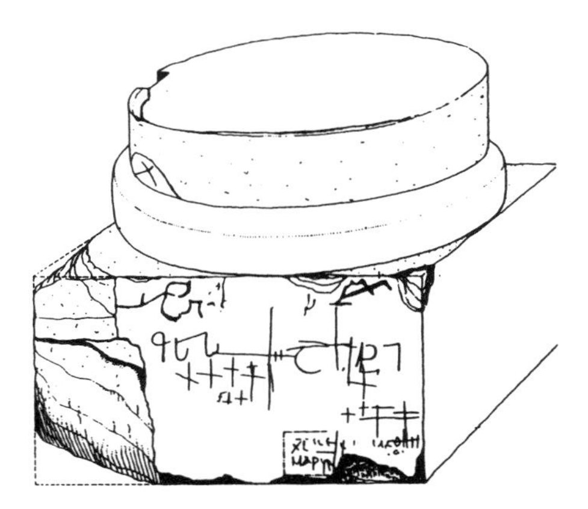

Illus. 94. Graffiti on a column of the synagogue church of Nazareth from the fourth century (according to E. Alliata, O.F.M.). Below right, in the designated square, it reads X (αιϱ) E MAPIA, *"Greetings, Mary" (see Lk 1:28).*

31. Simeon Bar Cleopas, Second Bishop of Jerusalem

I. Jesus' Cousin

Joseph of Nazareth had a brother called Cleophas (Κλεοφᾶς) or Clopas (Κλωπᾶς, קְלוֹפָּא),[1] who had a son called Simeon (Συμεών, שִׁמְעוֹן) or Simon (Σίμων), who became the second bishop of Jerusalem (*HE* 3.11). Simeon led the church of the Jews through the difficult period of the catastrophic war against Rome (A.D. 66–70). It was thanks to his efforts that the Jewish Christian community recovered and became a vibrant Christian community. Eusebius described it as "the very large church of the Jews" (μεγίστη ἐκκλησία ἀπὸ Ἰουδαίων συγκροτουμένη) that blossomed until the second destruction of the Holy City in A.D. 135.[2]

In the year A.D. 62 the Lord's brother James,[3] "the Just", had been killed in the temple through the machinations of the high priest Ananos, the son of Annas (pp. 392–93). An important witness about the development of the Early Christian Community after this martyrdom is the report of Hegesippos, the most reliable witness of the Apostolic period,[4] with his five books (ὑπομνήματα) written around A.D. 180 (*HE* 4.22:1). Unfortunately, today only fragments of these books remain. Hegesippos reports that after the death of James, the remaining surviving Apostles and disciples of the Lord met in one place: "They met together with those who were related by blood to the Lord, of whom

[1] Cf. R. RIESNER, "Kleopas", in *GBL*, 2nd ed. (1990), 2:794. [The name in English is also spelled Cleopas.]

[2] *Demonstratio Evangelica* 3.5 (GCS 23:131; Klijn-Reinink, 138).

[3] Cf. chapter 28, "James the Lord's 'Brother'" (pp. 380–93).

[4] Cf. L. HERRMANN, "La Familie du Christ d'après Hégésippe", *Revue de l'Université de Bruxelles* 42 (1936/1937): 387–94; B. GUSTAFSSON, "Hegesippus' Sources and His Reliability", *Texte und Untersuchungen* 78 (1961): 227–32.

many were still alive. Together they discussed who would merit taking the place of James. Unanimously they all voted for Simeon, the son of Cleopas who is mentioned in the Gospel [Lk 24:18; Jn 19:25], as worthy of the bishop seat with dignity. He was a cousin of the Redeemer" (*HE* 3.11).

In a parallel place Hegesippos reports: "After James, with the appellation 'the Just', had suffered the same martyrdom as the Lord, because of his teachings, a cousin of his, Simeon, the son of Cleopas, became bishop" (*HE* 4.22.4). In the literary sources there is some uncertainty as to whether the choice of Simeon Bar Cleopas occurred before or after the destruction of Jerusalem (cf. *HE* 3.11). Perhaps the problem is to be solved by the fact that the election took place soon after the death of James and after the destruction of Jerusalem (A.D. 70) and, after the return of the community from the areas beyond the Jordan, was confirmed a second time.

II. The Breaking Up of the Community

A monk named Alexander (540) describes Zion as the location of the election.[5] The consequences of this election seem to have been of great importance for the Jewish Christian community. Hegesippos reported that a certain Thebutis, who had counted on becoming bishop, rebelled because he was disappointed and insulted. This caused, according to Hegesippos, the first split of the Church, "which had been so far an intact virgin" (*HE* 4.22.4). Thebutis was therefore the first schismatic and also a heretic. What else might we say about Thebutis? (1) He must have been an important personality of the Early Church, if he considered himself as selectable. (2) He originally came from one of the seven Jewish sects, reports Hegesippos (*HE* 4.22.5). He was, thus, not, like the Apostles (see Acts 4:13), from the *am-ha'arez* (unskilled people of the country) but most probably from a certain group of trained teachers. (3) Eusebius describes seven Jewish sects, according to their attitude toward the tribe of Judah and Christ. Quoting from Hegesippos, Eusebius begins his description of the Jewish groups with the Essenes as the most positive and finishes by contrasting them with the Pharisees as the most extreme opponents (*HE* 4.22.7). It seems to suggest that Thebutis must have been in former times an important

[5] Baldi, 486.

Essene personality, an assumption that throws an interesting light on the position of the Essenes in the Early Church.[6]

The name Thebutis was not a common name and does not appear in the biblical literature, but it does appear in Flavius Josephus' *Jewish War* (*War* 6.387). Josephus mentions a Thebutis, the father of a priest named Jesus, who discovered hidden treasures following the fall of Jerusalem and acquired thereby Titus' favor and his own freedom. All this fits so well with the existence of the Essene quarter in Jerusalem[7] that I suggest that the Thebutis who was a rival to the Davidic Simeon and the priest Thebutis mentioned by Josephus were the same person.[8] Jesus, son of Thebutis, probably recovered the treasures from one of the hiding places that are mentioned in the Copper Scroll from Qumran (3Q15).[9]

If the above is correct, it provides an interesting perspective on the situation of the Jewish Christian church on the threshold of war against Rome. The rebellion of Thebutis was directed particularly against the strong influence of the Davidic family clan. One source of disagreement might have concerned the nature of leadership. Leadership, according to the Qumran doctrine, was always exercised by the priests. As the Temple Scroll reveals, even the king of Israel had to ask for their advice and benediction (11QTemple 56:20f.; 57:12f.; 58:18; 59:13–21). That applied also to the Davidian Messiah (4QpIs^{a} 161:22–24). Here also perhaps lies the source of the division of the Jewish Christians into the large church of the Nazoreans and the strongly Essene-influenced Ebionites (pp. 364–65). Did Thebutis become "Ebion" (Ἐβιών),[10] the archheretic and the founder of the Ebionites (Ἐβιωναῖοι)? Did their denial of the virgin birth and of the divinity of Jesus have its roots in a dispute with this family tradition? Did Luke, who discovered this tradition in the Jerusalem community (pp. 430–31), find it therefore necessary to expand Mark's Gospel and also include the history of Jesus' youth? It is quite possible that the emphasis in the Gospel on

[6] Cf. chapter 26, "The Essene Quarter and the Primitive Christian Community" (pp. 360–68), as well as chapter 32, "The Jerusalem Essenes, Barnabas and the Letter to the Hebrews" (pp. 415–22).

[7] Cf. chapter 15, "The Essene Quarter in Jerusalem" (pp. 192–219).

[8] "Sion III, 'Nea Sion'", *HlL* 111, nos. 2–3 (1979): 3–13 (at 11). Later, Prof. R. Riesner drew my attention to the fact that these correlations had already been made, i.e., by N. Hyldahl, "Hegesipps Hypomnemata", *Studia Theologica* 14 (1960): 70–113 (at 97).

[9] Cf. chapter 12, "The Copper Scroll of Qumran" (pp. 159–68).

[10] Cf. Epiphanius, *Panarion* 30.1.1—30.3 (GCS 25:333–380; Klijn-Reinink, 174–93).

the virgin birth and of Jesus as God's Son were directed against Ebionite teachings that sought to deny this. In particular Luke might have had in mind an Ebionite teaching that stressed that Jesus had only been a product of a union between Mary and Joseph and that he was adopted as the Son of God only at his baptism (cf. Mk 1:9–11).

III. The Escape to Pella

In the year A.D. 66 the Jewish War against Rome broke out. We know that at least one part of the Essene community participated in this war (*War* 2.151, 567). It is reported that the Jewish Christian community left Jerusalem and fled across the Jordan.[11] But why did they flee? Perhaps one reason was a response to the split in the Primitive Community following the activities of Thebutis and his extreme Essene views. Perhaps the departure was also caused by persecution following the execution of James. The reason was surely not that the Jewish Christians wanted to leave their compatriots in their national emergency. In my opinion, the principal reason was that the community expected the Parousia. There are indications for this in Mark 13, possibly the oracle mentioned by Eusebius (δι' ἀποκαλύψεως [*HE* 3.5.3]), which demanded an escape and is similar to the Parousia teaching in Mark (Mk 13:14ff.).

We have still another statement from an apocryphon that was written by an Essene-influenced Jewish Christian as a book of consolation, possibly during the period when the Jewish Christians were absent from Jerusalem. The book is known as the *Ascension of Isaiah*.[12] In a vision, Isaiah is shown the events that would take place among the community of God, of "the beloved" (Jesus), up to the war, which the godless king and mother murderer (Nero) would kindle against his people. The text seems to be directed against the activities of men such as Thebutis. Here are a few extracts:[13] "When the arrival of the

[11] Cf. Eusebius, *HE* 3.5.3; Epiphanius, *Panarion* 29.7.7 (GCS 25:330; Kijn-Reinink, 172); 30.2.7 (GCS 25:330; Klijn-Reinink, 176). For the reliability of the Pella tradition, cf. R. A. Pritz, *Nazarene Jewish Christianity* (Leiden: Brill, 1988), 122–27.

[12] Cf. P. Riessler, *Das altjüdische Schrifttum außerhalb der Bibel*, 2nd ed. (Heidelberg: Kerrle, 1966), 1300: "Die Himmelfahrt des Isaias ist die christliche Überarbeitung eines jüdischen, näherhin essenischen (2,11; 5,14) Werkes."

[13] *Ascen. Is.* 3:21—4:13 (E. Tisserant, *Ascension d'Isaïe* [Paris, 1909], 112–15). Cf. also J. H. Charlesworth, *The Old Testament Pseudepigrapha*, vol. 2 (New York: Doubleday, 1985), 161f.

Lord is approaching, there will be many different opinions. . . . People will strive after promotion . . . criminal presbyters and frivolous shepherds. . . . People will love money. . . . Believers who had seen the one who gave them hope, Jesus, the Messiah, and others who believed in him [without having seen him] will become a minority in those days, and they will flee from desert to desert in the expectation of his return."

"In the expectation of his return" is then the main motive for the exodus of the Primitive Community to Pella. Eusebius mentions this city in the Decapolis (*HE* 3.5.3) but actually provides only the area for the refuge (illus. 2), because they went "from desert to desert", probably in the mountains (Mk 13:14) of Gilead and Bashan, where later large communities of the Jewish Christians were living (pp. 173–74). We can imagine the cousin of the Lord hurrying from place to place, encouraging his Nazoreans to remain faithful and trying to heal the division during a very dangerous time. Meanwhile, the city of Jerusalem and the temple was reduced to ruins and ash under the onslaught of the destructive rage of the embittered Roman army. In the year A.D. 73 the last Jewish resistance in Masada was broken (*War* 7.252ff.).

IV. The Return to Jerusalem

The long-awaited Second Coming of the Lord had not arrived. Simeon Bar Cleopas gathered again his people around him and returned to Jerusalem to the place of the Primitive Community (*HE* 3.11). A later historian writes that the return had taken place in the fourth year of the reign of Vespasian (A.D. 73/74; see p. 336). It was at this time that the community began in earnest the building of a church. At the site of the destroyed "Last Supper room", a synagogue church was built whose remains are still visible today in the so-called Tomb of David.[14] It was at this time that the center for the Early Church was described as "Zion", and thus the west hill of Jerusalem was now understood as the location for the former City of David.

At this time the community around Simeon probably wrote a Hebrew Haggada about the life, youth and Passion of Jesus, which Luke then skillfully wove into his Gospel. The evangelist Luke demonstrates a very good knowledge of the topography of Jerusalem that is very detailed but very different from his incomplete knowledge of the north of the

[14] Cf. chapter 25, "The Apostolic Synagogue on Zion" (pp. 319–59).

country.[15] If this is the case, and he wrote from personal experience, he probably visited Jerusalem at the time when Simeon was the head of the church there. Then it is possible, as some authors believe,[16] that our Simeon is identical to the "other" Emmaus disciple (Lk 24:18), as this was suggested by Origen[17] and other writers (see *HE* 3.11; 3.32.4). If the Cleopas of the Emmaus story was his father, then Simeon and the community around him, who "were from the beginning eyewitnesses and ministers of the word" (Lk 1:2), were the very people that Luke carefully followed and recorded.

V. The Martyrdom

At the time of Emperor Vespasian (A.D. 69–79) and his son Domitian (A.D. 81–96), because of many rebellion attempts, there was a general persecution of the potential pretenders to the Jewish throne, particularly the descendants of David (*HE* 3.12, 20). Simeon initially escaped this persecution and reached the age of over one hundred (*HE* 3.32.3). But in the persecution of Domitian, two of Simeon's nephews, who had the Lord's brother Judas as their grandfather (Mk 6:3), were dragged before the imperial court in Rome (*HE* 3.20.1–6). After they had shown the emperor their calloused workers' hands, they were treated as poor insignificant peasants and were dismissed into their homeland of Galilee. There they took up prominent positions as witnesses to the faith and as Davidians.

Now a period of peace came to the Church (*HE* 3.32.6), during which the Christian faith was strengthened among the Jews. But the followers of traditional Judaism, led by the Pharisaic rabbinate, reorganized themselves and regarded the Nazoreans of Simeon as dangerous rivals, and this led finally to a complete break. In Jamnia,[18] on the coastal plain, the Pharisees established a new center for Judaism, and the scholars came to a decision to add to their daily prayers in the synagogue the so-called eighteen-prayer request, a prayer against the Nazoreans. This prayer was called *birkat ha-minim*, the "heretic's blessing". The Jewish Christians, who up to this date had more or less

[15] Cf. chapter 33, "Luke and Jerusalem" (pp. 423–32).

[16] Cf. T. Zahn, *Das Evangelium des Lucas* (Leipzig: Deichert, 1920), 710–13.

[17] *Contra Celsum* 2.62–68 (PG 11:893–901; GCS 2:184–89f.).

[18] Cf. R. Riesner, "Jabne/Jabneel", in *GBL*, 2nd ed. (1990), 2:637f.

been tolerated in the synagogue, were thereby completely excluded. The break between the Jewish Christian Nazoreans and the Rabbinic Jews was thus final and would never heal.

The end of Simeon Bar Cleopas, this great leader of the Primitive Community in Jerusalem, is reported to us by the Jewish Christian historical writer Hegesippos (*HE* 3.32), who was born probably around this time in Palestine. Hegesippos writes that under Emperor Trajan (A.D. 98–117) in some cities there were renewed rebellions by the Jewish people, which caused a persecution of the descendants of the royal lineage of the Jews. Simeon now was betrayed by other Jews as the cousin of the Lord, and the accusation was made "that he descended from David and was a Christian" (*HE* 3.32.3). For this reason he was placed in court under the proconsul Atticus. Although he was tortured for many days, he kept his faith. Everybody, even the proconsul, was surprised how such an old man could bear so much suffering.

When all art of persuasion and torture had failed, the command was given to crucify him. His authority had up to then, as Hegesippos says, kept "the Church as a pure, unstained virgin", and "those who sought to undermine the godly teaching of salvation kept themselves hidden away at that time, still in darkness" (*HE* 3.32.7). The Davidic family, which had traditionally retained faith in the virgin birth and the preexistence of the Son of God, by this time received the Gospels of Luke and Matthew (pp. 431–32), which demonstrate an anti-Ebionite perspective. Only with the death of Simeon was ended the "holy choir of the Apostles and that lineage that had paid tribute with their own ears and listened to the godly wisdom" (*HE* 3.32.8). But already in his time the Jewish Christian community had divided into the large Nazorean church and the Ebionite heretics. With this the crisis of the second century began. The Lord gave to his cousin a long life, so that he could be a witness and guard over the true records, in order to "seal finally his testimony by a death that was similar to the one of the Lord" (*HE* 3.32.2). The tomb of Simeon was on the slope of the Mount of Olives, and his feast day is celebrated on February 18. In the crypt of the Dormition Abbey on Zion, there is a stained glass window that commemorates the second bishop of Jerusalem, who from there led the Jewish Christian church.

32. The Jerusalem Essenes, Barnabas and the Letter to the Hebrews

I. *Essenes in Jerusalem?*

Several authors have expressed the opinion that there may have been an Essene monastery somewhere on the southwest hill (today's Mount Zion) at the time of the second temple. P. Seidensticker, for instance, in a much-discussed article, wrote that "surely such a group as [the Essenes] existed in Jerusalem, because there is a gate with their name (*Bell. Jud.* 5.4.2 [*War* 5.145]), in the proximity of which they probably had a monastery."[1] E. Schürer, P. Volz and M.J. Lagrange shared this opinion, and in his large commentary on Josephus' *Bellum judaicum*, O. Michel also expressed a similar view.[2]

Excavations undertaken at the southwest corner of Mount Zion by the Theological Faculty of the Dormition Abbey in partnership with the Israeli archaeologists Doron Chen and Shlomo Margalit succeeded in unearthing Seidensticker's Essene Gate,[3] and the investigations of the ritual bath structures plus other buildings near to it seem to confirm the opinion held by the researchers above: the reference to the Essene Gate, built in the early Herodian period into what was the existing town wall, suggests the emergence of an Essene settlement at that time.[4] Indeed, this bears out the theory that following the destruction of their monastery by fire in 37 B.C. and an earthquake in 31 B.C., the Qumran community was resettled in Jerusalem. Only later, at the

[1] "Die Gemeinschaftsform der religiösen Gruppen des Spätjudentums und der Urkirche", *SBFLA* 9 (1958/1959): 94–198 (at 129).

[2] *De bello judaico—Der jüdische Krieg: Griechisch und Deutsch*, vol. 2, pt. 1 (Munich: Kösel, 1963), 246, n. 41.

[3] Cf. B. Pixner, D. Chen and S. Margalit, "Mount Zion: The 'Gate of the Essenes' Reexcavated", *ZDPV* 105 (1989): 85–95.

[4] Cf. chapter 15, "The Essene Quarter in Jerusalem" (pp. 192–219).

time of Archelaus (4 B.C.–A.D. 6), was the monastery reestablished at Qumran as a second colony. This secondary settlement was completely destroyed in A.D. 68 in the Great War against Rome. Undoubtedly, then, in the first two-thirds of the first century A.D., there existed in the Holy City an Essene group, which the War Scroll from Qumran calls the "community [עֵדָה (*edah*)] in Jerusalem" (1QM 3:10f.).

II. *Life at the Monastery of the Essenes*

Herod the Great personally admired the Essenes, and following his victory over the Hasmoneans in 37 B.C. he granted them certain special privileges, including the opportunity to build their quarter in the southwest corner of Jerusalem, according to their halakha. The majority of the Essenes dwelling in the Holy City were probably priests and Levites but also some non-Levites, who belonged to the community and also had to fulfill the priestly purity regulations as God's "kingdom of priests" (Ex 19:6). For these Essenes, all of Jerusalem was the "camp of God" (מַחֲנֶה לֹאֵ [cf. 1QM 4:9]) but particularly their community, where they believed that the spirit of God dwelled. They visited the temple and seem even to have sent offerings (*Ant.* 18.19), but they did not sacrifice anything in person as they believed that the temple was contaminated by a secularized priesthood (p. 34). As much as possible they isolated themselves from the external world in order to await the arrival of two Messiahs and purified themselves by taking daily purity baths and eating communal "holy meals". In the "land of Damascus" they had made "a new alliance with God" (cf. Jer 31:31ff.; CD 6:19; 7:18–20) (p. 175), under the leadership of the "Teacher of Righteousness" (מוֹרֵה הַצֶּדֶק).

The daily routine of the Essenes was divided into three parts: a third of their day they dedicated to prayer, a third to writing and study, and a third to manual work (1QS 6:6–8). They welcomed the sunrise as a symbol of the triumph of the godly light with prayer and the singing of hymns (*War* 2.128). What differentiated the Essene groups, both the monks and the existing family communities, from most of the other Jews was the observation of their own solar feast calendar of 364 days, i.e., 52 × 7 days, aligned with the sun. For the sake of reconciliation, after a few years, a full week was added. Their celebrations always fell on a certain weekday: the Passover feast was on a Wednesday; the Sunday after the "week of unleavened bread" was always the celebration of wave offering; the Sunday fifty days later was Pentecost. On the seventh day after that was the celebration of new wine, and again seven days later on Sunday was the celebration of the new oils. The Temple Scroll from Qumran has given new insight into the Essene calendar of feasts (11QTemple 13:8—29:2).[5]

The Essenes were very hospitable to well-meaning or sympathetic strangers and provided visitors with their own guesthouses (*War* 2.125). Philo and Josephus respected the group greatly because of their holy lifestyle (pp. 195–96). The ordinary people called them *chassidim* (חֲסִידִים) in Hebrew and *chassayya'* (חַסַיָּא) in Aramaic, i.e., "the pious ones", from which the terms "Essenes" (Ἐσσηνοί) and "Esseias" (Ἐσσαῖοι) are derived. In monastic centers such as Qumran and probably in Jerusalem too, they lived under a *mebakker* (מְבַקֵּר), i.e., an overseer, who was usually a priest (cf. 1QS 6:3ff.; CD 13:2ff.). When Jesus spoke of "eunuchs who have made themselves eunuchs for the sake of the kingdom of heaven" (Mt 19:12), he could have been referring to a contemporary example (p. 190).

III. The Essene Settlement and the Primitive Community

One of the best-established facts of Jerusalem topography is that the Primitive Community developed on today's Mount Zion and therefore in close proximity to the Essene settlement.[6] Is contact between the Essene *machaneh* (camp) and the first Christian community suggested in the New Testament? Perhaps Jesus and his disciples, although definitely not Essenes themselves, had contact with them.[7] There is a possible reference in the report of the search for a place for the Last Supper (Mk 14:12–16 / Lk 22:7–15). Jesus had a premonition of his fate in the year A.D. 30 and held the Passover feast in the guesthouse of the Jerusalem Essene settlement. Thus Mrs. A. Jaubert[8] was correct in her statement that Jesus celebrated the last Passover feast according to the Essene calendar.

The place of the Last Supper on Zion became then the cradle of Christianity (Acts 13), and it had contacts with the Essene

[5] Cf. Y. Yadin, *The Temple Scroll*, vol. 1, *Introduction* (Jerusalem: Israel Exploration Society, 1983), 89–136. New evidence comes from a long unpublished text *Miqsat Ma^{c}ase ha-Torah* (4QMMT). Cf. A. Rabinovich, "Words of Light", *Jerusalem Post*, June 14, 1985, 6.

[6] Cf. chapter 25, "The Apostolic Synagogue on Zion" (pp. 319–59).

[7] Cf. chapter 18, "The Last Supper of Jesus" (pp. 239–49).

[8] *La date de la Cène* (Paris: Gabalda, 1957).

settlement.[9] Whatever the exact historical background for their activities at Pentecost were (Acts 2), one thing seems definite: a large group of these "pious ones" (cf. Acts 2:5), who had met in Jerusalem for the Feast of Pentecost, accepted the faith (pp. 361–63). The Essene calendar became an essential structure for the developing Church year, with Sunday as the main focus. The social structure of the Primitive Community was influenced by the Essene practice of sharing goods (Acts 2:44f.; 4:32). Many authors are convinced that those "great many of the priests [who] were obedient to the faith" (Acts 6:7) came from the Essene priest community,[10] and there are certainly many indications that there was within the Early Church a circle of former Essene priests who sought to carry out their previously adopted monastic ideals, but as Christians.

IV. The First Readers of the Letter to the Hebrews

With this background in mind, many modern authors believe that such a community was the intended recipient of the Letter to the Hebrews; in particular, Professor Y. Yadin of the Hebrew University in Jerusalem was fascinated by the possibility that the recipients of this letter must have been Essene priests.[11] Something similar is also expressed by H. Kosmala in his book concerning the relations between the Essenes and early Christianity.[12] Significantly too, G. W. Buchanan, professor at the Wesley Theological Seminary in Washington, D.C., in a comprehensive commentary in the Anchor Bible series, believes that the readers of the letter belonged to a strict Levitical and monastic community that aspired to a particularly high perfectionist ideal.[13] The purpose of the letter would have been to remind the discouraged group to stay steadfast and loyal to Christ. The fascinating cult of the temple in Jerusalem exercised a considerable attraction to the Levitical groups, and these were in danger of losing their faith in Christ. The author of

[9] Cf. in this volume, esp. chapter 26, "The Essene Quarter and the Primitive Christian Community" (pp. 360–68).

[10] Cf. the literature in nn. 11–13.

[11] "The Dead Sea Scrolls and the Epistle to the Hebrews", in *Aspects of the Dead Sea Scrolls*, Scripta Hierosolymitana 4 (Jerusalem: Magnes Press, 1958), 36–55.

[12] *Essener—Hebräer—Christen: Studien zur Vorgeschichte der frühchristlichen Verkündigung* (Leiden: Brill, 1959), 1–43.

[13] *To the Hebrews*, Anchor Bible 36 (Garden City, N.Y.: Doubleday, 1972), 257.

the letter sets them the ideal of Christ as the high priest according to the order of Melchizedek (Gen 14:17–24; Ps 110:4; cf. Heb 7:1–4). He praises their service for the "holy ones" in the Early Church and "in serving the saints" (Heb 6:10).

Buchanan is further convinced that the Letter to the Hebrews was written at a time when the temple service was still in full course: "In fact there is nothing at all in the homily 'To the Hebrews' ... to require a post–A.D. 70 composition."[14] Other authors are in agreement with Buchanan, who dates the epistle to around A.D. 65. At that time the Lord's "brother" James had just been killed (cf. Heb 13:7), and the Jerusalem community went through some great difficulties outwardly and inwardly.[15] Buchanan believes that the author was also a celibate monk and one of the "leaders" (Heb 13:7: ἡγουμένοι) of the resident groups in Jerusalem, probably including sympathetic believers and their families (Heb 13:4).[16]

Although the author never described himself or his readers as celibate monks, such a fact, according to Buchanan, can be discerned in the way the letter is expressed. Thus members were called "brothers", or "holy brothers", as is usual in monastic communities (Heb 3:1, 12; 7:5; 8:11; 10:19). The writer stresses the importance of the work and the love of one another (Heb 6:10; 10:24). He reminds them of their heavenly appointment (Heb 3:1; 9:7; 12:10, 14), the necessity for obedience (Heb 12:6f., 10f.) and their ideal of purity (Heb 2:14; 9:13). The entire membership is described in a way similar to the Essene community (הָרַבִּים [*ha-rabbim*]),[17] with the expression of "the many" (Heb 12:15: οἱ πολλοί). However, less convincing is the statement of "absolute sinlessness" demanded by Buchanan,[18] which could not have been taken seriously by someone outside of a monastic community: no one was allowed to have a bad and disbelieving heart (Heb 3:12); no one was allowed to turn back (Heb 4:11); all must be sanctified (Heb 12:14f.); and if one decides to leave, to separate, he was not allowed to return (Heb 6:6). Their ideal may not have been the Levitical priesthood but rather Christ as the high priest, who was without family (Heb 7:13) and fault (Heb 7:26).

[14] Ibid.

[15] Cf. chapter 31, "Simeon Bar Cleopas, Second Bishop of Jerusalem" (pp. 408–14).

[16] *To the Hebrews* (see n. 13), 264.

[17] This linguistic usage is common in the Community Rule (1QS), in the thanksgiving hymns (1QH) and in the Damascus Document.

[18] *To the Hebrews* (see n. 13), 256.

V. Barnabas and the Letter to the Hebrews

Some modern authors, such as J. A. T. Robinson,[19] are of the opinion that the author of the Letter to the Hebrews was Barnabas, as was testified by Tertullian[20] and Gregory of Elvira.[21] Actually, Barnabas was an outstanding Levite from a Cypriot family (Acts 4:36; 11:24). His sister Mary, the mother of John Mark, had made her house available to the Primitive Community for prayer meetings (Acts 12:12). Barnabas had sold his field and had followed the strict sharing of goods in the community (Acts 4:37). He seemed to have lived as a celibate, like Paul (1 Cor 9:6). The Jerusalem Apostles gave him the new name Barnabas to replace his former name Joseph (Acts 4:36), i.e., "son of the prophecy" (בַּר נְבוּאָה) or also "son of comfort" (בַּר נְוָחָא [cf. Heb 13:22: λόγος τῆς παρακλήσεως]). After his Cyprus mission in the company of Mark (Acts 15:39), Barnabas could have led this Jerusalem Christian group of monks as their "abbot" and teacher.

Taking up the thesis of Buchanan about this Christian Levitical community, I make the following proposal. There are many indications that this group had its monastery possibly outside of the first and second walls of Jerusalem (illus. 58), in the so-called Golgotha area. More recent excavations in the Armenian Crecor chapel[22] seem to show that after the building of the "third wall" by Agrippa I (ca. A.D. 43) some building activity took place on the rock of Golgotha (illus. 79). It would then be possible that Hebrews 13:12f. would also have a topographical-historical background: "So Jesus also suffered outside the gate in order to sanctify the people through his own blood. Therefore let us go forth to him outside the camp [ἔξω τῆς παρεμβολῆς], bearing abuse for him." The readers are to go from the "camp" of the walled Holy City (pp. 209f.) to the rock of Golgotha, which at the time of the crucifixion of Jesus was located outside the city, in the proximity of the excavated Gennath Gate (pp. 303–8). Also, with this particular reference, the author was able to develop his convincing cross and high-priest theology.

[19] *Redating the New Testament* (London: SCM Press, 1977), 200–220.

[20] *De pudicitia* 20 (PL 2:1021).

[21] *Tractatus Origenis* (ed. P. Battifol [Paris, 1900], 108).

[22] Unfortunately, there are only a few reports: C. Katsimbinis (with F. Diaz), "The Uncovering of the Eastern Side of the Hill of Calvary", *SBFLA* 27 (1977): 197–208; F. Diaz, "Golgotha: La recherche archeologique", *MB* 33 (1984): 28–36.

Since the beginning of the twentieth century, Mount Zion has been the site of a Benedictine monastic community (p. 398). For them, the Christian Chassidic monastery, with its adjoining community (Heb 10:25: ἐπισυναγωγή) and their exemplary leader, provides a model. The message of the Letter to the Hebrews is just as relevant today, despite new challenges, as an encouragement to remain faithful. On a stained leather scroll from the first cave of Qumran, a benediction was found with a blessing used by the Essene priests (1QS 2:2–4), and this probably often rang out on Mount Zion during the days of Jesus:

The Lord bless you with everything good
and protect you above all from everything bad.
May he illuminate your heart with insight of life
and give you graceful knowledge about the eternal.
He raises his benevolent face over you to the eternal peace.
Amen.

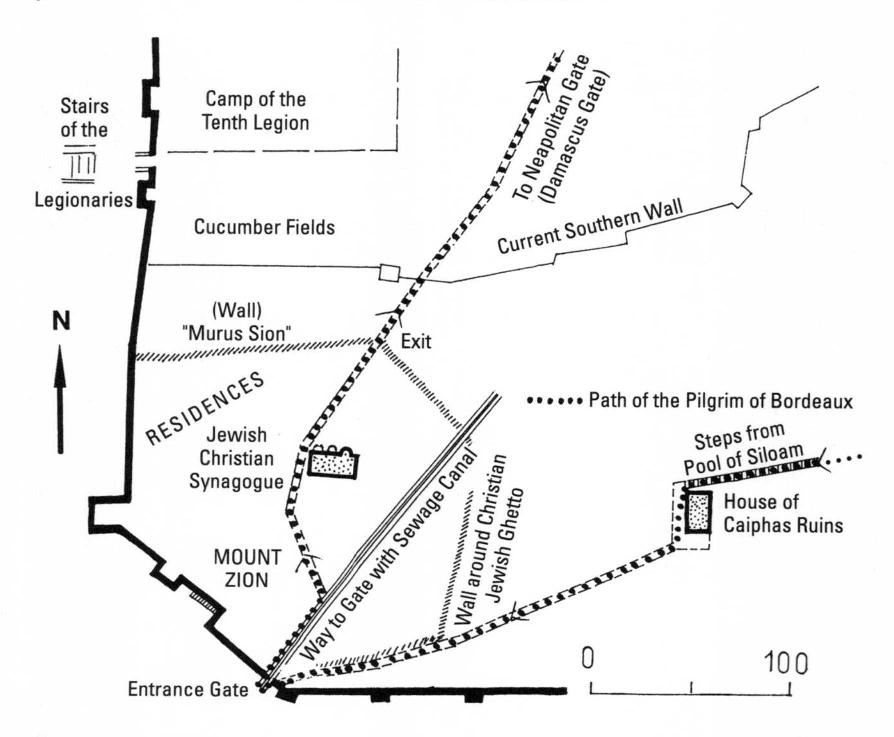

Illus. 95. Map of the southwest hill of Jerusalem in the first to the fourth centuries (according to D. Chen and B. Pixner, 1994).
Wall (murus Sion)*, third to fourth centuries*

33. Luke and Jerusalem

There is a surprising discovery in the geographical data that Luke provides. The author of Luke and Acts demonstrates an intimate knowledge of the topography of the Holy City and its surroundings, but this contrasts with the information he provides about the areas in the north of the country. This can be explained only if Luke personally knew Jerusalem and had visited it at least once.

When we consider the "we" reports of Acts, we can identify the personal memories of the author. Since the last journey to Jerusalem belongs to the "we" reports (Acts 20–21), the author must have visited the Apostle Paul together with the "Lord's brother" James (Acts 21:15–18). If this "we" report by the author is considered literally, as is believed by many, then the intimacy of the author with the topography of Jerusalem can be proven. In his Gospel, for which Luke used Mark's Gospel and a collection of sayings for his sources he edited the material in such a way that his detailed knowledge of the Jerusalem area is obvious, but it is clear that he lacks such precise data for the north of the country. This contrast cannot be explained simply by a consideration of the sources that he used because we would expect the same accuracy for the north as is demonstrated for Jerusalem. Acts also reveals a writer with a precise knowledge of the Holy City and the area along the road from Jerusalem to Caesarea by the coast. I wish to consider here in greater detail two of Luke's reports that are situated in Jerusalem and its surroundings: the entrance of Jesus to the Holy City and the capture of Paul.

I. Detailed Knowledge of Jerusalem and Its Surroundings

1. The Entrance of Jesus into Jerusalem

For the entrance into Jerusalem, Jesus came with his disciples from Jericho (Lk 19:1, 11). He naturally used the old Roman road from

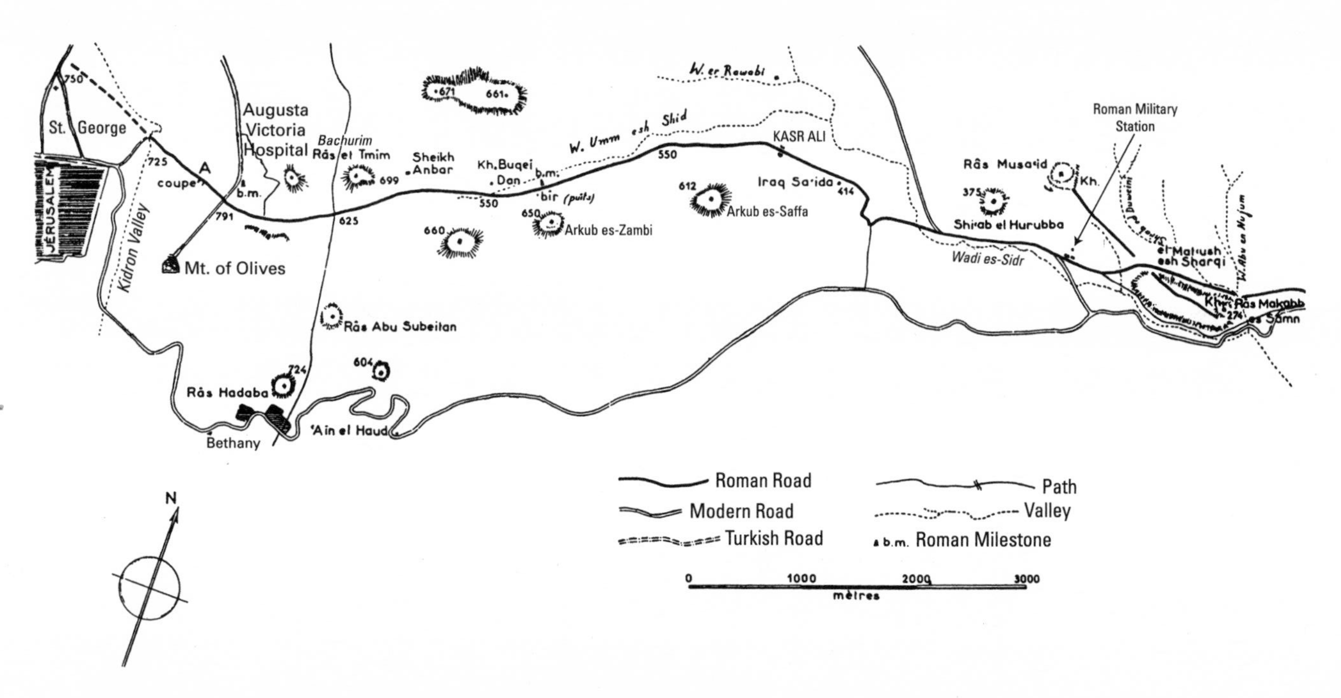

Illus. 96. The Roman road from Jericho to Jerusalem (according to R. Beauvery, 1957).

Jericho to Jerusalem,[1] which leads across the "saddle" of Ma^{c}ale Adummim, where today an Arab caravansary presents itself as the "lodging house of the good Samaritan". The road goes past the Roman military station of the Wadi es-Sidr, across the saddle of Kasr Ali, and along the north slope of the ridges Arkub es-Saffa and es-Zambi, where even today ancient milestones can be found lying about. The road then continues up to the hollow south of Bachurim,[2] then south of today's Protestant August a Victoria Hospice and finally across the Mount of Olives (illus. 53). The Pilgrim of Piacenza also used this path in about A.D. 570 while traveling from Jericho, passing the village Baorin (Bachurim) and other villages along the route in order to reach Bethany on the southeastern slope of the Mount of Olives.[3]

On the eastern slope of the Mount of Olives, the Roman road crossed the so-called old "way of sanctuaries", which connected Beersheba, Hebron, Mamre, Bethlehem, Rama, Bethel and Shilo. This is the path that Jesus took in order to reach, through the saddle of Bethphage,[4] the village of Bethany. From Bethphage, a path branches off; this takes a route across the southern slope of the Mount of Olives and then ascends, past Gethsemane, across the Kidron Valley to the Temple Mount. According to the Synoptics, Jesus selected this path (Mt 21:1 / Mk 11:1 / Lk 19:29) in order to ceremonially enter Jerusalem. According to John, he had come from Ephraim (Jn 12:1), today's es-Taybe,[5] across Bethany[6] to Jerusalem (Jn 12:12ff.). Luke follows Mark's report. After Jesus had left the Roman road in the company of his disciples, he took the path to Bethphage (Lk 19:29), which was on the eastern mountainside, of the Mount of Olives. He had to cross a small wadi. Bethphage lay south of it. When Jesus said to his disciples: "Go into the village opposite" (Mt 21:2 / Mk 11:2 / Lk 19:30), he was referring to Ras Haddad, which lies north of the wadi. The donkey was fetched from Bethphage by two of the disciples and brought to Jesus.

[1] Cf. R. Beauvéry, "La route romaine de Jerusalem à Jericho", *RB* 64 (1957): 72–101.

[2] Cf. 1 Sam 25:44; 2 Sam 3:16; 16:5; 17:18; 23:31; 1 Kings 2:8; and Josephus, *Ant.* 7.225.

[3] *Itinerarium* 16: "Ascendentibus nobis de montana in Hierusolima [from Jericho] non longe ab Hierusolima venimus in Baorin, deinde ad sinistram ad oppida Oliveti montis in Bethania ad monumentum Lazari" (Geyer, 107; Baldi, 1961).

[4] Cf. R. Riesner, "Betfage", in *GBL*, 2nd ed. (1990), 1:196.

[5] Cf. R. Riesner, "Ephraim", in *GBL*, 2nd ed. (1990), 1:322. [About this biblical place there is more research available by K. H. Fleckenstein, *Eine Stadt namens Ephraim (Johannes 11:54): Eine geschichtlich-geographische Untersuchung* (Lizentiatsthese Jerusalem, 1987).]

[6] Cf. chapter 17, "Bethany by Jerusalem—an Essene Settlement?" (pp. 227–38).

Until this point in the text, it was possible to state that the topographical background for Luke's Gospel came from a Marcan source. But from this point onward, Luke improves Mark's narrative with extra topographical details that expand his primary sources. Following the ascent to the Mount of Olives, there is a change as Luke writes: "As he was now drawing near, at the descent [κατάβασις] of the Mount of Olives, the whole multitude of the disciples began to rejoice and praise God with a loud voice for all the mighty works that they had seen" (Lk 19:37). The road ran at that time probably south of Eleona's cave (pp. 233–34), then across the area of the garden of the Mount of Olives and the present cemetery of the White Fathers.[7] The path initially drops gradually, and the upper city and the temple become progressively visible. Even today on the Mount of Olives, there are many stones lying around, and it is here that the author sets Jesus' argument with some Pharisees: "If these [the disciples] were silent, the very stones would cry out" (Lk 19:40). Following this there is a further topographical observation: "And when he drew near and saw the city he wept over it" (Luke 19:41). The author here knows that the city is not immediately visible from the road of the Mount of Olives. Only someone who had visited the area could write like this. The description demonstrates personal knowledge of the area. If Luke had written his Gospel sitting behind a desk in Antioch, he could not have given such a detail.

2. *The Capture of Paul*

Luke demonstrates a remarkable intimacy with the local conditions with the report about the capture of Paul in the temple (Acts 21:27–40). The riot he describes, where Asiatic Jews had plotted against the Apostle, must have occurred in the Court of the Israelites close to the sacrificial altar, because the Ephesian Trophimus could not have entered the Court of the Gentiles. Paul was seized there by the furious crowd and dragged through probably one of the northern gates. The "gates" were then closed (Acts 21:30), in order

[7] Because the empress mother Helen, in the years following A.D. 326, built over the Eleona cave, where the disciples received their teaching, a large church (Baldi, 385ff.), the paths could have been moved. At the time of Jesus, there were not many houses on the Mount of Olives, according to the Babylonian Talmud (*Pesachim* 14a) but fields that were regularly plowed.

to keep the crowd away from the sacred area. Perhaps that also happened in order to prevent Paul from returning to the altar, because touching the altar's horns would have allowed him to request asylum.

Outside, in the Court of the Gentiles, Paul ran the risk of being lynched by the furious crowd. But a report of the riot had reached the tribune of the cohort high in the Antonia castle[8] on the northwest corner of the temple square (Acts 21:31). The officer, with soldiers and centurions, hurried down to them (Acts 21:32), took Paul into protective custody and escorted him into the barracks. The castle Antonia (pp. 267–69) was used by the authorities as a military fortress, in order to control the activities in the temple, as Josephus reported (*Ant.* 15.292, 403–9). The Antonia, which stood on a rock that still exists today, was connected with the temple area by an outside staircase (ἀνάβαθμοι [Acts 21:35]). Since the crowd was pushing and pressing against Paul and the stairs, he had to be carried by the soldiers. When the Apostle had reached the highest step and the gates of the barracks were held open (Acts 21:34), he asked to be allowed to speak to the people. Standing on the stairway steps (Acts 21:40), Paul indicated to the crowd in the court to be quiet and gave his speech in Hebrew.

Flavius Josephus also describes these outside staircases, which gave the soldiers of the Antonia free access to the temple area. According to his report, the colonnade around the temple square was interrupted by the adjoining building of the Antonia fortress. Up to the Antonia there were two sets of stairs (καταβάσεις), one on each side, down which the guards could descend (*War* 5.243). As with the description of the entry scene, so also here, the data provided concerning the special architectural peculiarities of the temple and castle building demonstrates a well-informed local knowledge.

One could perhaps suggest that the source material that was at the author's disposal included very detailed place references. It is to be noted, however, that Luke possessed similar textual source material for Galilee and the remaining northern part of Palestine. But his own limited knowledge of the north seems to lack the sort of detail that is to be found here. This can be demonstrated in the following three examples.

[8] Cf. R. Riesner, "Antonia", in *GBL*, 2nd ed. (1990), 1:68.

II. Luke's Unsatisfactory Knowledge of the North

1. The Villages of Nazareth and Nain

Luke probably did not have his own local knowledge of Nazareth, which, according to the archaeological excavations, was at the time of Jesus hardly more than a hamlet[9] that probably belonged to the larger village of Japhia[10] (illus. 12). Nazareth is not mentioned elsewhere in either the Bible or any other contemporary literature. Nevertheless, Luke calls it generously πόλις (*polis*), a town, in Galilee (Lk 1:26; 2:4, 39) and writes that this town was built on a mountain (Lk 4:29), from its edge. Jesus was almost thrown down by its inhabitants (ἤγαγον αὐτὸν ἕως ὀφρύος τοῦ ὄρους ἐφ' οὗ ἡ πόλις ᾠκοδόμητο). Nazareth was situated on a small spur of a hill, of about 500 m on a north-south direction, which had steep slopes in some places. But probably Luke would hardly have described it as a mountain if he had known Nazareth himself. The description that Luke provides does not fit the local situation. A later local tradition located the mountain of the "fall" more than 2 km away, on the mountain Dshebel el-Kafze,[11] south of Nazareth, which is a rocky height above the plain of Jezreel. Luke also calls the small Galilean village of Nain[12] a πόλις, and he imagines it has a town wall, at whose gate (πύλη) Jesus raised the son of a widow from the dead (Lk 7:12).

2. The Feeding of the Five Thousand

While we could notice that, in the report of Jesus entering Jerusalem, Luke improves the Marcan text with his own local knowledge, twice he interpreted the Marcan data in Galilee differently from Mark. Mark, who reports two feeding miracles (and is followed by Matthew in this), has the first on the west bank, and the second one on the east bank, of Lake Gennesaret.[13] In Mark, Jesus takes a long walk (illus. 13),

[9] Cf. B. BAGATTI, *Excavations in Nazareth*, vol. 1, *From the Beginning till the XII Century*, SBFCMa 17 (Jerusalem: Franciscan Printing Press, 1969).

[10] Josephus, *Life* 230, calls it one of the biggest villages of Galilee; cf. R. RIESNER, "Jafia", in *GBL*, 2nd ed. (1990), 2:641.

[11] Baldi, 40f.; cf. also C. KOPP, *Die heiligen Stätten der Evangelien*, 2nd ed. (Regensburg: Pustet, 1964), 124–29.

[12] Cf. R. RIESNER, "Nain", in *GBL*, 2nd ed. (1990), 2:1022f.

[13] Cf. chapter 4, "Jesus' Routes around the Sea of Galilee" (pp. 53–76, esp. pp. 63–75).

which was also a spiritual journey.[14] From Capharnaum he goes to the "lonely place" (ἔρημος τόπος [Mk 6:31]), Tabgha, where the feeding of the five thousand occurred.[15] After the failed attempt by the disciples to reach Bethsaida, they landed in Gennesaret (Mk 6:53). There the abolishment of the *kashruth*, the Jewish food regulations (Mk 7:1–23), took place. Then they continued on their way into the Gentile area of Tyre and Sidon, where Jesus included the Gentiles in his mission: "Even the dogs under the table eat the children's crumbs" (Mk 7:28). Finally they reached the area of the Decapolis (Mk 7:31) after walking via a circular route across the Golan. At the lake, according to Matthew (Mt 15:29), the second feeding took place, on a hill (Mk 8:1–10). Jesus was with the crowd, which had already been with him three days, in a lonely area (ἐρημία [Mk 8:4]). The best location for this is probably Sheikh Chader (today Tell Hadar), a hill at the lakeshore, north of Kursi, which has traces of Israeli and early Arab settlements (pp. 68–70).

Luke seems to condense the miracle report. A reason for the omission of Mark 6:45—8:26 could be because of the abolishment of the *kashruth* (kosher regulations), which, according to the tradition that Luke regarded as the most accurate, came by the experiences of Peter in Joppa and Caesarea (Acts 10). Only one Marcan topographical detail concerning the feeding miracle narrative is included in Luke: Bethsaida (Lk 9:10). According to Mark, Jesus gives the order to his disciples following the first feeding to go ahead, across the lake, to the other side with the boat, to Bethsaida (Mk 6:46). In the past, as is still the case today, the Jordan's flow marked the boundary between the west and east banks. The place from which the disciples departed must have been on the west bank, which traditionally is called "Seven Springs" (Tabgha). Since the journey was not possible because of the strong wind, they landed in Gennesaret (Mk 6:53), which was at the foot of Tell Kinneret (Arabic el-ᶜOreimeh).[16] Luke's report does not include either the incident at Bethsaida or the one at Gennesaret, and he states that the miraculous feeding occurred in close proximity to Bethsaida, as he says: "He took them and withdrew apart to a city called Bethsaida" (Lk 9:10). Thus the evangelist describes the first

[14] Cf. also B. Pixner, *With Jesus through Galilee according to the Fifth Gospel* (Collegeville, Minn.: Liturgical Press, 1996).

[15] Cf. chapter 5, "Tabgha, the *Eremos* of Jesus" (pp. 77–99).

[16] Cf. R. Riesner, "Genezareth (Ort)", in *GBL*, 2nd ed. (1990), 1:439.

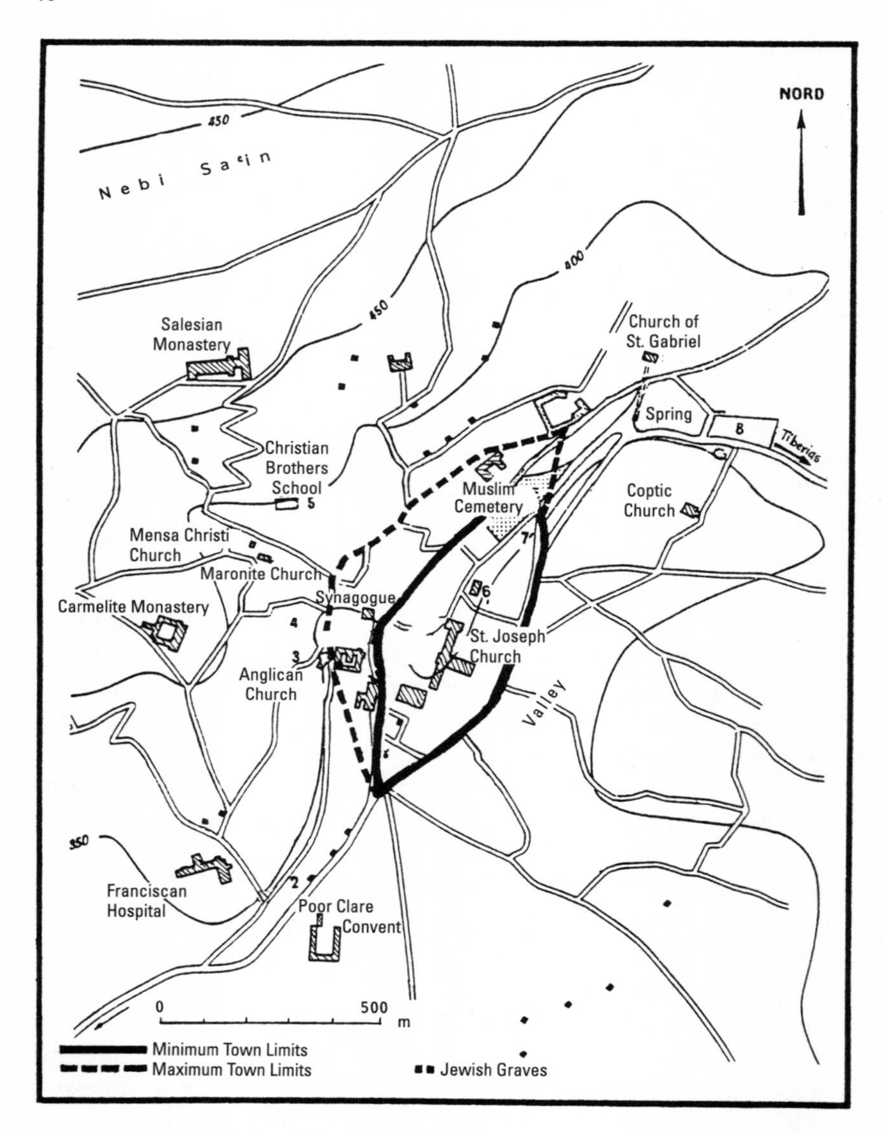

Illus. 97. Nazareth. The boundaries of the village during the New Testament period are indicated.

feeding in the geographical context of the second feeding. In John 6, only one feeding is reported, on a hill on the east bank of the lake (Jn 6:1–3). Only that uninhabited area offered an analogy to the desert migration of the tribes of Israel (cf. Jn 6:31).

3. The Departure to Jerusalem

Luke seems to have described the departure to Jerusalem, important for his understanding of Jesus' last journey, without any local knowledge and uses the topographical data very freely. In Mark 9:30 it says: "They went on from there and passed through Galilee." Luke might have used this Marcan statement as a starting point for his own narrative, but he makes the rather confusing geographical remark: "On the way to Jerusalem, Jesus was going through the region between Samaria and Galilee" (διὰ μέσον Σαμαρείας καὶ Γαλιλαίας [Lk 17:11]). It is difficult to imagine an actual route that would reflect this statement.

III. Luke and His Jerusalem Sources

This unequal treatment of the source material regarding the topography of Jerusalem and Galilee can be best explained if we consider that Luke possessed personal knowledge of Jerusalem in contrast to his knowledge for the north of the Holy Land. If Antioch was the homeland of the third evangelist, as is accepted by many commentators, then it was easier for him to visit Jerusalem. Luke needed to get on only one ship to go to Caesarea in order to go from there to Jerusalem. That journey would have taken only a few days. If Luke's intention was, as he states in the prologue to his Gospel, "investigating everything carefully from the very first" (Lk 1:3), then it is to be expected that he undertook such a journey, in order to question the best-informed members of the Primitive Community for the source material for his Gospel.

The prominent men of the community included at that time members of Jesus' relatives, including James, the Lord's "brother", who was the first leader of the Jerusalem community.[17] After James' martyrdom in the year A.D. 62, Simeon Bar Cleopas was selected as his successor; he was a cousin of Jesus and an eyewitness of the events around him.[18] In this family group, important traditions were treasured that went back to Mary, who had lived and died on Zion in Jerusalem.[19] The traditions of these Nazoreans about the virgin birth of Jesus in Bethlehem, reported in a Hebrew Haggada, were part of the christological dispute with the Ebionite branch of the Jewish Christian community.

[17] Cf. chapter 28, "James the Lord's 'Brother'" (pp. 380–93).
[18] Cf. chapter 31, "Simeon Bar Cleopas, Second Bishop of Jerusalem" (pp. 408–14).
[19] Cf. chapter 30, "Mary on Zion" (pp. 398–407).

Up to this point, perhaps the little-known fact of the virgin birth of Jesus in Bethlehem was probably communicated to the author of the third Gospel by members of this Davidian family group, and by his inclusion of this into his Gospel it became known to the wider Christian community.[20] Luke's visit to Jerusalem and his personal knowledge of its environment therefore plays a central role in his Gospel and in Acts.[21]

Supplement: In Nazareth the Jewish Christians possessed two sacred places during the Byzantine period. Under the Church of Saint Joseph, Jewish baptizing installations have been discovered that have links to a Jewish ritual bath (J. Briend, *L'Église judéo-chrétienne de Nazareth* [Jerusalem: Franciscan Printing Press, 1975], 48–64). A synagogue church of the fourth century has been discovered under the new basilica (illus. 6), which was aligned to the traditional place of the annunciation of Mary (Lk 1:26–38) (E. Alliata, "Il luogo dell'Annunziazione a Nazaret", in A. Strus, *Maria nella sua terra* [Cremisan and Bethlehem, 1989], 25–33). At the base of a column, the angel's greeting is scratched: X[AIP]E MAPIA, "Greetings, favored one" (Lk 1:28) (illus. 94). For further information on excavations in Nazareth, see also G. Kroll, *Auf den Spuren Jesu*, 11th ed. (Stuttgart: Katholisches Bibelwerk, 2002), 79–92; R. Riesner, "Nazarener/ Nazareth", in *GBL*, 2nd ed. (1990), 2:1030–37; and idem, "Nazarener/ Nazareth", in M. Görg and B. Lang, *Neues Bibel Lexikon*, vol. 2 (Solothurn and Duesseldorf: Benziger und Patmos, 1995), 908–12. For information on background to the tradition, see R. Riesner, "Luke's Special Tradition and the Question of a Hebrew Gospel Source", *Mishkan* 20 (1994): 44–52; and idem, "James' Speech (Acts 15:13–21), Simeon's Hymn (Lk 2:29–32), and Luke's Sources", in J. B. Green and M. Turner, *Jesus of Nazareth—Lord and Christ* (Grand Rapids and Carlisle: Eerdmans and Paternoster, 1994), 263–78.

[20] Matthew, the author of the other childhood history, which essentially agrees with Luke's, might have based his writing on the other branch of Jesus' family, which resided in Kochaba in the south Syrian area of Batanea (p. 191).

[21] This study was written in 1982. To the author's satisfaction, the highly regarded exegete M. Hengel published a year later an article with much more detail but similar results ("Der Historiker Lukas und die Geographie Palästinas in der Apostelgeschichte", *ZDPV* 99 [1983]: 147–83).

APPENDIX I

Timeline of Jesus' Public Ministry

1. An Attempted Chronology

Time	*Event*	*Source*
A.D. 26–28	Public ministry of John the Baptist in the area of the Jordan River.	Mk 1:4; Lk 3:2f.
January A.D. 28	Baptism of Jesus in the Jordan River near Jericho. Forty days in the desert.	Mk 1:9–12
March 28	John is baptizing in Batanea in a tributary of the Jordan River, the Cherith (Jarmuk). Jesus is introduced to disciples of John at Bethany beyond the Jordan. Jesus goes with his first disciples to the wedding at Cana.	Jn 1:28—2:2
	Jesus stays with family and disciples for a time in Capharnaum.	Jn 2:12
April 28	Passover in Jerusalem. The cleansing of the temple draws attention to Jesus from Essene groups, as well as from the Galilean Pharisee Nicodemus. Jesus does not rely on these people.	Jn 2:13—3:21
Summer 28	Jesus preaches and his disciples baptize in Judea. John baptizes by the springs of Aenōn near Salem, south of Beth Shean.	Jn 3:22–23
Autumn 28	John stands up against Herod Antipas and is thrown into prison. Jesus returns via Samaria to Galilee.	Mt 14:3f.; Mk 6:17; Jn 4:1f.

November 28	With the arrest of John, Jesus begins his own mission.	Mt 4:12
	Jesus finds two pairs of brothers, Simon and Andrew, and James and John, while they are fishing at Tabgha (Magadan) and calls them to become disciples.	Mt 4:18ff.; Mk 1:16ff.
Winter 28/29	The beginning of Jesus' ministry in Capharnaum. Preaching in neighboring villages; news of his miracles and of his message spreads. Choosing of the Twelve.	Mk 1:21ff.
January/ February 29	Large crowds while preaching in the area of Tabgha.	Mt 4:23; 5:1ff.; Mk 4:1ff.
February 29	First crossing to the Gentile Decapolis. Storm on the lake. Cure of the possessed man in Kursi (the Decapolis). Because of the loss of the swine, Jesus must leave the area (Hippene), but the cured man makes Jesus known in the Decapolis.	Mk 6:1; Lk 4:16ff.
March 29	Crisis at Nazareth. Jesus is rejected by his Nazarene kinsmen.	Mk 6:1; Lk 4:16ff.
	Jesus' disciples preach in the villages.	Lk 4:16ff.
	Execution of John the Baptist.	*Ant.* 18.116–19; Mk 6:27
	Jesus is suspected of being a new John the Baptist.	Mk 6:14
April 29	The people follow: the first miracle of feeding (feeding the Jews) in Magadan (Tabgha). The crossing to Bethsaida goes wrong because of the strong east wind (*sharkiyeh*).	Mk 6:33ff.
	Jesus walks on the water and lands with the disciples in Gennesaret. They journey through the villages to the north.	Mk 6:48ff.
	Crossing the frontier to Phoenicia, Jesus reaches out to the Gentiles through the healing of the daughter of the Syro-Phoenician woman and decides to go again to the Decapolis.	Mk 7:24ff., 31

Date	Event	Reference
Summer 29	After a long journey through the region of Tyre and Sidon, Jesus passes Caesarea Philippi and reaches the Hippene (Afeka, Hippos) via the Golan.	Mk 7:31ff.
	Cure of the deaf-mute. Many people of the Decapolis (Gentiles) gather around him on a hill by the lake (Tell Hadar). Three days of teaching and healing. Feeding the Gentiles because the baskets of food brought along for the journey had run out. Return of Jesus to Magadan (Dalmanutha).	Mk 7:31–37; Mt 15:29–39; Mk 8:1–4
	Crisis in Capharnaum. Sign of Jonah.	Mt 16:1–4
	Discourse on the bread of life, in the synagogue.	Jn 6:26–59
	Desertion by many of his followers.	Jn 6:60f.
September 29	Feast of Tabernacles in Jerusalem (?).	Jn 7:2ff.
October 29	Journey north: instruction of the apostles.	Mk 8:13—9:33
	Crossing from Capharnaum to Bethsaida.	Mk 8:13–21
	Cure of the blind man (symbolic healing).	Mk 8:22–26
	Journey to Caesarea Philippi. Peter confesses Jesus as the Messiah. Correction of the disciples' messianic aspirations. First prediction of the Passion; tension.	Mk 8:27–33
	Transfiguration on the high mountain (Hermon).	Mk 9:2ff.
	Cure of the epileptic young man.	Mk 9:14–29
	Return to Galilee. Second prediction of the Passion.	Mk 9:30–32
	Return to Capharnaum.	Mk 9:33
November 29	Warning: threat of danger from Herod Antipas.	Lk 13:31ff.
	Jesus leaves Galilee.	Mt 19:11
	The group travels to "Judea on the other side of the Jordan" (Batanea). [Or first they go to the Feast of Hanuka in Jerusalem and then on to Batanea.]	Mk 10:1; Jn 10:22f., 40–42

Winter 29/30	In Batanea. Further activity in the territory of Philip unhindered by threat of violence.	Mk 10:1; Jn 10:42
	Discourse on marriage and eunuchs for the sake of the Kingdom of God.	Mk 10:2ff.
	Jesus and the children.	Mk 10:13–16
	Jesus is a guest at the home of Mary and Martha (?).	Lk 10:38ff.
	The rich young man.	Mk 10:17f.
February/ March 30	Jesus travels along the Jordan Valley. Third prediction of the Passion. Jesus goes on to Jericho with the Twelve and then up to Jerusalem.	Mk 10:32ff.
April 30	Death and Resurrection of Jesus.	
April/May 30	Appearances of Jesus in Galilee—on the lakeside and on the mountain near Capharnaum. This last appearance on the Heremus Height was probably also the occasion when "he appeared to five hundred brethren at one time."	Mk 14:28; Mt 28:16ff.; Jn 21:1ff.; 1 Cor 15:6

II. Explanation for the Chronology

This chronology follows Mark's Gospel, with the addition of the dates from John's Gospel. In the framework of the three Passover feasts mentioned by John, Mark's material can be added, if careful attention is paid to the narrative and in particular the details that are provided, such as description of vegetation, wind, climate and fishing.

1. Three Passover Feasts in John's Gospel

[Three Passover feasts are mentioned in John's Gospel:]

a. Passover while John the Baptist was still alive (Jn 2:13, 23) in the year 28. Luke mentions that the Baptist appeared in the fifteenth year of the hegemony (i.e., actual reign)[1] of the emperor Tiberius (Lk 3:1) in the whole region of Jordan (Lk 3:3; Jn 1:28; 3:23) as a wandering preacher. That means 26/27. The first of John's Passovers would therefore have been in 28. This is consistent with the objection

[1] Cf. A. Strobel, "Zeitrechnung", in *Biblisch-historisches Handwörterbuch*, vol. 3 (Göttingen: Vandenhoeck und Ruprecht, 1966), 2211–28 (at 2222f.).

made by the people: "It has taken forty-six years to build this temple, and will you raise it up in three days?" (Jn 2:20). The year 18 B.C. is generally taken to be the start of the temple building by Herod: 18 + 28 = 46.

b. Passover at the time of the first miracle of the feeding of the multitude (Jn 6:4) in the year 29.

c. Passover at the time of the Passion (Jn 13:1) in the year 30.

2. *Vegetation*

[Important references to vegetation include the following:]

a. A herd of swine can find pasture on the hillside over the lake only between February and April (cf. Mk 5:11).

b. First miracle of the feeding of the multitude (April 29): they sat down in groups on green grass (Mk 6:37; Jn 6:10).

c. Second miracle of the feeding (Summer 29): the grass had died off in the meantime and the four thousand sat down on the earth or on rocks (cf. Mk 8:6).

d. The journey through the cornfields (Mk 2:23; Mt 12:1) and the rubbing of the ears of corn must have been in May/June, perhaps during the journey from the lake into the neighborhood of Tyre.

3. *Winds*

Different winds blow over the lake at different times of the year. In the summer the afternoon west wind (Arabic *gharbiyeh*) cools off the intense summer heat somewhat but causes no storms. In winter and spring the east wind (Arabic: *sharkiyeh)* can be dangerous and often results in sudden storms.[2]

a. The storm on the lake—February 29 (cf. Mk 4:35–41).

b. The strong east wind prevented the disciples from reaching the appointed destination of Bethsaida at the mouth of the Jordan, in spite

[2] Cf. M. NUN, *The Sea of Galilee and Its Fishermen in the New Testament* (En Gev: Kibbutz En Gev, 1989), 52–57.

of hard rowing—March/April 29: "He saw that they were distressed in rowing, for the wind was against them" (Mk 6:48).

4. *Climate*

For the pilgrimage to Jerusalem, three or four days were needed.[3] In general, pilgrims followed the Jordan Valley only during the cool season. In summer, because of the almost unbearable heat in the valley, travelers followed the mountain route, in spite of the dangers that Samaritans posed.[4]

a. In Winter 28 Jesus walked through the valley to John the Baptist, who was baptizing near Jericho. (This is also the traditional liturgical date in the Eastern and Western churches for the baptism of Jesus.)

b. Jesus traveled home from Jerusalem through Samaria—October 28 (cf. Jn 4:3–4).

c. Final journey of Jesus to Jerusalem through Jericho—February–March 30 (cf. Mk 10:48).

5. *Fishing*

In the cool months the fishermen of Capharnaum throw their nets near the beach of Tabgha, where once there was a small harbor (Peter's harbor). The tilapia ("Peter's fish"), being a tropical species, suffers from the winter cold. Attracted by water from the warm springs at Tabgha (Seven Springs), large shoals of these fish gather in the area. In winter and spring heavy catches can be made.

a. Calling of the disciples—November 28. The sons of Zebedee and of Jonas formed a partnership. They had come, together with the hired laborers, from fishing on the open water to land. While the one group got the nets ready for the next expedition, Peter and Andrew attempted to catch more fish in the shallow water with their casting nets. Jesus went past and called them (cf. Mk 1:16–20).

b. Appearance of Jesus after the Resurrection on the shore of Tabgha—April/May 30. The plentiful haul of fish (cf. Jn 21:1ff.).

[3] Cf. J. Jeremias, *Jerusalem zur Zeit Jesu*, 3rd ed. (Göttingen: Vanderhoeck und Ruprecht, 1962), 68.

[4] Cf. G. Dalman, *Orte und Wege Jesu*, 3rd ed. (Gütersloh: Bertelsmann, 1924), 222–56.

APPENDIX II

A Possible Chronology of the Events of Passion Week

In chapter 18, I expressed my opinion that Jesus celebrated the Last Supper and the Passover meal according to the Essene calendar, i.e., on Tuesday night. I am indebted to Professor Eugen Ruckstuhl (who died in 1996) for the following Passion chronology.[1]

The Night from Tuesday to Wednesday

1. Jesus' Last Supper on Tuesday night
2. Jesus' arrest on the Mount of Olives at midnight
3. Jesus' interrogation by Annas
4. Denial of Jesus by Peter in the yard of the high priest's palace
5. Ridiculing of Jesus by the high priest's servants

Wednesday, during the Day

6. Court hearing by the High Council in the official council building in the morning
7. Preparation of the Jewish complaint against Jesus
8. Submission of the complaint scripts and the beginning of the Roman hearing for the following morning
9. Second night for Jesus in the custody of the high priest

[1] "Zur Chronologie der Leidensgeschichte Jesu", in *Jesus im Horizont der Evangelien* (Stuttgart: Katholisches Bibelwerk, 1988), 101–84 (at 116f.).

Thursday

10. Second sitting of the High Council in the early hours of the morning

11. Jesus handed over to Pilate

12. Opening of the Roman proceedings; oral accusations by the Jewish hierarchy against Jesus

13. Interlude in front of the tetrarch Herod Antipas

14. Negotiation in front of Pilate in the afternoon

15. Fixing for a second day of negotiation

16. Jesus in detention at the palace of the governor

Friday

17. Conclusion of the Roman proceedings in connection with the Barabbas trial; sentencing of Jesus to death on the cross

18. Ridiculing of Jesus by the Roman soldiers

19. Jesus' crucifixion in the course of the morning

20. Jesus' death around three o'clock

APPENDIX III

Bibliography of the Writings of Bargil Pixner, O.S.B.

1. Publications 1976–2008

1976

"An Essene Quarter on Mount Zion?" In *Studia Hierosolymitana in onore di P. Bellarmino Bagatti* vol. 1, *Studi archeologici*, 245–85. SBFCMa 22. Jerusalem: Franciscan Printing Press, 1976. Also published as a monograph.

1979

"Noch einmal das Prätorium: Versuch einer neuen Lösung". *ZDPV* 95 (1979): 56–86.

"Sion III, 'Nea Sion': Topographische und geschichtliche Untersuchung des Sitzes der Urkirche und seiner Bewohner". *HlL* 111, nos. 2–3 (1979): 3–13.

"Where Was the Original Via Dolorosa?" *CNfI* 27 (1979): 7–10, 51–53. [French: "À la recherche du tracé original de la Via Dolorosa". *Nouvelles chrétiennes d'Israël* 27, no. 1 (1979): 8–11, 40f.]

with D. Chen and S. Margalit. "Har Zijon". *Hadashot Arkheologiyot* 72 (1979): 28f. [In Modern Hebrew.]

1980

"The Pit of Jeremiah Rediscovered?" *CNfI* 27 (1980): 118–21, 148.

1981

"Das Essenerquartier in Jerusalem und dessen Einfluß auf die Urkirche". *HlL* 113, nos. 2–3 (1981): 3–14.

with D. Chen and S. Margalit. "Har Zijon". *Hadashot Arkheologiyot* 77 (1981): 26f. [In Modern Hebrew.]

with G. Hintlian and A. van der Heyden. *The Glory of Bethlehem*. Jerusalem, 1981. [German: *Bethlehem, du schöne* . . . Neuhausen-Stuttgart, n.d.]

1982

"Wo lag Bethsaida? Eine Studie". *HIL* 114, nos. 2–3 (1982): 25–31.

"Jakobus der Herrenbruder". In J. G. Plöger and J. Schreiner, *Heilige im heiligen Land*, 146–52. Würzburg: Echter, 1982.

"Simeon Bar-Kleophas, zweiter Bischof von Jerusalem". Ibid., 300–304.

"Putting Bethsaida-Julias on the Map". *CNfI* 11 (1982): 165–70.

with D. Chen and S. Margalit. "Har Zijon". *Hadashoth Arkheologiyot* 80, no. 1 (1982): 30f. [In Modern Hebrew.] [English: "Mt. Zion". *ESI* 1 (1982): 57.]

with others. "Restoration at Kursi: The Site of the Healing of the Man with the Unclean Spirit" *CNfI* 11 (1982): 170–72.

1983

"Unravelling the Copper Scroll Code: A Study on the Topography of 3Q15". *RQ* 11 (1983): 323–66.

with S. Margalit. "Har Zijon". *Hadashot Arkheologiyot* 82 (1983): 45f. [In Modern Hebrew.] [English: "Mt. Zion". *ESI* 2 (1983): 57.]

1984

"Auf dem ras haddad setzte sich Jesus auf den Esel: Lukas kannte Jerusalem persönlich". *Entschluß* 39, nos. 9–10 (1984): 31–33.

1985

"Bethsaïda". *MB* 38 (1985): 30.

"The Miracle Church of Tabgha on the Sea of Galilee". *BA* 48 (1985): 196–206.

"Les routes de Jésus autour du lac". *MB* 38 (1985): 15f.

"Searching for the New Testament Site of Bethsaida". *BA* 48 (1985): 207–16.

"La synagogue de Capharnaüm". *MB* 38 (1985): 23–28.

"Tabgha". *MB* 38 (1985): 32–36.

"Tabgha on Lake Gennesareth—the Eremos of Jesus". Special issue, *CNfI* (June 1985): 18–26.

"Une hypothèse au sujet d'el Araj". *MB* 38 (1985): 31.

with S. Margalit. "Mt. Zion". *ESI* 4 (1985): 56f.

1986

"Der Sitz der Urkirche wird zum neuen Zion: Die bauliche Entwicklung auf dem Südwesthügel Jerusalems bis zum Jahre 415 n. Chr." In Dormition Abbey (Jerusalem), *Festschrift des theologischen Studienjahres der Dormition Abbey Jerusalem für Abt Dr. Laurentius Klein, O.S.B.*, 65–76. St. Ottilien: EOS, 1986.

"Tabgha, der Eremos des Herrn". Ibid., 35–47.

1987

"Was the Trial of Jesus in the Hasmonean Palace? A New Solution to a Thorny Topographical Problem of Jerusalem". In A.L. Eckardt, *Jerusalem—City of Ages*, 66–88. New York and London: American Professors for Peace in the Middle East, 1987.

"Wege Jesu um den See Gennesaret". *HlL* 119, nos. 2–3 (1987): 1–14.

1988

"Jarmuk". In *GBL* 2: 648. Wuppertal and Gießen, 1988.

with R. Riesner. "Kochaba". Ibid., 2:801f.

1989

"Maria sul Sion dopo la risurrezione". In A. Strus, *Maria nella sua terra*, 11–23. Cremisan and Bethlehem, 1989.

"Salzstadt". In *GBL*, 3:1324. Wuppertal and Gießen, 1989.

"Sechacha". Ibid., 3:1418.

"Wann fuhr Jesus mit dem Boot?" *Die Zukunft* 2 (December 1989): 30.

with D. Chen and S. Margalit. "Mount Zion: The 'Gate of the Essenes' Re-excavated". *ZDPV* 105 (1989): 85–95, plates 8–16.

"The History of the 'Essene Gate' Area". *ZDPV* 105 (1989): 96–104.

1990

"The Apostolic Synagogue on Mount Zion". *BAR* 17, no. 3 (1990): 16–35, 60.

"Church of the Apostles on Mt. Zion". *Mishkan* 13 (1990): 27–42.

"Traditionen und Legenden um Tabgha". Special issue, *HlL* 122, nos. 2–3 (1990): 1–14.

1991

"Maria im Hause Davids". *Geist und Leben* 64 (1991): 41–51.

"Wege des Messias und Stätten der Urkirche: Jesus und das Judenchristentum im Licht neuer archäologischer Erkenntnisse". Edited by R. Riesner. SBAZ 2. Gießen: Brunnen, 1991.

1992

"Archäologische Beobachtungen zum Jerusalemer Essener-Viertel und zur Urgemeinde". In B. Mayer, *Christen and Christliches in Qumran?* 89–113. Eichstätter Studien, N.F., 32. Regensburg: Pustet, 1992.

"Copper Scroll". In D. N. Freedman, *Anchor Bible Dictionary*, 1:1133f. New York: Doubleday, 1992.

"The Jerusalem Essenes, Barnabas and the Letter to the Hebrews". In Z. J. Kapera, *Intertestamental Essays in Honour of Józef Tadeusz Milik*, 167–78. Qumranica Mogilanensia 6. Cracow: Enigma Press, 1992.

Mit Jesus durch Galiläa nach dem fünften Evangelium. Rosh Pinna, Israel: Corazin, 1992. [English: *With Jesus through Galilee according to the Fifth Gospel*. Collegeville, Minn.: Liturgical Press, 1996.]

"Praetorium". In D. N. Freedman, *Anchor Bible Dictionary*, 5:445–47.

1993

"Die historische Via Dolorosa: Ein Gang durch die Geschichte des Kreuzweges Jesu". *Im Land der Bibel* 38, no. 1 (1993): 6–15.

"Der Norden Israels erschließt die biblischen Hintergründe neu: Gespräch mit Pater Bargil Pixner". In W. R. Schmidt, *Wenn Engel reisen: Eine Expedition durch Israel*, 36–52. Gütersloher Taschenbücher 1302. Gütersloh: Gütersloher Verlagshaus, 1993.

with D. Chen and S. Margalit. "Sh^{e}ridej bijzurijm mishlahej tequfot bejt ri'shon mitachat l^{e}sh^{e}'ar ha-'esajjim b^{e}har zijjon". *Qadmoniot* 26 (1993): 33–37. [In Modern Hebrew.]

1994

with D. Chen and S. Margalit. "Mount Zion: Discovery of Iron Age Fortifications below the Gate of the Essenes". In H. Geva, *Ancient Jerusalem Revealed*, 76–81. Jerusalem: Israel Exploration Society, 1994.

1996

"Mit Jesus in Jerusalem: Seine ersten und letzten Tage in Judäa". Rosh Pinna: Corazin, 1996. [English: *With Jesus in Jerusalem: His First and Last Days in Judea*. Rosh Pinna: Corazin, 1996.]

Wege des Messias und Stätten der Urkirche: Jesus und das Judenchristentum im Licht neuer archäologischer Erkenntnisse. Edited by R. Riesner. 3rd exp. ed. SBAZ 2. Gießen: Brunnen, 1996.

1997

"Betsaida—Zehn Jahre später". *HlL* 130, no. 3 (1997): 1–16.

"Jerusalem's Essene Gateway: Where the Community Lived in Jesus' Time". *BAR* 23, no. 3 (1997): 22–31, 64–66.

"Jesus and His Community between Essenes and Pharisees". In J. H. Charlesworth and L. L. Johns, *Hillel and Jesus: Comparisons of Two Major Religious Leaders*, 193–224. Minneapolis: Fortress, 1997.

2001

"Nazoreans on Mount Sion (Jerusalem)". In S. C. Mimouni and F. S. Jones, *Le judéo-christianisme dans tous ses états: Actes du Colloque de Jérusalem, 6–10 juillet 1998*, 289–316. Paris: Cerf, 2001.

2002

"Jerusalem". In M. Ben-Dov, *Historical Atlas of Jerusalem*, ix–xi. New York: Continuum International Publishing Group, 2002.

2006

"Jesus and the Two Feast-Calendars". *Qumran Chronicle* 14, nos. 3–4 (2006): 101–17.

"Mount Zion, Jesus, and Archaeology". In J. H. Charlesworth, *Jesus and Archaeology*, 209–322. Grand Rapids and Cambridge: Eerdmans, 2006.

2008

After Jesus: The First Century of Christianity in Jerusalem. Edited by Elizabeth McNamer. Chicago: Paulist Press, 2008.

APPENDIX IV

Jerusalem Sketch and Other Illustrations

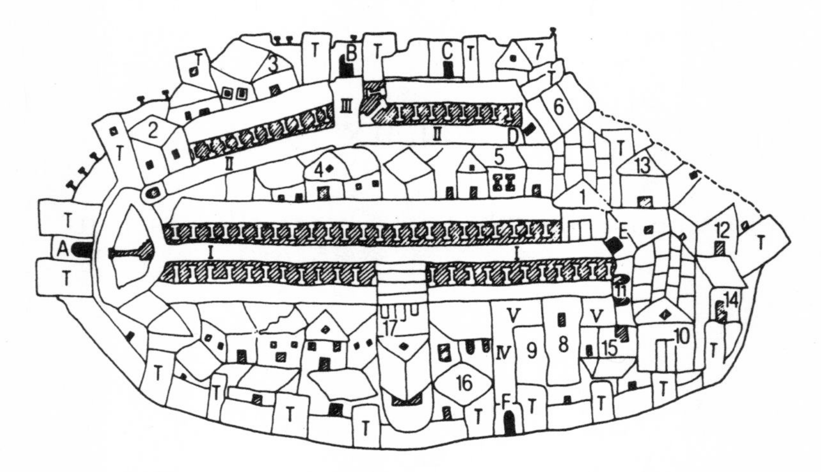

Illus. 98. Sketch of Jerusalem as pictured on the Madaba Mosaic Map (from G. Kroll).

A *Neapolitan Gate—Damascus Gate—Bab el-Amud*
B *Benjamin's Gate—Stephen's Gate—Mary's Gate*
C *Porta speciosa—Susa Gate—Golden Gate*
D *Jermiah's cistern*
E *Zion Gate*
F *Jaffa Gate—Bab el-Chalil*
T *Towers*
I *Main Street and Market Street—Cardo Maximus*
II *Via Triumphalis—Tarik el-Wad—Valley Road*
III *Tarik Bab Sitti Marjam—Start of the Via Dolorosa*
IV *Decumanus—Street of the Tenth Legion*
V *Street of the church of Zion*
1 *New Church of the Mother of God—Sancta Maria Nea*
2 *Palace of the empress Eudocia*
3 *Church of Bethesda*
4 *Sts. Cosmas and Damian (?)*
5 *Sancta Sophia—church of the Praetorium*
6 *Steps to the Siloam pool*
7 *Basilica of the Cross—pinnacle of the temple*
8 *"Tower of David"—Tower of Phasael*
9 *Tower of Mariamne*
10 *Basilica of Zion [Hagia Sion]*
11 *Gate entrances*
12 *St. Peter in Gallicantu—Caiaphas' House*
13 *Church of Siloam*
14 *Last Supper Room*
15 *Sts. Kyros and John*
16 *Baptistry*
17 *Church of the Holy Sepulchre*

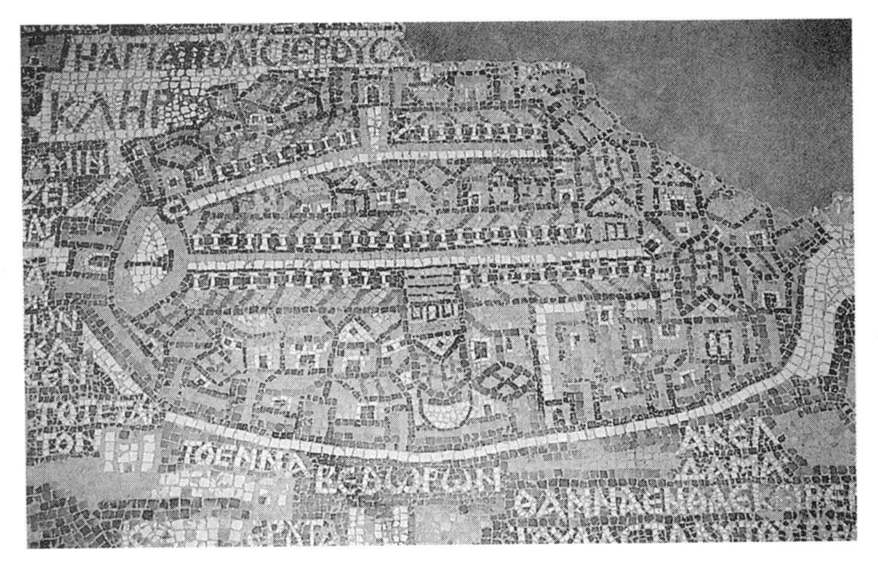

Plate 1. The Madaba Mosaic Map of Jerusalem.

Plate 2. The mosaic in the apse of the church Sancta Pudentiana in Rome.

Plate 3a. View from the Heremus grotto (Tabgha) on Lake Gennesaret to Tiberias in the southwest.

Plate 3b. The early Byzantine limestone synagogue of Capharnaum. Underneath [the limestone wall], one can clearly see the structure of a basalt wall that belongs to an older synagogue church.

Plate 4a. Bargil Pixner in el-Aradj (Bethsaida in Galilee?) with architectural finds, which belong to a synagogue or a church.

Plate 4b. Bethsaida-Julias—excavation of a building from the Hellenistic-Roman period.

Plate 5a. Kursi—view from the hanging chapel (grave cave of the possessed?) above the Byzantine monastery in the direction of northwest of Lake Gennesaret and the plain of Bethsaida.

*Plate 5b. Kursi—plastered wall in the proximity of the hanging chapel with Jewish Christian symbols in a branch pattern (*nezer *in Isaiah 11:1).*

Plate 6a. Essene Gate: Underneath the big threshold of the Byzantine Gate, one can see the plaster tiles of the Herodian street; to the left inside the city, one can see the early Herodian sewage canal.

Plate 6b. Essene Gate: Under the Byzantine threshold is constructed in two stone layers the gate from the time of Aelia Capitolina (murus Sion?)*, and below the tiles of the Herodian street. To the left is the flank stone of the New Testament Essene Gate.*

Plate 7a. Southwest hill of Mount Zion—double Jewish ritual baths outside the New Testament town wall.

*Plate 7b. Bethany—large Jewish ritual bath in the monastery of the St. Vincent nuns. Above right is the rock reservoir ('ozar sar*ᶜ*a').*

Plate 8a. View from the place of the New Testament Praetorium (rock cliff Gabbatha), above the square in front of the Western Wall [Wailing Wall] of the temple (today's Dome of the Rock).

Plate 8b. Mount Zion—the lower layers of large reused Herodian stones in the wall of the "Last Supper room", the remains of a Jewish Christian synagogue of the pre-Byzantine period. On the right, one can see the arch of the cloister of the former gothic Franciscan monastery.

Table of Maps and Illustrations

Illustrations, continued *Page*

Illustrations, continued *Page*

Illustrations, continued Page

Illustrations, continued *Page*

Illustrations, continued *Page*

Plates *Page*

Plates, continued *Page*

SCRIPTURE INDEX

OLD TESTAMENT

NEW TESTAMENT

INDEX OF PLACES

Note: Page numbers in italics refer to maps and illustrations.

INDEX OF PERSONS

INDEX OF SUBJECTS

Note: Page numbers in italics refer to maps and illustrations.